Philosophy in America

*FROM THE PURITANS TO JAMES*

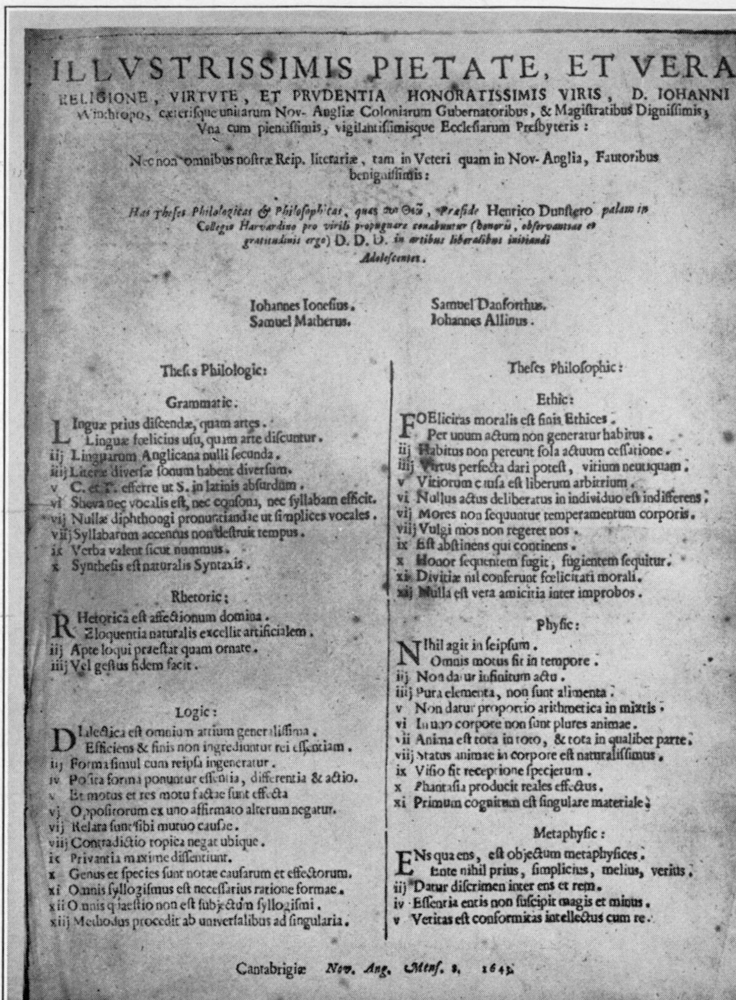

# ILLVSTRISSIMIS PIETATE, ET VERA RELIGIONE, VIRTVTE, ET PRVDENTIA HONORATISSIMIS VIRIS, D. IOHANNI

Winthropo, cæterisque unitarum Nov- Angliæ Coloniarum Gubernatoribus, & Magistratibus Dignissimis, Vna cum pientissimis, vigilantissimisque Ecclesiarum Presbyteris:

Nec non omnibus nostræ Reip. literariæ, tam in Veteri quam in Nov- Anglia, Fautoribus benignissimis:

*Has Theses Philologicas & Philosophicas, quas* σὺν Θεῷ, *Præside* Henrico Dunstero *palam in Collegio Harvardino pro viribus propugnare conabuntur (honoris, observantiae et gratitudinis ergo)* D. D. D. *in artibus liberalibus initiandi Adolescentes.*

Iohannes Ionesius. Samuel Danforthus.
Samuel Matherus. Iohannes Allinus.

## Theses Philologic:

### Grammatic.

Linguæ prius discendæ, quam artes.
Linguæ fœlicius usu, quam arte discuntur.
iij Linguarum Anglicana nulli secunda.
iiij Literæ diversæ sonum habent diversum.
v C. et T. efferre ut S. in latinis absurdum.
vi Sheva nec vocalis est, nec consona, nec syllabam efficit.
vij Nullæ diphthongi pronuntiandæ ut simplices vocales.
viij Syllabarum accentus non destruit tempus.
ix Verba valent sicut nummus.
x Synthesis est naturalis Syntaxis.

### Rhetoric;

Rhetorica est affectionum domina.
Eloquentia naturalis excellit artificialem.
iij Apte loqui praestat quam ornate.
iiij Vel gestus fidem facit.

### Logic:

Dialectica est omnium artium generalissima.
Efficiens & finis non ingrediuntur rei essentiam.
iij Forma simul cum reipsa ingeneratur.
iv Posita forma ponuntur essentia, differentia & actio.
v Et motus et res motu factae sunt effecta
vj Oppositorum ex uno affirmato alterum negatur.
vij Relata sunt sibi mutuo causae.
viij Contradictio topica negat ubique.
ix Privantia maxime dissentiunt.
x Genus et species sunt notae causarum et effectorum.
xi Omnis syllogismus est necessarius ratione formae.
xii Omnis quaestio non est subjectum syllogismi.
xiij Methodus procedit ab universalibus ad singularia.

## Theses Philosophic:

### Ethic:

FOElicitas moralis est finis Ethices.
Per unum actum non generatur habitus.
iij Habitus non pereunt sola actuum cessatione.
iiij Virtus perfecta dari potest, vitium neutiquam.
v Vitiorum causa est liberum arbitrium.
vi Nullus actus deliberatus in individuo est indifferens.
vij Mores non sequuntur temperamentum corporis.
viij Vulgi mos non regeret nos.
ix Est abstinens qui continens.
x Honor sequentem fugit, fugientem sequitur.
xi Divitiæ nil conferunt fœlicitati morali.
xij Nulla est vera amicitia inter improbos.

### Physic:

Nihil agit in seipsum.
Omnis motus fit in tempore.
iij Non datur infinitum actu.
iiij Pura elementa, non sunt alimenta.
v Non datur proportio arithmetica in mixtis.
vi In uno corpore non sunt plures animae.
vii Anima est tota in toto, & tota in qualibet parte.
viij Status animae in corpore est naturalissimus.
ix Visio fit receptione specierum.
x Phantasia producit reales effectus.
xi Primum cognitum est singulare materiale.

### Metaphysic:

ENs qua ens, est objectum metaphysices.
Ente nihil prius, simplicius, melius, verius.
iij Datur discrimen inter ens et rem.
iv Essentia entis non suscipit magis et minus.
v Veritas est conformitas intellectus cum re.

Cantabrigiæ *Nov. Ang. Mens.* 8, 1643.

HARVARD THESES OF 1643

THE CENTURY PHILOSOPHY SERIES
STERLING P. LAMPRECHT, EDITOR

# PHILOSOPHY IN AMERICA

## *FROM THE PURITANS TO JAMES*

With Representative Selections

BY

Paul Russell Anderson
LAKE ERIE AND OBERLIN COLLEGES

AND

Max Harold Fisch
WESTERN RESERVE UNIVERSITY

*D. APPLETON-CENTURY COMPANY*
INCORPORATED
NEW YORK LONDON

349

Printed in the United States of America

# Editor's Introduction

History of development of civilization in the United States has received in recent years increasing attention in the educational programs of our colleges and universities. To an extent this increasing attention has been due to a desire to place American culture in a more just relation to other vital and more traditional studies. It has not, I think, been a mark of parochialism or of preference for the more immediate and more local aspects of human affairs. It has not meant any diminution in recognition of the wide and deep indebtedness of American culture to its classical and European sources. Rather it has occurred conjointly with a realization of the present involvement of America in the intricate course of events across the entire world. Understanding of the physical and intellectual forces that have made American civilization in the past is part and parcel of the effort to orient American life wisely and effectively in a world to which determination of American policy can not but be of crucial and universal concern.

The present book is a contribution to the needed materials for a proper grasp of the history of ideas in the United States. Many of the early documents which exhibit phases of this history have long been unavailable except in research centers and to limited numbers of students. Some of these documents are here offered to all who wish to read them. The selection of these documents has been made, I think, with care and discrimination of their importance. But the book is more than a group of selections. It is also a history of the development of philosophy in the United States. In the introductions to the successive selections are given accounts of the intellectual trends which the selections illustrate, of the various waves of European influence which came one after another to our American shores, of the situations in our own land to which the American thinkers were directing their attention, and of the impact of ideas upon future developments to which they contributed. One problem which the authors of the present book had to solve was of course that of elimination. Much more was worthy of inclusion than limitations of space permitted. Enough has been included, however, to give a clear story of the main currents of American thought in its philosophical expressions. Emphasis has been upon the desirability of making available certain documents that can be little known because they are inaccessible at present. The earlier portions of the book especially, and all of it to a great extent, will prove of considerable interest to students of American literature and history, to students of political theory and sociology; for in this country, as often elsewhere, philosophy has been integral to the general life of the nation. In all fields of interest the purpose of the present book has been to supplement existing resources instead of to duplicate these resources; and hence the book comes as a timely as well as competent addition to the study and understanding of the intellectual history of the United States.

STERLING P. LAMPRECHT
General Editor

Amherst, Massachusetts

# Table of Contents

PART II

THE AGE OF REASON



PART III

TRANSCENDENTALISM AND EVOLUTION

## PART IV

## THE EMERGENCE OF CONTEMPORARY ISSUES

# Preface

American culture can hardly be understood without consideration of its origin; at the same time it is something more than just a geographical reëstablishment of European culture and its thoughtful expression something more than just a restatement of European ideas. American culture and thought have been decidedly influenced by their European antecedents, but they have also expressed attitudes and sentiments towards the essential problems of human existence in a form that is at once peculiar to and influential upon the American scene. To study this heritage is to deepen our understanding of the forces which have molded our civilization in the past and which continue to do so today.

The importance of American philosophy is evidenced by the number of works which have already appeared in the field. I. Woodbridge Riley's *American Philosophy: the Early Schools,* a pioneer work of spade-digging, his *American Thought,* a general summary, H. G. Townsend's *Philosophical Ideas in the United States,* a more selective interpretation, and Herbert W. Schneider's *The Puritan Mind,* together with a number of other volumes of more limited scope, all have their appropriate place in the study of American philosophy. Histories of American thought are now printed in German, French and Czech, and philosophy on this side of the Atlantic is receiving attention in general histories of philosophy.

The present volume is not intended as a final compendium of American philosophy. Its purpose is that of providing a running account of the Odyssey of the American mind from the time when America was but a land of colonies until the time when all agree American thought became as independent as philosophy ever is in a developed civilization. It was deemed advisable to let American philosophers speak for themselves in large part and then to add interpretive summaries and bibliographical suggestions to make further study of the key figures somewhat easier. The men chosen are thought to be representative rather than inclusive.

It would have been helpful perhaps to continue the story up to the present time but reason for not doing this can be seen in the hazardous task of doing justice to the variety of twentieth-century thought without extending the content of the volume beyond bounds. The least arbitrary stopping point short of the present seemed to be marked by Baldwin's *Dictionary of Philosophy and Psychology* (1901–02) in which the movements of thought up to that time were given definitive, though summary, statement. Accordingly the authors have confined their selections to thinkers whose basic ideas had been formulated and made public before 1900. For those who wish to go beyond the extent of the present volume, D. S. Robinson's *Anthology of Recent Philosophy* will be found to be very helpful.

It has been contended by some that much thought in America can hardly be called philosophical, the assumption being that there is a hard and fast line which distinguishes that thought which is to be called "philosophical" from other types of human discourse. It is equally possible to go to the other extreme by accepting any opinion as philosophical which gains acceptance by virtue either of its capacity to convince or its power to attract. With neither of these points of view are the authors in complete agreement. There are undoubtedly distinctions to be made between philosophy, science, theology, religion and art; but it must also be recognized that there are no hard and fast lines which separate them. Philosophy often lurks in the most unsuspected corners. The act of frowning upon what has passed for philosophy in the minds of others may often be an index of one's own partiality more than anything else. In a technical sense, a number of the figures included here would hardly be designated "philosophers" today. On the other hand, to sort out the technical philosophical issues from the thoughts of men in other periods when the distinctions between philosophy and allied fields of interest were even less clear than they are now, and in the process to disregard their more general reflective judgments, would be more an expression of what we feel and think than an explanation of why others felt and thought the way they did.

The authors have collaborated closely in selecting and interpreting the materials which are included. The burden of writing was naturally divided, Professor Anderson being responsible for chapters V–XIV, XVI–XVIII, and XXII and Professor Fisch responsible for chapters I–IV, XV, XIX–XXI, and XXIII.

Bibliographical materials are to be found in two places: for the individual men dealt with in the body of the volume, they have been included along with the materials about and by each figure; for the various periods and for other figures deserving consideration, they have been placed at the end of the volume. The lists in both cases are selective, but they will at least indicate where the most helpful materials are to be found.

The authors are grateful to the following: Dr. G. Adolf Koch for his help in choosing the selections from Ethan Allen; Professors Sterling P. Lamprecht, Herbert W. Schneider, H. G. Townsend, Harold A. Larrabee, Walter S. Gamertsfelder, Charles Hartshorne, Perry Miller, Gail Kennedy, J. D. Lewis, Robert S. Fletcher and Drs. Charles M. Wiltse and Thomas H. Johnson, whose suggestions and thoughtful criticisms—even those we have been unable to follow—have been of considerable value in determining the extent and content of this volume.

# *PART I*

# Colonial Thought

# I
# Introduction

In any survey of philosophy in the American colonies, a distinction must be made between that of the schools and that of the public platform, pulpit and press. The former was inherited and conservative; the latter had some degree of independence from the start because its source and focus was in the problems of life as they arose in the colonies.

The colleges were chiefly for the sons of the upper classes—merchants, landed gentry, clergy of the established churches, lawyers and officials. With only one clear exception, they were founded and in part maintained by religious bodies, and their primary purpose was the preservation of religious orthodoxy and the established order in church, state, and economic life. Their conservative function was supported by a conservative curriculum, beginning with the ancient languages and classics, grammar and rhetoric, passing on to logic and natural philosophy, and concluding with ethics and metaphysics. The doctrinal point of departure was Aristotle, as interpreted by the medieval schoolmen and made easy and safe by seventeenth-century textbook writers, with a slow infiltration of modern science and a still slower one of modern philosophy. The method, too, was medieval: lectures, textbooks, notebooks for the intake; "disputations" for the outgo, looking toward the defense of commencement theses. All of this was in Latin in the seventeenth century, with gradual displacement by English in the eighteenth.[1]

Candidates for the ministry went on to the master's degree, with but little formal instruction and no residence requirement. The *quaestiones* they disputed at commencement were largely metaphysical and theological, in the Aristotelian tradition. Among the most popular were those dealing with the creation and destruction of the universe. An almanac for 1666 has preserved for us what appears to be a translation of a master's commencement argument on the *quaestio* whether it is possible

[1] See the frontispiece for a commencement thesis sheet; Morison: *Harvard in the Seventeenth Century* for details of the Harvard curriculum; and Walsh: *Education of the Founding Fathers* for the other colleges.

that the world should have been created from eternity.[2] The terms in which the problem is conceived go back to Aristotle and Thomas Aquinas.

Textbooks were imported. Prior to the American Revolution, only three philosophical textbooks are known to have been written, printed, and used as college texts in the English-speaking colonies. The first of these was an elementary manual of Cartesian logic reduced to scholastic form, compiled by William Brattle, tutor at Harvard from 1685 to 1697. After circulating in manuscript copies for half a century, this was printed at Boston in 1735 and again in 1758, and was used as a textbook at Harvard until 1765. The second was Samuel Johnson's *Elements of Philosophy,* printed at Philadelphia by Benjamin Franklin in 1752, and used as a text at the College of Philadelphia and at King's College in New York City (later the University of Pennsylvania and Columbia University). The third was a mediocre *Essay on the Nature and Foundation of Moral Virtue and Obligation,* by Thomas Clap, printed at New Haven in 1765 and used as a text at Yale, of which Clap was rector from 1740 to 1766. If with textbooks we include treatises, there will be only one addition to make: Jonathan Edwards's *On the Freedom of the Will,* printed at Boston in 1754, and used by student request as the ethics text at Yale for a few years beginning in 1762.

Of the major philosophers of the seventeenth century and the first half of the eighteenth—Bacon, Descartes, Hobbes, Spinoza, Locke, Leibniz, Berkeley, Hume—only Locke was seriously studied at first hand in the colonial colleges. At Yale his *Essay concerning Human Understanding* was read almost continuously from 1719 to 1825, and at Harvard from 1743 or earlier until 1841. The most widely studied moral philosophers were Henry More (*Enchiridion Ethicum,* 1666) and Francis Hutcheson (*Inquiry into the Original of our Ideas of Beauty and Virtue,* 1725), intellectual and aesthetic intuitionists respectively. Hutcheson was the founder of the Scottish school of common-sense realism, which was to become the orthodox philosophy in our colleges in the nineteenth century.

In terms of colonial interest in and contributions to the academic branches of systematic philosophy as they now stand—metaphysics, logic (including epistemology or theory of knowledge), ethics (including political and social philosophy), aesthetics, and philosophy of religion—it must be said that there was relatively little interest in abstract speculation for its own sake—in metaphysics, epistemology,

[2] Reproduced below, pp. 28–9.

aesthetics, or even in pure science. The focus of reflection was upon the moral government of the universe, and even here the great questions of God's sovereignty and man's freedom, God's purpose and man's destiny, did not become acute until the Great Awakening of 1734–50, when theological differences first became divisive. Up to that time, the chief occasions for philosophic reflection were the practical problems of the government of church and state. Aesthetics was non-existent except for Edwards's notes on "Excellency," which remained in manuscript form until the nineteenth century. The philosophy of religion as it is now understood was represented only by Edwards's *Religious Affections* (1746). Metaphysics came into sharp focus only in Edwards's manuscript notes on the mind and on natural science (c. 1716–20), Franklin's *Dissertation on Liberty and Necessity, Pleasure and Pain* (1725), and Johnson's *Elements of Philosophy* (1752), though it cropped up also in Colden's *The Principles of Action in Matter* (1751). No original work was done in logic, and it is doubtful if anyone but Edwards really sensed the difficulties involved in the theory of knowledge. Logic was a tool, not a problem; it prescribed the rules for the game of disputation.

In the foundations of ethics, however, there was a genuine and widespread interest in the eighteenth century, and it was at this point that the growing independence of philosophic speculation was most sharply challenged by the champions of orthodoxy. Cotton Mather confided to his diary on June 28, 1716, that

> There are some very unwise Things done, about which I must watch for Opportunities, to bear public Testimonies. One is the Employing of so much Time upon *Ethicks* in our Colledges. A vile Peece of Paganism.[3]

Such an Opportunity presented itself a decade later in his *Manuductio ad Ministerium: Directions for a Candidate for the Ministry,* and this is the testimony he bore:

> As for ETHICKS. . . . It is all over a *Sham;* It presents you with a *Mock-Happiness;* It prescribes to you *Mock Vertues* for the coming at it: And it pretends to give you a Religion without a CHRIST, and a *Life* of PIETY without a *Living Principle;* a *Good Life* with no other than *Dead Works* filling of it. It is not amiss for you, to know what this *Paganism* is; and therefore you may, if you please, bestow a short Reading upon a *Golius,* or a *More:* But be more of a *Christian,* than to look on the *Enchiridion* of the Author last mentioned, as, *Next the Bible, the best Book in the World.*[4]

[3] *Massachusetts Historical Society Collections.* Seventh Series. 8 (1912) 357.
[4] 1726. Sec. 33.

By that time Jonathan Edwards had already outlined in his notes on "Excellency" the theory of ethics which he was later to develop at length in *The Nature of True Virtue* (published posthumously in 1765), and Franklin had just printed his *Dissertation* in London. This pamphlet, or at least the printing of it, he shortly decided was "another Erratum," which he proceeded to correct in his *Articles of Belief and Acts of Religion* (1728), *Dialogues between Philocles and Horatio* (1730), and a projected "Art of Virtue," which he never published but of which he later gave an extended account in his *Autobiography*. We have already referred to Clap's textbook of ethics (1765) and to Johnson's *Elements* (1752), but it should be added that the second part of the latter had been separately published in 1746 as *A New System of Morality*. Johnson sent a copy of this to Cadwallader Colden, who replied with a manuscript "First Principles of Morality," which Johnson annotated and returned, but which was never printed. Johnson's successor as President of King's College, Myles Cooper, published a compendium of ethics in 1774, but the Revolution swept it into deserved oblivion.

A word may be said of natural science. In the seventeenth century there were astronomical observers like John Winthrop, Jr., and Thomas Brattle. In the eighteenth there were naturalists like the Bartrams of Philadelphia. Some fifteen colonists were elected fellows of the Royal Society of London between 1663 and 1773. Significant work was constantly being done in the way of discovery, observation and classification, but nowhere was there any sign of interest in scientific theory for its own sake, save in Edwards's unpublished notes on natural science and in the writings of Cadwallader Colden. Scientific knowledge was valued for purposes of religious edification or practical use. The edificatory interest in the seventeenth century ran to the collecting of "remarkable providences"; in the eighteenth, to admiration of the wisdom of God manifest in the order of nature. In Cotton Mather's *The Christian Philosopher* (1721) the transition is nearly complete, but even he never quite lost the medieval conception that there was no natural law which God might not set aside at any time. The practical interest in science is well represented by Franklin's "Proposal for Promoting Useful Knowledge among the British Plantations in America," a circular letter which led to the organization of The American Philosophical Society in 1744. Half a century earlier President Increase Mather and the Fellows of Harvard College had circulated "Certain Proposals" for the collecting of "remarkables, but still well attested with credible and sufficient witnesses." This was Harvard's only corporate act during the Mather administration, and the contrast between the two sets of proposals is instructive.

| 1694 | 1743 |
|---|---|
| The things to be esteemed *memorable* are especially all *unusual accidents* in the *Heaven* or *earth* or *water:* all wonderful *deliverances* of the distressed: *mercies* to the godly! *judgments* on the wicked; . . . with *apparitions, possessions, inchantments,* and all extraordinary things wherein the existence and agency of the *invisible world* is more sensibly demonstrated.[5] | That the subjects of the correspondence be: . . . new methods of curing or preventing diseases; . . . new mechanical inventions for saving labour; . . . new methods of improving the breed of useful animals; . . . and all philosophical experiments that let light into the nature of things, tend to increase the power of man over matter, and multiply the conveniences or pleasures of life.[6] |

We come now to the heart of colonial thought, the development in political theory from the aristocratic or theocratic philosophy of the Puritans to the democratic natural rights philosophy of the Age of Reason. The Puritans brought with them a variant of Calvinism known as the Federal or Covenant Theology. The Covenant of Works had been broken by Adam, the "federal" head of the race, and the penalty for his default was legally imputed to his descendants, each of whom was born bankrupt. God, their creditor, in view of their helpless insolvency, offered through Christ a new Covenant, that of Grace, in which justification was based on faith, not works. God elected those whom He would thus save, but moral effort and appropriation of the means of grace were the evidence of faith and the basis for assurance of election.

The Covenant of Grace immediately united each recipient of grace to God, and mediately it united all the saints in the invisible church of the elect. But the means of grace was administered by the church visible, of which it was the duty of every saint to become a member. As Thomas Hooker of Connecticut put it, the saints constituted the *matter* of the visible church, but its *form* was a mutual covenant. Besides the Covenant of Grace, therefore, there was the Church Covenant by which the visible political union of saints was constituted. Unfortunately, with the utmost vigilance it was difficult so to order the church visible that no saints were excluded and no sinners admitted. For this among other reasons the two covenants had to be kept dis-

[5] Mather: *Magnalia Christi Americana.* Int. to bk. VI.
[6] Franklin: *Writings.* II, 229–30.

tinct in theory, though for most practical purposes they were presumed to coincide.

In New England at least there was still another Covenant, not merely in theory but also in practice: the Civil Covenant by which the government of the state was established. During the later seventeenth and the eighteenth centuries there was to be a revival and intensive development of the social compact theory of the basis of governmental authority, led by such thinkers as Hobbes, Pufendorf, Locke, and Rousseau. They were to assume either an actual historical or an implicit contract for every sovereign government, a contract to which each new citizen automatically became a party. Meanwhile, in the American colonies from the Mayflower Compact of 1620 to the Federal Constitution of 1787, the theory was being provided with a series of case histories, a dozen or so of them antedating the first classical statement of the theory in its modern form in Hobbes's *Leviathan* (1651). These compacts, formally drawn up and signed, were doubtless inspired less by theoretical considerations than by the exigencies of frontier life, but their chief model in early New England was the Church Covenant. In fact, as the Church Covenant gave visible form to the Covenant of Grace, so the Civil Covenant gave power to the Church Covenant; and thus all three tended in practice to be identified.

The democratic implications which were later found in these compacts, both church and civil, were not there for the original covenanters, as the following considerations will make clear.

1. Many of the early compacts were imposed upon the colonists by their leaders for purposes of discipline and morale.

2. Though "the people" elected their officers in church and state, they controlled not the offices but only the gateway to them. Magistrates as well as ministers and elders owed their offices and duties to God, and only their election to the people.

3. "The people" were only the minority of chosen "freemen," who in Massachusetts had to be not merely property holders but members of an approved congregational church, i. e., "saints" who had given evidence of election by God to the Covenant of Grace. They were selected from above by the General Court or by a magistrate empowered to choose freemen.

4. Though the religious requirement was less strict in Connecticut than in Massachusetts, there was no essential difference in theory. In his famous Election Sermon of 1638, Thomas Hooker did, to be sure, lay it down that the people, "who have power to appoint officers and magistrates, it is in their power, also, to set the bounds and limita-

tions of the power and place unto which they call them." But the people had this power only "by God's own allowance," and it "therefore must not be exercised according to their humours, but according to the blessed will and law of God"; they must "choose *in* God and *for* God." [7]

5. There was no belief in equal rights, at least as the doctrine came to be expressed later. The government in Massachusetts was called by Governor Winthrop a "mixed aristocracy," and by Minister John Cotton a theocracy, and the slanderous charge of its being a democracy was expressly guarded against by both. In Cotton's words:

> Democracy, I do not conceyve that ever God did ordeyne as a fitt government eyther for church or commonwealth. If the people be governors, who shall be governed? As for monarchy, and aristocracy, they are both of them clearely approoved, and directed in scripture, yet so as referreth the soveraigntie to himselfe, and setteth up Theocracy in both, as the best forme of government in the commonwealth, as well as in the church. . . .
>
> Bodine confesseth, that though it be *status popularis,* where a people choose their owne governors; yet the government is not a democracy, if it be administered, not by the people, but by the governors, whether one (for then it is a monarchy, though elective) or by many, for then (as you know) it is aristocracy.[8]

6. Religious toleration, inseparable from any modern conception of democracy, was even farther from their thoughts. Both in the first authoritative exposition of the theocratic philosophy in *A Model of Church and Civil Power* (1634) and in the Cambridge Platform (1648), the preliminary distinction between church and state was virtually annulled by making the magistrates responsible for enforcing both tables of the law—the first four commandments stating man's duties to God, as well as the other six stating his duties to his fellows.

> The end of the Magistrate's office, is not only the quiet and peaceable life of the subject, in matters of righteousness and honesty, but also in matters of godliness, yea of all godliness.[9]

In effect, as we have said, the Civil Covenant existed to give power to the Church Covenant; and under such a scheme religious diversity would be equivalent to anarchy. It is not surprising, therefore, that Nathaniel Ward, author-in-chief of the first code of laws established in New England, "The Body of Liberties" (1641), found no place for

[7] *Collections of the Connecticut Historical Society* I (1860) 20–1.

[8] Letter to Lord Say and Seal (1636). Miller and Johnson: *The Puritans.* 209–10, 211.

[9] Cambridge Platform. XVII, 6.

liberty of conscience. In his *Simple Cobler of Aggawam* (1647) he gave dissenters fair notice to expect only "free Liberty to keep away from us, and such as will come to be gone as fast as they can, the sooner the better." [10] How much of this religious intolerance was due to the class interest of the clergy is hard to say.

Behind the political philosophy of the theocracy there was a metaphysics, best represented by Urian Oakes's Artillery Election Sermon, *The Soveraign Efficacy of Divine Providence,* in 1677, expounding with great care and completeness the doctrine of divine concurrence with the operation of natural or "second" causes.[11] Half a century later, Cotton Mather, in his *Manuductio ad Ministerium* (1726), spoke of God as "the Universal Cause producing those Effects, whereof the Creatures are but what One may call, The Occasional Causes." [12] In his *Coheleth: A Soul Upon Reflection* (1720) he had stated the more restricted form of the doctrine, with which the term occasionalism is associated in the history of philosophy.

> The *Body,* which is *Matter* in such and such a *Figure,* cannot Affect the *Immaterial* SOUL, nor can the SOUL, which has no *Figure,* Command the *Body;* But the Great GOD having established certain *Laws,* that upon such and such *Desires* of the SOUL, the *Body* shall be so and so Commanded, HE 'tis, who by His *Continual Influx* does Execute His own *Laws;* 'Tis to His *Continual Influx* that the *Effects* are owing.[13]

But if this divine concurrence worked generally throughout nature, it worked in a higher sense in the Christian Commonwealth. As John Davenport expressed it in his Election Sermon of 1669:

> In regular actings of the creature, God is the first Agent: there are not two several and distinct actings, one of God, another of the People: but in one and the same action, God, by the Peoples suffrages, makes such an one Governour, or Magistrate, and not another.[14]

The substance of the Puritan social philosophy, we may conclude, was control from above through instruments chosen from below, with God's concurrence in the choice as well as in the control. This control extended not merely to matters of civil and ecclesiastical polity, and of personal and family morality, but to every phase of social life, including the economic. A typical example of its operation in business

[10] Miller and Johnson: op. cit. 227.

[11] Selection below, pp. 30–3.

[12] Sec. 9.

[13] 5.

[14] *Publications of the Colonial Society of Massachusetts* 10 (1907). P. 6 of the engraved reproduction which follows p. 6 of the volume.

may be found in the case of Robert Keaine, in which John Cotton laid down the medieval doctrine of just price.[15] The policy of Puritan New England was not to stimulate individual economic enterprise, but to regulate it. If the accumulation of wealth was not despised, if within limits it was even approved, there was no glorification or idealization of it; like all other secular pursuits, it was to be subordinated to spiritual ends. It was in fact one of the professed motives of colonization to found a society in which economic life could be directed from the start by moral and religious ideals. What may fairly be charged against the Puritans is that the spirit of their regulations was repressive and legalistic rather than humanitarian, and that they were curiously insensitive to the effects of economic exploitation upon the lower classes. For that kind of social conscience it was necessary to wait a century and more for John Woolman, the Quaker saint of New Jersey,[16] and in New England itself until the reform movements associated with transcendentalism in the nineteenth century. The more secular conception of wealth as a social product which the state may not merely tax for its own maintenance but appropriate for the general welfare, is first clearly formulated in one of the later utterances of Benjamin Franklin.

All Property, indeed, except the Savage's temporary Cabin, his Bow, his Matchcoat, and other little Acquisitions, absolutely necessary for his Subsistence, seems to me to be the Creature of public Convention. Hence the Public has the Right of Regulating Descents, and all other Conveyances of Property, and even of limiting the Quantity and the Uses of it. All the Property that is necessary to a Man, for the Conservation of the Individual and the Propagation of the Species, is his natural Right, which none can justly deprive him of: But all Property superfluous to such purposes is the Property of the Publick, who, by their Laws, have created it, and who may therefore by other Laws dispose of it, whenever the Welfare of the Publick shall demand such Disposition. He that does not like civil Society on these Terms, let him retire and live among Savages. He can have no right to the benefits of Society, who will not pay his Club towards the Support of it.[17]

From this digression into economics we return to trace the later stages in the theory of the relations (1) between church and state and (2) between the magistrates and "the people." The inevitable though constantly resisted tendencies, beginning almost immediately after the settlement of the colonies and continuing, in spite of occasional reaction, throughout the colonial period and beyond it, were these: (1)

[15] See Winthrop's account. Below, pp. 20–2.

[16] Selection below, pp. 42–5.

[17] *Writings.* IX, 138.

the secularization of the state and the increase of religious liberty, with a consequent decline in the power and influence of the clergy in American life, and a balancing rise in that of the lawyers; (2a) the widening of the popular basis of government by lowering and finally dropping the religious and (much later) the property requirement for citizenship, so that "we the people" became an ever larger minority of the total population, though always remaining a minority; and (2b) the establishment of constitutional limits to the authority of the magistrates, and constitutional checks upon the exercise of it. We shall consider Roger Williams as a pioneer in the separation of church and state, and John Wise and Jonathan Mayhew as representing successive stages in the growth of democratic thought.

With a fairly successful six-year experiment in religious liberty behind him in Rhode Island, Williams published in 1644 his great indictment of *The Bloudy Tenent of Persecution.* Against the theocracies of New England and the milder theocracy of old England, he maintained that state and church were two institutions radically different in nature and purpose, and that it was absolutely essential both to the purity of religion and to the peace of the state that there should be not merely toleration but equal liberty for all forms of religion and establishment of none. From the state's point of view, a church was merely one of the many civil corporations which it was bound impartially to protect, but no one of which was essential to its existence, or even to its integrity. From the church's point of view, on the other hand, the proper interests of religion could not be promoted, but only frustrated, by civil subsidy or compulsion.

> An Arme of Flesh, and Sword of Steele cannot reach to cut the darknesse of the Mind, the hardnesse and unbeleefe of the Heart, and kindely operate upon the Soules affections to forsake a long continued Fathers worship, and to imbrace a new, though the best and truest. This worke performes alone that sword out of the mouth of Christ, with two edges. . . .[18]

Though the divorce of state and church has had consequences some of which he would have sought to avoid if he could have foreseen them, Williams seems to have recognized from the start, at least in principle, the cardinal limitation of his great doctrine of "soul liberty." The magistrates ought not to interfere in matters of religion, he argued even before the beginning of the Rhode Island experiment, *"otherwise than in such cases as did disturb the public peace."* [19] But after nearly

[18] *Bloudy Tenent.* Narragansett Club edition. 354.
[19] Winthrop: *History of New England.* I, 193.

twenty years of practical experience of the problems of government, he gave classic expression to that limitation in his famous Ship of State analogy.[20]

It is only just to add that, though the government of Rhode Island was somewhat more democratic than that of Connecticut, as that of Connecticut was slightly more democratic than that of Massachusetts, democracy in our sense was as far from being an article of faith with Williams as with Hooker, or even with Cotton. Williams's real concern, like theirs, was for the purity of religion, and he differed only in his judgment as to how it was to be secured. For all his headlong career through Puritanism, Separatism, Anabaptism, and all the shades of Seekerism, which led Cotton to call him "the most prodigious Minter of Exorbitant Novelties in New England," he remained like them a Calvinist in theology, and there was no seventeenth-century latitudinarianism or eighteenth-century humanitarianism in his soul. So much of what he said has so modern a ring, that it is disconcerting to find his clearest statement of the doctrine of popular sovereignty in the most Calvinistic argument in all our colonial literature.[21] It stands there not as a conclusion to be defended on its own account, but as a premise from which to conclude the necessary separateness of church and state. Since the magistrates had only such powers as the people delegated to them, if a power to control the churches of Christ were included, the people must have got it from Christ; but this was absurd, he argued, since it would be equivalent to turning over the church to "Satan himself, by whom all peoples naturally are guided." Therefore, the magistrates have no such power.

With John Wise of Chebacco we enter at last the main stream of seventeenth and eighteenth-century political thought. Though a Harvard graduate and a minister, he was the son of an indentured servant, retained the lay point of view of the lower middle class, and was a life-long champion of popular causes. In 1705 an association of Boston and Cambridge ministers made certain proposals which threatened the autonomy of the local churches. Wise retorted first with satire in *The Churches' Quarrel Espoused* (1710), and then with a learning which he had not fully mastered in *A Vindication of the Government of New England Churches* (1717). In the latter, after arguing in the first of five "demonstrations" that the Christian churches of the first three centuries, which derived their constitution from the Apostles and therefore from God, were congregational, and thus es-

[20] Below, pp. 27–8.
[21] Below, pp. 26–7.

tablishing a divine pedigree for the similar churches of New England, he proceeded in the second to "inquire into the *natural reason* of the constitution of those churches we have been comparing." It was apparent to him that

> the reason of the constitution of these and the primitive churches, is really and truly owing to the original state and liberty of mankind, and founded peculiarly in the *light of nature*.
>
> The divine establishment in providence of the fore-named churches, in their order, is apparently the royal assent of the supreme monarch of the churches, to the grave decisions of reason in favor of man's *natural state of being and original freedom* . . . as though wise and provident *nature* by the dictates of right reason excited by the moving suggestions of humanity, and awed with the just demands of *natural liberty, equity, equality,* and principles of self-preservation, originally drew up the scheme, and then obtained the royal approbation.[22]

Thus Wise went back of the primitive church, back of the apostles, back in a sense even of the Divine Founder, to a natural order which He could not but recognize. Men were no longer bowing before the inscrutable decrees of Calvin's God, but gazing steadily upon those truths of reason before which God himself must bow. If there were still some traces of the Divine Lawgiver in the demonstration "from the light of nature" that followed, that was because Wise found them in the German jurist Pufendorf, from whom he copied it almost verbatim, though with so much abridgment and rearrangement as to make it seem nearly at home in his own more racy pages. Pufendorf was greatly exercised by the problem of sovereignty; as he could conceive no civil law without a sovereign power behind it, so the law of nature required a sovereign to give it the "force and authority" of law. Though God no longer made the laws, he gave them his *imprimatur,* and he still applied the sanctions. Wise's argument, however, proceeded from Pufendorf's premises to a conclusion from which Pufendorf would have shrunk: that of the various forms of government democracy "is as agreeable with the light and laws of nature as any other whatever . . . and more accommodated to the concerns of religion than any other."

There was but one more step to take, and the cardinal principles of the philosophy of the Revolution would all be stated. That step, the basing of the right of revolution itself upon the law of nature, was clearly and decisively taken by Jonathan Mayhew in his sermon on the centennial anniversary of the beheading of Charles I.[23] The doctrines of separation of church and state, of popular sovereignty, of

[22] 1860 edition. 25. Italics ours.

[23] Selection below, pp. 40–2.

government by consent, of the common safety, utility and happiness as the sole end of government, were here perhaps for the first time knit together and carried to their logical conclusions. No one of these, of course, was original with Mayhew. As he put it some sixteen years later in his thanksgiving sermon on the repeal of the Stamp Act:

> Having been initiated in youth in the doctrines of civil liberty as they were taught by such men as Plato, Demosthenes, Cicero, and other renowned persons among the ancients, and such as Sydney and Milton, Locke and Hoadley among the moderns, I liked them; they seemed rational.[24]

We have traveled far from the Bible Commonwealth of Mayhew's forbears. Wise could still say that "revelation is nature's law in a fairer and brighter edition." [25] In Mayhew's time it was already becoming respectable to think that the law of nature was itself the only revelation above suspicion. The quadrennial Dudleian lectureship at Harvard, begun in 1755, was giving a certain prestige to "natural religion." The colonists, who had at first stood for their rights as "English men," as Wise did against Governor Andros in 1687 before he found the law of nature in Pufendorf, were now demanding with John and Samuel Adams the rights of the British constitution founded in the law of nature; failing which, they were soon to exercise the natural rights of man.

[24] *The Snare Broken.* 1766.
[25] Op. cit. 26.

# II

# College, Church, State and Society

## A MODEL OF CHURCH AND CIVIL POWER [1]

### *The End of Both These Powers*

A. The common and last end of both is Gods glory, and Mans eternall felicitie.

B. The proper end:

1. Of Commonwealth, is the procuring, preserving, increasing of externall and temporall peace and felicitie of the State in all Godlines and Honestie, I *Tim.* 2.1–2.

2. Of the Church, a begetting, preserving, increasing of internall and spirituall peace and felicity of the Church, in all godlinesse and honesty, *Isaiah* 2.3–4 and 9.7. So that Magistrates have power given them from Christ in matters of Religion, because they are bound to

[1] An act of the Massachusetts General Court of March 4, 1634, entreated "the elders and brethren of every church within this jurisdiction, that they will consult & advise of one uniforme order of discipline in the churches, agreeable to the Scriptures, and then to consider howe farr the Magistrates are bound to interpose for the preservation of that uniformity & peace of the churches." The "Model" seems to have been the result. It is not known to have been printed except in the latter half of Williams's *Bloudy Tenent,* with his criticisms interspersed. He attributes it to "Mr. Cotton and the Ministers of New-England." Cotton denied any share in its composition, but much of its most characteristic phraseology may be found in his acknowledged writings. A preamble states the problem; the first chapter argues that civil peace and prosperity depend upon "the vigilant administration of the holy Discipline of the Church"; the second that "the delinquencie of either party [church or state] calleth for the exercise of the power of terrour from the other part." Chapters III and IV and part of V are reproduced above. Chapter VI considers how far the church is subject to civil law; VII, in what order the magistrate may punish a church or church-member "that offendeth his lawes"; VIII–XIII, the magistrate's powers in the gathering of churches, in the providing of church officers, in matters of doctrine and worship, in censures of the church, and in public assemblies of the churches; XIV, "what power particular churches have particularly over magistrates"; XV, "in what cases churches must proceed with magistrates in case of offense." The last chapter (XVI) argues that freemen as well as magistrates must be chosen from among church members (i. e., members in full communion). This document has the interest of being the first mature attempt to deal systematically with the fundamental problem of the theocracy. Selections taken from *Publications of the Narragansett Club* 3 (1867) 232–3, 247–9, 254–6.

see that outward peace be preserved, not in all ungodlinesse and dishonesty (for such peace is Satanicall) but in all godlinesse and honesty, for such peace God aymes at. And hence the Magistrate is *custos* of both the Tables of godlinesse, in the first of Honesty, in the second for Peace sake. Hee must see that honesty be preserved within his jurisdiction, or else the subject will not be *bonus Civis.* Hee must see that godlinesse as well as honesty be preserved, else the subject will not be *bonus vir,* who is the best *bonus civis.* Hee must see that godlinesse and honesty be preserved, or else himselfe will not bee *bonus Magistratus.*

## *The Proper Meanes of Both These Powers to Attaine Their Ends*

### A. THE CIVILL POWER

The proper meanes whereby the Civill Power may and should attaine its end, are onely Politicall, and principally these Five.

1. The erecting and establishing what forme of Civill Government may seeme in wisedome most meet, according to generall rules of the Word, and state of the people.[2]

2. The making, publishing, and establishing of wholesome Civill Lawes, not onely such as concerne Civill Justice, but also the free passage of true Religion: for, outward Civill Peace ariseth and is maintained from them both, from the latter as well as from the former: Civill peace cannot stand intire, where Religion is corrupted, 2 *Chron.* 15.3, 5–6, *Judg.* 8. And yet such Lawes, though conversant about Religion, may still be counted Civill Lawes, as on the contrary, an Oath doth still remaine Religious, though conversant about Civill matters.

3. Election and appointment of Civill officers, to see execution of those Lawes.

4. Civill Punishments and Rewards, of Transgressors and Observers of these Lawes.

5. Taking up Armes against the Enemies of Civill Peace.

### B. THE SPIRITUALL POWER

The meanes whereby the Church may and should attaine her ends, are only ecclesiasticall, which are chiefly five.

[2] See what Williams made of this. Below, pp. 26–7.—Editor's note.

1. Setting up that forme of Church Government only, of which Christ hath given them a pattern in his Word.

2. Acknowledging and admitting of no Lawgiver in the Church, but Christ, and the publishing of his Lawes.

3. Electing and ordaining of such officers onely, as Christ hath appointed in his Word.

4. To receive into their fellowship them that are approved, and inflicting Spirituall censures against them that offend.

5. Prayer and patience in suffering any evill from them that be without, who disturbe their peace.

So that Magistrates, as Magistrates, have no power of setting up the Forme of Church Government, electing Church officers, punishing with Church censures, but to see that the Church doth her duty herein. And on the other side, the Churches as Churches, have no power (though as members of the Commonweale they may have power) of erecting or altering formes of Civill Government, electing of Civill officers, inflicting Civill punishments (no not on persons excommunicate) as by deposing Magistrates from their Civill Authoritie, or withdrawing the hearts of the people against them, or their Lawes, no more than to discharge wives, or children, or servants, from due obedience to their husbands, parents, or masters: or by taking up armes against their Magistrate, though he persecute them for Conscience: for though members of Churches who are publique officers also of the Civill State, may suppress by force the violence of Usurpers, as *Iehoiada* did *Athaliah,* yet this they doe not as members of the Church, but as officers of the Civill State.

## *Concerning the Magistrates Power in Making of Lawes*

A. They have power to publish and apply such Civill Lawes in a State as either are exprest in the Word of God in *Moses* Judicialls (to wit, so far as they are of generall and morall equity, and so binding all Nations in all Ages) to bee deducted by way of generall consequence and proportion from the word of God.

For in a free State no Magistrate hath power over the bodies, goods, lands, liberties of a free people, but by their free consents. And because free men are not free Lords of their owne estates, but are onely stewards under God, therefore they may not give their free consents to any Magistrate to dispose of their bodies, goods, lands, liberties at large as themselves please, but as God (the soveraigne Lord of all) alone. And because the Word is a perfect rule as wel of righteousnes as of holines, it will be therfore necessary that neither the people give consent, nor that the Magistrate take power to dispose of the bodies, goods, lands, liberties of the people, but according to the Lawes and Rules of the Word of God.

B. In making Lawes about civill and indifferent things about the Commonweale:

1. He hath no power given him of God to make what laws he please, either in restraining from, or constraining to the use of indifferent things, because that which is indifferent in its nature, may sometimes bee inexpedient in its use, and consequently unlawfull, I *Cor.* 2.5, it having been long since defended upon good ground, *Quicquid non expedit, quatenus non expedit, non licet.*

2. He hath no power to make any such Lawes about indifferent things, wherein nothing good or evill is shewne to the people, but onely or principally the meere authority or wil of the imposer for the observance of them, *Colos.* 2.21–2, I *Cor.* 7.23, compared with *Ephes.* 6.6.

It is a prerogative proper to God to require obedience of the sonnes of men, because of his authority and will.

The will of no man is *Regula recti,* unlesse first it bee *Regula recta.*

It is an evill speech of some, that in some things the will of the Law, not the *ratio* of it, must be the Rule of Conscience to walke by; and that Princes may forbid men to seeke any other reason but their authority, yea when they command *frivola* & *dura.* And therefore it is the duty of the Magistrate in all lawes about indifferent things, to shew the Reasons, not onely the Will, to shew the expediency, as well as the indifferency of things of that nature.

For we conceive in Lawes of this nature, it is not the will of the Lawgiver onely, but the Reason of the Law which bindes. *Ratio est Rex Legis,* & *Lex est Rex Regis.* . . .

* * *

---

* * *

## JOHN WINTHROP

1588–1649

### [*John Cotton Expounds Commercial Ethics*] (1639) [3]

At a general court holden at Boston, great complaint was made of the oppression used in the country in sale of foreign commodities; and Mr. Robert Keaine, who kept a shop in Boston, was notoriously above others observed and complained of; and, being convented, he was charged with many particulars; in some, for taking above six-pence in the shilling profit; in some above eight-pence; and, in some small things, above two for one; and being hereof convict, (as appears by the records,) he was fined 200, which came thus to pass: The deputies considered, apart, of his fine, and set it at 200; the magistrates agreed but to 100. So, the court being divided, at length it was agreed, that his fine should be 200, but he should pay but 100, and the other should be respited to the further consideration of the next general court. By this means the magistrates and deputies were brought to an accord, which otherwise had not been likely, and so much trouble might have grown, and the offender escaped censure. For the cry of the country was so great against oppression, and some of the elders and magistrates had declared such detestation of the corrupt practice of this man (which was the more observable, because he was wealthy and sold dearer than most other tradesmen, and for that he was of ill report for the like covetous practice in England, that incensed the deputies very much against him). And sure the course was very evil, especial circumstances considered: 1. He being an ancient professor of the gospel: 2. A man of eminent parts: 3. Wealthy, and having but one child: 4. Having come over for conscience' sake, and for the advancement of the gospel here: 5. Having been formerly dealt with and admonished, both by private friends and also by some of the magistrates and elders, and having promised reformation; being a member of a church and commonwealth now in their infancy, and under the curious observation of all churches and civil states in the world. These added much aggravation to his sin in the judgment of all men of understanding. Yet most of the magistrates (though they discerned of the offence clothed with all these circumstances) would have been more moderate in their censure: 1. Because there was no law in

[3] Savage, James (editor): Winthrop, John: *The History of New England from 1630 to 1649*. Boston: Little, Brown and Co., 1853. I, 377–82.

force to limit or direct men in point of profit in their trade. 2. Because it is the common practice, in all countries, for men to make use of advantages for raising the prices of their commodities. 3. Because (though he were chiefly aimed at, yet) he was not alone in this fault. 4. Because all men through the country, in sale of cattle, corn, labor, etc., were guilty of the like excess in prices. 5. Because a certain rule could not be found out for an equal rate between buyer and seller, though much labor had been bestowed in it, and divers laws had been made, which, upon experience, were repealed, as being neither safe nor equal. 6. Lastly, and especially, because the law of God appoints no other punishment but double restitution; and, in some cases, as where the offender freely confesseth, and brings his offering, only half added to the principal.

After the court had censured him, the church of Boston called him also in question, where (as before he had done in the court) he did, with tears, acknowledge and bewail his covetous and corrupt heart, yet making some excuse for many of the particulars, which were charged upon him, as partly by pretence of ignorance of the true price of some wares, and chiefly by being misled by some false principles, as 1. That, if a man lost in one commodity, he might help himself in the price of another. 2. That if, through want of skill or other occasion, his commodity cost him more than the price of the market in England, he might then sell it for more than the price of the market in New England, etc.

These things gave occasion to Mr. Cotton, in his public exercise the next lecture day, to lay open the error of such false principles, and to give some rules of direction in the case.

Some false principles were these:—

1. That a man might sell as dear as he can, and buy as cheap as he can.

2. If a man lose by casualty of sea, etc., in some of his commodities, he may raise the price of the rest.

3. That he may sell as he bought, though he paid too dear, etc., and though the commodity be fallen, etc.

4. That, as a man may take the advantage of his own skill or ability, so he may of another's ignorance or necessity.

5. Where one gives time for payment, he is to take like recompense of one as of another.

The rules for trading were these:—

1. A man may not sell above the current price, i. e., such a price as is usual in the time and place, and as another (who knows the worth

of the commodity) would give for it, if he had occasion to use it; as that is called current money, which every man will take, etc.

2. When a man loseth in his commodity for want of skill, etc., he must look at it as his own fault or cross, and therefore must not lay it upon another.

3. Where a man loseth by casualty of sea, or, etc., it is a loss cast upon himself by providence, and he may not ease himself of it by casting it upon another; for so a man should seem to provide against all providences, etc., that he should never lose; but where there is a scarcity of the commodity, there men may raise their price; for now it is a hand of God upon the commodity, and not the person.

4. A man may not ask any more for his commodity than his selling price, as Ephron to Abraham, the land is worth thus much.

The cause being debated by the church, some were earnest to have him excommunicated; but the most thought an admonition would be sufficient. Mr. Cotton opened the causes, which required excommunication, out of that in 1 Cor. 5.11. The point now in question was, whether these actions did declare him to be such a covetous person, etc. Upon which he showed, that it is neither the habit of covetousness, (which is in every man in some degree,) nor simply the act, that declares a man to be such, but when it appears, that a man sins against his conscience, or the very light of nature, and when it appears in a man's whole conversation. But Mr. Keaine did not appear to be such, but rather upon an error in his judgment, being led by false principles; and, beside, he is otherwise liberal, as in his hospitality, and in church communion, etc. So, in the end, the church consented to an admonition.

Upon this occasion a question grew, whether an admonition did bar a man from the sacrament, etc. Of this more shall be spoken hereafter.

## [*Speech on Liberty and Authority*] (1645) [4]

. . . The great questions that have troubled the country, are about the authority of the magistrates and the liberty of the people. It is yourselves who have called us to this office, and being called by you, we have our authority from God, in way of an ordinance, such as hath the image of God eminently stamped upon it, the contempt and viola-

[4] Before the General Court of Massachusetts, the lower house of which had impeached Winthrop for exceeding his magisterial authority. He was tried, acquitted, and reseated. He then "asked leave for a little speech, which was to this effect," as recorded in his *History of New England from 1630 to 1649*. II, 279–82. His opening remarks are here omitted.

tion whereof hath been vindicated with examples of divine vengeance. I entreat you to consider, that when you choose magistrates, you take them from among yourselves, men subject to like passions as you are. Therefore when you see infirmities in us, you should reflect upon your own, and that would make you bear the more with us, and not be severe censurers of the failings of your magistrates, when you have continual experience of the like infirmities in yourselves and others. We account him a good servant, who breaks not his covenant. The covenant between you and us is the oath you have taken of us, which is to this purpose, that we shall govern you and judge your causes by the rules of God's laws and our own, according to our best skill. When you agree with a workman to build you a ship or house, etc., he undertakes as well for his skill as for his faithfulness, for it is his profession, and you pay him for both. But when you call one to be a magistrate, he doth not profess nor undertake to have sufficient skill for that office, nor can you furnish him with gifts, etc., therefore you must run the hazard of his skill and ability. But if he fail in faithfulness, which by his oath he is bound unto, that he must answer for. If it fall out that the case be clear to common apprehension, and the rule clear also, if he transgress here, the error is not in the skill, but in the evil of the will: it must be required of him. But if the case be doubtful, or the rule doubtful, to men of such understanding and parts as your magistrates are, if your magistrates should err here, yourselves must bear it.

For the other point concerning liberty, I observe a great mistake in the country about that. There is a twofold liberty, natural (I mean as our nature is now corrupt) and civil or federal. The first is common to man with beasts and other creatures. By this, man, as he stands in relation to man simply, hath liberty to do what he lists; it is a liberty to evil as well as to good. This liberty is incompatible and inconsistent with authority, and cannot endure the least restraint of the most just authority. The exercise and maintaining of this liberty makes men grow more evil, and in time to be worse than brute beasts: *omnes sumus licentia deteriores*. This is that great enemy of truth and peace, that wild beast, which all the ordinances of God are bent against, to restrain and subdue it. The other kind of liberty I call civil or federal, it may also be termed moral, in reference to the covenant between God and man, in the moral law, and the politic covenants and constitutions, amongst men themselves. This liberty is the proper end and object of authority, and cannot subsist without it; and it is a liberty to that only which is good, just, and honest. This liberty you are to stand for, with the hazard (not only of your goods, but) of your lives, if need be. Whatsoever crosseth this, is not authority, but a distemper thereof. This liberty is maintained and exercised in a way of subjection to authority; it is of the same kind of liberty wherewith Christ hath made us free. The woman's own choice makes such a man her husband; yet being so chosen, he is her lord, and she is to be subject to him, yet in a way of liberty, not of bondage; and a true wife accounts her subjection her honor and freedom, and would not think her condition safe and free, but in her subjection to her husband's authority. Such is the liberty of the church under the authority of Christ, her king and husband; his yoke is so easy and sweet to her as a bride's ornaments; and if through frowardness or wantonness, etc., she shake it off, at any time, she is at no rest in her spirit, until she take it up again; and whether her lord smiles upon her, and embraceth her in his arms, or whether he frowns, or rebukes, or smites her, she apprehends the sweetness of his love in all, and is refreshed, supported, and instructed by every such dispensation of his authority over her. On the other side, ye know who they are that complain of this yoke and say, let us break their bands, etc., we will not have this man to rule over us. Even so, brethren, it will be between you and your magistrates. If you stand for your natural corrupt liberties, and will do what is good in your own eyes, you will not endure the least weight of authority, but will murmur, and oppose, and be always striving to shake off that yoke; but if you will be satisfied to enjoy such civil and lawful liberties, such as Christ allows you, then will you quietly and cheerfully submit unto that authority which is set over you, in all the administrations of it, for your good. Wherein, if we fail at any time, we hope we shall be willing (by God's assistance) to hearken to good advice from any of you, or in any other way of God; so shall your liberties be preserved, in upholding the honor and power of authority amongst you.

* * *

---

* * *

# ROGER WILLIAMS

1604–1683

## [*Theses*] (1644) [5]

Fifthly, All *Civill States* with their *Officers* of *justice* in their respective *constitutions* and *administrations* are proved *essentially Civill,* and therefore not *Judges, Governours* or *Defendours* of the *Spirituall* or *Christian state* and *Worship.*

. . . . .

Tenthly, An inforced *uniformity* of *Religion* throughout a *Nation* or *civill state,* confounds the *Civill* and *Religious,* denies the principles of Christianity and civility, and that *Jesus Christ* is come in the Flesh.

Eleventhly, The permission of other *consciences* and *worships* then a state professeth, only can (according to God) procure a firme and lasting *peace,* (good *assurance* being taken according to the *wisedome* of the *civill state* for *uniformity* of *civill obedience* from all sorts.)

Twelfthly, lastly, true *civility* and *Christianity* may both flourish in a *state* or *Kingdome,* notwithstanding the *permission* of divers and contrary *consciences,* either of *Iew* or *Gentile.*

## [*Civil Peace is Consistent with Religious Liberty*] (1644) [6]

The *Church* or *company* of *worshippers* (whether true or false) is like unto a Body or Colledge of *Physitians* in a *Citie;* like unto a *Corporation, Society,* or *Company* of *East-Indie* or *Turkie-Merchants,* or any other *Societie* or *Company* in *London:* which Companies may hold their *Courts,* keep their *Records,* hold *disputations;* and in matters concerning their *Societie,* may dissent, divide, breake into *Schismes* and *Factions,* sue and implead each other at the *Law,* yea wholly breake up and dissolve into pieces and nothing, and yet the *peace* of the *Citie* not be in the least measure impaired or disturbed; because the *essence* or being of the *Citie,* and so the *well-being* and *peace* thereof is essentially distinct from those particular *Societies;* the *Citie-Courts, Citie-Lawes, Citie-punishments* distinct from theirs. The *Citie* was before them, and stands absolute and intire, when such a *Corporation*

[5] *The Bloudy Tenent of Persecution,* in *Publications of the Narragansett Club* 3 (1867) 3–4.

[6] Ibid. 73–4.

or *Societie* is taken down. For instance further, The *City* or *Civill state* of *Ephesus* was essentially distinct from the *worship* of *Diana* in the Citie, or of the *whole city*. Againe, the *Church* of *Christ* in *Ephesus* (which were Gods people, converted and call'd out from the *worship* of that *City* unto *Christianitie* or *worship* of *God* in *Christ*) was distinct from both.

Now suppose that *God* remove the *Candlestick* from *Ephesus,* yea though the *whole Worship* of the *Citie of Ephesus* should be altered: yet (if men be true and honestly ingenuous to *Citie-covenants, Combinations* and *Principles*) all this might be without the least impeachment or infringement of the Peace of the *City* of *Ephesus.*

Thus in the Citie of *Smirna* was the Citie it selfe or Civill estate one thing, The Spirituall or Religious state of *Smirna,* another; The Church of *Christ* in *Smirna,* distinct from them both; and the *Synagogue* of the *Jewes* . . . distinct from all these. And notwithstanding these spirituall oppositions in point of *Worship* and *Religion,* yet heare we not the least noyse (nor need we, if Men keep but the Bond of *Civility*) of any *Civil breach,* or *breach* of *Civill peace* amongst them: and to persecute Gods people there for Religion, that only was a breach of Civilitie it selfe.

## [*State Control Means Control by Satan*] (1644) [7]

First, whereas they say, that the *Civill Power* may erect and establish what *forme* of *civill Government* may seeme in *wisedome* most meet, I acknowledge the *proposition* to be most true, both in it self, and also considered with the end of it, that a *civill Government* is an *Ordinance* of *God,* to conserve the *civill peace* of people, so farre as concernes their *Bodies* and *Goods,* as formerly hath beene said.

But from this *Grant* I infer, (as before hath been touched) that the *Soveraigne, originall,* and *foundation* of *civill power* lies in the *people,* (whom they must needs meane by the *civill power* distinct from the *Government* set up.) And if so, that a People may erect and establish what *forme* of *Government* seemes to them most meete for their *civill condition:* It is evident that such *Governments* as are by them erected and established, have no more *power,* nor for no longer time, then the *civill power* or people consenting and agreeing shall betrust them with. This is cleere not only in *Reason,* but in the experience of all *common-*

[7] Ibid. 249–50. "They" are "Mr. Cotton and the Ministers of New-England." See above, p. 17.

*weales,* where the people are not deprived of their *naturall freedome* by the power of *Tyrants.*

And if so, that the Magistrates receive their power of governing the Church, from the People; undeniably it followes, that a *people,* as a *people,* naturally considered (of what *Nature* or *Nation* soever in *Europe, Asia, Africa* or *America*) have fundamentally and originally, as men, a power to governe the *Church,* to see her doe her *duty,* to correct her, to redresse, reforme, establish, &c. And if this be not to pull *God* and *Christ,* and *Spirit* out of *Heaven,* and subject them unto *naturall,* sinfull, inconstant men, and so consequently to *Sathan* himselfe, by whom all *peoples* naturally are guided, let *Heaven* and *Earth* judge.

## [*Liberty of Conscience Has Limits*] (1655) [8]

That ever I should speak or write a tittle, that tends to such an infinite liberty of conscience, is a mistake, and which I have ever disclaimed and abhorred. To prevent such mistakes, I shall at present only propose this case: There goes many a ship to sea, with many hundred souls in one ship, whose weal or woe is common, and is a true picture of a commonwealth, or a human combination or society. It hath fallen out sometimes, that both papists and protestants, Jews, or Turks, may be embarked in one ship; upon which supposal I affirm, that all the liberty of conscience, that ever I pleaded for, turns upon these two hinges—that none of the papists, protestants, Jews, or Turks, be forced to come to the ship's prayers or worship, nor compelled from their own particular prayers or worship, if they practice any. I further add, that I never denied, that notwithstanding this liberty, the commander of this ship ought to command the ship's course, yea, and also command that justice, peace and sobriety, be kept and practiced, both among the seamen and all the passengers. If any of the seamen refuse to perform their services, or passengers to pay their freight; if any refuse to help, in person or purse, towards the common charges or defence; if any refuse to obey the common laws and orders of the

[8] A letter to the town of Providence, which he had found threatened with anarchy on his return from England in 1654. This is Williams's reply, as "President," to a circular by William Harris, chronic agitator, arguing "That it is blood-guiltiness and against the rule of the Gospel to execute judgment upon transgressions against the private and public weal." Harris was not silenced; next year he was still maintaining "that he that can say it is his conscience, ought not to yield subjection to any human order among men." The text of Williams's letter is taken from *Publications of the Narragansett Club* 6 (1874) 278–9.

ship, concerning their common peace or preservation; if any shall mutiny and rise up against their commanders and officers; if any should preach or write that there ought to be no commanders or officers, because all are equal in Christ, therefore no masters nor officers, no laws nor orders, nor corrections nor punishments;—I say, I never denied, but in such cases, whatever is pretended, the commander or commanders may judge, resist, compel and punish such transgressors, according to their deserts and merits. This if seriously and honestly minded, may, if it so please the Father of lights, let in some light to such as willingly shut not their eyes.

* * *

---

* * *

## A MASTER'S *QUAESTIO* (1664) [9]

### [*The World's Eternity Is an Impossibility*]

Impious, Blasphemous, and detractive from the transcendent excellency of the Divine Majesty, have been the bold assertions of men unacquainted with, and unguided by the Spirit or Truth of him who is *Amen, the God of Truth.* Among other their malepert and audicious attempts, they endeavour to enthrone the *World* with the *Antient of Dayes,* to extend a Minute to Eternity, and coequalize a point with him *cujus centrum est ubique et circumferentia nullibi?* Affirming some that *the World was,* others that *the World could be from Eternity.* Which beside the many Scriptural demonstrations founded upon the αὐτὸς ἔφη of Truth itself, Reason presuming none so unreasonable as to maintain the *former,* presents the World with these Arguments to disprove the *latter,* drawn from these four *Topicks:* 1. *A parte creantis.* 2. *A parte creaturae.* 3. *A Natura creationis.* 4. *A Natura Aeternitatis.*

1. *A parte creantis,* because God could not produce by creation, or an external act, a Being coeternal with himself; not to imply any

[9] Apparently a translation of Joseph Whiting's argument on the *quaestio "Utrum Mundus potuerit creari ab Aeterno"* at Harvard commencement, 1664. Printed in Flint, Josiah: *An Almanack or, Astronomical Calculations for the Ensuing Year 1666.* Cambridge, Mass., 1666. Reprinted with notes and comment in Morison: *Harvard in the Seventeenth Century.* I, 277–9. By permission of Harvard University Press.

impotency in the Omnipotent, but rather to express his Infinite perfection, whose perfect Nature admits of no jarring contradictions: nor hath he made *impossibilities* the object of his power. For that an efficient should extrinsecally produce *another entity* contemporary, much more coeternal with it self, implies a contradiction.

2. *A parte creaturae,* though Reason nor Religion will not permit the least *Iota* of detraction from the Almighty, who is *Jehovah,* giving Being to all things, to assert that his Infinite power is not eternal and unchangeable, which is *Deus potens, aeternus et immutabilis:* Yet 'tis true and certain, the *Creature,* or rather *Nothing,* which was its first Principle, could not admit a possibility of Being from Eternity; (*In esse subjectivo non objectivo*) for the *Divine Idea* (If I speak in the dialect of some learned and pious) being God contemplating himself as imitable in the creatures fabrick, or as it were capable to receive the impression of the *Image* or *Vestigium* of those divine perfections which were in himself; it follows that whatever perfection was eminently in God, and the creature was Analogically capable of, was according to divine wisedome expressed (for otherwise the *Idea* or *Exemplar* would not have been consentaneous to the τὸ πραττόμενον. But Eternity not being communicated to any created Being, implies that it is no communicable property, so that though we grant *Potentia, Conveniens in Deo,* to be a creator from eternity, yet the incommunicability of Eternity to the subject, inferrs an impossibility of its external existence.

3. *A Natura creationis,* then creation would not be distinguished from providential conservation, *a creature* might be *ens et non ens* created, and preserved, in the same moment. *Nam creatio ponit non presupponit objectum sed conservatio praesupponit non ponit subjectum.*

4. *A natura Aeternitatis.* For Eternity admits no parenthesis of time, *Aeternitas est interminabilis existentiae possessio.* So that to make the World Eternal is to assert it cosubstantial with *ens primum,* to call the creature Creator, to confound the Truth in contradictions and to give the effect one of the incommunicable properties of its Cause.

* * *

---

* * *

## URIAN OAKES

1631–1681

### *The Soveraign Efficacy of Divine Providence*
(1677) [10]

Prop. 6. *The great God hath the absolute and infallible Determination of the Successes and Events of all the Operations & Undertakings of created Agents & Second Causes, in his own Power.* His Counsel and soveraign Will appoints what they shall be, and his Providence (which is not determined by any Second Cause: but is the Determiner of them all) Executes accordingly. And it must needs be so, if you consider these two Particulars,

I. *God is the Absolute First Cause, and Supream Lord of all.* Of Him, and to Him, and through Him are all Things, *Rom.* 11.36. He that understands any thing of God indeed, knows this to be a Truth. Here we might be large; as they that are acquainted with the Doctrine of *Creation* and *Providence,* in *Conservation* and *Gubernation* of all Things, will readily apprehend: for here we might shew you, 1. That God is the absolute first Cause of all the causal power and virtue that is in Creatures. He gives them power to act, furnisheth them with a Sufficiency for their Operations. He gives Swiftness to the Runner; Skill, and Strength, and Courage to the Souldier. 2. That He supports, and continues the active power of the creature. He continues Swiftness, Wisdom, Strength, Courage, as He pleaseth. If He withdraw, all is gone. The Swift is lame, or slow-footed, the Strong is weak & timorous, the Wise is foolish and besotted, the man of Skill, is a meer Bungler at any thing. 3. That He doth by a *previous Influx* excite and stirre up, and actuate the active power of the Creature, and set all the wheels agoing. For the most operative, active created Virtue, is not a *pure Act:* but hath some *Potentiality* mixed with it; and therefore cannot put forth it self into Action, unless it be set agoing by the *first Cause.* And the creature cannot be the absolute *first Cause* of any *physical action.* In Him we live, and move, *Act.* 17.28. Again. 4. That He determines and applyes Second Causes to the Objects of their Actions. When they stand, as it were, *in Bivio,* as it is said of *Nebuchadnezzar,* when he was marching with his Army He *stood at the parting of the way, at the head of the two wayes, to use*

[10] Artillery Election Sermon at Cambridge, September 10, 1677. Printed in Boston, 1682. 15–20.

*Divination,* as doubting which way he had best to march; whether to *Jerusalem,* or some other way, *Ezek.* 21.21, 22. Then the Lord casts the Scale and the Lot, & determines them this way, and not another. He doth not only stir up Second Causes to act at large, and set them agoing, and leave it to their own Inclination, whither they shall go, & what they shall do: but He leads them forth, and determines them to this, or that Object. 5. That He *cooperates,* and workes *jointly* with Second Causes, in producing their Effects. As He *predetermins* Second Causes, so He *concurres* with them in their Operations. And this *Praedetermination,* and *Concurse* is so necessary; that there can be no real Effect produced by the Creature without it. And it is a Truth also, that when God Improves Second Causes for the production of any Effect, He so concurres with them, that He doth withall most immediately, intimously, and without Dependence upon these Causes by which He acts, produce the *Entity,* or *Esse* of the Effect. If this be considered, it will appear that created Agents, are as it were, God's Instruments, that act as they are acted by Him; and cannot move of themselves. The busy, bustling, proud *Assyrian* was so, *Is.* 10.15. 6. *That all the Ataxy, Disorder, Irregularity, moral Evil that is found in the Actions of Rational Agents, is by His Permission.* If it were not the Pleasure of God to permit it, no Sin should be in the World, nor in the Actions of Men. Though there is no *Legal* Permission, or allowance of it; (for the Law of God forbids it) yet there is a *Providential* Permission of it. God could have kept it out of his World. 7. *That He limits and sets Bounds to the Actions of Second Causes: what they shall do, and how farre they shall proceed in this or that way.* He set bounds to Satan, when he had Commission to afflict *Job.* He limits, and restrains the Eruptions of the Wrath & Rage of the Churches Adversaries, *Ps.* 76.10. He sets bounds to the sinfull Actions of Men: He regulates and governs all the Actions of Second Causes, as to time, place, degrees, and all manner of Circumstances. He is not the *Author:* but He is the *Orderer* of Sin it self. 8. *That He serves Himself, and his own Ends of all Second Causes.* He makes them all in all their Operations subservient to his own Designs: and that not only natural, but rational Agents, that act by Counsel. And not only such of them as are his professed willing Servants. Many serve God's ends beside their Intentions, and against their wills. I will do this and that saith God, by the *Assyrian, howbeit he meaneth not so,* Is. 10.6, 7. Wicked men and Devils do God's will against their own will, and beside their Intentions. *Ye thougt Evil against me* (saith *Joseph* to his Brethren) *but God meant it for good &c.* Gen. 50.20. God elicites what good He pleases out of the actions of his Creatures. Whatever this or that Agent proposeth to himself, yet God alwayes attaineth His Ends. He serves Himself of the very Sins of his Creatures, and brings good out of them. He makes that which is not *Bonum honestum,* to be *Bonum conducibile:* and though Sin is not good; yet, as God orders the matter, it is good, in order to many holy Ends, that Sin should be in the World, as *Austin observes.* 9. *That He useth means in themselves* unfit, *and improves Agents of themselves* insufficient, *to bring about his own Purposes & produce marveilous Effects.* Yea, and it is as easy with Him to do any thing by weak and insufficient, as by the ablest & most accomplished Instruments. *There is no restraint to the Lord to Save by many, or by few.* 1 Sam. 14.6. *It is nothing with Him to help, whether with many, or with them that have no power.* 2. Chron. 14.11. Despicable Instruments, sometimes, do great Things in His Hand. 10. *That He renders the aptest means ineffectual, and the Undertakings of the most sufficient Agents unsuccessful, when He pleases.* He hath a *Negative Voice* upon all the Counsels and Endeavours, and Active Power of the Creature. He can stop the Sun in its course, and cause it to withdraw its shining; He can give check to the Fire, that it shall not burn; & to the hungry Lions, that they shall not devour: and He can order it so, that the men of might shall *sleep their sleep, and not find their Hands.* He can break the Ranks of the most orderly Souldiers, take away courage from the stoutest hearts, send a pannick Fear into a mighty Host, and defeat the Counsels of the wisest Leaders and Conducters. He can blow upon, and blast the likeliest Undertakings of the ablest Men. In a word: the Lord being the Absolute First Cause, and supream Governour of all his Creatures, and all their Actions; though He hath set an Order among his Creatures, this shall be the cause of that effect, &c. yet He himself is not tied to that Order; but Interrupts the course of it, when He pleases. The Lord reserves a Liberty to Himself to interpose, and to Umpire matters of Success and Event, contrary to the Law and common Rule of Second Causes. And though He ordinarily concurreth with Second Causes according to the Law given and Order set; yet sometimes there is in his Providence a Variation and Digression. Though He hath given Creatures power to act; and Man, to act as *a Cause by Counsel,* and hath furnished him with active Abilities; yet He hath not made any Creature *Master of Events;* but reserves the Disposal of Issues, and Events to Himself. Herein the absolute Soveraignty and Dominion of God appears.

II. *Otherwise, the Lord might possibly suffer real Disappointment, and be defeated of his Ends in some Instances.* He might be cross'd in his Designs, if any of his Creatures could doe what they will, without absolute Dependence upon Him. He could not be sure of his Ends, & what He designs in the World, if He had not command of all Events that may further or hinder them. If there were any active power in Creatures that He cannot controll; or any one event that is out of his Reach, and absolutely in the Creature's power, exempted from his providential Command, it would be possible that He might be defeated of his Ends, and so far unhappy, as to his *voluntary Happiness,* which results from his having his *Pleasure done* in the World, and compassing all his Ends in the works of Creation and Providence. God hath made all Things, ruleth all Things, and manageth all Things according to the Counsel of his Will, in a way of subserviency to Himself, and his own Occasions: which He could not do universally and infrustrably, if He had not the absolute and infallible Determination of all Events in his own Hand. *But His Counsel shall stand, and He will do all his Pleasure:* Is. 46.10.

* * *

---

* * *

## JOHN WISE

1652–1725

### [*Principles of Civil Knowledge*] (1717) [11]

### [IMMUNITIES OF MAN IN A STATE OF NATURAL BEING]

I

The prime immunity in Man's State, is that he is most properly the Subject of the Law of Nature. . . . That which is to be drawn from

[11] *A Vindication of the Government of New England Churches.* Boston, 1717. 34–50. Against current threats to the autonomy of local congregations, Wise justifies the congregational form of church government as settled by the Cambridge Platform (1649). His book is divided into five "Demonstrations": (I) from the practice of the first three Christian centuries; (II) from the Light of Nature; (III) from Holy Scripture; (IV) from the Noble and Excellent Nature of the Constitution itself; (V) from the dignity which the providence of God has put upon it, in the first three centuries, and in seventeenth century New England. The second demonstration first deduces

Man's Reason, following from the true Current of that Faculty, when unperverted, may be said to be the Law of Nature. . . . So that the meaning is, when we acknowledge the Law of Nature to be the dictate of Right Reason, we must mean that the Understanding of Man is endowed with such a power, as to be able, from the contemplation of Humane Condition to discover a necessity of Living agreeably with this Law; and likewise to find out some Principle, by which the Precepts of it may be clearly and so solidly Demonstrated. The way to discover the Law of Nature in our own state, is by a narrow Watch, and accurate Contemplation of our Natural Condition and propensions. . . .

. . . Man is a Creature extremely desirous of his own Preservation; of himself he is plainly Exposed to many Wants, unable to secure his own safety and Maintenance without Assistance of his fellows; and he is also able of returning Kindness by the furtherance of mutual Good; but yet Man is often found to be Malicious, Insolent, and easily Provoked, and as powerful in Effecting mischief as he is ready in designing it. Now that such a Creature may be Preserved, it is necessary that he be Sociable; that is, that he be capable and disposed to unite himself to those of his own species, and to Regulate himself towards them, that they may have no fair Reason to do him harm; but rather incline to promote his Interests, and secure his Rights and Concerns. This then is a fundamental law of nature, that every man as far as in him lies, do maintain a Sociableness with others, agreeable with the main end and disposition of humane Nature in general. For this is very apparent, that Reason and Society render Man the most potent of all Creatures. And Finally, from the principles of sociableness it follows as a fundamental Law of Nature, that man is not so wedded to his own Interest, but that he can make the Common good the mark of his aim; and hence he becomes Capacitated to enter into a Civil State by the Law of Nature; for without this property in Nature, viz. Sociableness, which is for Cementing of parts, every Government would soon moulder and dissolve.

## II

The Second Great Immunity of Man is an Original Liberty Instampt upon his Rational Nature. He that intrudes upon this Liberty,

---

"the principles of civil knowledge" from the law of nature, and then applies them to ecclesiastical affairs. The selections here printed are taken from the first part of this demonstration.

Violates the Law of Nature. In this Discourse I shall wave the Consideration of Mans Moral Turpitude but shall view him Physically as a Creature which God has made and furnished essentially with many Ennobling Immunities, which render him the most August Animal in the World, and still, whatever has happened since his Creation, he remains at the upper-end of Nature, and as such is a Creature of a very Noble Character. For as to his dominion, the whole frame of the Lower Part of the Universe is devoted to his use, and at his Command; and his Liberty under the Conduct of Right Reason is equal with his trust. Which Liberty may be briefly Considered, Internally as to his Mind, and Externally as to his Person.

1. The Internal Native Liberty of Man's Nature in general implies, a faculty of Doing or Omitting things according to the Direction of his Judgment. But in a more special meaning, this Liberty does not consist in a loose and ungovernable Freedom, or in an unbounded License of Acting. Such License is disagreeing with the condition and dignity of Man, and would make Man of a lower and meaner Constitution than Bruit Creatures; who in all their Liberties are kept under a better and more Rational Government by their Instincts. Therefore, as Plutarch says, *Those persons only who live in Obedience to Reason, are worthy to be accounted free: They alone live as they Will, who have learnt what they ought to Will.* So that the True Natural Liberty of man, such as really and truly agrees to him must be understood, as he is Guided and Restrained by the Tyes of Reason and Laws of Nature; all the rest is Brutal, if not worse.

2. Man's External Personal, Natural Liberty, antecedent to all Human parts or Alliances, must also be considered. And so every Man must be conceived to be perfectly in his own Power and disposal, and not to be controuled by the Authority of any other. And thus every Man must be acknowledged equal to every Man, since all Subjection and all Command are equally banished on both sides; and considering all Men thus at Liberty, every Man has a Prerogative to Judge for himself, *viz.* What shall be most for his Behoof, Happiness, and Well-being.

## III

The Third Capital Immunity belonging to Man's Nature, is an equality amongst Men; Which is not to be denyed by the Law of Nature, till Man has Resigned himself with all his Rights for the sake of a Civil State; and then his Personal Liberty and Equality is to be cherished and preserved to the highest degree, as will consist with all just distinctions amongst Men of Honor, and shall be agreeable with the publick Good. . . .

. . . And though as *Hensius* paraphrases upon *Aristotle's* Politicks to this Purpose, *viz. Nothing is more suitable to Nature, than that those who Excel in Understanding and Prudence, should Rule and Controul those who are less happy in those Advantages,* &c. Yet we must note, that there is room for an answer, scil. That it would be the greatest absurdity to believe, that Nature actually Invests the Wise with a Sovereignty over the weak; or with a Right of forcing them against their Wills; for that no Sovereignty can be Established, unless some Human Deed or Covenant Precede: Nor does natural fitness for government make a man presently governor over another; for that as *Ulpian* says, *by a natural right all men are born free;* and Nature having set all Men upon a level and made them equals, no servitude or subjection can be conceived without Inequality; and this cannot be made without Usurpation or Force in Others, or voluntary Compliance in those who resign their Freedom, and give away their degree of Natural Being.

## [TRANSITION FROM A NATURAL TO A CIVIL STATE]

. . . in the latter State many great Disproportions appear, or at least many obvious Distinctions are soon made amongst men, which Doctrine is to be laid open under a few heads.

### I

Every man, considered in a Natural State, must be allowed to be Free and at his Own Dispose; yet to suit mans inclinations to Society, and in a peculiar manner to gratify the Necessity he is in of Public Rule and Order, he is impelled to enter into a Civil Community; and divests himself of his Natural Freedom, and puts himself under Government, which, Amongst other things, comprehends the power of Life and Death over him, together with Authority to Injoyn him some things to which he has an Utter Aversation, and to prohibit him other things for which he may have as strong an inclination; so that he may be often, under this authority, obliged to sacrifice his Private for the Public Good. So that though Man is inclined to Society, yet he is driven to a Combination by Great Necessity. For that the true and leading cause of Forming Governments and yielding up Natural Liberty, and throwing man's Equality into a Common Pile to be new cast by the rules of Fellowship, was really and truly to Guard themselves against the Injuries men were liable to interchangeably; for none so good to Man as Man, and yet none a Greater Enemy. So that,

II

The first Humane Subject and Original of Civil Power is the People. For as they have a Power every man over himself in a Natural State, so upon a Combination they can and do bequeath this power unto Others; and settle it according as their United Discretion shall Determine. For that this is very plain, that when the Subject of Sovereign Power is quite extinct, that Power returns to the People again. And when they are free, they may set up what Species of Government they please; or if they rather incline to it, they may subside into a State of Natural Being, if it be plainly for the best. . . .

III

The formal Reason of Government is the Will of a Community yielded up and surrendered to some other Subject, either of one particular Person or more, Conveyed in the following manner.

Let us conceive in our Mind a multitude of Men, all Naturally Free and Equal; going about voluntarily to Erect themselves into a new Common-wealth. Now their Condition being such, to bring themselves into a Politick Body they must needs Enter into divers Covenants.

1. They must Interchangeably each Man Covenant to joyn in one lasting Society, that they may be capable to concert the measures of their safety, by a Publick Vote.

2. A Vote or Decree must then nextly pass to set up some particular species of Government over them. And if they are Joyned in their first Compact upon absolute Terms to stand to the Decision of the first Vote concerning the Species of Government: Then all are bound by the Majority to acquiesce in that Particular Form thereby settled, though their own private Opinion incline them to some other Model.

3. After a decree has specified the Particular form of Government, then there will be need of a New Covenant, whereby those on whom Sovereignty is conferred, engage to take care of the Common Peace and Welfare. And the Subjects on the other hand, to yield them faithful Obedience. In which covenant is Included that Submission and Union of Wills, by which a State may be conceived to be but one Person. So that the most proper Definition of a Civil State, is this, viz. A Civil State is a Compound Moral Person, whose Will (united by those covenants before passed) is the Will of all; to the end it may Use and

Apply the strength and riches of Private Persons towards maintaining the Common Peace, Security, and Well-being of all. Which may be conceived as though the whole State was now become but one Man; in which the aforesaid Convenants may be supposed under God's providence to be the Divine *Fiat,* Pronounced by God, let us make man. . . .

## THE FORMS OF A REGULAR STATE

are three only, which Forms arise from the proper and particular Subject in which the Supream Power Resides. As,

### I

A Democracy, which is when the Sovereign Power is Lodged in a Council consisting of all the Members, and where every member has the Priviledge of a Vote. This Form of Government appears in the greatest part of the World to have been the most Ancient. For that Reason seems to shew it to be the most probable, that when Men (being Originally in a condition of Natural Freedom and Equality) had thoughts of joyning in a Civil Body, would without question be inclined to Administer their common affairs by their common Judgment, and so must necessarily to gratify that Inclination establish a Democracy; neither can it be rationally imagined that Fathers of Families, being yet Free and Independent, should in a moment or little time take off their long delight in governing their own Affairs, & Devolve all upon some single Sovereign Commander; for that it seems to have been thought more Equitable that what belonged to all should be managed by all, when all had entered by Compact into one Community. . . .

A democracy is then Erected, when a Number of Free Persons do Assemble together in Order to enter into a Covenant for Uniting themselves in a Body: And such a Preparative Assembly hath some appearance already of a Democracy; it is a Democracy in *Embrio,* properly in this Respect, that every Man hath the Privilege freely to deliver his Opinion concerning the Common Affairs. Yet he who dissents from the Vote of the Majority is not in the least obliged by what they determine, till by a second Covenant a Popular Form be actually Established; for not before then can we call it a Democratical Government, *viz.* Till the right of determining all matters relating to the publick Safety is actually placed in a General Assembly of the whole People; or by their own Compact and Mutual Agreement,

Determine themselves the proper Subject for the Exercise of Sovereign Power. And to compleat this State, and render it capable to Exert its Power to answer the End of a Civil State; These Conditions are necessary.

1. That a certain Time and Place be assigned for Assembling.

2. That when the Assembly be orderly met, as to Time and Place, that then the Vote of the Majority must pass for the Vote of the whole Body.

3. That Magistrates be appointed to Exercise the Authority of the whole for the better dispatch of Business, of every day's Occurrence; who also may with more Mature diligence, search into more Important Affairs; and if in case any thing happens of greater Consequence, may report it to the Assembly; and be peculiarly Serviceable in putting all Publick Decrees into Execution, Because a large Body of People is almost useless in Respect of the last Service, and of many others as to the more Particular Application and Exercise of Power. Therefore it is most agreeable with the Law of Nature, that they Institute their Officers to act in their Name, and Stead.

II

The second Species of Regular Government, is an Aristocracy, and this is said then to be Constituted when the People or Assembly, United by a first Covenant, and having thereby cast themselves into the first rudiments of a State; do then by Common Decree, Devolve the Sovereign Power, on a Council consisting of some Select Members; and these having accepted of the Designation, are then properly invested with Sovereign Command; and then an Aristocracy is formed.

III

The Third Species of a Regular Government, is a Monarchy, which is settled when the Sovereign Power is conferred on some one worthy Person. It differs from the former, because a Monarch, who is but one Person in Natural as well as in Moral Account, & so is furnished with an Immediate Power of Exercising Sovereign Command in all Instances of Government; but the fore named must needs have Particular Time and Place assigned; but the Power and Authority is Equal in each.[12]

[12] Wise concludes with a paragraph on mixed governments, of which "possibly the fairest in the World is that which has a Regular Monarchy, (in Distinction to what is Despotick) settled upon a Noble Democracy as its Basis."—Editor's note.

* * *

---

* * *

## JONATHAN MAYHEW

1720–1766

### [*The Right of Revolution*] (1750) [13]

We may very safely assert these two things in general, without undermining government: One is, that no civil rulers are to be obeyed when they enjoin things that are inconsistent with the commands of God. All such disobedience is lawful and glorious; particularly if persons refuse to comply with any *legal establishment of religion,* because it is a gross perversion and corruption—as to doctrine, worship, and discipline—of a pure and divine religion, brought from heaven to earth by the Son of God,—the only King and Head of the Christian church,—and propagated through the world by his inspired apostles. All commands running counter to the declared will of the Supreme Legislator of heaven and earth are null and void, and therefore disobedience to them is a duty, not a crime. Another thing that may be asserted with equal truth and safety is, that no government is to be submitted to at the expense of that which is the sole end of all government—the common good and safety of society. Because, to submit in this case, if it should ever happen, would evidently be to set up the means as more valuable and above the end, than which there cannot be a greater solecism and contradiction. The only reason of the institution of civil government, and the only rational ground of submission to it, is the common safety and utility. If, therefore, in any case, the common safety and utility would not be promoted by submission to government, but the contrary, there is no ground or motive for obedience and submission, but for the contrary.

Whoever considers the nature of civil government, must indeed be sensible that a great degree of implicit confidence must unavoidably be placed in those that bear rule: this is implied in the very notion of authority's being originally a trust committed by the people to

[13] *A Discourse concerning Unlimited Submission and Non-Resistance to the Higher Powers.* Boston, 1750. This selection appears as a footnote on pp. 86–7 of the reprint in Thornton, J. Wingate: *The Pulpit of the American Revolution.* Boston, 1860.

those who are vested with it,—as all just and righteous authority is. All besides is mere lawless force and usurpation; neither God nor nature having given any man a right of dominion over any society independently of that society's approbation and consent to be governed by him. Now, as all men are fallible, it cannot be supposed that the public affairs of any state should be always administered in the best manner possible, even by persons of the greatest wisdom and integrity. Nor is it sufficient to legitimate disobedience to the higher powers that they are not so administered, or that they are in some instances very ill-managed; for, upon this principle, it is scarcely supposable that any government at all could be supported, or subsist. Such a principle manifestly tends to the dissolution of government, and to throw all things into confusion and anarchy. But it is equally evident, upon the other hand, that those in authority may abuse their trust and power to such a degree, that neither the law of reason nor of religion requires that any obedience or submission should be paid to them; but, on the contrary, that they should be totally discarded, and the authority which they were before vested with transferred to others, who may exercise it more to those good purposes for which it is given. Nor is this principle, that resistance to the higher powers is in some extraordinary cases justifiable, so liable to abuse as many persons seem to apprehend it. For, although there will be always some petulant, querulous men in every state,—men of factious, turbulent, and carping dispositions, glad to lay hold of any trifle to justify and legitimate their caballing against their rulers, and other seditious practices,—yet there are, comparatively speaking, but few men of this contemptible character. It does not appear but that mankind in general have a disposition to be as submissive and passive and tame under government as they ought to be. Witness a great, if not the greatest, part of the known world, who are now groaning, but not murmuring, under the heavy yoke of tyranny! While those who govern do it with any tolerable degree of moderation and justice, and in any good measure act up to their office and character by being public benefactors, the people will generally be easy and peaceable, and be rather inclined to flatter and adore than to insult and resist them. Nor was there ever any *general* complaint against any administration, which lasted long, but what there was good reason for. Till people find themselves greatly abused and oppressed by their governors, they are not apt to complain; and whenever they do, in fact, find themselves thus abused and oppressed, they must be stupid *not* to complain. To say that subjects in general are not proper judges when their governors oppress them and play the tyrant, and when they defend their rights, administer justice impartially, and promote the public welfare, is as great treason as ever man uttered. 'T is treason, not against one *single* man, but the state—against the whole body politic; 't is treason against mankind, 't is treason against common sense, 't is treason against God. And this impious principle lays the foundation for justifying all the tyranny and oppression that ever any prince was guilty of. The people know for what end they set up and maintain their governors, and they are the proper judges when they execute their trust as they ought to do it;—when their prince exercises an equitable and paternal authority over them; when from a prince and common father he exalts himself into a tyrant; when from subjects and children he degrades them into the class of slaves, plunders them, makes them his prey, and unnaturally sports himself with their lives and fortunes.

* * *

---

* * *

## JOHN WOOLMAN

1720–1772

### *A Plea for the Poor* (1763) [14]

While our minds are prepossessed in favour of Customs distinguishable from perfect purity, we are in danger of not attending with singleness to that Light which opens to our view the nature of Universal Righteousness.

In the affairs of a thick setled Country are variety of Useful Employments, besides tilling the Earth: that for some men to have no more Land than is necessary to build on, and to answer the Ocasions relative to the Family may consist with Brotherhood: & from the various gifts which God hath bestowed on those employ'd in Husbandry, for some to possess, & occupy much more than others, may

[14] Ch. 13 of a tract written under this title in 1763 but first published in 1793 under the title *A Word of Remembrance and Caution to the Rich.* Taken from Gummere, Amelia M. (editor): *The Journal and Essays of John Woolman.* New York, 1922. 424–7. By permission of The Macmillan Company, publishers. Cf. the abridged reprint in Fabian Society Tract No. 79, 1897, in the introduction to which Woolman was called "the John the Baptist of the Gospel of Socialism."

likewise. But where any on the Strength of their possessions, demand such Rent or Interest as necessitates those who hire of them, to a closer Application to business than our Merciful Father designed for us, this puts the wheels of perfect brotherhood out of order, and leads to employments, the promoting of which belongs not to the Family of Christ, Whose Example in all part, being a pattern of wisdom, so the Plainness & Simplicity of his outward appearance, may well make us ashamed to Adorn our Bodies in costly Array, or treasure up Wealth by the least Opression.

The Soyl yields us Support, and is profitable for man; & though some possessing a larger share of these profits than others, may consist with the Harmony of true Brotherhood, yet that the poorest people who are Honest, so long as they remain Inhabitants of the Earth are entitled to a certain portion of these profits, in as clear & absolute a sense as those who Inherit much, I believe will be agreed to by those whose hearts are Enlarged with Universal Love.

The first people who Inhabited the Earth, were the first who had possession of the Soyl. The Gracious Creator & Owner of it, gave the Fruits thereof for their Use. And as one generation passed away, another came & took possession, and thus through many Ages, Innumerable multitudes of people have been supplied by the Fruits of the Earth. But our Gracious Creator is as absolutely the owner of it as he was when he first formed it out of nothing, before man had possession of it. And though by Claims grounded on prior possession great inequality appears amongst men, yet the instructions of the Great Proprietor of the Earth, are necessary to be attended to in all our proceedings, as possessors or Claimers of the profits of Soyl. The steps of a good man are ordered of the Lord and those who are thus guided, whose hearts are enlarged in his Love, give directions concerning their possessions agreeably thereto; and that Claim which stands on Universal Righteousness is a good Right, but the Continuance of that Right depends on properly applying the profits thereof.

The word *Right,* is commonly used relative to our possessions. We say, a *Right* of propriety to such a Dividend of a Province; or a clear indisputable *Right* to the Land within such certain Bounds. Thus this word is continued as a remembrancer of the Original intent of Dividing the Land by Boundaries, and implies, that it was designed to be Equitably or Rightly divided: to be divided according to Righteousness. In this, that is, in Equity and Righteousness, consists the Strength of our Claims. If we trace an Unrighteous claim, & find gifts or Grants to be proved by sufficient seals & Witnesses, this gives not the Claimant a *Right:* for that which is Oposite to Righteousness is wrong, and the nature of it must be changed before it can be *Right.*

Suppose twenty free men professed followers of Christ, discovered an Island unknown to all other people, and that they with their Wives, Independent of all others took possession of it, and dividing it Equitably made Improvements, & Multiplied. Suppose these first possessors, being generally Influenced by true Love, did with paternal regard look over the increasing condition of the Inhabitants, and near the end of their lives, gave such directions concerning their respective possessions, as best suited the convenience of the whole, and tended to preserve Love & Harmony, & that their successors in the continued increase of people, generally followed their Pious examples, and pursued means the most effectual to keep Oppression out of their Island: But that one of these first settlers, from a fond attachment to one of his numerous Sons, no more deserving than the rest, gives the chief of his Lands to him, and by an Instrument sufficiently witnessed, strongly expresses his mind and Will.

Suppose this Son being Landlord to his Brethren & Nephews, demands such a portion of the Fruits of the Earth, as may supply him & his Family and some others; and that these others, thus supplied out of his Store, are Employed in adorning his Buildings with curious Engravings and Paintings, preparing Carriages to ride in, Vessels for his House, Delicious Meats, fine-wrought Apparel & Furniture, all suiting that distinction lately arisen between him & the other Inhabitants, And that, having the absolute disposal of these numerous Improvements, his Power so increaseth, that in all conferences relative to the publick Affairs of the Island, these plain, Honest men who are Zealous for Equitable Establishments, find great difficulty in proceeding agreeably to their Righteous Inclinations, while he stands in Oposition to them.

Suppose he from a fondness for one of his Sons, joyned with a desire to continue this Grandeur under his own name, confirms chief of his possessions to him, and thus, for many Ages, on near a twentieth part of this Island, there is one great Landlord, and the rest, poor Oppressed people; To some of whom, from the manner of their Education, joyned with a notion of the greatness of their predecessors, Labour is disagreeable; who therefore, by artful applications to the weakness, unguardedness, and Corruption of others, in striving to get a living out of them, increase the difficulties amongst them; while the Inhabitants of other parts, who guard against Oppression, and with one Consent train up their Children in plainness, frugality and useful labour, live more harmonious.

If we trace the claim of the ninth or tenth of these great landlords down to the first possessor, & find the Claim supported throughout by Instruments strongly drawn and witnessed, after all we could not admit a belief into our Hearts that he had a *Right* to so great a portion of Land, after such a numerous increase of Inhabitants.

The first possessor of that twentieth part, held no more we suppose than an Equitable portion; but when the Lord, who first gave these twenty men possession of this Island, unknown to all others, gave being to numerous people, who Inhabited this twentieth part, whose natures required the Fruits thereof for their sustenance, this Great Claimer of the Soyl could not have a *Right* to the whole, to dispose of it in gratifying his irregular desires: but they, as Creatures of the Most High God, possessor of Heaven & Earth, had a *Right* to part of what this Great Claimer held, though they had no Instruments to confirm their *Right*.

Thus Oppression in the extreme appears terrible: but oppression in more refined appearances, remains to be Oppression; and where the smallest degree of it is cherished it grows stronger and more extensive: that to labour for a perfect redemption from this spirit of Oppression, is the Great Business of the whole family of Christ Jesus in this world.

# III

## Samuel Johnson

1696–1772

Born in Guilford, Conn. A.B., Collegiate School at Saybrook (Yale), 1714; tutor at Guilford, 1715; at New Haven, 1716–20; A.M., 1717. Minister at West Haven, 1720–22. Went to England to take orders in the Church of England, 1722, and received M.A. from Oxford and Cambridge. Missionary of the Church of England at Stratford, Conn., 1723–54. Philosophical correspondence with Berkeley, 1729–30. Oxford, D.D., 1743. Correspondence with Colden, 1744–53. Declined Franklin's invitation to head College of Philadelphia (University of Pennsylvania), 1752. President of King's College (Columbia University), 1754–63. Again minister at Stratford from 1764 until his death.

Johnson may almost be said to have been a philosopher of one book, drafted in his senior year at college, recast, expanded and radically revised over a period of forty years, brought to completion and published in 1752, and subjected to further though minor revisions through the remaining twenty years of his life. It was a textbook, and breathed the spirit of perhaps the most pedagogically-minded of all American philosophers before W. T. Harris. The first drafts evidenced his mastery of the scholastic system it had taken him four years to absorb; a little later they grew out of his work as college tutor; in his middle years they were intended for the use of his sons; then for textbook use in the rising colleges of the middle colonies; and finally for his grandsons. Though his college teaching was confined to two short periods, one as tutor at Yale, the other, after an interval of thirty-five years, as President of King's College, he could write to Franklin in 1752 that in the preceding thirty-eight years he had seldom been without pupils of one sort or another, and then never for more than half a year at a time. He gave early Yale its first injection of modern thought; he influenced the plans for the College of Philadelphia; he was the founder and first president of King's College; and his son, William Samuel Johnson, was the first president of Columbia College, its successor after the Revolution.

The successive drafts of his textbook reflected the influences under which Johnson's thought developed: the medieval scholasticism which was standard fare in the colonial colleges; the "new learning" of Bacon, Newton and Locke; Anglican divinity; Berkeley; and (alas!) Hutchinsonianism. The first four "editions" were written in Latin, the rest in English. The fourth (1714) was a manuscript Encyclopedia of Philosophy in the form of nearly thirteen hundred Latin theses under the heads of logic, grammar, rhetoric, arithmetic, geometry, physics and theology. There was no trace of seventeenth century physics or astronomy, nor even of Copernicus, but only, as he later confessed, "a curious cobweb of distributions and definitions." The next draft (1716) abandoned the thesis form, carried a new classification of studies, a Baconian heading, and some traces of recent science and philosophy, though fewer than we should expect from his having read the *Advancement of Learning* "like one at once emerging out of the glimmer of twilight into the full sunshine of open day." Four years later (1720) a revision and expansion of the logic section of the Encyclopedia resulted from his experience as a tutor and his efforts to substitute his newly discovered Newton and Locke for Ptolemy and the schoolmen. After that there was a longer interval, during which his deeper interests, which were religious and moral, not logical and scientific, asserted themselves; and the two decisive events of his life occurred: he went over to the Church of England (1722), and he met George Berkeley (1729). From then on he worked at the ethical and metaphysical sections of his book, developing in the former a theological utilitarianism on the basis of the Arminian and deistic "religion of nature" so congenial to Anglican divines, and in the latter the idealism of his guide, philosopher and friend. After three published revisions of the entire Encyclopedia in outline (1731, 1743, 1744), he brought out the completed ethics separately as *A New System of Morality* in 1746; and finally, in his *Elementa Philosophica* (1752), dedicated to Berkeley, the metaphysics, logic and ethics appeared together, accompanied by a new outline of the Encyclopedia to show their relations to the other studies.

When Berkeley came to America in 1729, he was the greatest living philosopher. For many years thereafter he had no serious rival save David Hume, whose *Treatise of Human Nature* (1739–40) fell stillborn from the press, and whose star did not begin to rise until shortly before Berkeley's death in 1753. Johnson, from Berkeley's recognition of him in 1729–31, had no American peer as a philosopher in the academic sense. Yet Berkeley's writings were never adopted for study in any colonial college, Johnson's textbook was used for only a few years in Philadelphia and New York and dropped before his death, and idealism (except as it served as a background for the Edwardian theology) made no impression on American thought. Besides the external causes in the general drift toward the Age of Reason, in which any form of philosophical idealism might have been submerged, there were in Berkeley and Johnson themselves two causes, or two aspects of a single cause, for this lack of influence. (1) They were identified with institutions and projects, educational and religious, which even in sympathetic and still more in hostile minds overshadowed their philosophy and prevented its being fairly considered on its merits. (2) In their own thinking, science and philosophy were subservient to religion.

(1) Impressed by the sickness of the body politic in England, of which the wild speculation culminating in the disastrous failure of the South Sea Scheme was but one of many symptoms, Berkeley first wrote in 1721 an *Essay towards Preventing the Ruin of Great Britain,* and then, dreaming an American utopia

> Where men shall not impose for truth and sense
> The pedantry of courts and schools,

he planned a college in the Bermudas, with the twofold object of "the reformation of manners among the English in our western plantations, and the propagation of the gospel among the American savages." He was promised a grant from an unused fund originally intended for the support of four bishops in America. When he arrived in Rhode Island to establish a base of supplies, he was Dean of Derry and the highest ranking officer of the Church of England who had yet set foot in America, and Johnson was its only representative in Connecticut. This would have brought them together even if the Dean had not also been a philosopher whose most important book the missionary to the Puritans had recently read.

Johnson became a convert to Berkeley's philosophy in part because he was already a convert to his church, and in part also because his imagination was fired by what was, in effect, the design of a national university; for Bermuda had been chosen as being approximately equidistant from all the English colonies in North America. And not merely its location, but also its establishment under Anglican auspices would make it a force for unity in a land of bickering sects where, as the Dean put it, "all agree in one point, that the Church of England is the second best." [1] Soon after settling at Newport, however, Berkeley was convinced of the impracticability of a site so far out at sea. Johnson thought he would finally have fixed on New York City, and probably regarded the founding of King's College there a generation later as at least a partial fulfilment of Berkeley's dream. In the meantime Johnson had never ceased to labor for the establishment of an American episcopate, and during his presidency he proposed a political counterpart of these educational and religious unifying forces, in the form of a colonial union with a viceroy and a council composed of representatives from each colony, to meet annually in New York. There is a certain irony in the present position of Columbia University, the largest in the country, dominating its educational system and giving direction to its political and economic policies, but with a very different philosophy, of which the pragmatism of John Dewey is a characteristic expression. The next largest university also has a connection, though a more tenuous one, with Berkeley. When the trustees of the University of California, who had long sought in vain for the right name for their new university town, stood in 1866 by Founders Rock on the campus looking through the Golden Gate, one of their number, Frederick Billings, is said to have exclaimed:

> Let the name be Berkeley. The great philosopher and poet came from England to America to cast in his lot with us in the advancement of learning here, in the faith of his great verse, "Westward the course of empire takes its way." He went home saddened and frustrated. The westward course of learning in America has here reached its westernmost point; and let us honor his memory and hallow this soil by here bestowing his name.[2]

The new university was to become, through the teaching of Royce, Howison and Adams, one of the country's leading centers of philosophical idealism. But that was in the unguessed future, and Berkeley's institutional loyalties were in the forgotten past. It was no longer remembered that when in 1731 "he went home saddened and frustrated" by the failure of the promised support from England, his choice of Yale for his most liberal benefactions was inspired not merely by Johnson's connection with it but also by Johnson's assurance that it was more likely than Harvard to turn Episcopalian. It was no longer remembered that when he endowed it with land and money for prizes and scholarships, he stipulated that the awards should be made "upon

[1] Fraser, A. C.: *Life and Letters of George Berkeley.* Oxford, 1871. 160.

[2] *New England Quarterly* 3 (1930) 44–5. It is not likely that Billings used these words. See W. W. Ferrier: *The Story of the Naming of Berkeley.* Berkeley, 1929.

examination by the Rector with a minister of the Church of England"—which of course meant Johnson. The needy college had anxiously scrutinized his deed of gift and his boxes of books for indications of a design to proselyte; it had ended by paying lip service to its benefactor and ignoring his philosophy. Nor did Johnson's *Elementa* fare much better than Berkeley's *Principles*. Shortly after its introduction at Philadelphia, Franklin wrote to its author, "I have heard of no exceptions yet made to your work, nor do I expect any, unless to those parts that savor of what is called *Berkeleyanism*, which is not well understood here." [3] Only at Princeton did idealism have even a temporary vogue, and it was vigorously stamped out by Witherspoon upon his arrival there in 1768.

So far we have considered the way in which the connection of Berkeley and Johnson with the Church of England, their ambitions for its advancement in America, and their projects for a national college and a national assembly, tended to overshadow and prejudice their philosophical doctrines. Our literary and philosophic historians have tended politely to ignore the fact that our culture is a dissenting and not a catholic one, which neither Catholic nor Anglican authoritarianism, nor any movement of thought intimately associated with either, has ever decisively influenced. Such an association was one of the obstacles to the reception of early idealism, and the nineteenth century idealism of Emerson, Harris, Royce and Howison succeeded better in part because it had no such entangling alliance.

(2) These institutional affiliations and plans might not have been so fatal, however, if science and philosophy had not been so completely subservient to religion in their own minds, and so obviously so in their writings. A passage from Johnson's Autobiography is revealing on this point. Berkeley's idealism, he wrote,

> not only gave new incontestible proofs of a deity, but moreover the most striking apprehensions of his constant presence with us and inspection over us, and of our entire dependence on him and infinite obligations to his most wise and almighty benevolence. On these accounts (as well as to inure one to a close and exact way of thinking) Mr. Johnson wished his works might be thoroughly studied and well considered; especially his wonderfully ingenious theories of vision as well as his *Principles* and *Dialogues*, in which he has plainly outdone both Mr. Locke and Sir Isaac in some particulars. While the Dean was at Rhode Island he composed his *Minute Philosopher*, wherein he elegantly and powerfully confutes the infidels in every shape, under

[3] Reprinted from Schneider, Herbert, and Carol, *Samuel Johnson, President of King's College*, II, 328.

feigned names, in several beautiful and genteel dialogues after the manner of Plato.[4]

There can be no doubt that the chief value of Berkeley's idealism, both for himself and for Johnson, was the new support it offered to religion, less doubtful than that which Locke and Newton had seemed to promise. It was a weapon against scepticism, an assurance not merely of God's existence and general providence, but of his "constant presence." To appreciate the full significance of this fact, we must set it against the background of the general movement of thought in the seventeenth century.

As David Hume later put it, "the fundamental principle" of the new or modern philosophy of Galileo, Descartes, Newton and Locke was the distinction between the primary and the secondary qualities of matter. The former were those which belonged to bodies in their own right: solidity, size, shape, mass, position in space and time, motion or rest. The latter were effects in consciousness produced by the operation of other bodies on our own, directly or through some medium: effects such as color, sound, smell, taste, warmth and cold. No character in bodies themselves bore even the remotest resemblance to any of these secondary qualities; there was nothing in nature corresponding to them except the power in bodies, by virtue of their primary qualities, to produce these sensations in us. The primary qualities and their variations could be exhaustively stated in mathematical terms, and seventeenth century mathematicians like Descartes, Pascal, Fermat, Newton and Leibniz developed the mathematical techniques required for the purpose. By the simple device of reading the secondary qualities out of it, nature had been rendered transparent to our intelligence; the laws of nature were reduced to laws of motion, and the simplicity of the formulas by which these could be represented testified to a God who, like Plato's, "always geometrized."

Reduced to such terms, the universe seemed even more orderly than before, and more obviously presupposed an ordering intelligence. The rapid success of the new science gave a new prestige to as much of religious belief as could be made to seem directly deducible from it. This minimum came to be regarded as that which was common to all religions, independent of special revelation, tradition or authority. The remainder of Christian belief continued to receive lip service but tended to drop into subordinate position, and by "freethinkers" even to be discredited. Unfortunately, however, this minimum of belief, which

[4] Reprinted from Schneider, Herbert, and Carol, *Samuel Johnson, President of King's College,* I, 25–6.

went by the name of deism, seemed to devout and thoughtful Christians quite inadequate as an interpretation of their own religious experience. The absolute regularity of nature with only its primary qualities, suggested not a Sustaining Presence but a Creator who had designed the cosmic machine with such skill and imposed His wise laws upon it with so unerring a touch, that it continued to operate according to them without further intervention on His part. The scientist might therefore safely leave God out of his reckoning, the philosopher might dispose of Him with a courteous gesture, and even the pious would hardly look for daily news from so distant a deity.

This "bifurcation of nature," as Whitehead has recently called it, has been abundantly justified by the successes of modern science; but it has been the scandal of modern philosophy. Against it and the deism which followed in its wake, Berkeley's idealism was the first great protest. The secondary qualities, he argued, were inseparable from the primary and equally integral to nature. Color was no more subjective than extension or shape, motion no more objective than sound. There was no material "substance" in which the primary qualities might inhere, or which might "act" upon our minds to evoke the secondary qualities there. The only "substances" were minds, spirits, subjects; only they were causes; only they could be said to "act." The so-called primary qualities, as well as the secondary, existed only in or for minds; all alike were ideas or immediate objects of sense perception; their *esse* was *percipi,* as that of minds was, so far, *percipere*. Obviously, however, we were not the causes of our own ideas; they were presented to us immediately and afresh every moment by God; nature was simply the continuing and constant system of ideas which He presented to finite minds like ours. The sequence of ideas was such that some became signs of others; visual ideas in particular were signs of all the others. Science was the systematic study of this "divine visual language."

Clearly it was this new philosophic rationale of the sense of God's immediate presence which most appealed to Johnson's mind, already vaguely disturbed by the directions in which thinkers inspired by Locke and Newton were moving. Nevertheless, he had a certain reverence for these men as having wrought his emancipation from scholasticism, and his sense of the logical weaknesses in their positions was not so acute as Berkeley's. On the other hand, he retained enough of his original scholasticism to prevent his going all the way with his new master's polemic against abstract ideas, and to make him realize that putting God in the place of material substance was not enough to constitute a system of philosophy. The most obvious deficiency in

Berkeley's early idealism was its failure to make provision for the certainties of the intellect as adequate as that which it made for the data of sense. Johnson was already familiar with the tradition which could best supply this lack, for he had made the acquaintance of Plato, Cudworth, Norris, Malebranche and Fénelon. Perhaps partly under the stimulus of Johnson's difficulties and suggestions, Berkeley himself moved in that direction in his *Siris,* but it remained for Johnson to coordinate the two forms of idealism, the Platonic and the Berkeleyan, in a single system of thought in his *Elementa,* which has therefore an honorable though minor place of its own in the history of philosophy.

But there was another and for Johnson a more fatal deficiency. Berkeley's ethics was not well developed and stood in no obvious relation to his metaphysics, and Johnson was left with the deistic utilitarianism which he had worked out in his *New System of Morality.*[5] In its reprinting as the second part of his *Elementa* it was clearly only an addition to and not a systematic completion of the first part. Disturbed by that logical discontinuity, and shaken by a series of disasters and bereavements which culminated in the death of his younger son, Johnson finally fell back upon a movement on the lunatic fringe of eighteenth century thought. In 1757 he wrote to his surviving son:

> I confess Dr. Clarke etc. had led me far many years ago into the reasoning humor now so fashionable in matters of religion, from which I bless my God I was happily reclaimed . . . by Hutchinson, whose system I have been now more thoroughly canvassing from the Hebrew scriptures . . . in regard to the philosophical as well as the theological part, and to my unspeakable satisfaction am much convinced it is in both entirely right.[6]

John Hutchinson had contrived to find in Genesis not only a literal history of the world but an introduction to all science. By substituting other vowels in the traditional Hebrew text, he elicited from it a refutation of the Newtonian cosmology which he called *Moses' Principia* (1724). In 1750 Johnson read all twelve volumes of Hutchinson's newly collected works, and capitulated with only minor reservations. Colden and Berkeley (whose crochet had taken the humaner form of tar water) mildly deprecated this aberration, and other correspondents told him that Hutchinson was a humbug and his theories groundless, but Johnson persisted. Long known as one of the leading Hebrew scholars in the country, he now became obsessed with the study of it,

[5] This was largely derived from Wollaston's *The Religion of Nature Delineated.* Wollaston's influence on his thinking was second only to Berkeley's.

[6] Reprinted from Schneider, Herbert, and Carol, *Samuel Johnson, President of King's College,* I, 270.

and his last publication (1771) was a grammar designed for the instruction of children in English and Hebrew together. This little volume contained in an appendix the final revision in outline of the Encyclopedia he had first drafted nearly sixty years before; and it carried on the title page a scholastic motto in which he now saw a Hutchinsonian profundity: *Grammatica est Janitrix Sapientiae!*

## REFERENCES


Schneider, Herbert and Carol (editors): *Samuel Johnson, President of King's College: His Career and Writings.* 4 vols. New York: Columbia University Press, 1929. (Bibliography and chronological index in vol. IV; philosophical writings in vol. II with an introduction by H. W. Schneider, "The Mind of Samuel Johnson.")

Beardsley, E. Edwards: *Life and Correspondence of Samuel Johnson, D.D.* New York, 1873.

Chandler, Thomas Bradbury: *The Life of Samuel Johnson: with an Appendix Containing Many Original Letters.* New York, 1805.

Hoernle, R. F. Alfred: *Idealism as a Philosophy.* New York: George H. Doran Co., 1927. (Contains a good account of the meanings of the term "idea" in philosophy and of the relations between Berkeley's idealism and the Platonic theory of ideas.)

Hornberger, Theodore: "Samuel Johnson of Yale and King's College: A Note on the Relation of Science and Religion in Provincial America," *New England Quarterly* 8 (1935) 378–97.

Rand, Benjamin: *Berkeley's American Sojourn.* Cambridge: Harvard University Press, 1932.

Riley, I. Woodbridge: *American Philosophy: the Early Schools.* New York: Dodd, Mead and Co., 1907. 63–125.

Tyler, Moses Coit: *Three Men of Letters.* New York: G. P. Putnam's Sons, 1895. (Ch. I, "George Berkeley and his American Visit.")

Wild, John: *George Berkeley, A Study of His Life and Philosophy.* Cambridge: Harvard University Press, 1936. (Pp. 311–19 analyze the philosophic correspondence between Johnson and Berkeley.)


* * *

---

* * *

## CORRESPONDENCE WITH BERKELEY [7]

### *Johnson to Berkeley, September 10, 1729*

7. Some of us are at a loss to understand your meaning when you speak of archetypes. You say the beings of things consists in their being perceived. And that things are nothing but ideas, that our ideas have no unperceived archetypes, but yet you allow archetypes to our ideas when things are not perceived by our minds; they exist in, i. e., are perceived by, some other mind. Now I understand you, that there is a two-fold existence of things or ideas, one in the divine mind, and the other in created minds; the one archetypal, and the other ectypal; that, therefore, the real original and permanent existence of things is archetypal, being ideas in *mente Divinâ,* and that our ideas are copies of them, and so far forth real things as they are correspondent to their archetypes and exhibited to us, or begotten in us by the will of the Almighty, in such measure and degrees and by such stated laws and rules as He is pleased to observe; that, therefore, there is no unperceived substance intervening between the divine ideas and ours as a medium, occasion or instrument by which He begets our ideas in us, but that which was thought to be material existence of things is in truth only ideal in the divine mind. Do I understand you right? Is it not therefore your meaning, that the existence of our ideas (i. e., the ectypal things) depends upon our perceiving them, yet there are external to any created mind, in the all-comprehending Spirit, real and permanent archetypes (as stable and permanent as ever matter was thought to be), to which these ideas of ours are correspondent, and so that (tho' our invisible and tangible ideas are *toto coelo* different and distinct things, yet) there may be said to be external to my mind, in the divine mind, an archetype (for instance of the candle that is before me) in which the originals of both my visible and tangible ideas, light, heat, whiteness, softness, etc. under such a particular cylindrical

[7] Reprinted from Schneider, Herbert, and Carol, *Samuel Johnson, President of King's College,* II, 266–9; 275–81; 282–4. By permission of Columbia University Press. Besides the introductory and concluding remarks of each letter, we omit the first six sections of Johnson's first letter because (as he stated in his second) they represented not his own difficulties but those of his acquaintances; and we omit Berkeley's reply because the part of it which has been preserved refers entirely to these first six sections of Johnson's letter. What remains, therefore, consists of two formulations of Johnson's personal understanding of and difficulties with Berkeley's early idealism, and Berkeley's comments at a stage in his own development half way between that early idealism and the more Platonic idealism of his *Siris.*

figure, are united, so that it may be properly said to be the same thing that I both see and feel?

8. If this, or something like it might be understood to be your meaning, it would seem less shocking to say that we don't see and feel the same thing, because we can't dispossess our minds of the notion of an external world, and would be allowed to conceive that, tho' there were no intelligent creature before Adam to be a spectator of it, yet the world was really six days in *archetypo,* gradually proceeding from an informal chaotic state into that beautiful show wherein it first appeared to his mind, and that the comet that appeared in 1680 (for instance) has now, tho' no created mind beholds it, a real existence in the all-comprehending spirit, and is making its prodigious tour through the vast fields of ether, and lastly that the whole vast congeries of heaven and earth, the mighty systems of worlds with all their furniture, have a real being in the eternal mind antecedent to and independent on the perception of created spirit, and that when we see and feel, etc., that that almighty mind, by his immediate *fiat,* begets in our minds (*pro nostro modulo*) ideas correspondent to them, and which may be imagined in some degree resemblances of them.

9. But if there be archetypes to our ideas, will it not follow that there is external space, extention, figure and motion, as being archetypes of our ideas, to which we give these names. And indeed for my part I cannot disengage my mind from the persuasion that there is external space; when I have been trying ever so much to conceive of space as being nothing but an idea in my mind, it will return upon me even in spite of my utmost efforts, certainly there must be, there can't but be, external space. The length, breadth, and thickness of any idea, it's true, are but ideas; the distance between two trees in my mind is but an idea, but if there are archetypes to the ideas of the trees, there must be an archetype to the idea of the distance between them. Nor can I see how it follows that there is no external absolute height, bigness, or distance of things, because they appear greater or less to us according as we are nearer or remote from them, or see them with our naked eyes, or with glasses; any more than it follows that a man, for instance, is not really absolutely six foot high measured by a two foot rule applied to his body, because divers pictures of him may be drawn some six, some four, some two foot long according to the same measure. Nobody ever imagined that the idea of distance is without the mind, but does it therefore follow that there is no external distance to which the idea is correspondent, for instance, between Rhode Island and

Stratford? Truly I wish it were not so great, that I might be so happy as to have a more easy access to you, and more nearly enjoy the advantages of your instructions.

10. You allow spirits to have a real existence external to one another. Methinks, if so, there must be distance between them, and space wherein they exist, or else they must all exist in one individual spot or point, and as it were coincide with one another. I can't see how external space and duration are any more abstract ideas than spirits. As we have (properly speaking) no ideas of spirits, so, indeed, neither have we of external space and duration. But it seems to me that the existence of these must unavoidably follow from the existence of those, insomuch that I can no more conceive of their not being than I can conceive of the non-existence of the infinite and eternal mind. They seem as necessarily existent independent of any created mind as the Deity Himself. Or must we say there is nothing in Dr. Clarke's argument *a priori,* in his demonstration of the being and attributes of God, or in what Sir Isaac Newton says about the infinity and eternity of God in his *Scholium Generale* to his *Principia?* I should be glad to know your sense of what those two authors say upon this subject.

11. You will forgive the confusedness of my thoughts and not wonder at my writing like a man something bewildered, since I am, as it were, got into a new world amazed at everything about me. These ideas of ours, what are they? Is the substance of the mind the *substratum* to its ideas? Is it proper to call them modifications of our minds? Or impressions upon them? Or what? Truly I can't tell what to make of them, any more than of matter itself. What is the *esse* of spirits? —you seem to think it impossible to abstract their existence from their thinking. *Princ.* p. 143. sec. 98. Is then the *esse* of minds nothing else but *percipere,* as the *esse* of ideas is *percipi?* Certainly methinks there must be an unknown somewhat that thinks and acts, as difficult to be conceived of as matter, and the creation of which, as much beyond us as the creation of matter. Can actions be the *esse* of any thing? Can they exist or be exerted without some being who is the agent? And may not that being be easily imagined to exist without acting, *e. g.,* without thinking? And consequently (for you are there speaking of duration) may he not be said *durare, etsi non cogitet,* to persist in being, tho' thinking were intermitted for a while? And is not this sometimes fact? The duration of the eternal mind, must certainly imply some thing besides an eternal succession of ideas. May I not then conceive that, tho' I get my idea of duration by observing the succession of

ideas in my mind, yet there is a *perseverare in existendo,* a duration of my being, and of the being of other spirits distinct from, and independent of, this succession of ideas.

## *Johnson to Berkeley, February 5, 1730*

. . . And of all the particulars I troubled you with before, there remain only these that I have difficulty about, *viz.,* archetypes, space and duration, and the *esse* of spirits. And indeed these were the chief of my difficulties before. . . .

1. . . . I believe I expressed myself unworthily about archetypes in my 7th and 8th articles, but upon looking back upon your *Dialogues,* and comparing again three or four passages I can't think I meant any thing different from what you intended.

You allow, *Dial.* p. 74 "That things have an existence distinct from being perceived by us" (i. e., any created spirits), "and that they exist in, i. e., are perceived by, the infinite and omnipresent mind who contains and supports this sensible world as being perceived by him." And p. 109, "That things have an existence exterior to our minds, and that during the intervals of their being perceived by us, they exist in another (i. e., the infinite) mind"; from whence you justly and excellently infer the certainty of his existence, "who knows and comprehends all things and exhibits them to our view in such manner and according to such rules as he himself has ordained." And p. 113, "That, e. g., a tree, when we don't perceive it, exists without our minds in the infinite mind of God." And this exterior existence of things (if I understand you right) is what you call the archetypal state of things. p. 150.

From these and the like expressions, I gathered what I said about the archetypes of our ideas, and thence inferred that there is exterior to us, in the divine mind, a system of universal nature, whereof the ideas we have are in such a degree resemblances as the Almighty is pleased to communicate to us. And I cannot yet see but my inference was just; because according to you, the idea we see is not in the divine mind, but in our own. When, therefore, you say sensible things exist in, as understood by, the infinite mind I humbly conceive you must be understood that the originals or archetypes of our sensible things or ideas exist independent of us in the infinite mind, or that sensible things exist *in archetypo* in the divine mind. The divine idea, therefore, of a tree suppose (or a tree in the divine mind), must be the original or archetype of ours, and ours a copy or image of His (our ideas images of His, in the same sense as our souls are images of Him) of which there may be several, in several created minds, like so many several pictures of the same original to which they are all to be referred.

When therefore, several people are said to see the same tree or star, etc., whether at the same or at so many several distances from it, it is (if I understand you) *unum et idem in Archetypo,* tho' *multiplex et diversum in Ectypo,* for it is as evident that your idea is not mine nor mine yours when we say we both look on the same tree, as that you are not I nor I you. But in having each our idea being dependent upon and impressed upon by the same almighty mind, wherein you say this tree exists, while we shut our eyes (and doubtless you mean the same also, while they are open), our several trees must, I think be so many pictures (if I may so call them) of the one original, the tree in the infinite mind, and so of all other things. Thus I understand you not indeed that our ideas are in any measure adequate resemblances of the system in the divine mind, but however that they are just and true resemblances or copies of it, so far as He is pleased to communicate His mind to us.

2. As to space and duration, I do not pretend to have any other notion of their exterior existence than what is necessarily implied in the notion we have of God; I do not suppose they are any thing distinct from, or exterior to, the infinite and external mind; for I conclude with you that there is nothing exterior to my mind but God and other spirits with attributes or properties belonging to them and ideas contained in them.

External space and duration therefore I take to be those properties or attributes in God, to which our ideas, which we signify by those names, are correspondent, and of which they are the faint shadows. This I take to be Sir Isaac Newton's meaning when he says, *Schol. General. Deus—durat semper et adest ubique et existendo semper et ubique, durationem et spacium, eternitatem et infinitatem constituit.* And in his *Optics* calls space *as it were God's boundless sensorium,* nor can I think you have a different notion of these attributes from that great philosopher, tho' you may differ in your ways of expressing or explaining yourselves. However it be, when you call the Deity infinite and eternal, and in that most beautiful and charming description, *Dial.* p. 71, etc., when you speak of the *abyss of space and boundless extent beyond thought* and imagination, I don't know how to understand you any otherwise than I understood Sir Isaac, when he uses the like expressions. The truth is we have no proper ideas of

God or his attributes, and conceive of them only by analogy from what we find in ourselves; and so, I think we conceive His immensity and eternity to be what in Him are correspondent to our space and duration.

As for the *punctum stans* of the Schools, and the *to nun* of the Platonists, they are notions too fine for my gross thoughts; I can't tell what to make of those words, they don't seem to convey any ideas or notions to my mind, and whatever the matter is, the longer I think of them, the more they disappear, and seem to dwindle away into nothing. Indeed, they seem to me very much like abstract ideas, but I doubt the reason is because I never rightly understood them. I don't see why the term *punctum stans* may not as well at least, be applied to the immensity as the eternity of God; for the word *punctum* is more commonly used in relation to extension or space than duration; and to say that a being is immense, and yet that it is but a point, and that its duration is perpetual without beginning or end, and yet that it is but a *to nun,* look to me like a contradiction.

I can't therefore understand the term *to nun* unless it be designed to adumbrate the divine omnisciency or the perfection of the divine knowledge, by the more perfect notion we have of things present than of things past; and in this sense it would imply that all things past, present, and to come are always at every point of duration equally perfectly known or present to God's mind (tho' in a manner infinitely more perfect), as the things that are known to us are present to our minds at any point of our duration which we call *now.* So that with respect to His equally perfect knowledge of things past, present or to come, it is in effect always now with Him. To this purpose it seems well applied and intelligible enough, but His duration I take to be a different thing from this, as that point of our duration which we call *now,* is a different thing from our actual knowledge of things, as distinguished from our remembrance. And it may as well be said that God's immensity consists in His knowing at once what is, and is transacted in all places (e. g., China, Jupiter, Saturn, all the systems of fixed stars, etc.) everywhere, however so remote from us (tho' in a manner infinitely more perfect), as we know what is, and is transacted in us and about us just at hand; as that His eternity consists in this *to nun* as above explained, i. e., in His knowing things present, past and to come, however so remote, all at once or equally perfectly as we know the things that are present to us *now.*

In short our ideas expressed by the terms immensity and eternity are only space and duration considered as boundless or with the negation of any limits, and I can't help thinking there is something analogous to them without us, being in and belonging to, or attributes of, that glorious mind, whom for that reason we call immense and eternal, in whom we and all other spirits, *live, move and have their being,* not all in a point, but in so many different points, places or *alicubis,* and variously situated with respect one to another, or else as I said before, it seems as if we should all coincide one with another.

I conclude, if I am wrong in my notion of eternal space, and duration, it is owing to the rivetted prejudices of abstract ideas; but really when I have thought it over and over again in my feeble way of thinking, I can't see any connection between them (as I understand them) and that doctrine. They don't seem to be any more abstract ideas than spirits, for as I said, I take them to be attributes of the necessarily existing spirit; and consequently the same reasons that convince me of his existence, bring with them the existence of these attributes. So that of the ways of coming to the knowledge of things that you mention, it is that of inference or deduction by which I seem to know that there is external infinite space and duration because there is without me a mind infinite and eternal.

3. As to the *esse* of spirits, I know Descartes held the soul always thinks, but I thought Mr. Locke had sufficiently confuted this notion, which he seems to have entertained only to serve an hypothesis. The Schoolmen, it is true, call the soul *Actus* and God *Actus purus;* but I confess I could never well understand their meaning perhaps because I never had opportunity to be much versed in their writings. I should have thought the schoolmen to be of all sorts of writers the most unlikely to have had recourse to for the understanding of your sentiment because they of all others, deal the most in abstract ideas; tho' to place the very being of spirits in the mere act of thinking, seems to me very much like making abstract ideas of them.

There is certainly something passive in our souls, we are purely passive in the reception of our ideas; and reasoning and willing are actions of something that reasons and wills, and therefore must be only modalities of that something. Nor does it seem to me that when I say [something] I mean an abstract idea. It is true I have no idea of it, but I feel it; I feel that it is, because I feel or am conscious of the exertions of it; but the exertions of it are not the thing but the modalities of it distinguished from it as actions from an agent, which seems to me distinguishable without having recourse to abstract ideas.

And, therefore, when I suppose the existence of a spirit while it does not actually think, it does not appear to me that I do it by supposing an abstract idea of existence, and another of absolute time. The existence of John asleep by me, without so much as a dream is not an abstract idea. Nor is the time passing the while an abstract idea, they are only partial considerations of him. *Perseverare in existendo* in general, without reflecting on any particular thing existing, I take to be what is called an abstract idea of time or duration; but the *perseverare in existendo* of John is, if I mistake not, a partial consideration of him. And I think it is as easy to conceive of him as continuing to exist without thinking as without seeing.

Has a child no soul till it actually perceives? And is there not such a thing as sleeping without dreaming, or being in a *deliquium* without a thought? If there be, and yet at the same time the *esse* of a spirit be nothing else but its actual thinking, the soul must be dead during those intervals; and if ceasing or intermitting to think be the ceasing to be, or death of the soul, it is many times and easily put to death. According to this tenet, it seems to me the soul may sleep on to the resurrection, or rather may wake up in the resurrection state, the next moment after death. Nay I don't see upon what we can build any natural argument for the soul's immortality. I think I once heard you allow a principle of perception and spontaneous motion in beasts. Now if their *esse* as well as ours consists in perceiving, upon what is the natural immortality of our souls founded that will not equally conclude in favor of them? I mention this last consideration because I am at a loss to understand how you state the argument for the soul's natural immortality; for the argument from thinking to immaterial and from thence to indivisible, and from thence to immortal don't seem to obtain in your way of thinking.

If *esse* be only *percipere,* upon what is our consciousness founded? I perceived yesterday, and I perceive now, but last night between my yesterday's and today's perception there has been an intermission when I perceived nothing. It seems to me there must be some principle common to these perceptions, whose *esse* don't depend on them, but in which they are, as it were, connected, and on which they depend, whereby I am and continue conscious of them.

Lastly, Mr. Locke's argument (B. 2. Ch. 19. Sec. 4.) from the intention and remission of thought, appears to me very considerable; according to which, upon this supposition the soul must exist more or have a greater degree of being at one time than at another, according as it thinks more intensely or more remissly.

I own I said very wrong when I said I did not know what to make of ideas more than of matter. My meaning was, in effect, the same as I expressed afterwards about the substance of the soul's being a somewhat as unknown as matter. And what I intended by those questions was whether our ideas are not the substance of the soul itself, under so many various modifications, according to that saying (if I understand it right) *Intellectus intelligendo fit omnia?* It is true, those expressions (modifications, impressions, etc.) are metaphorical, and it seems to me to be no less so, to say that ideas exist in the mind, and I am under some doubt whether this last way of speaking don't carry us further from the thing, than to say ideas are the mind variously modified; but as you observe, it is scarce possible to speak of the mind without a metaphor.

## *Berkeley to Johnson, March 24, 1730*

[1.] I have no objection against calling the ideas in the mind of God, archetypes of ours. But I object against those archetypes by philosophers supposed to be real things, and to have an absolute rational existence distinct from their being perceived by any mind whatsoever, it being the opinion of all materialists that an ideal existence in the divine mind is one thing, and the real existence of material things another.

[2.] As to space, I have no notion of any but that which is relative. I know some late philosophers have attributed extension to God, particularly mathematicians; one of whom, in a treatise *de Spacio reali,* pretends to find out fifteen of the incommunicable attributes of God in space. But it seems to me, that they being all negative, he might as well have found them in nothing; and that it would have been as justly inferred from space being impassive, uncreated, indivisible, etc., that it was nothing, as that it was God.

Sir Isaac Newton supposeth an absolute space different from relative, and consequent thereto, absolute motion, different from relative motion; and with all other mathematicians, he supposeth the infinite divisibility of the finite parts of this absolute space; he also supposeth material bodies to drift therein. Now, though I do acknowledge Sir Isaac to have been an extraordinary man and most profound mathematician, yet I cannot agree with him in these particulars. I make no scruple to use the word space, as well as other words in common use, but I do not mean thereby a distinct absolute being. For my meaning I refer you to what I have published.

By the *to nun* I suppose to be implied that all things past and to come are actually present to the mind of God, and that there is in Him no change, variation, or succession—a succession of ideas I take to constitute time and not to be only the sensible measure thereof, as Mr. Locke and others think. But in these matters every man is to think for himself, and speak as he finds. One of my earliest inquiries was about time, which led me into several paradoxes that I did not think fit or necessary to publish, particularly into the notion that the resurrection follows next moment to death. We are confounded and perplexed about time. (1) Supposing a succession in God. (2) Conceiving that we have an abstract idea of time. (3) Supposing that the time in one mind is to be measured by the succession of ideas in another. (4) Not considering the true use and ends of words, which as often terminate in the will as the understanding, being employed rather to excite influence, and direct action than to produce clear and distinct ideas.

3. That the soul of man is passive as well as active I make no doubt. Abstract general ideas was a notion that Mr. Locke held in common with the Schoolmen, and I think all other philosophers; it runs through his whole book *Of Human Understanding*. He holds an abstract idea of existence, exclusive of perceiving and being perceived. I cannot find I have any such idea, and this is my reason against it. Descartes proceeds upon other principles. One square foot of snow is as white as one thousand yards; one single perception is as truly a perception as one hundred. Now any degree of perception being sufficient to existence, it will not follow that we should say one existed more at one time than another, any more than we should say one thousand yards of snow are whiter than one yard. But after all, this comes to a verbal dispute. I think it might prevent a good deal of obscurity and dispute to examine well what I have said about abstraction, and about the true use of sense and significancy of words, in several parts of these things that I have published, though much remains to be said on that subject.

You say you agree with me that there is nothing within your mind but God and other spirits, with the attributes or properties belonging to them, and the ideas contained in them. This is a principle or main point from which, and from what I had laid down about abstract ideas, much may be deduced. But if in every inference we should not agree, so long as the main points are settled and well understood, I should be less solicitous about particular conjectures. I could wish that all the things I have published on these philosophical subjects were read in the order wherein I published them, once to take the design and connection of them, and a second time with a critical eye, adding your own thought and observation upon every part as you went along.

* * *

---

* * *

# ELEMENTA PHILOSOPHICA [8]

## *Of the Mind in General, Its Objects and Operations*

**The Design.**

1. It is my design in the following essay, to trace out, in as short a compass as I can, the several steps of the mind of man, from the first impressions of sense, through the several improvements it gradually makes, till it arrives to that perfection and enjoyment of itself, which is the great end of its being. In order to which, it will first be expedient to define what we mean by the human mind, and to give some account of its various objects, powers and operations, and the principles and rules by which they are to be conducted in attaining to the knowledge of truth, which is the business of that science which is called Logic, or The Art of Thinking or Reasoning; the foundation of which is the *philosophia prima,* which is also called metaphysics and ontology, or the doctrine of the general notion of being, with its various properties and affections, and those applied in general both to body and spirit. And as truth and good are nearly allied, being in effect but the same thing under different considerations; this will pave the way towards the attainment of that supreme good, in the choice and enjoyment of which consists our highest happiness; the particular consideration of which is the business of ethics, or moral philosophy, which is the art of pursuing our highest happiness by the universal practice of virtue.

**The Definition of Mind.**

2. The word mind or spirit, in general, signifies any intelligent active being; which notion we take from what we are conscious of in ourselves, who know that we have within us a principle of conscious perception, intelligence, activity and self-exertion; or rather, that each of us is a conscious, perceptive, intelligent, active and self-exerting being: and by reasoning and analogy from ourselves we apply it to all other minds or intelligences besides, or superior to us; and (removing all limitations and imperfections) we apply it even to that Great Supreme Intelligence, who is the universal Parent of all created spirits, and (as far as our words and conceptions can go) may be defined, an infinite Mind or Spirit, or a Being infinitely intelligent and active. But by the human mind,

[8] Reprinted from Schneider, Herbert, and Carol, *Samuel Johnson, President of King's College,* II, (ch. I) 372–80. By permission of Columbia University Press.

we mean that principle of sense, intelligence and free activity, which we feel within ourselves, or rather feel ourselves to be, furnished with those objects and powers, and under those confinements and limitations, under which it hath pleased our great Creator to place us in this present state.

**Of the Union of Body and Mind.**

3. We are, at present, spirits or minds connected with gross, tangible bodies, in such a manner, that as our bodies, can perceive and act nothing but by our minds, so, on the other hand, our minds perceive and act by means of our bodily organs. Such is the present law of our nature, which I conceive to be no other than a mere arbitrary constitution or establishment of Him that hath made us to be what we are. And accordingly I apprehend that the union between our souls and bodies, during our present state, consists in nothing else but this law of our nature, which is the will and perpetual fiat of that infinite Parent Mind, who made, and holds our souls in life, and in whom we live, and move, and have our being, *viz.* that our bodies should be thus acted by our minds, and that our minds should thus perceive and act by the organs of our bodies, and under such limitations as in fact we find ourselves to be attended with.

**Definition of Idea, Notion, etc.**

4. The immediate object of these our perceptions and actions we call ideas; as this world has been commonly defined and used by the moderns, with whom it signifies any immediate object of the mind in thinking, whether sensible or intellectual, and so is, in effect, synonymous with the word thought, which comprehends both. Plato, indeed, by the word idea, understood the original exemplar of things, whether sensible or intellectual, in the eternal mind, conformable to which all things exist; or the abstract essences of things, as being originals or archetypes in that infinite intellect, of which our ideas or conceptions are a kind of copies. But perhaps, for the more distinct understanding ourselves upon this subject, it may be best to confine the word idea to the immediate objects of sense and imagination, which was the original meaning of it; and to use the word notion or conception, to signify the objects of consciousness and pure intellect, tho' both of them may be expressed by the general term thought; for these are so entirely, and *toto coelo* different and distinct one from the other, that it may be apt to breed confusion in our thoughts and language, to use the same word promiscuously for them both; tho' we are indeed generally obliged to substitute sensible images and the words annexed to them,

to represent things purely intellectual; such, for instance, are the words, spirit, reflect, conceive, discourse, and the like.

**The Original of our Ideas.**

5. Our minds may be said to be created mere *tabulae rasae; i. e.,* they have no notices of any objects of any kind properly created in them, or concreated with them; yet I apprehend that in all the notices they have of any kind of objects, they have an immediate dependence upon the Deity, as really as they depend upon Him for their existence; *i. e.,* they are no more authors to themselves of the objects of their perceptions, or the light by which they perceive them, than of the power of perceiving itself; but that they perceive them by a perpetual intercourse with that great Parent Mind, to whose incessant agency they are entirely passive, both in all the perceptions of sense, and in all that intellectual light by which they perceive the objects of the pure intellect. Notwithstanding which, it is plain from experience, that in consequence of these perceptions they are entirely at liberty to act, or not to act, and all their actions flow from a principle of self-exertion. But in order the better to understand these things, I must more particularly define these terms. And, as all the notices we have in our minds derive to them originally from (or rather by means of) these two fountains, sense and consciousness, it is necessary to begin with them.

**Of the Senses.**

6. By sense, we mean, those perceptions we have of objects *ab extra,* or by means of the several organs of our bodies. Thus, by feeling or touch, we perceive an endless variety of tangible objects, resistance, extension, figure, motion, hard, soft, heat, cold, &c. By sight we perceive light and colors, with all their endlessly various modifications, red, blue, green, &c. By hearing, we perceive sounds: by tasting, sapors: by smelling, odors, &c. These are called simple ideas. And of these, sorted out into a vast variety of fixed combinations, or compound ideas, distinct from each other, and in which they are always found to co-exist, consists every sort and individual body in nature, such as we call man, horse, tree, stone, apple, cherry, &c. And of all these various distinct combinations or compounds, connected together in such a manner as to constitute one most beautiful, useful and harmonious whole, consists what we call universal nature, or the entire sensible or natural world.

**In Which we Are Passive.**

7. In the perception of these ideas of objects of sense, we find our minds are merely passive, it not being in our power (supposing our organs rightly disposed and situated) whether we will see light and colors, hear sounds, etc.

We are not causes to ourselves of these perceptions, nor can they be produced in our minds without a cause; or (which is the same thing) by any imagined unintelligent, inert, or unactive cause (which indeed is a contradiction in terms) from whence it is demonstration that they must derive to us from an Almighty, intelligent active cause, exhibiting them to us, impressing our minds with them, or producing them in us; and consequently (as I intimated) it must be by a perpetual intercourse of our minds with the Deity, the great Author of our Beings, or by His perpetual influence or activity upon them, that they are possessed of all these objects of sense, and the light by which we perceive them.

**Ideas of Sense not Pictures, but the Real Things.**

8. These ideas or objects of sense are commonly supposed to be pictures or representations of things without us, and indeed external to any mind, even that of the Deity himself, and the truth or reality of them is conceived to consist in their being exact pictures of things or objects without us, which are supposed to be the real things. But as it is impossible for us to perceive what is without our minds, and consequently, what those supposed originals are, and whether these ideas of ours are just resemblances of them or not; I am afraid this notion of them will lead us into an inextricable scepticism. I am therefore apt to think that these ideas, or immediate objects of sense, are the real things, at least all that we are concerned with, I mean, of the sensible kind; and that the reality of them consists in their stability and consistence, or their being, in a stable manner, exhibited to our minds, or produced in them, and in a steady connection with each other, conformable to certain fixed laws of nature, which the great Father of Spirits hath established to Himself, according to which He constantly operates and affects our minds, and from which He will not vary, unless upon extraordinary occasions, as in the case of miracles.

**Instanced in Things Visible and Tangible.**

9. Thus, for instance, there is a fixed stable connection between things tangible and things visible, or the immediate objects of touch and sight, depending, as I conceive, immediately upon the permanent, most wise and almighty will and fiat of the great creator and preserver of the world. By which, neither can it be meant, that visible objects are pictures of tangible objects (which yet is all the sense that can be made of our ideas of sense being images of real things without us) for they are entirely different and distinct things; as different as the sounds, triangle, and the figure signified by it; so different that a man born blind, and made to see, could have no more notion that a visible globe

hath any connection with a tangible globe, by mere sight, without being taught, than a Frenchman that should come in England, and hear the word, man, could imagine, without being taught, that it signified the same thing with the word, *homme,* in his language. All that can be meant by it, therefore, is, that, as tangible things are the things immediately capable of producing (or rather, being attended with) sensible pleasure or pain in us, according to the present laws of our nature, on account of which they are conceived of as being properly the real things; so the immediate objects of sight or visible things, are always, by the same stable law of our nature, connected with them, as signs of them, and ever correspondent and proportioned to them; visible extension, figure, motion, &c. with those of the tangible kind, which go by the same names; and so in the compounds or combinations of them; the visible man, horse, tree, stone, &c. with those of the tangible kind, signified by the same names.[9]

**Of Archetypes.**

10. Not that it is to be doubted but that there are archetypes of these sensible ideas existing, external to our minds; but then they must exist in some other mind, and be ideas also as well as ours; because an idea can resemble nothing but an idea; and an idea ever implies in the very nature of it, relation to a mind perceiving it, or in which it exists. But then those archetypes or originals, and the manner of their existence in that eternal mind, must be entirely different from that of their existence in our minds; as different, as the manner of His existence is from that of ours: in him they must exist, as in original intellect; in us, only by way of sense and imagination; and in Him, as originals; in us only as faint copies; such as he thinks fit to communicate to us, according to such laws and limitations as he hath established, and such as are sufficient to all the purposes relating to our well-being, in which only we are concerned. Our ideas, therefore, can no otherwise be said to be images or copies of the archetypes in the eternal mind, than as our souls are said to be images of Him, or as we are said to be made after his image.[10]

**Of Consciousness, Imagination and Memory.**

11. Thus much for sense.—By consciousness is meant, our perception of objects *ab intra,* or from reflecting or turning the eye of our mind inward, and observing what passeth within itself; whereby we know that we perceive all those sensible objects and their connections, and all the pleas-

[9] See Bp. Berkeley's Theories of Vision, Principles of Human Knowledge, and Three Dialogues.

[10] See on this head, Norris's Ideal World. Part I.

ures and pains attending them, and all the powers and faculties of our minds employed about them. Thus I am conscious that I perceive light and colors, sound, odors, sapors, and tangible qualities with all the various combinations of them; and that of these, some give me, or rather are attended with pain or uneasiness, others with pleasure or ease, and the comfortable enjoyment of myself. I find moreover, that when I have had any perception or impression of sense, I retain a faint image of it in my mind afterwards, or have a kind of internal sense or remembrance of it; as having seen the sun, a flower, a horse, or a man, I retain the image of their figure, shape, color, &c. afterwards. Thus I have now a faint idea of the sun at midnight, and of a rose in winter: I know how such a tree, such a horse, or such a man looks, tho' I have neither of them before my eyes. This power of mind is called imagination and memory, which implies a consciousness of the original impression (tho' indeed the word memory may imply the recollection of intellectual as well as sensible objects, but chiefly those by means of these, which is also called reminiscence) and these ideas of the imagination may be truly said to be images or pictures of the ideas or immediate objects of sense. We are moreover conscious of a power whereby we can not only imagine things as being what they really are in nature, but can also join such parts and properties of things together, as never co-existed in nature, but are mere creatures of our minds, or chimeras; as the head of a man with the body of an horse, etc. which must also be referred to the imagination, but as influenced by the will.

**Of the Pure Intellect and its Acts.**

12. But besides these powers of sense and imagination, we are conscious of what is called the pure intellect, or the power of conceiving of abstracted or spiritual objects, and the relations between our several ideas and conceptions, and the various dispositions, exertions and actions of our minds, and the complex notions resulting from all these; of all which we cannot be properly said to have ideas, they being entirely of a different kind from the objects of sense and imagination, on which account I would rather call them notions or conceptions. And they are either simple, such as perception, consciousness, volition, affection, action, &c., or complex, as spirit, soul, god, cause, effect, proportion, justice, charity, &c. And of all these, and what relates to them, consists the entire spiritual or moral world. But in order the better to understand or conceive of these, it is necessary more particularly to pursue and explain these intellectual and active powers, whereof we are conscious within ourselves; such as, 1. The simple apprehension of objects, and

their several relations, connections and dependencies, arising from our comparing our ideas and conceptions one with another. 2. Judging of true or false, according as things appear to agree or disagree, to be connected or not connected one with another; and 3. Reasoning or inferring one thing from another, and methodising them according to their connections and order: all which are the subject of logics. To which succeed, 1. Affecting or disaffecting them according as they appear good or bad, agreeable or disagreeable to us, *i. e.,* attended with pleasure or uneasiness. 2. Willing or nilling, choosing or refusing according as we affect or disaffect them. 3. Liberty of acting, or forbearing to act in consequence of the judgment and choice we have made of them: all which are the subject of ethics. It is necessary to define all these terms, and give some account of these several acts and exertions of our minds (which, as well as those of sense, consciousness, imagination and memory above-mentioned, are only so many modifications of them) in order to what is next to follow.

**Of Intellectual Light or Intuitive Evidence.**

13. But before I proceed, I would, in order thereunto, first observe, that no sooner does any object strike the senses, or is received in our imagination, or apprehended by our understanding, but we are immediately conscious of a kind of intellectual light within us (if I may so call it) whereby we not only know that we perceive the object, but directly apply ourselves to the consideration of it, both in itself, its properties and powers, and as it stands related to all other things. And we find that as we are enabled by this intellectual light to perceive these objects and their various relations, in like manner as by sensible light we are enabled to perceive the objects of sense and their various situations;[11] so our minds are as passive to this intellectual light, as they are to sensible light, and can no more withstand the evidence of it, than they can withstand the evidence of sense. Thus I am under the same necessity to assent to this, that I am or have a being, and that I perceive and freely exert myself, as I am of assenting to this, that I see colors or hear sounds. I am as perfectly sure that $2 + 2 = 4$, or that the whole is equal to all its parts, as that I feel heat or cold, or that I see the sun when I look full upon it in the meridian in a clear day; *i. e.,* I am intuitively certain of both. This intellectual light I conceive of as it were a medium of knowledge, as sensible light is of sight: in both there is the power of perceiving, and the object perceived; and this is the medium by which I am enabled to know it. And this light is one, and common to all intelligent beings, and enlighteneth alike

[11] This is Plato's Doctrine, in his Rep. 6 &c.

every man that cometh into the world, a Chinese or Japanese, as well as an European or American, and an angel as well as a man: by which they all at once see the same thing to be true or right in all places at the same time, and alike invariably in all times, past, present, and to come.

**Whence it is Derived.**

14. Now if it be asked, whence does this light derive, whereby all created minds at once perceive, as by a common standard, the same things alike to be true and right. I answer, I have no other way to conceive how I come to be affected with this intuitive intellectual light, whereof I am conscious, than by deriving it from the universal presence and action of the Deity or a perpetual communication with the great father of lights,[12] or rather his eternal word and spirit, exhibiting and impressing. For I know I am not the author of it to myself, being passive and not active with regard to it, tho' I am active in consequence of it. Therefore, tho' I cannot explain the manner how I am impressed with it (as neither can I that of sense) I do humbly conceive that God does as truly and immediately enlighten my mind internally to know these intellectual objects, as he does by the light of the sun (his sensible representative) enable me to perceive sensible objects. So that those expressions are indeed no less philosophical than devout, that God is light, and in his light we see light. And this intuitive knowledge, as far as it goes, must be the first principles, from which the mind takes its rise, and upon which it proceeds in all its subsequent improvements in reasoning, and discovering both truth in speculation, and right in action; so that this intellectual light must be primarily and carefully attended to, if we would avoid and be secure from either error or vice. Nor must this manner of thinking be suspected to savor of enthusiasm, it being the settled course or law of nature, according to which the great parent mind enlighteneth us; and that in things, in their own nature capable of clear evidence; whereas enthusiasm implies an imaginary, as revelation is a real and well-attested adventitious light, above and beyond the settled law or course of nature, discovering truths not otherwise knowable, and giving directions, or enjoining rules of action in things arbitrary, or matters of mere institution. And from this intuitive intellectual light it is (as I conceive) that we derive what we call taste and judgment, and, with

[12] See the Archbishop of Cambray, on this Subject, in his Demonstration of the Existence of God. And Norris or Malbranche & Cudworth's Int. Syst. [True Intellectual System of the Universe] p. 736. Ed. 1743, and his Eternal and Immutable Morality, p. 250–60.

respect to morals, what some call the moral sense or the conscience, which are only a sort of quick intuitive sense or apprehension of the decent and amiable, of beauty and deformity, of true and false, and of right and wrong, or duty and sin: and it is the chief business of culture, art and instruction, to awaken and turn our attention to it, and assist us in making deductions from it.

# IV

# Jonathan Edwards

1703–1758

Born in East Windsor, Conn. Yale, A.B., 1720; A.M., 1723; tutor, 1724; resigned, 1726, to assist his grandfather, Solomon Stoddard, minister of the Congregational church at Northampton, Mass. Became sole minister on his grandfather's death, 1729. Dismissed, 1750. Settled in Stockbridge, Mass., as minister of the local church and missionary to the Indians, 1751. Chosen President of the College of New Jersey (Princeton), 1757. Died of inoculation for smallpox a few weeks after assuming office.

Edwards's career falls naturally into three periods: (I) the young idealist, (II) the precipitator, psychological analyst, and apologist of the Great Awakening, and (III) the protagonist of Calvinism against Arminianism and deism.

## I

At the age of fourteen, in his second year at college, Edwards read John Locke's *Essay concerning Human Understanding* (1690), enjoying a far higher pleasure in the perusal of its pages "than the most greedy miser finds, when gathering up handfuls of silver and gold, from some newly discovered treasure." [1] It was probably under the stimulus of Locke that he projected and began making notes for a treatise on the mind and another on natural science.

Like Berkeley a decade earlier, but in apparent ignorance of him, Edwards in these "Notes on the Mind" asserted the ideality of the physical world: minds or spirits were the only substances. In many details, however, his system differed from that in the writings Berkeley had so far published: he found room for abstract ideas or universals, for instance,[2] and his spiritual pluralism verged on pantheism.

As to *Bodies,* we have shown in another place, that they have no proper Being of their own. And as to *Spirits,* they are the communica-

[1] *Works.* I, 30.

[2] Ibid. I, 684–6. §§ 41–3.

tions of the Great Original Spirit; and doubtless, in metaphysical strictness and propriety, He *is,* as there is none else. He is likewise Infinitely Excellent, and all Excellence and Beauty is derived from him, in the same manner as all Being. And all other Excellence is, in strictness, only a shadow of His.[3]

This is something that Edwards did not learn from Locke, and would not have learned from Berkeley if he had read him. The truth is that Edwards was from the first an idealist not merely in the Berkeleyan sense, resolving the material universe into ideas whose being consisted in their being perceived, but in the sense of the great Platonic tradition which Berkeley did not fully enter until his *Siris* (1744): an idealism which conceives all that is apprehended by the senses to be only a shadow or intimation of a reality to be apprehended by thought. This latter aspect owed something to that immense storehouse of Platonism, Ralph Cudworth's *The True Intellectual System of the Universe* (1678), which he had been reading along with Locke. But both aspects have their roots in Edwards's own religious experiences, beginning before his reading of either Locke or Cudworth, and resembling those of the mystics generally, but with three distinguishing features: (1) an absence of the imagery of sex love, remarkable in one who was as thrilled as any Christian mystic ever was by the Song of Songs; (2) an aesthetic sense of God's "excellency," both as it was in Himself and as it shone forth in nature; and (3) a melting of his earlier objections to "the doctrine of God's sovereignty, in choosing whom he would to eternal life, and rejecting whom he pleased," which "used to appear like a horrible doctrine to me," but which now "very often appeared exceeding pleasant, bright, and sweet."[4]

One of the first objections to which any assertion of the ideality of the physical world lays itself open is that it dissolves nature into atomic and momentary bits of sensation, and thus belies not merely the objectivity but also the continuity and permanence of the world as we know it. The theory seems better accommodated to the aspects of change than to those of order and stability in nature. The way in which Edwards met this objection is perhaps the most interesting feature of his exposition of the theory.

But it may be asked, How do those things exist, which have an actual existence, but of which no created mind is conscious?—For instance, the Furniture of this room, when we are absent, and the room is shut up, and no created mind perceives it; How do these things exist?—I answer . . . in short, That the existence of these things is in God's

[3] *Works.* I, 700. § 45, sec. 8.
[4] Ibid. I, 60.

supposing of them, in order to the rendering complete the series of things, (to speak more strictly, *the series of ideas,*) according to his own settled order, and that harmony of things, which he has appointed. —The supposition of God, which we speak of, is nothing else but God's acting, in the course and series of his exciting ideas, as if they, (the things supposed,) were in actual idea.[5]

And indeed the secret lies here: That which truly is the Substance of all Bodies, is *the infinitely exact, and precise, and perfectly stable Idea, in God's mind, together with his stable Will that the same shall gradually be communicated to us, and to other minds, according to certain fixed and exact established Methods and Laws:* or in somewhat different language, *the infinitely exact and precise Divine Idea, together with an answerable, perfectly exact, precise and stable Will, with respect to correspondent communications to Created Minds, and effects on their minds.*[6]

The notes raised all the fundamental problems of philosophy—metaphysics, philosophy of religion, theory of knowledge, aesthetics, ethics. Only the philosophy of the state and of society were slighted. But the systematic treatise in which all these problems were to be discussed in relation to one another and to his fundamental idealism, was never written. In the books he did write, the problems appeared one by one, but almost invariably in connection with and overshadowed by some theological controversy. A representative example may be found in the problem of personal identity, made acute for Edwards by his belief in the absolute sovereignty of God. Two paragraphs of the "Notes on the Mind" dealt with it,[7] the earlier accepting, the later criticizing, Locke's doctrine that identity of person consisted in identity of consciousness. The implications of the later paragraph were developed in the last book which Edwards prepared for the press, *The Great Christian Doctrine of Original Sin Defended* (1758).[8] One of the objections there met was that "the appointing Adam to stand, in this affair, as the moral *head* of his posterity, and so treating them as one with him, as standing or falling with him," was "altogether *improper,* as it implies *falsehood,* viewing and treating those as one which indeed are not one, but entirely *distinct.*" His answer exhibited his philosophic powers at their height, but the essence of it was that there was no difference in principle between the "arbitrary constitution" of God which united us with Adam and that which united us with our own past selves.

[5] *Works.* I, 671. § 40. See the exposition in terms of atomism in § 34, pp. 669–70.

[6] Ibid. I, 674. § 13.

[7] Ibid. I, 680–1. §§ 11, 72.

[8] See the selection below, pp. 90–6.

But why was the treatise on the mind never written? There is no evidence that he ever abandoned the fundamental position taken in his notes; though never expressly stated and defended, it was implicit in all his writings—in fact, at the end of the selection to which we have just been referring. Nor is it likely that he found, or would have found, the difficulty of constructing a consistent system on that basis an insuperable one.[9] A close reading of his Diary and Resolutions (1722–25) suggests rather that as he pursued his study of theology, and as he entered upon the ministry, his energies were increasingly focused upon preparing for his appointed rôle of physician and surgeon of souls by probing the depths of his own religious experience. He was resolved,

> Whenever I do any conspicuously evil action, to trace it back, till I come to the original cause; and then, both carefully to endeavor to do so no more, and to fight and pray with all my might against the original of it. . . . Constantly, with the utmost niceness and diligence, and the strictest scrutiny, to be looking into the state of my soul. . . . I think it a very good way, to examine dreams every morning when I awake; what are the nature, circumstances, principles, and ends of my imaginary actions and passions in them; in order to discern what are my prevailing inclinations, &c. . . . As a help against that inward shameful hypocrisy . . . not in the least to endeavor to smother over what is in my heart, but to bring it all out to God and my own conscience. By this means, I may arrive at a greater knowledge of my own heart. . . . The very thing I now want, to give me a clearer and more immediate view of the perfections and glory of God, is as clear a knowledge of the manner of God's exerting himself, with respect to Spirits and Mind, as I have of his operations concerning Matter and Bodies.[10]

Edwards was, in fact, turning from philosophy to moral and religious psychology, with an acute sense of the momentous character of the issues of spiritual life and death that hung upon the discoveries to be made, and of the uncertainty that he should live to make them. "My time is so short, that I have not time to perfect myself in all studies: Wherefore resolved, to omit and put off, all but the most important and needful studies." [11] He had already, in his "Notes on the Mind," reached the conclusion that the denial of material substance had no practical consequences for religion or for science. His principles did not

[9] *Works*. VII, 264 is not really an admission to the contrary.
[10] Ibid. I, 69, 71, 84, 92, 105.
[11] Ibid. I, 94.

at all make void Natural Philosophy, or the science of the Causes or Reasons of corporeal changes; For to find out the reasons of things, in Natural Philosophy, is only to find out the proportion of God's acting. And the case is the same, as to such proportions, whether we suppose the World only mental, in our sense, or no.

And again:

It is just all one, as to any benefit or advantage, any end that we can suppose was proposed by the Creator, as if the Material Universe were existent in the same manner as is vulgarly thought. For the corporeal world is to no advantage but to the spiritual; and it is exactly the same advantage this way or the other, for it is all one, as to any thing excited in the mind.[12]

For the purposes of Edwards's life work, therefore, a completed and consistent system of philosophy was a spendthrift luxury. Having satisfied his own mind on general principles, he abandoned his investigations in natural science and its metaphysical and epistemological foundations, and from his first publication in 1731 until his death, he appeared before the world as evangelist, psychologist of religion, and theologian; bringing to whatever he did the equipment of a philosopher, but often apologizing for the philosophical digressions into which he was led for the clarification of theological issues.

## II

When Edwards became his grandfather's colleague in the church at Northampton in 1726, the discipline of the New England churches was no longer what it had been in the seventeenth century. In the Cambridge Platform of 1648 (III, 2) it had been agreed that the children of members of the Church Covenant were also members, but on coming of age must make public confession of regeneration by grace before being admitted to Holy Communion. When the time came, however, the many who could not lay claim to any experience of conversion nevertheless regarded themselves as members by right of birth, and asked to have their own children baptized in turn. To save itself from extinction without complete surrender of discipline, the church allowed the unconverted of the second and following generations to remain in the church but excluded them from the Lord's Supper—a compromise that came to be called the Half-Way Covenant. Edwards's grandfather, Solomon Stoddard, had gone a step farther. Arguing that Holy Communion was not primarily a privilege of the elect but a means of salvation, he began in 1704 to extend it to those

[12] *Works.* I, 669–70. § 34.

of the unregenerate who led good moral lives. The result was that church membership soon ceased to be anything but a badge of respectability, and the time was ripe for just such a revival of genuine religious piety as Edwards's searchings of soul had prepared him to initiate. Edwards revived the preaching of the Calvinistic doctrines of the total depravity of man, the necessity of supernatural grace for his salvation, and God's election of whom He pleased; but he employed a psychology of his own in his portrayal of the all-important differences between a truly religious and a merely moral life. As the Great Awakening, which began in his own church in 1734 and spread rapidly through the colonies, gathered momentum, he kept vigilant watch over all its manifestations, analyzed and recorded them with great skill and care, and elaborated the distinctions between truly "gracious affections" and the welter of hysterics, false sentimentality and delusive enthusiasm that accompanied the movement.

The inevitable reaction came. The ideal of piety and purity that Edwards held before his people proved in the end to be as far above their understanding as their attainment, and when he attempted to make that ideal the standard of admission to full communion, he was dismissed. For the history of American thought, however, the movement left a lasting monument in his *Treatise concerning Religious Affections* (1746), in which William James was to find "admirably rich and delicate description," critical acumen in the sifting of evidence, and "an elaborate working out" of the pragmatic test in matters of religion.[13]

## III

The leading opponents of the Great Awakening were deists and Arminians, and Edwards became convinced not merely that their theological views were responsible for the opposition, but that the spread of them would be fatal to the cause of vital religion. The doctrine of a self-determining will in particular was "almost inconceivably pernicious"; it tended to prevent all dependence upon God, to "encourage the sinner in present delays and neglects, and embolden him to go on in sin, in a presumption of having his own salvation at all times at his command"; indeed, it destroyed the very notion of conversion itself. The denial of man's total depravity and corruption, moreover, led to an increasing loss of the sense of sin. When a minister labored to convince his audience of their real guilt and sinfulness in

[13] James, William: *The Varieties of Religious Experience.* New York: Longmans, Green and Co., 1902. 20, 202 n. 2, 239.

the sight of God, they thought, perhaps, of "some instances of lewd behaviour, lying, dishonesty, intemperance, profaneness, &c.," but "the grand principles of iniquity, constantly abiding and reigning," were all overlooked.[14] As early as 1747, therefore, while still at Northampton, Edwards was planning a series of tracts or treatises on the various points of conflict between Arminian and Calvinist theology; and as soon as the routine of his work was well established at Stockbridge, he set himself to writing,

> . . . endeavoring also to bring the late great objections and outcries against Calvinistic divinity . . . to the test of the strictest reasoning; and particularly that great objection. . . That the Calvinistic notions of God's moral government are contrary to the common sense of mankind.[15]

In 1754 he published *A Careful and Strict Enquiry into the Modern Prevailing Notions of that Freedom of Will which is supposed to be Essential to Moral Agency, Vertue and Vice, Reward and Punishment, Praise and Blame;* and at the time of his death in 1758 his *The Great Christian Doctrine of Original Sin Defended* was passing through the press. It was the former of these that established Edwards's international reputation as a theologian, and led Dugald Steward to say in 1821:

> There is, however, one metaphysician of whom America has to boast, who, in logical acuteness and subtility, does not yield to any disputant bred in the universities of Europe. I need not say, that I allude to Jonathan Edwards.[16]

More profound and more original, however, were his essays "The End for which God created the World" and "The Nature of True Virtue," written in 1755 and published in 1765 by his disciple Samuel Hopkins. In these essays his speculative genius frees itself at last from the toils of controversy, returns to the themes and even to the language and imagery of his early "Notes on the Mind," and envisions a universe like that of Plotinus or Spinoza:

> In the creature's knowing, esteeming, loving, rejoicing in, and praising God, the glory of God is both *exhibited* and *acknowledged;* his fulness is *received* and *returned*. Here is both an *emanation* and *remanation*. The refulgence shines upon and into the creature, and is reflected back to the luminary. The beams of glory come from God, and are something of God, and are refunded back again to their original.[17]

[14] *Works*. I, 558–63.
[15] Ibid. I, 497–8.
[16] *Collected Works*. Edited by Sir William Hamilton. I (1877) 424–5.
[17] *Works*. III, 84.

Edwards's immediate and lasting influence on American thought, however, was due almost entirely to his great polemical treatises. His revived Calvinism, modified by his own religious psychology, was systematized by Hopkins, and under the name of "The New England Theology" continued to dominate Congregational and Presbyterian theological seminaries until the last quarter of the nineteenth century. His influence in his own century may be roughly gauged by comparing Hopkins's *System of Doctrines* (1793) with the first folio of theology published in America, Samuel Willard's *Compleat Body of Divinity* (1726), delivered between 1688 and 1707 as a course of two hundred and fifty expository lectures on the Westminster Shorter Catechism.

## REFERENCES

Dwight, Sereno E. (editor): *The Works of President Jonathan Edwards.* 10 vols. New York: 1829–30. (First volume contains *Life* by Dwight, and notes on the mind and natural science.)

Allen, A. V. G.: *Jonathan Edwards.* Boston: Houghton Mifflin Co., 1889.

Carpenter, F. I.: "The Radicalism of Jonathan Edwards," *New England Quarterly* 4 (1931) 629–44.

Curtis, M. M.: "Kantian Elements in Jonathan Edwards," in *Festschrift für Heinze.* Berlin, 1906.

Faust, C. H., and Johnson, T. H.: *Jonathan Edwards.* Representative Selections, with Introduction, Bibliography, and Notes. Cincinnati: American Book Co., 1935. (Annotated bibliography, systematic account of Edwards's thought in its historical setting, and adequate selections for further study.)

Foster, Frank Hugh: *A Genetic History of the New England Theology.* Chicago: University of Chicago Press, 1907.

Haroutunian, Joseph: "Jonathan Edwards: a Study in Godliness," *Journal of Religion* 11 (1931) 400–19.

———: *Piety versus Moralism: The Passing of the New England Theology.* New York: Henry Holt and Co., 1932.

McGiffert, A. C.: *Jonathan Edwards.* New York: Harper and Brothers, 1932.

Riley, I. Woodbridge: *American Philosophy: the Early Schools.* New York: Dodd, Mead and Co., 1907. 126–87.

Schneider, H. W.: *The Puritan Mind.* New York: Henry Holt and Co., 1930.

Smyth, Egbert C.: "Some Early Writings of Jonathan Edwards," *Proceedings of the American Antiquarian Society* n.s. 10 (1895) 212–47; 11 (1896) 251–2.

———: "Jonathan Edwards' Idealism," *American Journal of Theology* 1 (1897) 950–64.

Townsend, H. G.: *Philosophical Ideas in the United States.* Cincinnati: American Book Co., 1934. 35–62.

* * *

---

* * *

## EXCELLENCY [18]

There has nothing been more without a definition, than *Excellency;* although it be what we are more concerned with, than any thing else whatsoever: yea, we are concerned with nothing else. But what is this Excellency? Wherein is one thing excellent, and another evil; one beautiful, and another deformed? Some have said that all Excellency is *Harmony, Symmetry,* or *Proportion;* but they have not yet explained it. We would know, Why Proportion is more excellent than Disproportion: that is, why Proportion is pleasant to the mind, and Disproportion unpleasant? Proportion is a thing that may be explained yet further. It is an *Equality,* or *Likeness of ratios;* so that it is the Equality, that makes the Proportion. Excellency therefore seems to consist in *Equality.* Thus, if there be two perfect *equal* circles, or globes, together, there is something more of beauty than if they were of *unequal,* disproportionate magnitudes. And if two *parallel* lines be drawn, the beauty is greater, than if they were *obliquely* inclined without proportion, because there is equality of distance. And if betwixt two parallel lines, two equal circles be placed, each at the same distance from each parallel line, as in Fig. 1, the beauty is greater,

1 2 3 4

than if they stood at irregular distances from the parallel lines. If they stand, each in a perpendicular line, going from the parallel lines, (Fig. 2,) it is requisite that they should each stand at an equal distance from the perpendicular line next to them; otherwise there is no beauty. If there be three of these circles between two parallel lines, and near to a perpendicular line run between them, (Fig. 3,) the most beautiful form perhaps, that they could be placed in, is in an equilateral

[18] "Notes on the Mind," secs. 1, 45; in *Works.* I, 693–6, 699–702.

triangle with the cross line, because there are most equalities. The distance of the two next to the cross line is equal from that, and also equal from the parallel lines. The distance of the third from each parallel is equal, and its distance from each of the other two circles is equal, and is also equal to their distance from one another, and likewise equal to their distance from each end of the cross line. There are two equilateral triangles: one made by the three circles, and the other made by the cross line and two of the sides of the first protracted till they meet that line. And if there be another like it, on the opposite side, to correspond with it and it be taken altogether, the beauty is still greater, where the distances from the lines, in the one, are equal to the distances in the other; also the two next to the cross lines are at equal distances from the other two; or, if you go crosswise, from corner to corner. The two cross lines are also parallel, so that all parts are at an equal distance, and innumerable other equalities might be found.

This simple Equality, without Proportion, is the lowest kind of Regularity, and may be called Simple Beauty. All other beauties and excellencies may be resolved into it. Proportion is Complex Beauty. Thus, if we suppose that there are two points, A B, placed at two inches distance, and the next, C, one inch farther; (Fig. 1,) it is

Fig. 1

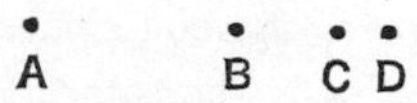

A B C D

Fig. 2

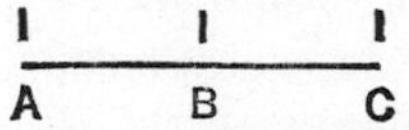

A B C

requisite, in order to regularity and beauty, if there be another, D, that it should be at half an inch distance; otherwise there is no regularity, and the last, D, would stand out of its proper place; because now the relation that the space C D, bears to B C, is equal to the relation that B C, bears to A B; so that B C D, is exactly similar to A B C. It is evident, this is a more complicated excellency than that which consisted in Equality, because the terms of the relation are here complex, and before were simple. When there are three points set in a right line, it is requisite, in order to regularity, that they should be set at an equal distance, as A B C, (Fig. 2,) where A B, is similar to B C, or the relation of C to B, is the same as of B to A. But in the other are three terms necessary in each of the parts, between which, is the relation, B C D, is as A B C: so that here more simple beauties are omitted, and yet there is a general complex beauty: that is, B C is not as A B, nor is C D as B C, but yet, B C D is as A B C. It is requisite that the consent or regularity of C D to B C, be omitted, for the sake of the harmony of the whole. For although, if C D was perfectly equal to B C, there would be regularity and beauty with respect to them two; yet, if A B be taken into the idea, there is nothing but confusion. And it might be requisite, if these stood with others, even to omit this proposition, for the sake of one more complex still. Thus, if they stood with other points, where B stood at four inches distance from A, C at two from B, and D at six from C: the place where D must stand in, if A, B, C, D, were alone, viz. one inch from C, must be so as to be made proportionate with the other points beneath;

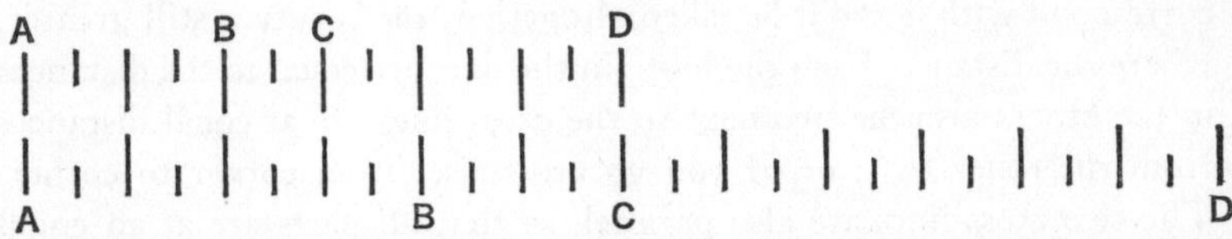


So that although A, B, C, D, are not proportioned, but are confusion among themselves; yet taken with the whole they are proportioned and beautiful.

All beauty consists in similarness or identity of relation. In identity of relation consists all likeness, and all identity between two consists in identity of relation. Thus, when the distance between two is exactly equal, their distance is their relation one to another, the distance is the same, the bodies are two; wherefore this is their correspondency and beauty. So bodies exactly of the same figure, the bodies are two, the relation between the parts of the extremities is the same, and this is their agreement with them. But if there are two bodies of different shapes, having no similarness of relation between the parts of the extremities; this, considered by itself, is a deformity, because being disagrees with being, which must undoubtedly be disagreeable to perceiving being: because what disagrees with Being, must necessarily be disagreeable to Being in general, to every thing that partakes of Entity, and of course to perceiving being; and what agrees with Being, must be agreeable to Being in general, and therefore to perceiving being. But agreeableness of perceiving being is pleasure, and disagreeableness is pain. Disagreement or contrariety to Being, is evidently an approach to Nothing, or a degree of Nothing; which is nothing else but disagreement or contrariety of Being, and the greatest and only evil: And Entity is the greatest and only good. And by how much more perfect Entity is, that is without mixture of Nothing, by so much the more Excellency. Two beings can agree one with another in nothing else but Relation; because otherwise the notion of their twoness (duality,) is destroyed, and they become one.

And so, in every case, what is called Correspondency, Symmetry, Regularity, and the like, may be resolved into Equalities; though the Equalities in a beauty, in any degree complicated, are so numerous, that it would be a most tedious piece of work to enumerate them. There are millions of these Equalities. Of these consist the beautiful shape of flowers, the beauty of the body of man, and of the bodies of other animals. That sort of beauty which is called Natural, as of vines, plants, trees, etc. consists of a very complicated harmony; and all the natural motions, and tendencies, and figures of bodies in the Universe are done according to proportion, and therein is their beauty. Particular disproportions sometimes greatly add to the general beauty, and must necessarily be, in order to a more universal proportion:—So much equality, so much beauty; though it may be noted that the quantity of equality is not to be measured only by the number, but the intenseness, according to the quantity of being. As bodies are shadows of being, so their proportions are shadows of proportion.

The pleasures of the senses, where harmony is not the object of judgment, are the result of equality. Thus in Music, not only in the proportion which the several notes of a tune bear, one among another, but in merely two notes, there is harmony; whereas it is impossible there should be proportion between only two terms. But the proportion is in the particular vibrations of the air, which strike on the ear. And so, in the pleasantness of light, colours, tastes, smells and touch, all arise from proportion of motion. The organs are so contrived that, upon the touch of such and such particles, there shall be a regular and harmonious motion of the animal spirits.

Spiritual harmonies are of vastly larger extent: i. e. the proportions are vastly oftener redoubled, and respect mere beings, and require a vastly larger view to comprehend them; as some simple notes do more affect one, who has not a comprehensive understanding of Music.

The reason, why Equality thus pleases the mind, and Inequality is unpleasing, is because Disproportion, or Inconsistency, is contrary to Being. For Being, if we examine narrowly, is nothing else but Proportion. When one being is inconsistent with another being, then Being is contradicted. But contradiction to Being, is intolerable to perceiving being, and the consent to Being, most pleasing.

Excellency consists in the *Similarness* of one being to another—not merely Equality and Proportion, but any kind of Similarness—thus Similarness of direction. Supposing many globes moving in right lines, it is more beautiful, that they should move all the same way, and according to the same direction, than if they moved disorderly; one, one way, and another, another. This is an universal definition of Excellency:—*The Consent of Being to Being,* or *Being's Consent to Entity.* The more the Consent is, and the more extensive, the greater is the Excellency.

How exceedingly apt are we, when we are sitting still, and accidentally casting our eye upon some marks or spots in the floor or wall, to be ranging of them into regular parcels and figures: and, if we see a mark out of its place, to be placing of it right, by our imagination; and this, even while we are meditating on something else. So we may catch ourselves at observing the rules of harmony and regularity, in the careless motions of our heads or feet, and when playing with our hands, or walking about the room.

. . . . . .

1. When we spake of Excellence in Bodies, we were obliged to borrow the word, *Consent,* from Spiritual things; but Excellence in and among Spirits is in its prime and proper sense, Being's consent to Being. There is no other proper consent but that of *Minds,* even of their Will; which, when it is of Minds towards Minds it is *Love,* and when of Minds towards other things, it is *Choice.* Wherefore all the Primary and Original beauty or excellence, that is among Minds, is Love; and into this may all be resolved that is found among them.

2. When we spake of External excellency, we said, that *Being's consent to Being,* must needs be agreeable to *Perceiving Being.* But now we are speaking of Spiritual things, we may change the phrase, and say, that *Mind's love to Mind* must needs be lovely to *Beholding Mind;* and Being's love to Being, in general, must needs be agreeable to Being that perceives it, because itself is a participation of Being, in general.

3. As to the proportion of this Love;—to greater Spirits, more, and to less, less;—it is beautiful, as it is a manifestation of love to Spirit or Being in general. And the want of this proportion is a deformity, because it is a manifestation of a defect of such a love. It shows that it is not Being, in general, but something else, that is loved, when love is not in proportion to the Extensiveness and Excellence of Being.

4. Seeing God has so plainly revealed himself to us; and other minds are made in his image, and are emanations from him; we may judge what is the Excellence of other minds, by what is his, which we have shown is Love. His Infinite Beauty, is His Infinite mutual Love of Himself. Now God is the Prime and Original Being, the First and Last, and the Pattern of all, and has the sum of all perfection. We may

therefore, doubtless, conclude, that all that is the perfection of Spirits may be resolved into that which is God's perfection, which is Love.

5. There are several degrees of deformity or disagreeableness of dissent from Being. One is, when there is only merely a dissent from Being. This is disagreeable to Being, (for Perceiving Being only is properly Being.) Still more disagreeable is a dissent to very excellent Being, or, as we have explained, to a Being that consents in a high degree to Being, because such a Being by such a consent becomes bigger; and a dissenting from such a Being includes, also, a dissenting from what he consents with, which is other Beings, or Being in general. Another deformity, that is more odious than mere dissent from Being, is, for a Being to dissent from, or not to consent with, a Being who consents with his Being. It is a manifestation of a greater dissent from Being than ordinary; for the Being perceiving, knows that it is natural to Being, to consent with what consents with it, as we have shown. It therefore manifests an extraordinary dissent, that consent to itself will not draw its consent. The deformity, for the same reason, is greater still, if there be dissent from consenting Being. There are such contrarieties and jars in Being, as must necessarily produce jarring and horror in perceiving Being.

6. Dissent from such Beings, if that be their fixed nature, is a manifestation of Consent to Being in General; for consent to Being is dissent from that, which dissents from Being.

7. Wherefore all Virtue, which is the Excellency of minds, is resolved into *Love to Being;* and nothing is virtuous or beautiful in Spirits, any otherwise than as it is an exercise, or fruit, or manifestation, of this love; and nothing is sinful or deformed in Spirits, but as it is the defect of, or contrary to, these.

8. When we speak of Being in general, we may be understood of the Divine Being, for he is an Infinite Being: therefore all others must necessarily be considered as nothing. As to *Bodies,* we have shown in another place, that they have no proper Being of their own. And as to *Spirits,* they are the communications of the Great Original Spirit; and doubtless, in metaphysical strictness and propriety, He is, as there is none else. He is likewise Infinitely Excellent, and all Excellence and Beauty is derived from him in the same manner as all Being. And all other Excellence, is, in strictness only, a shadow of his. We proceed, therefore, to show how all Spiritual Excellence is resolved into Love.

9. As to God's Excellence, it is evident it consists in the *Love of himself;* for he was as excellent, before he created the Universe, as he is now. But if the Excellence of Spirits consists in their disposition

and action, God could be excellent no other way at that time; for all the exertions of himself were towards himself. But he exerts himself towards himself, no other way, than in infinitely loving and delighting in himself; in the mutual love of the Father and the Son. This makes the Third, the Personal Holy Spirit, or the Holiness of God, which is his Infinite Beauty; and this is God's Infinite Consent to Being in general. And his love to the creature is his Excellence, or the communication of Himself, his complacency in them, according as they partake of more or less of Excellence and beauty, that is of holiness, (which consists in love;) that is according as he communicates more or less of his Holy Spirit.

10. As to that Excellence, that Created Spirits partake of; that it is all to be resolved into Love, none will doubt, that knows what is the Sum of the Ten Commandments; or believes what the Apostle says, That Love is the fulfilling of the Law; or what Christ says, That on these two, loving God and our neighbor, hang all the Law and the Prophets. This doctrine is often repeated in the New Testament. We are told that the End of the Commandment is Love; that to Love, is to fulfil the Royal Law; and that all the Law is fulfilled in this one word, Love.

11. I know of no difficulties worth insisting on, except pertaining to the spiritual excellence of Justice; but enough has been said already to resolve them. Though Injustice is the greatest of all deformities, yet Justice is no otherwise excellent, than as it is the exercise, fruit and manifestation of the mind's love or consent to Being; nor Injustice deformed any otherwise, than as it is the highest degree of the contrary. Injustice is not to exert ourselves towards any Being as it deserves, or to do it contrary to what it deserves, in doing good or evil, or in acts of Consent or Dissent. There are two ways of deserving our Consent, and the acts of it: (By *deserving* any thing, we are to understand *that the nature of being requires it:*) By extensiveness and excellence; and by consent to that particular being. The Reason of the deformity of not proportioning our consent, and the exercise of it, may be seen in paragraphs 3 and 5. As to the beauty of Vindictive Justice, see paragraph 6.

12. 'Tis peculiar to God, that he has beauty *within himself*, consisting in Being's consenting with his own Being, or the love of himself, in his own Holy Spirit. Whereas the excellence of others is in loving others, in loving God, and in the communications of his Spirit.

13. We shall be in danger, when we meditate on this love of God to himself, as being the thing wherein his infinite excellence and love-

liness consists, of some alloy to the sweetness of our view, by its appearing with something of the aspect and cast of what we call self love. But we are to consider that this love includes in it, or rather is the same as, a love to every thing, as they are all communications of himself. So that we are to conceive of Divine Excellence as the Infinite General Love, that which reaches all, proportionally, with perfect purity and sweetness; yea, it includes the true Love of all creatures, for that is his Spirit, or which is the same thing, his Love. And if we take notice, when we are in the best frames meditating on Divine Excellence, our idea of that tranquility and peace, which seems to be overspread and cast abroad upon the whole Earth, and Universe, naturally dissolves itself, into the idea of a General Love and Delight, every where diffused.

14. Conscience is *that Sense the Mind has of this Consent:* Which Sense consists in the Consent of the Perceiving Being, to such a General Consent; (that is of such perceiving Beings, as are capable of so general a perception, as to have any notion of Being in general;) and the Dissent of his mind to a Dissent from Being in general. We have said already, that it is naturally agreeable to Perceiving Being that Being should consent to Being, and the contrary disagreeable. If by any means, therefore, a particular and restrained love overcomes this General Consent;—the foundation of that Consent yet remaining in the nature, exerts itself again, so that there is the contradiction of one consent to another. And as it is naturally agreeable to every Being, to have being consent to him; the mind, after it has thus exerted an act of dissent to Being in general, has a sense that Being in general dissents from it, which is most disagreeable to it. And as he is conscious of a dissent from Universal Being, and of that Being's dissent from him, wherever he is, he sees what excites horror. And by inclining or doing that, which is against his natural inclination as a Perceiving Being, he must necessarily cause uneasiness, inasmuch as that natural inclination is contradicted. And this is the *Disquiet of Conscience.* And, though the Disposition be changed, the remembrance of his having so done in time past, and the idea being still tied to that of himself, he is uneasy. The notion of such a dissent any where, as we have shown is odious; but the notion of its being in himself, renders it uneasy and disquieting. But when there is no sense of any such dissent from Being in general, there is no contradiction to the natural inclination of Perceiving Being. And when he reflects, he has a sense that Being in general doth not dissent from him; and then there is *Peace of Conscience;* though he has a remembrance of past dissentions with nature. Yet if by any means it be possible, when he has the idea of it, to conceive of it as not be-

longing to him, he has the same Peace. And if he has a sense not only of his not dissenting, but of his consenting to Being in general, or Nature, and acting accordingly; he has a sense that Nature, in general, consents to him: he has not only *Peace,* but *Joy, of mind,* wherever he is. These things are obviously invigorated by the knowledge of God and his Constitution about us, and by the light of the Gospel.

* * *

---

* * *

## [PERSONAL IDENTITY] [19]

Some things are *entirely distinct,* and *very diverse,* which yet are so united by the established law of the Creator, that by virtue of that establishment, they are in a sense *one.* Thus a *tree,* grown great, and a hundred years old, is *one* plant with the little *sprout,* that first came out of the ground from whence it grew, and has been continued in constant succession; though it is now so exceeding *diverse,* many thousand times bigger, and of a very different form and perhaps not one atom the very same: Yet God, according to an established law of nature, has in a constant succession communicated to it many of the same qualities, and most important properties, as if it were *one.* It has been his pleasure to constitute an union in these respects, and for these purposes, naturally leading us to look upon all as *one.*—So the *body* of *man* at forty years of age, is *one* with the *infant-body* which first came into a world, from whence it grew; though now constituted of different substance, and the greater part of the substance probably changed scores (if not hundreds) of times: And though it be now in so many respects exceeding diverse, yet God, according to the course of nature which he has been pleased to establish, has caused that in a certain method it should communicate with that *infantile* body, in the same life, the same senses, the same features, and many the same qualities, and in union with the same soul; and so, with regard to these purposes, it is dealt with by him as *one* body. Again the *body* and *soul* of a man are *one,* in a very different manner, and for different purposes. Considered in themselves, they are exceeding different beings, of a nature as diverse as can be conceived; and yet, by a very peculiar divine con-

[19] *The Great Christian Doctrine of Original Sin Defended,* in *Works.* II, 549–56 (omitting footnote on 553–4).

stitution, or law of nature, which God has been pleased to establish, they are strongly united, and become *one,* in most important respects; a wonderful mutual communication is established; so that both become different parts of the *same man.* But the union and mutual communication they have, has existence, and is entirely regulated and limited, according to the sovereign pleasure of God, and constitution he has been pleased to establish.

And if we come even to the *personal identity* of created intelligent beings, though this be not allowed to consist *wholly* in what Mr. Locke supposes, i. e. *Same consciousness;* yet I think it cannot be denied, that this is one thing essential to it. But it is evident, that the communication or continuance of the same consciousness and memory to any subject, through successive parts of duration, depends wholly on a divine establishment. There would be no necessity that the remembrance and ideas of what is past should continue to exist, but by an arbitrary constitution of the Creator.—If any should here insist that there is no need of having recourse to any such *constitution,* in order to account for the continuance of the *same consciousness;* and should say, that the very *nature* of the soul is such as will sufficiently account for it, its ideas and consciousness being retained, according to the *course of nature:* Then let it be remembered, who it is that gives the soul this nature; and let that be remembered, which Dr. T. says of the course of nature, before observed; denying, that "the course of nature is a proper active cause, which will work and go on by itself without God, if he lets and permits it;" saying, "that the course of nature, separate from the agency of God, is no cause, or nothing;" and affirming, that "it is absolutely impossible, the course of nature should continue itself, or go on to operate by itself, any more than produce itself; and that God, the original of all being, is the *only cause* of all natural effects." Here is worthy also to be observed, what Dr. Turnbull says of the laws of nature, as cited from Sir Isaac Newton. "It is the will of the mind that is the *first cause,* that gives subsistence and efficacy to all those *laws,* who is the *efficient cause* that produces the *phaenomena,* which appear in analogy, harmony and agreement, according to these *laws.*" And, "the same principles must take place in things pertaining to *moral,* as well as natural philosophy."

From these things it will clearly follow, that identity of *consciousness* depends wholly on a law of *nature;* and so, on the sovereign *will* and *agency of* GOD. And therefore, that personal identity, and so the derivation of the pollution and guilt of past sins in the same person, depends on an arbitrary divine *constitution;* and this, even though we should allow the same consciousness not to be the only thing which constitutes oneness of person, but should, besides that, suppose sameness of substance requisite. For, if same consciousness be *one thing* necessary to personal identity, and this depends on God's sovereign *constitution,* it will still follow, that personal identity depends on God's sovereign *constitution.*

And with respect to the identity of created substance itself, in the different moments of its duration, I think we shall greatly mistake, if we imagine it to be like that absolute, independent identity of the FIRST BEING, whereby he is *the same yesterday, to-day, and for ever.* Nay, on the contrary, it may be demonstrated, that even this oneness of created substance existing at different times, is a merely *dependent* identity; dependent on the pleasure and sovereign constitution of him who *worketh all in all.* This will follow from what is generally allowed, and is certainly true, that God not only created all things, and gave them being at first, but continually preserves them, and upholds them in being. This being a matter of considerable importance, it may be worthy here to be considered with a little attention. Let us inquire therefore, in the first place, whether it be not evident, that God does continually, by his immediate power, *uphold* every created substance in being; and then let us see the *consequence.*

That God does, by his immediate power, *uphold* every created substance in being, will be manifest, if we consider that their present existence is a *dependent* existence, and therefore is an *effect* and must have some *cause;* and the cause must be one of these two; either the *antecedent existence* of the same substance, or else the *power* of the *Creator.* But it cannot be the *antecedent existence* of the same substance. For instance, the existence of the body of the *moon,* at this present moment cannot be the *effect* of its existence at the last foregoing moment. For not only was what existed the last moment, no active cause, but wholly a passive thing; but this also is to be considered, that no cause can produce effects in a *time and place* in which itself is *not.* It is plain, nothing can exert itself, or operate, *when* and *where* it is not existing. But the moon's past existence was neither *where* nor *when* its present existence is. In point of *time,* what is *past* entirely ceases when *present* existence begins; otherwise it would not be *past.* The past moment has ceased, and is gone when the present moment takes place; and no more *co-exists* with it, than any other moment that had ceased twenty years ago. Nor could the past existence of the particles of this *moving body* produce effects in any *other place,* than where it then was. But its existence at the present moment, in every point of it, is in a different *place* from where its existence was at the last preceding moment. From these things I suppose it will certainly follow, that the present existence, either of this, or any other created substance, cannot be an effect of its past existence. The existences (so to speak) of an effect, or thing dependent, in different parts of space or duration, though ever so near one to another, do not at all *co-exist* one with the other; and therefore are as truly different effects, as if those parts of space and duration were ever so far asunder. And the prior existence can no more be the proper cause of the new existence, in the next moment, or next part of space, than if it had been in an age before, or at a thousand miles distance, without any existence to fill up the intermediate time or space. Therefore the existence of created substances, in each successive moment, must be the effect of the *immediate* agency, will, and power of GOD.

If any shall insist upon it, that their present existence is the effect or consequence of past existence, according to the *nature* of things; that the established *course of nature* is sufficient to *continue* existence once given; I allow it. But then it should be remembered, *what* nature is in created things; and *what* the established *course* of nature is; that, as has been observed already, *it is nothing, separate from the agency of God;* and that, as Dr. T. says, GOD, *the original of all being, is the ONLY cause of all natural effects.* A father, according to the course of nature, begets a child; an oak, according to the course of nature, produces an acorn, or a bud; so according to the course of nature, the former existence of the trunk of the tree is followed by its new or present existence. In the one case, and the other, the new effect is consequent on the former, only by the *established laws* and *settled course of nature;* which is allowed to be nothing but the continued immediate efficiency of GOD, according to a *constitution* that he has been pleased to establish. Therefore, according to what our author urges; as the child and the acorn which come into existence according to the *course of nature,* in consequence of the prior existence and state of the parent and the oak, are truly *immediately* created by God; so must the existence of each created person and thing, at each moment, be from the immediate *continued* creation of God. It will certainly follow from these things, that God's *preserving* of created things in being, is perfectly equivalent to a *continued creation,* or to his creating those things out of nothing at *each moment* of their existence. If the continued existence of created things be wholly dependent on God's preservation, then those things would drop into *nothing,* upon the ceasing of the present moment, without a new exertion of the divine power to cause them to exist in the following moment. If there be any who own that God *preserves* things in being, and yet hold that they would continue in being without any further help from him after they once have existence; I think, it is hard to know what they mean. To what purpose can it be, to talk of God *preserving* things in being, when there is *no need* of his preserving them? Or to talk of their being *dependent* on God for continued existence, when they would of themselves continue to exist, without his help; nay, though he should wholly withdraw his sustaining power and influence?

It will follow from what has been observed, that God's upholding of created substance, or causing of its existence in each successive moment, is altogether equivalent to an *immediate production out of nothing,* at each moment. Because its existence at this moment is not merely in part from *God,* but wholly from him; and not in any part, or degree, from its *antecedent existence.* For, to suppose that its antecedent existence *concurs* with God in *efficiency,* to produce some *part* of the effect, is attended with all the very same absurdities, which have been shewn to attend the supposition of its producing it *wholly.* Therefore the antecedent existence is nothing, as to any proper influence or assistance in the affair: And consequently *God* produces the effect as much from *nothing,* as if there had been nothing *before.* So that this effect differs not at all from the first creation, but only *circumstantially;* as, in *first* creation there had been no such act and effect of God's power *before;* whereas his giving existence afterwards, *follows* preceding acts and effects of the same kind, in an established order.

Now, in the next place, let us see how the *consequence* of these things is to my present purpose. If the existence of created *substance,* in each successive moment, be wholly the effect of God's immediate power in *that* moment, without any dependence on prior existence, as much as the first creation out of *nothing,* then what exists at this moment, by this power, is a *new effect;* and simply and absolutely considered, not the same with any past existence, though it be like it and follows it according to a certain established method.[20] And there is no identity

[20] When I suppose, that an effect which is produced every moment by a new action or exertion of power, must be a *new* effect in each moment, and not absolutely and numerically the same with that which existed in preceding moments, what I intend may be illustrated by this example. The lucid colour or brightness of the *moon,* as we look steadfastly upon it, seems to be a *permanent* thing, as though it were perfectly the same brightness continued. But indeed it is an effect produced every moment. It ceases, and is renewed, in each successive point of time; and so becomes altogether a *new* effect at each instant; and no one thing that belongs to it is numerically the same that existed in the preceding moment. The rays of the sun, impressed on that

or oneness in the case, but what depends on the *arbitrary* constitution of the Creator; who by his wise sovereign establishment so unites these successive new effects, that he *treats them as one,* by communicating to them like properties, relations, and circumstances; and so leads us to regard and treat them as *one.* When I call this an *arbitrary constitution,* I mean that it is a constitution which depends on nothing but the *divine will;* which divine will depends on nothing but the *divine wisdom.*[21] In this sense, the whole *course of nature,* with all that belongs to

---

body, and reflected from it, which cause the effect, are none of them the same: The impression made in each moment on our sensory, is by the stroke of *new* rays: And the sensation excited by the stroke is a new effect, an effect of a *new* impulse. Therefore the brightness or lucid whiteness of this body is no more numerically the same thing with that which existed in the preceding moment, than the *sound* of the wind that blows now is individually the same with the sound of the wind that blew just before; which, though it be like it, is not the same, any more than the agitated *air,* that makes the sound, is the same; or than the *water* flowing in a river, that now passes by, is individually the same with that which passed a little before. And if it be thus with the brightness or colour of the moon, so it must be with its *solidity,* and every thing else belonging to its substance, if all be, each moment, as much the immediate effect of a *new* exertion or application of power.

The matter may perhaps be in some respects still more clearly illustrated thus.—The *images* of things in a *glass,* as we keep our eye upon them, seem to remain precisely the same, with a continuing perfect identity. But it is known to be otherwise. Philosophers well know, that these images are constantly *renewed,* by the impression and reflection of *new* rays of light; so that the image impressed by the former rays is constantly vanishing, and a *new* image impressed by *new* rays every moment, both on the glass and on the eye. The image constantly renewed, by new successive rays, is no more numerically the same, than if it were by some artist put on anew with a pencil, and the colours constantly vanishing as fast as put on. And the new images being put on *immediately* or instantly, do not make them the same, any more than if it were done with the intermission of an *hour* or a *day.* The image that exists this moment, is not at all *derived* from the image that existed the last preceding moment: for, if the succession of new *rays* be intercepted by something interposed between the object and the glass, the image immediately ceases; the *past existence* of the image has no influence to uphold it, so much as for one moment. Which shews, that the image is altogether new-made every moment; and strictly speaking, is in no part numerically the same with that which existed the moment preceding. And truly so the matter must be with the *bodies* themselves, as well as their images. They also cannot be the same, with an absolute identity, but must be wholly renewed every moment, if the case be as has been proved, that their present existence is not, strictly speaking, at all the effect of their past existence; but is wholly, every instant, the effect of a new agency, or exertion of the powerful cause of their existence. If so, the existence caused is every instant a new effect, whether the cause be *light* or immediate *divine power,* or whatever it be.

[21] Returning to this point on p. 558 Edwards adds: "The wisdom which is exercised in these constitutions appears in these two things.—First, in a

it, all its laws and methods, constancy and regularity, continuance, and proceeding, is an *arbitrary constitution.* In this sense, the continuance of the very being of the world and all its parts, as well as the manner of continued being, depends entirely on an *arbitrary constitution.* For it does not at all *necessarily* follow, that because there was sound, or light, or colour, or resistance, or gravity, or thought, or consciousness, or any other dependent thing the last moment, that therefore there shall be the like at the next. All dependent existence whatsoever is in a constant flux, ever passing and returning; renewed every moment, as the colours of bodies are every moment renewed by the light that shines upon them; and all is constantly proceeding from GOD, as light from the sun. *In him we live, and move, and have our being.*

---

beautiful analogy and harmony with *other* laws or constitutions, especially relating to the same subject; and secondly, in the good ends obtained, or useful consequences of such a constitution."—Editor's note.

# V

# Cadwallader Colden

1688–1776

Born in Ireland of Scotch ancestry, the son of a minister. B.A., Edinburgh, 1705. Declined opportunity to enter ministry. Studied medicine at Edinburgh and London. Emigrated to Philadelphia to practice medicine, 1710. Moved to New York, 1718. Gave up medicine to become surveyor-general, 1719. Served on Governor's Council. Lieutenant governor, 1761–76. Wrote on history, mathematics, botany and medicine. Died in Flushing, L. I.

Colden's intellectual interests, like those of most eighteenth century savants, were varied. His first publication, *The History of the Five Indian Nations Depending on the Province of New York,* was an immediate success. His experimental work in botany was rewarded when Linnaeus had much of his material published and gave the name Coldenia to a new plant he had discovered. He was widely known for his work on cancer and the control of epidemics. An early paper of his on animal secretion was read by Dr. Halley before the Royal Society. His correspondents included such well-known scientific figures as Linnaeus, Gronovius, Euler and Franklin. He invented a process now known as stereotyping and was one of the first men to suggest the formation of a learned society in America, an idea which was finally brought to fruition by Franklin. His lasting fame will hardly be what he had hoped for, but he does stand out not only as one of the prominent leisure-time scientists of the period but as a thinker through whose mind filtered the chief cross-currents of the day.

Newtonian physics was the starting point for Colden's philosophy. As he said in the preface to his only published philosophical work, *The Principles of Action in Matter,*

Though the author has presumed, in some material points, to differ in opinion from the great sir *Isaac Newton,* and to point out some errors he has fallen into, (and what man never fell into any error?) yet no man can have a greater opinion of sir *Isaac's* wonderful sagacity and accuracy in discovering the most hidden truths, than the author has: this work it self will shew what great advantage has been made of sir *Isaac's* discoveries.

Although his parents were religious, his thought never bore the imprint of religious preconceptions. While actively engaged in political affairs during the major part of his life, he considered politics a means, not an end. Science was his great intellectual love. Newton was the symbol for science and hence he started with Newton.

The law of gravitation and the mechanistic implications of Newton's work were epoch-making in significance. Colden was the first American to study Newton thoroughly. He attempted to offer a satisfactory explanation for gravitation where he felt Newton had failed. That he was convinced he had done this is evidenced by literal statement as well as by the tone of his writings. He estimated his own contribution in relation to Newtonian gravitation by saying, "In this tract the author presumes to think, that he has discovered the cause of this apparent attraction, and from which all the phaenomena in gravitation evidently follow, as necessary consequences." [1] When he had prepared copy for another edition of the book in 1762 (which never materialized), he sent it for criticism to Robert Whyte, Professor of Medicine at Edinburgh, requesting if it be unsuitable for publication that it be placed in the library "for I am perswaded they [its pages] will some time or other be found to contain the true Principles of Physical Knowledge and to be of real use." [2]

Colden took a phenomenalistic position. Newton had made a distinction between physical laws and metaphysical explanation of those laws; Colden accepted this distinction but went on to deny the possibility of knowing the ultimate nature of things. Matter, as a substance, was unknowable. All that we could know of it was what it appeared to be in action. Efficient causes could be known, but of ultimate causes man was to remain forever ignorant. When writing to William Popple he said,

> Our knowledge of the powers in nature can only be attained by an accurate observation of the phenomena or effects produced by them and from thence collecting the general rules or laws which these powers observe in producing their effects in different circumstances. We thereby have obtained all the knowledge of nature which can be obtained by our faculties.[3]

[1] *The Principles of Action in Matter.* Preface.
[2] *The Colden Letter Books.* I, 168.
[3] *The Letters and Papers of Cadwallader Colden.* VI, 197.

Holding rather consistently to this phenomenalistic viewpoint Colden attempted to describe the action of matter. Matter was of three types, each type possessing functions of its own. First was resisting matter whose primary function was the prevention of movement; it was impenetrable. Second was moving matter whose primary function was movement; it was penetrable by itself but impenetrable by resisting matter. Third was elastic matter whose primary function was to serve as a medium for communicating the actions of resisting and moving matter; aether, as this elastic matter was called, was alternately penetrable and impenetrable. All objects possessing quantity and shape, insofar as they were known to us, were material and were to be understood on the basis of mathematical and mechanical principles and in terms of the three types of matter. The physical world was to be interpreted in terms of the mechanics of energy, not in terms of essences or final causes. Colden was inclined toward hylozoism but here, as elsewhere, his proximity to an historic position served as an omen of restraint rather than as a suggestion of conversion.

Colden's position on the nature of mind, or intelligence, was not entirely clear. He expressed opposition to considering mind a quality of matter and, on the other hand, to making matter so subservient to mind as to be meaningless. Although he never developed his philosophy of the immaterial as he said he would, he did say enough to indicate a dualistic leaning. The immaterial, or spirit, was different from matter because it served a different function. Colden was out of sympathy with the tendency to believe that motion, or action, was caused by the influence of mind, or intelligence, on matter. At the same time, he felt that to give intelligence to matter would be to suggest that matter possessed will; this would invalidate the mathematical approach to nature. Accepting the mathematical approach he felt it necessary to conceive of intelligence as a mode of action different from the action of matter and hence suggestive of another type of existence.

Colden and Samuel Johnson carried on an interesting correspondence on the subject of the relationships of mind and matter. Johnson, a follower of Berkeley, had kept Colden supplied with the Irish sage's writings hoping that Colden would ultimately accept the idealistic position. Colden was rather unimpressed by Berkeley's position for he could not conceive of matter as passive. He pointed out to Johnson that whatever existed had to be active and that matter could be active without possessing intelligence. Johnson, always inclined to smooth over their differences, suggested that perhaps Colden was speaking only figuratively, that he probably did not mean to say that matter possessed its own power of movement and that he would possibly agree that motion was imparted to matter by an intelligent agent separate from it. Colden replied that he could not conceive of anything which did not have some action of its own and that to attribute all immediate action to an intelligent agent would not only invalidate scientific analysis but would also destroy the foundations of morality, for under such circumstances no human action could be morally evil. In his reply, Johnson professed his inability to conceive of action without intelligence. He contended that Colden's statement that "perfect intelligence will not act in contradiction to the action of matter" should read "will not in the settled course of things act in contradiction to the laws He hath established according to which He wills matter to act." The upshot of this correspondence was that Colden finally accepted the idea of an intelligent creator of nature who gave matter the direction of its action but who in no sense interfered with matter in the performance of that action. In the revision of his *First Causes of Action in Matter,* printed under the title *The Principles of Action in Matter,* he added a chapter (included below) entitled "Of the Intelligent Being, and of the Formation and Duration of the Several Systems in the Universe" in which he dealt with intelligent agents. Colden's Intelligent Creator was thus an afterthought, inspired by Johnson for the most part and forced on him by the necessity of explaining the orderliness of nature and intelligence in man. He promised a careful treatment of intelligence at a later date but it was never forthcoming. He never went over to the position of Berkeley but he was forced into a dualism from which it was not easy to escape.

Colden's philosophy was indeed a compromise. Influenced by many thinkers he was a thorough-going disciple of none. He was sympathetic to Hobbesian psychology and materialism but to him the mind was more than a series of physiological reactions and matter hardly the substance Hobbes had made it. He was close to Leibniz in assigning activity to physical objects, but he denied that they had intelligence. He followed the realistic approach of the English empiricists but he could not accept its resultant subjectivism. He approached the deism which Priestley and Cooper expressed later yet he did not, like them, make mind homogeneous with matter. Colden was rather typically American, being inspired by ideas peculiarly European in origin but reconstructing them in a heterogeneous system of his own. Colden's importance lies more in what he imported and in what he inspired than in what he created.

## REFERENCES

Colden, Cadwallader: *The Principles of Action in Matter, the Gravitation of Bodies, and the Motion of the Planets, Explained from those Principles.* London, 1751. (This was a revision of *An Explication of the First Causes of Action in Matter, and of the Cause of Gravitation.* New York, 1745; London, 1746. It was again revised in 1762 but this revision was not printed. Two copies of the 1751 edition in the possession of the New York Historical Society contain notations and additions, one of them in Colden's handwriting, evidently used in the preparation of the revision.)

———: *The Colden Letter Books.* 2 vols. New York: Collections of the New York Historical Society, 1876–77.

———: *The Letters and Papers of Cadwallader Colden.* 9 vols. New York: Collections of the New York Historical Society, 1917–23, 1934–35. (Esp. vol. I which contains an introduction on Colden's intellectual interests and vol. III which contains the correspondence between Colden and Samuel Johnson. This correspondence is also included in Schneider, Herbert and Carol (editors): *Samuel Johnson, President of King's College: His Career and Writings.* II, 285–305. A list of Colden's unpublished manuscripts in the possession of the New York Historical Society is included in vol. VII, 359–76. A number of these are of scientific and philosophic interest.)

Ingraham, Charles A.: "A Great Colonial Executive and Scholar—Cadwallader Colden," *Americana* XIX (1925) 295–314.

Keys, Alice M.: *Cadwallader Colden: A Representative Eighteenth Century Official.* New York: Columbia University Press, 1906. (Esp. ch. I, "A Colonial Savant.")

Riley, I. Woodbridge: *American Philosophy: the Early Schools.* New York: Dodd, Mead and Co., 1907. 329–72.

* * *

---

* * *

# THE PRINCIPLES OF ACTION IN MATTER, THE GRAVITATION OF BODIES, AND THE MOTION OF THE PLANETS, EXPLAINED FROM THOSE PRINCIPLES [4]

## *Of the Principles of Action in Matter*

### SECT. I

### OF THE ESSENTIAL PROPERTIES AND DIFFERENCES OF THINGS

1. We have no knowledge of substances, or of any being, or of any thing, abstracted from the action of that thing or being. All our knowledge of things consists in the perception of the power, or force, or property, or manner of acting of that thing; that is, of the action of that thing on our senses, or of the effects of that thing on some other thing, whose action affects, or is the object of our senses, and in the perception of the relations or ratios of these actions to each other. For if any thing produce no alteration in our senses, it is impossible for us to know that any such thing exists: and every effect must be produced by some cause, or by some action.

2. Every thing, that we know, is an agent, or has a power of acting: for as we know nothing of any thing but its action, and the effects of that action, the moment any thing ceases to act it must be annihilated as to us: we can have no kind of idea of its existence. Any thing, which produces any effect or alteration in another thing, must either have its power and force of itself, or its action must be the effect of some other cause, and consequently it is not a primary agent: but in this place I only consider primary agents, and such must continually exert their force and energy. For it seems a contradiction in terms that any thing should obstruct or oppose its own force or energy: consequently every thing exerting of itself any power or force must be continually acting. Whatever stops be supposed to happen in its action, they can only be the effects of some opposite power or force, acting at the same time, and of superior or equal force in that instance, by which, tho' it continue to exert its power, its action is stopt, or rendered ineffectual.

3. If the idea or conception, which the action of any thing excites in us, be such, that at the same time we perceive that the thing itself, endowed with this power of acting, must be of some shape, or that it

[4] Ch. I, 1–29; ch. VII, 157–67.

may be divided into parts, that its power or force may be increased by addition of parts, or lessened by the taking away of part, it is then conceived to be of some quantity. And every thing which is conceived to be of some quantity, is commonly called *matter.*

4. But if the action of any thing do not excite in us any perception of its being of any quantity, or of any form or shape, or of its consisting of any parts, or that its force or action can be increased or lessened by the addition or taking away of part, that thing commonly goes under the name of an *immaterial* substance, or of *spirit.*

5. Now from this manner of considering things, I hope to shew, that we may have as clear and distinct an idea or conception of spirit, as we can have of matter: and that all the difficulties or absurdities, which many have fallen into, arise from an error in the conceptions of the power, force, energy, or manner of acting, and which are commonly called the properties or qualities of things; or from the confusion which arises by the using of different terms, or words to express things, which in themselves are not different. The property, or quality of any thing, is nothing else but the action of that thing: and the different qualities or properties of any thing or substance are no other than the different actions or manner of acting of that thing. For we can have no idea or conception of the property or quality of any thing excited in us, but by the action of that thing: unless it can be supposed, that an effect is produced without a cause, and that a cause can be conceived without action. Therefore,

6. The differences of things (so far at least as we can know) consists in their different actions, or manner of acting. And if the actions of several things be such, as that we evidently perceive, that they cannot proceed from the same power or force, or kind of power or force, such things are said to be in their *nature* different, or *essentially* different. The essence of things or of substances, so far as we can discover it, consists in the power, or force, or manner of acting of those things.

It remains then, in the first place, to consider the several powers of those things, which we conceive as consisting of some quantity, and which are commonly called matter. Afterwards the action of the immaterial powers, or of intelligent beings, may be considered.

## SECT. II

## OF THE FORCE OF RESISTING, OR *VIS INERTIAE* OF SIR *ISAAC NEWTON*

1. The most obvious property or quality in things which are the objects of, or affect our senses, is that property by which they resist or affect our sense of touch; and which is sometimes called the tangible quality of things. This was first consider'd as a force or power by Sir *Isaac Newton,* under the Name of *vis inertiae,* or that power or force by which any thing resists or opposes any alteration of the state in which it is: and it is so generally observed, that it is commonly accounted a permanent essential property of all matter.

2. That this is a real or positive power or force, is evident from these obvious and constant observations of the manner of exerting its power. First, this power is sometimes greater, at other times less; it may be augmented by an addition of more force, or of more parts, and it may be lessen'd by taking away of part: for example, a ball of twenty pounds weight resists a greater force than a ball of ten pounds, or of one pound. But a meer negative power, or passive power, as some call it, that is, an unactive power, cannot be augmented or lessened; because it is a negation of all power and action, and is truly a *non entity.* And next, the thing or being which exerts this force, is truly an agent or power, whose principles of action is in itself independent of the force or action of any other thing: because its force is exerted in opposing and lessening the force and action of every other thing, and therefore cannot receive its force and action from that which it opposes or resists.

3. Nothing of motion enters the conception of the action of this power. For in the motion the action is directed from one point to another, and its force or action is exerted in one only direction: It has no force in the opposite direction, or in any other line of direction, except in one. If then in the action of resistance, or of the *vis inertiae,* there were any kind of motion, it would resist motion only when their directions are opposite, and could not resist when their directions tend towards the same point. But the resisting power opposes motion equally in all directions, and therefore we cannot conceive any thing of motion, in the action of resisting. And this power equally resists motion, whether itself be put in motion by any other power, or be at rest. For if two quantities of the resisting matter or power be put in motion, and the one be greater, or resists more than the other, when both at rest, that

quantity which resisted most when at rest, will likewise resist most when in motion. It is evident from constant observation, that motion no way encreases or lessens the force or action of resistance, and consequently that it does not consist in motion.

4. The thing, substance, or being, endowed with the power of resisting, or the *vis inertiae,* is truly an agent, exerting a certain kind of action, whereby it persists in its present state, and opposes and lessens the action of every other agent that can change that state. It exerts its force equally in all directions, and in a manner peculiar to itself, different from all other natural agents or powers.

5. Power, force, and action, are so essential to the conception of resisting, that the denying of it necessarily includes a contradiction in terms. For the power of resisting either does something or nothing; if it do any thing, it acts; if it do nothing, it does not resist in contradiction to what is supposed. Therefore that resisting is acting, may be reckoned among the self-evident maxims, which cannot be denied without falling into an absurdity.

6. Nothwithstanding this, we are so accustomed from our infancy to join motion to the idea of all action, that it is difficult for us to conceive any kind of action without it. But a little reflection may discover, that this is occasioned by a continued faulty connection of ideas, which ought not to be joined together. When a man thinks, he certainly does something; then thinking is acting, or is a kind of action: but this action cannot be conceived as either moving or resisting, it is a kind of action of a peculiar kind, differing from all other kinds of action.

7. This kind of reasoning, however, is by some not thought sufficient, unless the *modus,* or manner of acting in the resisting power, be explained; otherwise, it is thought the words *resisting power* are words without a meaning, and signify no more than an occult quality, a deceitful or cunning covering of our ignorance. On this occasion it is necessary to observe, that though I cannot explain the manner of acting when I think, yet I hope none will deny that I think: but I say further, we cannot explain the action of any simple power, no not the action of moving, though no man doubts of his knowing what motion is. When the moving power puts any quantity of matter into motion, what conception have we of its manner of acting? If it be said to be pushing or pressing the thing which it moves, I must ask again, what idea have we of pushing or pressing different from moving? Have we any other idea, than that the moving thing communicates the action of moving to the thing which it pushes, presses, or moves? Till the action of moving be explained by some other action than that of mov-

ing, I shall presume to say, that we have as clear and distinct a conception of the manner of acting in resisting, as of the manner of acting in moving: that is, that the resisting thing communicates its action to the thing on which it acts. We have no idea of any thing but of action, and all ideas arise from the communication of some kind of action to the thinking being: simple ideas arise from the action of simple powers, and complex ideas from the complicated actions of several simple powers. No simple idea can be explained; no definition or explication can give a blind man any idea of colours, or a deaf man of sounds: and the explication of complex ideas is, the shewing of what simple ideas they are compounded.

8. It is generally concluded, that the force of resistance is in proportion to the quantity of matter, or of the resisting thing, because a greater quantity of resisting matter requires a greater force to move it. But it must be observed, that in considering the resisting power, there are two ways of considering it as quantity, *viz.* the quantity of extension or its bulk, and the quantity of its force. When we say two powers, producing the same effect, are equal, we then mean only the quantity of force; but two different quantities in bulk may have the same force. There may therefore be different species of this resisting matter, in which the proportions of their force to their bulk may be different: and as these different proportions may be infinite in number, the different species of resisting matter may be infinitely different. No experiment, which determines the force of two different agents to be equal, does, for that reason, determine that their bulk is so likewise. The absolute force therefore of any quantity of resisting matter may be compounded of the degree of resisting, with which each particle is endowed, and the quantity or number of particles.

From Sir *Isaac Newton's* discovery of the infinitely different species of light, it is possible there may be as many different species of the resisting matter; and if there be, we may hope, that a method may be discovered to demonstrate this. Before Sir *Isaac's* discovery, light was generally thought to be homogeneous: and yet he has so clearly demonstrated the contrary, that none can doubt of its being the very reverse, that it consists of an infinite variety of species. Could any man have imagined, that this discovery, which had avoided all the curious researches of philosophers to his day, was made by so simple and common a contrivance as a triangular glass prism? Glass and prisms had been in use many ages, and in all that time it was never imagined that any such discovery could be made. Who then can say what discoveries may be made, when such another genius as Sir *Isaac Newton's* shall appear in the world?

9. Some object that no agent or active power can be conceived void of intelligence, or that all active powers or agents must be intelligent, or conscious of their own actions. I perceive no necessity of joining the ideas of acting and intelligence together, since they are separate and distinct ideas. I observe, I think, every day multitudes of action, without that the idea of intelligence is necessarily connected with those actions. They, who perceive the necessity of this connection, must shew it, and till that be done, we must delay the further consideration of this objection, till the nature of intelligent beings shall be considered and explained.

10. From the action of resisting we receive the idea of impenetrability; for by this action, the action of every other thing, by which it is supposed that it may be penetrated, is opposed: and as nothing of motion or change of place enters the idea of resisting, no other thing can be penetrated by the resisting power. How great the force of resisting is in the least particles, which compose any quantity of the resisting matter, will be more clearly shewn afterwards.

## SECT. III

## OF MOTION, OR THE MOVING POWER

1. We daily observe that some things move, or pass from one place to another: the power of resistance is so very different from that of moving, that they can in no manner be conceived as the effects of the same agent, or of the same cause. We likewise observe, that some things in motion lose their motion; that the same things again, or other things at rest, acquire motion; and that things moving with a small velocity, acquire a great velocity; this motion must then either be by some power, or force, or agency, in the moving thing itself, or it must be the effect of some other power or agent: this other thing must of itself be an agent, and has the power of moving essential to it, or it must be put in motion by a third thing, and so on: we must then at last rest in something, to which the power of moving is essential, or we must allow that an effect can be produced without a cause. This thing then, to which motion is essential, which moves by its own natural power or force, must be an agent, which has its active principle in itself. When we see a small spark gradually set a large city all in a flame, can any man imagine that there is no more motion in all the parts of the city thus

in a flame, than there was in the small spark which first began the fire? That there is no more power, or force, or action, in this prodigious fire, than there was in the scarce distinguishable spark which perhaps first began it? If there be not supposed something mixed with the materials of the city thus all in fire, which has a power in itself of moving, all the prodigious force or action of motion in the city in fire, must be supposed in the little spark which first began the fire; for nothing can give what it has not. In like manner, when a small spark sets fire to a quantity of gun-powder, by which castles, and the greatest weights are moved, the little spark cannot be supposed to have had in it all the force of motion, which is discovered from its effects to be in the gun-powder. These and innumerable other phaenomena, evidently shew, that some things are self-moving agents, and which ever move, unless hinder'd by the superior force of resisting matter; and that as soon as the resisting power is removed, the self-moving power immediately recovers its motion.

2. Tho' it be evident, from the idea we have of motion, that it can only exert its force in one direction, in passing in a streight line from one point to another; yet it is equally susceptible of any direction: and its assuming one direction rather than another, or its changing its direction, is only from the opposition of some resisting power. For this reason gun-powder in open air exerts its force chiefly upwards, because in that direction it meets with the least resistance: but gun-powder confin'd in a gun-barrel, meets with resistance in every direction, except in that parallel to the bore of the gun-barrel, and therefore exerts its force in the direction of the bore of the barrel.

3. In considering motion purely of itself, abstractedly from any other power or agent, we can conceive nothing but the degree of swiftness or velocity with which it moves, and the direction of its motion. Velocity, from the swiftness to the slowest we can imagine, may be divided into any number of degrees: so that as to its velocity it may be consider'd as consisting of some quantity. But besides this, we can conceive motion, or the moving thing, as confin'd within certain bounds, and consequently of some shape or extension. It may then be divided into parts or particles: then if one particle, moving with a certain velocity, have any determin'd force or power, then two particles must have twice that force, moving with the same velocity, and three particles thrice that force. So that the absolute force of the moving agent or thing is compounded of the velocity, and the quantity of the moving thing.

4. Since then the resisting and moving powers are so contrary to each other in their nature, resisting motion and self-moving, that it is im-

possible to conceive them both essential to the same thing, we must be careful then not to attribute these essentially different modes of action to the same agent: and since we cannot conceive impenetrability without resistance, there is nothing in our conception of the action of motion which renders two quantities of the moving thing impenetrable as to each other; tho' as before observed, from the nature of the resisting power, the resisting and moving things must be mutually impenetrable to each other.[5] If then two quantities or particles of the moving thing were to meet each other in opposite or different directions, they not only could not stop each other's motion, but likewise could not alter each other's direction. For it is impossible to conceive how motion can stop or destroy motion, or that the direction of motion can be alter'd without resistance; but resistance, as before proved, cannot exist in the same power with motion, being contradictory to each other.

5. I am sensible how difficult it is to form proper conceptions of the action of the moving power, abstracted from the resisting power, because we commonly form our ideas of motion from resisting matter in motion. In order to remove these difficulties, let us suppose, that two quantities of matter meet, one of the moving agent, the other of the resisting, what will happen? If the resisting power be greater or equal to the moving power, it will stop the action of the moving power and both remain at rest; tho' the force or endeavour to move still remain in the moving power: but if the moving power be stronger or greater than the resisting, then the moving power will only lose part of its motion, and both will move together with the remaining force of motion or velocity. This becomes a compound quantity, endowed with both motion and resistance.

6. Again suppose, that this united quantity of the moving and resisting agents be by some means separated, the moving matter will, the moment after it is separated from the resisting matter, recover its first or original action of moving, or its whole motion; and the resisting matter will continue its motion in the same manner, or with the same velocity it did when joined with the moving matter, and this by its power of resistance; for this power consists in persevering in whatever state it is in, and in opposing all change of that state. As the degree of velocity with which it moves is the state in which every part of that resisting matter is in at that time, the force of resisting all change, or persisting in that state in two different quantities, moving with the same velocity, will be as the several quantities of resisting matter in each; and in different quantities moving with different velocities, as

[5] Sect. 2. par. 10.

the respective velocities multiplied into their quantities of resisting matter. This force is by Sir *Isaac Newton* called *momentum,* and is by him rightly distinguished from motion or velocity; for it is a complicated, not a simple power, and arises from the joint action of agents essentially different in their natures and manner of acting. Any quantity of resisting matter, moving thus by the action of the moving power communicated to it, loses the whole, or some part of its motion, every time it meets with any other quantity of resisting matter, and never of itself recovers that motion again. The laws of this communicated motion in resisting matter, being most common to our observation, are well described; but the laws by which the primary agents act are little understood, tho' they be the true causes of all the phaenomena or appearances in nature, and therefore deserve the trouble of further inquiry. I hope in another place more particularly to describe the moving power, and to shew that there is such a thing distinct from all other things, which come under the observation of our senses. I hope to shew, that as the resisting power is the proper object or cause in our sense of feeling, so the moving power is the proper object or cause of seeing; or as the tangible qualities of things arise from the resisting power, so the visible qualities arise from the moving power.

## SECT. IV

## OF THE ELASTIC POWER, OR OF AETHER

1. Nothing can act where it is not; and therefore nothing can communicate its action to any other thing, which is at a distance from it, but by the intervention or communication of some middle thing or *medium,* which extends from the one thing to the other. As the hand, for example, cannot communicate action to a ball it does not touch, but by the intervention of a stick, or other thing between the hand and the ball. We perceive that the sun communicates some kind of action to all the planets, which circulate round it, by which they are retain'd in their orbits, or gravitate towards it: So likewise we observe, that the earth communicates action to bodies at a distance from it, by which they gravitate towards the earth. There must then be some *medium,* some middle thing, by which the sun and the earth communicate action to other things, at a distance from them. This cannot be by an emanation of some kind of virtue, as some imagine; because any kind of emanation supposes motion from the thing which emits the virtue to the thing on which the virtue exerts its force; but it is impossible to conceive that any motion from a thing, can cause a motion to that

thing. If then we desire to inquire into the causes producing the several phaenomena or appearances in nature, it becomes necessary to discover the nature of this medium, by which things communicate their action at a distance. It is called *aether* by Sir *Isaac Newton* and other philosophers; and all suppose the existence of such a thing.

2. The nature then of aether is to receive the action of any thing to which it is contiguous, and to communicate the same action to any other thing at a distance, to which it is likewise contiguous. And since the aether receives and communicates action at all distances, and every point of the aether must receive the action, and react, or communicate that action; as when that hand strikes a ball by the means of a stick, every particle of the stick receives the action of the hand, and communicates it from the one end to the other.

3. Since aether cannot be conceived to act or receive action where it is not, however small the distance be, all the several parts or points of aether which receive and communicate action must be contiguous to each other, or there cannot be the least distance between the points of aether. This may not seem necessary in communicating motion, yet in communicating any other action, which has no motion, it is necessary that the parts be contiguous.

4. Consequently the receiving action, to the greatest distance that it extends, must be at the same instant in every part or point, in the most distant as well as the nearest. As we see the motion communicated at one end of a stick, or any other thing, whose parts are contiguous, or not separated, is in the same moment communicated from the one end of the stick to the other, whatever the length thereof.

5. The aether receives the action of resisting matter, as well as moving, and communicates the action, which it receives, from every point to every thing contiguous to that point, by a kind of expansive action proceeding in all directions from each point, as a center. And the force of expansion or reaction, in each point, is every where observed to be equal to the force of action communicated to that point. As the idea of this expansive power is commonly taken from elastic bodies, whose parts, if they by any force be compressed nearer to each other, restore themselves to their former place, with a force equal to that which compressed them, the aether is frequently called an elastic fluid.

6. Since then the aether expands or reflects the action of resistance in all directions, in a direction opposite to the direction in which it received the action of the resisting thing, as well as in the same direction, they cannot both act in the same instant, because both their actions are resisting and equal in that instant, or destructive of each other's action,

consequently they must act by fits and turns, that is, while the resisting power is in action, the aether is in a fit of receiving action, or of inaction; and while the aether is in a fit of reaction, the resisting power is in a fit of inaction, alternately by turns; so likewise as the reaction of resistance in aether is destructive or negative to the action of motion, the moving thing must likewise act by fits, or by alternate turns of action and inaction. And since impenetrability is the consequence or effect of resistance only,[6] aether is only impenetrable during its fit of reacting resistance, at other times it is penetrable by the moving thing which has no power of resisting. This is curiously observed by Sir *Isaac Newton* in his Optics in the passage on light.

7. Now it is plain, that the elastic or expansive force of the aether; cannot be the effect of the resisting agent: for the whole power of the resisting agent is exerted in its preserving its present state: but the idea of this includes a perpetual endeavor of change by a kind of expansion. Again, the resisting power is exerted in opposing, lessening, and rendering ineffectual all motion; but this power, by its reaction, preserves the motion impressed upon it in its full force, and communicates the motion to every thing round it by expanding the action received in all directions. Neither can it be the effect of the moving power, for the moving power exerts its action only in one direction, but this power exerts its action in every direction from every point. This then must be a force or power essentially different both from the resisting and moving agents for the effects of this power cannot be produced by either of these simply, or by both jointly. The whole manner of acting in this power is singular and peculiar to itself; and yet it exerts no kind of action without the concurrence of some other power, and in their absence and ceasing to act it is in a state of inaction; and though it in no manner receives its power of expanding or reflecting the action from any power, yet it imitates the manner of acting of every power whose action it receives.

8. The resisting power is negative to every other power, as well as the moving power, it lessens the elastic power of the aether as to its reflecting or expanding motion; therefore in whatever degree the action of resistance is communicated to the aether, in the same degree is its action of expanding or reflecting motion lessened. But the moving and elastic powers being no way negative or resisting to each other, they no way lessen each others action.

9. Elastic force has been usually attributed to the shape of the parts which compose the elastic body. They are supposed to be spiral springs,

[6] Sect. 2. par. 10. and Sect. 3. par. 4.

like watch springs. But why a spiral shape, or any shape, or arrangement of the parts of any thing, should give it any power, which it had not before, is to me inconceivable. Common observation makes it manifest, that a spiral of lead is as little elastic as a strait line of lead.

10. Though this power, by which the aether expands or reflects, and conveys the action of any other power to any distance, be called elastic by Sir *Isaac Newton,* and other philosophers, yet the action of the elastic aether must not be conceived as in any manner similar to that of elastic bodies, such as a ball of ivory; but as a kind of action singular and peculiar to itself, and which cannot be explained by any similitude to the action of any other thing or power, no more than the actions of resisting and thinking can be explained by moving. Therefore if one should imagine that the aether consists of innumerable small globules (as of ivory) whose parts being pressed together rebound with the same force with which they were compressed, he would have no conception of the elastic action which I mean. The actions of all first principles, and the ideas of them, must be simple, nothing of shape, or of parts, or of number, or of any thing like composition can enter into the conception of these simple powers; for otherwise they cannot be simple. In any conception of globules, they must be conceived as consisting of parts, which being pressed nearer to each other, endeavor to separate again: and as this cannot be conceived, without motion, such elastic power can never reflect or continue any other action but that of moving. It is true, that in machines, and such like aggregates, there is a kind of compound action, which none of its parts have separately, and by this the machine, or aggregate, becomes a kind of unity (or *τό ἕν*, as the *Greeks* express it) for its essence is destroyed by division, and it no longer remains the same thing: but every one easily perceives, that no machine can be a simple being, or its action simple, but is the complication of several simple actions. The manner of acting in machines can therefore be explained by discovering the simple actions of which they are compounded: but the actions of simple powers, as before observed, cannot be explained.

11. Since the aether has no other action but what it receives, either from the resisting or moving power, and we have no idea of any thing but what we receive from its action, we must conceive aether as quantity, in the same manner we do resisting or moving matter; because it can receive a greater or less degree of force or action from the resisting or moving agent; and consequently its reaction, in which its peculiar power consists, may be greater or less. If quantity then be the distinguishing character of matter, the aether must be a species of it.

12. We have before shewn, that impenetrability is a necessary consequence of resistance,[7] and therefore that the aether in the reaction of the resisting power must likewise be impenetrable, and that it must by fits and turns be penetrable and impenetrable.[8] It may then be objected, that, if the aether be thus by fits and turns penetrable and impenetrable, resisting matter must be so likewise, for, as it has been before shewn, that resisting matter exerts its action of resistance by fits and turns. But if it be considered, that while the resisting power is in its fit of inaction, the aether is in its fit of action or reaction of the resisting action, then any moving thing, by which action only any other thing can be penetrated, is stopped by the resisting action of the aether, and moving thing can never act upon, or pass through or penetrate the resisting matter, but while it is in its act of resisting, and consequently can never pass or penetrate it. It may be likewise objected, that we cannot conceive things to be different without conceiving them at the same time to occupy different place. In answer to this I must repeat, what has been several times before said, viz.: We have no idea or conceptions of substances or of things themselves, nor have we any conception in what manner substances or things exert their action, our ideas are only excited by the actions of things on our senses. If then any thing cease to act in such a manner as can oppose the action of another thing, there is nothing in our conception to hinder their being both in one place. So that truly we may conceive, that the resisting thing or the resisting matter cannot be in the same place with any other thing, because it opposes the action of every other thing by which that thing can penetrate it. There is nothing in the action of moving to destroy motion, and therefore there is nothing in the conception of motion, without joining resistance to it, to shew that two moving quantities cannot be in the same place. There is a great deal of reason to think, from the phaenomena of light, that any quantity of light is penetrable by another quantity of light, or that the rays or particles of light are mutually penetrable by each other, every the least particle of an opaque body reflects the rays of light, the distance between the points, which reflect light, is less than can be distinguished by the best microscope: there must then be above a million of these points in a square inch. Every one of these reflect rays of light in all directions, and therefore they must cross each other in innumerable places. Therefore every inch of a great room, for example, has innumerable points reflecting rays of light, which cross each other.

[7] Sect. 2. par. 10.
[8] Sect. 4. par. 6.

If then the rays or particles of light be impenetrable to each other, they must meet and oppose each others motions and change each others directions in innumerable places, by which such confusion must arise, that nothing could be seen distinctly. It is likewise observed, that tho' an infinite number of rays from all the points of a large burning glass, and that all of them intersect each other in the focus, yet the motion or direction of motion of not any of them is impeded or alter'd by their thus meeting and intersecting each other.

13. All the disputes that happen among men, who have nothing else in view beside the discovery of truth, arise from the faulty conception they have of things, by our ideas being not true or perfect images of the things they are supposed to represent: whenever the argument on both sides is loaded with such difficulties that we know not how to extricate ourselves, it is from thence evident that we have not perfect conceptions of the things about which the dispute arises. Of this sort is the dispute about a *vacuum,* whether there can be any place in nature absolutely void. If we can have no conception of an absolute void, we cannot affirm that it is, or is not; and what conceptions can a man have of a place void of every thing, and of which nothing can be affirm'd? We cannot affirm any thing of it, for the moment we do, it must be something, and if it be any thing, then that thing exists in that place, and the place is not void in contradiction to what would be prov'd. It is evident, from what was before said, that all the parts of the aether are contiguous, or no void space between them, except where their place is taken up by resisting matter, and if so there can be no *vacuum.* Sir *Isaac Newton* and his followers on the contrary think there must be a *vacuum,* and their reason is, that all matter has the *vis inertiae* or the force of resisting. If it were so, then the supposition of a *vacuum* would become absolutely necessary; for without it there could be no motion. If all matter were equally endowed with the power of resistance, as Sir *Isaac* supposes, the supposition of a *vacuum* becomes necessary; but if it be true, as I think I have prov'd, that there are different species of matter, and that only one species has the power of resisting, and that this (as will appear upon the least reflection) is by far the least part of the universe, all the difficulties as to motion on the supposition of space being everywhere full, vanish.

14. It follows then from the whole of what precedes, that the species of matter above describ'd are agents, or acting principles: that each hath a power or force peculiar to itself, differing from the others in its essence and manner of acting. Whether there be any more species of matter is not easy to determine, tho' most of the ancients agree in

this number. That these three are essentially different I can make no doubt. If there be any other species of matter, it must likewise be an active principle. For this reason some of the ancient philosophers asserted that all nature is alive, that is, all nature is active. Try to describe matter without power, force, or action, the whole description must consist of negatives, that is, it must be the description of *nothing:* and then it very certainly follows, that nothing or no-being exists nowhere. The word *matter,* when it represents a meer passive being without power, force, or action, or property, is synonimous to the word *nothing:* Perhaps the chemists aim at the same thing I do, in the three principles they establish, viz. *salt, sulphur,* and *mercury.* By salt they may intend resisting matter, by the action of which parts of matter (as may be hereafter shewn) are kept in union; by sulphur they mean the moving matter; and by mercury the aether by which the action of other matter is (as by a messenger) carried to any distance, or because, like *Mercury* or *Proteus,* it imitates the action of the other species of matter. But it is beside my present purpose to enquire into the opinions of philosophers.

15. I shall only now add, that I suppose that this our earth, and all upon it, which affect our sense of touch, the planets, and every thing commonly called body, to consist chiefly of resisting matter: that all space between these great bodies, and likewise the interstices between the parts or particles which compose them, are filled with aether: that the moving matter (as light) is every where passing thro' the spaces fill'd with aether; consequently that the space fill'd with aether and light is vastly greater than the space fill'd with resisting matter or body. If then I can shew, that the most general phaenomena in nature, and such as have hitherto puzzled the philosophers of all ages, can be explain'd and made easy to our conceptions, from the actions of the different species of matter as the cause of those phaenomena, it will be a further and stronger proof of what has been advanc'd, and will at the same time shew the use of what I attempt to teach. I shall next proceed to explain some of those general phaenomena, and to shew how they arise from the actions of these different species of matter. But before I proceed, I believe the reader will not be displeased that I take notice of one thing, by which it will appear, that the sagacious Sir *Isaac Newton* had the strong scent of something like this which I call aether. What I mean is his last paragraph in his *Principia,* and which, without doubt, he inserted to excite others to pursue the scent which he was forced to leave; his words translated into English are.

"I might now add something of a most subtile spirit, which pervades all gross bodies, and is hidden in them, by the power and action of which the smallest bodies attract each other, while within the smallest distance, and by the force thereof cohere together; by the force of this spirit electric bodies act, both in attracting and repelling small bodies near them; by its power and action light is emitted, reflected, refracted, and inflected, and bodies are heated, and all sensation in animals and their voluntary motion is perform'd by the vibration of this spirit, continued from the external organs of the senses of the brain to the muscles, through the solid fibres of the nerves. But these things cannot be explain'd in a few words, neither am I furnished with sufficient experiments to determine and shew the laws, which govern this spirit in its actions."

## *Of the Intelligent Being, and of the Formation and Duration of the Several Systems in the Universe*

1. The elementary parts of matter, or the smallest parts of which matter is supposed or imagined to be compounded, must have one single simple action, for it cannot be imagined that a complication of different actions can arise from one simple uncompounded thing. The alledging of it seems to involve a contradiction, as it supposes both a multiplicity and a unity at the same time. Thus we see, that the mixed rays of light after they are separated and become simple or single, let them be reflected or refracted, or agitated in any manner, still produce one simple colour, and always are in the same degree refrangible, as is demonstrated in Sir *Isaac Newton's* Optics.

2. The elementary parts of matter act uniformly, necessarily and invariably, always in the same manner, and with the same degree of force. Whatever differences are in their actions, they arise from their different quantities, or from the opposite, or mixed, or complicated action of the same or different kinds of matter. For otherwise this action could not be the object of mathematical enquiry, which with the greatest certainty determines the actions of matter, from their several quantities, and from the ratios these quantities have to each other.

3. Nothing in the action of matter can induce one to think that its action proceeds from any sense, perception, intelligence or will, or that sense or will can be essential to matter, or that they are naturally involved or complicated with the actions of matter: for our ideas of the action of matter are perfect and compleat, though it were supposed that sense, perception, intelligence, or will, existed no where but in ourselves.

4. Then since we cannot doubt of the existence of sense of perception, intelligence and will, they must be the action, operations, or properties of some kind of being distinct from what is commonly called matter. There is nothing in the actions of motion, resistance or elasticity, that raises in our minds any idea of sense, perception, intelligence or will; otherwise we could not conceive any machine, for example a mill, without at the same time conceiving that it may have some degree of sense of perception, or intelligence or will.

5. There is nothing then in the idea of the actions of matter, by which the parts of it can form themselves into any kind of regular system, with any view to serve any purpose or end; neither is there any thing in any system of matter that we know, which necessarily supposes an existence of that system, or without which we cannot imagine matter to exist. We cannot conceive any thing essential to matter, whereby such a quantity of matter (for example) must exist in that part of space where the sun now exists, that it should contain such proportion of resisting matter, and such another proportion of resisting matter, and such another proportion of light: that the most resisting parts of matter should be collected into the sun; that it should be of a globular figure, etc. Or why matter of a different power of resisting from what is in the planets, would be collected into the comets; or why one part of matter should be collected and placed in another order, as to form an animal, another part in such another order as to form a vegetable or plant. If there be nothing in the actions of matter to do this, then it must be done by something different from matter.

6. That the diameter of the equator of the sun and planets is longer than their axes, cannot be caused by their rotation: for the rotation on their axes must presuppose, that the diameters of their equators are longer than their axes, otherwise there can be nothing to determine the rotation to be on their axes, that is to say, on that particular axis. It cannot be done by chance, for chance is a nonentity, it is only our ignorance of the cause: again, if the greater length of the equatorial diameters were caused by the rotation, they must continually increase; for if they be supposed once to increase by the rotation, the velocity in the equator must likewise increase, and the gravitation, by which the parts are retain'd, decrease; therefore the shape and figure of the planets is caused by some other agent, besides the action of matter in the planets. If the equatorial diameter were not longer than the axis, the axis could not be inclined to the plane of the orbit, and thereby none of the planets could have the different seasons of summer and winter; and thereby could not be replenished with such variety of animals

and plants, whose constitutions require different climates and different seasons; therefore the figure of the sun and planets is shaped with a certain view to serve a certain purpose.

7. Suppose a planet were placed any where in the plane of the sun's equator infinitely extended, there is nothing in the actions of the sun or of the planet, in the action of light or resistance, or in the reaction by the aether of these actions, to determine the first motion of the planets towards the east rather than towards the west; this determination at first is absolutely indifferent from those causes, it must then proceed from some other cause, and which has a view or purpose in its actions: for if some of the planets moved to the east and others to the west, their motions would be more frequently disturbed, and become more irregular, by their coming more frequently into the nearest distance one with another, than when all of them move from west to east.

8. Again, the mean distances of the comets are so far from the sun, that there can be nothing to determine their motion, to east or west, to north or south, or to any intermediate point. Yet it is remarkable, that none of them move nearly in the plane of the ecliptic, if they did not pass very near some of the planets, and by their great attraction, and by the heat of their atmospheres, occasion great disorder, if not destruction, among the planets.

9. All these discover foresight, design, and purpose, of which innumerable other instances may be given, in every part of the universe that comes within our knowledge. The more knowledge we have of any thing, the more intelligence we discover in its formation; but I confine myself to my present subject. The more common instances have again and again been taken notice of by others.

10. It follows then, that the first formation of all kinds of material systems, the greatest and the least, was made by some intelligent being; that some being form'd the grand solar system, the more particular system of this earth, and all the small systems on it, whether animal, vegetable, or mineral: that the same intelligent being governs the great and small, each according to its nature, as is most conducive for the well-being of every individual, and of the universal system of nature.

11. We have no idea of substances; we have as little knowledge of the substance of material beings as of intelligent ones; we have no idea of the thing in which the power of resisting, or of moving or of reacting, subsists, as little as we have of the being in which intelligence subsists: but we may have ideas of the actions or operations of intelligence, as we have of the actions of matter, or as we have of motion or resistance.

12. The essential or characteristic distinction between the material agent and the intelligent agent is this: the material agents act always uniformly, and in all directions, they have no power in themselves to increase their force of action, or to determine it to one direction more than to another, all alteration in their action or in the direction of them is made by something external, which for that reason is called an *efficient cause,* they have no will, purpose, view, or design in their action. But the intelligent being determines and directs its own actions, by the purpose, design, or view which it has, and therefore its actions are said to be determin'd or directed by *final causes,* and this direction by final causes is called the *will;* therefore in all actions of intelligent beings, which are likewise called *moral actions,* the intention, purpose, or will, is principally to be considered. This is the guiding principle in morality, policy, and religion.

13. The actions of intelligent beings cannot be the object of mathematical inquiry. For quantity, and the ratios of quantities, is the sole object of mathematics, but there can be nothing of quantity in design, intention, or will. Therefore any inquiry into the actions of an intelligent agent must be on different principles, from what are used in an inquiry into the actions of matter. But frequently our ideas arise from the complicated actions of intelligent and material agents, in which case, a mixture of mathematical and metaphysical principles become necessary in our inquiries.

14. The intelligent agent never acts in opposition or contradiction to the material agents; for if it did, nothing but confusion, contradiction and absurdity could ensue: and there could be no need or use of machinery, or of a certain order and disposition of the parts of matter in the several systems, which compose the universe. But the intelligent either so disposes of the parts of the system, that their complicated actions shall serve the purpose, which the intelligent being has in forming of the systems: or where the action of the material agent is not determined, by any thing external to it, and its action is indifferent to any direction, in such case the intelligent being gives the action such direction, as best suits its own purpose; and this without any contradiction or opposition to the action of matter. This seems to be the case, in the voluntary actions of animals. It seems probable, that the aether contained in the nerves has its elasticity equal through the whole length; and therefore, as thereby any action is easily and equally communicated from the external to the internal extremity, or from the internal to the external, the mind can direct or stop the reaction at pleasure. But

these things I see only with a very glimmering light. The manner of animal motion is among the dark things hereafter to be discovered. But this seems self-evident, that perfect intelligence, or wisdom, will not, and consequently never can act in contradiction to the action of matter, otherwise any thing may be absurd, and there would be no distinction between truth and falsehood.

15. The parts of every system have some general reference or connection with one single point, by which they become a kind of unity, or one system. This reference is commonly, if not always, done by means of the aether. Thus all actions, by the increasing elasticity of the aether in its several distances from the sun, are reacted to the sun's center. In like manner all actions within the sphere of the earth's system, are all reacted to the earth's center. In the animal and vegetable systems, there is one part in the system with which all the parts of the system have some kind of communication. Whatever new part is added, so that it becomes united in the common reference, becomes part of the same system. When any part is so far removed, as to have no farther reference to or communication with the common or principal point, it is no longer a part of that system. So that the identity of the system does not consist in the identity of the parts, nor in the identity of its place in space, or with respect to other systems, but in the common reference of the part to the same point. While the communication of action between the principal point and parts of the system remain perfect, the systematical action, or health and life of the system, remains perfect. When that communication is lessened or disordered, the system becomes irregular or sick. When this communication is cut off from any part, that part dies; when the communication in general ceases, the system is dissolved, and consequently the union between the system and the intelligent being ceases. For after this it is not properly a system, when there can be no communication of action between the principal point and the whole system, or between the system and its parts, or between the system and the intelligent being.

16. No time can be supposed, when no system of matter did exist. For if it be not consistent with perfect intelligence, or wisdom, that material systems do exist, they cannot in any time be improper; or that if in wisdom it be necessary that they do exist, it cannot be consistent with wisdom that they do not. This is to be understood as to systems in the universal; for as to this or the other individual system, as any one or two bears no proportion to an infinite number, the existence of any one individual cannot increase or diminish the fitness or unfitness of

the whole. Therefore there may have been a time when the present solar system did not exist, and the distance of time or duration from its first existence to the present time may be finite, and consequently it may be of any quantity of finite duration to the present time.

17. That every particular system has had a beginning, and will have an end, seems highly probable from this, that all the smaller systems, such as those of animals and vegetables, have a beginning and an end, and their durations are of various lengths: so likewise the great systems must also have their periods of existence. For as the small systems naturally cease and are dissolved, by the decay of that fermentation, which gives them action or life; so the great systems must necessarily suffer some such decay. For example, the motion in this solar system is continued and preserved by the perpetual emission of light; now this store of light in the sun must at last be spent, since there are no evident means continually to supply the perpetual waste of light. When this defect happens, the consequences are very evident, and that they do happen frequently in one or another solar system, appears probable from the disappearing of some of the fixed stars.

18. But it seems probable, that light or other waste in the sun may be supplied from the comets. For as the light of the sun decays, some one or other of the comets, which approach nearer the sun, may in their perihelion unite with the sun, and thereby a new quantity of matter be added to it, and a new fermentation be raised. This may be the more probable, because it is observed, nature has contrived means in all systems to recruit their waste for some time, till at last, the waste being greater than the recruit, a total dissolution ensues.

19. Nature, or more properly speaking, the infinite intelligent *Archeus,* has ordered so, that, since the several individual systems must in time fail, from their natural constitution, this defect is supplied by the generation of new and similar systems, the constant method of doing which is by fermentation, under the direction of the intelligent agent. So, supposing that all the comets, planets, and other parts of the solar system, by the failure of light in the sun, should at any time be united with the sun; then a chaos or confused mixture of the heterogeneous parts of matter must ensue; and thereby an extraordinary fermentation, during which the *Archeus* forms a new solar system, and a new heaven and a new earth may be produced. This conjecture seems to be confirmed by the appearing of new stars, and reappearing of some which before had disappeared.

20. The duration of all the solar systems probably is infinite, in respect to the duration of any small system on this earth, whose period

we know; and yet the duration of the solar systems may be infinitely small, in respect to the duration of the universe.

The *Egyptian* priests, and *Pythagoras* from these, seem to have had speculations of this sort, which they delivered in mystic terms to the people, and explained clearly to the initiated only.

# VI

## Benjamin Franklin

1706–1790

Born in Boston. Although his family wanted him to be a minister, he entered his father's business of candle-making because of economic necessity. Later became apprentice to his brother James, a printer, for whose newspaper he wrote anonymously but effectively, 1718–23. Moved to Philadelphia and followed trade of printing, 1723. Served as printer in London where he met many of the leading characters of the day, 1724–26. Bought *Pennsylvania Gazette,* 1729, and established his own printing shop. Began *Poor Richard's Almanack,* 1732. Served in England as envoy and in France as commissioner. Signer of Declaration of Independence. First postmaster-general under Confederation. Helped found American Philosophical Society and Academy of Philadelphia. Discovered relationship between lightning and electricity and invented numerous practical devices. Awarded degrees by Harvard, Yale, Oxford and St. Andrews. Member of numerous learned societies. Died in Philadelphia.

One of Poor Richard's maxims was, "Employ thy time well if thou meanest to gain leisure." Benjamin Franklin, to whom we are indebted for much practical wisdom of this sort, followed his own advice by employing his time and energy in economic and political affairs to such an extent that he soon came to deplore the lack of leisure which he so much desired in order to pursue his scientific and philosophical interests. As early as 1752 he had occasion to write an envious letter to Cadwallader Colden congratulating him on his prospect of "passing the remainder of life in philosophic retirement." In later years he continued to express this sentiment when writing to numerous other friends such as Lord Kames, Giambattista Beccaria and Joseph Priestley, but unfortunately the leisure to produce a *magnum opus,* or whatever else he may have had in mind, was never permitted him. His fame, therefore, has been largely based on his inventive genius, his shrewd financial powers, his political sagacity, and his practical worldly wisdom. Some would discount Franklin as a philosopher because he soon disowned the only metaphysical treatise he ever published and because he never developed a systematic presentation of his thought. Although this position is defensible, Franklin was a philosopher at heart and his philosophical writings, however meagre, had considerable effect upon his own activities and upon the thought of others; they therefore merit the study of anyone interested in observing a characteristic expression of the transition which took place in American thought from the Calvinism of New England to the humanism of the middle Atlantic and southern colonies. Franklin was bred on New England Calvinism, soon found himself reacting against it, and gradually became one of the exponents of the free, but none the less moral, order so characteristic of the American Age of Reason.

Franklin's rejection of Calvinism was neither complete nor conclusive, although according to his own words it occurred quite early in life. He had been thoroughly indoctrinated with Calvinism in the family circle and in the family pew at Cotton Mather's church and although he felt he had fairly definitely broken away from Mather's orthodoxy he retained certain overtones of Calvinism through life. In religion he held to belief in a providential God although this was not a strong conviction nor one about which he had particularly clear ideas. Late in life he expressed the opinion that arguments against the doctrine of providence struck at the very foundation of religion and he often indicated that he considered his own career as somehow influenced by a kindly deity. In ethics the influence of Mather was strong. He wrote to Samuel Mather (son of Cotton Mather) in 1784 saying,

> When I was a boy, I met with a book, entitled "Essays to do Good," which I think was written by your father. It had been so regarded by a former possessor, that several leaves of it were torn out; but the remainder gave me such a turn of thinking, as to have an influence on my conduct through life; for I have always set a greater value on the character of a *doer of good,* than on any other kind of reputation; and if I have been, as you seem to think, a useful citizen, the public owes the advantage of it to that book.[1]

Franklin's emphasis upon discipline is largely attributable to his Puritan background. Although influenced strongly by the prophets of the Age of Reason who emphasized the essential goodness of man, Franklin never lost sight of man's tendency toward evil. Writing to Joseph Priestley he said,

> Men I find to be a Sort of Beings very badly constructed, as they are generally more easily provok'd than reconcil'd, more dispos'd to do Mischief to each other than to make Reparation, much more easily

[1] From A. H. Smyth, editor. The Writings of Benjamin Franklin. IX, 208. The Macmillan Company, publishers.

deceiv'd than undeceiv'd, and having more Pride and even Pleasure in killing than in begetting one another. . . .[2]

Mather's *Essays to Do Good,* along with Defoe's writings, led Franklin to conceive the doing of good to others as a part of man's duty. Mather, of course, was a believer in charity, Franklin in humanitarianism, but the altruism involved in both had a common source.

Although Franklin's background was Calvinistic, he was equally influenced by Newtonianism and the philosophical and social implications to which the popularized versions of Newtonianism led. Franklin's weaning away from Calvinism was assisted by numerous authors whom he had early read. Shaftesbury, Locke, Anthony Collins, Tillotson, Xenophon, the Port Royal *Art of Thinking* and the *Spectator,*—these were the major sources of his heterodoxy. Reading excerpts from the Boyle Lectures, Franklin was more moved by the quotations he read from the deists than he was by the arguments against deism which the authors had advanced. Xenophon and the *Art of Thinking* provided him with a method of reasoning, the *Spectator* with a style of writing, and the others with representative examples of where such reasoning led. The major conclusion at which he arrived on the basis of such reading was that the outpourings of revelation and scriptural authority were either to be renounced in favor of reason or else accepted because they were reasonable rather than because they were revealed. At all events, reason was henceforth to remain the arbiter of truth; Franklin had come to accept one of the basic tenets of the Age of Reason.

Armed with an essentially rationalistic, although later with a more empirical, method Franklin shifted from the religious determinism of Calvinism to scientific determinism. This change is apparent in *A Dissertation on Liberty and Necessity, Pleasure and Pain,* published in England at the age of nineteen after he had been setting up Wollaston's *The Religion of Nature Delineated* with which he felt he could not completely agree. He accepted Wollaston's emphasis upon reason and his basic argument for the existence of God, but he could not see how Wollaston, or anyone else, could argue at one and the same time for an omnipotent, omniscient God on the one hand and for man's moral freedom and a clear-cut distinction between good and evil on the other. By this time just as enamored of the Newtonian mechanical world as the English deists were, he still retained enough of his Calvinistic heritage to favor a consistent determinism rather than to hold a fence-warming position which would permit him to speak of an all-powerful,

[2] *Writings.* VIII, 451,

all-wise God and free creatures in the same breath. Franklin thus argued that whatever God did was infinitely wise and good. Evil could not exist; pleasure and pain equalized one another; therefore, by implication, the present was just as acceptable as the past or the future because it was the best that could possibly be. Franklin published only one hundred copies of this treatise, gave a few copies to his friends and then, disliking it, burned all the remaining copies but one. This did not stop its circulation, however, as a second edition was published in 1733, seemingly without Franklin's knowledge. However disconcerting the book was to Franklin himself, it brought him new acquaintances among enthusiastic Newtonians (particularly Henry Pemberton) and allied him with the deism which they espoused. He expressed this position in *Articles of Belief and Acts of Religion* which he wrote three years later in Philadelphia and which he used for his own private devotions. Here he emphasized the seeming remoteness of God and the relative unimportance of man although he bridged the gulf between God and man by introducing an order of subordinate deities. He used the typical deistic argument for God, pointing to the orderliness and harmony of nature as proof of an infinite creator of order and harmony. He recommended the reading of Ray, Blackmore and Fénelon, typical exponents of deism. To Franklin the physical world was still a concourse of immutable natural laws but his psychological determinism had weakened. He emphasized the value of "moral virtue," and included a prayer of petition, asking God to assist his "Continual Endeavours and Resolutions of eschewing Vice and embracing Virtue."

It was Franklin's own particular experience of the moral problem which led him to reject the *Dissertation*. In the *Autobiography,* he stated that on the basis of the injustice of his friends Collins, Ralph and Keith to him and his own injustice to Vernon and Miss Read (later his wife), "I began to suspect that this Doctrine tho' it might be true, was not very useful." [3] After expressing the feeling that he had fallen into error in his reasoning, he went on to say, "I grew convinc'd that *Truth, Sincerity* and *Integrity* in Dealings between Man and Man, were of the utmost Importance to the Felicity of Life, and I form'd written Resolutions (w[ch] still remain in my Journal Book) to practice them everwhile I lived." [4] In 1730 he wrote another pamphlet in which he defended free will on the basis of the existence of prayer, but it was never printed and subsequently lost.

[3] *Writings.* I, 296.
[4] Ibid.

Writing to Benjamin Vaughan in 1779 concerning this period of his life he said, "The great Uncertainty I found in metaphysical Reasonings disgusted me, and I quitted that kind of Reading and Study for others more satisfactory." [5] He remained true to the goddess of reason, but reason understood more as an intelligent guide in human affairs than as aiming at a logically consistent system of truth. Theology and morality were divorced, and henceforth personal and social problems were to be viewed on an essentially human stage which had as its background a setting of natural laws.

The remainder of Franklin's career was given over to scientific, political and moral interests. In science he sought for laws governing physical nature, and his electrical discoveries and theories permitted him to be honored among his fellow men as a second Newton. He stressed the practical efficacy of scientific knowledge more than Newton did, but he followed the Newtonian principles of scientific investigation, a combination of observation and hypothesis. It was this Newtonian background which served as a basis for his subsequent economic, educational, political and moral thoughts. His defense of agrarianism and free trade were outgrowths of his viewing economic laws as on a plane with physical laws. His educational ideas were based on his faith in reason and intellectual progress. His belief in natural rights was dependent upon his faith in the natural orderliness of human as well as cosmic relations. His moral philosophy was likewise a product of his attempt to look upon human affairs as amenable to the laws of nature. Writing to Joseph Priestley in 1780 he said,

> I always rejoice to hear of your being still employ'd in experimental Researches into Nature, and of the Success you meet with. The rapid Progress *true* Science now makes, occasions my regretting sometimes that I was born too soon. . . . O that moral Science were in as fair a way of Improvement, that Men would cease to be Wolves to one another, and that human Beings would at length learn what they now improperly call Humanity! [6]

Morality he regarded as a science, but a science of means, not ends.[7] Franklin has often been regarded as a typical exponent of American success, parading the values of wealth and industry for the sake of themselves. This misunderstanding is due to the failure to recognize the character of the audience for which Franklin wrote and the real significance of his moral philosophy. Most of his readers were products

[5] *Writings.* VII, 412.

[6] Ibid. VIII, 9.

[7] For enlargement on this point see Schneider, "The Significance of Benjamin Franklin's Moral Philosophy."

of a frontier civilization which stressed such values as wealth, independence and industry. What Franklin sought to do was to tell them how to achieve those values, or any other values which might be set up as ends worth realizing. He held that the values which human beings consciously and unconsciously seek changed but that the means for attaining those ends were less fugitive and fleeting. Assuming a scientific structure in morality Franklin urged upon his contemporaries certain rules of habit and action which he felt were preconditions of a satisfactory pursuit of any end whatsoever. Franklin was less a moralist in the sense of telling people what to do than he was a successful moral guide in suggesting how it could be done. In a letter to Joseph Priestley in 1772 he said, "In the Affair of so much Importance to you, I cannot for want of sufficient Premises, advise you *what* to determine, but if you please I will tell you *how*." [8] He went on to advise his own method of listing arguments pro and con and then evaluating them one by one. While he felt it was difficult to arrive at quantitative judgments as precise as those in algebra he went on to say, "I have found great Advantage from this kind of Equation, in what may be called *Moral* or *Prudential Algebra*." [9] Franklin was always interested in helping others to get things done. His attitude was, "Tell me what end you are seeking and I will help you find the way to achieve it." That his scientific approach to ethics might be furthered he suggested the formation of a "Society of the Free and Easy" to provide that constant cross-fertilization of minds out of which the greatest of scientific knowledge in any field ultimately comes. This, like a number of other suggestions Franklin made, never came to fruition.

We have thus seen how the Puritan virtues came to be interpreted when detached from Calvinism and associated with the naturalistic spirit of the Age of Reason. Franklin was a fascinating transitional figure who carried with him much of the force of the winds of doctrine current in his age. With men of his character and inclinations a new period of thought began.

## REFERENCES

Franklin, Benjamin: *A Dissertation on Liberty and Necessity, Pleasure and Pain.* London, 1725. Reproduced from the first edition by the Facsimile Text Society, New York, 1930. (Included in

[8] *Writings.* V, 437.
[9] Ibid. V, 438.

I. Woodbridge Riley, *American Philosophy: the Early Schools.* 571–80.)

———: *A Lecture on the Providence of God in the Government of the World,* in Jared Sparks: *The Works of Benjamin Franklin.* 10 vols. Boston, 1836–40. II, 525 ff. (Authorship questionable.)

———: *Articles of Belief and Acts of Religion.* 1728. (In almost all editions of his writings.)

———: *Dialogues between Philocles and Horatio.* 1730. (In almost all editions of his writings.)

———: *Autobiography.* 1771–88. (In almost all editions of his writings. A critical edition is to be published soon by the Huntington Library.)

Smyth, A. H. (editor): *The Writings of Benjamin Franklin.* Collected and Edited with a Life and Introduction. 10 vols. New York: The Macmillan Company. 1905–07.

Baumgarten, Eduard: *Benjamin Franklin.* Frankfurt am Main: Vittorio Klostermann, 1937. (Vol. I of *Die geistigen Grundlagen des amerikanischen Gemeinwesens.*)

Bruce, W. C.: *Benjamin Franklin, Self-Revealed: A Biographical and Critical Study Based Mainly on His Own Writings.* 2 vols. New York: G. P. Putnam's Sons, 1917.

Crane, V. W.: *Benjamin Franklin, Englishman and American.* Baltimore: Williams and Wilkins Co., 1936. (Esp. ch. II, "Franklin as a Social Philosopher.")

Faÿ, Bernard: *Franklin, the Apostle of Modern Times.* Boston: Little, Brown and Co., 1929.

Mott, F. L. and Jorgenson, C. E.: *Benjamin Franklin.* Representative Selections, with Introduction, Bibliography and Notes. Cincinnati: American Book Co., 1936. (Has excellent bibliography.)

Parton, James: *Life and Times of Benjamin Franklin.* 2 vols. New York, 1864.

Riley, I. Woodbridge: *American Philosophy: the Early Schools.* New York: Dodd, Mead and Co., 1907. 229–65.

Schneider, H. W.: "The Significance of Benjamin Franklin's Moral Philosophy," *Studies in the History of Ideas.* 3 vols. New York: Columbia University Press. II (1925) 291 ff.

Van Doren, Carl: *Benjamin Franklin.* New York: Viking Press, 1938.

* * *

---

* * *

## A DISSERTATION ON LIBERTY AND NECESSITY, PLEASURE AND PAIN [10]

Sir, I have here, according to your Request, given you my *present* Thoughts of the *general State of Things* in the Universe. Such as they are, you have them, and are welcome to 'em; and if they yield you any Pleasure or Satisfaction, I shall think my Trouble sufficiently compensated. I know my Scheme will be liable to many Objections from a less discerning Reader than your self; but it is not design'd for those who can't understand it. I need not give you any Caution to distinguish the hypothetical Parts of the Argument from the conclusive: You will easily perceive what I design for Demonstration, and what for Probability only. The whole I leave entirely to you, and shall value my self more or less on this account, in proportion to your Esteem and Approbation.

### *Sect. I. Of Liberty and Necessity*

I. *There is said to be a* First Mover, *who is called* God, *Maker of the Universe.*

II. *He is said to be all-wise, all-good, all powerful.*

These two Propositions being allow'd and asserted by People of almost every Sect and Opinion; I have here suppos'd them granted, and laid them down as the Foundation of my Argument; What follows then, being a Chain of Consequences truly drawn from them, will stand or fall as they are true or false.

III. *If He is all-good, whatsoever He doth must be good.*

IV. *If He is all-wise, whatsoever He doth must be wise.*

The Truth of these Propositions, with relation to the two first, I think may be justly call'd evident; since, either that infinite Goodness will act what is ill, or infinite Wisdom what is not wise, is too glaring a Contradiction not to be perceiv'd by any Man of common Sense, and deny'd as soon as understood.

[10] This selection (the complete work) was taken from the reproduction of the first edition by the Facsimile Text Society. New York, 1930.

V. *If He is all-powerful, there can be nothing either existing or acting in the Universe* against *or* without *his Consent; and what He consents to must be good, because He is good; therefore* Evil *doth not exist.*

*Unde Malum?* has been long a Question, and many of the Learned have perplex'd themselves and Readers to little Purpose in Answer to it. That there are both Things and Actions to which we give the Name of *Evil,* is not here deny'd, as *Pain, Sickness, Want, Theft, Murder,* &c, but that these and the like are not in reality *Evils, Ills, or Defects* in the Order of the Universe, is demonstrated in the next Section, as well as by this and the following Proposition. Indeed, to suppose any Thing to exist or be done, *contrary* to the Will of the Almighty, is to suppose him not almighty; or that Something (the Cause of *Evil*) is more mighty than the Almighty; an Inconsistence that I think no One will defend: And to deny any Thing or Action, which he consents to the existence of, to be good, is entirely to destroy his two Attributes of *Wisdom* and *Goodness.*

*There is nothing done in the Universe,* say the Philosophers, *but what God either does, or* permits *to be done.* This, as He is Almighty, is certainly true: But what need of this Distinction between *doing* and *permitting?* Why, first they take it for granted that many Things in the Universe exist in such a Manner as is not for the best, and that many Actions are done which ought not to be done, or would be better undone; these Things or Actions they cannot ascribe to God as His, because they have already attributed to Him infinite Wisdom and Goodness; Here then is the Use of the Word *Permit;* He *permits* them to be done, *say they.* But we will reason thus: If God permits an Action to be done, it is because he wants either *Power,* or *Inclination* to hinder it; in saying he wants *Power,* we deny Him to be *almighty;* and if we say He wants *Inclination* or *Will,* it must be either because He is not Good, or the Action is not *evil,* (for all Evil is contrary to the Essence of *infinite Goodness.*) The former is inconsistent with his before given Attribute of Goodness, therefore the latter must be true.

It will be said, perhaps, that *God permits evil Actions to be done, for* wise *Ends and Purposes.* But this Objection destroys itself; for whatever an infinitely good God hath wise Ends in suffering to *be,* must be good, is thereby made good, and cannot be otherwise.

VI. *If a Creature is made by God, it must depend upon God, and receive all its Power from Him; with which Power the Creature can do nothing contrary to the Will of God, because God is Almighty;*

*what is not contrary to His Will, must be agreeable to it; what is agreeable to it, must be good, because He is Good; therefore a Creature can do nothing but what is good.*

This Proposition is much to the same Purpose with the former, but more particular; and its Conclusion is as just and evident. Tho' a Creature may do many Actions which by his Fellow Creatures will be nam'd *Evil,* and which will naturally and necessarily cause or bring upon the Doer, certain *Pains* (which will likewise be call'd *Punishments;*) yet this Proposition proves, that he cannot act what will be in itself really Ill, or displeasing to God. And that the painful Consequences of his evil Actions (*so call'd*) are not, as indeed they ought not to be, *Punishments* or Unhappinesses, will be shewn hereafter.

Nevertheless, the late learned Author of *The Religion of Nature,* (which I send you herewith) has given us a Rule or Scheme, whereby to discover which of our Actions ought to be esteem'd and denominated *good,* and which *evil:* It is in short this, "Every Action which is done according to *Truth,* is good; and every Action contrary to Truth, is evil: To act according to Truth is to use and esteem every Thing as what it is, &c. Thus if A steals a Horse from B, and rides away upon him, he uses him not as what he is in Truth, *viz.* the Property of another, but as his own, which is contrary to Truth, and therefore *evil.*" But, as this Gentleman himself says, (Sect. I. Prop. VI.) "In order to judge rightly what any Thing is, it must be consider'd, not only what it is in one Respect, but also what it may be in any other Respect; and the whole Description of the Thing ought to be taken in:" So in this Case it ought to be consider'd, that A is naturally a *covetous* Being, feeling an Uneasiness in the want of B's Horse, which produces an Inclination for stealing him, stronger than his Fear of Punishment for so doing. This is Truth likewise, and A acts according to it when he steals the Horse. Besides, if it is prov'd to be a *Truth,* that A has not Power over his own Actions, it will be indisputable that he acts according to Truth, and impossible he should do otherwise.

I would not be understood by this to encourage or defend Theft; 'tis only for the sake of the Argument, and will certainly have no *ill Effect.* The Order and Course of Things will not be affected by Reasoning of this Kind; and 'tis as just and necessary, and as much according to Truth, for B to dislike and punish the Theft of his Horse, as it is for A to steal him.

*VII. If the Creature is thus limited in his Actions, being able to do only such Things as God would have him to do, and not being able to refuse doing what God would have done; then he can have no such Thing as Liberty, Free-will, or Power to do or refrain an Action.*

By *Liberty* is sometimes understood the Absence of Opposition; and in this Sense, indeed, all our Actions may be said to be the Effects of our Liberty: But it is a Liberty of the same Nature with the fall of a heavy Body to the Ground; it has Liberty to fall, that is, it meets with nothing to hinder its Fall, but at the same Time it is necessitated to fall, and has no Power or Liberty to remain suspended.

But let us take the Argument in another View, and suppose ourselves to be, in the common sense of the Word, *Free Agents*. As Man is a Part of this great Machine, the Universe, his regular Acting is requisite to the regular moving of the whole. Among the many Things which lie before him to be done, he may, as he is at Liberty and his Choice influenc'd by nothing, (for so it must be, or he is not at Liberty) chuse any one, and refuse the rest. Now there is every Moment something *best* to be done, which is alone then *good,* and with respect to which, every Thing else is at that Time *evil.* In order to know which is best to be done, and which not, it is requisite that we should have at one View all the intricate Consequences of every Action with respect to the general Order and Scheme of the Universe, both present and future; but they are innumerable and incomprehensible by any Thing but Omniscience. As we cannot know these, we have but as one Chance to ten thousand, to hit on the right Action; we should then be perpetually blundering about in the Dark, and putting the Scheme in Disorder; for every wrong Action of a Part, is a Defect or Blemish in the Order of the Whole. Is it not necessary then, that our Actions should be over-rul'd and govern'd by an all-wise Providence?—How exact and regular is every Thing in the *natural* World! How wisely in every Part contriv'd! We cannot here find the least Defect! Those who have study'd the mere animal and vegetable Creation, demonstrate that nothing can be more harmonious and beautiful: All the heavenly Bodies, the Stars and Planets, are regulated with the utmost Wisdom! And can we suppose less Care to be taken in the Order of the *moral* than in the *natural* System? It is as if an ingenious Artificer, having fram'd a curious Machine or Clock, and put its many intricate Wheels and Powers in such a Dependance on one another, that the whole might move in the most exact Order and Regularity, had nevertheless plac'd in it several other Wheels endu'd with an independent *Self-Motion,* but ignorant of the general Interest of the Clock; and these would every now and then be moving wrong, disordering the true

Movement, and making continual Work for the Mender: which might better be prevented, by depriving them of that Power of Self-Motion, and placing them in a Dependance on the regular Part of the Clock.

*VIII. If there is no such Thing as Free-Will in Creatures, there can be neither Merit nor Demerit in Creatures.*

*IX. And therefore every Creature must be equally esteem'd by the Creator.*

These Propositions appear to be the necessary Consequences of the former. And certainly no Reason can be given, why the Creator should prefer in his Esteem one Part of His Works to another, if with equal Wisdom and Goodness he design'd and created them all, since all Ill or Defect, as contrary to his Nature, is excluded by his Power. We will sum up the Argument thus, When the Creator first design'd the Universe, either it was His Will and Intention that all Things should exist and be in the Manner they are at this Time; or it was his Will they should *be* otherwise in a different Manner: To say it was His Will Things should be otherwise than they are, is to say Somewhat hath contradicted His Will, and broken His Measures, which is impossible because inconsistent with his Power; therefore we must allow that all Things exist now in a Manner agreeable to His Will, and in consequence of that are all equally Good, and therefore equally esteem'd by Him.

I proceed now to shew, that as all the Works of the Creator are equally esteem'd by Him, so they are, as in Justice they ought to be, equally us'd.

## *Sect. II. Of Pleasure and Pain*

*I. When a Creature is form'd and endu'd with Life, 'tis suppos'd to receive a Capacity of the Sensation of Uneasiness or Pain.*

It is this distinguishes Life and Consciousness from unactive unconscious Matter. To know or be sensible of Suffering or being acted upon is *to live;* and whatsoever is not so, among created Things, is properly and truly *dead.*

All *Pain* and *Uneasiness* proceeds at first from and is caus'd by Somewhat without and distinct from the Mind itself. The Soul must first be acted upon before it can re-act. In the Beginning of Infancy it is as if it were not; it is not conscious of its own Existance, till it has receiv'd the first Sensation of *Pain;* then, and not before, it begins to feel itself, is rous'd, and put into Action; then it discovers its Powers and Faculties, and exerts them to expel the Uneasiness. Thus is the Machine set on work; this is Life. We are first mov'd by *Pain,* and the whole succeeding Course of our Lives is but one continu'd Series of Action with a View to be freed from it. As fast as we have excluded one Uneasiness another appears, otherwise the Motion would cease. If a continual Weight is not apply'd, the Clock will stop. And as soon as the Avenues of Uneasiness to the Soul are choak'd up or cut off, we are dead, we think and act no more.

II. *This Uneasiness, whenever felt, produces* Desire *to be freed from it, great in exact proportion to the Uneasiness.*

Thus is *Uneasiness* the first Spring and Cause of all Action; for till we are uneasy in Rest, we can have no Desire to move, and without Desire of moving there can be no voluntary Motion. The Experience of every Man who has observ'd his own Actions will evince the Truth of this; and I think nothing need be said to prove that the *Desire* will be equal to the *Uneasiness,* for the very Thing implies as much: It is not *Uneasiness* unless we desire to be freed from it, nor a great *Uneasiness* unless the consequent Desire is great.

I might here observe, how necessary a Thing in the Order and Design of the Universe this *Pain* or *Uneasiness* is, and how beautiful in its Place? Let us but suppose it just now banish'd the World entirely, and consider the Consequence of it: All the Animal Creation would immediately stand stock still, exactly in the Posture they were in the Moment Uneasiness departed; not a Limb, not a Finger would henceforth move; we should all be reduc'd to the Condition of Statues, dull and unactive: Here I should continue to sit motionless with the Pen in my Hand thus—and neither leave my Seat nor write one Letter more. This may appear odd at first View, but a little Consideration will make it evident; for 'tis impossible to assign any other Cause for the voluntary Motion of an Animal than its *uneasiness* in Rest. What a different Appearance then would the Face of Nature make, without it! How necessary is it! And how unlikely that the Inhabitants of the World ever were, or that the Creator ever design'd they should be, exempt from it!

I would likewise observe here, that the VIIIth Proposition in the preceding Section, viz. *That there is neither Merit nor Demerit,* &c. is here again demonstrated, as infallibly, tho' in another manner: For since *Freedom from Uneasiness* is the End of all our Actions, how is it possible for us to do any Thing disinterested?—How can any Action be meritorious of Praise or Dispraise, Reward or Punishment, when the natural Principle of *Self-Love* is the only and the irresistible Motive to it?

III. *This* Desire *is always fulfill'd or satisfy'd.*

In the *Design* or *End* of it, tho' not in the *Manner:* The first is requisite, the latter not. To exemplify this, let us make a Supposition; A Person is confin'd in a House which appears to be in imminent Danger of Falling, this, as soon as perceiv'd, creates a violent *Uneasiness,* and that instantly produces an equal strong *Desire,* the *End* of which is *freedom from the Uneasiness,* and the *Manner* or Way propos'd to gain this *End,* is *to get out of the House.* Now if he is convinc'd by any Means, that he is mistaken, and the House is not likely to fall, he is immediately freed from his *Uneasiness,* and the *End* of his Desire is attained as well as if it had been in the *Manner* desir'd, viz. *leaving the House.*

All our different Desires and Passions proceed from and are reducible to this one Point, *Uneasiness,* tho' the Means we propose to ourselves for expelling of it are infinite. One proposes *Fame,* another *Wealth,* a third *Power,* &c. as the Means to gain this *End;* but tho' these are never attain'd, if the Uneasiness be remov'd by some other Means, the *Desire* is satisfy'd. Now during the Course of Life we are ourselves continually removing successive Uneasinesses as they arise, and the *last* we suffer is remov'd by the *sweet Sleep* of Death.

IV. *The fulfilling or Satisfaction of this Desire, produces the Sensation of* Pleasure, *great or small in exact proportion to the* Desire.

*Pleasure* is that Satisfaction which arises in the Mind upon, and is caus'd by, the accomplishment of our *Desires,* and by no other Means at all; and those Desires being above shewn to be caus'd by our *Pains* or *Uneasinesses,* it follows that *Pleasure* is wholly caus'd by *Pain,* and by no other Thing at all.

V. *Therefore the Sensation of* Pleasure *is equal, or in exact proportion to the Sensation of* Pain.

As the *Desire* of being freed from Uneasiness is equal to the *Uneasiness,* and the *Pleasure* of satisfying that Desire equal to the *Desire,* the *Pleasure* thereby produc'd must necessarily be equal to the *Uneasiness* or *Pain* which produces it: Of three Lines, A, B, and C, if A is equal to B, and B to C, C must be equal to A. And as our *Uneasi-*

*nesses* are always remov'd by some Means or other, it follows that *Pleasure* and *Pain* are in their Nature inseparable: So many Degrees as one Scale of the Ballance descends, so many exactly the other ascends; and one cannot rise or fall without the Fall or Rise of the other: 'Tis impossible to taste of *Pleasure,* without feeling its preceding proportionate *Pain;* or to be sensible of *Pain,* without having its necessary Consequent *Pleasure:* The *highest Pleasure* is only Consciousness of Freedom from the *deepest Pain,* and Pain is not Pain to us unless we ourselves are sensible of it. They go Hand in Hand; they cannot be divided.

You have a View of the whole Argument in a few familiar Examples: The *Pain* of Abstinence from Food, as it is greater or less, produces a greater or less *Desire* of Eating, the Accomplishment of this *Desire* produces a greater or less *Pleasure* proportionate to it. The *Pain* of Confinement causes the *Desire* of Liberty, which accomplish'd, yields a *Pleasure* equal to that *Pain* of Confinement. The *Pain* of Labour and Fatigue causes the *Pleasure* of Rest, equal to that *Pain.* The *Pain* of Absence from Friends, produces the *Pleasure* of Meeting in exact proportion, &c.

This is the *fixt Nature* of Pleasure and Pain, and will always be found to be so by those who examine it.

One of the most common Arguments for the future Existence of the Soul, is taken from the generally suppos'd Inequality of Pain and Pleasure in the present; and this, notwithstanding the Difficulty by outward Appearances to make a Judgment of another's Happiness, has been look'd upon as almost unanswerable: but since *Pain* naturally and infallibly produces a *Pleasure* in proportion to it, every individual Creature must, in any State of *Life,* have an equal Quantity of each, so that there is not, on that Account, any Occasion for a future Adjustment.

Thus are all the Works of the Creator *equally* used by him; and no Condition of Life or Being is in itself better or preferable to another: The Monarch is not more happy than the Slave, nor the Beggar more miserable than *Croesus.* Suppose A, B, and C, three distinct Beings; A and B, animate, capable of *Pleasure* and *Pain,* C an inanimate Piece of Matter, insensible of either. A receives ten Degrees of *Pain,* which are necessarily succeeded by ten Degrees of *Pleasure:* B receives fifteen of *Pain,* and the consequent equal Number of *Pleasure:* C all the while lies unconcern'd, and as he has not suffer'd the former, has no right to the latter. What can be more equal and just than this? When the Accounts come to be adjusted, A has no Reason to complain that his Portion of *Pleasure* was five Degrees less than that of B, for his Portion of Pain was five Degrees less likewise: Nor has B any Reason to boast that his Pleasure was five Degrees greater than that of A, for his *Pain* was proportionate: They are then both on the same Foot with C, that is, they are neither Gainers nor Losers.

It will possibly be objected here, that even common Experience shews us, there is not in Fact this Equality: "Some we see hearty, brisk and cheerful perpetually, while others are constantly burden'd with a heavy Load of Maladies and Misfortunes, remaining for Years perhaps in Poverty, Disgrace, or Pain, and die at last without any Appearance of Recompence." Now tho' 'tis not necessary, when a Proposition is demonstrated to be a general Truth, to shew in what manner it agrees with the particular Circumstances of Persons, and indeed ought not to be requir'd; yet, as this is a common Objection, some Notice may be taken of it: And here let it be observ'd, that we cannot be proper Judges of the good or bad Fortune of Others; we are apt to imagine, that what would give us a great Uneasiness or a great Satisfaction, has the same Effect upon others: we think, for Instance, those unhappy, who must depend upon Charity for a mean Subsistence, who go in Rags, fare hardly, and are despis'd and scorn'd by all; not considering that Custom renders all these Things easy, familiar, and even pleasant. When we see Riches, Grandeur and a cheerful Countenance, we easily imagine Happiness accompanies them, when oftentimes 'tis quite otherwise: Nor is a constantly sorrowful Look, attended with continual Complaints, an infallible Indication of Unhappiness. In short, we can judge by nothing but Appearances, and they are very apt to deceive us. Some put on a gay chearful Outside, and appear to the World perfectly at Ease, tho' even then, some inward Sting, some secret Pain imbitters all their Joys, and makes the Ballance even: Others appear continually dejected and full of Sorrow; but even Grief itself is sometimes *pleasant,* and Tears are not always without their Sweetness: Besides, Some take a Satisfaction in being thought unhappy, (as others take a Pride in being thought humble,) these will paint their Misfortunes to others in the strongest Colours, and leave no Means unus'd to make you think them throughly miserable; so great a *Pleasure* it is to them *to be pitied;* Others retain the Form and outside Shew of Sorrow, long after the Thing itself, with its Cause, is remov'd from the Mind; it is a Habit they have acquir'd and cannot leave. These, with many others that might be given, are Reasons why we cannot make a true Estimate of the *Equality* of the Happiness and Unhappiness of others; and unless we could, Matter of Fact cannot be opposed to this Hypothesis. Indeed, we are sometimes apt to think, that the Uneasinesses we ourselves have had, outweigh our Pleasures; but the Reason is this, the Mind takes no Account of the latter, they slip away un-remark'd, when the former leave more lasting Impressions on the Memory. But suppose we pass the greatest part of Life in Pain and Sorrow, suppose we die by Torments and *think no more,* 'tis no Diminuation to the Truth of what is here advanc'd; for the *Pain,* tho' exquisite, is not so to the *last* Moments of Life, the Senses are soon benumm'd, and render'd incapable of transmitting it so sharply to the Soul as at first; She perceives it cannot hold long, and 'tis an *exquisite Pleasure* to behold the immediate Approaches of Rest. This makes an Equivalent tho' Annihilation should follow: For the Quantity of *Pleasure* and *Pain* is not to be measur'd by its Duration, any more than the Quantity of Matter by its Extension; and as one cubic Inch may be made to contain, by Condensation, as much Matter as would fill ten thousand cubic Feet, being more expanded, so one single Moment of *Pleasure* may outweigh and compensate an Age of *Pain.*

It was owing to their Ignorance of the Nature of Pleasure and Pain that the Antient Heathens believ'd the idle Fable of their *Elizium,* that State of uninterrupted Ease and Happiness! The Thing is intirely impossible in Nature! Are not the Pleasures of the Spring made such by the Disagreeableness of the Winter? Is not the Pleasure of fair Weather owing to the Unpleasantness of foul? Certainly. Were it then always Spring, were the Fields always green and flourishing, and the Weather constantly serene and fair, the Pleasure would pall and die upon our Hands; it would cease to be Pleasure to us, when it is not usher'd in by Uneasiness. Could the Philosopher visit, in reality, every Star and Planet with as much Ease and Swiftness as he can now visit their Ideas, and pass from one to another of them in the Imagination; it would be a *Pleasure* I grant; but it would be only in proportion to the *Desire* of accomplishing it, and that would be no greater than the Uneasiness suffer'd in the Want of it. The Accomplishment of a long and difficult Journey yields a great *Pleasure;* but if we could take a Trip to the Moon and back again, as frequently and with as much Ease as we can go and come from Market, the Satisfaction would be just the same.

The *Immateriality* of the Soul has been frequently made use of as an Argument for its *Immortality;* but let us consider, that tho' it should be allow'd to be immaterial, and consequently its Parts incapable of Separation or Destruction by any Thing material, yet by

Experience we find, that it is not incapable of Cessation of *Thought,* which is its Action. When the Body is but a little indispos'd it has an evident Effect upon the Mind; and a right Disposition of the Organs is requisite to a right Manner of Thinking. In a sound Sleep sometimes or in a Swoon, we cease to think at all; tho' the Soul is not therefore then annihilated, but *exists* all the while tho' it does not *act;* and may not this probably be the Case after Death? All our Ideas are first admitted by the Senses and imprinted on the Brain, increasing in Number by Observation and Experience; there they become the Subjects of the Soul's Action. The Soul is a mere Power or Faculty of *contemplating* on, and *comparing* those Ideas when it has them; hence springs Reason: But as it can *think* on nothing but Ideas, it must have them before it can *think* at all. Therefore as it may exist before it has receiv'd any Ideas, it may exist before it *thinks.* To remember a Thing, is to have the Idea of it still plainly imprinted on the Brain, which the Soul can turn to and contemplate on Occasion. To forget a Thing, is to have the Idea of it defac'd and destroy'd by some Accident, or the crouding in and imprinting of great variety of other Ideas upon it, so that the Soul cannot find out its Traces and distinguish it. When we have thus lost the Idea of any one Thing, we can *think* no more, or *cease to think,* on that Thing; and as we can lose the Idea of one Thing, so we may of ten, twenty, a hundred, &c. and even of all Things, because they are not in their Nature permanent; and often during Life we see that some Men, (by an Accident or Distemper affecting the Brain,) lose the greatest Part of their Ideas, and remember very little of their Past Actions and Circumstances. Now upon *Death,* and the Destruction of the Body, the Ideas contain'd in the Brain, (which are alone the Subjects of the Soul's Action) being then likewise necessarily destroy'd, the Soul, tho' incapable of Destruction itself, must then necessarily *cease to think* or *act,* having nothing left to think or act upon. It is reduc'd to its first inconscious State before it receiv'd any Ideas. And to cease to *think* is but little different from *ceasing to be.*

Nevertheless, 'tis not impossible that this same *Faculty* of contemplating Ideas may be hereafter united to a new Body, and receive a new Set of Ideas; but that will no way concern us who are now living; for the Identity will be lost, it is no longer that same *Self* but a new Being.

I shall here subjoin a short Recapitulation of the Whole, that it may with all its Parts be comprehended at one View.

1. *It is suppos'd that God the Maker and Governour of the Universe, is infinitely wise, good, and powerful.*

2. *In consequence of His infinite Wisdom and Goodness, it is asserted, that whatever He doth must be infinitely wise and good;*

3. *Unless He be interrupted, and His Measures broken by some other Being, which is impossible because He is Almighty.*

4. *In consequence of His infinite Power, it is asserted, that nothing can exist or be done in the Universe which is not agreeable to His Will, and therefore good.*

5. *Evil is hereby excluded, with all Merit and Demerit; and likewise all preference in the Esteem of God, of one Part of the Creation to another. This is the Summary of the first Part.*

Now our common Notions of Justice will tell us, that if all created Things are equally esteem'd by the Creator, they ought to be equally us'd by Him; and that they are therefore equally us'd, we might embrace for Truth upon the Credit, and as the true Consequence of the foregoing Argument. Nevertheless we proceed to confirm it, by shewing *how* they are equally us'd, and that in the following Manner.

1. *A Creature when endu'd with Life or Consciousness, is made capable of Uneasiness or Pain.*

2. *This Pain produces Desire to be freed from it, in exact proportion to itself.*

3. *The Accomplishment of this Desire produces an equal Pleasure.*

4. *Pleasure is consequently equal to Pain.*

From these Propositions it is observ'd,

1. *That every Creature hath as much Pleasure as Pain.*

2. *That Life is not preferable to Insensibility; for Pleasure and Pain destroy one another: That Being which has ten Degrees of Pain subtracted from ten of Pleasure, has nothing remaining, and is upon an equality with that Being which is insensible of both.*

3. *As the first Part proves that all Things must be equally us'd by the Creator because equally esteem'd; so this second Part demonstrates that they are equally esteem'd because equally us'd.*

4. *Since every Action is the Effect of Self-Uneasiness, the Distinction of Virtue and Vice is excluded; and* Prop. VIII. *in* Sect. I. *again demonstrated.*

5. *No State of Life can be happier than the present, because Pleasure and Pain are inseparable.*

Thus both Parts of this Argument agree with and confirm one another, and the Demonstration is reciprocal.

I am sensible that the Doctrine here advanc'd, if it were to be publish'd, would meet with but an indifferent Reception. Mankind naturally and generally love to be flatter'd: Whatever sooths our Pride, and tends to exalt our Species above the rest of the Creation, we are pleas'd with and easily believe, when ungrateful Truths shall be with the utmost Indignation rejected. "What! bring ourselves down to an Equality with the Beasts of the Field! with the *meanest* part of the Creation! 'Tis insufferable!" But, (to use a Piece of *common* Sense) our *Geese* are but *Geese* tho' we may think 'em *Swans;* and Truth will be Truth tho' it sometimes prove mortifying and distasteful.

* * *

---

* * *

## AUTOBIOGRAPHY [11]

It was about this time I conceiv'd the bold and arduous project of arriving at moral perfection. I wish'd to live without committing any fault at any time; I would conquer all that either natural inclination, custom, or company might lead me into. As I knew, or thought I knew, what was right and wrong, I did not see why I might not always do the one and avoid the other. But I soon found I had undertaken a task of more difficulty than I had imagined. While my care was employ'd in guarding against one fault, I was often surprised by another; habit took the advantage of inattention; inclination was sometimes too strong for reason. I concluded, at length, that the mere speculative conviction that it was our interest to be completely virtuous, was not sufficient to prevent our slipping; and that the contrary habits must be broken, and good ones acquired and established, before we can have any dependence on a steady, uniform rectitude of conduct. For this purpose I therefore contrived the following method.

In the various enumerations of the moral virtues I had met with in my reading, I found the catalogue more or less numerous, as different writers included more or fewer ideas under the same name. Temperance, for example, was by some confined to eating and drinking, while by others it was extended to mean the moderating every other pleas-

[11] From A. H. Smyth, editor. *The Writings of Benjamin Franklin.* I, 326–31, 336–7, 339–42. By permission of The Macmillan Company, publishers. These selections refer to his thoughts in the early 1730's; the first two were written in 1784 and the third in 1788.

ure, appetite, inclination, or passion, bodily or mental, even to our avarice and ambition. I propos'd to myself, for the sake of clearness, to use rather more names, with fewer ideas annex'd to each, than a few names with more ideas; and I included under thirteen names of virtues all that at that time occurred to me as necessary or desirable, and annexed to each a short precept, which fully express'd the extent I gave to its meaning.

These names of virtues, with their precepts, were:

1. TEMPERANCE.

Eat not to dullness; drink not to elevation.

2. SILENCE.

Speak not but what may benefit others or yourself; avoid trifling conversation.

3. ORDER.

Let all your things have their places; let each part of your business have its time.

4. RESOLUTION.

Resolve to perform what you ought; perform without fail what you resolve.

5. FRUGALITY.

Make no expense but to do good to others or yourself; i. e., waste nothing.

6. INDUSTRY.

Lose no time; be always employ'd in something useful; cut off all unnecessary actions.

7. SINCERITY.

Use no hurtful deceit; think innocently and justly, and, if you speak, speak accordingly.

8. JUSTICE.

Wrong none by doing injuries, or omitting the benefits that are your duty.

## 9. MODERATION.

Avoid extreams; forbear resenting injuries so much as you think they deserve.

## 10. CLEANLINESS.

Tolerate no uncleanliness in body, cloaths, or habitation.

## 11. TRANQUILLITY.

Be not disturbed at trifles, or at accidents common or unavoidable.

## 12. CHASTITY.

Rarely use venery but for health or offspring, never to dulness, weakness, or the injury of your own or another's peace or reputation.

## 13. HUMILITY.

Imitate Jesus and Socrates.

My intention being to acquire the *habitude* of all these virtues, I judg'd it would be well not to distract my attention by attempting the whole at once, but to fix it on one of them at a time; and, when I should be master of that, then to proceed to another, and so on, till I should have gone thro' the thirteen; and, as the previous acquisition of some might facilitate the acquisition of certain others, I arrang'd them with that view, as they stand above. Temperance first, as it tends to procure that coolness and clearness of head, which is so necessary where constant vigilance was to be kept up, and guard maintained against the unremitting attraction of ancient habits, and the force of perpetual temptations. This being acquir'd and establish'd, Silence would be more easy; and my desire being to gain knowledge at the same time that I improv'd in virtue, and considering that in conversation it was obtained rather by the use of the ears than of the tongue, and therefore wishing to break a habit I was getting into of prattling, punning, and joking, which only made me acceptable to trifling company, I gave *Silence* the second place. This and the next, *Order,* I expected would allow me more time for attending to my project and my studies. *Resolution,* once become habitual, would keep me firm in my endeavors to obtain all the subsequent virtues; *Frugality* and Industry freeing me from my remaining debt, and producing affluence and independence, would make more easy the practice of Sincerity and Justice, etc., etc. Conceiving then, that, agreeably to the advice of

Pythagoras in his *Golden Verses,* daily examination would be necessary, I contrived the following method for conducting that examination.

I made a little book, in which I allotted a page for each of the virtues.[12] I rul'd each page with red ink, so as to have seven columns, one for each day of the week, marking each column with a letter for the day. I cross'd these columns with thirteen red lines, marking the beginning of each line with the first letter of one of the virtues, on which line, and in its proper column, I might mark, by a little black spot, every fault I found upon examination to have been committed respecting that virtue upon that day.

FORM OF THE PAGES

| TEMPERANCE | | | | | | | |
|---|---|---|---|---|---|---|---|
| *Eat Not to Dulness. Drink Not to Elevation.* | | | | | | | |
| | *S.* | *M.* | *T.* | *W.* | *T.* | *F.* | *S.* |
| T. | | | | | | | |
| S. | * | * | | * | | * | |
| O. | ** | * | * | | * | * | * |
| R. | | | * | | | * | |
| F. | | * | | | * | | |
| I. | | | * | | | | |
| S. | | | | | | | |
| J. | | | | | | | |
| M. | | | | | | | |
| C. | | | | | | | |
| T. | | | | | | | |
| C. | | | | | | | |
| H. | | | | | | | |

I determined to give a week's strict attention to each of the virtues successively. Thus, in the first week, my great guard was to avoid every the least offence against *Temperance,* leaving the other virtues to their

12 Dated July 1, 1733.—Editor's note.

ordinary chance, only marking every evening the faults of the day. Thus, if in the first week I could keep my first line, marked T, clear of spots, I suppos'd the habit of that virtue so much strengthen'd, and its opposite weaken'd, that I might venture extending my attention to include the next, and for the following week keep both lines clear of spots. Proceeding thus to the last, I could go thro' a course compleat in thirteen weeks, and four courses in a year. And like him who, having a garden to weed, does not attempt to eradicate all the bad herbs at once, which would exceed his reach and his strength, but works on one of the beds at a time, and, having accomplish'd the first, proceeds to a second, so I should have, I hoped, the encouraging pleasure of seeing on my pages the progress I made in virtue, by clearing successively my lines of their spots, till in the end, by a number of courses, I should be happy in viewing a clean book, after a thirteen weeks' daily examination.

. . . . . .

It will be remark'd that, tho' my scheme was not wholly without religion, there was in it no mark of any of the distinguishing tenets of any particular sect. I had purposely avoided them; for, being fully persuaded of the utility and excellency of my method, and that it might be serviceable to people in all religions, and intending some time or other to publish it, I would not have any thing in it that should prejudice any one, of any sect, against it. I purposed writing a little comment on each virtue, in which I would have shown the advantages of possessing it, and the mischiefs attending its opposite vice; and I should have called my book THE ART OF VIRTUE,[13] because it would have shown the means and manner of obtaining virtue, which would have distinguished it from the mere exhortation to be good, that does not instruct and indicate the means, but is like the apostle's man of verbal charity, who only without showing to the naked and hungry how or where they might get clothes or victuals, exhorted them to be fed and clothed.—James ii. 15, 16.

But it so happened that my intention of writing and publishing this comment was never fulfilled. I did, indeed, from time to time, put down short hints of the sentiments, reasonings, etc., to be made use of in it, some of which I have still by me; but the necessary close attention to private business in the earlier part of my life, and public business since, have occasioned my postponing it; for, it being connected

[13] Nothing so likely to make a man's fortune as virtue.

in my mind with *a great and extensive project,* that required the whole man to execute, and which an unforeseen succession of employs prevented my attending to, it has hitherto remain'd unfinish'd.

In this piece it was my design to explain and enforce this doctrine, that vicious actions are not hurtful because they are forbidden, but forbidden because they are hurtful, the nature of man alone considered; that it was, therefore, every one's interest to be virtuous who wish'd to be happy even in this world; and I should, from this circumstance (there being always in the world a number of rich merchants, nobility, states, and princes, who have need of honest instruments for the management of their affairs, and such being so rare), have endeavoured to convince young persons that no qualities were so likely to make a poor man's fortune as those of probity and integrity.

. . . . . .

Having mentioned *a great and extensive project* which I had conceiv'd, it seems proper that some account should be here given of that project and its object. Its first rise in my mind appears in the following little paper, accidentally preserv'd, viz.:

*Observations* on my reading history, in Library, May 19th, 1731.

"That the great affairs of the world, the wars, revolutions, etc., are carried on and affected by parties.

"That the view of these parties is their present general interest, or what they take to be such.

"That the different views of these different parties occasion all confusion.

"That while a party is carrying on a general design, each man has his particular private interest in view.

"That as soon as a party has gain'd its general point, each member becomes intent upon his particular interest; which, thwarting others, breaks that party into divisions, and occasions more confusion.

"That few in public affairs act from a meer view of the good of their country, whatever they may pretend; and, tho' their actings bring real good to their country, yet men primarily considered that their own and their country's interest was united, and did not act from a principle of benevolence.

"That fewer still, in public affairs, act with a view to the good of mankind.

"There seems to me at present to be great occasion for raising a United Party for Virtue, by forming the virtuous and good men of all nations into a regular body, to be govern'd by suitable good and wise rules, which good and wise men may probably be more unanimous in their obedience to, than common people are to common laws.

"I at present think that whoever attempts this aright, and is well qualified, can not fail of pleasing God, and of meeting with success.

B.F."

Revolving this project in my mind, as to be undertaken hereafter, when my circumstances should afford me the necessary leisure, I put down from time to time, on pieces of paper, such thoughts as occurr'd to me respecting it. Most of these are lost; but I find one purporting to be the substance of an intended creed, containing, as I thought, the essentials of every known religion, and being free of every thing that might shock the professors of any religion. It is express'd in these words, viz.:

"That there is one God, who made all things.

"That he governs the world by his providence.

"That he ought to be worshiped by adoration, prayer, and thanksgiving.

"But that the most acceptable service of God is doing good to men.

"That the soul is immortal.

"And that God will certainly reward virtue and punish vice, either here or hereafter."

My ideas at that time were, that the sect should be begun and spread at first among young and single men only; that each person to be initiated should not only declare his assent to such creed, but should have exercised himself with the thirteen weeks' examination and practice of the virtues, as in the before-mentioned model; that the existence of such a society should be kept a secret, till it was become considerable, to prevent solicitations for the admission of improper persons, but that the members should each of them search among his acquaintance for ingenuous, well-disposed youths, to whom, with prudent caution, the scheme should be gradually communicated; that the members should engage to afford their advice, assistance, and support to each other in promoting one another's interests, business, and advancement in life; that, for distinction, we should be call'd *The Society of the Free and Easy:* free, as being, by the general practice and habit of the virtues, free from the dominion of vice; and particularly by the practice of industry and frugality, free from debt, which exposes a man to confinement, and a species of slavery to his creditors.

This is as much as I can now recollect of the project, except that I communicated it in part to two young men, who adopted it with some enthusiasm; but my then narrow circumstances, and the necessity I was under of sticking close to my business, occasion'd my postponing the further prosecution of it at that time; and my multifarious occupations, public and private, induc'd me to continue postponing, so that it has been omitted till I have no longer strength or activity left sufficient for such an enterprise; tho' I am still of opinion that it was a practicable scheme, and might have been very useful, by forming a great number of good citizens; and I was not discourag'd by the seeming magnitude of the undertaking, as I have always thought that one man of tolerable abilities may work great changes, and accomplish great affairs among mankind, if he first forms a good plan, and, cutting off all amusements or other employments that would divert his attention, makes the execution of that same plan his sole study and business.

# *PART II*

# The Age of Reason

# VII
## Introduction

Franklin's birth in Boston and death in Philadelphia were symbols of the change which took place during his lifetime. When he was born, Boston was the center of American culture and thought, the Puritan theocracy was still in the ascendency, the world was viewed as a divine plenum and man's concern was to fulfil his God-appointed destiny. When he died, Philadelphia was the center of culture and thought, deism of one sort or another held the stage, the world was thought to be controlled by immutable laws and man's desire was to achieve happiness. No intellectual upheaval marked the change; a convergence of religious and social forces over two-thirds of a century slowly brought about the shift.

By the middle of the eighteenth century, the New England theocratic viewpoint with its Calvinistic theology was losing hold. Disagreement had arisen among the clergy, argument often reaching the point where charges and counter-charges were made. The control of the state by the church had been supplanted by a more secular view of society. The individualism of Protestantism aided in the disintegration of the early colonial world-view, for the right of individual judgment came to be exercised in questioning, and even rejecting, the Puritan mode of life and thought. The Great Awakening, emotional rather than rational, spread throughout the country, led by such men as Jonathan Edwards; this substitution of emotional for rational and revealed certainty led to further diversity of opinion and questioning. Likewise, within the circle of the orthodox and near-orthodox there was a growing substitution of natural for supernatural evidences of the existence of God. Cotton Mather, for example, in *The Christian Philosopher* (1721) used the argument from design almost exclusively.

The nascent individualism of New England led to a new viewpoint in the economic sphere. The Puritans had stressed the virtues of hard work; thrift, enterprise and discipline, virtues of real benefit in a frontier civilization. They served so successfully in fact that men became enamored of economic well-being. The more secure the mundane appeared, the less necessary the spiritual seemed to be. Economic victory gave man greater faith in himself. The natural independence of the frontier mind was an additional influence working in the same direction.

Contact with thought from abroad aided the shift to a new point of view. The first impulse came through the works of independent English thinkers, many of which were available in the early part of the century. Newton, who was largely known through secondary sources, presented a picture of a mechanical world which shook man's faith in an active deity who was the efficient cause of physical events. Locke, who was more widely read than any other single figure, offered an empirical approach to reality in place of authority. The writings of English deists such as Blount, Clarke, Wollaston, Shaftesbury, Collins and Bolingbroke, men who had taken Newton and Locke seriously, were available in numerous libraries by the middle of the eighteenth century and had been read earlier by many. Contact with British troops during the French and Indian War helped acquaint the Americans with ideas current in England at the time. Later in the century, when relations with England became strained, French sources came to be read. By the 1780's French was being introduced quite widely in schools and colleges. The writings of Cabanis, Condillac, Condorcet, Diderot, Holbach, La Mettrie, Volney and Voltaire were available and were on the whole more radical than the English sources; their influence was greatest in the South. The change taking place in American thought paralleled that in English and French thought, although its effect was noticeable later. Even without inspiration from abroad, the shift in American thought would undoubtedly have taken place, although still later, for it was the inevitable outcome of a changing social order and scientific advancement. As it happened, however, the Americans did borrow heavily from both the English and the French, selecting those ideas which satisfied the inclinations of their own minds.

We have already seen that departure from traditional Calvinism was on the way in the Colonial period. This process was considerably accelerated during the Age of Reason through deism, certain elements of which were mildly suggested by theologians early in the century but whose real importance came to be felt after the Revolution. It is somewhat difficult to enumerate the tenets of deism because of the diversity of opinion among those who shared the position. In general, however, the deists regarded God as a first cause but conceived of nature as based upon lawful principles; they rejected miracles. They looked upon nature as a revelation of God's beneficence. They conceived the universe to be orderly and man rational. They regarded reason as the primary source of truth and rejected authority, both ecclesiastic and Biblical. They emphasized living the good life, conceiving of immortality, if they believed in it, as of secondary importance. Deism was more than a sum-total of these beliefs, however; it was an attitude of mind, optimistic and confident, free and untrammeled, humanitarian and moral. The most widely-read deistic book was Thomas Paine's *Age of Reason* (1794). Although a naturalized citizen, Paine's comparatively late and short residence here hardly entitles him to be regarded as an American thinker though the *Age of Reason* has ever since been the Bible of freethinkers in this country. Ethan Allen's *Reason the Only Oracle of Man* (1784) was the earliest of the major deistic books and demonstrates the deistic reaction to traditional Calvinism. Allen went further than many deists, vigorously defending anticlericalism which was its most radical expression. Elihu Palmer's *Principles of Nature* (1801 or 1802) was an excellent later expression of a similar viewpoint. Deism was at its height at the end of the eighteenth century. By this time deistic societies had been established in many of the larger cities and periodicals such as *The Temple of Reason, The Theophilanthropist* and *Prospect, or View of the Moral World* were being published, although neither the societies nor the periodicals lasted long.

Republicanism was the dominant political movement in the Age of Reason. Conservative clergy, in their desire to stamp out deistic thinking, resorted to the common practice of calling names. They associated deism with infidelity, atheism, immorality and republicanism. The latter association was as inaccurate as the others. Some deists were republicans but others were not, and vice versa. The major reason for linking the two was the dislike on the part of aristocratic Calvinism for republicanism in politics, a feeling which was nearly as strong as its hatred for deism in religion. Republicanism represented the desire of man to view political organization on a naturalistic basis. Newtonianism in physics soon developed into naturalism in the social sciences. If physical nature were to be understood in terms of natural law, so were society and man. In political theory men spoke of natural rights. The gradual shift of this point of view through men like John Wise and Jonathan Mayhew has already been noted. Political economy began to be talked about and later introduced into the classroom. Adam Smith's laws of economics came to be widely accepted. This whole tendency developed because men were now seeking to understand things on the basis of natural law; as deism was the religion of nature so the natural rights philosophy was the politics of nature. When the Revolution came, men's minds were turned toward both the purpose and structure of government. Opinion was not uniform. Conflict arose over the proper structure for government, such problems as representation, the divisions of government and the duties of the various branches receiving attention. There was concern over the technique of government; witness, for example, the Hamilton-Jefferson controversy over industrial and agricultural protection. No problems, however, were of greater importance than those of the class aims of government and the source of final power. Were all men equal by virtue of natural existence or was equality to be understood as a relative right, to apply differently to the various strata in society? Were the masses to determine for themselves in what their own greatest happiness might consist or was their destiny to be determined for them by a superior minority? Two major schools developed in regard to these problems; one might be called the aristocratic and the other the democratic. John Adams and John Taylor represented these opposing points of view. There were many important men who had much to do with moulding opinion in the early years of independence, such men as James Wilson, John Dickinson, Alexander Hamilton and James Madison, but nowhere is the clash over the ultimate class aims of government better exemplified than in the Adams-Taylor controversy.

The Age of Reason was humanistic. Man's happiness in the here and now was of primary concern. His relations with his fellow men were looked upon as more important than his relations with God. There was a growing interest in social welfare, as is demonstrated by the increase in hospitals and the interest in the slave population. Emphasis was placed upon education and learning. The gentleman-scholar was held in high esteem. Practical wisdom was regarded more highly than metaphysical dexterity. Tolerance, cosmopolitanism, common sense,—these were values to be sought. No man better represented the typical spirit of the period than Thomas Jefferson.

The humanistic spirit of the Age of Reason soon led to the study of the nature of man. Man was regarded as a product of nature rather than as a creation of the divine. Medicine and physiology combined to develop this naturalistic picture of his existence. His body, his mind, and his soul came to be looked upon as homogeneous, not as temporarily connected entities which had been so united by God. Differences between men were regarded as basically environmental. Disease, illness, even mental deficiencies could be cured through environmental techniques. The ordinary hazards of human existence were not looked upon as divinely imposed punishment or discipline but rather as natural obstacles to be overcome. Joseph Priestley, Thomas Cooper,

Benjamin Rush and Joseph Buchanan (*Philosophy of Human Nature,* 1812) were influential in developing the picture of homogeneous man. Priestley was perhaps better known than the others because of his fame in chemistry but, since he spent only the last ten years of his life here and did most of his important writing before he came, he, like Paine, can hardly be regarded as an American philosopher. Cooper, who was born in England but who emigrated at a much earlier age, can more properly be regarded as an American and he is of additional interest because he manifests the influence of French physiology on American soil. Cooper was led on to a materialistic position; Rush and Buchanan were inclined to reconcile physiological science with more or less orthodox religion.

Morality was emphasized throughout the Age of Reason, but it was a morality which in large part was divorced from traditional theology. Morality was interpreted in a variety of ways, from Allen's morality of reasonableness to the Scotch common-sense position of Witherspoon and Smith; its most characteristic expression is perhaps to be found in Jefferson, who demonstrated the shift from the Hebraic to the Greek attitude. In the Age of Reason, men were less interested in a strict, legal interpretation of morality, and more in an attitude of decency and fair play. Man was regarded as basically good and gifted with reason; no fear need be felt for his ultimate moral fate. The Quakers were influential in furthering this interest in morality although their moral ideal was conceived as a part of spiritual existence.

The optimism expressed over man's moral destiny was one aspect of the belief in progress which was common during the period. Natural events were not to be feared for nature was beneficent. Man was not depraved; he was not only good but had unlimited possibilities. The idea of universal progress, which was later to be associated with the doctrine of evolution, particularly in its religious interpretation, found expression.

As the Age of Reason gradually penetrated the common mind, orthodox opposition increased. By the last decade of the eighteenth century and the first decade of the nineteenth, organized religion was making a concentrated attack upon the whole character and spirit of the Age of Reason. Timothy Dwight's poem, *Triumph of Infidelity* (1788), his *The Nature, and Danger, of Infidel Philosophy* (1798), Uzal Ogden's *Antidote to Deism* (1795) and John Foster's *Infidelity Exposed, and Christianity Recommended* (1802) were typical vitriolic attacks upon the religious tendency of the period. Their spirits enkindled to defeat the enemy of traditional religion, the orthodox enlisted all the ammunition at their disposal for the battle. Pamphleteering, pulpit manifestos and the like had much to do with weaning away the rank and file from the deistic temper characteristic of the period. With attacks from the orthodox, no unanimity within and a rationalistic position not always appealing to ordinary men, the Age of Reason was on the wane by the early nineteenth century. It lingered on, however. As late as the third decade, Thomas Cooper published his treatise on *The Metaphysical and Physiological Arguments in Favor of Materialism.* What happened was that neither the proponents of deism nor its extremely orthodox objectors won the battle. A process of give and take resulted in a path of reconciliation which tempered orthodoxy but which also largely displaced the Age of Reason. Important in this middle-of-the-way position was Scotch realism which succeeded in getting its first real foothold in America at Princeton. Hutcheson, the founder of the common-sense school, was read during the second quarter of the eighteenth century, but the first real champion of the position was John Witherspoon who drove out an incipient wave of Berkeleyan immaterialism when he arrived in 1768 to become president of Princeton. He passed the mantle on to his son-in-law and successor, Samuel Stanhope Smith, who is perhaps the best example of Scotch realism become American. The influence of the movement extended from the application of its common-sense epistemology to political problems (evidenced, for example, by James Wilson's lectures on law delivered at the College of Philadelphia in 1790–91) through its more general interpretation by such men as Smith, Samuel Miller and Frederick Beasley until in the nineteenth century it had become the orthodox philosophy taught in the colleges and had as its leaders such men as James McCosh. Realism was not opposed to empirical science; Smith, for example, was somewhat of a scientist himself. On the other hand, its doctrine of common-sense when applied to morality and religion became a defense of reasonable orthodoxy. What the realists did was to attempt to reconcile traditional religion on the one hand with empirical knowledge on the other. At first this tendency was not given great backing by the orthodox, but as they were slowly won over orthodoxy became revised and deism was largely overshadowed.

The deistic spirit was not completely lost, however. Through such men as William Ellery Channing and Theodore Parker many deistic tenets passed over into American Unitarianism. The naturalism of the Age of Reason was eclipsed by transcendentalism only to reappear when the evolution controversy came to the fore in the middle of the century.

# VIII
# Ethan Allen
## 1737–1789

Born in Litchfield, Conn. Forced by his father's death to abandon plans for college and to support his family. Served in French and Indian War, 1757. Engaged in farming, mining, manufacturing and real estate. Mainly interested in New Hampshire Grants (Vermont) from 1770 on. Made Colonel Commandant of Green Mountain Boys, 1770. Led in capture of Fort Ticonderoga, 1775, but was made prisoner a few months later and sent to England. Freed on exchange of prisoners, 1778. Given brevet colonel's commission by Washington. Presented Vermont claims to Continental Congress. Made brigadier general of Vermont militia, 1779. Regarded as virtual dictator in Vermont throughout controversies with New Hampshire, New York, the Continental Congress and the British. Died near Colchester, Vt.

Ethan Allen is known primarily as a rebel patriot. He spent the best years of his life as leader of the Green Mountain Boys of Vermont, clashing first with the New Yorkers while Cadwallader Colden was lieutenant governor, later capturing Fort Ticonderoga from the English and continuing intermittent skirmishes with the New Yorkers until the last few years of his life. When not engaged in battle or preparing for it he used his pen as an instrument of propaganda in the service of his adopted state. *A Concise Refutation of the Claims of New-Hampshire and Massachusetts-Bay, to the Territory of Vermont* (1780) and *The Present State of the Controversy between the States of New-York and New-Hampshire on the one part, and the State of Vermont on the other* (1782) were typical of Allen's pamphlets, aimed as they were to stir the people of Vermont to action. His philosophic work was also characteristic of his rebellious nature, for it expressed the protest of the independent frontier mind against traditional Calvinism.

Early in life Allen began to revolt against accepted dogma. He grew up under the influence of Arminian teachings which offered a broader basis for salvation than did Calvinism. He rejected the doctrine of original sin quite early, and under the influence of Thomas Young (1731–77), a traveling physician and an independent thinker with whom he was closely associated at Salisbury, his heterodoxy grew; by his later teens he had become a religious radical. Just what books Allen read is uncertain, but Young was well acquainted with English deism and passed this influence on to him. Charles Blount, English deist, was often a subject of conversation, but whether importance should be attached to the similarity in titles of Blount's *The Oracles of Reason* and Allen's subsequent *Reason the Only Oracle of Man* is questionable.[1] It is doubtful whether Allen ever read any of the English deistic literature; his own word as given in the preface to *Reason the Only Oracle* would indicate that he did not. In any case, Young provided him with the essential spirit of free thought, if not with primary sources, and gave him superficial knowledge of authors from Plutarch to Locke. According to the traditional story, Allen and Young made notes on their conversations and agreed that later on they would publish them; in case of the prior death of either, the survivor was to fulfil the agreement. Thus, to continue the story, Allen acquired notes from Young's family after his mentor's death and completed the volume; it appeared in 1784.[2] Allen's own story is told in the preface to his book.

> In my youth I was much disposed to contemplation, and at my commencement in manhood, I committed to manuscript such sentiments or arguments, as appeared most consonant to reason, least through the debility of memory my improvement should have been less gradual: This method of scribbling I practiced for many years, from which I experienced great advantages in the progression of learning and knowledge. . . .
>
> The Bible and a Dictionary have been the only books, which I have made use of, since I have been correcting my old manuscripts, and making the following composition; though in those manuscripts I had copied sundry passages from certain authors, many years prior to the completion of the subsequent discourse, which the reader will find transcribed with proper quotations.

Whatever the particular circumstances surrounding the final publication of the book, Allen's youthful radicalism combined with his distaste for Jonathan Edwards's sermons (some of which he read while he was in Northampton), his scepticism amidst the emotional fervor

[1] Allen actually used the expression "Oracles of Reason" for his page-headings.

[2] One writer has recently argued that Allen was guilty of plagiarism, basing his case largely upon variations in literary style and the use of technical vocabulary with which Allen was probably not well acquainted. See Anderson, G. P.: "Who Wrote 'Ethan Allen's Bible'?" Considering Allen's own story, however, changes in style might well be accounted for on the basis of his using notes made earlier in life.

created by the Great Awakening, and his frontier existence developed in him the characteristic spirit of the revolt against Puritanism.

The weapon which Allen used against orthodoxy was reason. Largely in the tradition of British empiricism, Allen held that we start with the senses upon which we are dependent for our ideas. Reason stood above sensation, however, correcting its deficiencies and pursuing its implications. The mind, therefore, could deal with abstract ideas and attain to rational knowledge of nature and to knowledge of the existence of God. He praised the results of the use of reason in philosophy, history and the various sciences and deplored the prevalence of superstition in religion. He held that

> if mankind would dare to exercise their reason as freely on those divine topics, as they do in the common concerns of life, they would, in a great measure rid themselves of their blindness and superstition, gain more exalted ideas of God and their obligations to him and to one another, and be proportionably delighted and blessed with the views of his moral government, make better members of society, and acquire many powerful incentives to the practice of morality, which is the last and greatest perfection that human nature is capable of.[3]

Reason was a God-given faculty; through its possession man was God-like. It offered the closest approximation to truth of which man was capable. Although man might err because of his finitude, he could also arrive at real certainty. As he said, "though human reason cannot understand every thing, yet in such things, which it does understand, its knowledge which is acquired by reasoning, is as true and certain, as the divine knowledge may be supposed to be."[4] The doctrine of the depravity of human reason was self-destructive, and it was incredible in the creature of a benevolent, rational God.

Allen attacked authority of every kind. Faith, he held, was less a gift of God than reason; it was secondary to reason, valid when based upon reason and treacherous when it contradicted reason. Tradition was fallible, often detrimental because of unreflective acceptance, and meaningful only when rational. The clergy were to be challenged since they defended tradition and revelation. He referred to the Catholics as "Holy Cheats," regarded the decline of witchcraft as an omen of the passing of the priesthood, and thought it "highly probable that the improvement of succeeding generations, in the knowledge of nature, and science, will exalt the reason of mankind, above the tricks and impostures of Priests, and bring them back to the religion of nature and

[3] *Reason the Only Oracle.* 24–5.

[4] Ibid. 183–4. Below, p. 176.

truth." [5] The Bible was fallible on numerous counts, one of these being its lack of authenticity; it had suffered from changes in the process of transmission even if the original text had been verbally inspired (which Allen would not admit). In order to understand his additional criticisms of the Bible and revealed religion we must turn to other aspects of his philosophical position upon which his criticisms were based. Suffice it to say at this point, however, that Allen was an unremitting critic of any tendency which he felt was opposed to reason.

It is indicative of what Allen meant by reason that he argued for the existence of God largely on an *a posteriori* basis; he was more consistent here than elsewhere, however, for he often resorted to *a priori* solutions of other problems. He said the axis of the whole book was his attempt to give a correct idea of God, "for the superstructure of our religion will be proportionate to the notions we entertain of the divinity whom we adore." [6] According to Allen, the observed fact of man's dependence pointed to the existence of a God on whom he depended. The succession of causes in nature necessitated a self-existent cause. Harmony and order within nature indicated a designer. Motion implied the existence of an activating force. The providential character of nature was evidence of a benevolent deity. In conventional deistic fashion he maintained that "the knowledge of nature is the revelation of God." [7]

Allen regarded the universe as a harmonious machine, the medium through which God expressed Himself to man. Of the final nature of God man could know little. Since our mental powers were limited in contrast to the omniscience of God, our knowledge of deity was restricted to our knowledge of His manifestations in and through nature. These manifestations were always beneficent to man. Allen said, "we are morally sure, that of all possible plans, infinite wisdom must have eternally adopted the best, and infinite goodness have approved it, and infinite power perfected it." [8] He therefore conceived of God as a self-existent cause, revealed as providential in the orderliness of the physical world and as wise and just through the moral nature of man. Nature was His creation, lawful and beneficent, the best of all possible worlds. This optimistic view was the natural outgrowth of Newtonian physics, Lockean psychology and the deistic view which accompanied them.

Armed thus with a natural theology as well as with what he considered an empirical epistemology, Allen attacked many orthodox be-

[5] *Reason the Only Oracle.* 456.
[6] Ibid. 27. Below, p. 167.
[7] Ibid. 30. Below, p. 169.
[8] Ibid. 82.

liefs. Against a finite creation he defended an infinite creation. He argued that since God was eternal and infinite, creation must also be eternal and infinite. There must have been an eternal creation else God could not have eternally manifested His attributes and demonstrated His providence. Accepting the existence of an orderly world he rejected revelations. They were questionable because they were always limited in spatial and temporal extent, were absolute and hence not adaptable to changes in social circumstances, were made known through the ignorant rather than through the well informed, and were often contradictory. He contended they were impossible because they were above nature rather than based on nature, and unintelligible because man's knowledge was limited to the natural and rational. He made the Bible a special object of criticism, attacking among other things the Mosaic account of creation and the visions of the apostles. Prophecy was not defensible since man could not communicate with spiritual beings. Miracles were impossible since they contradicted the laws of nature. He argued that since God was perfect and had created the laws of nature they had to be perfect. The existence of miracles would upset the Newtonian world of law and order. Belief in miracles he classed with superstition and witchcraft, all of which declined with the advance of knowledge.

Allen's rejection of predestination, election and imputation resulted in large part from his belief in free will. He held that man must be free else either God would be responsible for moral evil or no moral evil could be said to exist. Likewise reward and punishment would be meaningless if man's actions were "passive" rather than active. Allen regarded man as a responsible agent, capable of doing good and tempted to do evil. Man was responsible for whatever moral evil existed and would be punished for it either here or in the hereafter just as he would be rewarded for the good he did. Predestination he rejected because it took responsibility away from man. Election also invalidated responsibility and necessitated belief in eternal reward and punishment. Imputation made the individual the victim of others' sins rather than the free agent of his own.

Virtue and vice were man's primary concern, according to Allen. He was realistic enough to see the importance of evil but at the same time he was confident of the ultimate triumph of virtue. Like the majority of deists Allen believed in immortality, principally as a stimulus for moral living. He argued that belief in immortality gave man a higher opinion of God's justice, that it was universally accepted by mankind and that God was powerful enough to provide for the continuous development of those things which were good. As man was on trial in this life, so he would continue to be on trial in the life to come. Whether any sensorium would be necessary for the soul's existence was debatable, but that the soul continued after death there could be no reasonable doubt. The ultimate aim of God was to exalt moral existence and provide for a higher stage of being. Virtue in this life would bring us commensurate satisfaction through the contemplation of virtue in the next; vice would bring us temporary remorse in the world to come. Allen contended that the future life would be an indefinite series of stages, each preparatory to the next, in which even the sinner would have opportunity to better his state. What these future states might be in detail was beyond human comprehension, yet goodness and happiness would ultimately prevail.

Allen was conscious of his religious radicalism. He was rather inclined to accept the designation of "Deist," although he was not sure of its appropriateness. He said in the preface to *Reason the Only Oracle,* "In the circle of my acquaintance (which has not been small) I have generally been denominated a Deist, the reality of which I never disputed, being conscious I am no Christian, except mere infant baptism makes me one; and as to being a Deist, I know not strictly speaking, whether I am one or not, for I have never read their writings." Allen was perhaps more certain of what he was not than of what he was, for the whole tone of his writing was critical rather than constructive. His book was well received by the freethinkers, bitterly criticized by the orthodox. On March 2, 1786 Allen wrote to St. John de Crèvecoeur, "The Clergy of this Country reprobate the work and anathematize the writer of it." [9] President Timothy Dwight of Yale, Jared Sparks, who became president of Harvard in 1849, and others condemned it. It had considerable influence, however, as the first important deistic publication in America. Thomas Paine, whose *Age of Reason* came out ten years later, was accused of pilfering his ideas from Allen.[10] Referred to as "Ethan Allen's Bible," the book had as much influence as the Bible with some, although its effect was greatly diminished by a fire in 1788 which destroyed the copies remaining in the hands of the printer.[11]

In *An Essay on the Universal Plenitude of Being and on the Nature and Immortality of the Human Soul and Its Agency* (written about 1787 and intended as an appendix to *Reason the Only Oracle*) Allen

[9] *Records of the Governor and Council of Vermont.* III, 390.

[10] Pell: *Ethan Allen.* 254.

[11] The orthodox regarded this fire as an "act of God."

sought to expand his thought on the nature of the soul and to strengthen his case for immortality and free will. In his earlier work, despite his professed allegiance to *a posteriori* reasoning, he often depended on *a priori* evidence; in the proposed appendix he appealed directly to intuitive certainty, arguing for immortality and free will on much the same basis as did the Scotch realists. His use of intuition, however, was restricted to his argument for the soul's being and agency, not extended to include knowledge of physical nature or of right and wrong and hence not necessarily contradicting his previous emphasis upon external reason. The most interesting aspects of this later work were his exposition of the doctrine of a universal plenum of being and his argument that the soul, in order to exist at all, must have a place in this plenum and be substantial, though not material. Allen was probably the first exponent in the American Age of Reason of this typical concept of eighteenth-century European thought, which was the metaphysical basis for the optimistic viewpoint expressed during the period. By means of this concept Allen absolved God of the responsibility for moral evil, arguing that man, the creator of evil, had to be created by God in order to complete the chain of being.

> Probably we are the most selfish, oddest, and cunningest medley of beings, of our size, in the universe. However to compleat the general schale of being, it seems to have been requisite, that the link of being called man, must have been, and since under the Divine government, we have a positive existence, we can not ultimately fail, of being better than not to have been.[12]

All in all, Allen gave a fairly clear presentation of the deistic position. The concept of a more or less absentee deity, natural law, reason, reliance upon man's innate capacities, moral living, inevitable progress—these beliefs he shared with most deists. He lacked the humanitarian zeal of some, was less optimistic than others, made reason internal as well as external whereas many thought of it as purely external, yet he was as typical as any other single individual of the deistic spirit of the period.

## REFERENCES

Allen, Ethan: *Reason the Only Oracle of Man; or a Compenduous System of Natural Religion. Alternately Adorned with Confutations of a variety of Doctrines incompatible to it; Deduced from the most exalted Ideas which we are able to form of the Divine and Human Characters, and from the Universe in General.*

[12] *The Historical Magazine* 2 (1873) 82.

Bennington, Vt., 1784. (An abridged edition was published in New York in 1836 and another in Boston in 1854.)

———: "An Essay on the Universal Plenitude of Being and on the Nature and Immortality of the Human Soul and Its Agency" (written about 1787), *The Historical Magazine, and Notes and Queries concerning the Antiquities, History and Biography of America.* Third series. 1 (1872–73) 193–6, 274–82, 330–3; 2 (1873) 29–32, 76–82.

Anderson, George P.: "Who Wrote 'Ethan Allen's Bible'?", *New England Quarterly* 10 (1937) 685–96.

Conway, Moncure D.: "Ethan Allen's Oracles of Reason," *Open Court* 6 (1892) 3119–21.

Doten, Dana: "Ethan Allen's 'Original Something'," *New England Quarterly* 11 (1938) 361–6.

Gohdes, Clarence: "Ethan Allen and His *Magnum Opus*," *Open Court* 43 (1929) 129–51.

Hall, Henry: *Ethan Allen, the Robin Hood of Vermont.* New York: D. Appleton and Co., 1892.

Koch, G. Adolf: *Republican Religion: The American Revolution and the Cult of Reason.* New York: Henry Holt and Co., 1933. (Esp. ch. I, "Ethan Allen, Freethinking Revolutionist.")

Pell, John: *Ethan Allen.* Boston: Houghton Mifflin Co., 1929.

———: "Ethan Allen's Literary Career," *New England Quarterly* 2 (1929) 585–602.

Rife, Clarence W.: "Ethan Allen, an Interpretation," *New England Quarterly* 2 (1929) 561–84.

Riley, I. Woodbridge: *American Philosophy: the Early Schools.* New York: Dodd, Mead and Co., 1907. 46–58.

Schantz, B. T.: "Ethan Allen's Religious Ideas," *Journal of Religion* 18 (1938) 183–217.

Sparks, Jared: *Life of Ethan Allen.* Vol. I, *The Library of American Biography.* Boston, 1834.

* * *

---

* * *

## REASON THE ONLY ORACLE OF MAN [13]

### *Of the Being of a God*

The Laws of Nature having subjected mankind to a state of absolute dependence on something out of, and manifestly beyond themselves, or the compound exertion of their natural powers, gave them the

[13] Edition of 1784. Ch. I, sec. II, 25–31; ch. III, sec. III, 130–6; ch. V, sec. I, 177–85; ch. VII, secs. IV–V, 262–9; ch. XIV, sec. III, 472–7.

first conception of a superior principle existing; otherwise they could have had no possible conception of a superintending power. But this sense of dependency, which results from experience and reasoning on the facts, which every day cannot fail to produce, has uniformly established the knowledge of our dependence to every of the species who are rational, which necessarily involves or contains in it the idea of a ruling power, or that there is a GOD, which ideas are synonimous.

This is the first glimpse of a Deity, and powerfully attracts the rational mind to make farther discoveries, which, through the weakness of human reasonings opens a door for errors and mistakes respecting the divine essence, though there is no possibility of our being deceived in our first conceptions of a superintending power. Of which more will be observed in its order.

The globe with its productions, the planets in their motions, and the starry heavens in their magnitudes, surprize our senses, and confound our reason, in their munificent lessons of instruction concerning GOD, by means whereof we are apt to be more or less lost in our ideas of the object of divine adoration, though at the same time every one is truly sensible that their being and preservation is from GOD. We are too apt to confound our ideas of GOD with his works, and take the latter for the former. Thus barbarous and unlearned nations have imagined, that inasmuch as the sun in its influence is beneficial to them in bringing forward the spring of the year, causing the production of vegetation, and food for their subsistence, that therefore it is their GOD: while others have located other parts of creation, and ascribe to them the prerogatives of God; and mere creatures and images have been substituted to be Gods by the wickedness or weakness of man, or both together. It seems that mankind in most ages and parts of the world have been fond of corporeal Deities with whom their outward senses might be gratified, or as fantastically diverted from the just apprehension of the true God, by a supposed supernatural intercourse with invisible and mere spiritual beings, to whom they ascribe divinity, so that through one means or other, the character of the true God has been much neglected, to the great detriment of truth, justice and morality in the world; nor is it possible, that mankind can be uniform in their religious opinions, or worship God according to knowledge, except they can form a consistent arrangement of ideas of the Divine character. This therefore shall be the great object of the following pages, to which all others are only subordinate; for the superstructure of our religion will be proportionate to the notions we entertain of the divinity whom we adore. A sensibility of mere dependence includes an idea of something, on which we depend (call it by what name we will) which has a real existence, in as much as a dependency on nonentity is inadmissible, for that the absence or non-existence of all being could not have caused an existence to be. But should we attempt to trace the succession of the causes of our dependence, they would exceed our comprehension, though every of them, which we could understand, would be so many evidences (of the displays) of a God. Although a sense of dependency discloses to our minds the certainty of a Supreme Being, yet it does not point out to us the object, nature or perfections of that being; this belongs to the province of reason, and in our course of ratiocination on the succession of causes and events. Although we extend our ideas retrospectively ever so far upon the succession, yet no one cause in the extended order of succession, which depends upon another prior to itself, can be the independent cause of all things: nor is it possible to trace the order of the succession of causes back to that self-existent cause, inasmuch as it is eternal and infinite, and therefore cannot be traced out by succession, which operates according to the order of time, consequently can bear no more proportion to the eternity of God, than time itself may be supposed to do, which has no proportion at all; as the succeeding arguments respecting the eternity and infinity of God will evince. But notwithstanding the series of the succession of causes cannot be followed in a retrospective succession up to the self-existent or eternal cause, it is nevertheless a perpetual and conclusive evidence of a God. For a succession of causes, considered collectively, can be nothing more than effects of the independent cause, and as much dependent on it, as those dependent causes are upon one another; so that we may with certainty conclude that the system of nature, which we call by the name of natural causes, is as much dependent on a self-existent cause, as an individual of the species in the order of generation is dependent on its progenitors for existence. Such part of the series of nature's operations, which we understand, has a regular and necessary connection with, and dependence on its parts, which we denominate by the names of cause and effect. From hence we are authorised from reason to conclude, that the vast system of causes and effects are thus necessarily connected, (speaking of the natural world only) and the whole regularly and necessarily dependent on a self-existent cause; so that we are obliged to admit an independent cause, and ascribe self-existence to it, otherwise it could not be independent, and consequently not a God. But the eternity or manner of the existence of a self-existent and independent being is to all finite capacities utterly incomprehensible; yet this is so far from an objection against the reality of such a being, that it is essentially necessary to support the evidence of it; for if we could comprehend that being, whom we call God, he would not be God, but must have been finite, and that in the same degree as those may be supposed to be, who could comprehend him; therefore so certain as God is, we cannot comprehend his essence, eternity or manner of existence. This should always be premised, when we assay to reason on the being, perfection, eternity and infinity of God, or his creation and providence. As far as we understand nature, we are become acquainted with the character of God; for the knowledge of nature is the revelation of God. If we form in our imagination a compeduous idea of the harmony of the universe, it is the same as calling God by the name of harmony, for there could be no harmony without regulation, and no regulation without a regulator, which is expressive of the idea of a God. Nor could it be possible, that there could be order or disorder, except we admit of such a thing as creation, and creation contains in it the idea of a creator, which is another appellation for the Divine Being, distinguishing God from his creation. Furthermore there could be no proportion, figure or motion without wisdom and power; wisdom to plan, and power to execute, and these are perfections, when applied to the works of nature, which signify the agency or superintendency of God. If we consider nature to be matter, figure and motion, we include the idea of God in that of motion; for motion implies a mover, as much as creation does a creator. If from the composition, texture, and tendency of the universe in general, we form a complex idea of general good resulting therefrom to mankind, we implicitly admit a God by the name of good, including the idea of his providence to man. And from hence arises our obligation to love and adore God, because he provides for, and is benificent to us: abstract the idea of goodness from the character of God, and it would cancel all our obligations to him, and excite us to hate and detest him as a tyrant; hence [it] is, that ignorant people are superstitiously misled into a conceit that they hate God, when at the same time it is only the idol of their own imagination, which they truly ought to hate and be ashamed of; but were such persons to connect the ideas of power, wisdom, goodness and all possible perfection in the character of God, their hatred toward him would be turned into love and adoration.

## *Human Liberty, Agency and Accountability, Cannot Be Attended with Eternal Consequences, Either Good or Evil*

From what has been argued in the foregoing section, it appears, that mankind in this life are not agents of trial for eternity, but that they will eternally remain agents of trial. To suppose that our eternal circumstances will be unalterably fixed in happiness or misery, in consequence of the agency or transactions of this temporary life, is inconsistent with the moral government of God, and the progressive and retrospective knowledge of the human mind. God has not put it into our power to plunge ourselves into eternal woe and perdition; human liberty is not so extensive, for the term of human life bears no proportion to eternity succeeding it; so that there could be no proportion between a momentary agency, (which is liberty of action,) or probation, and any supposed eternal consequences of happiness or misery resulting from it. Our liberty consists in our power of agency, and cannot fall short of, or exceed it, for liberty is agency itself; or is that by which agency or action is exerted; it may be, that the curious would define it, that agency is the effect of liberty, and that liberty is the cause, which produces it; making a distinction between action and the power of action: be it so, yet agency cannot surpass its liberty; to suppose otherwise, would be the same as to suppose agency without the power of agency, or an effect without a cause; therefore as our agency does not extend to consequences of eternal happiness or misery, the power of that agency, which is liberty, does not. Sufficient it is for virtuous minds, while in this life, that they keep *"Consciences void of offence towards God and toward man."* And that in their commencement in the succeeding state, they have a retrospective knowledge of their agency in this, and retain a consciousness of a well spent life. Beings thus possessed of a habit of virtue, would enjoy a rational felicity beyond the reach of physical evils, which terminate with life; and in all rational probability would be advanced in the order of nature to a more exalted and sublime manner of being, knowledge and action, than at present we can conceive of, where no joys or pains can approach, but of the mental kind; in which elevated state, virtuous minds will be able, in a clearer and more copious manner than in this life, to contemplate the superlative beauties of moral fitness; and with extatic satisfaction enjoy it, notwithstanding imperfection and consequently agency, proficiency and trial, of some kind or other, must everlastingly continue with finite minds.

And as to the vicious, who have violated the laws of reason and morality, lived a life of sin and wickedness, and are at as great a remove from a rational happiness as from moral rectitude; such incorigible sinners, at their commencing existence in the world of spirits, will undoubtedly have opened to them a tremendous scene of horror, self-condemnation and guilt, with anguish of mind; the more so, as no sensual delights can there (as in this world) divert the mind from its conscious guilt; the clear sense of which will be the more pungent, as the mind in that state will be greatly enlarged, and consequently more capaciously susceptible of sorrow, grief and conscious woe, from a retrospective reflection of a wicked life, yet we have reason to hope and believe through the wisdom of the divine government, they may in some limited period of duration have a contrition for and detestation of sin and vanity, the procuring cause of their punishment, and be reclaimed from viciousness and restored to virtue and happiness; but liable to transgression, and future misery, in consequence of an imperfect nature, eternally subjected to agency and trial, and consequently to alternate happiness and misery, which must be the case with all intelligent probationary beings. But after all our researches, the insufficiency of the human understanding, to discover the œconomy of the divine government, over the moral world, is so great, that we can determine but very little about the manner of its rewards and punishments, or of the extent of them; except that they cannot be perpetual or eternal; but on the other hand will be as temporary and interchangeable as the virtue and vice of moral agents. Nevertheless, from the arguments which we have deduced from the wisdom and goodness of God in his creation and providence, we may with rational certainty conclude, that moral goodness and happiness will ultimately be victorious over sin and misery, which will undoubtedly be more conspicuously so in the future stages of our immortality; so that there will be a far greater plentitude of the former than of the latter; to which the latter finally is made subservient, for otherwise we could not account for the wisdom and goodness of God in his creation, providence or moral government.

The endless disproportion between the cogitations and agency of the human mind, in this momentary life, may, with great propriety, be urgent against an everlasting fixedness of the condition of happiness or misery, after this life is ended; merely in consequence of the agency of this. Our conceptions themselves are progressive; we think by succession, and our ideas, in their operations, are numerical, and by nature subject to number; each individual idea has its circumscription, and the whole, collectively considered, would make but a limited knowledge; and the more inconsiderably so, as it is most probable, that not one hundredth part of our reflections, from infancy to old age, are worthy to be denominated knowledge; by reason of their fictitious and incoherent rudeness; so that when we contemplate on the endlessness of eternity, our cogitations are lost in its infinitude; for neither numbers, quantity, admeasurement, or any possible motion, or comparison of cogitations, or of things, can possibly co-extend with it; and consequently human liberty, or agency and accountability, in their progressive exertions, can bear no manner of proportion or connection with an eternity of rewards or punishments; for the nature of our liberty, agency and accountability is but finite, and therefore can no otherwise operate but by succession, and cannot be attended with eternal consequences, any more than succession itself can comprize eternity. We may therefore with a well grounded judgment determine, that neither the virtues or vices of human life, can be attended with eternal consequences of good or evil; inasmuch as such endless consequences, necessarily imply an infinite disproportion between them and human agency: but the truth of the matter is, our liberty, and therefore our accountability, cannot exceed the limits of our cogitations and knowledge; this is the circumference in which our liberty can exercise itself, and this is the boundary of its agency; and although eternal probation is necessarily connected with the eternal existence of finite minds, yet the merits or demerits of an everlasting probation, has its various operations forever on the mind, existing in the conscience, and causing it to be alternately happy or miserable, in such proportions, and periods, as conformity or nonconformity to moral rectitude, in our eternal probation, will admit.

The policy of human governments has demanded, that corporeal punishments should be inflicted on the violaters of their laws, *to wit,* the whip, the halter, the gibbit, and the like; from these and from the ideas of physical evils, which are common to us in this life, it seems, that most of mankind form to themselves an arrangement of ideas of the manner of God's punishing incorrigible sinners in the world to come. The idea of fire and brimstone is, in this part of the world, their main apprehension, to which they unite the evils of a guilty conscience, in as much as mental, as well as physical evils, with their divers modes of sufferings, are common to them in this life: but it should be considered, that death puts a final end to physical evils, except these our mortal bodies are to be raised and re-united to their respective souls; which if admitted, they must unavoidably suffer death a second time, and such as may be supposed to be cast into hell-fire (in the vulgar sense) would suffer a second dissolution instantly, unless their resurrection bodies are supposed to be of the salamander kind. And thus a physical suffering, instead of being eternal, would be but for a moment, or at most but temporary; and if we suppose those resurrection bodies will be able to endure fire, it must be likewise supposed, that it would be their proper element, and consequently that they would be happy in it; as so intense a heat would destroy such bodies, whose qualities may be supposed to be opposed [to] it.

## *Speculations on the Doctrine of the Depravity of Human Reason*

In the course of our speculations on divine providence we proceed next to the consideration of the doctrine of the depravity of human reason; a doctrine derogatory to the nature of man, and the rank and character of being which he holds in the universe, and which, if admitted to be true, overturns knowledge and science and renders learning, instruction and books useless and impertinent; inasmuch as reason, depraved or spoiled, would cease to be reason; as much as the mind of a raving madman would of course cease to be rational: admitting the depravity of reason, the consequence would unavoidably follow, that as far as it may be supposed to have taken place in the minds of mankind, they could be no judges of it, in consequence of their supposed depravity; for without the exercise of reason, we could not understand what reason is, which would be necessary for us previously to understand, in order to understand what it is not; or to distinguish it from that which is its reverse. But for us to have the knowledge of what reason is, and the ability to distinguish it from that which is depraved, or is irrational, is incompatible with the doctrine of the depravity of our reason. Inasmuch as to understand what reason is, and to distinguish it from that which is marred or spoiled, is the same to all intents and purposes, as to have, exercise and enjoy, the principle of reason itself, which precludes its supposed depravity: so that it is impossible for us to understand what reason is, and at the same time determine that our reason is depraved; for this would be the same as when we know that we are in possession and exercise of reason, to determine that we are not in possession or exercise of it.

It may be, that some, who embrace the doctrine of the depravity of human reason, will not admit, that it is wholly and totally depraved, but that it is in a great measure marred or spoiled. But the foregoing arguments are equally applicable to a supposed depravity in part, as in the whole; for in order to judge whether reason be depraved in part, or not, it would be requisite to have an understanding, of what reason may be supposed to have been, previous to its premised depravity; and to have such a knowledge of it, would be the same as to exercise and enjoy it in its lustre and purity; which would preclude the notion of a depravity in part, as well as in the whole; for it would be utterly impossible for us to judge of reason undepraved and depraved, but by comparing them together. But for depraved reason to make such a comparison, is contradictory and impossible; so that, if our reason had been depraved, we could not have had any conception of it any more than a beast. Men of small faculties in reasoning cannot comprehend the extensive reasonings of their superiors, how then can a supposed depraved reason, comprehend that reason which is uncorrupted and pure? to suppose that it could, is the same as to suppose that depraved and undepraved reason is alike, and if so there needs no further dispute about it.

There is a manifest contradiction in applying the term *depraved,* to that of reason, the ideas contained in their respective difinitions will not admit of their association together, as the terms convey heterogeneous ideas; for reason spoiled, marred, or robbed of its perfection, ceaseth to be rational, and should not be called reason; inasmuch as it is premised to be depraved, or degenerated from a rational nature; and in consequence of the depravation of its nature, should also be deprived of its name, and called subterfuge, or some such-like name, which might better define its real character.

Those who invalidate reason, ought seriously to consider, *"Whether they argue against reason with or without reason; if with reason, then they establish the principle, that they are labouring to dethrone:"* but if they argue without reason, (which, in order to be consistent with themselves, they must do) they are out of the reach of rational conviction, nor do they deserve a rational argument.

We are told that the knowledge of the depravity of reason, was first communicated to mankind by the immediate inspiration of God. But inasmuch as reason is supposed to be depraved, what principle could there be in the human irrational soul, which could receive or understand the inspiration, or on which it could operate, so as to represent, to those whom it may be supposed were inspired, the knowledge of the depravity of (their own and mankind's) reason (in general:) For a rational inspiration must consist of rational ideas; which pre-supposes, that the minds of those who were inspired, were rational, previous to such their inspiration; which would be a downright contradiction to the inspiration itself; the import of which was to teach the knowledge of the depravity of human reason, which without reason could not be understood, and with reason it would be understood, that the inspiration was false.

Will any advocates for the depravity of reason suppose, that inspiration ingrafts or super-adds the essence of reason itself, to the human mind? admitting it to be so, yet such inspired persons could not understand any thing of reason, before the reception of such supposed inspiration; nor could such a premised inspiration, prove to its possessors, or receivers, that their reason had ever been depraved. All that such premised inspired persons could understand, or be conscious of, respecting reason, would be after the inspiration may be supposed to have taken effect, and made them rational beings, and then instead of being taught by inspiration, that their reason had been previously depraved, they could have had no manner of consciousness of the existence or exercise of it, 'till the imparting the principle of it by the supposed energy of inspiration; nor could such supposed inspired persons communicate the knowledge of such a premised revelation to others of the species, who for want of a rational nature, could not be supposed, *on this position,* to be able to receive the impressions of reason.

That there are degrees in the knowledge of rational beings, and also in their capacities to acquire it, cannot be disputed, as it is so very obvious among mankind. But in all the retrospect gradations from the exalted reasonings of a Locke or a Newton, down to the lowest exercise of it among the species, still it is reason, and not depraved; for a less degree of reason by no means implies a depravity of it, nor does the imparting of reason argue its depravity, for what remains of reason, or rather of the exercise of it, is reason still. But there is not, and cannot be such a thing as depraved reason, for that which is rational is so, and for that reason cannot be depraved, whatever its degree of exercise may be supposed to be.

A blow on the head, or fracture of the perecranium, as also palsies and many other casualties that await our sensorium; retard, and in some cases wholly prevent the exercise of reason, for a longer, or shorter period; and sometimes through the stage of human life; but in such instances as these, reason is not depraved, but ceases in a greater or less degree, or perhaps wholly ceases its rational exertions or operations; by reason of the breaches, or disorders of the organs of sense, but in such instances, wherein the organs become rectified, and the senses recover their usefulness, the exercise of reason returns; free from any blemish or depravity. For the cessation of the exercise of reason, by no means depraves it.

There is in God's infinite plentitude of creation and providence, such an infinite display of reason, that the most exalted finite rational beings, fall infinitely short of the comprehension thereof. For though the most inconsiderable rational beings, who can discern any truth at all, bear a resemblance or likeness to God, as well as every rational nature of whatever degree in the scale of being, yet neither the greatest or least of them can bear any manner of proportion to God; inasmuch as no possible degree of reason or knowledge, can bear any proportion to that reason and knowledge, which is eternal and infinite, as has been before argued. And though human reason cannot understand every thing, yet in such things, which it does understand, its knowledge which is acquired by reasoning, is as true and certain, as the divine knowledge may be supposed to be: for to more than understand a thing, speaking of that particular, is impossible even to omniscience itself. For knowledge is but knowledge, and that only whether it is in the divine mind, or ours, or in any other intelligencies; therefore knowledge is not imperfect; for a knowledge of any thing is the same as to have right ideas of it, or ideas according to truth, and as all knowledge of things in general must be predicated on truth, it will agree in the divine or human mind.

From what has been argued on this subject, in this and the preceeding chapters, it appears, that reason is not, and cannot be depraved, but that it bears a likeness to divine reason, is of the same kind, and in its own nature as uniform as truth, which is the test of it; though in the divine essence, it is eternal and infinite, but in man it is eternal only, as it respects their immortality, and finite, as it respects capaciousness. Such people, as can be prevailed upon to believe, that their reason is depraved, may easily be led by the nose, and duped into superstition at the pleasure of those, in whom they confide, and there remain from generation to generation: for when they throw by the law of reason, *the only one* which God gave them to direct them in their speculations and duty, they are exposed to ignorant or insiduous teachers, and also to their own irregular passions, and to the folly and enthusiasm of those about them, which nothing but reason can prevent or restrain: Nor is it a rational supposition that the commonality of mankind would ever have mistrusted, that their reason was depraved, had they not been told so, and it is whispered about, that the first insinuation of it was from the Priests; (though the Arminian Clergymen in the circle of my acquaintance have exploded the doctrine.) Should we admit the depravity of reason, it would equally affect the priesthood, or any other teachers of that doctrine, with the rest of mankind; but for depraved creatures to receive and give credit to a depraved doctrine, started and taught by depraved creatures, is the greatest weakness and folly imaginable, and comes nearer a proof of the doctrine of a total depravity, than any arguments which have ever been advanced in support of it.

## *Rare and Wonderful Phaenomenae No Evidence of Miracles, nor Are Diabolical Spirits Able to Effect Them, or Superstitious Traditions to Confirm Them, nor Can Ancient Miracles Prove Recent Revelations*

There has been so much detection of the artifice, juggle and imposture of the pretenders to miracles, in the world, especially in such parts where learning and science have prevailed, that it should prompt us to be very suspicious of the reality of them; even without entering into any lengthy arguments from the reason and nature of things to evince the utter impossibility of their existence in the creation and providence of God.

We are told, that the first occasion and introduction of miracles into the world, was to prove the divine authority of revelation, and the mission of its first teachers; be it so; upon this plan of evincing the divinity of revelation, it would be necessary that its teachers should always be vested with the power of working miracles; so that when their authority or the infallibility of the revelation which they should teach, should at any time be questioned, they might work a miracle; or that in such a case God would do it; which would end the dispute, provided mankind were supposed to be judged of miracles which may be controverted. However, admitting that they are possible, and mankind in the several generations of the world to be adequate judges of them, and also that they were necessary to support the divine mission of the first promulgators of revelation, and the divinity which they taught; from the same parity of reasoning miracles ought to be continued to the succeeding generations of mankind, co-extensive with its divine authority, or that of its teachers. For why should we in this age of the world be under obligation to believe the infallibility of revelation, or the heavenly mission of its teachers, upon less evidence than those of mankind who lived in the generations before us? For that which may be supposed to be a rational evidence, and worthy to gain the belief and assent of mankind at one period of time, must be so at another; so that it appears, from the sequel of the arguments on this subject, that provided miracles were requisite to establish the divine authority of revelation originally, it is equally requisite that they be continued to the latest posterity, to whom the divine legislator may be supposed to continue such revelation as his law to mankind.

Furthermore, should we admit the divine mission and authority of the first promulgators of revelation, and the reality of the miracles they wrought, or that God may be supposed to have wrought, as a confirmation of the revelation they then promulgated; yet we cannot for certain determine but that their successors have since corrupted it, and altered it to answer their own sinister designs, and thereby provoke God to withdraw from them the power of working miracles, or to have ceased to work miracles himself, to the intent that they might not obtrude spurious revelations on mankind. For any miraculous works, which may be premised to have been anciently wrought, to evince the divine authority of the first manuscript copies of revelation can bear no testimony to revelation, as we have it according to the present translation, or to the divine mission of the present clergy. Though admitting miracles to have been wrought in the primitive times of the promulgation of revelation, for its then support, and the support of the religion they then taught, it would have been evidential of the divine mission of its first promulgators, but these are matters of speculation to us, and particularly concerned those ages in which revelation may be supposed to have been taught in its purity, and confirmed by miracles; as they supposed, who were the first converts to it, and who are said to have seen and believed; and when this generation is favoured with a miraculous confirmation of the divine mission of our present clergy, and of the authenticity of our present revelation, as it has been handed down to us th[r]ough the complicated revolutions of the world, and the vicissitudes of human learning, by miracles wrought in open day light, not only of the fun, but of learning and science (the latter of which the primitive believers had not the advantage of) it will be early enough for us to subscribe to the divine mission of the one, or divinity, or infallibility of the other.

Nothing is more evident to the understanding part of mankind, than that in those parts of the world where learning and science has prevailed, miracles have ceased; but in such parts of it as are barbarous and ignorant, miracles are still in vogue; which is of itself a strong presumption that in the infancy of letters, learning and science, or in the world's non-age, those who confided in miracles, as a proof of the divine mission of the first promulgators of revelation, were imposed upon by fictitious appearances instead of miracles.

Furthermore, The author of Christianity warns us against the impositions of false teachers, and describes the signs of the true believers, saying "And these signs shall follow them that believe, in my name shall they cast out devils, they shall speak with new tongues, they shall take up serpents, and if they drink any deadly thing it shall not hurt them, they shall lay hands on the sick and they shall recover." These are the express words of the founder of Christianity, and are contained in the very commission, which he gave to his eleven Apostles, who were to promulgate his gospel in the world; so that from their very institution it appears, that when the miraculous signs, therein spoken of, failed, they were to be considered as unbelievers, and consequently no faith or trust to be any longer reposed in them or their successors. For these signs were those which were to perpetuate their mission, and were to be continued as the only evidences of the validity and authenticity of it, and as long as these signs followed, mankind could not be deceived in adhearing to the doctrines which the Apostles and their successors taught; but when the signs failed, their divine authority ended. Now if any of them will drink a dose of deadly poison, which I could prepare, and it does not "hurt them," I will subscribe to their divine authority, and end the dispute; not that I have a disposition to poison any one, but nor do I suppose that they would dare to take such a dose as I could prepare for them, which, if so, would evince, that they were unbelievers themselves, though they are extremely apt to censure others for unbelief which according to their scheme is a damnable sin.

## *Miracles Could not Be Instructive to Mankind*

Should we admit the intervention of Miracles, yet they could not enlarge our ideas of the power of God. For that to unmake nature universally, and to impress it with new and opposite laws from those of its eternal establishment, could require no greater exertion of power, than that which is Omnipotent, and which must have been exerted in the eternal creation, regulation and support of the universe. But any supposed miraculous alteration of nature, must imply mutability in the wisdom of God; and therefore is inadmisable. Should God miraculously raise a dead person to life again, would the restoring life argue a greater exertion of power in God than in first giving existence to that life? surely it could not. From all which we infer, that miracles cannot inlarge our ideas of the power of God. We proceed next to enquire, what advantages could accrue to mankind by them in the way of teaching and instruction? For this must be the great end proposed by them. That they cannot teach us any thing relative to the omnipotence of God, has been evinced; but that they militate against his wisdom: and furthermore, that they cannot prove the divine authority of written revelation, or the mission of its respective teachers to any country, people or nation, any farther or longer than the miraculous works are actually continued, has been sufficiently argued in the proceeding section. It remains farther to be considered, that they are incapable of instructing us in the subject-matter, doctrine, proposition or inference of any premised written revelation; or of giving us any insight into the precepts or injunctions thereof, or to communicate any sort of intelligence or knowledge respecting its contents. The premised, sudden and miraculous alterations of the common course of nature might astonish us; but such alterations or changes, do not evince that they have any thing to do with us, or we with them in the way of teaching and instruction: for truth and falsehood, right and wrong, justice and injustice, virtue and vice, or moral good and evil are in their distinct natures diametrically opposite to each other, and necessarily and eternally will remain so to be, and that, independent of miracles or revealed religion. It is by reason we investigate the knowledge of moral good and evil, it is that which lays us under a moral obligation, and it is not a miracle or revelation that can alter the moral rectitude of things, or prove that to be truth, which in its nature is not so. Therefore admitting ever so many miracles, and revelations, we should still have to recur to reason and argument, the old and only way of exploring truth and distinguishing it from falsehood, or understanding true religion from imposture or error. For though miracles might evince the divine mission of the clergy, and the divinity of the christian revelation, to us, were they in fact wrought in this enlightened age for that purpose, yet they are not calculated to expound or explain it, but would perplex and confound us, in our logical and doctrinal speculations, nature and reason being opposed to them as before argued. Such supposed miraculous changes in nature, would to us be mysterious, and altogether unintelligible, and consequently could not come within our deliberation on the right understanding, or comments on a supposed written revelation; the understanding of which, after all the bustle about miracles, must be investigated by reason: and revelation itself be either approved or disapproved by it. From the foregoing reasonings we infer, that miracles cannot be edifying or instructive to us; and though they are strenuously urged as a proof of the divine legation of the first promulgators of revelation, and their successors; nevertheless, where the premised miracles became extinct, their divine authority and the evidence of the infalibility of revelation, became extinct also.

## *Of the Importance of the Exercise of Reason, and Practice of Morality, in Order to the Happiness of Mankind*

The period of life is very uncertain, and at the longest is but short: a few years bring us from infancy to manhood, a few more to a dissolution; pain, sickness and death are the necessary consequences of animal life. Through life we struggle with physical evils, which eventually are certain to destroy our earthly composition; and well would it be for us did evils end here; but alas! moral evil has been more or less predominant in our agency, and though natural evil is unavoidable, yet moral evil may be prevented or remedied by the exercise of virtue. Morality is therefore of more importance to us than any or all other attainments; as it is a habit of mind, which, from a restrospective consciousness of our agency in this life, we should carry with us into our succeeding state of existence, as an acquired appendage of our rational nature, and as the necessary means of our mental happiness. Virtue and vice are the only things in this world, which, with our souls, are capable of surviving death; the former is the rational and only procuring cause of all intellectual happiness, and the latter of conscious guilt and misery; and therefore, our indispensible duty and ultimate interest is, to love, cultivate and improve the one, as the means of our greatest good, and to hate and abstain from the other, as productive of our greatest evil. And in order thereto, we should so far divest ourselves of the incumbrances of this world, (which are too apt to engross our attention) as to enquire a consistent system of the knowledge of religious duty, and make it our constant endeavour in life to act conformably to it. The knowledge of the being, perfections, creation and providence of GOD, and of the immortality of our souls, is the foundation of religion; which has been particularly illustrated in the four first chapters of this discourse. And as the Pagan, Jewish, Christian and Mahometan countries of the world have been overwhelmed with a multiplicity of revelations diverse from each other, and which, by their respective promulgators, are said to have been immediately inspired into their souls, by the spirit of God, or immediately communicated to them by the intervening agency of angels (as in the instance of the invisible Gabriel to Mahomet) and as those revelations have been received and credited, by far the greater part of the inhabitants of the several countries of the world (on whom they have been obtruded) as supernaturally revealed by God or Angels, and which, in doctrine and discipline, are in most respects repugnant to each other, it full evinces their imposture, and authorizes us, without a lengthy course of arguing, to determine with certainty, that not more than one if any one of them, had their original from God; as they clash with each other; which is ground of high probability against the authenticity of each of them.

A revelation, that may be supposed to be really of the institution of God, must also be supposed to be perfectly consistent or uniform, and to be able to stand the test of truth; therefore such pretended revelations, as are tendered to us as the contrivance of heaven, which do not bear that test, we may be morally certain, was either originally a deception, or has since, by adulteration become spurious. Furthermore, should we admit, that among the numerous revelations on which the respective priests have given the stamp of divinity, some one of them was in reality of divine authority, yet we could no otherwise, as rational beings, distinguish it from others, but by reason.

Reason therefore must be the standard, by which we determine the respective claims of revelation; for otherwise we may as well subscribe to the divinity of the one as of the other, or to the whole of them, or to none at all. So likewise on this thesis, if reason rejects the whole of those revelations, we ought to return to the religion of nature and reason.

Undoubtedly it is our duty, and for our best good, that we occupy and improve the faculties, with which our Creator has endowed us, but so far as prejudice, or prepossession of opinion prevails over our minds, in the same proportion, reason is excluded from our theory or practice. Therefore if we would acquire useful knowledge, we must first divest ourselves of those impediments; and sincerely endeavour to search out the truth; and draw our conclusions from reason and just argument, which will never conform to our inclination, interest or fancy; but we must conform to that if we would judge rightly. As certain as we determine contrary to reason, we make a wrong conclusion; therefore, our wisdom is, to conform to the nature and reason of things, as well in religious matters, as in other sciences. Preposterously absurd would it be, to negative the exercise of reason in religious concerns, and yet, be actuated by it in all other and less occurrences of life. All our knowledge of things is derived from God, in and by the order of nature, out of which we cannot perceive, reflect or understand any thing whatsoever; our external senses are natural and so are our souls; by the instrumentality of the former we perceive the objects of sense, and with the latter we reflect on them. And those objects are also natural; so that ourselves, and all things about us, and our knowledge collected therefrom, is natural, and not supernatural; as argued in the 6th chapter.

We may and often do, connect or arrange our ideas together, in a wrong or improper manner, for the want of skill or judgment, or through mistake or the want of application, or through the influence of prejudice; but in all such cases, the error does not originate from the ideas themselves, but from the composer; for a system, or an arrangement of ideas justly composed; always contain the truth; but an unjust composition never fails to contain error and falsehood. Therefore an unjust connection of ideas is not derived from nature, but from the imperfect composition of man. Misconnection of ideas is the same as misjudging, and has no positive existence, being merely a creature of the imagination; but nature and truth are real and uniform; and the rational mind by reasoning, discerns the uniformity, and is thereby enabled to make a just composition of ideas, which will stand the test of truth. But the fantastical illuminations of the credulous and superstitious part of mankind, proceed from weakness, and as far as they take place in the world, subvert the religion of REASON and TRUTH.

# IX

# Thomas Jefferson

1743–1826

Born in Shadwell, Albemarle County, Va. Secured early classical education under William Douglas and James Maury, beginning at age of nine. A.B., William and Mary College, 1762. Admitted to bar, 1767. Appointed county lieutenant of Albermarle, 1770, and surveyor of county, 1773. Member, House of Burgesses, 1769–75. Member Continental Congress. Wrote Declaration of Independence, 1776. Member, House of Delegates in Virginia, 1776–79. Governor of Virginia, 1779–81. Retired to Monticello where he wrote *Notes on Virginia,* 1781–83. Member of Congress, 1783. Minister to France, 1785–89. Secretary of State under Washington, 1790–94. Monticello, 1794–96. Vice President of the United States, 1796–1800. President, 1800–08. Retired to Monticello, 1809. Founder and first Rector of the University of Virginia. Died at Monticello, Va.

Thomas Jefferson had many and varied interests. He was well versed in law, having studied intensively for six years before presenting himself for admission to the bar. He read widely, acquainting himself with current literature as well as the classics. He advocated public education, emancipation of the slaves and religious freedom. He was an able farmer, studying soils, crop rotation and labor economy in order to develop a model farm. He was skilled in mathematics, botany and meteorology and had some knowledge of zoölogy, ethnology and astronomy. He was talented in music and anxious to make it an integral part of American culture. He planned Monticello and the University of Virginia, and left a collection of excellent architectural drawings. As a public servant, he held many positions of leadership, among them the highest elective positions in his own state and in the federal government.

While studying at William and Mary College, Jefferson's ability came to be recognized. More mature than other students, he was a constant companion of William Small who taught him philosophy and literature, George Wythe under whom he secured his legal training, and Governor Fauquier, the able and cultured governor of the colony. By the end of his Williamsburg sojourn his statesmanlike qualities and his liberalism were already in evidence. It might be said that Jefferson's two abiding interests were the enrichment of the life of the individual and the furtherance of social good which he conceived to be correlative values. His whole public career was dominated by the desire to apply intelligence to social problems. He sought intelligence not for what it would produce in terms of neatly-spun theories but rather for what practical values it could afford. This was perhaps nowhere better evidenced than in his attitude toward democracy. Democracy was not, for him, a final governmental philosophy but a workable one. He felt it would work in America because of the peculiar state of American civilization; he feared that it might not work effectively in Europe because the social conditions there were different. Jefferson was a relativist, holding that government, like all other institutions, was dependent upon the circumstances at a given time and place.[1] He believed in progress (even by revolution if necessary) for, like most thinkers in the Age of Reason, he regarded change and development as essential to the continued welfare of man.

In large part, Jefferson's emphasis was upon improving the status of man. He had confidence in man's integrity and ability. He said, "I cannot act as if all men were unfaithful because some are so. . . . I had rather be the victim of occasional infidelities, than relinquish my general confidence in the honesty of man." [2] The life of each and every man was to him of supreme worth. Wealth, position in society —these and other factors suggesting social stratification in no way detracted from the fundamental equality of man. Jefferson was an aristocrat in his own right and believed that an aristocracy of talent should ultimately rule but only because the common man in choosing his rulers would prefer intelligence to incompetence. Jefferson was always a friend of the common man, accepting his natural rights as the fundamental starting point for all reflection. He was eager to aid the human search for happiness in whatever direction it might lead.

Jefferson was a eudaemonist in morality as were many of the cultured men of his time. Happiness was to him the elixir which all men were seeking. It was to be achieved not through any authoritarian principles derived from religion but through the development of man's moral sense. In one respect, Jefferson divorced religion and morality, in that he believed a man could be moral without having a religion. In an-

1 "The excellence of every government is its adaptation to the state of those to be governed by it." *Writings.* XIV, 487.

2 Ibid. XIV, 43.

other respect, he made them one in that he argued that the only true value of religion lay in its moral results. True morality arose from the innate desire of man for the good. In holding this Jefferson was somewhat Socratic, accepting the general principle that man will do the good if he knows it.

When Jefferson speaks of a moral sense, however, it is not to be understood in terms of its contemporaneous Scotch interpretation even though he had personal contact with Scotch moral philosophy. The moral sense, he thought, would never arrive at final moral truth; it could attain only to moral truths relative to the social milieu in which a man lived. Morality would vary according to time, place, and circumstance. The moral sense, bred in a particular environment and reconditioned if necessary, would arrive at the principles of morality necessary for participation in that environment. Utility was the criterion by which the moral sense could ascertain the good and distinguish it from the evil. Jefferson conceived the good life to consist in the most successful adjustment of the individual to his environment. His attitude toward morality was never more clearly expressed than in a letter to his nephew, Peter Carr, in which he said,

> Man was destined for society. His morality, therefore, was to be formed to this object. He was endowed with a sense of right and wrong, merely relative to this. This sense is as much a part of his nature, as the sense of hearing, seeing, feeling; it is the true foundation of morality, and not the τὸ καλόν, truth, etc., as fanciful writers have imagined. The moral sense, or conscience, is as much a part of man as his leg or arm.[3]

Jefferson was partial to the Epicureans and Stoics. This was partly due to Bolingbroke's influence upon him but also partly due to the practical needs of life which these philosophies met. He called himself an Epicurean, not because he was a complete follower of Epicurus but because the ideal of tranquillity which Epicurus espoused was attractive to him. He was eclectic, seeking in the last years of his life to effect a reconciliation between Greek and Christian morality. He followed Epicurus and the Stoics for what they could provide in terms of peace of mind; he followed Jesus because he felt Jesus added a note of social morality lacking in Epicurus. In his *Syllabus of an Estimate of the Merit of the Doctrines of Jesus, Compared with Those of Others,* inspired by Joseph Priestley and sent in a letter to Benjamin Rush, he said:

[3] *Writings.* VI, 257.

His moral doctrines, relating to kindred and friends, were more pure and perfect than those of the most correct of the philosophers, and greatly more so than those of the Jews; and they went far beyond both in inculcating universal philanthropy, not only to kindred and friends, to neighbors and countrymen, but to all mankind, gathering all into one family, under the bonds of love, charity, peace, common wants and common aids.[4]

Jefferson's eudaemonism was essentially social. Man was not to seek his own happiness regardless of others but was to find it along with others. With Jefferson's moral philosophy in the background, it is much easier to understand his basic political ideas and the cultural program he advocated. Jefferson was the writer of the Declaration of Independence. He considered this, his struggle for religious freedom, and the founding of the University of Virginia as the three great contributions of his career. Locke had much influence on the political thought of eighteenth-century America but Locke had spoken of life, liberty and property as the three basic natural rights. Jefferson changed "property" to "the pursuit of happiness," an emphasis which brings out on the one hand the fact that men were not always agreed on what natural rights were and on the other hand that Jefferson, as well as Franklin and other early political thinkers in America, looked upon property as less defensible as a natural right than the eudaemonistic ideal. Jefferson never claimed originality for the principles of the Declaration, feeling that he was only putting down on paper the common sentiments of men. At the same time, the shift from Locke to the Declaration indicates that Jefferson, and probably many others as well, looked upon natural rights more as moral ideals than as invariable social laws. Jefferson never spent time seeking a metaphysical basis for natural rights; natural rights to him were the rights upon which reasonable men would agree. It hardly seemed reasonable to Jefferson to look upon property as a natural right; it was a right which men possessed because of their participation in society; he called this a civil right. This division of rights into natural and civil is nowhere better brought out than in the first selection included here, a selection which Chinard discovered in the Jeffersonian papers in Washington. In this selection, Jefferson defined a natural right as one which could be supported by man's individual power, a civil right as one supported only by society. Civil rights were those which came to a man because he contracted with others for mutual benefit when he became a member of society. Jefferson accepted the contract theory of

[4] *Writings*. X, 384–5.

the state in large part, the state being an organization for creating and preserving the rights of the individual. His conception of the social nature of man called for government by the people as well as for the people. He thought the perfect society would be without government, the next best would have the form of a pure democracy, but since these were both impracticable, he favored a society with a representative form of government. He looked upon government more or less as a necessary evil, but since it was necessary he wanted to insure the individual against encroachments upon his natural (reasonable) rights.

Jefferson held that there were two pillars of representative government. One of these was local government. He wanted local government to exercise the largest amount of power commensurate with practical efficiency. He favored state rights over against the federal government on the same basis: the rights of the individual were to come first and they could best be preserved when government was nearest to the people. The second pillar of representative government was education. Jefferson felt that democratic government could be most successful when the public was trained to accept the responsibilities of citizenship and organized in such a way as to develop a group of superior people capable of performing the more important tasks in society. Education was to provide greater happiness for people in three respects: personal development, preparation for citizenship and training for leadership. The system of education which Jefferson outlined sounds somewhat elementary viewed from our standpoint today, but it was an essential part of Jefferson's struggle to build the empire of man. His desire to eliminate religious teaching from the curriculum and to replace it with moral teaching in conformity with the common sentiments of man and to set up a system of state education available for all are landmarks in the history of education in America. Jefferson's thorough conviction that education was a social necessity is borne out by his persistent struggle to found the University of Virginia and his untiring service in the last years of his life as its Rector.

Just as Jefferson sought to free education from religious partisanship, he sought to free religion from political or ecclesiastical domination. He was born and reared an Episcopalian and was buried with the rites of that church, but his real religious opinions were far more in accord with the deistic sentiments of the period. In a letter to Benjamin Waterhouse in 1822, he defined the religion of Jesus as consisting of three cardinal points:

> 1. That there is one only God, and He all perfect. 2. That there is a future state of rewards and punishments. 3. That to love God with all thy heart and thy neighbor as thyself is the sum of religion.[5]

He was a bitter opponent of Calvinism, speaking of Athanasius and Calvin as "mere usurpers of the Christian name, teaching a counter-religion made up of the *deliria* of crazy imaginations. . . ."[6] He rejected the scriptural authority of the Bible and the authority of ecclesiastical institutions and constantly maintained that religion was a relationship between man and God and hence not to be interfered with by doctrinal or clerical authority. He was hopeful that the personal element in religion might be considered uppermost, praised the Quakers for the simplicity of their faith, and trusted "that there is not a *young man* now living in the United States who will not die an Unitarian."[7] Jefferson's personal religion was not distinctive, but his attitude toward religious freedom was important, for it was representative of his desire to protect the inalienable rights of man (of which he considered religious belief to be one) from being trammeled by social or political influences, no matter how righteous their motives might be. He conceived of religion as one of the fields in which government had no right to interfere. He said, "Our particular principles of religion are a subject of accountability to our God alone."[8] His opposition to Calvinism and to much other religious doctrine was an essential part of his opposition to any kind of authoritarianism or intolerance. He said, "We ought with one heart and one hand hew down the daring and dangerous efforts of those who would seduce the public opinion to substitute itself into that tyranny over religious faith which the laws have so justly abdicated."[9]

Jefferson's attitude toward slavery was another example of his desire never to permit infringement upon man's natural rights. There was no great agitation against slavery in Jefferson's day. Jefferson himself had between one and two hundred slaves. He felt himself obliged to operate his family economy on the basis of the prevailing system, but he never believed it to be just. His argument against slavery was based partly on the ill-effect upon children of cruelty to slaves, although his real opposition grew out of his feeling that slaves, as human beings, had natural rights just as did the white people. Jefferson was no agitator for immediate abolition of slavery, for he

[5] *Writings*. XV, 384.
[6] Ibid.
[7] Ibid. XV, 385.
[8] Ibid. XIV, 198.
[9] Ibid. X, 378.

saw the practical consequences of such action, but he did believe in gradual abolition and looked forward to the time when that peril to the rights of man would be eliminated.

Jefferson is not always regarded as a philosopher since no one product of his pen set forth his mature position on politics, morality or religion. His thoughts, however, did have a certain harmony. They all grew out of his one great interest, man, and the happiness which might result from intelligent ordering of his existence. He believed that reason, in the common sense meaning of that word, was man's most useful tool in achieving that happiness. Reason would arrive at a philosophy of social eudaemonism. Society would contribute to the individual's happiness by preserving his natural rights and by adding to these certain contributory civil rights. Religion would increase happiness by offering inspiration to lead the good life. Jefferson's philosophy was less explicit than implicit. He is entitled to consideration in philosophy because of the pragmatic effect of his whole career. He zealously sought the application of reason to the essential problems of human existence, and accepted utility as the test of the value of any speculative vision. He was not a philosopher because he wrote about his philosophy in orderly, systematic fashion, but rather because the ideas he expressed and the life he led were testimony to his essentially philosophic mind. It could be further argued that Jefferson is peculiarly fitted to be called a philosopher because he gave expression to indigenous sentiments and ideas which led to the development of a distinct culture. Americanism found an eloquent voice in Jefferson.

## REFERENCES

Bergh, A. L. (editor): *The Writings of Thomas Jefferson.* 20 vols. Washington: The Thomas Jefferson Memorial Association, 1903.

Adams, J. T.: *The Living Jefferson.* New York: Charles Scribner's Sons, 1936. (Deals with Jefferson and his conflict with Hamiltonian principles.)

Chinard, G.: *Thomas Jefferson, the Apostle of Americanism.* Boston: Little, Brown and Co., 1929.

Gould, W. D.: "The Religious Opinions of Thomas Jefferson," *Mississippi Valley Historical Review* 20 (1933) 191–209.

Honeywell, R. J.: *The Educational Work of Thomas Jefferson.* Vol. XVI, Harvard Studies in Education. Cambridge: Harvard University Press, 1931.

Prescott, F. C.: *Alexander Hamilton and Thomas Jefferson.* Representative Selections, with Introduction, Bibliography and Notes. Cincinnati: American Book Co., 1934.

Randall, H. S.: *Life of Thomas Jefferson.* 3 vols. New York, 1858.

Riley, I. Woodbridge: *American Philosophy: the Early Schools.* New York: Dodd, Mead and Co., 1907. 266–95.

* * *

---

* * *

## REFLECTIONS ON THE ARTICLES OF CONFEDERATION [10]

After I got home, being alone and wanting amusement I sat down to explain to myself (for there is such a thing) my Ideas of natural and civil rights and the distinction between them—I send them to you to see how nearly we agree.

Suppose 20 persons, strangers to each other, to meet in a country not before inhabited. Each would be a sovereign in his own natural right. His will would be his Law,—but his power, in many cases, inadequate to his right, and the consequence would be that each might be exposed, not only to each other but to the other nineteen.

It would then occur to them that their condition would be much improved, if a way could be devised to exchange that quantity of danger into so much protection, so that each individual should possess the strength of the whole number. As all their rights, in the first case are natural rights, and the exercise of those rights supported only by their own natural individual power, they would begin by distinguishing between those rights they could individually exercise fully and perfectly and those they could not.

Of the first kind are the rights of thinking, speaking, forming and giving opinions, and perhaps all those which can be fully exercised by the individual without the aid of exterior assistance—or in other words, rights of personal competency—Of the second kind are those of personal protection, of acquiring and possessing property, in the exercise of which the individual natural power is less than the natural right.

Having drawn this line they agree to retain individually the first Class of Rights or those of personal Competency; and to detach from their personal possession the second Class, or those of defective power and to accept in lieu thereof a right to the whole power produced by

[10] Taken from Chinard, *Thomas Jefferson.* 80–2. By permission of Little, Brown and Co. These thoughts were written after Jefferson had attended the meetings of Congress at which the Articles of Confederation were discussed. They provide the basis for his democratic political philosophy.

a condensation of all the parts. These I conceive to be civil rights or rights of Compact, and are distinguishable from Natural rights, because in the one we act wholly in our own person, in the other we agree not to do so, but act under the guarantee of society.

It therefore follows that the more of those imperfect natural rights, or rights of imperfect power we give up and thus exchange the more securely we possess, and as the word liberty is often mistakenly put for security M^r^ Wilson has confused his Argument by confounding the terms.

But it does not follow that the more natural rights of *every kind* we resign the more securely we possess,—because if we resign those of the first class we may suffer much by the exchange, for where the right and the power are equal with each other in the individual naturally they ought to rest there.

M^r^ Wilson must have some allusion to this distinction or his position would be subject to the inference you draw from it.

I consider the individual sovereignty of the States retained under the Act of Confederation to be of the second Class of rights. It becomes dangerous because it is defective in the power necessary to support it. It answers the pride and purpose of a few men in each state—but the State collectively is injured by it.

* * *

---

* * *

## NOTES ON VIRGINIA [11]

### *The Administration of Justice and the Description of the Laws?* [12]

Another object of the revisal is to diffuse knowledge more generally through the mass of the people. This bill proposes to lay off every county into small districts of five or six miles square, called hundreds, and in each of them to establish a school for teaching reading, writing, and arithmetic. The tutor to be supported by the hundred, and every

[11] *Writings.* II, (query XIV) 203–8; (query XVIII) 225–8; (appendix) 300–3.

[12] This selection shows Jefferson's intense interest in education as one of the chief means of increasing human happiness. The law he here favors was not passed, but this excerpt formed the basis for his later *Plan for Elementary Schools,* 1817.

person in it entitled to send their children three years gratis, and as much longer as they please, paying for it. These schools to be under a visitor who is annually to choose the boy of best genius in the school, of those whose parents are too poor to give them further education, and to send him forward to one of the grammar schools, of which twenty are proposed to be erected in different parts of the country, for teaching Greek, Latin, geography, and the higher branches of numerical arithmetic. Of the boys thus sent in any one year, trial is to be made at the grammar schools one or two years, and the best genius of the whole selected, and continued six years, and the residue dismissed. By this means twenty of the best geniuses will be raked from the rubbish annually, and be instructed, at the public expense, so far as the grammar schools go. At the end of six years' instruction, one-half are to be discontinued (from among whom the grammar schools will probably be supplied with future masters) and the other half, who are to be chosen for the superiority of their parts and disposition, are to be sent and continued three years in the study of such sciences as they shall choose, at William and Mary College, the plan of which is proposed to be enlarged, as will be hereafter explained, and extended to all the useful sciences. The ultimate result of the whole scheme of education would be the teaching all the children of the State reading, writing, and common arithmetic; turning out ten annually, of superior genius, well taught in Greek, Latin, geography, and the higher branches of arithmetic; turning out ten others annually, of still superior parts, who, to those branches of learning, shall have added such of the sciences as their genius shall have led them to; the furnishing to the wealthier part of the people convenient schools at which their children may be educated at their own expense. The general objects of this law are to provide an education adapted to the years, to the capacity, and the condition of every one, and directed to their freedom and happiness. Specific details were not proper for the law. These must be the business of the visitors entrusted with its execution. The first stage of this education being the schools of the hundreds, wherein the great mass of the people will receive their instruction, the principal foundations of future order will be laid here. Instead, therefore, of putting the Bible and Testament into the hands of the children at an age when their judgments are not sufficiently matured for religious inquiries, their memories may here be stored with the most useful facts from Grecian, Roman, European and American history. The first elements of morality too may be instilled into their minds; such as, when further developed as their judgments advance in strength, may teach them how to work out their own greatest happiness, by showing them that it does not depend on the condition of life in which chance has placed them, but is always the result of a good conscience, good health, occupation, and freedom in all just pursuits. Those whom either the wealth of their parents or the adoption of the State shall destine to higher degrees of learning, will go on to the grammar schools, which constitute the next stage, there to be instructed in the languages. The learning Greek and Latin, I am told, is going into disuse in Europe. I know not what their manners and occupations may call for; but it would be very ill-judged in us to follow their example in this instance. There is a certain period of life, say from eight to fifteen or sixteen years of age, when the mind like the body is not yet firm enough for laborious and close operations. If applied to such, it falls an early victim to premature exertion; exhibiting, indeed, at first, in these young and tender subjects, the flattering appearance of their being men while they are yet children, but ending in reducing them to be children when they should be men. The memory is then most susceptible and tenacious of impressions; and the learning of languages being chiefly a work of memory, it seems precisely fitted to the powers of this period, which is long enough, too, for acquiring the most useful languages, ancient and modern. I do not pretend that language is science. It is only an instrument for the attainment of science. But that time is not lost which is employed in providing tools for future operation; more especially as in this case the books put into the hands of the youth for this purpose may be such as will at the same time impress their minds with useful facts and good principles. If this period be suffered to pass in idleness, the mind becomes lethargic and impotent, as would the body it inhabits if unexercised during the same time. The sympathy between body and mind during their rise, progress and decline, is too strict and obvious to endanger our being misled while we reason from the one to the other. As soon as they are of sufficient age, it is supposed they will be sent on from the grammar schools to the university, which constitutes our third and last stage, there to study those sciences which may be adapted to their views. By that part of our plan which prescribes the selection of the youths of genius from among the classes of the poor, we hope to avail the State of those talents which nature has sown as liberally among the poor as the rich, but which perish without use, if not sought for and cultivated. But of all the views of this law none is more important, none more legitimate, than that of rendering the people the safe, as they are the ultimate, guardians of their own liberty. For this purpose the reading in the first stage, where *they* will receive their whole education, is proposed, as has been said, to be chiefly historical. History, by apprising them of the past, will enable them to judge of the future; it will avail them of the experience of other times and other nations; it will qualify them as judges of the actions and designs of men; it will enable them to know ambition under every disguise it may assume; and knowing it, to defeat its views. In every government on earth is some trace of human weakness, some germ of corruption and degeneracy, which cunning will discover, and wickedness insensibly open, cultivate, and improve. Every government degenerates when trusted to the rulers of the people alone. The people themselves, therefore, are its only safe depositories. And to render even them safe, their minds must be improved to a certain degree. This indeed is not all that is necessary, though it be essentially necessary. An amendment of our constitution must here come in aid of the public education. The influence over government must be shared among all people. If every individual which composes their mass participates of the ultimate authority, the government will be safe; because the corrupting the whole mass will exceed any private resources of wealth; and public ones cannot be provided but by levies on the people. In this case every man would have to pay his own price. The government of Great Britain has been corrupted, because but one man in ten has a right to vote for members of parliament. The sellers of the government, therefore, get nine-tenths of their price clear. It has been thought that corruption is restrained by confining the right of suffrage to a few of the wealthier of the people; but it would be more effectually restrained by an extension of that right to such members as would bid defiance to the means of corruption.

Lastly, it is proposed, by a bill in this revisal, to begin a public library and gallery, by laying out a certain sum annually in books, paintings, and statues.

## *The Particular Customs and Manners that May Happen to Be Received in that State?* [13]

It is difficult to determine on the standard by which the manners of a nation may be tried, whether *catholic* or *particular*. It is more difficult for a native to bring to that standard the manners of his own nation, familiarized to him by habit. There must doubtless be an un-

[13] This selection indicates Jefferson's interest in emancipation as a necessary accompaniment of the acceptance of belief in natural rights.

happy influence on the manners of our people produced by the existence of slavery among us. The whole commerce between master and slave is a perpetual exercise of the most boisterous passions, the most unremitting despotism on the one part, and degrading submissions on the other. Our children see this, and learn to imitate it; for man is an imitative animal. This quality is the germ of all education in him. From his cradle to his grave he is learning to do what he sees others do. If a parent could find no motive either in his philanthropy or his self-love, for restraining the intemperance of passion towards his slave, it should always be a sufficient one that his child is present. But generally it is not sufficient. The parent storms, the child looks on, catches the lineaments of wrath, puts on the same airs in the circle of smaller slaves, gives a loose to the worst of passions, and thus nursed, educated, and daily exercised in tyranny, cannot but be stamped by it with odious peculiarities. The man must be a prodigy who can retain his manners and morals undepraved by such circumstances. And with what execration should the statesman be loaded, who, permitting one-half the citizens thus to trample on the rights of the other, transforms those into despots, and these into enemies, destroys the morals of the one part, and the *amor patriae* of the other. For if a slave can have a country in this world, it must be any other in preference to that in which he is born to live and labor for another; in which he must lock up the faculties of his nature, contribute as far as depends on his individual endeavors to the evanishment of the human race, or entail his own miserable condition on the endless generations proceeding from him. With the morals of the people, their industry also is destroyed. For in a warm climate, no man will labor for himself who can make another labor for him. This is so true, that of the proprietors of slaves a very small proportion indeed are ever seen to labor. And can the liberties of a nation be thought secure when we have removed their only firm basis, a conviction in the minds of the people that these liberties are of the gift of God? That they are not to be violated but with His wrath? Indeed I tremble for my country when I reflect that God is just; that his justice cannot sleep forever; that considering numbers, nature and natural means only, a revolution of the wheel of fortune, an exchange of situation is among possible events; that it may become probable by supernatural interference! The Almighty has no attribute which can take side with us in such a contest. But it is impossible to be temperate and to pursue this subject through the various considerations of policy, of morals, of history natural and civil. We must be contented to hope they will force their way into every one's mind. I think a change already perceptible, since the origin of the present revolution. The spirit of the master is abating, that of the slave rising from the dust, his condition mollifying, the way I hope preparing, under the auspices of heaven, for a total emancipation, and that this is disposed, in the order of events, to be with the consent of the masters, rather than by their extirpation.

## *An Act for Establishing Religious Freedom Passed in the Assembly of Virginia in the Beginning of the Year 1786* [14]

Well aware that Almighty God hath created the mind free; that all attempts to influence it by temporal punishments or burdens, or by civil incapacitations, tend only to beget habits of hypocrisy and meanness, and are a departure from the plan of the Holy Author of our religion, who being Lord both of body and mind, yet chose not to propagate it by coercions on either, as was in his Almighty power to do; that the impious presumption of legislators and rulers, civil as well as ecclesiastical, who, being themselves but fallible and uninspired men, have assumed dominion over the faith of others, setting up their own opinions and modes of thinking as the only true and infallible, and as such endeavoring to impose them on others, hath established and maintained false religions over the greatest part of the world, and through all time; that to compel a man to furnish contributions of money for the propagation of opinions which he disbelieves, is sinful and tyrannical; that even the forcing him to support this or that teacher of his own religious persuasion, is depriving him of the comfortable liberty of giving his contributions to the particular pastor whose morals he would make his pattern, and whose powers he feels most persuasive to righteousness, and is withdrawing from the ministry those temporal rewards, which, proceeding from an approbation of their personal conduct, are an additional incitement to earnest and unremitting labors for the instruction of mankind; that our civil rights have no dependence on our religious opinions, more than our opinions in physics or geometry; that, therefore, the proscribing any citizen as unworthy the public confidence by laying upon him an incapacity of being called to the offices of trust and emolument, unless he profess or renounce this or that religious opinion, is depriving him

[14] Jefferson's belief in natural rights involved the strong conviction that religious freedom should be unhampered. This act Jefferson regarded as one of his great contributions to mankind. It was heralded abroad as well as in the United States.

injuriously of those privileges and advantages to which in common with his fellow citizens he has a natural right; that it tends also to corrupt the principles of that very religion it is meant to encourage, by bribing, with a monopoly of worldly honors and emoluments, those who will externally profess and conform to it; that though indeed these are criminal who do not withstand such temptation, yet neither are those innocent who lay the bait in their way; that to suffer the civil magistrate to intrude his powers into the field of opinion and to restrain the profession or propagation of principles, on the supposition of their ill tendency, is a dangerous fallacy, which at once destroys all religious liberty, because he being of course judge of that tendency, will make his opinions the rule of judgment, and approve or condemn the sentiments of others only as they shall square with or differ from his own; that it is time enough for the rightful purposes of civil government, for its officers to interfere when principles break out into overt acts against peace and good order; and finally, that truth is great and will prevail if left to herself, that she is the proper and sufficient antagonist to error, and has nothing to fear from the conflict, unless by human interposition disarmed of her natural weapons, free argument and debate, errors ceasing to be dangerous when it is permitted freely to contradict them.

*Be it therefore enacted by the General Assembly,* That no man shall be compelled to frequent or support any religious worship, place, or ministry whatsoever, nor shall be enforced, restrained, molested, or burdened in his body or goods, nor shall otherwise suffer on account of his religious opinions or belief; but that all men shall be free to profess, and by argument to maintain, their opinions in matters of religion, and that the same shall in nowise diminish, enlarge, or affect their civil capacities.

And though we well know this Assembly, elected by the people for the ordinary purposes of legislation only, have no power to restrain the acts of succeeding assemblies, constituted with the powers equal to our own, and that therefore to declare this act irrevocable would be of no effect in law, yet we are free to declare, and do declare, that the rights hereby asserted are of the natural rights of mankind, and that if any act shall be hereafter passed to repeal the present or to narrow its operation, such act will be an infringement of natural right.

* * *

---

* * *

## TO THOMAS LAW, ESQ.[15]

Poplar Forest, June 13, 1814.

DEAR SIR,—The copy of your Second Thoughts on Instinctive Impulses, with the letter accompanying it, was received just as I was setting out on a journey to this place, two or three days distant from Monticello. I brought it with me and read it with great satisfaction, and with the more as it contained exactly my own creed on the foundation of morality in man. It is really curious that on a question so fundamental, such a variety of opinions should have prevailed among men, and those, too, of the most exemplary virtue and first order of understanding. It shows how necessary was the care of the Creator in making the moral principle so much a part of our constitution as that no errors of reasoning or of speculation might lead us astray from its observance in practice. Of all the theories on this question, the most whimsical seems to have been that of Wollaston, who considers *truth* as the foundation of morality. The thief who steals your guinea does wrong only inasmuch as he acts a lie in using your guinea as if it were his own. Truth is certainly a branch of morality, and a very important one to society. But presented as its foundation, it is as if a tree taken up by the roots, had its stem reversed in the air, and one of its branches planted in the ground. Some have made the *love of God* the foundation of morality. This, too, is but a branch of our moral duties, which are generally divided into duties to God and duties to man. If we did a good act merely from the love of God and a belief that it is pleasing to Him, whence arises the morality of the Atheist? It is idle to say, as some do, that no such being exists. We have the same evidence of the fact as of most of those we act on, to wit: their own affirmations, and their reasonings in support of them. I have observed, indeed, generally, that while in Protestant countries the defections from the Platonic Christianity of the priests is to Deism, in Catholic countries they are to Atheism. Diderot, D'Alembert, D'Holbach, Condorcet, are known to have been among the most virtuous of men. Their virtue, then, must have had some other foundation than the love of God.

The *τὸ καλόν* of others is founded in a different faculty, that of taste, which is not even a branch of morality. We have indeed an innate sense of what we call beautiful, but that is exercised chiefly on subjects addressed to the fancy, whether through the eye in visible

[15] *Writings.* XIV, 138–44. This and the following letter to William Short deal with Jefferson's moral philosophy.

forms, as landscape, animal figure, dress, drapery, architecture, the composition of colors, etc., or to the imagination directly, as imagery, style, or measure in prose or poetry, or whatever else constitutes the domain of criticism or taste, a faculty entirely distinct from the moral one. Self-interest, or rather self-love, or *egoism,* has been more plausibly substituted as the basis of morality. But I consider our relations with others as constituting the boundaries of morality. With ourselves we stand on the ground of identity, not of relation, which last, requiring two subjects, excludes self-love confined to a single one. To ourselves, in strict language, we can owe no duties, obligation requiring also two parties. Self-love, therefore, is no part of morality. Indeed it is exactly its counterpart. It is the sole antagonist of virtue, leading us constantly by our propensities to self-gratification in violation of our moral duties to others. Accordingly, it is against this enemy that are erected the batteries of moralists and religionists, as the only obstacle to the practice of morality. Take from man his selfish propensities, and he can have nothing to seduce him from the practice of virtue. Or subdue those propensities by education, instruction or restraint, and virtue remains without a competitor. Egoism, in a broader sense, has been thus presented as the source of moral action. It has been said that we feed the hungry, clothe the naked, bind up the wounds of the man beaten by thieves, pour oil and wine into them, set him on our own beast and bring him to the inn, because we receive ourselves pleasure from these acts. So Helvetius, one of the best men on earth, and the most ingenious advocate of this principle, after defining "interest" to mean not merely that which is pecuniary, but whatever may procure us pleasure or withdraw us from pain, (*de l'esprit* 2, 1,) says, (ib. 2, 2,) "The humane man is he to whom the sight of misfortune is insupportable, and who to rescue himself from this spectacle is forced to succor the unfortunate object." This indeed is true. But it is one step short of the ultimate question. These good acts give us pleasure, but how happens it that they give us pleasure? Because nature hath implanted in our breasts a love of others, a sense of duty to them, a moral instinct, in short, which prompts us irresistibly to feel and to succor their distresses, and protests against the language of Helvetius, (ib. 2, 5,) "what other motive than self-interest could determine a man to generous actions? It is as impossible for him to love what is good for the sake of good, as to love evil for the sake of evil." The Creator would indeed have been a bungling artist, had he intended man for a social animal, without planting in him social dispositions. It is true they are not planted in every man, because there is no rule without exceptions; but it is false reasoning which converts exceptions into the general rule. Some men are born without the organs of sight, or of hearing, or without hands. Yet it would be wrong to say that man is born without these faculties, and sight, hearing, and hands may with truth enter into the general definition of man.

The want or imperfection of the moral sense in some men, like the want or imperfection of the senses of sight and hearing in others, is no proof that it is a general characteristic of the species. When it is wanting, we endeavor to supply the defect by education, by appeals to reason and calculation, by presenting to the being so unhappily conformed, other motives to do good and to eschew evil, such as the love, or the hatred, or rejection of those among whom he lives, and whose society is necessary to his happiness and even existence; demonstrations by sound calculation that honesty promotes interest in the long run; the rewards and penalties established by the laws; and ultimately the prospects of a future state of retribution for the evil as well as the good done while here. These are the correctives which are supplied by education, and which exercise the functions of the moralist, the preacher, and legislator; and they lead into a course of correct action all those whose disparity is not too profound to be eradicated. Some have argued against the existence of a moral sense, by saying that if nature had given us such a sense, impelling us to virtuous actions, and warning us against those which are vicious, then nature would also have designated, by some particular earmarks, the two sets of actions which are, in themselves, the one virtuous and the other vicious. Whereas, we find, in fact, that the same actions are deemed virtuous in one country and vicious in another. The answer is, that nature has constituted *utility* to man, the standard and test of virtue. Men living in different countries under different circumstances, different habits and regimens, may have different utilities; the same act, therefore, may be useful, and consequently virtuous in one country which is injurious and vicious in another differently circumstanced. I sincerely, then, believe with you in the general existence of a moral instinct. I think it the brightest gem with which the human character is studded, and the want of it as more degrading than the most hideous of the bodily deformities. I am happy in reviewing the roll of associates in this principle which you present in your second letter, some of which I had not before met with. To these might be added Lord Kaims, one of the ablest of our advocates, who goes so far as to say, in his Principles of Natural Religion, that a man owes no duty to which he is not urged by some impulsive feeling. This is correct, if referred to the standard of general feeling in the given case, and not to the feeling of a single individual. Perhaps I may misquote him, it being fifty years since I read his book.

The leisure and solitude of my situation here has led me to the indiscretion of taxing you with a long letter on a subject whereon nothing new can be offered you. I will indulge myself no farther than to repeat the assurances of my continued esteem and respect.

* * *

---

* * *

## TO WILLIAM SHORT [16]

Monticello, October 31, 1819.

DEAR SIR,—Your favor of the 21st is received. My late illness, in which you are so kind as to feel an interest, was produced by a spasmodic stricture of the ileum, which came upon me on the 7th inst. The crisis was short, passed over favorably on the fourth day, and I should soon have been well but that a dose of calomel and jalap, in which were only eight or nine grains of the former, brought on a salivation. Of this, however, nothing now remains but a little soreness of the mouth. I have been able to get on horseback for three or four days past.

As you say of yourself, I too am an Epicurian. I consider the genuine (not the imputed) doctrines of Epicurus as containing everything rational in moral philosophy which Greece and Rome have left us. Epictetus indeed, has given us what was good of the Stoics; all beyond, of their dogmas, being hypocrisy and grimace. Their great crime was in their calumnies of Epicurus and misrepresentations of his doctrines; in which we lament to see the candid character of Cicero engaging as an accomplice. Diffuse, vapid, rhetorical, but enchanting. His prototpye Plato, eloquent as himself, dealing out mysticisms incomprehensible to the human mind, has been deified by certain sects usurping the name of Christians; because, in his foggy conceptions, they found a basis of impenetrable darkness whereon to rear fabrications as delirious, of their own invention. These they fathered blasphemously on Him whom they claimed as their Founder, but who would disclaim them with the indignation which their caricatures of His

[16] *Writings.* XV, 219–24.

religion so justly excite. Of Socrates we have nothing genuine but in the Memorabilia of Xenophon; for Plato makes him one of his Collocutors merely to cover his own whimsies under the mantle of his name; a liberty of which we are told Socrates himself complained. Seneca is indeed a fine moralist, disfiguring his work at times with some Stoicisms, and affecting too much of antithesis and point, yet giving us on the whole a great deal of sound and practical morality. But the greatest of all the reformers of the depraved religion of His own country, was Jesus of Nazareth. Abstracting what is really His from the rubbish in which it is buried, easily distinguished by its lustre from the dross of His biographers, and as separable from that as the diamond from the dunghill, we have the outlines of a system of the most sublime morality which has ever fallen from the lips of man; outlines which it is lamentable He did not live to fill up. Epictetus and Epicurus give laws for governing ourselves, Jesus a supplement of the duties and charities we owe to others. The establishment of the innocent and genuine character of this benevolent Moralist, and the rescuing it from the imputation of imposture, which has resulted from artificial systems,[17] invented by ultra-Christian sects, unauthorized by a single word ever uttered by Him, is a most desirable object, and one to which Priestley has successfully devoted his labors and learning. It would in time, it is to be hoped, effect a quiet euthanasia of the heresies of bigotry and fanaticism which have so long triumphed over human reason, and so generally and deeply afflicted mankind; but this work is to be begun by winnowing the grain from the chaff of the historians of His life. I have sometimes thought of translating Epictetus (for he has never been tolerably translated into English) by adding the genuine doctrines of Epicurus from the Suntagma of Gassendi, and an abstract from the Evangelists of whatever has the stamp of the eloquence and fine imagination of Jesus. The last I attempted too hastily some twelve or fifteen years ago. It was the work of two or three nights only, at Washington, after getting through the evening task of reading the letters and papers of the day. But with one foot in the grave, these are now idle projects for me. My business is to beguile the wearisomeness of declining life, as I endeavor to do, by the delights of classical reading and of mathematical truths, and by the consolations of a sound philosophy, equally indifferent to hope and fear.

[17] E. g. The immaculate conception of Jesus, His deification, the creation of the world by Him, His miraculous powers, His resurrection and visible ascension, His corporeal presence in the Eucharist, the Trinity, original sin, atonement, regeneration, election, orders of Hierarchy, etc.

I take the liberty of observing that you are not a true disciple of our master Epicurus, in indulging the indolence to which you say you are yielding. One of his canons, you know, was that "That indulgence which presents a greater pleasure, or produces a greater pain, is to be avoided." Your love of repose will lead, in its progress, to a suspension of healthy exercise, a relaxation of mind, an indifference to everything around you, and finally to a debility of body, and hebetude of mind, the farthest of all things from the happiness which the well-regulated indulgences of Epicurus ensure; fortitude, you know, is one of his four cardinal virtues. That teaches us to meet and surmount difficulties; not to fly from them like cowards; and to fly, too, in vain, for they will meet and arrest us at every turn of our road. Weigh this matter well; brace yourself up; take a seat with Correa, and come and see the finest portion of your country, which, if you have not forgotten, you still do not know, because it is no longer the same as when you knew it. It will add much to the happiness of my recovery to be able to receive Correa and yourself, and prove the estimation in which I hold you both. Come, too, and see our incipient University, which has advanced with great activity this year. By the end of the next, we shall have elegant accomodations for seven professors, and the year following the professors themselves. No secondary character will be received among them. Either the ablest which America or Europe can furnish, or none at all. They will give us the selected society of a great city separated from the dissipations and levities of its ephemeral insects.

I am glad the bust of Condorcet has been saved and so well placed. His genius should be before us; while the lamentable, but singular act of ingratitude which tarnished his latter days, may be thrown behind us.

I will place under this a syllabus of the doctrines of Epicurus, somewhat in the lapidary style, which I wrote some twenty years ago; a like one of the philosophy of Jesus, of nearly the same age, it is too long to be copied. *Vale, et tibi persuade carissimum te esse mihi.*

*Syllabus of the doctrines of Epicurus.*

*Physical.*—The Universe eternal.

Its parts, great and small, interchangeable.

Matter and Void alone.

Motion inherent in matter which is weighty and declining.

Eternal circulation of the elements of bodies.

Gods, an order of beings next superior to man, enjoying in their sphere, their own felicities; but not meddling with the concerns of the scale of beings below them.

*Moral.*—Happiness the aim of life.

Virtue the foundation of happiness.

Utility the test of virtue.

Pleasure active and In-do-lent.

In-do-lence is the absence of pain, the true felicity.

Active, consists in agreeable motion; it is not happiness, but the means to produce it.

Thus the absence of hunger is an article of felicity; eating the means to obtain it.

The *summum bonum* is to be not pained in body, nor troubled in mind.

i. e. In-do-lence of body, tranquillity of mind.

To procure tranquillity of mind we must avoid desire and fear, the two principal diseases of the mind.

Man is a free agent.

Virtue consists in 1. Prudence. 2. Temperance. 3. Fortitude. 4. Justice.

To which are opposed, 1. Folly. 2. Desire. 3. Fear. 4. Deceit.

# X

# John Taylor and John Adams

1753–1824 1735–1826

John Taylor. Born in Caroline County, Virginia. Raised by Edmund Pendleton, famous lawyer. Attended William and Mary College, 1770–72. Studied law under Pendleton. Began legal practice, 1774. Major in Revolutionary army. Member of Virginia legislature along with Thomas Jefferson, Patrick Henry, John Marshall and John Breckenridge, 1779–85 and 1796–1800. United States Senator for three short periods. Defender of agrarianism and state rights. Died in Hazelwood, Caroline County.

John Adams. Born in Braintree, Mass. A.B., Harvard, 1755. Taught school at Worcester, expecting to become minister, 1755–57. Turned to practice of law, 1758. Delegate to first Continental Congress, 1774. Commissioner to France, 1778. Negotiated treaties with France and England, 1779. Appointed Ambassador to Court of St. James, 1785. Vice President of the United States, 1789–96. President, 1796–1800. Died in Quincy.

Belief in natural law increased as the eighteenth century wore on. Accepting at first the lawfulness of physical events men soon began to search for the laws governing human nature and social events. Encouraged by the writings of such men as Locke, Collins, Harrington, Shaftesbury, Adam Smith and Hume, American thought became newly orientated. The transition which took place led to deism in religion, eudaemonism in morality and republicanism in politics. Men came to regard God as a first cause who had created the natural world but who never interfered with its lawful procedure. They looked upon morality as a search for human happiness rather than as a quest for divine grace. They viewed political events as natural happenings in a social drama rather than as ominous signs of divine intervention or control. The philosophy of natural rights took form as the political counterpart of faith in the orderliness of nature. This philosophy was translated into practical terms in the Declaration of Independence, the Constitution of the United States, and in the constitutions of the various states.

Most of the political literature of the age was polemical rather than philosophical in nature. It was a period of storm and stress. It was more necessary to get things done than to have ideas presented systematically and logically. Thomas Paine's *Common Sense* was a typical political product of the time; Patrick Henry was a typical personality. The reformer and orator were more highly regarded than the political theorist. Jefferson has been regarded as the intellectual father of the Revolution, but his political thoughts were scattered through his writings, ranging from the Declaration of Independence and *Notes on Virginia* to incidental comments in his voluminous correspondence. Despite the practical motive of the age, however, it is well to remember that the fathers of the American system of government worked with political ideas and that those ideas took a fairly systematic form with some of the more erudite and scholarly men of the period. Two of these men were John Adams and John Taylor.

Superficial study of the period has led many to believe that the fathers of our country were in fundamental agreement over the purpose of government and that their only point of disagreement was the structure of government by which that purpose was to be achieved. As a matter of fact, there was much argument before and after the writing of the Constitution over the nature of government, so much that at times it appeared as if the job of uniting the various factions was almost hopeless. Three of the issues which stood out were the relations between the state and federal governments, the structure of each of these, and the interpretation of the principles upon which government was based. The third of these is the one of greatest philosophic importance. On the one side were those who contended that nature provided for the rise of a superior class in any society and that this class should rule, although it should concern itself with the good of the many. On the other side were those who contended that men were born equal and that the many should have final authority, even though they were represented by the few. The former position was taken by John Adams; those who held this position were the aristocrats of the day and they sided with British conservatism. The latter position was taken by John Taylor; those who shared this view were the democrats and they were seeking a more distinctive basis for American government.[1]

[1] While the selections included here from Taylor and Adams were printed in the second decade of the nineteenth century, the argument which they represent was at its height twenty years earlier. By the time Taylor's book appeared, Adams was defending a dying cause, Taylor the increasingly popular point of view.

John Adams became an important political figure at the age of thirty when he opposed the famous Stamp Act. He became an influential political thinker ten years later when he sketched his ideas on government in a letter to Richard Henry Lee of Virginia. He was subsequently asked to print *Thoughts on Government* (1776) which was a rewriting of his letter to Lee and which, although printed anonymously, was known to have been written by him. It had considerable effect upon the members of the Continental Congress. From that time on, serving with Jefferson on a committee to draft the Declaration (although Jefferson wrote it), writing the constitution for the state of Massachusetts (finally adopted in 1780), representing his state and nation abroad in difficult diplomatic rôles, and later serving as President of the United States for one term, Adams was regarded as a powerful force in political life. His *Defense of the Constitutions of Government of the United States of America,* in which he leaned heavily on historical data, was the most comprehensive statement of his political viewpoint. It appeared in 1787 while he was in England and was inspired by an attack of Turgot upon the theory of balances expressed in the various state constitutions. Turgot believed in concentrated authority; Adams, a strong believer in authority divided between executive, legislative and judicial branches of government, rose to defend the system of balances; before he had disposed of Turgot he had written three volumes and had dealt with almost every political problem which had arisen in the history of the western world. Written in odd moments in the midst of a hurried life, it contained many errors, but it was a remarkably erudite work for the age in which he lived.

The political philosophy of Adams was basically rooted in the reign of law which the Age of Reason accepted. To Adams, politics was a "divine science." In writing to Samuel Adams he said, "We have human nature, society and universal history to observe and study, and from these we may draw all the real principles which ought to be regarded." [2] In that same letter he criticized philosophers for having failed to base their political views on the factual evidence to be found in nature and history. He was desirous of casting the light of natural law and historical experience upon existing problems; he felt that an inductive study of history would reveal definite laws for human society and precise systems for its governance. He came to believe that the system of government which he was advocating was on the plane of scientific knowledge. He said in the conclusion to the first volume of the *Defense,* "By the authorities and examples already recited, you

[2] *Works.* VI, 416.

will be convinced that three branches of power have an unalterable foundation in nature; that they exist in every society natural and artificial; and that if all of them are not acknowledged in any constitution of government, it will be found to be imperfect, unstable, and soon enslaved. . . ."[3] There is small room for wonder, then, that Adams gave such an air of finality to his opinions. He carried into his philosophy of government the mind of the New England Puritan. This New England background was responsible for numerous emphases in his thought, one being his strong inclination to favor the English constitutional system with its aristocratic bias.

Aristotle's division of government into three basic types, monarchy, aristocracy and democracy, was largely followed by Adams. While he often contradicted in conversation what he had said in writing, and vice versa, it seems quite clear that Adams was never a strong believer in government by the many. Adams's basic interest in a balance of power was his hope that it, as a mixed form of government, would keep the one, the few and the many (which represented Aristotle's three types of government) from preying upon each other. He wanted a lower chamber to represent the many (but even here he wanted relatively high property qualifications for membership), an upper chamber to represent the few (with a high property qualification, at least if one may judge from the Massachusetts constitution which he wrote), and an executive to check them both. He held that it was a fundamental law of politics that an aristocratic group would arise within society, that it should not be allowed to dominate the one or the many, but that it had a better right to rule than either the one or the many alone. He wrote to Samuel Adams saying that a republic was a government "in which the people have collectively, or by representation, an essential share in the sovereignty."[4] In his answer, Samuel Adams retorted that "an essential share in the sovereignty" was not sufficient for a republic, that the whole sovereignty must be in the hands of the people, and that everyone who seriously supported a republic believed the same. John Adams was ever fearful that the masses would ruin good government and actually expected the time would come when the members of the upper chamber and even the executive would be selected for life and perhaps placed on an hereditary basis in order to save the country from the masses. Universal suffrage was never in his mind, and his system of balanced power was aimed partly at preventing the many from getting the upper hand. He was an aristocrat, not be-

[3] *Works*. IV, 579.
[4] Ibid. VI, 415.

cause he wanted a clear-cut aristocracy to rule but because his republic was tainted with aristocratic preferences and sentiments.

Southern thinkers especially were opposed to the thesis that nature provided for the production of an aristocratic class. Franklin, Jefferson, Rush, Cooper, Taylor and others could not accept Adams's lukewarm democracy. They were interested in clearing the slate and breaking with the English system which provided for definite orders within society. In this regard they were much more sympathetic with the English radicals (Thomas Cooper was originally one of these) while Adams sided with the English conservatives. Taylor was a good spokesman for the group, not because of his reputation as a public figure but because of his innate thoughtfulness and his more or less systematic approach.

Taylor wrote several volumes of considerable importance in early political controversy. His *Arator* was a series of essays espousing the agricultural ideal. His *Construction Construed, and Constitutions Vindicated* was a strong defense of state rights. His *Tyranny Unmasked* was a powerful diatribe against the protective tariff which he felt was a form of governmental favoritism and was destructive of state rights. His *New Views of the Constitution* was a general interpretation of the Constitution and an able analysis of the pitfalls of government. Taylor's ideas, as expounded in these volumes, were highly respected by the members of the Virginia school of thought. Jefferson rarely commended any books but he took occasion to praise Taylor's. Other men such as James Madison, James Monroe and John Quincy Adams, although they differed from him on minor issues, all looked upon Taylor as one of the ablest political theorists of the period. None of his books had more lasting importance, although some of them had more immediate appeal, than *An Inquiry into the Principles and Policy of the Government of the United States*. It was in this that he challenged Adams's aristocratic theory and defended a more equalitarian theory of government and society.

The idea of natural aristocracy was repellent to Taylor. He was as strong a believer in social law as was Adams but his interpretation of that law was different. To him equality was not to be understood as equality of opportunity but as equality of moral rights and duties. Aristocracy was an artificial, not a necessary or desirable order. Whether defended by superstition, ignorance, conquest, pope or patronage (which he felt was the basis of existing aristocratic sentiment), aristocracy was always a device cloaking the selfish desire of special interests. He felt the defenders of aristocracy in America were clinging to the skirts of a fated monarchical system of classes, best exemplified in the government of England. He held that nature provided for a body of independent citizens with equal rights before the law. Government was not set up by nature, a nation was; government was the means by which the nation achieved social good.

The basic issue to Taylor was whether the many were to rule with the few as their agents or whether the few were to be given power to determine the fate of the many. He defended the right of the states to instruct their congressmen, for he felt that unless sovereignty were clearly resident in the many government would soon become tyrannical and exclusive. Taylor was no more against the abuse of government than Adams, but he felt that abuse was to be prevented not by setting up a system of orders, but by recognizing sovereignty as resident in the people and by dividing power in government. Taylor thought Adams conceived of the form of government as well as sovereignty to be rooted in nature; on this he could not agree. He thought the object of government to be the welfare of the people, based on the natural desire for self-preservation; its forms should be in fundamental accord with this moral principle, but the form was of secondary importance and not itself based upon nature. As he said, "To contend for forms only, is to fight for shadows."[5] He felt that the government of the United States should not be understood in terms of a hybrid conglomeration of monarchy, aristocracy and democracy, but in terms of the moral ideal it sought.

> Monarchy, aristocracy, and democracy, appeared to the author to be inartificial, rude, and almost savage political fabricks; and the idea of building a new one with the materials they could afford, seemed like that of erecting a palace with materials drawn from Indian cabins. He thought that then respectable commentators, in making the attempt, had allowed little or nothing new or pre-eminent to the policy of the United States; had overlooked both the foundation and the beautiful entablature of its pillars; and had left mankind still enchanted within the magic circle of the numerical analysis.[6]

He was a strong believer in division of power and advocated measures to prevent any one branch of government or any one individual from acquiring too much power: such measures, for example, as a law preventing the reelection of the President and an interpretation of the Constitution which would prohibit the Supreme Court from judging peculiarly intra-state suits. He wanted division of power, however,

[5] *Construction Construed, and Constitutions Vindicated.* 13.

[6] *An Inquiry into the Principles and Policy of the Government of the United States.* "To the Publick."

rather than a balance of power. Division of power meant to him a device for preventing tyranny or control by special interests, balance of power a system whereby different classes within society had a voice in government. He contended that a balance of power suggested natural inequality whereas a division of power prevented inequality because it recognized sovereignty as resident in the people.

Adams, in line with his egotistical and temperamental qualities, did not accept Taylor's criticisms. He contended Taylor misunderstood the whole motive of his book, often misinterpreted him, and introduced problems which had never been broached by him. Nevertheless he recognized Taylor's importance and even complimented him on some of the ideas he expressed in the volume, a thing which Adams rarely did. He received the volume in sections. The answers which he made in the letters to Taylor were based upon the first pages of Taylor's book, included here under the section heading, "Aristocracy." It is very questionable if Adams ever read Taylor's complete volume due to his advancing years but he was still active enough to restate some of his own ideas in clearer form than that in which they had originally appeared. Adams and Taylor could never get together. Their varying interpretations of natural law as applied to social life served as a barrier too great to be overcome. In 1824 Taylor wrote a very gracious letter to Adams in which he said he wanted to go on record as paying tribute to one who had played such an important part in the early struggles of the country. Adams answered this letter, saying Taylor had completely misunderstood him, and again added a few defensive remarks, a letter quite lacking in the generosity and graciousness so characteristic of Taylor. The southern gentleman had engaged in battle with a temperamental Puritan, the southerner remaining a gentleman and the Puritan defending to his dying days the ideas in which he believed.

## REFERENCES

### JOHN TAYLOR

Taylor, John: *A Defense of the Administration of Thomas Jefferson.* Washington, 1804. (Printed under pseudonym, "Curtius.")

———: *Arator: Being a Series of Agricultural Essays, Practical and Political.* Columbia, S. C., 1813.

———: *An Inquiry into the Principles and Policy of the Government of the United States.* Fredericksburg, Va., 1814.

———: *Construction Construed, and Constitutions Vindicated.* Richmond, Va., 1820.

Taylor, John: *Tyranny Unmasked.* Washington, 1822.
———: *New Views of the Constitution of the United States.* Washington, 1823.
Mudge, Eugene T.: *The Social Philosophy of John Taylor of Caroline.* New York: Columbia University Press, 1939.
Simms, H. H.: *Life of John Taylor: The Story of a Brilliant Leader in the Early Virginia State Rights School.* Richmond, Va.: William Byrd Press, 1932.
Wright, B. F.: "The Philosopher of Jeffersonian Democracy," *American Political Science Review* 22 (1928) 870–92.

JOHN ADAMS

Adams, C. F.: *The Works of John Adams, Second President of the United States: with a Life of the Author, Notes and Illustrations.* Boston: Little, Brown and Co., 1850–56.
Adams, J. T.: *The Adams Family.* Boston: Little, Brown and Co., 1930.
Chinard, Gilbert: *Honest John Adams.* Boston: Little, Brown and Co., 1933.
Morse, J. T., Jr.: *John Adams.* Boston: Houghton Mifflin Co., 1885.
Walsh, C. M.: *The Political Science of John Adams: a Study in the Theory of Mixed Government and the Bicameral System.* New York: G. P. Putnam's Sons, 1915.

* * *

---

* * *

JOHN TAYLOR

# AN INQUIRY INTO THE PRINCIPLES AND POLICY OF THE GOVERNMENT OF THE UNITED STATES [7]

## *Aristocracy*

Mr. Adams's political system, deduces government from a natural fate; the policy of the United States deduces it from moral liberty. Every event proceeding from a motive, may, in a moral sense, be termed natural. And in this view, "natural" is a term, which will cover all human qualities. Lest, therefore, the terms "natural and moral" may not suggest a correct idea of the opposite principles, which have produced rival political systems, it is a primary object to ascertain the sense in which they are here used.

[7] Sec. I, 1–8; sec. II, 75–8, 80–4; sec. VI, 435–43.

Man, we suppose to be compounded of two qualities, distinguishable from each other; matter and mind. By mind, we analyze the powers of matter; by matter we cannot analyze the powers of mind. Matter being an agent of inferior power to mind, its powers may be ascertained by mind; but mind being an agent of sovereign power, there is no power able to limit its capacity. The subject cannot be an adequate menstruum for its own solution. Therefore, as we cannot analyze mind, it is generally allowed to be a supernatural quality.

To the human agencies, arising from the mind's power of abstraction, we apply the term "moral;" to such as are the direct and immediate effect of matter, independent of abstraction, the terms "natural or physical." Should Mr. Adams disallow the application of this distinction to his theory, by saying, that when he speaks of natural political systems, he refers both to man's mental and physical powers, and includes whatever the term "moral" can reach; I answer, that it is incorrect to confound in one mass the powers of mind and body, in order to circumscribe those of mind, by applying to the compound, the term "natural," if it is impossible for mind to limit and ascertain its own powers.

Whether the human mind is able to circumscribe its own powers, is a question between the two modern political parties. One (of which Mr. Adams is a disciple) asserts that man can ascertain his own moral capacity, deduces consequences from this postulate, and erects thereon schemes of government—right, say they, because natural. The other, observing that those who affirm the doctrine, have never been able to agree upon this natural form of government; and that human nature has been perpetually escaping from all forms; considers government as capable of unascertained modification and improvement, from moral causes.

To illustrate the question; let us confront Mr. Adams's opinion "that aristocracy is natural, and therefore unavoidable," with one "that it is artificial or factitious, and therefore avoidable." He seems to use the term "natural" to convey an idea distinct from moral, by coupling it with the idea of fatality. But moral causes, being capable of human modification, events flowing from them, possess the quality of freedom or evitation. As the moral efforts, by which ignorance or knowledge are produced, are subjects themselves of election, so ignorance and knowledge, the effects of these moral efforts, are also subjects of election; and ignorance and knowledge are powerful moral causes. If, therefore, by the term "natural" Mr. Adams intended to include "moral," the idea of "fatality" is inaccurately coupled with it; and if he resigns this idea, the infallibility of his system, as being natural, must also be resigned.

That he must resign his political predestination, and all its consequences, I shall attempt to prove, by shewing, that aristocracies, both ancient and modern, have been variable and artificial; that they have all proceeded from moral, not from natural causes; and that they are evitable and not inevitable.

An opinion "that nature makes kings or nobles" has been the creed of political fatalists, from the commencement of the sect; and confronts its rival creed "that liberty and slavery are regulated by political law." However lightly Mr. Adams may speak of Filmer, it is an opinion in which they are associated, and it is selected for discussion, because by its truth or falsehood, the folly or wisdom of the policy of the United States is determined.

In the prosecution of these objects, frequent use will be made of the word "aristocracy," because the ideas at present attached to it, make it more significant than any other.

Mr. Adams rears his system upon two assertions: "That there are only three generical forms of government; monarchy, aristocracy and democracy, of which all other forms are mixtures; and that every society naturally produces an order of men, which it is impossible to confine to an equality of rights." Political power in one man, without division or responsibility, is monarchy; the same power in a few, is aristocracy; and the same power in the whole nation, is democracy. And the resemblance of our system of government to either of these forms, depends upon the resemblance of a president or a governor to a monarch; of an American senate, to an hereditary order; and of a house of representatives, to a legislating nation.

Upon this threefold resemblance Mr. Adams has seized, to bring the political system of America within the pale of the English system of checks and balances, by following the analysis of antiquity; and in obedience to that authority, by modifying our temporary, elective, responsible governors, into monarchs; our senates into aristocratical orders; and our representatives, into a nation personally exercising the functions of government.

Whether the terms "monarchy, aristocracy and democracy," or the one, the few, and the many, are only numerical; or characteristic, like the calyx, petal and stamina of plants; or complicated, with the idea of a balance; they have never yet singly or collectively been used to describe a government, deduced from good moral principles.

If we are unable to discover in our form of government, any resemblance of monarchy, aristocracy or democracy, as defined by ancient writers, and by Mr. Adams himself, it cannot be compounded of all, but must be rooted in some other political element; whence it follows, that the opinion which supposes monarchy, aristocracy and democracy, or mixtures of them, to constitute all the elements of government, is an error, which has produced a numerical or exterior classification, instead of one founded in moral principles.

By this error, the moral efforts of mankind, towards political improvement, have been restrained and disappointed. Under every modification of circumstances these three generical principles of government, or a mixture of them, have been universally allowed to comprise the whole extent of political volition; and whilst the liberty enjoyed by the other sciences, has produced a series of wonderful discoveries; politics, circumscribed by an universal opinion (as astronomy was for centuries) remained stationary from the earliest ages, to the American revolution.

It will be an effort of this essay to prove, that the United States have refuted the ancient axiom, "that monarchy, aristocracy and democracy, are the only elements of government," by planting theirs in moral principles, without any reference to those elements; and that by demolishing the barrier hitherto obstructing the progress of political science, they have cleared the way for improvement.

Mr. Adams's system promises nothing. It tells us that human nature is always the same: that the art of government can never change; that it is contracted into three simple principles; and that mankind must either suffer the evils of one of these simple principles, as at Athens, Venice, or Constantinople; or those of the same principles compounded, as at London, Rome, or Lacedemon. And it gravely counts up several victims of democratic rage, as proofs, that democracy is more pernicious than monarchy or aristocracy. Such a computation is a spectre, calculated to arrest our efforts, and appal our hopes, in pursuit of political good. If it be correct, what motives of preference between forms of government remain? On one hand, Mr. Adams calls our attention to hundreds of wise and virtuous patricians, mangled and bleeding victims of popular fury; on the other, he might have exhibited millions of plebeians, sacrificed to the pride, folly and ambition of monarchy and aristocracy; and, to complete the picture, he ought to have placed right before us, the effects of these three principles commixed, in the wars, rebellions, persecutions and oppressions of the English form, celebrated by Mr. Adams as the most perfect of the mixed class of governments. Is it possible to convince us, that we are compelled to elect one of these evils? After having discovered principles of government, distinct from monarchy, aristocracy or democracy, in the experience of their efficacy, and the enjoyment of their benefits; can we be persuaded to renounce the discovery, to restore the old principles of political navigation, and to steer the commonwealth into the disasters, against which all past ages have pathetically warned us? It is admitted, that man, physically, is "always the same;" but denied that he is so, morally. Upon the truth or error of this distinction, the truth or error of Mr. Adams's mode of reasoning and of this essay, will somewhat depend. If it is untrue, then the cloud of authorities collected by him from all ages, are irrefutable evidence, to establish the fact, that political misery is unavoidable; because man is always the same. But if the moral qualities of human nature are not always the same, but are different both in nations and individuals; and if government ought to be constructed in relation to these moral qualities, and not in relation to factitious orders; these authorities do not produce a conclusion so deplorable. The variety in the kinds and degrees of political misery, is alone conclusive evidence of distinct degrees of moral character, capable of unknown moral efforts.

Supposing that none of Mr. Adams's quotations had been taken from poetical and fabulous authors; that no doubt could exist of the truth of those furnished by ancient historians; and that they had not been dexterously selected to fit an hypothesis; yet their whole weight would have depended upon the similarity of moral circumstances, between the people of America, and those of Greece, Italy, Switzerland, England, and a multitude of countries, collected from all ages into our modern theatre.

Do the Americans recognize themselves in a group of Goths, Vandals, Italians, Turks and Chinese? If not, man is not always morally the same. If man is not always morally the same, it is not true that he requires the same political regimen. And thence a conclusion of considerable weight follows, to overthrow the ground-work of Mr. Adams's system; for by proving, if he had proved it, that his system was proper for those men, and those times, resorted to by him for its illustration, he proves that it is not proper for men and times of dissimilar moral characters and circumstances.

The traces of intellectual originality and diversity; the shades and novelties of the human character, between the philosopher and the savage; between different countries, different governments, and different eras; exhibit a complexity, which the politician and philologist have never been able to unravel. Out of this intellectual variety, arises the impossibility of contriving one form of government, suitable for every nation; and also the fact, that human nature, instead of begetting one form constantly, demonstrates its moral capacity, in the vast variety of its political productions.

Having apprized the reader, by these general remarks, of the political principles to be vindicated or assailed in this essay; and that an effort will be made to prove, that the policy of the United States is rooted in moral or intellectual principles, and not in orders, clans, or casts, natural or factitious; this effort must be postponed, until the way is opened to it, by a more particular review of Mr. Adams's system. To this, therefore, I return.

He supposes "that every society must *naturally* produce an aristocratical order of men, which it will be impossible to confine to an equality of rights with other men." To determine the truth of this position, an inquiry must be made into the mode by which these orders have been produced in those countries, placed before us by Mr. Adams, as objects of terror or imitation.

In order to understand the question correctly, it is proper to hear Mr. Adams state it himself. Throughout his book, it is constantly appearing, as constituting the great principle upon which his system is founded; but here it can only appear in a quotation, selected as concise, explicit and unequivocal.

These sources of inequality, [says he] which are common to every people, and can never be altered by any, *because they are founded in the constitution of nature;* this *natural* aristocracy among mankind, has been dilated on, because it is a fact essential to be considered in the constitution of a government. It is a body of men which contains the greatest collection of *virtues and abilities* in a free government; *the brightest ornament and glory of a nation; and may always be made the greatest blessing of society, if it be judiciously managed in the constitution.* But if it is not, it is always the most dangerous; nay it may be added, it never fails to be the destruction of the commonwealth. What shall be done to guard against it? There is but one expedient yet discovered, to avail the society of all the benefits from this body of men, which they are capable of affording, and at the same time prevent them from undermining or invading the public liberty; *and that is to throw them all, or at least the most remarkable of them, into one assembly together, in the legislature;* to keep all the executive power entirely out of their hands, as a body; *to erect a first magistrate over them invested with the whole executive authority;* to make them dependant on that executive magistrate for all public executive employments; to give that magistrate a negative on the legislature, by which he may defend both himself and the people from all their enterprises in the legislature; and to erect on the other side of them, an impregnable barrier against them, *in a house of commons fairly, fully, and adequately representing the people,* who shall have the power of negativing all their attempts at encroachments in the legislature, and of withholding both from them *and the crown* all supplies, by which they may be paid for their services in executive offices, or even the public service carried on to the detriment of the nation.[8]

This is the text on which it is proposed to comment; incidentally considering several of the arguments, by which its doctrine is defended, without the formality of frequent quotations. It contains the substance of Mr. Adams's system, and is evidently the English form of government, excepting an equal representation of the people, in the proposed house of commons.

## *The Principles of the Policy of the United States, and of the English Policy*

Before we proceed to the consideration of the policy of the United States, it is necessary to discover a political analysis, founded in some moral principle; because government is as strictly subject to the moral, as a physical being is to the physical laws of nature. Persons are not principles; and hence the operations of monarchy, aristocracy and democracy (governments founded in persons) are fluctuating; generally evil, but sometimes good; whereas the effects of a moral principle are ever the same. Mr. Adams, however, adopts the ancient analysis of governments, asserts that it comprises all their generical forms, and adds "that every society naturally produces an order of men, which it is impossible to confine to an equality of rights;" and he erects his system upon the foundations of this ancient analysis, and of a natural or unavoidable aristocracy. If society cannot exist without aristocracy, (as it cannot, if aristocracy is natural to society,) then democracy and monarchy cannot be generical forms of government, unless they can exist without society or with aristocracy. This disagreement between the ancient analysis, and a system bottomed upon it, at the threshold of their association; and Mr. Adams's idea that one of his generical forms of government was a natural consequence of society, without contending that the others were, excited doubts of the correctness of that analysis. If monarchy, aristocracy and democracy are all natural or generical forms of government, nature has determined on Mr. Adams's mixed government, and his labours in favour of her will, were super-

[8] Adams's Def. P. 116–117—vol. i. 3d Philadelphia edition.

fluous; but if either of these forms is artificial, it could not be natural or generical, and an invention of one form by the human intellect, is no proof that it is unable to invent another. The terms monarchy, aristocracy and democracy, convey adequate ideas of particular forms of government, but they are insufficient for the purpose of disclosing a government which will certainly be free and moderate, since the effects of each depend on the administration of wise and good, or of weak and wicked men: and all are therefore founded in the same principle, however differing in form. This both suggests a doubt of the soundness of the ancient analysis, and a solution of the phenomenon "that all these natural or generical forms of government should produce bad effects." The effects of these three forms are bad, because they are all founded on one principle, namely, an irresponsible undivided power; and that principle is bad. We want an analysis, distinguishing governments in point of substance, and not limited to form.

The moral qualities of human nature are good and evil. An analysis founded in this truth, however general, can alone ascertain the true character, and foretell the effects of any form of government, or of any social measure. Every such form and measure must have a tendency to excite the good or the evil moral qualities of man; and according to its source, so will be its tendency with moral certainty.

The strongest moral propensity of man, is to do good to himself. This begets a propensity to do evil to others, for the sake of doing good to himself. A sovereignty of the people, or self-government, is suggested by the first moral propensity; responsibility, division, and an exclusion of monarchy and aristocracy, by the second.

Self love, being the strongest motive to do evil to others, as well as good to ourselves, will operate as forcibly to excite an individual or a faction to injure a nation for advancing self good, as to excite a nation to preserve its own happiness. Therefore, whilst national self government, is founded in the strongest moral quality for producing national good; every other species of government, is founded in the strongest moral quality for producing national evil.

The objection to this analysis is, that nations may oppress individuals or minorities. An imperfection does not destroy comparative superiority; and should one be found in a form of government bottomed upon the quality of a nation's love for itself, it will not diminish the defects of forms, bottomed upon the self love of individuals or minorities, if these are as likely to oppress majorities, as majorities are to oppress these.

The quality, self love, stimulates in proportion to the good or gratification in view. This prospect to an individual or minority, having power to extract good or gratification from a nation, must be infinitely more alluring, than to a nation, having power to extract good or gratification from an individual or a minority; and as the excitement to injure others, for gratifying ourselves, will be in proportion to the extent of the gratification, it follows, that an individual or minority will be infinitely more likely to oppress a nation for self gratification, than a nation, for the same end, to oppress an individual or minority.

The certainty with which moral inferences flow from moral causes, is illustrated by a computation of the cases, in which the quality of self love, has induced nations to oppress individuals, or individuals to oppress nations. The anomaly of a nation's becoming a tyrant over an individual, would be nearer to the character of prodigy, than even that of monarchy or aristocracy, preferring national good or gratification, to its own.

It is from the want of some test, to determine whether a form of government, or law, is founded in the good or evil qualities of man, that the disciples of monarchy, aristocracy and democracy, have entered into the field of controversy, with so much zeal. Each, though blinded to the defects of the system he defends, from education, habit, or a supposed necessity of enlisting under one, clearly discerns the defects of the system espoused by his adversary; and despises him for a blindness, similar to his own. That monarchy, aristocracy and democracy will all make men miserable, is universally assented to, by two out of the three members of this analysis itself; and a contrary effect from either, is allowed by two to one to be out of the common course of events. A violation of the relation between cause and effect, awakens the admiration of mankind, whenever a good moral effect proceeds from a government founded in evil moral qualities.

It is not enough for the illustration of our analysis, that a good effect from either monarchy, aristocracy or democracy, is by this majority considered as a phenomenon; a few reasons, accounting for it according to the principles of that analysis, will be added.

Monarchy and aristocracy, have the strongest tendency of any conceivable human situation, to excite the evil moral quality, or propensity, of injuring others for our own benefit, both by the magnitude of the temptation, and the power of reaching it. A long catalogue of evil moral qualities, are included in this. These forms of government are therefore founded in the evil moral qualities of man, and it is unnatural that evil moral qualities, should produce good moral effects.

. . . . . .

The inherent evil nature of monarchy, aristocracy and democracy, can only furnish a solution of the fact, testified by all history, "that each separately, any two, and the three however mingled, have uniformly produced evil effects, which have driven mankind into a multitude of exchanges and modifications." From all, disappointment has issued, because good effects could not be extracted from evil principles. At length, all philosophers, politicians and learned men have been taught by experience to unite in one opinion. They universally agree, that monarchy, aristocracy and democracy, acting separately, will produce evil to nations; they agree, that any two will operate oppressively; and they also agree that the three, however blended, excluding the modern idea of representation, will also operate oppressively. Is it then possible; that the ancient analysis of political systems, which separately or combined, presented only a form of government now universally acknowledged to be bad, could have been correct?

From a belief that a political analysis does exist, capable of arranging all forms of government into two classes; one rooted in good, and the other in evil moral qualities; and that monarchy, aristocracy and democracy, singly or united, belong to the latter class; the idea has been brought before the reader preparatory to arguments designed to prove, that the civil policy of the United States must be assigned to the first class; that it is of course at enmity with Mr. Adams's mixture of monarchy, aristocracy and representation; but that certain of its details and laws, are at enmity with its essential principles, for want of some distinct analysis as a test to ascertain their nature and effects. A position contended for is, "that political temptations, which propel to vice, are founded in evil moral principles."

The reader is solicited for the last time, to keep in mind, that in this essay, the term "democracy" means "a government administered by the people," and not "the right of the people to institute a government, nor the responsibility of magistrates to the people." The contrast of the ancient analysis between its three forms of government, is imperfect unless democracy is thus understood, since the two terms opposed to it, are used to specify governments, as numerically administered. Monarchy and aristocracy mean, governments administered by one or a few, and not a right in one or a few to institute a government, and make it responsible to the institutor. Democracy also meant, a government administered by the people personally. The distinction is considered as useful, for relieving the mind from an association, between the sovereignty of the people, and the evils produced by a nation's exercising the functions of government.

Let us now take up the thread of this essay. I have endeavoured to prove that aristocracy is artificial and not natural; that the aristocracies of superstition and landed wealth, have been destroyed by knowledge, commerce and alienation; that a new aristocracy has arisen during the last century from paper and patronage, of a character so different from titled orders, as not to be compressible within Mr. Adams's system; and that his system is evidently defective, in having silently past over this powerful aristocracy, now existing in England.

By the civil policy of the United States, I mean the general and state constitutions, as forming one system. Most of the state constitutions existed when Mr. Adams wrote, and no new principles have been introduced by those since created. The differences among them all, consist only in modifications of the same principles. As immaterial is the anachronism of applying Mr. Adams's reasoning to the general constitution, because if his system is inimical to that, it must have been more so to the state constitutions he professed to defend; as in that, the executive and senatorial lines are drawn with a stronger pencil than in those.[9]

Mr. Adams's system simply is, "that nature will create an aristocracy, and that policy ought to create a king, or a single, independent executive power, and a house of popular representatives, to balance it."

Let one of the state constitutions speak for the rest. That of Massachusetts declares, that

all men are born free and equal. [That] no man, or corporation, or association of men, have any other title to obtain advantages, or particular and exclusive privileges, distinct from those of the community, than what arises from the consideration of services, rendered to the publick. And this title being, *in nature,* neither hereditary, nor transmissible to children, or descendants, or relations by blood, the idea of a man born a magistrate, law-giver or judge, is absurd and unnatural. [That] the people have the sole and exclusive right of governing themselves. [That] government is instituted for the common good, for the protection, safety, prosperity, and happiness of the people; and not for the profit, honour, or private interest of any one man, family, or class of men. [And that] in order to prevent those, who are vested with authority, from becoming oppressors, the people have a right, at such periods, and in such manner, as they shall establish by their frame of government, to cause their publick officers to return to private life; and to fill up vacant places, by certain and regular elections and appointments.

[9] Adams's Def. 3 v. 187 and 426.

Two principles are clearly expressed by them all; one, that every person in authority is responsible and removable; the other, that talents, virtue, and political power, are not inheritable.

These principles are precisely levelled at the opinions, that monarchy is divine, and nobility natural; the first asserted by Filmer, the last by Mr. Adams. And they treat the idea of hereditary power, contended for by Mr. Adams, as *"absurd and unnatural."* [10]

The constitutions build their policy upon the basis of human equality —"all men are born free and equal;" and erect the artificial inequalities of civil government, with a view of preserving and defending the natural equality of individuals. Mr. Adams builds his policy upon the basis of human inequality by nature—"aristocracy is natural;" and proposes to produce an artificial level or equality, not of individuals, but of orders, composed of individuals naturally unequal. Yet the disciples of the balance, accuse the republicans of levelism.

It is necessary to affix a correct idea to the term "equality," contended for by the constitutions, and denied by Mr. Adams. They do not mean an equality of stature, strength or understanding, but an equality of moral rights and duties. The constitutions admit of no inequality in these moral rights and duties, excepting that produced by temporary and responsible power, conferred "for the common good." Mr. Adams contends for a natural inequality of moral rights and duties, in contending for a natural aristocracy. The constitutions establish the inequalities of temporary and responsible power, with a view of maintaining an equality of moral rights and duties among the individuals of society; and Mr. Adams proposes orders, with a view of maintaining his natural inequality among men, by balancing or equalising the rights of orders.

The constitutions consider a nation as made of individuals; Mr. Adams's system, as made of orders. Nature, by the constitutions, is considered as the creator of men; by the system, of orders. The first idea suggests the sovereignty of the people, and the second refutes it; because, if nature creates the ranks of the one, the few and the many, the nation must be compounded of these ranks; and one rank, politically, is the third part of a nation. These ranks composing the nation, have of course a power to alter the form of government at any time, without consulting the people, because the people do not constitute the nation. An illustration of this idea has several times occurred in the English practice of Mr. Adams's system.

[10] Mr. Adams calls Filmer's notions "ABSURD AND SUPERSTITIOUS." Vol. 1. 7.

## *The Good Moral Principles of the Government of the United States*

The project of hereditary systems, is to destroy the morals of one part of a community by power, in order to preserve the morals of the rest, by despotism. Hence it is compelled to multiply punishments for crimes which it causes; and to defend itself against punishment, for having caused the crimes which it punishes. It corrupts the morals of the few, under pretence of restraining the vices of the many; and this corruption is a source of more vice than it restrains.

Our policy takes a wider range. It is not so miserably defective, as to make one part of a nation worse, for the sake of making another better. It considers government as intended to improve the manners and happiness of the whole nation; and instead of leaving half its work undone, proposes to finish it, by providing for the manners and happiness of those who govern, as well as of those who are governed. It applies the reason for civil government, not partially, but generally; not to particular orders, but to nations; not to individuals, but to totals. This reason simply is, that the restraint of accountableness, improves the manners and happiness of mankind. Unable to see a distinction in nature, between man and man, our system has made that happy discovery, by which the salutary restraint of accountableness, may be extended to every individual of a nation. Instead of leaving some men to the guidance of an uncontrolled will or in a state of nature, it subjects all to law; and instead of sublimating the evil qualities of human nature, to their highest degree of acrimony, by power unrestrained, it subjects it in as well as out of office to government. It does not attempt to prevent a viper from biting by irritation.

Whether man is naturally virtuous or vicious, is a question, furnishing however determined, no just argument in favour of hereditary systems. If the most transcendent virtue is hardly proof against the seduction of exorbitant power, these systems, in their own defence, ought to prove, that mankind are by nature virtuous. If he is vicious, his restraints ought to be multiplied in proportion to his power to do mischief; if virtuous, it strengthens the reasons derived from self love, for leaving moral power, where nature has placed physical.

Estimated by its sympathies, human nature discloses a vast preponderance of virtuous sensations. It spontaneously shrinks from an expression of rage, and is drawn towards one of joy; whilst ignorant of the cause of either; because one is an emblem of vice, and the other of virtue.

Horrible or impious, as the atomical philosophy may be, it cannot be more so, than the idea of a natural depravity in man, rendering him unfit for self government. One doctrine assails the existence of a God; the other, his power or goodness. If man, the noblest creature of this world; if mind, the noblest attribute of this creature; are both incorrigibly imperfect; the inference that the world itself is a bad work, is unavoidable. Man's case is hopeless. If he is the creature of malignity or imbecility, and doomed to be governed by fiends, naturally as bad, and artificially made worse than himself, where is his refuge? Shall he fly to the hereditary system, which teaches him to despair; or adhere to one, which inspires him with hope? The hereditary system which having almost exclusively exercised the office of forming the human character since the creation of the world, very gravely urges as a reason in favor of its regimen, that its work is detestable.

Upon this wretch, man, however wicked he may be, nature has unequivocally bestowed one boon. This blessing, the hereditary system proposes to deprive him of; our policy uses it as the principle of civil government; it is the right of self preservation. No other government, ancient or modern, has fairly provided for the safety of this right. In all others, it is fettered by compounds of orders or separate interests; by force or by fraud. Between governments which leave to nations the right of self preservation, and those which destroy it, we must take our stand, to determine on which side the preference lies. A coincident view of happiness and misery, will presently transform this line, into a wide gulf, on the farther side of which, we shall behold the governed of all other nations, expressing their agonies. Shall we go to them, because they cannot come to us?

The restraint of governours, or the laws impressed on them by the nation, termed political, in this essay, constitutes the essential distinction between the policy of the United States, and of other countries. Machiavel, in deciding that a "free government cannot be maintained, when the people have grown corrupt;" and in admitting monarchy, "to be the proper corrective of a corrupt people," has reasoned from false principles to false conclusions, because he had not discerned this distinction. He supposes orders proper to maintain liberty, whilst the people are virtuous; and that they are hurtful, when the people become corrupt; and taking it for granted, that liberty cannot exist without virtue, nor without orders, he dooms all nations to orders or to monarchy. If vicious, he saddles them with political orders; if virtuous, with an avenger instead of a reformer. History has neither related, nor fable feigned, that monarchs or demons reform the wicked committed to their durance. His errour lay in an utter ignorance of restraining governments. He never considered whether a corrupt nation might not establish a free political system, as avaricious mercantile partners establish just articles of partnership; and that it would be the interest of the majority to do so, because slavish political systems, inevitably prey upon majorities; nor whether this interest, united with common sense, would not induce majorities, since they cannot be lasting tyrants themselves, to absolve themselves from tyranny. Orders and national virtue united, says Machiavel, produce liberty; but if virtue disappears, liberty ceases. Others, split up this dogma. Virtue, say they, will produce liberty; and without it, liberty cannot exist. Orders, says Mr. Adams, will produce liberty. If in the case of the compound dogma of Machiavel, virtue and liberty disappear, whilst orders remain, the orders were not the cause of the liberty. If the virtue and liberty remain, after orders disappear, as in America, the orders caused neither the virtue nor the liberty. And if orders will produce liberty, according to Mr. Adams, the necessity for virtue to preserve liberty does not exist.

This confusion arises from the substitution of moral artifice, which may be good or bad, for good moral principles. Virtue, or moral goodness, may overpower an evil moral artifice, and for a short space preserve national liberty, against the assaults of a bad form of government. National virtue, pervading both the governours and people, like individual virtue, is a sponsor for happiness; and whilst political writers tell us that an assembly of good moral principles, embraced by the term virtue, will produce their natural effects, they say nothing in favour of evil moral artifices. The general acknowledgement of the capacity of good moral principles to correct a bad form of government, is a vast encouragement to expect from them a capacity to correct bad governours; and hence our policy has resorted to the good and virtuous moral principle of responsibility, or a strong code of political law, which can exist and operate upon governours, if the nation understands its interest, at whatever degree of virtue or corruption it may be stationed, in fact or in theory.

If orders (a moral artifice) should become corrupt, they are then, says Machiavel, hurtful to liberty; and he recommends one of these corrupt orders, a king, as a cure for the hurt. Bolingbroke observes, "Instead of wondering that so many kings, unfit and unworthy to be trusted with the government of mankind, appear in the world, I have been tempted to wonder that there are any tolerable;"[11] and "a patriot king is a kind of miracle."[12] If the moral artifice, "orders," should become corrupt, Machiavel's remedy is Bolingbroke's miracle. These are ranked among the first class of political writers. "Nothing can restrain the propensity of orders to hurt liberty, but virtue," says Machiavel. "Good kings are not to be expected by the laws of nature," says Bolingbroke. Yet they concur in favour of orders. Each decides against his own reasoning, because both being enslaved to the old tenet of the one, the few and the many, neither contemplated the abolition of orders or monarchy, nor the invention of a sound restraint upon the vices of governments, now practically illustrated in every state in the Union. In fact, neither of them saw the difference between a moral artifice, and a moral principle. Bolingbroke's alternative, of an elective or hereditary monarch, is unnecessary, because both are evil moral artifices, which may be superseded by a political system, founded in good moral principles. If inconveniences appear in the United States on the election of presidents, it will only demonstrate that we have approached too near to the moral artifice, called an elective monarchy, and that we ought to recede from this bad moral artifice, nearer to the good moral principle of a division of power. Neither of these writers entertained the least idea of a policy founded in fixed and good moral principles, and have only laboured like Bayes, in his dance of the sun, the moon and the earth, to invent new postures for the triumvirate of the old political analysis.

Bolingbroke says, "that absolute stability, is not to be expected in any thing human; all that can be done, therefore, to prolong the duration of a good government, is to draw it back, on every favorable occasion, to the *first good principles* on which it was founded." Does he mean by carrying a government back to *good principles,* to carry it back to monarchy, aristocracy, democracy, or to some mixture of them? Such was not his meaning, because these human contrivances are not principles themselves, but founded in, or deduced from principles. And whether either, or any mixture of two or all, is founded in good or bad moral principles, is the immemorial subject of political controversy. If he did not mean that a decaying government should seek for regeneration in some one of these human contrivances, the moral nature of which remained to be tried by the test of principles; or that the test was its own subject; he has explicitly admitted the existence of

[11] Patriot King. 88.
[12] 117.

a political analysis, both the ancestor and judge of the ancient analysis of governments, and also of every conceivable form which can be invented. Upon this anterior analysis, the policy of the United States is founded. We resort to it as the test by which to discover whether either member of the old forms of government, or any mixture of them, is good or bad. It is not a fluctuating, but permanent tribunal. Its authority is divine, and its distinctions perspicuous. And if it shall supersede the erroneous idea, that mankind are manacled down to monarchy, aristocracy or democracy, as the only principles of government, the effect of diminishing the instability of human affairs, by a resort to unchangeable principles, may be fairly anticipated.

Without considering "good principles," as distinct from forms of government, a return to them, for political regeneration, could not convey a single idea. A government may commence in monarchy, aristocracy or democracy, and degenerate from either to another. Recessions to and from all forms of government may take place, and therefore these forms could not be intended by "good principles," because these fluctuating recessions would, under that idea, make all forms good, and all bad.

The inability of the old analysis to define a good form of government, and its destitution of some beacon by which to steer back to the harbour of safety, from an ocean of corruption, is thus apparent. It only tells mankind, when unhappy under monarchy, aristocracy or democracy, to go back from one to another, or to some mixture of them. Whereas the analysis of this essay, by arranging governments according to the principles in which they are founded, discloses the mode of their preservation in a state of purity, and also the way to restore that purity whenever it is impaired.

Although the idea of going back to *first good principles* has been repeated into a maxim, it is seldom honestly explained or applied; nor has it ever been confessed, that the phrase explodes the old, and suggests a more correct analysis of governments. Its correctness and power is illustrated, by supposing that sedition laws, or a chartered stock aristocracy, are deviations from our *first good principles*. How is the deviation to be discovered? By launching into the ocean of the old analysis and its mixtures? No. By bringing it to the test of the new analysis, founded in moral principles. If it is thus discovered, how are nations to return to their *first good principles?* By taking refuge in monarchy, aristocracy, democracy, or a mixture of them? No. By repealing laws deviating from its *first good principles*. One of these illustrations will also serve to display the errour and fraud of the artifice, by which mankind have been persuaded to subscribe to the following syllogism—"Man cannot possess free government, unless he is virtuous; but he is vicious; therefore he cannot possess free government"—so ingeniously invented, and so comfortably recommended in all ages, by patriotick kings, ministers and nobles. Now if the banking system is a mode, however ingenious, of oppressing a majority, that majority, however corrupt, may remove the oppression. And if the corruption itself, shall have been chiefly produced by the oppressing system, as is generally the case, then the removal of the oppression, is the true remedy for the corruption. Not so, say Machiavel and Montesquieu; virtue being gone, freedom has fled beyond the reach of a nation, and oppression or monarchy is the remedy.

The interest of a vicious majority to remove oppression from itself, is as strong as if it was virtuous; and the coincidence between its interest and reformation, is a foundation for an honest politician to build on. If avarice and fraud are propagated by laws for amassing wealth at the expense of a majority, the pecuniary interest of this majority to destroy these laws, is the strongest ground for effecting a reformation of the corrupt manners they have produced. And the just laws of a vicious majority, in self defence, will have a wide influence in the re-establishment of virtue; whereas no corrupt minority whatever, composed either of orders or separate interests, can be actuated by self interest to enact just laws, the best restorers of good manners.

There are two considerations which sustain this reasoning. First, that man is more prone to reason than to errour. Secondly, that he is more prone to self love than to self enmity. Notwithstanding the first propensity, every man, however wise, is liable to err; and an occasional errour of a wise man may ruin a nation. The general propensity of the whole species, will usually impress its own character, upon a general opinion, and is undoubtedly less liable to errour, than the conclusions of an individual. It is safer to confide in this propensity, than in individual infallibility. One exists, the other does not. One is ever honest, the other often knavish. The force of self love, is as strong in majorities, as in an individual, but its effect is precisely contrary. It excites one man to do wrong, because he is surrounded with objects of oppression; and majorities to do right, because they can find none. Their errours of judgment are abandoned, so soon as they are seen, whilst the despotism of one man is more strongly fortified for being discovered. The old analysis intrusts great power to individuals and minorities; and provides no mode of controlling their natural vicious propensities. Our policy deals out to them power more sparingly, and superadds a sovereign, whose propensity is towards reason, and whose self interest is an excitement to justice. Such is the competitor of the sovereign of the old analysis, of which even its advocate, Bolingbroke, admits, that a good one would be a miracle. To avoid reasons, so strong in favour of our species of sovereignty, kings, nobles, and even mobs, have claimed a divine right to govern, because there existed no ground between the right of self government and authority from God. It was obvious, that a nation, like an individual, could never become a tyrant over itself, and therefore all abuses of good moral principles, whether in the form of the ancient analysis, or of the modern aristocracy of paper and patronage, find means to control and defeat national self government, either by the impiety of fathering tyranny upon God, or by the fraud of admitting but evading its pretensions. And though it is at length confessed, that nations have a right to destroy tyrants, the difficulty of finding a tyrant willing to be destroyed, remains. Monarchy, aristocracy, hierarchy, patronage, and ambition, still urge every plea, however false, which transient circumstances may render plausible; even the paper aristocracy of the United States, though constructed of republicans, would surrender the sanctity of tyrannical kings, to secure a sanctity for tyrannical charters; and whilst it strives to find refuge for the latter, under some good word, joins in dragging the former from under the throne of God himself.

* * *

---

* * *

## JOHN ADAMS

# LETTERS TO JOHN TAYLOR OF CAROLINE, VIRGINIA IN REPLY TO HIS STRICTURES ON SOME PARTS OF "THE DEFENSE OF THE AMERICAN CONSTITUTIONS"[13]

## I

SIR,—I have received your *Inquiry* in a large volume neatly bound. Though I have not read it in course, yet, upon an application to it of

[13] Written from April 15, 1814 on. *Works.* VI, (letter I) 447–9; (V) 456–8; (XII) 471–2; (XXI, XXII) 491–6; (XXVI) 504–6; (XXXII) 518–21.

the *Sortes Virgilianae*, scarce a page has been found in which my name is not mentioned, and some public sentiment or expression of mine examined. Revived as these subjects are, in this manner, in the recollection of the public, after an oblivion of so many years, by a gentleman of your high rank, ample fortune, learned education, and powerful connections, I flatter myself it will not be thought improper in me to solicit your attention to a few explanations and justifications of a book that has been misunderstood, misrepresented, and abused, more than any other, except the Bible, that I have ever read.

In the first words of the first section, you say, "Mr. Adams's political system deduces government from a *natural* fate; the policy of the United States deduces it from *moral* liberty."

This sentence, I must acknowledge, passes all my understanding. I know not what is meant by fate, nor what distinction there is, or may be made or conceived, between a natural and artificial, or unnatural fate. Nor do I well know what *"moral liberty"* signifies. I have read a great deal about the words *fate* and *chance;* but though I close my eyes to abstract my meditations, I never could conceive any idea of either. When an action or event happens or occurs without a cause, some say it happens by chance. This is equivalent to saying that chance is no cause at all; it is nothing. Fate, too, is no cause, no agent, no power; it has neither understanding, will, affections, liberty, nor choice; it has no existence; it is not even a figment of imagination; it is a mere invention of a word without a meaning; it is a nonentity; it is nothing. Mr. Adams most certainly never deduced any system from chance or fate, natural, artificial, or unnatural.

Liberty, according to my metaphysics, is an intellectual quality; an attribute that belongs not to fate nor chance. Neither possesses it, neither is capable of it. There is nothing moral or immoral in the idea of it. The definition of it is a self-determining power in an intellectual agent. It implies thought and choice and power; it can elect between objects, indifferent in point of morality, neither morally good nor morally evil. If the substance in which this quality, attribute, adjective, call it what you will, exists, has a moral sense, a conscience, a moral faculty; if it can distinguish between moral good and moral evil, and has power to choose the former and refuse the latter, it can, if it will, choose the evil and reject the good, as we see in experience it very often does.

"Mr. Adams's system," and "the policy of the United States," are drawn from the same sources, deduced from the same principles, wrought into the same frame; indeed, they are the same, and ought never to have been divided or separated; much less set in opposition to each other, as they have been.

That we may more clearly see how these hints apply, certain technical terms must be defined.

1. Despotism. A sovereignty unlimited, that is,—the *suprema lex,* the *summa potestatis* in one. This has rarely, if ever, existed but in theory.

2. Monarchy. Sovereignty in one, variously limited.

3. Aristocracy. Sovereignty in a few.

4. Democracy. Sovereignty in the many, that is, in the whole nation, the whole body, assemblage, congregation, or if you are an Episcopalian you may call it if you please, *church,* of the whole people. This sovereignty must, in all cases, be exerted or exercised by the whole people assembled together. This form of government has seldom, if ever, existed but in theory; as rarely, at least, as an unlimited despotism in one individual.

5. The infinite variety of mixed governments are all so many different combinations, modifications, and intermixtures of the second, third, and fourth species or divisions.

Now, every one of these sovereigns possesses intellectual liberty to act for the public good or not. Being men, they have all what Dr. Rush calls a *moral faculty;* Dr. Hutcheson, a *moral sense;* and the Bible and the generality of the world, *a conscience.* They are all, therefore, under moral obligations to do to others as they would have others *do to them;* to consider themselves born, authorized, empowered for the good of society as well as their own good. Despots, monarchs, aristocrats, democrats, holding such high trusts, are under the most solemn and the most sacred moral obligations, to consider their trusts and their power to be instituted for the benefit and happiness of their nations, not their nations as servants to them or their friends or parties. In other words, to exert all their intellectual liberty to employ all their faculties, talents, and power for the public, general, universal good of their nations, not for their own separate good, or the interest of any party.

In this point of view, there is no difference in forms of government. All of them, and all men concerned in them,—all are under equal moral obligations. The intellectual liberty of aristocracies and democracies can be exerted only by votes, and ascertained only by ayes and noes. The sovereign judgment and will can be determined, known, and declared, only by majorities. This will, this decision, is sometimes determined by a single vote; often by two or three; very rarely by a large majority; scarcely ever by a unanimous suffrage. And from the impossibility of keeping together at all times the same number of voters, the majorities are apt to waver from day to day, and swing like a pendulum from side to side.

Nevertheless, the minorities have, in all cases, the same intellectual liberty, and are under the same moral obligations as the majorities.

In what manner these theoretical, intellectual liberties have been exercised, and these moral obligations fulfilled, by despots, monarchs, aristocrats, and democrats, is obvious enough in history and in experience. They have all in general conducted themselves alike.

But this investigation is not at present before us.

## V

When your new democratical republic meets, you will find half a dozen men of independent fortunes; half a dozen, of more eloquence; half a dozen, with more learning; half a dozen, with eloquence, learning, and fortune.

Let me see. We have now four-and-twenty; to these we may add six more, who will have more art, cunning, and intrigue, than learning, eloquence, or fortune. These will infallibly soon unite with the twenty-four. Thus we make thirty. The remaining seventy are composed of farmers, shopkeepers, merchants, tradesmen, and laborers. Now, if each of these thirty can, by any means, influence one vote besides his own, the whole thirty can carry sixty votes,—a decided and uncontrolled majority of the hundred. These thirty I mean by aristocrats; and they will instantly convert your democracy of ONE HUNDRED into an aristocracy of THIRTY.

Take at random, or select with your utmost prudence, one hundred of your most faithful and capable domestics from your own numerous plantations, and make them a democratical republic. You will immediately perceive the same inequalities, and the same democratical republic, in a very few of the first sessions, transformed into an aristocratical republic; as complete and perfect an aristocracy as the senate of Rome, and much more so. Some will be beloved and followed, others hated and avoided by their fellows.

It would be easy to quote Greek and Latin, to produce a hundred authorities to show the original signification of the word *aristocracy* and its infinite variations and application in the history of ages. But this would be all waste water. Once for all, I give you notice, that whenever I use the word *aristocrat,* I mean a citizen who can command or govern two votes or more in society, whether by his virtues, his talents, his learning, his loquacity, his taciturnity, his frankness, his reserve, his face, figure, eloquence, grace, air, attitude, movements, wealth, birth, art, address, intrigue, good fellowship, drunkenness, debauchery, fraud, perjury, violence, treachery, pyrrhonism, deism, or atheism; for by every one of these instruments have votes been obtained and will be obtained. You seem to think aristocracy consists altogether in artificial titles, tinsel decorations of stars, garters, ribbons, golden eagles and golden fleeces, crosses and roses and lilies, exclusive privileges, hereditary descents, established by kings or by positive laws of society. No such thing! Aristocracy was, from the beginning, now is, and ever will be, world without end, independent of all these artificial regulations, as really and as efficaciously as with them!

Let me say a word more. Your democratical republic picked in the streets, and your democratical African republic, or your domestic republic, call it which you will, in its first session, will become an aristocratical republic. In the second session it will become an oligarchical republic; because the seventy-four democrats and the twenty-six aristocrats will, by this time, discover that thirteen of the aristocrats can command four votes each; these thirteen will now command the majority, and, consequently, will be sovereign. The thirteen will then be an oligarchy. In the third session, it will be found that among these thirteen oligarchs there are seven, each of whom can command eight votes, equal in all to fifty-six, a decided majority. In the fourth session, it will be found that there are among these seven oligarchs four who can command thirteen votes apiece. The republic then becomes an oligarchy, whose sovereignty is in four individuals. In the fifth session, it will be discovered that two of the four can command six-and-twenty votes each. Then two will have the command of the sovereign oligarchy. In the sixth session, there will be a sharp contention between the two which shall have the command of the fifty-two votes. Here will commence the squabble of Danton and Robespierre, of Julius and Pompey, of Anthony and Augustus, of the white rose and the red rose, of Jefferson and Adams, of Burr and Jefferson, of Clinton and Madison, or, if you will, of Napoleon and Alexander.

This, my dear sir, is the history of mankind, past, present, and to come.

## XII

You "are unable to discover in our form of government any resemblance of aristocracy."

As every branch of executive authority committed or intrusted exclusively to one, resembles and is properly called a monarchical power, and a government, in proportion as its powers, legislative or executive, are lodged in one, resembles monarchy, so whatever authority or power of making or executing laws is exclusively vested in a few is properly called aristocratical; and a government, in proportion as it is constituted with such powers, resembles aristocracy.

Now, sir, let me ask you, whether you can discover no "resemblance of aristocracy in our form of government?" Are not great, very great, important, and essential powers intrusted to a few, a very few? Thirty-four senators, composed of two senators from each state, are an integral part of the legislature, which is the representative sovereignty of seven or eight millions of the people in the United States. These thirty-four men possess an absolute negative on all the laws of the nation. Nor is this all. These few, these very few, thirty-four citizens only in seven or eight millions, have an absolute negative upon the executive authority in the appointment of all officers in the diplomacy, in the navy, the army, the customs, excises, and revenues. They have, moreover, an absolute negative on all treaties with foreign powers, even with the aboriginal Indians. They are also an absolute judicature in all impeachments, even of the judges. Such are the powers in legislation, in execution, and in judicature, which in our form of government are committed to thirty-four men.

If in all these mighty powers and "exclusive privileges" you can "discover no resemblance of aristocracy," when and where did any resemblance of aristocracy exist? The Trigintivirs of Athens and the Decemvirs of Rome, I acknowledge, "resembled aristocracy" still more. But the lords of parliament in England do not resemble it so much. Nor did the nobility in Prussia, Germany, Russia, France, or Spain, possess such powers. The Palatines in Poland indeed!

How are these thirty-four senators appointed? Are they appointed by the people? Is the constitution of them democratical? They are chosen by the legislatures of the several states. And who are the legislatures of these separate states? Are they the people? No. They are a selection of the *best men* among the people, made by the people themselves. That is, they are the ἄριστοι of the Greeks. Yet there is something more. These legislatures are composed of two bodies, a senate and a house of representatives, each assembly differently constituted, the senate more nearly "resembling aristocracy" than the house. Senators of the United States are chosen, in some states, by a convention of both houses; in others, by separate, independent, but concurrent votes. The senates in the former have great influence, and often turn the vote; in the latter, they have an absolute negative in the choice.

Here are refinements upon refinements of "resemblances of aristocracy," a complication of checks and balances, evidently extended beyond any constitution of government that I can at present recollect. Whether an exact balance has been hit, or whether an exact balance will ever be hit, are different questions. But in this I am clear, that the nearer we approach to an exact balance, the nearer we shall approach to "moral liberty," if I understand the phrase.

We have agreed to be civil and free. In my number thirteen, I will very modestly hint to you my humble opinion of the point where your principal mistake lies.

## XXI

The corporeal inequalities among mankind, from the cradle and from the womb to the age of Oglethorpe and Parr, the intellectual inequalities from Blackmore to Milton, from Crocker to Newton, and from Behmen to Locke, are so obvious and notorious, that I could not expect they would have been doubted. The moral equality, that is, the innocence, is only at the birth; as soon as they can walk or speak, you may discern a moral inequality. These inequalities, physical, intellectual, and moral, I have called sources of a natural aristocracy; and such they are, have been, and will be; and it would not be dangerous to say, they are sources of all the artificial aristocracies that have been, are, or will be.

Can you say that these physical, intellectual, and moral inequalities produce no inequalities of influence, consideration, and power in society?

You say, "upon the truth or error of this distinction, the truth or error of Mr. Adams's mode of reasoning, and of this essay, will somewhat depend." I know not whether I ought not to join issue with you upon this point. State the question or questions, then, fairly and candidly between us.

1. Are there, or are there not physical, corporeal, material inequalities among mankind, from the embryo to the tomb?

2. Are there, or are there not intellectual inequalities from the first opening of the senses, the sight, the hearing, the taste, the smell, and the touch, to the final loss of all sense?

3. Are there not moral inequalities, discernible almost, if not quite, from the original innocence to the last stage of guilt and depravity?

4. From these inequalities, physical, intellectual, and moral, does

there or does there not arise a natural aristocracy among mankind? or, in other words, some men who have greater capacities and advantages to acquire the love, esteem, and respect of their fellow men, more wealth, fame, consideration, honor, influence, and power in society than other men?

When, where, have I said that men were always morally the same? Never, in word or writing. I have said,—

1. There is an inequality of wealth.

2. There is an inequality of birth.

3. There are great inequalities of merit, talents, virtues, services, and reputations.

4. There are a few in whom all these advantages of birth, fortune, and fame, are united.

I then go on to say, "these sources of inequality, common to every people, founded in the constitution of nature a natural aristocracy, etc. etc."

Now, sir, let me modestly and civilly request of you a direct and simple answer to the three foregoing questions. Ay or no; yea or nay. You and I have been so drilled to such answers that we can have as little difficulty in promising them as in understanding them; at least, unless we have become greater proficients in pyrrhonism, than we were when we lived together. When I shall be honored with your yea or nay to those three questions, I hope I shall know the real questions between us, and be enabled to confess my error, express my doubts, or state my replication.

But, sir, let me ask you why you direct your artillery at me alone? at me a simple individual *"in town obscure, of humble parents born?"* I had fortified myself behind the intrenchments of Aristotle, Livy, Sidney, Harrington, Dr. Price, Machiavel, Montesquieu, Swift, etc. You should have battered down these strong outworks before you could demolish me.

The word *"crown,"* which you have quoted from me in your eighth page, was used merely to signify the *executive authority*. You, sir, who are a lawyer, know that this figure signifies nothing more nor less. "The prince" is used by J. J. Rousseau, and by other writers on the social compact, for the same thing. Had I been blessed with time to revise a work which is full of errors of the press, I should have noted this as an erratum, especially if I had thought of guarding against malevolent criticism in America. I now request a formal erratum; page 117 at the bottom, dele "crown," and insert "executive authority."

In your eighth page, you begin to consider my natural causes of aristocracy.

1. "Superior abilities." Let us keep to nature and experience. Is there no such thing as genius? Had Raphael no more genius than the common sign-post painters? Had Newton no more genius than even his great master, that learned, profound, and most excellent man, Dr. Barrow? Had Alexander no more genius than Darius? Had Caesar no more than Catiline, or even than Pompey? Had Napoleon no more than Santerre? Has the Honorable John Randolph no more than Nimrod Hughes and Christopher Macpherson? Has every clerk in a counting-house as great a genius for numbers as Zorah Colburne, who, at six years of age, demonstrated faculties which Sanderson and Newton never possessed in their ripest days? Is there in the world a father of a family who has not perceived diversities in the natural capacities of his children?

These questions deserve direct answers. If you allow that there are natural inequalities of abilities, consider the effects that the genius of Alexander produced! They are visible to this day. And what effect has the genius of Napoleon produced? They will be felt for three thousand years to come. What effect have the genius of Washington and Franklin produced? Had these men no more influence in society than the ordinary average of other men? Genius is sometimes long lived; and it has accumulated fame, wealth, and power, greater than can be commanded by millions of ordinary citizens. These advantages are sometimes applied to good purposes, and sometimes to bad.

## XXII

When superior genius gives greater influence in society than is possessed by inferior genius, or a mediocrity of genius, that is, than by the ordinary level of men, this superior influence I call natural aristocracy. This cause, you say, is "fluctuating." What then? it is aristocracy still, while it exists. And is not democracy "fluctuating" too? Are the waves of the sea, or the winds of the air, or the gossamer that idles in the wanton summer air, more fluctuating than democracy? While I admit the existence of democracy, notwithstanding its instability, you must acknowledge the existence of natural aristocracy, notwithstanding its fluctuations.

I find it difficult to understand you, when you say that "knowledge and ignorance are fluctuating." Knowledge is unchangeable; and ignorance cannot change, because it is nothing. It is nonentity. Truth is one, uniform and eternal; knowledge of it cannot fluctuate any more than itself. Ignorance of truth, being a nonentity, cannot, surely, become entity and fluctuate and change like Proteus, or wind, or water. You sport away so merrily upon this topic, that I will have the pleasure of transcribing you. You say, "the aristocracy of superior abilities will be regulated by the extent of the space between knowledge and ignorance; as the space contracts or widens, it will be diminished or increased; and if aristocracy may be thus diminished, it follows that it may be thus destroyed."

What is the amount of this argument? Ignorance may be destroyed and knowledge increased *ad infinitum*. And do you expect that all men are to become omniscient, like the almighty and omniscient Hindoo, perfect Brahmins? Are your hopes founded upon an expectation that knowledge will one day be equally divided? Will women have as much knowledge as men? Will children have as much as their parents? If the time will never come when all men will have equal knowledge, it *seems* to follow, that some will know more than others; and that those who know most will have more influence than those who know least, or than those who know half way between the two extremes; and consequently will be aristocrats. "Superior abilities," comprehend abilities acquired by education and study, as well as genius and natural parts; and what a source of inequality and aristocracy is here! Suffer me to dilate a little in this place. Massachusetts has probably educated as many sons to letters, in proportion to her numbers, as any State in the Union, perhaps as any nation, ancient or modern. What proportion do the scholars bear to the whole number of people? I wish I had a catalogue of our Harvard University, that I might state exact numbers. Say that, in almost two hundred years, there have been three or four thousand educated, from perhaps two or three millions of people. Are not these aristocrats? or, in other words, have they not had more influence than any equal number of uneducated men? In fact, these men governed the province from its first settlement; these men have governed, and still govern, the state. These men, in schools, academies, colleges, and universities; these men, in the shape of ministers, lawyers, and physicians; these men, in academies of arts and sciences, in agricultural societies, in historical societies, in medical societies and in antiquarian societies, in banking institutions and in Washington benevolent societies, govern the state, at this twenty-sixth of December, 1814. The more you educate, without a balance in the government, the more aristocratical will the people and the government be. There never can be, in any nation, more than one fifth—no, not one tenth of the men, regularly educated to science and letters. I hope, then, you will acknowledge, that "abilities" form a DISTINCTION and confer a privilege, in fact, though they give no peculiar rights in society.

2. You appear, sir, to have overlooked or forgotten one great source of natural aristocracy, mentioned by me in my Apology, and dilated on in subsequent pages, I mean BIRTH. I should be obliged to you for your candid sentiments upon this important subject. Exceptions have been taken to the phrase *well born;* but I can see no more impropriety in it than in the epithets *well bred, well educated, well brought up, well taught, well informed, well read, well to live, well dressed, well fed, well clothed, well armed, well accoutred, well furnished, well made, well fought, well aimed, well meant, well mounted, well fortified, well tempered, well fatted, well spoken, well argued, well reasoned, well decked, well trimmed, well wrought,* or any other *well* in common parlance.

And here, sir, permit me, by way of digression, to remark another discouragement to honest political literature, and the progress of real political science. If a *well-meant* publication appears, it is instantly searched for an unpopular word, or one that can be made so by misconstruction, misrepresentation, or by any credible and imposing deception. Some ambitious, popular demagogue gives the alarm,—"heresy?" Holy, democratical church has decreed that word to be "heresy!" Down with him! And, if there was no check to their passions, and no balance to their government, they would say, *à la lanterne! à la guillotine! roast him! bake him! boil him! fry him!* The Inquisition in Spain would not celebrate more joyfully an *auto-da-fé.*

Some years ago, more than forty, a writer unfortunately made use of the term *better sort.* Instantly, a popular clamor was raised, and an odium excited, which remains to this day, to such a degree, that no man dares to employ that expression at the bar, in conversation, in a newspaper, or pamphlet, no, nor in the pulpit; though the "baser sort" are sufficiently marked and distinguished in the New Testament, to prove that there is no wrong in believing a "better sort." And if there is any difference between virtue and vice, there is a "better sort" and a worse sort in every human society.

With sincere reverence, let me here quote one of the most profound philosophical, moral, and religious sentiments that ever was expressed: —*"We know not what spirit we are of."*

## XXVI

In page 10, you say, "Mr. Adams has omitted a cause of aristocracy in the quotation, which he forgets not to urge in other places, namely, —exclusive wealth." This is your omission, sir, not mine. In page 109, vol. i. I expressly enumerated, "inequality of wealth" as one of the causes of aristocracy, and as having a natural and inevitable influence in society. I said nothing about "exclusive" wealth. The word "exclusive," is an interpolation of your own. This you acknowledge to be, "by much the most formidable with which mankind have to contend;" that is, as I understand you, superior wealth is the most formidable cause of aristocracy, or of superior influence in society. There may be some difficulty in determining the question, whether distinctions of birth, or distinctions of property, have the greatest influence in the world? Both have very great influence, much too great, when not restrained by something besides the passions or the consciences of the possessors. Were I required to give an answer to the question, my answer would be, with some diffidence, that, in my opinion, taking into consideration history and experience, birth has had, and still has, most power and the greatest effects; because conspicuous birth is hereditary; it is derived from ancestors, descends to posterity, and is inalienable. Titles and ribbons, and stars and garters, and crosses and legal establishments, are by no means essential or necessary to the preservation of it. The evidences of it are in history and records, and in the memories and hearts they remain, and it never fails to descend to posterity as long as that posterity furnishes any one or more whose talents and virtues can support the reputation of the name. Birth and wealth are commonly so entangled together, from an emperor down to a constable or tithing-man, that it is difficult to separate them so distinctly as to place one in one scale, and the other in an opposite scale, to ascertain in grains and scruples the preponderance. The complaint of Theognis, that pelf is sometimes preferred to blood, was, and is true; and it is also true that beauty, wit, art, disposition, and "winning ways," are more successful than descent; yet, in general, I believe this prevails oftener than any of the others. I may be mistaken in this opinion; but of this I am certain; that it always has the same weight, when it is at all considered. You must recur, Mr. Taylor, to Plato's republic and the French republic, destroy all marriages, introduce a perfect community of women, render it impossible to know, or suspect, or conjecture one's own father or mother, son or daughter, brother or sister, uncle or aunt, before you can annihilate all distinctions of birth. I conclude, therefore, that birth has naturally and necessarily and unavoidably some influence, more or less, in human society. Will you say it has none? I have a right, sir, to an answer to this question, yea or nay. You have summoned me before the world and posterity, in my last hours, by your voluminous criticisms and ratiocinations, which gives me a right to demand fair play. On my part, I promise to answer any question you can state, by an affirmative, negative, or doubt, without equivocation. Property, wealth, riches, although you allow them to be a cause of aristocracy in your tenth page, yet you will not permit this cause to be "ascribed to nature." But why not? If, as I have heard, "the shortest road to men's hearts is down their throats," this is surely a natural route. Hunger and thirst are natural wants, and the supplies of them are natural. Nature has settled the point, that wood and stones shall not invigorate and enliven them like wine. Suppose one of your southern gentlemen to have only one hundred thousand acres of land. He settles one thousand tenants with families upon it. If he is a humane, easy, generous landlord, will not his tenants feel an attachment to him? will he not have influence among them? will they not naturally think and vote as he votes? If, on the contrary, he is an austere, griping, racking, rack-renting tyrant, will not his tenants be afraid to offend him? will not some, if not all of them, pretend to think with him, and vote as he would have them, upon the same principle as some nations have worshipped the devil, because they knew not into whose hands they might fall? Now, sir, my argument is this. If either the generous landlord or the selfish landlord can obtain by gratitude or fear only one vote more than his own from his tenants in general, he is an aristocrat, whether his vote and those of his dependents be beneficial or maleficial, salutary or pestilential, or fatal to the community.

I remember the time, Mr. Taylor, when one thousand families depended on Mr. Hancock for their daily bread; perhaps more. All men allowed him to be punctual, humane, generous. How many of the heads of these families would naturally be inclined to vote with and for Mr. Hancock? Could not Mr. Hancock command, or at least influence one vote, besides his own? If he could, he was an aristocrat, according to my definition and conscientious opinion. Let me appeal now to your own experience. Are there not in your own Caroline County, in Virginia, two or three, or four, five or six, eight or ten great planters, who, if united, can carry any point in your elections? These are every one of them aristocrats, and you, who are the first of them, are the most eminent aristocrat of them all.

## XXXII

A few words more concerning the characters of literary men. What sort of men have had the conduct of the presses in the United States for the last thirty years? In Germany, in England, in France, in Holland, the presses, even the newspapers, have been under the direction of learned men. How has it been in America? How many presses, how many newspapers have been directed by vagabonds, fugitives from a bailiff, a pillory, or a halter in Europe?

You know it is one of the sublimest and profoundest discoveries of the eighteenth century, that knowledge is corruption; that arts, sciences, and taste have deformed the beauty and destroyed the felicity of human nature, which appears only in perfection in the savage state,—the children of nature. One writer gravely tells us that the first man who fenced a tobacco yard, and said, "this is mine," ought instantly to have been put to death; another as solemnly says, the first man who pronounced the word "dieu," ought to have been despatched on the spot; yet these are advocates of toleration and enemies of the Inquisition.[14]

I never had enough of the ethereal spirit to rise to these heights. My humble opinion is, that knowledge, upon the whole, promotes virtue and happiness. I therefore hope that you and all other gentlemen of property, education, and reputation will exert your utmost influence in establishing schools, colleges, academies, and universities, and employ every means and opportunity to spread information, even to the lowest dregs of the people, if any such there are, even among your own domestics and John Randolph's serfs. I fear not the propagation and dissemination of knowledge. The conditions of humanity will be improved and ameliorated by its expansion and diffusion in every direction. May every human being,—man, woman, and child,—be as well informed as possible! But, after all, did you ever see a rose without a briar, a convenience without an inconvenience, a good without an evil, in this mingled world? Knowledge is applied to bad purposes as well as to good ones. Knaves and hypocrites can acquire it, as well as honest, candid, and sincere men. It is employed as an engine and a vehicle to propagate error and falsehood, treason and vice, as well as truth, honor, virtue, and patriotism. It composes and pronounces, both panegyrics and philippics, with exquisite art, to confound all distinctions in society between right and wrong. And if I admit, as I do, that truth generally prevails, and virtue is, or will

[14] *Vide* Rousseau and Diderot *Passim.*

be triumphant in the end, you must allow that honesty has a hard struggle, and must prevail by many a well-fought and fortunate battle, and, after all, must often look to another world for justice, if not for pardon.

There is no necessary connection between knowledge and virtue. Simple intelligence has no association with morality. What connection is there between the mechanism of a clock or watch and the feeling of moral good and evil, right or wrong? A faculty or a quality of distinguishing between moral good and evil, as well as physical happiness and misery, that is, pleasure and pain, or, in other words, a CONSCIENCE,—an old word almost out of fashion,—is essential to morality.

Now, how far does simple, theoretical knowledge quicken or sharpen conscience? La Harpe, in some part of his great work, his Course of Literature, has given us an account of a tribe of learned men and elegant writers, who kept a kind of office in Paris for selling at all prices, down to three livres, essays or paragraphs upon any subject, good or evil, for or against any party, any cause, or any person. One of the most conspicuous and popular booksellers in England, both with the courtiers and the citizens, who employed many printers and supported many writers, has said to me, "the men of learning in this country are stark mad. There are in this city a hundred men, gentlemen of liberal education, men of science, classical scholars, fine writers, whom I can hire at any time at a guinea a day, to write for me for or against any man, any party, or any cause." Can we wonder, then, at any thing we read in British journals, magazines, newspapers, or reviews?

Where are, and where have been, the greatest masses of science, of literature, or of taste? Shall we look for them in the church or the state, in the universities or the academies? among Greek or Roman philosophers, Hindoos, Brahmins, Chinese mandarins, Chaldean magi, British druids, Indian prophets, or Christian monks? Has it not been the invariable maxim of them all to deceive the people by any lies, however gross? "Bonus populus vult decipi; ergo decipiatur."

And after all that can be done to disseminate knowledge, you never can equalize it. The number of laborers must, and will forever be so much more multitudinous than that of the students, that there will always be giants as well as pygmies, the former of which will have more influence than the latter; man for man, and head for head; and, therefore, the former will be aristocrats, and the latter democrats, if not Jacobins or *sans culottes*.

These morsels, and a million others analogous to them, which will easily occur to you, if you will be pleased to give them a careful mastication and rumination, must, I think, convince you, that no practicable or possible advancement of learning can ever equalize knowledge among men to such a degree, that some will not have more influence in society than others; and, consequently, that some will always be aristocrats, and others democrats. You may read the history of all the universities, academies, monasteries of the world, and see whether learning extinguishes human passions or corrects human vices. You will find in them as many parties and factions, as much jealousy and envy, hatred and malice, revenge and intrigue, as you will in any legislative assembly or executive council, the most ignorant city or village. Are not the men of letters,—philosophers, divines, physicians, lawyers, orators, and poets,—all over the world, at perpetual strife with one another? Knowledge, therefore, as well as genius, strength, activity, industry, beauty, and twenty other things, will forever be a natural cause of aristocracy.

# XI

## Thomas Cooper

### 1759–1839

Born in Westminster, England. Matriculated at Oxford, 1779, but took no degree because of failure to sign the Thirty-Nine Articles. Studied anatomy in London and attended patients at Manchester. Turned to law and business due to father's influence, although he carried on chemical studies at the same time. Nominated by Joseph Priestley and others for membership in Royal Society but failed of election due to radical beliefs. Attacked because of ardent reforming zeal, he emigrated to America with son of Priestley and settled near Northumberland, Pa., 1793. Practiced law and medicine. State judge, 1804–11. Professor of Chemistry at Dickinson College, 1811–15, University of Pennsylvania, 1816–19, and South Carolina College (University of South Carolina) where he was President, 1821–34. Established first medical school and insane asylum in South Carolina. One of the early teachers of political economy in the United States. Staunch defender of state rights. Wrote on chemistry, politics and religion. Died in Columbia, S. C.

Cooper was one of the most vigorous polemical writers of his day and as such was forever in the heat of controversy involving his position, his reputation and his life. Being impetuous he often left himself open to the charge of inconsistency. Although a strong abolitionist in England he held slaves seemingly with no compunction in South Carolina. While a thorough advocate of moderation he often flared up vehemently. Even though a staunch individualist he defended necessitarianism with great zeal. While John Adams's reference to him as one possessing a "rash hot head" may have indicated as much of Adams's character as it did of Cooper's, undoubtedly much of Cooper's effectiveness was diminished because of his harsh argumentativeness. He left England when it appeared a trial for seditious activities and slander of the King was imminent. He became a judge in Pennsylvania but found it difficult to be impartial and was subsequently removed. When Jefferson suggested him as the most valuable man to be secured for the new University of Virginia, there was much opposition to appointing him, although this was not the only reason why he went elsewhere. As President of South Carolina College (now the University of South Carolina) he was constantly under attack for his political and religious views and on one occasion he was publicly tried for corrupting the youth of the state. It is to Cooper's credit, however, that the versatility of his mind and the breadth of his learning were always sufficient to assure him safe journey over the stormy seas of his career.

The enemies Cooper made probably outnumbered his friends, but two of the friendships he developed, those with Thomas Jefferson and Joseph Priestley, are worthy of particular mention. Jefferson and Cooper were brought together by Priestley. The high opinion which Jefferson acquired of the South Carolina sage was never shaken. He valued Cooper's political and social opinions as highly as those of any man with whom he continuously corresponded. He appreciated Cooper's aid in the election of 1800 and he frequently asked for his opinion on important issues while he was President. He was bitterly disappointed that Cooper was not connected with the University of Virginia.[1] He was swayed by Cooper's *Scripture Doctrine of Materialism* and appreciative of his *View of the Metaphysical and Physiological Arguments in Favor of Materialism*. Cooper's relations with Priestley are more important for our purposes here, however, since it was Priestley above all others who influenced Cooper. Their association began in England where they were attracted to each other by virtue of mutual interests. Priestley, Cooper's senior by twenty-six years, had considerable influence upon the formulation of Cooper's ideas, but he can hardly be said to have inspired them, for the seeds of unconventionality were already present in Cooper's mind before he met Priestley. Priestley was an outstanding nonconformist in religion preaching Unitarianism to his dying day, a capable scientist who was world-renowned, and a political reformer. Political radicalism brought Priestley and Cooper together, materialism passed from Priestley to Cooper, and theology divided them although they accepted disagreement here as nothing more than a friendly difference. Cooper

[1] Writing to General Robert Taylor on May 16, 1820, Jefferson said, "I do sincerely lament that untoward circumstances have brought on us the irreparable loss of this professor, whom I have looked to as the cornerstone of our edifice. I know of no one who could have aided us so much in forming the future regulations for our infant institution; and although we may perhaps obtain from Europe equivalents in science, they can never replace the advantages of his experiences, his knowledge of the character, habits, and manners of our country, his identification with its sentiments and principles, and high reputation he has obtained in it generally." *Writings*. XV, 256.

came to the United States with Priestley's son the year before Priestley arrived, and lived with Priestley for several years in Northumberland, Pa. He never departed far from Priestley's philosophy, although in this, as in all matters, his independence can hardly be questioned. English materialism was inclined toward religious radicalism, French materialism was usually more thoroughgoing and anticlerical. In America, Priestley represented the former, Cooper the latter, partly due to the influence of French physiology which he studied and taught.

The *Arguments in Favor of Materialism* contained the most explicit statement of Cooper's materialistic position. One of the essays in his *Tracts* (1789) was a defense of materialism. *Arguments in Favor of Materialism* was a revision of this early essay and along with *The Scripture Doctrine of Materialism* came out anonymously in Philadelphia in 1823.[2] For Cooper, physiology was the starting point for metaphysical analysis; without that point of departure he felt metaphysics was liable to be nothing but "a mere collection of sophisms, and a science of grammatical quibbling." [3] Metaphysics, to Cooper, should be kept as close to demonstrative knowledge as possible. He said, "True metaphysics, like every other branch of philosophy, can only be founded on an accurate observation of facts, and as these gradually become substituted for mere names, our real knowledge will improve." [4] He was a bitter opponent of the Scotch realists, Reid, Beattie and Oswald.[5] He felt they disregarded physiology, had never read Hartley carefully, and therefore had produced nothing but a "young gentlemen and lady's philosophy." He was opposed to innate ideas and questioned knowledge

[2] He felt it dangerous to have them published in South Carolina at the time, although in 1831 he added them to his translation of Broussais: *On Irritation and Insanity* which was published in his home state.

[3] Cooper wrote this when analyzing Priestley's metaphysical thought. *Memoirs of Dr. Joseph Priestley*. I, 295.

[4] Ibid. I, 316–7.

[5] "But Messrs. Reid, Oswald, Beattie, Dugald Stewar[t], and Thomas Brown, have had their day. They are favorites with the clergy, for they are of the orthodox school of ideology; they are ontologists and psychologists; they offend no popular prejudices; they run counter to no clerical doctrines; they express due horror at the tendencies of heterodox metaphysics; their style of writing is for the most part good, frequently marked by elegance and taste; while the dogmatism that pervades their pages of inanity is well calculated to impose upon the numerous class of readers who are content to read without thinking. But the progress of accurate physiology, has destroyed them: the thinking part of the public which ultimately gives the tone to the much larger part that does not think, is wearied with toiling through pages after pages of figurative words and phrases without distinct meaning, and calls aloud for facts in the matter, and precision in the language." *Outline of the Association of Ideas,* in Broussais: *On Irritation and Insanity.* 380.

which did not result from the impressions of external objects upon the senses. He thought man was a biological organism whose abilities and qualities were to be understood in terms of physiological principles. Whatever distinguished man from the brute was a difference of degree, not of quality.

Cooper's frequent missiles directed at Scotch realism were a part of his continual and consistent opposition to belief in an immaterial soul. Eighteenth-century materialism was the bitter enemy both of immaterialism and of any form of Cartesian dualism. This opposition was natural considering the strong physiological bias of materialism. Cooper showered bitter invectives upon those who held that man's soul was somehow different in essence from his body, that it was attached to his body for the brief space of earthly existence and then became detached at death to move on to a secure and lasting immortality. He accused those who held this position of cherishing superstitions, of trafficking fraud, and of being defended by civil authorities who thought such falsehood would support morality.

In his attack upon immaterialism Cooper opposed the dualistic metaphysics which often went with it. The soul was no separate form of existence; neither was matter the inactive, extended stuff which the immaterialists had made it. He accepted the contemporaneous materialistic position which held matter to be extended, but which gave to it certain active qualities such as attraction and repulsion. Cooper was less interested in developing this theory than he was in defending it. In his analysis of Priestley's metaphysical position (which meant in large part Priestley's philosophy of human nature) he suggested that the best way of proving the materialistic position was not to define the properties of matter but rather to demonstrate that there were no properties with which matter was not coextensive. Part of his technique, therefore, was to prove his own case by showing how his opponents were wrong. In his more positive presentation, his arguments were based upon a physiological interpretation of man rather than upon a more inclusive materialistic interpretation of the whole of nature.

Mental phenomena, according to Cooper, consisted of sensations and ideas. A sensation he defined as "an impression made by some external object on the Senses." [6] He went on, "the motion thus excited is propagated along the appropriate nerve, until it reaches the Sensory in the Brain, and it is there and there only, felt or *perceived.*" [7] An

[6] In Broussais: *On Irritation and Insanity.* 314 n.
[7] Ibid.

idea he spoke of as "a motion in the Brain, excited there either by the laws of association to which that organ is subject, or by some accidental state of the system in general, or that organ in particular, without the intervention of an impression on the Senses ab extra as the cause of it. Such a motion being similar to a sensation formerly excited, and being also felt or perceived is the correspondent *Idea.*"[8] Mental phenomena were dependent upon physiological processes, affected by disease, accident, sleep, or death. They were an outgrowth of the organization within nature, not the result of an immaterial existence separate from nature. Thoughts were dependent upon the functions of the body which nature provided, not the creation of man or of a supermundane existence. The will he explained as the force which calls into action the voluntary muscles, dependent upon given inclinations, desires and wants. To speak of man in this light led Cooper to accept determinism. He could not accept man as a free agent, creating, choosing, willing as if in a vacuum. Thought and will were equally determined by the structure of nature and although seemingly less enshackled than in animal species were only apparently so because of the greater complexity of man's existence.

Cooper's rejection of the soul as a separate existence led him to deny the possibility of immortality on any natural basis. Nevertheless, he accepted it on the basis of scriptural authority, probably to protect himself from attacks by the clergy. Immortality was to take place through resurrection, just as in the case of Jesus, and to be acquired by the grace of God. It could not be the continuance of the soul without the body since soul and body were inseparable; hence resurrection was the only possibility for life after death. This position, along with most of Cooper's other religious ideas, was dictated more by expediency than by conviction. Cooper was not convinced of the necessity of belief in God. He felt the essence of religion was to lead the good life which he held an atheist could do as well as a theist. Public opinion and common interest were sufficiently strong incentives to make the good life worthwhile. He was anticlerical and afforded the clergy reason to resent his vitriolic criticisms of their profession. He charged them with bias and with permitting their opinions to be dictated by the beliefs they were paid to extol. He felt the whole clerical profession was set up to offer comfort and ease to those who entered its sacred precincts. A large portion of ecclesiastical thought was to him falsehood parading as truth. He looked upon the clerical profession as a deterrent to progress and as a screen against truth.

[8] In Broussais: *On Irritation and Insanity.* 314–5.

He said, "If the people do not keep the *Clergy* under control, they will bring the people into abject slavery, and keep them there." [9] *The Scripture Doctrine of Materialism,* a tract intended to prove his essential Christianity, was on the whole more a defense of his materialistic doctrines than an exposition of accepted religion.

Cooper was essentially a believer in free speech. In Socratic fashion he looked upon the expression of opinion and its subsequent sifting as one of the safest means of protecting truth from tradition, bias, ignorance and superstition. No idea was too sacred to question, no citadel of truth too secure to be attacked. His openness and candor kept him in the public eye and made him subject to constant criticism, but these were psychological counterparts of the confidence and optimism of the Age of Reason of which he was a characteristic example. His materialism was soon to be overshadowed by the transcendentalism of New England and the Scotch realism he so abhorred, only to recur later on in the nineteenth century as the biological basis of his theory came to be more thoroughly accepted.

## REFERENCES


Cooper, Thomas: *Tracts: Ethical, Theological and Political.* Warrington, England, 1789.

———: *Memoirs of Dr. Joseph Priestley, to the Year 1795, Written by Himself: with a Continuation, to the Time of his Decease, by his Son, Joseph Priestley: and Observations on his Writings, by Thomas Cooper, President Judge of the Fourth District of Pennsylvania; and the Rev. William Christie.* 2 vols. Northumberland, Pa., and London, 1806. (Esp. vol. I, appendix no. 2, "Of Dr. Priestley's Metaphysical Writings.")

———: *Lectures on the Elements of Political Economy.* Columbia, S. C., 1826.

——— (trans.): F. J. V. Broussais: *On Irritation and Insanity: to which are Added two Tracts on Materialism and an Outline of the Association of Ideas.* Columbia, S. C., 1831. (The two tracts referred to are *The Scripture Doctrine of Materialism* and *A View of the Metaphysical and Physiological Arguments in Favor of Materialism,* both originally published anonymously in Philadelphia, 1823.)

Kelley, Maurice: *Additional Chapters on Thomas Cooper.* University of Maine Studies, Second Series, No. 15. In *The Maine Bulletin* 33 (1930) 1–92. (Ch. III gives a good account of Cooper's early ideas as expressed in *Tracts.*)

Malone, Dumas: *The Public Life of Thomas Cooper.* New Haven:


[9] In Broussais: *On Irritation and Insanity.* 326.

Yale University Press, 1926. (Esp. chs. I, VII, and XI. Good bibliography.)

Riley, I. Woodbridge: *American Philosophy: the Early Schools.* New York: Dodd, Mead and Co., 1907. 407–20.

* * *

---

* * *

# A VIEW OF THE METAPHYSICAL AND PHYSIOLOGICAL ARGUMENTS IN FAVOR OF MATERIALISM [10]

## *The Argument in Favor of the Separate Existence of an Immaterial Soul Joined with and Placed in the Human Body, Is as Follows*

Man consists of a body, which, when living, exhibits a peculiar organization, and certain phenomena connected with it, termed intellectual; such as perception, memory, thinking or reasoning, and willing or determining. When the body ceases to live, it becomes decomposed into carbon, azote, hydrogen, oxygen, phosphorus, and lime; and perhaps another substance or two: all of them similar to what we find in the inanimate material bodies around us. We differ from them, so far as we can judge by our senses, in no way, but in possessing a peculiar organization which those bodies have not. But as no configuration or disposition of the particles of which our bodies are composed, can amount to any thing more than varieties of position—varieties of matter and motion, we have no reason to ascribe perception, memory, thought, or will, to any form of matter and motion, however varied. From matter and motion, nothing but matter and motion can result. The phenomena of intellect are too dissimilar to allow us to consider them as the result of, or as varieties of matter and motion. We must, therefore, recur to some other principle as the source of intellect; and that cannot be the body. It must be something different from mere matter and motion, something immaterial, something that has no relation to matter; that something, be it a separate being, or a separate principle, is the Soul. Will any arrangement of carbon, azote, hydrogen and oxygen produce a syllogism? Having no

[10] In Broussais: *On Irritation and Insanity.* 335–47, 350–4.

relation to matter, being essentially immaterial, this source of intellect is not, like matter, liable to decomposition and decay: it is therefore immortal: it dies not when the body dies. It puts a future state therefore, out of doubt, for it lives when the body is no more.

Such are the views generally taken of this question by those who believe in the separate existence of an immaterial *Soul* as the cause and origin of all the phenomena termed mental or intellectual. With them, it is absurd to ascribe the sublime fictions of poetry, or the sublimer disquisitions of Newton and La Place, to a mere arrangement of assimilated particles of the grossest kind; possessing, before their entrance into the body, and when thrown by the exhalent vessels out of it, nothing approaching the nature of intellect under any of its denominations.

In the present view of the subject, all arguments of a theological nature are excluded. They can be considered apart: and they are to the full as difficult of solution, as the arguments deduced from natural phenomena; and are productive of as much practical discrepancy.

The Immaterialists of modern days are led on still further. They say that the tendency to organization itself, and all the results of that tendency, must have been originally imparted and communicated to inert matter, which could not have assumed this tendency by any effort of its own. That organization, life, and the properties connected with life, as feeding, digestion, assimilation, excretion, &c. as well as the phenomena termed intellectual, cannot arise from any known property of matter as such; and therefore must have been originally impressed by that Being to whom all creation is to be ascribed. That the phenomena termed intellectual, are clearly distinguishable from the other phenomena of living organized matter—they are peculiar to the human species—not to be accounted for from the common properties of organization or life, and are therefore owing to a separate and distinct communication from the author of our common existence. That not being ascribable to any form of organization, or to be regarded as the result of it, they must of necessity be ascribed to some separate being of a different and superior nature from matter; destined during the present life to act by means of the bodily organs. This separate being is the *Soul*. It is granted that we are not to argue from the possibility of any thing, to its actual existence, (*a posse ad esse non valet consequentia,*) but when the phenomena cannot be explained by any known properties of organized or unorganized matter, we are of necessity driven to something else than—something beside matter—something which is not matter, to explain appearances that are not material.

I do not know how to state better, more fairly, or more forcibly, the views taken of this question by the writers who contend for the separate existence of the Soul, as a being perfectly immaterial, and by consequence incorruptible and immortal.

## *On the Other Hand*

The *Materialists,* who ascribe all the phenomena termed intellectual, to the body; and consider them as the properties of organized matter, the result of that organization—reason as follows:

Their arguments may be considered, as 1. *Metaphysical,* and 2. *Physiological.*

To begin with the FIRST class.

1. The only reason we have for asserting in any case that one thing is the property of another, is the certainty or universality with which we always find them accompanying each other. Thus, we say gold is ductile, because we have always found gold, when pure to be so. We assert that manure will nourish a plant—that muscular fibers are irritable—that the nerves are the instruments of sensation, &c. for the same reason. Let the reader sit down, and describe a mineral by its characters, and he will have no doubt of the truth of this assertion.

Moreover, finding by experience that every thing we see has some *cause* of its existence, we are induced to ascribe the constant concomitance of a substance and any of its properties, to some necessary connexion between them. Hence, therefore, *certainty and universality of concomitance is the sole ground of asserting or supposing a necessary connexion between two phenomena.* And we cannot help believing that like consequences will invariably follow like antecedents under like circumstances. For thus we reason: if two circumstances, or things, always present themselves to our observation accompanying each other —the one always preceding, the other always following—there must be some reason in the nature of things why it should be so.

There is a necessary connexion between such a structure as the nervous system in animals, and the property of sensation, or as it is often called, PERCEPTION [11]—the property of feeling, of being conscious of impressions made upon our senses. For there is precisely the same reason for making this assertion, as there can be for any other the most incontestable; namely, the certainty and universality wherewith (in a healthy state of the system) we observe perception and the

[11] The French writers call it conscience, *consciousness.* The English adopt *perception.*

nervous system accompany each other. The seat of perception, so far as we know from the facts of anatomy and physiology, is situated at the internal sentient extremity of the nerve impressed. But be it there or elsewhere, as it manifestly belongs to the nervous system, that is sufficient for the purpose. It must be somewhere. Let the reader according to his best judgment from known facts, place it where he thinks fit, and it will equally serve the purposes of my argument. Perception sensation, feeling, consciousness of impressions, (for all these terms have been used synonymously; I prefer the first,) is a property of the nervous apparatus belonging to animal bodies in health and life. When the sentient extremities of a nerve are excited or impressed, perception is the certain instantaneous result, as surely as the peculiar weight, color, ductility, and affinities of gold are the result of gold, when obtained pure. These properties are inseparable. You must define gold *by* them: in like manner, you must define the properties of the nervous system by perception—sensation.

I consider this argument as conclusive; unless it can be shewn *how* perception results necessarily from something distinct from, and independent of the nervous system; or that, whether this can be shewn or not, the assertion that perception does so result, implies a contradiction, and therefore is at all events inadmissible. As to the *how*—the mode and manner in which perception results from the stimulations of the nervous system—how or why it is, as we see it to be, a function of the brain—no one can pretend to shew or to explain; any more than we can shew or explain how an immaterial soul can act on a material body without having one property in common with it. In the first case we feel in ourselves, and we know by observing others, that perception, feeling, or consciousness is a function of that visible organ; but of the existence of a separate soul, we know nothing but by conjecture. We know that irritability and contractility are properties of the muscular fibre, but beyond the mere fact of its being thus, we know nothing. Can we explain the life and growth of a blade of grass?

That certainty and universality of concomitance is the sole ground for asserting a necessary connexion between two phenomena, or that the one is the result of the other, is so true, that if this be false, no argument from induction can possibly be true: for all proofs from induction imply the truth of this. And as no direct contradiction has ever been attempted to be shewn in the assertion that perception is the result of organization—as the matter of fact, so far as our senses can judge, is plainly so—and as no immaterialist has ever yet pretended to account *how* perception results from an immaterial rather than a material substance—there is nothing more requisite to prove that perception is really and truly the result of our organization. The argument then stands thus: Certainty and universality of concomitance between two or more phenomena, are the only direct reasons we have, for asserting or supposing a necessary connexion between them. The property of perception and a sound state of the nervous system under excitation, are certainly and universally concomitant. Therefore, this concomitance furnishes the only direct reason we have for asserting a necessary connexion between perception and the nervous system. But this reason is the same that we have for asserting a necessary connexion between any other phenomena whatever. Therefore, we have the same reason for asserting a necessary connexion between the property of perception and a sound state of the nervous system, as for asserting the same thing of any other phenomena whatever. It will be understood of course, that the nervous system must be excited, before the excitement can be perceived; and whether we adopt Hume's phraseology, or that of Dr. T. Brown in his Treatise on Cause and Effect, the argument will be exactly the same. In all cases, where the necessary connection between two phenomena is such, that the one is denominated a *property,* and the other the *subject* of which the first is a property, the property is universally deemed to result necessarily from the nature or essence of the subject to which it belongs. But as perception must be a property of something; and as it is uniformly connected with a sound state of the nervous system, perception is a property of that system, and results necessarily from the nature or essence thereof.

Such is the proper and direct proof of the doctrine of *Materialism;* which, so far as I am acquainted with the controversy, REMAINS UNANSWERED. But this doctrine will receive additional support, if the opposite doctrine of *Immaterialism* can be shewn impossible or improbable. I shall endeavour to do both.

## OF THE IMPOSSIBILITY OF THE EXISTENCE OF AN IMMATERIAL, INDISCERPTIBLE, IMMORTAL SOUL

2.—(a) The Soul hath *all* the properties of matter and no other; or it hath some properties *in common* with matter, and *some* that matter hath not; or it hath *no* property in common with matter.

In the first case, it is matter, and nothing else.

In the second case, it is partially material.

In the third case, it is in no respect of degree material. This the last case is the only one of the alternatives that the hypothesis of Immaterialism can consistently maintain: for in so far as the Soul is material, it will be discerptible, moral, and corruptible, as matter is.

(b) But let the Soul have no property in common with matter. Then I say: Nothing can act upon another but by means of some common property. Of this we have not only all the proof that induction of known and acknowledged cases can furnish, but that additional proof also which arises from the impossibility of conceiving how the opposite proposition *can* be true. You cannot erect the Colisoeum at Rome by playing Haydn's Rondeau. You cannot impel a ray of light by the mace of a billiard table, and so on. This proposition is every where admitted, or assumed in treatises on natural philosophy.

But by the proposition, the Soul hath no property in common with matter. Whereas by the universal acknowledgement of Immaterialists, the Soul acts upon and by means of the material body; but it is a contradiction to suppose that the Soul can and cannot, does and does not, act upon the material body; and therefore, the hypothesis involving this contradiction must fall to the ground.

3. (a) Whatever we know, we know by means of its properties, nor do we, in any case, know certainly any thing but these. Gold is heavy, yellow, ductile, soluble in aqua regia, &c. Suppose gold deprived for an instant of all these properties—what remains, would it be gold? If it have other properties, it is another substance; if it have no properties remaining, it is nothing; for nothing is that which hath no properties. Hence, if any thing lose all its properties, it becomes nothing; it loses its existence.

(b) Now the existence of the soul is inferred like the existence of every thing else, from its supposed properties, which are the intellectual phenomena of the human being, perception,[12] memory, judgment, volition. But in all cases of *perfect* sleep—of the operation of a strong narcotic—of apoplexy—of swooning—of drowning where the vital powers are not extinguished—of the effects of a violent blow on the back of the head—and all other leipothymic affections—there is neither perception, memory, judgment or volition; that is, all the properties of the Soul are gone, are extinguished; therefore the Soul itself loses its existence for the time; all evidences and traces of its existence are lost; *pro hac vice,* therefore, and during the continuance of these derangements of the nervous system, the Soul is dead, for all its properties are actually extinguished. The Soul, therefore, is not immortal, and of consequence is not immaterial.

(c) This disappearance of all intellectual phenomena in consequence of the derangement of the nervous apparatus of the human system, is

[12] Feeling, Sensation, Consciousness, are the synonymous terms. T. C.

easily accounted for, if they be considered (as the Materialists consider them) no other than phenomena dependent upon the nervous system in its usual state of excitement by impressions *ab extra,* or motions dependent on the sensitive surfaces of the internal vicera, and an association originating *ab intra.* On this view of the subject, all is natural and explicable. But if these intellectual phenomena are the evidences and properties of a separate immaterial being (the Soul) then comes the insuperable difficulty—where is the subject itself when all its properties, all evidences of its existence are annihilated; though but for a day or an hour. A materialist can easily account for returning animation by renewed excitement from the unsuspended action of the functions of organic life.

4. (a) No laws of reasoning will free us from the bondage imposed by matters of fact. It is impossible to deny that all these intellectual phenomena, these peculiar properties of an immaterial Soul, these only evidences of its existence, are also properties of the body: for where there is no nervous apparatus, as in vegetables, they never appear; nor do they appear in the embryo or the infant, till the encephalon is developed; where the nervous system is deranged by violence, or by disease, or by medicine, these phenomena are also deranged, and even disappear; when the body dies and the nervous system with it, all these phenomena cease, and are irrevocably gone; we never possess after death, so far as our senses can inform us, the slightest evidence of the existence of any remaining being, which, connected with the body during life, is separated from it at death. This may be asserted, but there is not one solitary fact to prove it: when the body dies, no more perception, no more memory, no more volition. So far as we can see, these die with the body, and exhibit no proof of their subsequent existence. These phenomena are phenomena then of the body: if they be also phenomena of the Soul, then is the Soul also like the body, material; for it has properties in common.

(b) If it be said the Soul may exist after the body is dead and decomposed, I reply, the Soul may also not exist: one supposition is as good as the other. Remember, it is not allowable in fair argument to take for granted the existence of a thing, merely because it may possibly exist. If you assert its existence, you must prove your assertion. *Affirmantis est probare. A posse ad esse, non valet consequentia.*

(c) If any one shall say these properties are only *suspended* for the time, I would desire him to examine what idea he annexes to this suspension; whether it be any thing more or less than *they are made not to exist for the time.* Either no more is meant, or it is plainly opposed to matter of fact. Moreover if more *be* meant, it may easily be proved to involve the archetypal existence of abstract ideas; to approach to the Platonic absurdities modified by the pre-established harmony of Leibnitz, which, I apprehend, will not be considered as defensible at this day. It can also be shewn that such ulterior meaning will contradict the maxim *impossib[i]le est idem esse et non esse.*

(d) If any one shall say farther, "These mental phenomena are not constituent parts, but acts of the Soul, and evidences of its existence; so that the Soul may continue to exist when it no longer continues to act, or to act in this manner—that it does not follow that man's power of working is annihilated because he has lost the tools or instruments with which he has usually worked."—I reply: 1. That whenever the evidences of the existence of a thing arise from the nature and structure of the thing itself, they are synonymous with its properties. Such are the phenomena of thinking with respect to the Soul: they are confessedly of its very essence. I cannot give a plainer illustration than I have already given; let my reader, if he be a mineralogist, sit down and describe a mineral; and then let him suppose all his characters annihilated. 2. As these intellectual phenomena are *all* the evidences we have of the Soul's existence, when these are destroyed or extinguished, so is the conclusion drawn from them. When all the evidences of the existence of *life* fail, no one scruples to say that life itself is gone. 3. The instruments with which a man usually works, are only a *small part of, not all* the evidences of his power of working. Were he to lose his senses, and his hands, and his powers of volition, and of voluntary motion, which are also conjoint evidences of his power of working, every one would say he had lost that power; that is, it no longer existed. 4. It is equally legitimate to assert of gold, for instance, that what are termed its essential and characteristic properties are nothing more than acts and evidences of the existence of the substance gold, which *may* continue to exist, notwithstanding it no longer continues to exhibit any of those phenomena which are termed its properties, but are in fact only temporary evidences of its existence. Would any reasonable man acknowledge the justness of such an argument? 5. If this conclusion *a posse ad esse—a potentia ad actum*—from the remotest of all possibilities of existence, be allowed—then can any thing whatever be proved to exist in despite of all proof to the contrary. Would not a physician regard that man as a lunatic, who was seriously to say of a putrid dead body before them: "to be sure, none of the actions which are the evidences of life are exhibited at present, but life may exist notwithstanding?"

5.—(a) All relative terms imply the existence of their correlates: a man cannot be a father without having a child, a husband without a wife, &c. Hence when either of two relatives cease to exist, the other does so likewise.

(b) All those ideas which make up our idea of the Soul, or in other words, all those properties from whence we infer its existence, are relative; their correlates are ideas. Thus, there can be no *perception* without ideas to be perceived; no *recollection* without ideas to be remembered; no *judgment* without ideas to be compared; no *volition* without ideas of the object on which it is exerted.

(c) Locke has shewn that we have no innate ideas; that all our ideas are ideas of sensation or reflection; and that the ideas of reflection are no other than the operations of the mind on our ideas of sensation: that is, all our ideas proceed from, and are founded on the impressions made upon our senses. The doctrine of the ancient school was the same, *nil unquam fuit in intellectu, quod non prius erat in sensu,* including the internal as well as the external senses; which is not the less true for being acknowledged as true by the wisest men of antiquity.[13] I am

[13] That the best informed of *modern* writers hold the same doctrine, and that the whole phenomena termed mental are merely excitations of the nervous system perceived, I assert on the authority of Cabanis, of Bichat, of Blumenbach, of Richerand, of Magendie; as well as Hartley, Darwin, Priestl[e]y, and Lawrence. The elementary works of Bichat, Richerand, Blumenbach, and Magendie, being usually read in all our medical schools, I subjoin the references.

See Bichat, Phys. Res. (Dr. Watkins' Edit. 1809. Philad.) p. 105, prope finem. Richerand, (Dr. Chapman's Edit. 1813, Philad.) p. 390–392 and p. 400. Blumenbach, (Dr. Chapman's Edit. 1795, Philad.) p. 195 of Vol. 1. Magendie, (Dr. Revere's Edit. Baltim. 1822,) p. 102, 103. Broussais' sur l'irrit. et la Folie, p. 448.

The reader will find that the best informed and most approved elementary writers on physiology adopt the Latin axiom in the text verbatim, or in substance. So Haller, Phys. 556, describes a sensation as an affection of the brain perceived. Primae Lineae, Edinb. 1767.

No man is qualified to write on metaphysics and the phenomena of intellect, who is not well versed in physiology, a branch of knowledge in which the Scotch school of metaphysicians are sadly deficient.

I would not willingly include Dr. T. Brown in this tirade against his superficial and dogmatic predecessors. I agree with him, that power and causation are words only, and inseparable from the real and actual antecedents and consequents to which they relate: and that our belief of the invariable attendance of like consequents on like antecedents, under like circumstances, is rather intuitive than a process of reasoning. I much fear, however, he has not succeeded in obviating the difficulty of Hume's argument against miracles; for all that writer's argument applies to the introduction of new antecedants, the permanent character of the usual and natural course of phenomena; and the difficulty of establishing this introduction by testimony which remains just as before. Dr. Brown has substituted one form

aware the "faculties of the mind," the numberless brood of the Scotch metaphysicians. I cannot and will not condescend to reply to the dreadful nonsense on this subject assumed as true by Dr. Reid and Dr. Beattie, or to the shallow sophisms of Dr. Gregory, or the prolix pages of inanity of Dr. Dugald Stewart, or the ignorant hardihood of assertion of Dr. Barclay in his late inquiry. We are all before the public, and I am content. In the mean time, let the reader ask himself, how he could acquire ideas of vision without the eye and its apparatus—of odour without the nostrils—of taste without the papillae on the tongue and palate, &c. Let him say what ideas a man could have, all whose senses were entirely wanting. This is enough.

In fact, people begin to doubt whether a man can by any possibility, receive satisfactory evidence of the existence of any thing whatever, not cognizable by any of the human senses.

(d) But if all our ideas proceed from impressions made on our senses, as these are entirely corporeal, we never could have attained ideas without the body; that is, there would have been none of the phenomena of perception, recollection, judgment, or volition without the body; that is, there would have been none of those phenomena of thinking from whence we deduce the existence of the Soul—none of the properties of the Soul, without the body: in other words there would have been no Soul without the body. So that the commencement of the existence of the Soul depends on the commencement of the existence of the body. Such is matter of fact.

(e) But the Immaterialists say, the Soul is distinct from and independent of the body as to its existence: hence, it is both dependent and independent of the body: that is, it does not exist, for contradictions cannot co-exist.

## *THE IMMORTALITY,* A PARTE ANTE, *OF THE SOUL BEING NULL, LET US EXAMINE ITS IMMORTALITY* A PARTE POST

6[a]. (a) All impressions made on our senses can be traced up to the internal sentient extremity of the nerve impressed, and no further.

(b) When an impression has been made on our senses by means of

---

of defence for another, but he has not substantially altered the state of the case. Brown, however, is a clear sighted and able metaphysician, but of the Scotch school; whose characteristic is a dreadful ignorance of all physiological facts.

T. C.

external objects, we have the property of perceiving the effects of that impression at a distance of time, and after the original impression has ceased. This is *memory* and *recollection.* Hence, although all our ideas have been caused by impressions made on our senses originally, we may lose one or two of our senses, and yet remember the ideas which are the effect of the impressions formerly made on them.

(c) But ideas can no more be remembered without the nervous system, than they could have been caused originally without senses. All this is plain matter of fact.

(d) At death, however, not only all our senses are destroyed, (the only sources of original ideas) but the nervous system itself is destroyed, which is the *sine qua non* to the existence of ideas already caused. At death, therefore, all our ideas of every kind are destroyed.

(e) But there can be none of the properties of the Soul without ideas: for these are relates and correlates; and if all the properties of the Soul are destroyed, the Soul itself is destroyed.

(f) Therefore, whatever may be the case during the life of the body, the Soul did not exist previous thereto, and is destroyed when that is destroyed.

(g) And when it is considered that many circumstances during the life of the body may totally destroy for a time all the properties of the Soul, the little of existence that remains is hardly worth contending for.

(h) But when it is further considered, that the natural immortality of the Soul is supposed a necessary consequence of its immateriality, it will be a necessary consequence that this immaterial Soul does not exist at all.

6[b]. [(a)] If the Soul exist at all, it must exist somewhere, for it is impossible to frame to one's self an idea of any thing existing which exists no where, and yet whose operations are limited as to space.

(b) But if the Soul exist somewhere, by the terms it occupies space; and therefore is extended; and therefore has figure or shape, in common with matter.

(c) Moreover by the supposition of every Immaterialist (except Malbranche, Leibnitz, and Berkley) the Soul acts upon the body; that is upon matter. That is, it attracts and repels, and is attracted and repelled; for there is no conceivable affection of matter, but what is founded upon, and reducible to attraction and repulsion. If it be attracted and repelled, its re-action must be attraction and repulsion. This implies solidity.

(d) The Soul then possesses extension, figure, solidity, attraction, repulsion. But these comprise all the properties by which matter is characterized, and the Soul therefore, whatever else it be, is a material being.

(e) But it cannot be both material and immaterial at the same time, and therefore it does not exist.

7. Those truths which we derive from the evidence of our senses, carefully observed and sufficiently repeated, are more weighty than such as are mere deductions of reason and argument. If I feel that by beating a large stone with my fist I shall hurt my knuckles, I cannot doubt of that after a sufficient number of trials. If I find that a large quantity of strong wine will render me intoxicated, I cannot disbelieve the result of experience. I *see* that the mental phenomena are in fact connected with the organization of the human body, by means of the nervous apparatus which is a part of it. I know by observation and experience, that if you destroy that part of the nervous system which supplies any one of the organs of sense, as the optic nerve of the eye, the organs of that sense no longer supply me with the same feelings as before. All this is matter of fact, ascertainable in the same way that we ascertain the effect of a bottle of Madeira; by the use of our senses. About all this we can no more doubt, than about our existence. But what evidence can we possibly have of the existence of the Soul? It is not cognizable by any of our senses—by any of the common inlets of knowledge—it is, by the hypothesis, immaterial, it hath no relation to matter. By the very nature of it, we can have no sensible proof of its existence. It is an hypothesis, a supposed being, introduced to account for appearances manifestly connected with our bodily organs, which so far as we know, cannot take place without them, whether there be a Soul or not. This connexion we see, hear, feel, and know to exist, though we do not know exactly how to trace it. But the Soul has no existence for our senses—it is a being whose existence is assumed because the present state of knowledge does not enable us (perhaps) to account for the precise mode of connexion between intelligence and our nervous system. I shall by and by shew, that we are just as much at a loss to account for the growth of a blade of grass, or the life of a tree, as for the reasoning of an animal.

But let the reader reflect for a moment, and ask himself if this hypothetical introduction of an immaterial Soul to solve the difficulties that our inevitable ignorance produces, be not a manifest breach of the acknowledged axiom, *a posse ad esse non valet consequentia?* A mere refuge for present ignorance of a connexion which future knowledge may or may not unravel.

A THEORY EXPLAINS UNKNOWN FACTS by the laws and

properties of known facts. Newton applied the cause which makes a stone fall to the earth to the tendency of the planets toward the sun. Here was nothing new assumed to aid the reasoning. Had he said that as it was impossible to explain the tendency of the planets toward the sun, by any properties of the planets or the sun, and therefore it must be owing to some angel whose duty it was to impel the planets in their proper direction, this would have been HYPOTHESIS: just like our notions of the Soul to account for the phenomena of the body.

So that we not only have no direct and satisfactory evidence of the existence of the Soul, and from the presumed nature of it never can have, but the clear, direct, undeniable evidence of our senses is all the other way.

Is it not singular, moreover, that we cannot talk about this immaterial Soul, its existence, its properties, its mode of action, but in language suggested and borrowed from the bodily senses? Can we think or speak of immaterial beings in any other words or expressions than those which our senses have suggested to us, and which belong to our corporeal senses alone?

I see [says Mr. Hallet, in his discourses] a man move, and hear him speak for some years. From his speech, I certainly infer that he *thinks* as I do. I see, then, that a man is a being who thinks and acts. After some time, the man falls down in my sight, grows still and cold. He speaks and acts no more. As the only reason I had to believe that he did think, was his motion and speech, so now that they cease, I have lost the only way I had of proving that he had the power of thought. Upon this sudden death, the one visible thing, the one man, is greatly changed. Whence could I infer that the same *he* consists of two parts, and that the inward part continues to live and think, and flies away from the body, while the outward part ceases to live and move? It looks as if the *whole man* was gone, and that all his powers cease at the same time. So far as I can discern, his motion and thought die together.

The powers of thought, speech, and motion equally depend on the body, and run the same fate in case of men's declining old age. When a man dies through old age, I see his powers of motion and thought decay and die together, and each of them by degrees: [14] the moment he ceases to move and breath, he appears to cease to think too.

When I am left to mere reason, it seems to me, that my power of thought depends as much on my body, as my power of sight and hearing. I could not think in infancy. My powers of thought, of sight, and of feeling are equally liable to be obstructed by the body. A blow on the head has deprived a man of thought, who could yet see, and feel, and move. So that naturally the power of thinking seems to belong as much to the body, as any power of men whatsoever. Naturally there

[14] The Reader will recollect Gil Blas' Archbishop of Toledo.

appears no more reason to suppose a man can *think* out of the body than that he can hear sounds or feel cold out of the body.

If this be the case (which cannot be denied)—if there neither be in fact, nor from the nature of the thing ever can be, any direct evidence for the existence of an immaterial, distinct, independent Soul—still further, if all the direct and positive evidence that there can be of any thing whatever, all that the present case can in the nature of it admit, is *against* the existence of such a Soul—how strong, how absolutely irrefragable, how evident ought that reasoning to be, by which its existence is inferred! Even the possibility of its being fairly and honestly disputed, is a strong presumption against its conclusiveness. Who can fairly and honestly dispute the dependence of thought on the body?

8. I apprehend all the phenomena termed mental or intellectual, are explicable as phenomena of the body. Hartley, and Destut Tracey, the one in his first volume on Man, and the other in his Ideologie, have done it to my satisfaction. I cannot enter into their reasonings; they must speak for themselves. The public by and by will give to these authors that fair play which the orthodoxy of the moment will not concede to them.

9. We have not the slightest proof of any kind, that ideas can arise or can exist independently of corporeal organization. We have never known them so to exist. We know not, nor have we from facts the slightest reason to believe that they can. But the Soul itself has been invented to account for them. They are (by those who believe in a separate Soul) considered as essential to that being—the peculiar property and result of the Soul's operations. But where is the proof that ideas can exist in the Soul without the body? Where is thought when the body dies? Where was thought before the body began to exist? *De non apparentibus et non existentibus eadem est ratio.* All assertions are equally true concerning that which doth not exist, and that of whose existence there is no evidence.

Such are the arguments of an abstract and metaphysical nature, on which I ground my opinion that an immaterial, immortal Soul, separate from the body, does not and cannot exist: and it appears to me, from what has been said, that there is the same proof for the truth of the doctrine of *Materialism,* as that gold is heavy, ink black, water fluid, or any other indubitable assertion. Also, that there is the same proof that the opposite doctrine *cannot* be true, as that contradictory assertions cannot be both true.

[*Here Cooper includes a section devoted to the description of minerals, vegetables and animals and to the distinctions which can be made between them. This section adds little to his basic case for materialism and is hence omitted from these selections.*]

I proceed to my *second class* of arguments.

1. The propensity of the minute particles of quartz to unite together in a six-sided prism terminated by six-sided pyramids—of the zirconite to assume a tetrahedral prism terminated by tetrahedral pyramids—of the diamond and garnet to appear as dodecahedrons—of pyrites as a cube—of carbonate of lime as a rhomboid, &c. &c. so that their particles seek out an union with adjacent particles, not indiscriminate and promiscuous, but in the peculiar manner proper to form these figures—is either a property of the material particles themselves, or it is owing to some separate being or principle who impresses on the particles the necessary force in the necessary direction on each occasion. No one hitherto, however, has thought of ascribing this propensity but to some property belonging and essential to the particles themselves.

The arrangement of the nutritious matter taken in by a vegetable, in the peculiar form which that vegetable affects, and by which it is characterized, has usually been attributed to the effect of vegetable life as connected with vegetable organization. No one hitherto has advanced the hypothesis of a vegetable soul—distinct from the plant, but regulating and governing it—a being superior to, and surviving, the vegetable. Yet there is no more difficulty in supposing perception a property of a nervous system, or christallization of a mineral system. We see them all, like other properties, intimately and essentially connected, as antecedents and consequents, with the subject to which they are referred; and we refer them accordingly, as in all other cases of similar connexion. How is life of any kind the result of mere matter and motion? Yet the fact is undeniable. Does it not exist by stimulation?

We see in the human frame a nervous apparatus that is essentially connected with sensation and volition, and from which these properties arise—that serves no other purpose than to give birth to them—we see them in infancy in a state approaching to nonentity; forming gradually and slowly; growing with the growth of the being to which they belong, and improving by degrees—we see them vary in kind and intensity according to our education and the nature of the society in which we are thrown—we see them dependent for almost all their characters on the manner in which that part of the nervous system is excited ab extra; so that a man born and educated in Constantinople will have one set of impressions and associations, one habit of sensation and volition, and a man with a similar arrangement of nervous apparatus born and educated among the Quakers at Philadelphia will have another. All this is the result of generating causes extraneous to system—owing to specific peculiarities of excitement that causes the nervous apparatus to act in this manner rather than in that, and to assume different habits. I say, we see all this to be in every case, undeniable matter of fact. How then can we deny sensation and volition to be the result of the stimulated nervous system? There is the same connexion of phenomena, the same uniform result of that connexion, presenting no more difficulty in the case of sensation and volition, than in the case of glandular secretion; or animal heat; or muscular motion; or sanguification; or the secretion of resin in the pine, and the sugar in the maple from the same introsuscepted fluid. All the processes are equally inexplicable from any a priori arrangement of matter and motion known to us; all of them stand in equal need for explanation of an immaterial principle; for although we see clearly that these are the phenomena of an organized matter in each case, yet in no case can we explain the rationale by any of the known properties of other inorganized matter. Hence according to the psychological doctrines, we must resort to some distinct and superadded being; to the anima intellectualis; the anima sensitiva, and the anima vitalis of the ancients—or to the separate faculties of the Scotch school of metaphysics, a species of entities most accomodating, ready for all work, and always in waiting—or to some being of analogous existence to the immaterial Soul of the orthodox. For I assert, and appeal to matter of fact, that,

*There is exactly the same evidence that sensation or perception, and volition, are properties of the nervous apparatus of the human system, that there is of contractility being a property of muscular fiber, or sight the property of the eye.*

On the truth of this proposition, I should (were it necessary) be willing to rest the controversy. In the one case and the other, constant concomitance is the sole foundation for ascribing necessary connexion. If it be sufficient in any one of the cases, it is sufficient in all. It is not necessary that we should be able to explain the quomodo: it is enough that our senses, under careful observation, assure us of the fact. Future facts and the future improvement of the human intellect may enable our posterity to do that which our more imperfect knowledge will not enable us to accomplish: just as the present generation are able to explain what remained an enigma to their forefathers.

2. I have said above, that our perception, volition, and in fact our other intellectual faculties, begin from nothing in infancy, grow with our growth, improve with our experience, vary with our education, and differ, not merely as to the nervous systems excited, but in consequence of the habitual difference in the stimuli applied. Suppose the original intellect of two infants exactly the same; educate the one among the thieves of broad St. Giles in London, and the other among the best class of Philadelphia Quakers, would their intellect be the same at one and twenty? But is the Soul thus mouldable and changeable? Is the Soul infantile as well as the body?

3. If the intellectual phenomena depended entirely on the Soul, then we should be unable to produce, annihilate, alter, or modify them by any mere mode of action operating merely on the body. But

Our ideas are frequently produced and commonly modified by the internal state of our bodily organs, particularly of the internal viscera —and by the state and condition of our organic life: hence the phenomena of dreaming, of delirium, and the hallucinations of hypochondria; and the alterations produced in our sensations and ideas by our state of internal health. Our ideas also are produced and modified by substances exhibited to us acting medicinally; as by wine, by opium, by cantharides, &c. But as Judge Cooper has said in his Medical Jurisprudence, how can you exhibit a dose of glauber salts to the Soul?

If then sensations, ideas, reasonings, and volitions are produced, modified or extinguished, by the condition of the involuntary parts of our organic system—by disease—by medicine: if they be (as we know they are) greatly under the command of the physician who acts only on the body—are not these effects thus produced by means of the body, bodily effects? What has the Soul to do with them? Are not these effects, however, the only evidences of the Soul's existence—the essential, incommunicable properties of the Soul, according to the Immaterialists? Yet are they manifestly produced on the body; and so far as we can see, on the body alone, by means of material stimuli calculated to act solely on the body?

If it be said, the body is no more than the instrument of the Soul, which can only act according to the condition of that body with which it is connected, and when the body is altered, the intellectual phenomena which it is calculated to exhibit, are altered also—then it follows, from the evidences of what takes place, that the very nature of the Soul is altered by altering the condition of the body, and the Soul therefore is under the control of accident, of disease, of medicine, and may be just what a physician chooses to make it. For if a physician can control the intellectual phenomena of sensation, memory, judgment, and volition, (as he can) then are all the *essential* properties of the Soul itself subject to the articles of the Materia Medica, and slaves of the Pharmacopeia.

4. I have already said, that no phenomena of mere matter and motion —no principle of mechanical or chemical philosophy can account for the phenomena of life and stimulus—for digestion, assimilation, secretion, reproduction. These are just as difficult as sensation, memory, or volition: the interposition of an immaterial Soul is as necessary to vegetable life, as to the human faculties. If this be denied, shew me where and by whom they have been explained, or explain them if you can.

5. I appeal to any physician accustomed to cases of insanity; and I ask whether all the intellectual appearances in that disease are not manifestly the result of the morbid state of the bodily organs? Is not this the case from the most violent symptoms of mania, to that almost imperceptible obliquity, from which in some degree or other, hardly any of us are free? In fact, such as is the state of our system, such are the mental phenomena we exhibit; the latter are the result of the former. Can you put a male mind into a female body, or vice versa? Let a parent decide this question; he will answer at once, No. Can you put an old head on young shoulders? No.

If a morbid intellect be the result of a morbid state of the encephalon, then is a sane intellect the result of a sane state, for like reason: and the intellect is what the encephalon is.

6. But there are no mental phenomena exhibited by the human species that are not also exhibited by the brute species. The difference is concomitant with difference of organization. The superiority of the human being arises from his larger, more expanded, and more perfect cerebral apparatus; from his erect position; from the skill with which he can use his hands; and from the faculty of speech. These give rise to the manipulations of art, and to the preservation and propagation of knowledge. For want of these, one generation of brutes is little wiser than the preceding. There is with them no means of accumulating knowledge.

When a dog has lost his master, does he not seek him at the places his master has been accustomed to frequent? I know by oft repeated facts in my own case, that he does. Does not this imply memory, ratiocination, volition? So many volumes of instances of the sagacity of animals, particularly of the canine species, have been collected, and instances are so familiar, that I would not condescend to argue with a man who would have hardihood enough to deny it. All these are intellectual phenomena *of the same kind* with such as we exhibit; the difference is in complication, and degree only. They are evidences therefore of an immaterial, immortal, distinct Soul, producing them. What say you to the immortal Soul of an opossum or an oyster?

I see no possibility of denying the facts, or avoiding the conclusions; and I leave the difficulty to be overcome by those who choose voluntarily to encounter it.

Finally, I say, that the phenomena termed mental, have been so well explained by Hartley, Cabanis, and Destut Tracey, that no man conversant with their writings, can hesitate to allow this. I say it is not possible for a fair man, conversant with physiology, to deny, that a sensation from recent impression, and an idea from recollection, are motions in the brain (or common sensory) perceived. As all our intellectual phenomena consist of sensations or ideas, which are the materials and substrata of memory, judgment, and volition, all of them consist in motions communicated to the corporeal nervous system—to the common sensory; whether by external impression, by association, or by internal sympathetic action, (innervation.) They are, therefore, corporeal phenomena, and no more. Destut Tracey has shewn this so clearly, and so well explained the phenomena of memory, judgment, desire, volition, as mere names given to various states and conditions of our brain, that I do not expect any refutation will or can be given to the view of the subject he has taken. Orthodox Ontology is in the seat of authority now, but truth will prevail at last.

# XII
## Benjamin Rush

1745–1813

Born in Byberry, Pa. A.B., College of New Jersey (Princeton), 1760. Medical apprentice under John Redman, Philadelphia, 1760–61. M.D. under William Cullen, Edinburgh, 1768. Started practice of medicine in Philadelphia, 1769. Professor at College of Philadelphia and at University of Pennsylvania. Wrote first textbook on chemistry in America, 1770. Signer of Declaration of Independence. Surgeon general in Revolutionary army, 1777. One of the founders of Dickinson College, 1783. Established first free dispensary in America, 1786. Made treasurer of United States mint, 1797. Regarded as father of psychiatry. Advocated temperance and abolition of capital punishment and of slavery. Wrote voluminously on medicine and social reform. Died in Philadelphia.

Benjamin Rush's philosophic interests were only one aspect of a varied career. He was a physician, a reformer, a moralist, a churchman and a practical man of affairs. In medicine he was one of the leading men of his day.[1] In politics he was a supporter of republicanism and encouraged Paine to write *Common Sense,* even suggesting the title of the book. In morality he spared no effort to defend the conventional standards of the day as viewed from a religious standpoint. In religion he wanted to retain the faith of his ancestry and early training. In practical affairs his accomplishments ranged from the founding of colleges to the manufacture of money. Famous in large part for his medical attainments, he has often been misinterpreted as a typical representative of the Age of Reason. Actually he was a strange mixture of old and new, of religious orthodoxy and scientific learning.

At Edinburgh Rush became acquainted with Scotch realism and assimilated some of its principles without completely understanding their implications. One of these principles was the unity of knowledge. In *The Influence of Physical Causes upon the Moral Faculty* he pleaded for a recognition of the equality of science and religion. In his

[1] Rush Medical College, founded in 1837, was named in his honor; it is now affiliated with the University of Chicago.

numerous essays and addresses on educational themes he constantly reiterated the belief that science and learning, philosophy and religion all contribute to an understanding of the fundamental relationships, direct and indirect, between God, the world and man. Regarding religion and science, therefore, as complementary aids in understanding the mystery of existence he, like many others who have fought the same battle, was alternately inclined to sacrifice fact to belief and belief to fact. The result was compromise and indecisiveness. Wishing to be both scientific and religious, he became more religious in his science than scientific in his religion. Practical in his motives, he could be realistic without being a realist, materialistic without being a materialist, deterministic without being a determinist and deistic without being a deist. Conversant with the leading trends of his day, he absorbed something from all and ended with a philosophic eclecticism, the parts of which were imperfectly synthesized.

The philosophy of mind, often spoken of in Rush's day as metaphysics, was the focal point of his thinking, although here as elsewhere he was somewhat indecisive. Although for the most part leaning toward the homogeneous interpretation of man as presented by Priestley and Cooper, at times he thought of the mind as immaterial. Whether excitability was a quality or a substance or a sort of vital phlogiston, he never decided. He was satisfied to give a descriptive account of life without clearly defining its ultimate nature. This account formed the substance of his *Animal Life*. Here he conceived man to be dependent upon stimulation for bringing his powers into action. Every part of the body being endowed with excitability, both external and internal sources of stimulation worked upon it. As external stimuli he cited air, sound, odors, heat, exercise and the pleasures of the senses. As internal stimuli he listed food, drinks, chyle, blood, glands and the exercises of the faculties of the mind. Mental stimuli were equally influential along with physical ones. The "desire of life," for example, made it possible to live on for days without food. The "love of money" led to such extremes as occurred during the speculative boom in 1791 when a man became insane and died a few days later because he had won twelve thousand dollars. Other mental stimuli such as amusements, love of dress and of novelty, patriotism and religion had their appropriate effect. On the basis of these varied stimuli, he concluded that life is "as much an effect of impressions upon a peculiar species of matter, as sound is of the stroke of a hammer upon a bell, or music of the motion of the bow upon the strings of a violin." [2] He contended that without

[2] Below, p. 285.

these stimuli children would never develop and mental life as we know it would be non-existent. He hypostasized faculties in the mind as did the Scotch thinkers, developing a theory of numerous minds within one mind similar to that accepted by many later psychiatrists. Along with memory, imagination and understanding, he listed faith, the passions, the moral faculty, conscience and a sense of deity. In some places Rush implied that these faculties might be real parts of a soul, but in others he was more partial to a physical interpretation of them. At times he leaned toward psycho-physical parallelism, but his commoner view was that of interactionism, in an attempt, of course, to avoid placing too great weight upon either the psychical or the physical factors in existence.

The practical use to which he put his theories is Rush's greatest claim to fame. He has been considered the father of psychiatry in America. His book, *Medical Inquiries and Observations upon the Diseases of the Mind,* published in 1812, was regarded as the standard reference in the field for half a century. Emphasizing the important effect of environmental influences, physical and mental, upon the individual, he fought persistently for reform in the handling of criminals and the insane. His reform consisted in substituting therapeutic for punitive treatment, and was based upon a pathological point of view. He advocated the use of mental catharsis and of occupational therapy, both of which are timely even today. Many of his other cures, such as bloodletting, have long since been discounted, but he remains a pioneer in the field of psychiatry. Insanity in his day was viewed largely from a religious or magical point of view; he regarded it as a disease of the mind, caused either by physical or mental ailments or both. Excessive study, for example, could cause insanity just as well as a physical ailment; in any case the proper treatment was to substitute counteracting stimulants. He suggested treatment for the over-credulous and for the sceptical. In the case of the latter, in whom the believing faculty was inadequately nourished, proper mental diet, consisting of plain and simple ideas at first followed by more involved propositions later, would effect a cure.

Rush's thoughts on morality demonstrate rather clearly his compromising attitude. This comes out in his only real work on moral philosophy, *An Inquiry into the Influence of Physical Causes upon the Moral Faculty,* published in 1786. In order to properly understand this essay, however, it is necessary to keep in mind Rush's scrupulous attitude toward moral problems as reflected in numerous essays. He condemned the use of liquor and has been regarded as one of the founders of the temperance movement in the United States. He wrote on the bad effects of tobacco. In an address to ministers he enumerated various practices which he felt exerted a pernicious effect upon morals, naming such things as liquor, military service, fairs ("they tempt to extravagance, gaming, drunkenness and uncleanness"), a licentious press, horse-racing, cock-fighting, eating clubs and Sunday amusements.[3] In speaking of the proper education for college students he opposed the use of dormitories because he felt that young people would corrupt one another if they lived together. He praised the Methodists for banning sports in college and for not permitting "the healthy and pleasurable exercise of swimming . . . except in the presence of their masters." [4] It is little wonder, then, that in writing the *Influence of Physical Causes upon the Moral Faculty* Rush was careful not to permit his essay to be interpreted as destructive of accepted moral principles. He intended the essay to be a reinforcement of the obligations of morality and religion and frequently digressed to point out the restricted sense in which he wished his views to be understood. He said he did not want the essay to be interpreted as defending a materialistic view of the soul, even though it was his particular purpose to show how the moral faculty was influenced by physical causes. In his exposition he followed the Scotch common-sense philosophy in assuming man to be possessed of a distinct moral faculty separate from other faculties such as reason (Locke) and taste (Shaftesbury) and listed numerous specific factors which influence it such as climate, diet, hunger, disease, idleness, sleep, solitude and habit. He would not trust the moral faculty alone, however, and closed the essay by saying that the great necessity of the age was to build schools where proper instruction might be given the young to assure the development of the type of moral character desired. On the other hand, he would not trust reason, as did the deists, suggesting that "the boasted morality of the Deists is, I believe, in most cases the offspring of habits, produced originally by the principles and precepts of Christianity." [5] Here the emphasis was on habit, in other places it was on the moral faculty, but the key to his whole moral system was his religious orthodoxy. Like the Scotch and the Princeton realists, he had the best interests of orthodoxy at heart and hence kept his moral as well as his

[3] Refer to "An Address to the Ministers of the Gospel of Every Denomination in the United States, upon Subjects Interesting to Morals," *Essays, Literary, Moral and Philosophical.*

[4] Ibid. 60.

[5] *Influence of Physical Causes upon the Moral Faculty.* 28.

mental philosophy in leash, despite his professed allegiance to the facts of science as they related to human life.

Morality, therefore, was fundamentally dependent upon religion. So were political ideals. In one passage in his *Essays* he pointed out that Christian principles were the best defense of republicanism. His basic dependence upon religion was clarified in the revision he made of *Animal Life* in 1809. Here he shied away from the necessitarianism and materialism into which his scientific opinions had seemed to lead him earlier. He denied that matter had power of its own. He denied that animal life could be propelled by its own innate power. He elaborated at great length on how God had given life to Adam. He now refuted what might have been interpreted as a deistic position in the first edition by appealing, not to occasionalism but to a species of continualism. It is on the basis of this final plea for orthodoxy that his paper *On Liberty and Necessity,* intended as an appendix to *Animal Life,* is best understood. Here he argued for necessity from a Calvinistic and teleological viewpoint, defending free will of a sort at the same time. The position he took was somewhat ambiguous but it helped temper his materialistic leanings and keep him within the circle of the orthodox.

Rush's position was, therefore, a transitional one. He breathed the intellectual air of his age, borrowing from Scotch realism and English materialism and deism, but without sacrificing one to the others except as his desire to include all forced him to compromise. In compromising he was ambiguous but honest. His sincerity served as a prophylactic where consistency might otherwise have been more intellectually respectable.

## REFERENCES

Rush, Benjamin: *An Oration, Delivered before the American Philosophical Society, Containing an Inquiry into the Influence of Physical Causes upon the Moral Faculty.* Philadelphia, 1786.

———: *Essays: Literary, Moral and Philosophical.* Philadelphia, 1798.

———: *An Inquiry into the Cause of Animal Life,* published in *Medical Inquiries and Observations.* 4 vols. Third edition. Philadelphia, 1809. I, 1–99. (These lectures were originally printed in 1799 under the title *Three Lectures upon Animal Life.* They were revised when printed in the 1809 edition of *Medical Inquiries and Observations* and retained this form in subsequent editions.)

———: *Sixteen Introductory Lectures, to Courses of Lectures upon the Institutes and Practice of Medicine, with a Syllabus of the*

*Latter. To Which are Added Two Lectures upon the Pleasures of the Senses and of the Mind with an Inquiry into Their Proximate Cause.* Philadelphia, 1811.

———: *Medical Inquiries and Observations upon the Diseases of the Mind.* Philadelphia, 1812. (Not to be confused with the book entitled *Medical Inquiries and Observations.*)

———: *Letters and Thoughts.* (Unpublished manuscript in the Ridgway Library of the Library Company of Philadelphia.)

Biddle, Louis A. (editor): *A Memorial Containing Travels through Life or Sundry Incidents in the Life of Dr. Benjamin Rush.* Lanordie, Pa., 1905.

Goodman, Nathan G.: *Benjamin Rush: Physician and Citizen.* Philadelphia: University of Pennsylvania Press, 1934. (Esp. chs. XI–XIV. Also has excellent bibliography.)

Good, Harry G.: *Benjamin Rush and His Services to American Education.* Berne, Ind., 1918.

Lloyd, James H.: "Benjamin Rush and His Critics," *Annals of Medical History* 2 (1931) 470–5.

Riley, I. Woodbridge: *American Philosophy: the Early Schools.* New York: Dodd, Mead and Co., 1907. 421–53.

* * *

* * *

## AN INQUIRY INTO THE CAUSE OF ANIMAL LIFE [6]

### *Lecture I*

In beholding the human body, the first thing that strikes us, is its *life.* This, of course, should be the first object of our inquiries. It is a most important subject; for the end of all the studies of a physician is to preserve life; and this cannot be perfectly done, until we know in what it consists.

I include in animal life as applied to the human body, *motion, heat, sensation,* and *thought.* These four, when united, compose perfect life. It may exist without thought, sensation, or heat, but none of them can exist without motion. The lowest grade of life, probably exists in the absence of even motion, as I shall mention hereafter. I have preferred the term *motion* to those of oscillation and vibration which have been employed by Dr. Hartley in explaining the laws of

[6] Taken from revised edition, 1809, in *Medical Inquiries and Observations.* I, 6–12, 28–30; 72–8, 83–99. Bracketed portions are major additions which did not appear in the earlier editions of this work.

animal matter; because I conceived it to be more simple, and better adapted to common apprehension.

In treating upon this subject, I shall first consider animal life as it appears in the waking and sleeping states in a healthy adult, and shall afterwards inquire into the modification of its causes in the foetal, infant, youthful, and middle states of life, in certain diseases, in different states of society, in different climates, and in different animals.

[Before I proceed any further, I shall remark, that there are certain grades of matter; and that in all its forms it is necessarily quiescent, or in other words, possesses no self-moving power. Every form of it is moved by a force external to it, and each form has its appropriate or specific stimulus, or stimuli, from the waves that are moved by the wind, and the sand upon the sea shore which is moved by the waves, up to the human body which is moved by the stimuli to be mentioned presently. From this view of matter, I am naturally led to reject the common division of it into active and passive, or into substances that possess a power to move themselves, and into such as require a power to move them. I believe that animals, like water, earth and air, nay further, that the mind of man are all moved only by their appropriate stimuli; and that water, earth and air do not become more certainly quiescent from the abstraction of the causes that move them, than motion, heat, sensation and thought cease from the abstraction of impressions upon the human body. The only difference between what is called animated and inanimate matter consists in the stimuli which move the former, acting constantly, and in health, with uniformity; whereas the stimuli which act upon the latter, act occasionally and with intermission. However diversified the motions and effects of these stimuli may be, the causes of their motions are exactly the same.]

I shall begin, by delivering a few general propositions.

I. Every part of the human body (the nails and hair excepted) is endowed with sensibility, or excitability, or with both of them. By sensibility is meant the power of having sensation excited by the action of impressions. Excitability denotes that property in the human body, by which motion is excited by means of impressions. This property has been called by several other names, such as, irritability, contractibility, mobility, and stimulability.

I shall make use of the term excitability, for the most part, in preference to any of them. I mean by it, a capacity of imperceptible, as well as obvious motion. It is of no consequence to our present inquiries, whether this excitability be a quality of animal matter, or a substance.

The latter opinion has been maintained by Dr. Girtanner, and has some probability in its favor.

II. The whole human body is so formed and connected, that impressions made in the healthy state upon one part, excite motion, or sensation, or both, in every other part of the body. From this view, it appears to be a unit, or a simple and indivisible substance. Its capacity for receiving motion, and sensation, is variously modified by means of what are called the senses. It is external, and internal. The impressions which act upon it shall be enumerated in order.

III. Certain motions are voluntary, and others are performed in an involuntary manner.

IV. Different parts of the body possess different degrees of what has been called excitability, that is, different degrees of susceptibility to the action of the same stimuli upon them.

V. Life is the *effect* of certain stimuli acting upon the sensibility and excitability which are extended, in different degrees, over every external and internal part of the body. These stimuli are as necessary to its existence, as air is to flame. Animal life is truly (to use the words of Dr. Brown) "a forced state." I have said the *words* of Dr. Brown; for the opinion was delivered by Dr. Cullen in the University of Edinburgh, in the year 1766, and was detailed by me in this school, many years before the name of Dr. Brown was known as a teacher of medicine. It is true, Dr. Cullen afterwards deserted it; but it is equally true, I never did; and the belief of it has been the foundation of many of the principles and modes of practice in medicine which I have since adopted. In a lecture which I delivered in the year 1771, I find the following words, which are taken from a manuscript copy of lectures given by Dr. Cullen upon the institutes of medicine. "The human body is not an automaton, or self-moving machine; but is kept alive and in motion, by the constant action of stimuli upon it." In thus ascribing the discovery of the cause of life which I shall endeavour to establish, to Dr. Cullen, let it not be supposed I mean to detract from the genius and merit of Dr. Brown. To his intrepidity in reviving and propagating it, as well as for the many other truths contained in his system of medicine, posterity, I have no doubt, will do him ample justice, after the errors that are blended with them have been corrected, by their unsuccessful application to the cure of diseases.

Agreeably to our last proposition, I proceed to remark, that the action of the brain, the diastole and systole of the heart, the pulsation of the arteries, the contraction of the muscles, the peristaltic motion of the bowels, the absorbing power of the lymphatics, secretion, excretion, hearing, seeing, smelling, taste, and the sense of touch, nay more, thought itself, are all the effects of stimuli acting upon the organs of sense and motion. These stimuli have been divided into external and internal. The external are light, sound, odours, air, heat, exercise, and the pleasures of the senses. The internal stimuli are food, drinks, chyle, the blood, a certain tension of the glands, which contain secreted liquors, and the exercises of the faculties of the mind; each of which I shall treat in the order in which they have been mentioned.

[*Rush goes on to deal separately with the effect which external and internal stimuli have upon human life. The section is largely devoted to physiological considerations. Of interest philosophically is the part dealing with air. In this revised edition he gives first consideration to air among external stimuli, although it will be noted that it still retains fourth position in the list in the preceding paragraph. His main support for the importance he attaches to air is Biblical, not physiological. He argues that the life of man began when God animated the lifeless body and soul of Adam by dilating his nostrils and inflating his lungs with air. This offers additional evidence of Rush's tendency to mix religion with science.*

*After dealing with food and drinks, chyle, blood, and tension of the glands as four of the internal stimuli, he continues the lecture with the following section on the faculties of the mind.*]

V. The exercises of the faculties of the mind have a wonderful influence in increasing the quantity of human life. They all act by *reflection* only, after having been previously excited into action by impressions made upon the body. This view, of the *re-action* of the mind upon the body, accords with the simplicity of other operations in the animal economy. It is thus the brain repays the heart for the blood it conveys to it, by re-acting upon its muscular fibres. The influence of the different faculties of the mind is felt in the pulse, in the stomach, and in the liver, and is seen in the face, and other external parts of the body. Those which act most unequivocally in promoting life, are the understanding, the imagination, and the passions. Thinking belongs to the understanding, and is attended with an obvious influence upon the degree and duration of life. Intense study has often rendered the body insensible to the debilitating effects of cold and hunger. Men of great and active understandings, who blend with their studies temperance and exercise, are generally long lived. In support of this assertion, a hundred names might be added to those of Newton and Franklin. Its truth will be more fully established by attending to the state of human life in persons of an opposite intellectual character. The Cretins, a race of idiots in Valais in Switzerland, travellers tell us, are all short lived. Common language justifies the opinion of the stimulus of the understanding upon the brain, hence it is common to say of dull men, that they have scarcely ideas enough to keep themselves awake.

The imagination acts with great force upon the body, whether its numerous associations produce pleasure or pain. But the passions pour a constant stream upon the wheels of life. They have been subdivided into emotions and passions properly so called. The former have for their objects present, the latter, future good and evil. All the objects of the passions are accompanied with desire or aversion. To the former belong chiefly, hope, love, ambition, and avarice; to the latter, fear, hatred, malice, envy, and the like. Joy, anger, and terror, belong to the class of emotions. The passions and emotions have been further divided into stimulating and sedative. Our business at present is to consider their first effect only upon the body. In the original constitution of human nature, we were made to be stimulated by such passions and emotions only as have moral good for their objects. Man was designed to be always under the influence of hope, love, and joy. By the loss of his innocence, he has subjected himself to the dominion of passions and emotions of a malignant nature; but they possess, in common with such as are good, a stimulus which renders them subservient to the purpose of promoting animal life. It is true, they are like the stimulus of a dislocated bone in their operation upon the body, compared with the action of antagonist muscles stretched over bones, which gently move in their natural sockets. The effects of the good passions and emotions, in promoting health and longevity, have been taken notice of by many writers. They produce a flame, gentle and pleasant, like oil perfumed with frankincense in the lamp of life. There are instances likewise of persons who have derived strength, and long life from the influence of the evil passions and emotions that have been mentioned. Dr. Darwin relates the history of a man, who used to overcome the fatigue induced by travelling, by thinking of a person whom he hated. The debility induced by disease, is often removed by a sudden change in the temper. This is so common, that even nurses predict a recovery in persons as soon as they become peevish and ill-natured, after having been patient during the worst stage of their sickness. This peevishness acts as a gentle stimulus upon the system in its languid state, and thus turns the scale in favour of life and health.

The famous Benjamin Lay, of this state, who lived to be eighty years of age, was of a very irascible temper. Old Elwes was a prodigy of avarice, and every court in Europe furnishes instances of men who have attained to extreme old age, who have lived constantly under the dominion of ambition. In the course of a long inquiry, which I instituted some years ago into the state of the body and mind in old people, I did not find a single person above eighty, who had not possessed an active understanding, or active passions. Those different and opposite faculties of the mind, when in excess, happily supply the place of each other. Where they unite their forces, they extinguish the flame of life, before the oil which feeds it is consumed.

In another place I shall resume the influence of the faculties of the mind upon human life, as they discover themselves in the different pursuits of men.

## *Lecture III*

It remains now to mention certain mental stimuli which act nearly alike in the production of animal life, upon the individuals of all the nations in the world. They are,

1. The desire of life. This principle, so deeply and universally implanted in human nature, acts very powerfully in supporting our existence. It has been observed to prolong life. Sickly travellers by sea and land, often live under circumstances of the greatest weakness, till they reach their native country, and then expire in the bosom of their friends. This desire of life often turns the scale in favor of a recovery in acute diseases. Its influence will appear, from the difference in the periods in which death was induced in two persons, who were actuated by opposite passions with respect to life. Atticus, we are told, died of voluntary abstinence from food in five days. In Sir William Hamilton's account of the earthquake at Calabria, we read of a girl who lived eleven days without food, before she expired. In the former case, life was shortened by an aversion from it; in the latter, it was protracted by the desire of it. The late Mr. Brissot, in his visit to this city, informed me, that the application of animal magnetism (in which he was a believer) had in no instance cured a disease in a West India slave. Perhaps it was rendered inert, by its not being accompanied by a strong desire of life; for this principle exists in a more feeble state in slaves than in freemen. It is possible likewise the wills and imaginations of these degraded people may have become so paralytic, by slavery,

as to be incapable of being excited by the impression of this fanciful remedy.

2. The love of money sets the whole animal machine in motion. Hearts, which are insensible to the stimuli of religion, patriotism, love, and even of the domestic affections, are excited into action by this passion. The city of Philadelphia, between the 10th and 15th of August, 1791, will long be remembered by contemplative men, for having furnished the most extraordinary proofs of the stimulus of the love of money upon the human body. A new scene of speculation was produced at that time by the scrip of the bank of the United States. It excited febrile diseases in three persons who became my patients. In one of them, the acquisition of twelve thousand dollars in a few minutes, by a lucky sale, brought on madness which terminated in death in a few days.[7] The whole city felt the impulse of this paroxysm of avarice. The slow and ordinary means of earning money were deserted, and men of every profession and trade were seen in all our streets hastening to the coffee-house, where the agitation of countenance, and the desultory manners, of all the persons who were interested in this species of gaming, exhibited a truer picture of bedlam, than of a place appropriated to the transaction of mercantile business. But further, the love of money discovers its stimulus upon the body in a peculiar manner in the games of cards and dice. I have heard of a gentleman in Virginia who passed two whole days and nights in succession at a card table; and it is related in the life of a noted gamester in Ireland, that when he was so ill as to be unable to rise from his chair, he would suddenly revive when brought to the hazard table, by hearing the rattling of the dice.

3. Public amusements of all kinds, such as a horse race, a cockpit, a chase, the theatre, the circus, masquerades, public dinners, and tea parties, all exert an artificial stimulus upon the system, and thus apply the defect of the rational exercises of the mind.

4. The love of dress is not confined in its stimulating operation to persons in health. It acts perceptibly in some cases upon invalids. I have heard of a gentleman in South Carolina, who always relieved himself of a fit of low spirits by changing his dress; and I believe there are few people, who do not feel themselves enlivened, by putting on a new suit of clothes.

[7] Dr. Mead relates, upon the authority of Dr. Hales, that more of the successful speculators in the South-Sea Scheme of 1720 became insane, than of those who had been ruined by it.

5. Novelty is an immense source of agreeable stimuli. Companions, studies, pleasures, modes of business, prospects, and situations, with respect to town and country, or to different countries, that are *new,* all exert an invigorating influence upon health and life.

6. The love of fame acts in various ways; but its stimulus is most sensible and durable in military life. It counteracts in many instances the debilitating effects of hunger, cold, and labour. It has sometimes done more, by removing the weakness which is connected with many diseases. In several instances, it has assisted the hardships of a camp life, in curing pulmonary consumption.

7. The love of country is a deep seated principle of action in the human breast. Its stimulus is sometimes so excessive, as to induce disease in persons who recently migrate, and settle in foreign countries. It appears in various forms; but exists most frequently in the solicitude, labors, attachments, and hatred of party spirit. All these act forcibly in supporting animal life. It is because newspapers are supposed to contain the measure of the happiness or misery of our country, that they are so interesting to all classes of people. Those vehicles of intelligence, and of public pleasure or pain, are frequently desired with the impatience of a meal, and they often produce the same stimulating effects upon the body.[8]

8. The different religions of the world, by the activity they excite in the mind, have a sensible influence upon human life. Atheism is the worst of sedatives to the understanding and passions. It is the abstraction of thought from the most sublime, and of love from the most perfect of all possible objects. Man is as naturally a religious, as he is a social and domestic animal; and the same violence is done to his mental faculties, by robbing him of a belief in a God, that is done by dooming him to live in a cell, deprived of the objects and pleasures of social and domestic life. The necessary and immutable connection between the texture of the human mind, and the worship of an object of some kind, has lately been demonstrated by the atheists of Europe, who, after rejecting the true God, have instituted the worship of nature, of fortune, and of human reason; and, in some instances, with ceremonies of the most expensive and splendid kind. Religions are friendly to animal life, in proportion as they elevate the understanding, and act upon the passions of hope and love. It will readily occur to you, that Christianity when believed, and obeyed, according to its original consistency with itself, and with the divine attributes, is more

[8] They have been very happily called by Mr. Green in his poem entitled Spleen, "the manna of the day."

calculated to produce those effects, than any other religion in the world. Such is the salutary operation of its doctrines and precepts upon health and life, that if its divine authority rested upon no other argument, this alone would be sufficient to recommend it to our belief. How long mankind may continue to prefer substituted pursuits and pleasures, to this invigorating stimulus, is uncertain; but the time, we are assured, will come, when the understanding shall be elevated from its present inferior objects, and the luxated passions be reduced to their original order. This change in the mind of man, I believe, will be effected only by the influence of the Christian religion, after all the efforts of human reason to produce it, by means of civilization, philosophy, liberty, and government, have been exhausted to no purpose.

. . . . .

From a review of what has been said of animal life, in all its numerous forms and modifications, we see that it is as much an effect of impressions upon a peculiar species of matter, as sound is of the stroke of a hammer upon a bell, or music of the motion of the bow upon the strings of a violin. I exclude therefore the intelligent principle of Whytt, the medical mind of Stahl, the healing powers of Cullen, and the vital principle of John Hunter, as much from the body, as I do an intelligent principle from air, fire, and water.

[Upon the opinions of these different authors, I beg leave to add further, that they are all modifications of two errors held by Pythagoras and Epicurus. The former believed and taught what is called the transmigration of souls, that is, that the principle of life, rational and animal, was a kind of elementary body; that it never died; and that it passed from animals that perished, into other animal matter, and thereby imparted to it a soul, or what is called life. This opinion accords with the vital principle of Mr. Hunter and Dr. Girtanner, while the anima medica of Stahl accords with the doctrine taught by Epicurus, of the globe being animated by a principle called anima mundi. Both opinions substitute an intelligent and self-moving principle to the agency of a Supreme Being, in every part of his works. There is a third error connected with this subject, which it may not be improper to mention upon this occasion, and that is, that man consists of spirit, soul, and body . . . that his spirit resides in his brain, and is concerned only in intellectual and spiritual exercises . . . that his soul is diffused through every part of his body, and constitutes what is called his "soulish," or animal life. This pagan opinion seems to have tinctured some of the writings of St. Paul, who, though inspired by the Spirit of truth upon theological subjects, was left to follow the opinions of the world in matters of human learning. The doctrine I have delivered, obliges us to consider man as consisting and of two parts only; these, are, soul, or mind, and body. This view of the nature of man is simple, and accords alike with reason and revelation.

The speaking figures, which are conducted through our country as spectacles to amuse the vulgar, afford a striking illustration of the error of animal life depending upon a self-moving principle in the body. The voice is supposed to come from *within* the figure; whereas, it is certain it is conveyed there by the reflection of words pronounced by a person external to it.

I have often been struck with the similarity of the controversies upon the origin of moral obligation, of power, and of animal life, and with the similarity of their issue in a simple elementary truth, obvious to the most humble capacities. They were all believed to depend upon causes within themselves; but they are now rescued from an internal and placed upon an external basis. The origin of moral obligation, which was formerly ascribed to utility, to sympathy, and to the fitness of things, is now derived wholly from the will of God. The origin of power, which was derived for ages from divine or hereditary right, now rests exclusively upon the will of the people, while the origin of animal life, which has been, time immemorial, derived from a self-moving power, under the different names that have been mentioned, now reposes, probably for ever, upon external and internal impressions. By means of this doctrine, revelation and reason embrace each other, and Moses and the prophets shake hands with Dr. Brown, and all those physicians, who maintain the great and sublime truth which he has promulgated. Think of it, gentlemen, in your closets, and in your beds, and talk of it in your walks, and by your fire-sides. It is the active and wide-spreading seminal principle of all truth in medicine.]

It is no uncommon thing for the simplicity of causes to be lost in the magnitude of their effects. By contemplating the wonderful functions of life, we have strangely overlooked the numerous and obscure circumstances which produce it. Thus the humble but true origin of power in the people, is often forgotten in the splendor and pride of governments. It is not necessary to be acquainted with the precise nature of that form of matter, which is capable of producing life from impressions made upon it. It is sufficient for our purpose to know the fact. It is immaterial, moreover, whether this matter derive its power of being acted upon wholly from the brain, or whether it be in part inherent in animal fibres. The inferences are the same in favour of life being the effect of stimuli, and of its being as truly mechanical, as the movements of a clock from the pressure of its weights, or the passage of a ship in the water from the impulse of winds and tide.

The infinity of effects from similar causes, has often been taken notice of in the works of the Creator. It would seem as if they had all been made after one pattern. The late discovery of the cause of combustion has thrown great light upon our subject. Wood and coal are no longer believed to contain a principle of fire. The heat and flame they omit are derived from an agent altogether external to them. They are produced by a matter which is absorbed from the air by means of its decomposition. This matter acts upon the predisposition of the fuel to receive it, in the same way that stimuli act upon the human body. The two agents differ only in their effects. The former produces the destruction of the bodies upon which it acts, while the latter excite the more gentle and durable motions of life. Common language in expressing these effects is correct, as far as it relates to their cause. We speak of a coal of fire being *alive,* and of the *flame* of life.

The causes of life which I have delivered will receive considerable support, by contrasting them with the causes of death. This catastrophe of the body consists in such a change, induced on it by disease or old age, as to prevent its exhibiting the phaenomena of life. It is brought on,

1. By the abstraction of all the stimuli which support life. Death from this cause is produced by the same mechanical means, that the omission of sound from a violin is prevented by the abstraction of the bow from its strings.

2. By the excessive force of stimuli of all kinds. No more occurs here, than happens from too much pressure upon the strings of a violin, preventing its emitting musical tones.

3. By too much relaxation, or too weak a texture of the matter which composes the human body. No more occurs here, than is observed in the extinction of sound by the total relaxation or slender combination of the strings of a violin.

4. By an error in the place of certain fluid or solid parts of the body. No more occurs here, than would happen from fixing the strings of a violin upon its body, instead of elevating them upon its bridge.

5. By the action of poisonous exhalations, or of certain fluids vitiated

in the body, upon parts which emit most forcibly the motions of life. No more happens here, than occurs from enveloping the strings of a violin in a piece of wax.

6. By the solution of continuity, by means of wounds in solid parts of the body. No more occurs in death from this cause, than takes place when the emission of sound from a violin is prevented by a rupture of its strings.

7. Death is produced by a preternatural rigidity, and in some instances by an ossification of the solid parts of the body in old age, in consequence of which they are incapable of receiving and emitting the motions of life. No more occurs here, than would happen if a stick or pipe-stem were placed, in the room of catgut, upon the bridges of the violin. But death may take place in old age, without a change in the texture of animal matter, from the stimuli of life losing their effect by repetition, just as opium, from the same cause, ceases to produce its usual effects upon the body.

Should it be asked, what is that peculiar organization of matter, which enables it to emit life, when acted upon by stimuli, I answer, I do not know. [It is true, the votaries of chemistry have lately attempted to imitate it; but no arrangements of matter by their hands have ever produced a single living fibre, nor have any of their compounds produced a substance endowed with the properties of dead animal matter. Lavoissier laboured in vain to produce that simple animal substance we call bile. That the human body is composed of certain matters which belong to the objects of chemistry, there can be no doubt; but their proportions, and manner of aggregation, are unknown to us; nor are the products, when obtained by fire, the same in form, number, or proportion, which existed in the body in its living state. But admitting this medico-chemical theory of animal life to be demonstrated, it does not in the least degree militate against the doctrine which I have taught. Let us suppose a chemist to have discovered all the matters which compose an animal body, and to have arranged them in their exact order and proportions, they cannot in this situation assume the properties of life, without the impression of some agent upon them. A stimulus of some kind must give them activity. Even the matter of phosphorus is torpid, when confined in a phial. It requires the stimulus of air to impart to it its blazing life. It is remarkable, that some of the ancient philosophers had more correct ideas of the origin of animal life than some of our modern chemists. This is elegantly illustrated in the fable of Prometheus. He was unable, by any chemical combination, to animate his image of clay, until he stole fire, or an external stimulus from heaven, for that purpose. As well might we suppose thinking to be a chemical process, as motion and sensation. They are all alike the effects of impression. We think by force, as well as live by force. If any man doubt the truth of this assertion, let him suspend, for a moment, the operations of his mind, or, in other words, let him cease to think. As well might he attempt to stop the pulsation of his heart, by the action of his will, or to arrest the planets in their course, by holding up his finger. Here then let us limit our inquiries, and remain satisfied with facts which are obvious, and capable of application to all the useful purposes of medicine.]

The great Creator has kindly established a witness of his unsearchable wisdom in every part of his works, in order to prevent our forgetting him, in the successful exercises of our reason. Mohammed once said, "that he should believe himself to be a God, if he could bring down rain from the clouds, or give life to an animal." It belongs exclusively to the true God to endow matter with those singular properties, which enable it, under certain circumstances, to exhibit the appearances of life.

I cannot conclude this subject, without taking notice of its extensive application to medicine, metaphysics, theology, and morals.

The doctrine of animal life which has been taught exhibits, in the

First place, a new view of the nervous system, by discovering its origin in the extremities of the nerves on which impressions are made, and its termination in the brain. This idea is extended in an ingenious manner by Mr. Valli, in his treatise upon animal electricity.

2. It discovers to us the true means of promoting health and longevity, by proportioning the number and force of stimuli to the age, climate, situation, habits, and temperament of the human body.

3. It leads us to a knowledge of the causes of all diseases. These consist in excessive or preternatural excitement in certain parts, of the human body, accompanied *generally* with irregular motions, and induced by natural or artificial stimuli. The latter have been called very properly by Mr. Hunter, *irritants*. The occasional absence of motion in acute diseases is the effect only of the excess of impetus in their remote causes.

4. It discovers to us that the cure of all diseases depends simply upon the abstraction of stimuli from the whole, or from a part of the body, when the motions excited by them, are in excess; and in the increase of their number and force, when motions are of a moderate nature. For the former purpose, we employ a class of medicines known by the name of sedatives. For the latter, we make use of stimulants.

Under these two extensive heads are included all the numerous articles of the Materia Medica.

5. It enables us to reject the doctrine of innate ideas, and to ascribe all our knowledge of sensible objects to impressions acting upon an *innate* capacity to receive ideas. Were it possible for a child to grow up to manhood without the use of any of its senses, it would not possess a single idea of a material object; and as all human knowledge is compounded of simple ideas, this person would be as destitute of knowledge of every kind, as the grossest portion of vegetable, or fossil matter.

6. The account which has been given of animal life furnishes a striking illustration of the origin of human actions, by the impression of motives upon the will. As well might we admit an inherent principle of life in animal matter, as a self-determining power in this faculty of the mind. Motives are necessary, not only to constitute its *freedom,* but its *essence;* for, without them, there could be no more a will, than there could be vision without light, or hearing without sound. It is true, they are often so obscure as not to be perceived, and they sometimes become insensible from habit; but the same things have been remarked in the operation of stimuli, and yet we do not upon this account deny their agency in producing animal life. In thus deciding in favor of the necessity of motives to produce actions, I cannot help bearing a testimony against the gloomy misapplication of this doctrine by some modern writers. When properly understood, it is calculated to produce the most comfortable views of the divine government, and the most beneficial effects upon morals and human happiness.

7. There are errors of an impious nature, which sometimes obtain a currency, from being disguised by innocent names. The doctrine of animal life that has been delivered, is directly opposed to an error of this kind, which has had the most baneful influence upon morals and religion. To suppose a principle to reside necessarily and constantly in the human body, which acted independently of external circumstances, is to ascribe to it an attribute, which I shall not connect, even in language, with the creature man. Self-existence belongs only to God.

The best criterion of the truth of a philosophical opinion is, its tendency to produce exalted ideas of the Divine Being, and humble views of ourselves. The doctrine of animal life which has been delivered is calculated to produce these effects in an eminent degree; for

8. It does homage to the Supreme Being, as the governor of the universe, and establishes the certainty of his universal and particular providence. Admit a principle of life in the human body, and we open

a door for the restoration of the old Epicurean or atheistical philosophy which has been mentioned. The doctrine I have taught cuts the sinews of this error; for by rendering the *continuance* of animal life, no less than its commencement, the effect of the constant operation of divine power and goodness, it leads us to believe that the whole creation is supported in the same manner. [It leads us further to distinguish between the works of the Creator of the universe, and the works of a common architect. It has been supposed by some men, that the author of our world formed all its wonderful machinery as a man makes a clock, and, having wound it up, threw it out of his hands, and afterwards retired to rest, or employed himself in other acts of creating power, or if this were not the case, that he committed the care of his works to certain deputies, called nature in the inanimate, and vital principle in the animated parts of the globe. This idea is contrary to the whole tenor of revelation. The Being that created our world never takes his hand, nor his eye, for a single moment, from any part of it. He constantly

> Warms in the sun, refreshes in each breeze,
> Glows in the stars, blossoms in the trees,
> Lives through all life, extends through all extent,
> Spreads undivided, operates unspent.

His providence is one continued act of creating power. The sun rises (to use the words of a late elegant writer [9]) only because he says every morning, "let there be light." The moon and the stars supply the absence of the sun, only because he says every evening, "let there be lights in the firmament of heaven, to divide the day from the night." The seasons of spring and autumn return, only because he says, "let the earth bring forth grass, the herb yielding seed, and the fruit tree yielding fruit according to its kind;" and even man exists, only because he breathes into his nostrils the breath, or air, of life, not only at his birth, but every moment of his existence.]

9. The view that has been given of the dependent state of man for the blessing of life leads us to contemplate with very opposite and inexpressible feelings, the sublime idea which is given of the Deity in the scriptures, as possessing life "within himself." This divine prerogative has never been imparted but to one being, and that is the Son of God. This appears from the following declaration. "For as the Father hath life in himself, so hath he given to the Son to have life *within himself*." [10] To this plenitude of independent life we are to ascribe his being called the "life of the world," "the prince of life," and "life" itself, in the New Testament. These divine epithets, which are very

[9] Mr. Fawcett.
[10] John V. verse 26.

properly founded upon the manner of our Saviour's existence, exalt him infinitely above simple humanity, and establish his divine nature upon the basis of reason, as well as revelation.

10. We have heard that some of the stimuli, which produce animal life, are derived from the moral and physical evils of our world. From beholding these instruments of death thus converted by divine skill into the means of life, we are led to believe goodness to be the supreme attribute of the Deity, and that it will appear finally to predominate in all his works.

11. The doctrine which has been delivered is calculated to humble the pride of man, by teaching him his constant dependence upon his Maker for his existence, and that he has no pre-eminence, in his tenure of it, over the meanest insect that flutters in the air, or the humblest plant that grows upon the earth. What an inspired writer says of the innumerable animals which inhabit the ocean, may with equal propriety be said of the whole human race. "Thou sendest forth thy spirit, and they are created. Thou takest away their breath, they die, and return to their dust." Let us not complain of this tenure of our lives. By taking their capital out of our hands, and dealing it out to us according to our necessities, our benevolent Creator prevents our squandering it away without judgment or prudence, and thus becoming bankrupts in life as soon as we begin to exist.

12. Melancholy indeed would have been the issue of all our inquiries, did we take a final leave of the human body in its state of decomposition in the grave. Revelation furnishes us with an elevating and comfortable assurance that this will not be the case. The precise manner of its re-organization, and the new means of its future existence, are unknown to us. It is sufficient to believe the event will take place, and that, after it, the soul and body of man will be exalted, in one respect, to an equality with their Creator. They will be immortal.

Here, gentlemen, we close the history of animal life. I feel as if I had waded across a rapid and dangerous stream. Whether I have gained the opposite shore with my head clean, or covered with mud and weeds, I leave wholly to your determination.

* * *

---

* * *

## ON LIBERTY AND NECESSITY [11]

Is it not absurd to talk of *past* or *future* when we speak of the knowledge of the Deity? Can anything be *past* or *future* to a being who exists from eternity to eternity? Are not past, present, and future to *Him* one eternal *now?* Is not time a finite idea only, and past and future knowable only to finite beings? May not the moral actions of man then have appeared as complete to the Deity at the creation, as the *material* world? I see the objects of a plain before me as distinctly as if I was near it. My view of it has no influence on its form or distance. The same probably occurs to the Deity with respect to pre-existing actions. Imperfect man by *memory sees* past events, a wonderful power in a finite mind! May not a perfect being see future events in the same manner? They all have an existence in the eternal mind. *There is nothing* truly *new* in actions, any more than in truths *under the Sun.* There can be no contingency with the Deity,—all is fixed and immutable with Him,—cause and effect, *motive* and *action,* creation and preservation, all one simple object and act. Hence the death of our Lord is described "as the lamb slain from the foundation of the World." This event like all moral actions had its *completion* in His creation. Hence it is said 1000 years to Him are as one day, and he is not slack in his promises, as some count slack. Why? Because promise and fulfillment are with Him one and the same thing. The perfection of the Deity requires this solution of this doctrine. *Prescience* is only a human term, but like many others applied to the Deity in accomodation to our weak capacities. Prophesies are to him things present,—to us things to come, hence their great accuracy. It is improper and dishonourable to his glorious Oneness in existence as well as nature. It is impossible matters should be otherwise. Succession belongs only to man. God can do and know nothing in succession. So far for necessity. But all this is compatible with the most perfect liberty. The knowledge of God of actions flows from a perfect knowledge of the union between cause and effect in creation. All is

[11] *Letters and Thoughts.* 53–6. Rush intended this to be added to *An Inquiry into the Cause of Animal Life.*

still free. An artist can tell from the construction of a machine exactly its strokes and without touching it after its wheels are set in motion, although he still upholds it in his hand. We still live, move and have our being in *God*. To have just ideas on this subject we must often recur to the identity of God as to existence as well as to nature. "Known unto him are all his works" of moral actions as well as of nature "from the beginning." The moral actions are most important as they were intended to prepare the way for the display of his perfections on the cross. Nor does this idea destroy man's responsibility. He is still free. His liberty is essential to the necessity, otherwise his action would have no moral nature and could not be the object of pardon, and for this purpose alone evil existed. It must be free to be a crime and crimes existed, not for love of vindictive justice in endless punishment, but from the display of love in justice in endless and universal happiness. This removes all the fears and difficulties about moral necessity. It was necessary that man should fall. It was likewise necessary that he should be *free,* or he would not have fallen. Liberty and necessity are therefore both true, and both necessary to advance in due consistency all the glorious attributes of God. This union of liberty and necessity may be illustrated by a simple example. I require a perfect knowledge of a man's taste in building, and then convey secretly into his hands a plan of a house. Every bit of this man in building this house is foreknown by me, and yet no influence is exercised over his will. Here is necessity and liberty united. Hence we are led to explain a difficult passage in Genesis. Adam was good but did not know good 'till he knew evil; Christ knew good and evil at his creation; the latter by *imputation* as much as when he expiated it on the cross. Adam became like Christ ("or one of us") by eating the forbidden fruit. He knew evil by sad experience, and good from the promise of the seed of the woman bruising the serpents head. The fall was the gate which opened heaven to man. To talk of what man was or what he would have been had he never fallen is to talk without reason or Scripture. I consider all that has been written upon that subject as calvinistical romances, contrary and injurious to the wisdom and decrees of God. The glory of God by redemption was the end of man's creation. The fall of man was accessory for the display of this glory. It was the second stage (in man's conception) of the business, not the first as is usually represented. Evil then serves only to produce more good. Under all circumstances *existence* is an infinite blessing. To exist as a drop of water, to be the subject of creating goodness, to attract divine observation in any way is infinitely preferable to nonexistence. Adam was good, but knew little of God or good. The world was his portion, dominion given to him over it. Now God is given to man instead of the world.

# XIII

## Samuel Stanhope Smith

1750–1819

Born in Pequea, Lancaster County, Pa., the son of a clergyman. Studied classics in his father's academy. Graduated at Princeton, 1769. Aided his father in the academy, 1769–71. Taught classics and studied theology at Princeton, 1771–73. Missionary among Scotch-Irish in western section of Virginia, 1773–79. Founded Academy of Hampden-Sidney (later College of Hampden-Sidney), 1776. Married Ann Witherspoon, daughter of John Witherspoon, President of Princeton. Appointed Professor of Moral Philosophy at Princeton, 1779. President of Princeton, 1795–1812. Member, American Philosophical Society. Awarded honorary degrees by Yale and Harvard. Died in Princeton.

As the religious implications of the naturalism of the Age of Reason became clearer, opposition from the orthodox became more pronounced. By the beginning of the nineteenth century the conservatives in religion had marshaled their forces to stamp out what they regarded as infidelity. The colleges were an important ally in the crusade; no institution played a larger rôle than did Princeton with its teaching of realistic philosophy.

The writings of Scotch realists such as Hutcheson, Reid, Beattie and Oswald were read in the United States during the latter half of the eighteenth century. With the arrival of John Witherspoon, a follower of Reid and Beattie who became President of Princeton in 1768, the Scotch philosophy succeeded in acquiring a more or less permanent center of influence. At the time, Berkeley's idealism was current on the Princeton campus but it was not long before Witherspoon had supplanted it by the common-sense philosophy. In Princeton, and from Princeton throughout the middle colonies and beyond, it gradually gathered adherents until it was regarded by many as the typical American philosophy by the middle of the nineteenth century.[1]

[1] President James McCosh of Princeton, writing in the 1880's, spoke of realism as *the* American philosophy. See his *Realistic Philosophy: Defended in a Philosophic Series.* 2 vols. New York: Charles Scribner's Sons, 1887 (first published in 1882). Refer to introduction, "What an American Philosophy Should Be."

When Witherspoon arrived at Princeton Samuel Stanhope Smith was a student there, much enamored of idealism due to the influence of Joseph Periam, his instructor. Converted to realism by Witherspoon, he later taught moral philosophy at Princeton and became Witherspoon's successor as president. Although he borrowed heavily from Witherspoon as Cooper did from Priestley, his American birth of religious parents, his interest in science and his careful preparation of his lectures for publication combine to make him more representative of native realism.

It has been said that early realism and orthodoxy were allied. This assertion was more true of their joint opposition to common enemies than of their method of attack. While the Dwights and Fosters were more likely to resort to direct condemnation of their opponents and to authority for defense of their own position, the realists professed allegiance to the empirical approach of the deists and materialists they sought to defeat. To Smith, truth was unified; there was no real opposition between science and philosophy on the one hand and religion and theology on the other. At the same time, it is well to keep in mind that when opposition did develop between science or philosophy and religion, Smith made philosophy and science conform to religion. He wanted to achieve the same certainty in morality and religion as Newton had in physical science. Accepting nature as orderly, he sought to find principles of morality and religion by the same procedure used in discovering the laws of the physical world.

Smith divided philosophy into two branches, natural and moral. The first had to do with the physical world, the second with man. The same process of reasoning was to be followed in both, namely, observation followed by induction. Attempting to view man empirically, he concluded that man possessed two types of senses, external and internal. The external senses provided impressions of the physical world, the only basis we had for knowledge of that world. Impressions passed through the nerves and became ideas in the mind. Following Hartley, he held that ideas were brought together by association and were organized and synthesized by reason. While speaking of ideas, he defined his realistic position in the following manner:

And these ideas are, at the same time, accompanied with a conviction of the reality of external objects; which are conceived to exist independent of our perceptions of them, and distinct from the properties by which they are exhibited to the senses. It is the admission of this principle which distinguishes what may be called the *substantial,* from the *ideal* theory. The substantial philosophers acknowledge that

> the essence which gives support to the properties perceived by our senses, does not resemble any of these properties, and is not itself an immediate subject of sense.[2]

Smith held that the ultimate nature of the physical and spiritual were unknowable but that we could be certain of their existence through observation of their properties.

Internal sensations were divided into three classes: those relating to acts and sentiments of our own mind (such as the sensations of the existence of the soul or of God), those relating to the fine arts, and those relating to morality. Each of these classes was correlated with an appropriate internal sense. In regard to the finality of the sensations he said, "The general sentiments of human nature are always found to point to truth. They are intuitive perceptions resulting immediately from the bare inspection of their objects; or conclusions which force their evidence upon the mind, like the *first truths* of science, necessarily springing out of the comparison of our ideas." [3] Smith's emphasis upon the internal senses came not only from Reid, Beattie and Oswald with whose writings he had become acquainted under Witherspoon but also from Hutcheson and Shaftesbury. He attached particular importance to the moral sense, or faculty. It was the immediate source of knowledge of virtue and vice, good and bad. It was above custom and law, providing knowledge of intrinsic good and not merely temporary approval or disapproval of conduct.

> This sense is as much the natural and the only organ, (if that term may be applied to any of our principles of internal sensation) of the ideas of duty and of right, and their contraries, as the eye is of those of color, or the ear of sound. If we were void of this sense of morality, we might have from other principles in our nature, ideas of reasonableness, propriety, beauty, gracefulness in human actions; but of merit and demerit, of moral excellence, or of guilt we could have had no adequate conception.[4]

Backing up the existence of a moral sense were Smith's anthropological studies. *An Essay on the Causes of the Variety of Complexion and Figure in the Human Species* attempted to establish the existence of one human species and account for the differences between people on the basis of variations in climate, the state of society and the manner of living in various social groups. In this essay Smith followed early evolutionary thought, accepting the transmission of acquired characteristics and holding, with Lamarck, to the cumulative effect of

[2] *Lectures on Moral and Political Philosophy.* I, 145.
[3] *Principles of Natural and Revealed Religion.* 8.
[4] *Lectures on Moral and Political Philosophy.* I, 301.

variations caused by environmental influences. Despite his emphasis upon natural law as the cause of development, he held to the unity of species, for he felt in addition to being scientifically verifiable it was in accord with the scriptural doctrine of creation and essential to his argument for a moral sense. In *Lectures on Moral and Political Philosophy* he said, "The proof of the identity of the race, is essential to a just philosophy of human nature." [5] He held that if it could be established that there were more species than one, the moral sense would be variable; since there was only one species, the moral sense was common and universal.

Despite his confidence in the correctness of the judgments of the moral sense, Smith did not want his doctrine to be interpreted as defending anything as arbitrary as what we ordinarily call intuition. He recognized the possibility of doubt and difference of opinion and held that in such cases reason, experience and an extensive knowledge of human nature would add precision to our judgments.

> By giving this just extent to the moral faculty, we take off the chief force of the objections of those writers who deny its existence as a distinct power in our constitution, from an apprehension that the friends of that theory would raise it into an intuitive and universal arbiter of right and wrong in human action.—I conclude by observing that by such a fair and equitable use of reason as auxiliary to the moral sense, we shall often perceive the necessity of equal candor and caution in judging both of national manners and of individual conduct.[6]

The moral sense, aided by reason, would produce moral truths as certain in their sphere as scientific truths were in theirs.

In *An Essay on the Cause of the Variety of Complexion and Figure in the Human Species* Smith had approached dangerously close to the doctrine of mind-body homogeneity expounded by such men as Priestley and Cooper. He felt it necessary, therefore, to make clear that he regarded the mind as independent of the body, for if mind were but a complex development of body the internal senses would be derivatory rather than autonomous and the basis for moral and religious ideas would be insecure. He attacked the physiological theory which assumed material vibrations to be the cause of thought, arguing that the existence of such vibrations had not been conclusively established, that even if vibrations did exist there was no necessary connection between them and thought and that in all events vibrations could not explain the variety of thought.[7] In the selection included here from *Lectures on*

[5] I, 51.
[6] Ibid. I, 318.
[7] Refer to Riley: *American Philosophy: the Early Schools.* 507–8.

*Moral and Political Philosophy* Smith held that although the essences of mind and matter were unknowable their properties offered us sufficient evidence of their essential difference. He contended, furthermore, that to confuse matter and mind would be to destroy our strongest argument for deity (that based on the active intelligence of man), make us less grateful for our creation and take away the greatest incentive for moral living, namely, the belief in immortality. Granting that body affected mind he considered it no less certain that mind influenced body. Despite their interaction, however, he argued for the independence of mind from body.

He was equally anxious to show wherein he differed from the rigid determinist. In physical nature he accepted natural law and mechanical causation. In places he indicated that moral action was equally certain, although on a different basis. He said, "For to an omniscient Being, who is perfectly acquainted with the nature and influence of every motive, its combination, and co-action, with all other means, and with the peculiar temperament of each individual agent, moral effects are as certain, in their order, as the results of any physical causes whatever." [8] In order to avoid determinism he distinguished between certainty and necessity, arguing that there was a difference "between a thing *certainly* done by a free cause, and the same thing accomplished by an internal but unperceived force, so that it could not be otherwise than it is." [9] As the moral sense provided knowledge of virtue, so another internal sense made us certain of free will. He felt there was no inconsistency in believing in free will and in divine foreknowledge at the same time. He argued that just as a parent can oftentimes predict with assurance the act of his son in a particular situation, an omniscient God with knowledge of all inclinations, desires, habits and character could know exactly how each individual would act in every situation without interfering in any degree with the individual's free choice. To him physical events arose out of the mechanical action of matter and motion but moral action sprang from the "free laws of motive and volition." [10] He anticipated the contention of the necessitarian that motive determined action and that motive was in turn determined by forces not within our control.

> The proper effect of motive is to solicit and excite the mind, and to put it into a state of action. But I have a power within me which *determines* my choice, on a view more deliberate, or more rapid, of the

[8] *Principles of Natural and Revealed Religion.* 266.
[9] Ibid. 282.
[10] Ibid. 246.

motives before it. If you ask me to explain that power—I feel it—I am sensible that I exercise it—and, *in* the feeling and exercise I understand the act.[11]

The inner sense which assured us of free will also assured us of the existence of God and immortality. He said there were two types of argument for the existence of God, the scientific and the popular. The scientific, as presented by such a man as Samuel Clarke, appealed largely to those who spent much time in thought; the popular was direct and accessible to all.

The idea of God is one that can hardly be said to wait the slow process of reasoning and deduction; but forces itself irresistibly upon the mind from the contemplation of the works of nature, either in ourselves or in the universe around us. It is an instantaneous and almost intuitive impression, congenial with our nature, and that seems to form a part of our existence, till torn from it by vice, or the false refinements of philosophy.[12]

Again he said the existence of God was "more a sentiment than a deduction." [13] Smith stretched his concept of the internal senses to the extent of making them emotional, as well as rational, powers. In regard to immortality he admitted the value of certain rational arguments but again depended largely on inner perception for its existence. His view of immortality was reminiscent of Ethan Allen, for he argued that it provided for the continuous development of the individual.

In contrast to the divorce of morality from religion so common during the Age of Reason, Smith held that religion was the backbone of morality. Without religion, he felt, reasoning in morality would be nothing but a vindication of our passions. Even if religion led to superstition he said, "Superstition itself is preferable to atheism, a cold and selfish principle which destroys all certainty or obligation in morals; which first relaxes, and finally bursts asunder the bonds of society." [14] Revelation backed up moral and religious truths arrived at on the basis of the internal senses and filled in the gaps wherever doubt existed.

Smith's realism, although it permitted him to accept the naturalistic tendency of the Age of Reason in his science, was mainly used as a vindication of religion. Traditional religion became liberalized with him, however. The sting of such concepts as predestination and eternal damnation was removed. Science was made more respectable among the orthodox. Emphasis upon the internal senses rather than upon

[11] *Principles of Natural and Revealed Religion.* 283.
[12] *Sermons.* II, 40.
[13] Ibid. II, 53.
[14] Ibid. I, 327.

external authority made it easier for varied interpretations to develop. Smith defended religion but he changed it as well.

## REFERENCES

Smith, Samuel Stanhope: *An Essay on the Causes of the Variety of Complexion and Figure in the Human Species.* Second edition. New Brunswick, N. J., 1810. (First published in Philadelphia in 1787.)

———: *The Lectures, Corrected and Improved, which have been delivered for a Series of Years in the College of New Jersey; on the Subjects of Moral and Political Philosophy.* 2 vols. Trenton, N. J., 1812.

———: *A Comprehensive View of the Leading and Most Important Principles of Natural and Revealed Religion: Digested in such Order as to Present to the Pious and Reflecting Mind, a Basis for the Superstructure of the Entire System of the Doctrines of the Gospel.* New Brunswick, N. J., 1815.

———: *Sermons of Samuel Stanhope Smith: to which is Prefixed a Brief Memoir of his Life and Writings.* Newark, N. J., 1821. (The memoir was written by Frederick Beasley.)

Riley, I. Woodbridge: *American Philosophy: the Early Schools.* New York: Dodd, Mead and Co., 1907. 497–508.

* * *

---

* * *

# LECTURES ON MORAL AND POLITICAL PHILOSOPHY [15]

## *Lecture I*

Philosophy is an investigation of the constitution and laws of nature, both in the physical and moral world, as far as the powers of the human mind, unaided by the lights of revelation, are competent to discover them. In this enquiry we can proceed, with any reasonable prospect of arriving at truth, only by a careful and extensive induction of facts, whence we may hope ultimately, to attain to some acquaintance with the principles and causes of things. In the physical world, a minute and patient observation of the phenomena of nature, and, in the moral world, of the conduct of men, individually, and in their various social relations, is the only method by which we can gain any certain knowl-

[15] 9–27; 123–39.

edge of their constitution, or of the springs and laws of their action respectively. We are, evidently, not endued with powers by which we can immediately inspect their essence, and discern their intimate structure, and thence be able, antecedently to experience, to anticipate the effects of their action, either singly, or in any possible combination. In order to understand the works of an infinite mind, and to draw from them any useful information, a being so limited in his capacities as man, should be contented simply to observe their effects with attention, and carefully to remark how those effects are varied in different situations and connexions, whence only we can form general rules concerning their operation in all similar and analogous cases. The wisdom of modern science has justly excluded from philosophy all hypotheses, by which the operations of nature are attempted to be conjecturally explained. Indeed, when a mind so feeble in its powers, and circumscribed in its views, as that of man, attempts to explain by conjecture the infinite plans of the Deity, or to unfold *a priori,* as it is called in the language of the schools, the phenomena that result from their inscrutable structure, it is perhaps impossible that it should not err, or that it should approach even near the truth.—Let hypothesis have antecedently formed its conjecture on any phenomenon in nature, with which experiment has since made the philosopher in some degree acquainted; as, for example, on the manner in which the eye perceives objects by the rays of the sun; or on the laws of that spark which we elicit by friction from a cylinder of glass; no man can doubt but that, before the principles of optics were discovered, and the structure of the eye laid open by anatomical dissection; or before the science of electricity was explained, ten thousand conjectures might have been framed, and all should have been almost infinitely and equally distant from the actual fact. Experience, therefore, and a diligent and attentive observation of the course of nature, and of the actions of mankind in every variety of situation in which they may be placed, is the only legitimate means of attaining a competent knowledge of the laws of either the material, or the moral world. But when experience has once conducted us from effects up to their causes, we may, in analogous cases, be reconducted by the same means, from causes with which we have become acquainted, to the effects which may be expected in known situations, to result from them. For such conclusions, the constancy observed in nature affords us just grounds. We are taught by experience to expect a perfect uniformity of action in each cause, when placed precisely in the same circumstances; and from similar causes, in resembling situations, to look for similar effects. This tendency to uniform results we impute to some power in the cause, which, being essential to it, and belonging to its very constitution, will always operate in the same way, when not vitiated from within, or obstructed by some obstacle from without. We pronounce it to be a necessary consequence of a law of nature; and the regularity of action which obtains throughout all parts of the universal system, we ascribe to the uniform operation of established laws.—It is on this ground that we study human nature in our own hearts; and that history may be regarded as a volume of moral experiment.

Philosophy is divided into two great branches,—the natural and the moral. Nature, taken in its utmost extent, embraces the whole compass of things in the universe, whether corporeal or spiritual, physical or moral. But, in this division of the science, natural philosophy consists in an investigation of the constitution and the laws of the body; moral philosophy in an investigation of the constitution and laws of the mind, especially as it is endued with the power of voluntary action, and is susceptible of the sentiments of duty and obligation. Its chief end is to ascertain the principles, and the rule of duty, and to regulate conduct, both in our individual capacities, and in our social relations, whether domestic or civil. This is the object of our present enquiries. But in order to attain this end in any considerable degree of perfection, it will be necessary to enter into many important disquisitions concerning the constituent principles, the natural tendencies, and the moral relations of that sensible, rational, and moral being, who is the subject of duty.

In the universe there may be many orders of spirit, as there are many modifications of matter. We are, however, acquainted with two only; God and the human soul. And our knowledge of the former, which must necessarily be extremely imperfect, from the infinite distance at which we are placed from him, must be derived principally from our knowledge of the latter. But, although our conceptions of the divine mind must be far from reaching the perfection of his nature, it is important that, as far as the weakness of man is capable of comprehending the infinity of God, the ideas which we frame of him should be consistent with truth. For, the duty of all rational beings must have a reference to his will. And our nature having been formed by his almighty power, can then only be perfect, when it is evidently conformed to his design in our creation.

The science of moral philosophy, therefore, begins in the study of the human mind—its sensations, perceptions, and generally, its means of acquiring knowledge—its sentiments, dispositions and affections, and generally, its principles of action or enjoyment—its present state, and relations to other beings—its future hopes and fears. From an attentive examination of its various principles and powers, and from carefully remarking their operations either singly, or in combination with others, we may at length form a rational judgment of what man was intended, by his creator, to be, and thence deduce the law of his duty.

In this investigation, as has already been suggested, it is necessary to follow the method of analysis, and to reason from particular facts, collected by extensive and careful observation, to the general laws of the human mind. It occurs here as a natural enquiry, what is *a law* of nature? And, by what process are its laws to be collected?—The essential nature of things in which the laws of their action are founded, it has been already acknowledged, cannot be intuitively known to the weakness of the human understanding. But their laws, as far as it is requisite for the purposes of science, may be understood from a less perfect knowledge. The uniformity of a multitude of facts, arising from the action of any subject, indicates some principle or power in that subject, which, tho' unknown in its essence, we conclude, from our experience of the constancy of nature, will, in similar circumstances, always operate in the same way. This uniformity of effect, or rather, perhaps, the unknown but constant cause on which it depends, is denominated *a law of nature*. And the several classes of uniformities, which science has discovered in the system of the universe, are consequently ascribed to so many natural laws.[16] And when any fact or phenomenon occurs to our observation, it is said to be accounted for, or explained, as far as the human intellect is capable of explaining, or accounting for it, when it can be referred to some common and known class of similar facts.

This observation may be illustrated by a familiar example. The electric fluid, like all other principles of nature, is, in its essence, unknown. But the uniform effects resulting from it, in a vast variety of situations, are now well understood from repeated experiment. They are therefore denominated the laws of electricity. We wish then to explain the phenomenon of lightning. And by applying to it the same tests as to the principle of electricity, with the effects of which we are better acquainted, we find precisely the same results. We esteem it,

[16] For instance, the uniformities which we observe in magnetism, in the refractions of light, or in the passions and emotions of the human heart under the various circumstances naturally calculated to excite them, are called the laws of magnetism, or refraction, etc.

therefore, accounted for, as far as human sagacity can explain it, not by revealing its essential nature, which is inscrutable, but simply by referring it to the class of electric phenomena.

In the moral world, when we perceive, in all nations, that a bare inspection of the works of nature has led mankind to the acknowledgement of a Supreme Power which presides over the order of the whole, we justly infer that the belief of the existence of God is to be ascribed to an original law of our rational and moral nature. The parental affection, in like manner, and the social inclinations of our nature, which, in all nations and ages, and in similar circumstances, we see operating with great uniformity, we pronounce to be natural laws of our being.

Many resembling facts, therefore, indicate a law of nature. If any new fact, with which we have not before been acquainted, occurs to our observation, if it is found, in its properties, to coincide with any class of phenomena already known, it is supposed to be accounted for by referring it to that class. Otherwise it is called a solitary fact, which, of course, is left open to future enquiry.

Thus, in the moral, as in the natural world, by an attentive induction of fact, that is, by observing the operations of the human mind in every variety of situation in which it may be placed, in solitude, or in society, in prosperity, or in adversity, in its various relations, to our creator, or our fellow men, or in positions in which all the passions may be successively called into action, which observation may, with propriety, be stiled moral experiment, we arrive at length, at a knowledge of the laws of our moral nature.

The mind of man being intimately united with a corporeal system, receiving all its original informations, through the organs of the senses, and being in all its perceptions and emotions affected by the state of the body, this union is not to be neglected in the study of the mind. On the other hand, the reciprocal influences of these great component parts of human nature ought carefully to be regarded, that, both in our moral and physical studies, we may be able to discriminate the effects of their mutual action. By this means many false, and visionary notions which have sometimes mingled themselves with both morals and religion might be corrected. And superstition, particularly, which derives its gloomy, or fantastic reveries chiefly from certain bodily impressions, would lose its principal hold upon a weak imagination.

In entering on this science it will be requisite to examine if human nature be radically one under all the various appearances which it exhibits in different portions of the globe; or if, according to the opinion of certain philosophers, it is divided into different species which, in many points, possess only a faint resemblance of one another. If the human race is to be regarded as an assemblage of different species, that course of moral experiment, which has been already recommended as the necessary means of perfecting the science, would be fruitless. No certain and universal theory of duty could result from it. The laws of moral conduct, which we might collect from the most careful examination of our own nature, could not be applied with truth to those tribes of men who should be of foreign species. Not only would the principles of morals and religion deduced from human nature, as it exists at present in any nation, be different from those of every other people, but, at any future period in the same nation, by reason of the infinite migrations and mixtures of mankind, all past experience might be rendered uncertain, and all rules confounded, in proportion as the several races should be intermixed and blended. On the other hand, if the whole family of mankind be found to be racially one, notwithstanding the various external appearances under which it is presented to us in different climates, the same general laws of duty may be applied to them all, subject only to such modifications as shall be found to arise out of their respective states of society, or the diversity of their mutual relations.

In the philosophy of man the same rules ought to be observed which have been followed in natural philosophy ever since the age of the great Newton, with so much advantage to the science.

1. "That no law should be admitted on hypothesis but should rest solely on an induction of facts." Some reasons for this rule have been already assigned; particularly the feebleness of the human mind, and the contracted sphere within which its observation is necessarily limited. It is but lately since the science of moral philosophy has been freed from the disgrace and embarassment of hypothesis at its very entrance, in its enquiry concerning the manner in which we become acquainted with external objects by sensation. It was first laid down as a principle, that no material being can act where it is not. The question then arose how we perceive objects at a distance? To solve this difficulty recourse was had to the following hypothesis;—that every sensible object is continually emitting from its own body some images of itself in every direction, which the ancient philosophers denominated *ideas,* or *sensible species,* and that these aerial, gaseous, or almost spiritual images impinging upon the organ of sense communicated, by that impulse, a perception of their subject; or rather a ground of inferring its existence, from the vivacity of the impressions. Such was the doc-

trine of Aristotle, and from him of the whole peripatetic school. And there are some vestiges of it even in the philosophy of Locke, of which Berkeley and Hume availing themselves denied the existence of the material subject altogether, as being wholly unnecessary.[17] But let the mind be relieved from the philosophic delerium of hypothesis, and form her judgments on experience and fact, interpreted by plain common sense, and we must pronounce a totally different decision. Whatever medium, in the opinion of these philosophers, nature may employ to connect the object with the organ of sense, whether image, or idea, or any other sensible phantasm, it is, beyond a doubt, the object itself, not its idea, which is discerned by the sense, any image or phantasm in the case, being either unknown, or unperceived, and at the time wholly unthought of. An idea is merely a conception of the fancy, or the reminiscence of an absent object.

2. Another rule is, "that laws collected from an ample and accurate induction of facts should be deemed universal, till other facts occur to invalidate, or limit the conclusions which have been drawn from them."—Unless we could rely on this rule, the progress of science would be arrested almost at its commencement. Few are the conclusions which we could frame if it required a knowledge of facts strictly universal before we could admit a general consequence from induction. And the known analogy of nature is a sufficient and satisfactory ground of those general inferences embraced within the rule. On this foundation solely we build our knowledge of the constituent principles of human nature, the laws both of physical and moral action in man, and the acknowledged maxims of society, domestic and civil.

3. In the third place, "laws founded on a partial induction of facts should not be extended beyond the limits to which they are certainly known to apply."—The neglect of this rule is one of the principal causes of national antipathies, and of the bigotry of religious sects. From a few facts imperfectly observed a rash and unfair judgment is pronounced on a whole party, or a whole nation. With the same confident precipitancy have we sometimes heard the natives of Africa, who

[17] If, say they, according to the peripatetic hypothesis, or the metaphysic of Locke, the principles of which were generally acknowledged in the time of these philosophers, it be only the images or ideas of objects that we perceive, and not the objects themselves, what ground can there be to infer their existence? Ideas, it is confessed, may be impressed on a lively imagination without the presence of any external substance. And, agreeably to the scheme of Mr. Hume, the vivacity of the idea is the only criterion of truth. The reality of the material world, therefore, perishes by the fairest inference, since, according to the confession of its friends, it is not the object of our perceptions.

have been contemplated only in a state of savagism or of slavery, pronounced to be destitute of the best faculties of human nature; and the American continent judged to be unfriendly equally to corporeal vigor, and to mental talent. It is a rule, especially, by which we should rigorously examine the narratives of travellers, and of those writers who profess to exhibit comparative estimates of the characters of foreign nations, so seldom have they an opportunity of observing the interior of their manners; and so much more rarely do they possess the talent necessary to trace the causes of what they observe with philosophic accuracy, or the inclination to represent them with candor.

4. A fourth rule is, "that similar appearances should, because of the uniformity of nature, be referred, as far as possible, to the same causes."—On this rule we interpret the actions of men in all their various relations in different portions of the globe; and we find them to be the same as fathers, brothers, sons, as the members of a family, or of civil society.—We discern but one race throughout the whole.—To take another example from a peculiar department of our nature.—The belief of spectres, of the feats of witchcraft, and magic, and of those little tricky, or mischievous spirits, which are found among the traditionary tales of the vulgar in most of the modern countries in Europe, ought to be ascribed to the same principle, the force of a timid and ardent imagination unregulated by the science of nature, which anciently filled Egypt with magicians, and Assyria with soothsayers, and peopled the hills, the streams, and the skies of Greece with the objects of a superstitious veneration.

5. The last rule which I mention is, "that the testimony of our senses, and of all our simple perceptions, ought to be admitted as true, and no ulterior evidence be required of the reality, or the nature of the facts which they confirm."—The informations of the senses are intended to be ultimate. They are perfectly simple, and cannot, by any artifice of language, be rendered more obvious or clear. They are the first elements of our knowledge; and the only acquaintance which we can have with the nature of their objects is conveyed in the impression which they make upon the organ of perception.—This rule is of the more importance, because philosophers, of no inferior name, have appeared in modern times, as well as in the earlier ages of science, who have denied the certainty of our senses, and have reasoned concerning their operations with such excessive subtlety as to confound the most obvious and natural consequences resulting from their informations. While they have filled the rational and intellectual sphere with images, ideas, and sensible species, and other such shadowy forms

as substitutes for a material world, they have utterly denied the reality of body. Others carrying their temerity still farther, have denied the reality both of body and spirit; and have equally reduced the physical and the moral world to a mere train of fugitive, and unsubstantial ideas.

The object of the science of moral philosophy, as it is designed to be treated in this system, is not so much a minute and extensive detail of particular duties, which, from their multitude, and the innumerable modifications to which they are subject from the ever varying state of society, and the mutable situations and connexions in which men may be placed, would be too voluminous, as to propose such general *principles* as may enable a rational and reflecting mind to deduce the point of duty for itself, on every case as it arises in practice.

It is, manifestly, a science of primary dignity and importance, as it is intended to unfold the principles of human nature, and bring us more intimately acquainted with man, who is evidently the first object which deserves our consideration in this world, and for whom the world seems chiefly to have been formed. Thence it proceeds to investigate the laws of morality and duty in the various relations of life, and to cultivate the heart to virtue, which gives the supreme value to this, and to every science. Man it contemplates in his different powers and principles of action,—it considers him in his social capacities, as a member of a family,—as associated in a political community,—as a subject of civil government,—as a citizen of the world. It unfolds his infinitely important relations to the Deity; and endeavors to open his view on those immortal hopes which give the chief, if not the only value to rational existence, and add the greatest force to the obligations of duty and virtue.—The dignity and happiness of individuals, the prosperity of states, and the order and happiness of the world, are intimately connected with the practical knowledge of those truths at the cultivation and improvement of which this science aims. And, from the commencement of learning, it has occupied the profoundest attention and enquiry of the philosophic part of mankind in every age.

At the first view of this subject we are naturally inclined to conceive that the science of morals must be as clear and definite in its principles, and as obvious and certain in its conclusions, as they are important to the best interests of mankind. It seems not unreasonable to expect that the foundations of duty should be laid open even to a slight attention of the inquisitive mind. Yet, it is certain that no science has been embarassed with greater, or more numerous controversies. To this effect various causes have contributed their influence. Not only is it liable to obscurity and doubt, in common with other sciences, arising from the imbecility of human reason, from the love of hypothesis, and the vanity of system, from the difficulty of distinguishing many of the nicer operations of our own minds, and often from defect of patience and attention in examining and discriminating the subjects and the facts presented in it to our observation; but it is exposed to causes of peculiar obscurity and mistakes arising from the general depravity and corruption of human nature. To whatever source that corruption may have been imputed by various writers, there can be no doubt of its existence. The disorders of the world attest it; and every man perceives its principles, more or less powerfully, operating in his own heart. When incorporated by habit, into the moral state and affections of the soul, it must necessarily impart, in the same proportion, a false bias in judging of the general principles of the moral law, and especially of those particular details of the law which come most immediately in collision with the passions and manners of the individual.

Perhaps no philosopher has his judgment wholly exempted from some bias to modify the practical precepts of the moral law, according to his own peculiar character and habits, which cannot be done without extending in the same degree, an oblique influence to the theory of morals. It is, however, the sincere aim, and the gradual tendency of true philosophy to correct the errors of prejudice, and to dissipate the mists that shed themselves over the mind, in consequence of the prevalence of any dominant affection or passion. Much may be effected by candid, patient, and dispassionate enquiry in accomplishing this desirable end. It may be presumption to expect to arrive at truth on all the subjects of our research with complete and unhesitating conviction; on many, perhaps, we ought to rest satisfied with only probable evidence; yet, we ought ever to bear it in mind that, in our philosophical enquiries, we have as much reason to avoid the dangers of a weak and suspicious scepticism, as of a bold and positive dogmatism.

## *Lecture VI*

Having considered man as a species, and taken a cursory view of the properties which distinguish him from other species of animals, I proceed to consider him in his individual capacity, and briefly to explain the principles which enter into the composition of his nature, with reference chiefly to its moral destinations.—In his contemplating the nature of man, what first demands the attention of the philosopher, is its being a compound of body and mind. For whatever controversies may have arisen concerning the primary and ultimate essences of these respective substances, they are certainly, in the aggregates of their several qualities, as exhibited in the body and the soul of man, entirely diverse, if not opposite to one another. The body is a system of organs fitted for receiving the impressions of external objects in such a manner as to make their existence and their qualities sensible to the mind, and for acting upon them again as the mind's instrument. The mind is that external principle which is endowed with the faculty of perceiving, comparing, judging, and reasoning concerning things presented through the senses; and of directing our actions towards them.

With regard to the nature of the mind many disquisitions have been raised. And frequently with an injudicious boldness, which, leaving the plain but tedious road of experience and fact, plunges into the region of conjecture, where philosophy has often wandered, and perhaps, must always wander in inextricable error. Among other enquiries, it has been made a question whether the rational principle be essentially different from the principle of sensation common to man with the inferior animals; or be the same, with only the added power of reflecting on its own sensations, comparing them, and deriving from them another ultimate sensation which is called its judgment, induction, or conclusion.

Some ancient sects held the rational and sensitive powers in man to be seated in two totally distinct principles,—the one the *soul,* the principle of vitality, or sensation; the other the *spirit,* the principle of reason.[18] With this the philosophic opinion of St. Paul seems to coincide, when he divides the departments of human nature into those of the body, the *animal soul,* and the *rational spirit* or *mind.*—Most of the moderns esteem the rational and sensitive parts of our nature to be only different powers, inherent in the same simple essence, the *soul;* receiving their denominations from the objects to which they are applied, and the peculiar action of the soul with respect to them.—To take an example from color; the soul, in the act of sensation, simply receives the impression of this quality through the eye; in the exercise of its reasoning powers, it may enter into various enquiries concerning visible properties; as whether they are inherent in bodies, or are merely sensations in us? Whether these sensations have any resemblance to the objects which excite them, or are occasioned by some affections of matter which have no similarity to any sensation? Still the sensation, and the reasoning, are only different modes of acting of the same spiritual substance. On this diversity of opinion we may justly remark,

[18] This was the opinion particularly of the Pythagoreans and the Platonists.

that it is of small importance except to gratify a barren curiosity. When we attempt to pry into the essential constitution of things, a secret which nature hath placed beyond the reach of the human faculties, we dive into a bottomless ocean. We are not sufficiently acquainted with the nature of the inferior animals to know how far they possess the powers of comparison, or induction. And with regard to the spiritual part of our own nature, we know not its essence and texture. We cannot, in explaining its principles, go beyond the simple perceptions of consciousness. And when these are most carefully examined, we do not, in *reasoning* and *sensation,* perceive different agents, but only different exercises of the same sensible and intelligent nature.

But another question of higher moment, because it draws after it more important consequences, is: whether *mind* be essentially, or, in its primary principles, different from *matter;* and whether sensation and thought may not be the result of a certain organization of the body, producing a peculiar refinement of its secretions, and ultimately a sensitive state, and action of its nerves, and fluids?—That matter is capable of refinement and activity to an indefinite degree, there cannot remain a doubt, since light has been discovered to be a body; but, that it is susceptible of such a modification as is implied in sensation, and intelligence, must be mere hypothesis; and one that possesses very lame pretensions to probability, none of the sensible properties of matter, as far as experiments have ever been made upon it, having the smallest analogy to the operations of thought. On the true principles of philosophy, therefore, the opinion which confounds mind with matter ought to be rejected. A more serious objection lies against it in the mind of every good man; for, if we reduce the soul to the condition of perishable matter, the most reasonable foundation of gratitude to our creator for existence is removed; the most powerful encouragements to virtue, and restraints from vice, are effectually destroyed, when we lose the natural hopes, and apprehensions of a future being. But a consequence still more fatal results from the principle of the materialism of the soul; it annihilates the only basis on which can rationally rest the belief of a wise and intelligent creator of the universe. The ideas of a free, essentially active, and intelligent power presiding over the system of nature, can be derived only from the exercise of similar powers within our own minds. If that active, sensitive, and rational principle which we call the soul, be only an emanation of matter organized in a certain form, all our religious hopes, and duties, are merged in the gloom of an eternal fatality: we induce all the laws of a blind material necessity. For, if the human soul be only a refinement of the corporeal essence; or, in other words, a secretion from the fluids of the body, the divine mind, if we admit its existence at all, can only be conceived to be a result of the physical actions, or elemental secretions of the universal material system—the *anima mundi* of the ancients,—the effect, not the cause, of infinite, unintelligent matter. Some religious men, however, who have embraced the materialism of the soul, have endeavored to rescue themselves from these cheerless consequences by resting the hope of immortality, and the resurrection of the body, and the belief of a moral governor of the universe, on revelation. This appears to be a preposterous jumble of ideas. Certain it is, that the friends of this doctrine are generally enemies of revelation; and there can be little doubt of the tendency of its principles to atheism. No writer, perhaps, has carried these principles out, with more wit and talent, and I may add, with more audacity, to their ultimate, and legitimate consequences, than the French philosopher Helvetius. How they appear in the hands of a christian divine, who endeavors to guard them with all the efforts of his ingenuity from their immoral results, we may learn from Dr. Priestley's *Essay on Matter and Spirit*.

The doctrine, however, of the perfect and essential difference of mind from matter has ever been received by the greatest, and the most numerous class of philosophers, and seems to rest on the most solid and rational grounds. For, although their essences be not the objects of immediate and direct perception, yet their properties, by which alone we judge of the nature of things, present them to our understanding as being in every respect different, and contrary to one another. The properties of the one we discern only through the medium of the external senses; those of the other are perceived exclusively by the powers of internal sensation, or consciousness. These sensations furnishing the mind with perceptions which are primary and original, their difference, and the different natures of the subjects from which they are derived, can be indicated only in the perceptions themselves. By a law of our constitution, this is the ultimate evidence which we can enjoy on any subject. And when we compare together the properties of body and spirit, what have color, figure, extension, taste, smell, which belong to the former, in common with thought, volition, sympathy, affection, and other purely mental qualities and actions? Body, moreover, we perceive to be composed of parts, separable from, and movable among one another; but, in every act of the mind, we are conscious only of one simple, indivisible essence. The one is naturally inert, and set in movement only by extraneous impulse; the other is self-motive. The actions of the one are governed by mechanical laws;

the other is excited in its operations by laws which we perceive to be wholly variant in their nature from those which preside over the material world.—From this diversity, or rather opposition of properties, we infer, that the soul is not of the same substance, with the body; that the one cannot be a mere secretion or refinement from the other, the result of a peculiar organization, but that they are in their nature and essence, as in their properties, entirely distinct.

From the spiritual and immaterial nature of the soul arises what is called the *physical* proof of its immortality. The destruction of bodies is occasioned by the dissolution, or separation of their parts; or by that rigidity which grows, in time, upon their elastic organs, and, at length, stops their action. The perfect unity, and simplicity, of the spiritual essence, and its natural and inherent activity, seem to place it beyond the sphere of those causes of dissolution which have been ascribed to matter.—We are not, however, sufficiently acquainted with the nature of the soul to be sure that there may not be other causes which may finally produce an extinction of its active powers. We know that its actions appear to cease on the dissolution of the body. And although we discern no positive reason why it may not exist in a state of separation from the corporeal part of our frame, yet nothing but a direct revelation from the author of our being can ascertain a fact so desirable to all good men. There are, indeed, many moral probabilities of this truth, derivable from other sources, which have contributed to console the virtuous philosopher in other ages, before a clearer light arose to assist his reason. These shall be offered to your consideration in a future lecture. All that I can say of this physical speculation, is, that, although it offers to our reason no solid ground of confidence, it may be regarded as affording some corroboration to other arguments which find a more persuasive access to the heart.

An objection against the argument which we have just surveyed for the immateriality, and consequent immortality of the soul, has been derived from the fact of its being affected by all the changes of health in the body; and from the further fact of the reasoning faculty being sometimes wholly deranged by disease, or the malformation of some of its organs. Whence it is concluded that, as the soul is dependent for the regularity of its exercises on the state of the body, it derives its existence likewise from the same source; and that, with the cessation of the vital actions, all mental action will equally cease; and the soul will consequently perish in the dissolution of this corporeal system.—The converse of this reasoning will demonstrate its weakness; for it is not more certain that the sound and perfect exercises of the soul depend, in a great degree, upon the healthful state of the body, than that the health of the body is reciprocally affected by the state of the mind. But, would any man pretend to infer that the corporeal part of our nature is, therefore, an emanation from the spiritual, and dependent upon the latter for its existence?—From the intimate connexion established between the different parts of the same nature, we ought to expect to find a mutual influence exerted by each upon the other. The exercises of the soul ought especially to be exposed to derangement in their action from any disorders in the corporeal system, or any malformation of its parts. For, the body being the organ of all its sensations, notices, and informations, any error or disorder in these, by perverting, in the same degree, the materials and groundwork of its reasonings, must proportionably impair the clearness of its perceptions, and the justness of its conclusions.[19] It resembles a philosopher in his observatory, who is obliged to make use of defective instruments; or a man confined in a prison, who must form his judgment of all things passing around him from those erroneous means of intelligence to which alone he has access. His philosophic acuteness may remain as perfect as ever, but his primary information being false or incorrect, will throw a necessary error into all his reasonings. Whatever errors, therefore, the infirmity, or disorder of the corporeal organs may introduce into the exercises of the soul, it does not the less preserve unimpaired its title to that immateriality, rationality, simplicity, and immortality of essence which we have ascribed to it. This is certain, that, at the approach of death, when the bodily frame is weakest, but, at the same time, its movements, as frequently happens, are most regular and tranquil—least disturbed by disorderly impulses of the senses, the imagination, and the passions,—then the action of the soul has not rarely been found to be most vigorous and clear.

If the soul, in parting from the body at death, presents no sensible indications of itself in assuming a separate existence, this ought not to create any surprize, when we remember that a spiritual and immaterial

[19] Insane persons more frequently err, perhaps, by some fault in the organs of perception, and the impressions of objects that are conveyed to the imagination, than in the conclusions of the reasoning power founded upon these. The mind may be impaired in the clearness, consistency, steadiness and comprehensiveness of the view it takes of a subject; but commonly, its deductions are more consequential and consistent, than the premises and data, on which they are founded.—The reasoning faculty may be sound, while the organs of the senses and imagination are so disordered, as to occasion all its perceptions, and conclusions to be confused and false.—They may be disordered only on one point, or subject—sometimes they may be alternately healthful and diseased.

essence cannot be an object of the senses. Still less ought it to beget any doubt on the subject of a future existence, since there are even material influences of so fine and subtle a nature as to escape all detection of the senses, while they may be accumulated in, or abstracted from different bodies, in the largest quantities. Of these we need no other examples than the familiar ones of electricity and magnetism.

Having made these reflections on the spiritual and immaterial nature of the soul, and on the physical proof arising thence of its immortality, I shall conclude this lecture with presenting to you a brief outline of a scheme which, about half a century since, attracted great attention from the philosophic world, supported by the ingenious names of Berkeley bishop of Cloyne, in Ireland, and the celebrated David Hume of Scotland. As maintained by Berkeley it was opposed to the existence of matter, and as reformed and carried out to its ultimate consequences by Hume, it was equally hostile both to matter and spirit, filling the universe only with ideas.

The origin of this scheme is to be found in the ancient Aristotelian doctrine of ideas, revived by some of the most celebrated metaphysicians of modern times, and by none with greater authority than the profound and discriminating Locke. It was held almost as an axiom by these great men that *nothing can be perceived where it is not*. Therefore, the only way in which external objects are discerned, is by means of *images,* called *ideas,* or *sensible species,* sent forth on all sides from them, which, impinging on their proper organs, render those objects perceptible to sense. The sensible forms, or ideas of color, figure, sound, emanating from the visible and sonorous bodies around us, impart to us the only conceptions which we possess of these bodies. They are not the objects themselves which are perceived, but the images, forms, or ideas of them whence their existence is only inferred through the medium of ideas which have no resemblance to the things which they represent. In like manner, ideas of taste, odour, touch, although their objects are immediately present, and act by direct contact with the sense, have no similitude to the causes, or that constitution of bodies, by which they are produced. Yet, by a certain order of nature, they become signs of the existence of substances which are not themselves the objects of sense, and to which they are no way like.

These were received almost as undisputed principles of the metaphysical philosophy from the age of Des Cartes and Locke. Bishop Berkeley, at first, carried along with the stream of the general opinion, and embracing the system with unhesitating confidence, began to see, at length, ulterior consequences resulting from it, which the first moment had not presented.—If, according to the received philosophy, the ideas, or images in our own minds, are the whole of what we perceive; and if these ideas are only sensations in us, which, strictly and philosophically speaking, have no similitude to any external object, what right, demands this ingenious writer, have we to infer from these premises, the existence of *substances,* or *substrata,* for our ideas, which, it is acknowledged, are not themselves perceived? He concludes, therefore, that their existence is only a philosophical vision; and that ideas and sensations, which are all that we perceive, are all that exist, except the mind which perceives them. The mind, according to his system, is the only real existence in nature, wherein ideas and sensations follow one another in a certain order established by the Deity in the constitution of our nature. And this established order of ideas is the only sensible world with which we are acquainted. It is the only one which exists; and when it is not perceived it is nothing.

Mr. Hume, pleased with the ingenuity of this reasoning, and equally a disciple of Locke's doctrine of ideas, immediately perceived its tendency to annihilate the spiritual no less than the material world, according to men's vulgar notions, and to reduce all to mere ideas. The very same argument which the bishop employed against the existence of matter, he saw operated with equal force against the notion of spirit. According to the old philosophy, we have no perception of the nature of a spiritual substance, more than of a material. We perceive nothing but our own sensations, and ideas. Why then should we suppose that any thing else exists?—As Berkeley had pronounced body to be only a collection of co-existing ideas; Hume regarded the human soul as consisting of successive trains, or collections of ideas, of which self-consciousness is always one. And this habitual, or central idea, forming an essential part of each train, constitutes the identity of the human soul.

Such is a brief outline of the schemes of Berkeley and Hume, than whom two more acute metaphysicians never existed. And if the ancient system of ideas which attained almost oracular authority from the penetrating and discriminating genius of Mr. Locke, be admitted, the conclusions of these philosophers are irrefutable. The whole fabric, however, is too subtle, and too far removed from the apprehensions of common sense, to be true. The radical error of these visionary systems rests upon a principle which had long held the rank almost of an axiomatic truth in the schools of philosophy;—that the direct objects of the senses are not external things themselves, but only images, or ideas of those things. From this principle Hume and Berkeley have drawn the natural results, which were not foreseen by the philosophers who preceded them. But let the common apprehensions of mankind be received as truth;—that external things are the direct objects of our perceptions, which we contemplate through the medium of the impressions that they make upon the senses, and the whole foundation of the ideal theories is removed. Those theories, which were leading the mind to universal scepticism, were received, at first, with great éclat by the philosophers of Great-Britain, on account of the ingenuity of their authors. But when the charm of novelty began to subside, and the tendency of the principles more clearly to be discerned, the mind soon returned in a retrograde direction to the calm and rational dictates of the common feelings of mankind. A number of ingenious writers, especially in Scotland, soon appeared against these novel doctrines, who studiously labored to set this part of philosophy on its proper foundation—that common sense which it had deserted. In this field no writer has distinguished himself with greater zeal, ability, and success than Dr. Reid of Glasgow, first in his treatise on *the human mind,* and afterwards in his essays on the *intellectual,* and the *active powers of man.* He is particularly admirable for the clearness and comprehension of his views, and the perspicuity of his elucidation. To no author is this branch of science, not to Locke himself, more indebted for its approaches towards perfection.

[illegible] by the [illegible] [illegible] [illegible] [illegible] [illegible] [illegible] [illegible] [illegible] [illegible] These [illegible] [illegible] [illegible] [illegible] [illegible] [illegible] [illegible] [illegible] [illegible] [illegible] [illegible] [illegible] [illegible] [illegible] [illegible] [illegible] [illegible] [illegible] [illegible] [illegible] [illegible] [illegible] [illegible] Scotland, [illegible] against [illegible] [illegible] [illegible] of philosophy [illegible] [illegible] [illegible] [illegible] [illegible] [illegible] [illegible] [illegible] [illegible] [illegible] [illegible] [illegible] [illegible] [illegible] [illegible] [illegible] [illegible] [illegible] [illegible] [illegible] [illegible] [illegible] [illegible] [illegible] [illegible] [illegible] [illegible]

# *PART III*

# Transcendentalism and Evolution

# XIV
## Introduction

By the second quarter of the nineteenth century New England had largely regained the position of eminence in thought which it had lost to the middle colonies during the previous period. The Age of Reason had largely spent its energy. Reason was overshadowed by sentiment and intuition. The empirical study of nature was replaced by a poetic reading of nature. Deism was supplanted by a warm mysticism. Romantic in spirit, this new movement has generally gone by the name of transcendentalism; it was the expression of American romanticism.

While the Age of Reason had disintegrated as a movement much of its influence remained. Its liberality lived on through Unitarians such as Channing and Parker. Its reliance upon man, its doctrine of progress, its humanitarianism—these remained but were absorbed into an optimistic idealism and were given the status of intuitive inspirations rather than doctrines defensible by argument. The Age of Reason had not been popular in New England and had never dominated the New England scene. Instead, its concepts slowly penetrated the New England mind until, combined with nourishment which came indirectly from German and oriental sources and with the individualistic spirit of the growing economic order, they became assimilated in a new mode of thinking.

Knowledge of German thought came to America largely through the English, who hellenized it. Although the term transcendentalism came from Kant, the German thinkers were at first known through English sources such as Coleridge and Carlyle and their ideas were cherished more as opening vistas of thought than as fountains of truth. The appointment of Carl Follen as the first professor of German at Harvard in 1825 and study in Germany by such men as George Tichnor, Edward Everett, George Bancroft, Horace Mann and Henry James, Sr. afforded some first-hand knowledge of German thought. The French thinkers, Cousin and Jouffroy, who emphasized the spirituality of the mind, also influenced transcendentalism. James Marsh, President of the University of Vermont, gave impetus to the movement when he brought out in 1829 an American edition of Coleridge's

*Aids to Reflection,* which achieved the status of a textbook for the American romantics.

Transcendentalism was not an institutional development although many of its leading figures were originally Unitarians and some of them remained so. It was largely the product of a group of friendly independent thinkers and writers with Concord its chosen home. George Ripley, Frederick Henry Hedge, Bronson Alcott, Margaret Fuller, Theodore Parker, Henry Thoreau, Ralph Waldo Emerson,—these are names which stand out in the movement. It spread gradually to the Mississippi and beyond, followed here and led there by Alcott and Emerson on lecture tours. It found a wide range of literary expression, but one mind more than others, that of Emerson, gave it philosophical unity.

American romanticism rediscovered the life of the soul. It rejected the use of external reason in favor of an internal intuitive sense. It replaced analytical judgment by imaginative creation. Clear to the transcendentalist above all else was the existence of a soul free to contemplate spiritual and material entities, creating as it went visions of the harmony which pervaded all things. The transcendentalist accepted from Coleridge the three closely related distinctions between reason and understanding, genius and talent, imagination and fancy. The first came from Plato and from English Platonism, the second from German romanticism, and the third was largely developed by Coleridge himself. Reason no longer meant the enlightened common sense of the Age of Reason; it was an intuitive faculty which acquired truth directly. Man's mind was a sensitive vehicle through which truth flowed and out of which certainty came. The acquisition of knowledge was not a difficult observational trail to follow step by step; it was rather a pleasant experience to enjoy. Logic was no obstacle to be surmounted, for logic resulted from the natural clarity of man's intuitive powers. Truth was not remote; it was clear, direct and immediate. Emerson did acknowledge a discipline of the understanding, but the main drift of the whole romantic spirit was away from strict, logical principles of thought to free, easy scintillations of the mind.

The transcendentalist was not opposed to science but was rather uninterested in it except as it seemed to substantiate his vision of the essential harmony in things. The spirit of the age was monistic; it revolted against the dualistic tendencies of the Age of Reason, the severance of God from nature and of man from God. This does not mean that the transcendentalist disregarded nature; on the contrary, he not only talked about but praised and communed with it. His view of nature, however, was part of a synthetic picture. He fused the scientific idea of natural law with the religious idea of providence, arriving at an orderly and harmonious universe purposively moving toward the fulfilment of cosmic designs. His was no arbitrary combination of science and religion; it was rather an outgrowth of sensitiveness to a variety of thought currents prevalent in his day, currents which he intuitively absorbed into what was for him a natural harmony. His philosophy was mystical; unity was natural, plurality was derivative.

Transcendentalism served as a liberal religion. It was critical of Biblical authenticity without completely rejecting Biblical authority. It was not ecclesiastical, yet it preserved the emotion and spirituality essential for religion. It was a powerful leaven in the liberalizing of orthodoxy. In place of a God of wrath was a God of love; in place of man the sinner was man the divine organ; in place of election and eternal damnation were freedom and eternal blessedness.

A strong ethical note pervaded the movement. The cry for freedom which transcendentalism was so effective in expressing grew out of a craving for individual righteousness rather than Greek *eudaimonia* or the Golden Mean; it possessed the dominant spirit of Protestantism. The transcendentalists were too interested in the future to become absorbed in aesthetic or epicurean pleasures. In rejecting the old hell they turned to the task of making this world a heaven. Brook Farm, a transcendentalist haven for a time, was a result of this utopianism. But there was little sympathy with large-scale collectivism among the transcendentalists; the good life was to be achieved by each individual through the fulfilment of the divine powers with which God had endowed him. Economic individualism combined with Protestantism thus developed into intellectual and moral individualism.

Concurrent with transcendentalism and partly inspired by it was a growing maturity of democratic thought. Transcendentalism had not only been individualistic; it had glorified the individual. Emerson gave clear expression to democratic sentiments and has ever since been regarded as one of the intellectual fathers of democracy. Yet forces which were at work gave democracy an interpretation not in complete accord with the extreme individualism of transcendentalism. The more extensive the application of individualism the more acquisitive man became, necessitating reconsideration of democratic claims. Economic, class and sectional differences arose to check the belief in equality. Industrialism increased the dependence of each individual on others and emphasized the collective character of society. The transcendentalists had raised the hope for perfection but this came to be interpreted as meaning social as well as individual perfection. The result was that democracy came to be redefined, party or factional government was attacked and thought was enkindled on the problem of how democracy might be improved. The doctrine of natural rights was overshadowed by the concept of a social organism. Society was looked upon as the natural state of man rather than as the result of a contractual agreement, a movement in the direction of the Greek interpretation of the state. Government was looked upon as necessary, but not as necessarily evil. This new point of view held to the organic character of society in common with Hegelianism without being directly influenced by it. John Calhoun, despite his southern partiality, represented this tendency extremely well, as did Francis Lieber, an influential teacher and writer. Lieber's *Manual of Political Ethics* (1838–39) and *Treatise on Civil Liberty and Self-Government* (1853) were widely used as textbooks for a long period of years.

The influx of German immigrants during the second quarter of the nineteenth century afforded a more direct knowledge of German philosophy than the early transcendentalists possessed. One of the first men to introduce Hegel was Frederick A. Rauch, President of Franklin and Marshall College from 1836 to 1841. His book *Psychology: or, A View of the Human Soul; Including Anthropology* (1841) was a purer form of Hegelianism than anything which followed in the next generation. The St. Louis Movement, Hegelian in large part, came into being through the formation of the St. Louis Philosophical Society in 1866, but it will be dealt with in the next period since its national influence came to be felt later.

By the 1860's transcendentalism had run its course, although later idealism was in part a revival of it. The idea of evolution, acquiring empirical verification, began to assume importance in men's minds. It has been said, on the basis of the Comtean formulation of the three stages of human thought, that the idea of evolution in America was based upon theological concepts in the seventeenth century, upon metaphysical considerations in the eighteenth and upon positivistic, or scientific, bases in the nineteenth. Although this generalization may be somewhat too neat, it is true that the idea of evolution or development was not completely new to the philosophers of the mid-nineteenth century but had itself gone through a process of continual refinement. It was implicit in the concept of progress of which the philosophers of the Age of Reason were enamored. In the neoplatonic emanation theory accepted by the transcendentalists, the "return" was sometimes understood in an evolutionary sense. The idea was also implicit in the political concept of the state as a social organism. Its full impact was not felt, however, until geological and zoölogical research gave it an essentially empirical form. Lamarck, Lyell, Cuvier, Von Baer, Agassiz, Gray, Haeckel, Wallace and Darwin—these are the names which symbolize the growing interest in the empirical study and classification of species. When the attempt was made to offer an explanatory basis for this widening empirical knowledge of nature, philosophical consideration of the issues involved assumed importance. Serious concern over these issues can hardly be said to date much before the second half of the nineteenth century. Darwin's *Origin of Species* (1859) served as the final bell to summon the defenders of opposing views from their respective corners for the battle which was to ensue.

Up to this time, the prevailing leaning in American philosophy had been toward some form of supernaturalism, except for the period of the Age of Reason during which a half-hearted naturalism was temporarily in the limelight. The majority view from the Puritans to Harris had inclined toward *a priori* analysis, had been highly saturated with traditional religious tenets, and had seen the world in terms, either literally or figuratively, of certain axiomatic truths on the basis of which its system of thought had been constructed. Those sharing this view were inclined to adjust experience to reason and the natural world to the supernatural. Their cosmology was neat even if only hypothetically or symbolically true; this neatness was conducive to a certain smugness which made its exponents somewhat unreceptive to a new scientific point of view which sooner or later they were forced to confront. As the problems of organic and cosmic evolution came to the fore, however, the doctrinal framework of their system became more precisely defined. They were believers in special creation, accepting the thesis that God was the originator of whatever species appeared; this was, of course, acceptance of divine intervention, each new species being a miraculous creation of a providential deity. They believed in the permanance of species, holding that what God had created, nature could never change. They held that evolution or development within a species was possible, but they also held that transmutation of species was unproved and unsound. They thought in terms of a final cataclysm for all orders of nature which was, in a sense, a restatement of belief in a final judgment day. Louis Agassiz represented this general position and is a particularly interesting study because he combined it with an intense devotion to the empirical study of nature.

The new naturalism which this preformationist school opposed was the heir to eighteenth-century empiricism. Stifled for a time in the United States because it had neither an organization nor a sufficient number of enthusiastic devotees to further it, naturalism was given new life through the development of evolutionary concepts. Less tied to any particular ideology than their opponents, the naturalists were inclined toward a freer interpretation of new knowledge. The result was that they came to look upon Darwin as the empirical basis for their thinking and upon Spencer as the philosopher who gave it systematic form. They were partial to induction, somewhat inclined toward positivism (although they were not necessarily followers of Comte), and anxious to extend the concept of evolution to the largest possible realm. Against the principle of special creation they defended spontaneous generation; against the doctrine of the permanence of species they opposed transmutation; against the idea of a final cataclysm they defended natural selection and continuous development. John Fiske represented this school of thought and although not a scientist he was thoroughly acquainted with scientific developments and gave an able exposition of evolutionary thought.

The battle over evolution and its philosophical consequences was an indication of what was happening in philosophy by the second half of the nineteenth century. Philosophy was being weaned away from theology and religion and being nourished by science. After the industrial revolution science was pursued less for edification and for reinforcement of religion than for that practical ministry to the comforts and conveniences of life which Franklin had sought to promote. As science gained in prestige over religion and theology, philosophy, for long the handmaid of theology, could maintain its standing only by adjusting its methods and conclusions to those of science. This gave new direction to philosophical activity. The developing laboratory techniques of science inspired consideration of epistemological problems, scientific method and the concepts of science. John Bernhard Stallo's *General Principles of the Philosophy of Nature* (1848) and Albert Taylor Bledsoe's *The Philosophy of Mathematics* (1866) represent this tendency. More important than either of these was Chauncey Wright whose able analyses of evolutionary ideas and of scientific procedure mark him as one of the real forbears of contemporary naturalism. There were influential teachers during the period such as Francis Bowen of Harvard, Francis Wayland of Brown, Noah Porter of Yale, James McCosh of Princeton and Laurens Hickok of Union and Amherst, who were in the more traditional stream of thought; but the attention paid by philosophy to science stands out particularly because of the increasing importance it assumed in the period which followed.

# XV

# Ralph Waldo Emerson

1803–1882

Born in Boston. A.B., Harvard, 1821. Taught school and studied theology, 1821–28. Minister of Second Church in Boston, 1829–32. Traveled in Europe, 1833, visiting Coleridge, Carlyle and Wordsworth in England. Moved to Concord, 1834. Began professional lecturing, 1835. The Transcendental Club, 1836–50. Phi Beta Kappa oration, "The American Scholar," 1837. The Divinity School Address, 1838. *The Dial,* 1840–44; edited by Emerson 1842–44. Lectured in England and revisited Paris, 1848. Made lecture tours of the middle west almost annually, 1850–71. LL.D., Harvard, and elected Overseer by alumni, 1866. Harvard lectures on "The Natural History of Intellect," 1870–71. Traveled and lectured in California, 1871. Third visit to Europe, 1872. Concord School of Philosophy, 1879–87 (first planned by Emerson and Alcott in 1840). Died in Concord.

Emerson's position in American philosophy is unique; he escapes the categories of the historian of thought so completely that he has often been called, in the same estimate, both *the* American philosopher and scarcely a philosopher at all. George Santayana in 1898 thought him "not primarily a philosopher, but a Puritan mystic with a poetic fancy and a gift for observation and epigram." But Santayana's last word was that if Emerson was not a star of the first magnitude, he was certainly "a fixed star in the firmament of philosophy," and the only American one. William James, after a re-reading of all his works, could deliver a centenary address upon him in 1903 without once using the word philosopher; he was rather the seer, reporter, prophet and, above all, artist. But Harvard was then planning the first building in America to be devoted to philosophy, and the obvious name for it was Emerson Hall. In the same year John Dewey in Chicago called him "the one citizen in the New World fit to have his name uttered in the same breath with that of Plato," and thought the dawning century might well make it evident that he was not only a philosopher but *the* "Philosopher of Democracy." After James's death in 1910, and with the Emerson centenary safely past, Josiah Royce pronounced the soberer judgment that there were three representative American philosophers, each giving classic expression to a distinct stage of our culture—Edwards, Emerson, and James.[1]

Emerson was born just a century after Edwards, and there is a significant parallel between the movements of which they were the chief spokesmen—the Great Awakening of the seventeen-thirties and forties and the transcendentalism of the eighteen-thirties and forties. The former was a protest against the leveling and desiccation of religion in Puritan New England, the latter against "the pale negations of Boston Unitarianism." Both appealed to a heightened intuition involving the will and the affections as well as the intellect. Edwards made notes for a "Treatise on the Mind," and Emerson for a "Natural History of Intellect," in which their idealistic metaphysics and theory of knowledge were to be fully developed, and of which most of their published writings were but *disiecta membra.* Emerson was not unaware of the essential kinship underlying the obvious differences between the two movements. After 1790 he remarked there was in Massachusetts "not a book, a speech, a conversation, or a thought" until about 1820 when "the Channing, Webster, and Everett era" began; and then, as if to correct the former date, he added: "Edwards on the Will was printed in 1754."[2] The transcendental movement restored to New England the intellectual leadership it had lost to the middle states during the Age of Reason.

At Harvard's second centennial celebration in September, 1836, Emerson conferred with a few friends on the low state of religion and philosophy. In the previous year there had been some talk in his circle of starting a journal to be called *The Transcendentalist,* which later materialized as *The Dial.* For the time being they contented themselves with forming what came to be known as "The Transcendental Club." At its early meetings the discussion centered around "The American Genius—the causes which hinder its growth, giving us no first rate productions." The cause most obvious to them was "the reigning sensuous philosophy, dating from Locke, on which our Unitarian theology was based." The antidote had been proposed by James Marsh, President of the University of Vermont, in his "Preliminary Essay" to the American edition of Coleridge's *Aids to Reflection* in 1829. This and his edition of Coleridge's *The Friend* (1831) had been

[1] Royce, Josiah: *William James and Other Essays on the Philosophy of Life.* New York: The Macmillan Co., 1911. (See essays by Dewey, James and Santayana in reference list below.)

[2] *Journals.* VIII, 339.

reviewed at length by Emerson's companion Frederick Henry Hedge in *The Christian Examiner* for March, 1833. The essential point was the distinction between understanding and reason, which went back to Plato's *Republic*. It had been revived in the seventeenth century by the Cambridge Platonists, and again by Kant in the eighteenth. It was the key to the German idealists who followed Kant. Coleridge had made its establishment his later life's task, and Marsh was republishing his works in America to fix the attention of thinking men upon it.[3]

In the three years following Hedge's review, which Emerson regarded as "a living, leaping Logos," he had been exploring the implications of the distinction between understanding and reason. In 1834 he wrote to his brother Edward, "I think it a philosophy itself, and, like all truth, very practical." [4] By June, 1835, he had planned a book on "First Philosophy," in the notes for which he said regarding this same distinction, "A clear perception of it is the key to all theology, and a theory of human life." [5] The title "First Philosophy" was soon exchanged for another which we meet first in an essay of 1841: "Gladly would I unfold in calm degrees *a natural history of the intellect,* but what man has yet been able to mark the steps and boundaries of that transparent essence? " [6]

Precisely such a history, for all his deprecation of artificial system-building, was the life work which Emerson set for himself and never abandoned until after the failure of his final effort in 1871. But in his case there was a progressive loss of constructive power as over against a steady growth in the case of Edwards. The latter's return to the themes of his "Treatise on the Mind" just before assuming the presidency of Princeton, permits us to believe that with longer life he might have carried through his original design. But Emerson's painful attempts at composition in connection with his last series of lectures in 1870 and 1871 made it clear that he was no longer adequate to the task; and we must go back to the productions of his early maturity, and particularly to *Nature* (1836), "Circles" and "Intellect" (1841), and "Experience" (1844), for our best clues to the form the treatise would have taken if executed at the height of his powers. The first and last of these are examples of that "long logic" to which he referred in

[3] Cabot: *Memoir.* 245 ff. Gohdes, Clarence: "Alcott's 'Conversation' on the Transcendental Club and *The Dial,*" *American Literature* 3 (1931) 14–27. Nicolson, Marjorie H.: "James Marsh and the Vermont Transcendentalists," *Philosophical Review* 34 (1925) 28–50.

[4] Cabot: *Memoir.* 218.

[5] Below, p. 338.

[6] *Works.* II, 325.

"Intellect" as consisting in "the procession or proportionate unfolding of the intuition." [7] It is upon them that his reputation as a philosopher must rest.

Whatever the literary critics may say, the student of philosophy will find in Emerson's "Experience" his masterpiece. Struck off under the shadow of the spiritual crisis of his life, the death of his eldest son, it is the most original and audacious, the most densely packed and the swiftest, of all his essays. Though it owes nothing directly to Hegel, it has the histrionic flavor and the dialectic unity of that tragi-comic biography of human experience, *The Phenomenology of Mind* (1807).

> So much of our time is preparation, so much is routine, and so much retrospect, that the pith of each man's genius contracts itself to a very few hours. . . . We see young men who owe us a new world, so readily and lavishly they promise, but they never acquit the debt; they die young and dodge the account; or if they live they lose themselves in the crowd. . . . How strongly I have felt of pictures that when you have seen one well, you must take your leave of it; you shall never see it again. . . . We do what we must, and call it by the best names we can, and would fain have the praise of having intended the result which ensues. . . . The plays of children are nonsense, but very educative nonsense. So it is with the largest and solemnest things. . . . We live amid surfaces, and the true art of life is to skate well on them. . . . We must set up the strong present tense against all the rumors of wrath, past or to come. . . . The consciousness in each man is a sliding scale, which identifies him now with the First Cause, and now with the flesh of his body; life above life, in infinite degrees. . . . In liberated moments we know that a new picture of life and duty is already possible. . . . The new statement will comprise the scepticisms as well as the faiths of society, and out of unbeliefs a creed shall be formed. . . . The universe is the bride of the soul. All private sympathy is partial. . . . We permit all things to ourselves, and that which we call sin in others is experiment for us. . . . Thus inevitably does the universe wear our color, and every object fall successively into the subject itself. . . . The partial action of each strong mind in one direction is a telescope for the objects on which it is pointed. But every other part of knowledge is to be pushed to the same extravagance, ere the soul attains her due sphericity. . . . Illusion, Temperament, Succession, Surface, Surprise, Reality, Subjectiveness,—these . . . are the lords of life. I dare not assume to give their order, but I name them as I find them in my way. I know better than to claim any completeness for my picture. I am a fragment, and this is a fragment of me. . . .[8]

This was a far cry from the winged speculation, the morning freshness and clairvoyance of *Nature,* which was much closer in content as

[7] *Works.* II, 329.
[8] Ibid. III, 43–86.

well as in time to the first draft of the never finished *opus maximum,* and closer also to the characteristic temper and doctrine of transcendentalism. *Nature* is therefore the obvious choice to represent its period in American thought, whereas "Experience" anticipates the later idealism of Harris and Royce. The essential argument of *Nature* required for its construction the full three years following Hedge's review, and did not take final form until the book was nearly completed. It can be thrown into sharper relief by such abridgment as we have undertaken, and can in fact be detached altogether, as that of "Experience" cannot. Emerson had written two separate essays, "Nature" and "Spirit," in that order, and it was not until the middle of August, 1836, a month before publication, that he bridged the gap between the two with the section headed "Idealism." This was no stop-gap, however, but the settling into place of a possession of longer standing than anything else in the book. As he wrote to Margaret Fuller in 1841, "I know but one solution to my nature and relations, which I find in remembering the joy with which in my boyhood I caught the first hint of the Berkeleyan philosophy, and which I certainly never lost sight of afterwards." [9]

The problem of the book, "to what end is nature?," was the same as that of Edwards's *The End for which God created the World,* and the conclusion was not radically different, though Edwards started from God, and Emerson from man. After a few preliminary distinctions, Edwards had proceeded at once to show by "the dictates of reason" that God's last or ultimate end was the emanation of his own infinite fulness, an end in which God's glory and the creature's good were one. Emerson began with the most immediate and obvious ends which nature is empirically found to serve—the uses of nature, its ministries to man—under the heads of Commodity, Beauty, Language ("Every natural fact is a symbol of some spiritual fact"), and Discipline,—ends which the philosophically untutored would readily recognize. Then, by an appeal to Berkeleyan idealism, he reached the conclusion that "the noblest ministry of nature is to stand as the apparition of God," and that "all the uses of nature admit of being summed" in this. Here again, however, creator and creature were not to be opposed; "the Supreme Being does not build up nature around us, but puts it forth through us"; and again, "man has access to the entire mind of the Creator, is himself the creator in the finite." The apparition of God in nature was thus the revelation to man of his own high estate, an estate from which he had fallen and which he could recover only by the application to na-

[9] Cabot: *Memoir.* 478. Cf. 259 also.

ture of his entire force, reason as well as understanding. The final note was therefore one of prophecy rather than accomplished fact, and with Socratic reserve Emerson put into the mouth of his Orphic poet, Bronson Alcott: "The kingdom of man over nature, which cometh not with observation,—a dominion such as now is beyond his dream of God,—he shall enter without more wonder than the blind man feels who is gradually restored to perfect sight." [10]

The most interesting of all aspects of Emerson's intellectual development, and the one most intimately related to the general movement of thought during his long life, is his gradual shift from this neoplatonic doctrine of emanation and return, to the scientific theory of evolution. The decisive year seems to have been 1849. On Sunday, August 5, Bronson Alcott talked all day with Emerson in study and field about his doctrine of "genesis," and drew on his own journal page several chains and rings to show how all nature *descends* from man. Though Emerson had seemed to share Alcott's view when he wrote *Nature,* he now preferred to read Alcott's diagrams in an *ascending* sense, and on the same page he wrote the lines:

A subtle chain of countless rings
The next unto the farthest brings;
The eye reads omens where it goes,
And speaks all languages the rose;
And, striving to be man, the worm
Mounts through all the spires of form.[11]

Emerson was then engaged in correcting proofs for *Nature, Addresses and Lectures,* which was published on September 7. This volume included a second edition of *Nature,* which was also issued separately. In this edition he substituted the above lines for the motto of the original edition of 1836, which had read:

Nature is but an image or imitation of wisdom, the last thing of the soul; nature being a thing which doth only do, but not know.

PLOTINUS

The day after his long talk with Alcott, Emerson wrote in his own journal:

There are three degrees in philosophy. Plato came with geometry; that was one degree. Plotinus came with mythology, Zoroastrian or Magian illumination, etc., as exalted or stilted Plato: that was the second degree. But now comes my friend with palmistry, phrenology,

[10] *Works.* I, 77.

[11] Shepard, Odell: *Pedlar's Progress: The Life of Bronson Alcott.* Boston: Little, Brown and Co., 1937. 459.

mesmerism, and Davisian revelation: this is the third degree; and bearing the same relation to Plotinism which that bore to Platonism.[12]

Though Emerson the critic, respecting the sober science of the mid-nineteenth century, might thus deprecate the mythology and the exaltation of Plotinus, Emerson the seer and artist continued to speak the language of Plotinus, as he had in *Nature,* "The Over-Soul" and "The Poet." His own most exalted flight, at the end of "Illusions," published in the year after Darwin's *Origin of Species,* was taken on Plotinian wings:

> There is no chance and no anarchy in the universe. All is system and gradation. Every god is there sitting in his sphere. The young mortal enters the hall of the firmament; there is he alone with them alone, they pouring on him benedictions and gifts, and beckoning him up to their thrones. On the instant, and incessantly, fall snow-storms of illusions. He fancies himself in a vast crowd which sways this way and that and whose movement and doings he must obey: he fancies himself poor, orphaned, insignificant. The mad crowd drives hither and thither, now furiously commanding this thing to be done, now that. What is he that he should resist their will, and think or act for himself? Every moment new changes and new showers of deceptions to baffle and distract him. And when, by and by, for an instant, the air clears and the cloud lifts a little, there are the gods still sitting around him on their thrones,—they alone with him alone.[13]

## REFERENCES


Emerson, Ralph Waldo: *Complete Works.* Centenary Edition. 12 vols. Boston: Houghton Mifflin Co., 1903–04.

———: *Journals.* 10 vols. Boston: Houghton Mifflin Co., 1909–14.

———: *Letters.* 6 vols. New York: Columbia University Press, 1938.

Beach, Joseph Warren: "Emerson and Evolution," *University of Toronto Quarterly* 3 (1933–34) 474–97.

Cabot, James Elliot: *A Memoir of Ralph Waldo Emerson.* 2 vols. Boston: Houghton Mifflin Co., 1887. (The standard biography.)

Carpenter, Frederic Ives: *Emerson and Asia.* Cambridge: Harvard University Press, 1930.

———: *Ralph Waldo Emerson.* Representative Selections, with Introduction, Bibliography, and Notes. Cincinnati: American Book Co., 1934.

Dewey, John: "Emerson—The Philosopher of Democracy," *International Journal of Ethics* 13 (1902–03) 405–13.

Firkins, Oscar W.: *Ralph Waldo Emerson.* Boston: Houghton Mifflin Co., 1915.


[12] *Journals.* VIII, 37.

[13] *Works.* VI, 325.

Gray, Henry David: *Emerson: A Statement of New England Transcendentalism as Expressed in the Philosophy of its Chief Exponent.* Stanford University, Cal.: Stanford University Press, 1917. (Best exposition and criticism of Emerson's philosophy.)

Harris, William Torrey: "The Dialectic Unity in Emerson's Prose," *Journal of Speculative Philosophy* 18 (1884) 195–202.

Harrison, John Smith: *The Teachers of Emerson.* New York: Sturgis & Walton Co., 1910.

Hotson, Clarence Paul: "Sampson Reed, A Teacher of Emerson," *New England Quarterly* 2 (1929) 249–77.

James, William: *Memories and Studies.* New York: Longmans, Green and Co., 1912. (Ch. II, "Address at the Emerson Centenary.")

Santayana, George: *Interpretations of Poetry and Religion.* New York: Charles Scribner's Sons, 1900. (Ch. VIII, "Emerson.")

Woodberry, George Edward: *Ralph Waldo Emerson.* English Men of Letters Series. New York: The Macmillan Co., 1907.

* * *

---

* * *

## FIRST PHILOSOPHY [14]

The *first* Philosophy, that of mind, is the science of what *is,* in distinction from what *appears.* It is one mark of its laws that their enunciation awakens the feeling of the moral sublime, and *great men* are they who believe in them. They resemble great circles in astronomy, each of which, in what direction soever it be drawn, contains the whole sphere. So each of these seems to imply all truth. These laws are Ideas of the Reason, and so are obeyed easier than expressed. They astonish the Understanding, and seem to it gleams of a world in which we do not live.

[14] Two sets of extracts from Emerson's notes under this head have been published: one in Cabot's *Memoir,* 246–8; the other in *Journals,* III, 235–40. We follow the latter, except for reading "east" rather than "cast" in the last paragraph; but we add in footnotes two passages included by Cabot which are not in the *Journals.* Cabot assigns these notes to June, 1835; the editors of the *Journals* say they were "probably written in 1833." The *Journals* (III, 489–90) contain under date of June 10, 1835, a paragraph much like the first one here, but beginning "I endeavor to announce the laws of the First Philosophy." Comparison of these notes with other entries in May, June, and July of that year leads us to accept Cabot's date. See especially May 29, 30; June 4, 10, 20, 21; July 1, 2. Reprinted by permission of Houghton Mifflin Co.

Our compound nature differences us from God, but our Reason is not to be distinguished from the divine Essence. We have yet devised no words to designate the attributes of God which can adequately stand for the universality and perfection of our own intuitions. To call the Reason "ours" or "Human" seems an impertinence, so absolute and unconfined it is. The best we can say of God, we mean of the mind as it is known to us.[15] Thus when you say,

> The gods approve
> The depth, but not the tumult of the soul
> (A fervent, not ungovernable love),

the sublime in the sentiment is, that to the soul itself depth, not tumult, is desirable. When you say (Socrates said it), "Jupiter prefers integrity to charity," your finest meaning is the "soul prefers," etc. When Jesus saith, "Who giveth one of these little ones a cup of cold water shall not lose his reward," is not the best meaning the love at which the giver has arrived? And so on throughout the New Testament there is not a volition attributed to God considered as an external cause but gains in truth and dignity by being referred to the soul.

Reason, seeing in objects their remote effects, affirms the effect as the permanent character. The Understanding, listening to Reason, on the one side, which says *It is,* and to the senses on the other side, which say *It is not,* takes middle ground and declares *It will be.* Heaven is the projection of the Ideas of Reason on the plane of the understanding.[16]

Jesus Christ was a minister of the pure Reason. The beatitudes of the Sermon on the Mount are all utterances of the mind contemning the phenomenal world. "Blessed are the righteous poor, for theirs is the kingdom of heaven. Blessed are ye when men revile you," etc. The Understanding can make nothing of it. 'Tis all nonsense. The Reason affirms its absolute verity.

[15] In place of the rest of this paragraph, Cabot has the following: "Time and space are below its sphere; it considers things according to more intimate properties; it beholds their essence, wherein is seen what they can produce. It is in all men, even the worst, and constitutes them men. In bad men it is dormant, in the good efficient; but it is perfect and identical in all, underneath the peculiarities, the vices, and the errors of the individual. Compared with the self-existence of the laws of truth and right, of which he is conscious, his personality is a parasitic, deciduous atom. The Understanding is the executive faculty, the hand of the mind. It mediates between the soul and inert matter. It works in time and space, and therefore successively. The ideas of Reason assume a new appearance as they descend into the Understanding; they walk in masquerade."—Editor's note.

[16] Cabot adds: "The Understanding accepts the oracle, but, with its short sight not apprehending the truth, declares that in futurity it is so, and adds all manner of fables of its own."—Editor's note.

Various terms are employed to indicate the counteraction of the Reason and the Understanding, with more or less precision, according to the cultivation of the speaker. A clear perception of it is the key to all theology, and a theory of human life. St. Paul marks the distinction by the terms natural man and spiritual man. When Novalis says, "It is the instinct of the understanding to counteract the Reason," he only translates into a scientific formula the sentence of St. Paul, "The Carnal mind is enmity against God."

The mind is very wise, could it be roused into action. But the life of most men is aptly signified by the poet's personification, "Death in Life." We walk about in a sleep. A few moments in the year, or in our lifetime, we truly live; we are at the top of our being; we are pervaded, yea, dissolved by the Mind; but we fall back again presently. Those who are styled Practical Men are not awake, for they do not exercise the Reason; yet their sleep is restless. The most active lives have so much routine as to preclude progress almost equally with the most inactive. We bow low to the noted merchants whose influence is felt, not only in their native cities, but in most parts of the globe; but our respect does them and ourselves great injustice, for their trade is without system, their affairs unfold themselves after no law of the mind, but are bubble built on bubble without end; a work of arithmetic, not of commerce, much less of humanity. They add voyage to voyage, and buy stocks,—that they may buy stocks,—and no ulterior purpose is thought of. When you see their dexterity in particulars, you cannot overestimate the resources of good sense; and when you find how empty they are of all remote aims, you cannot underestimate their philosophy.

The man of letters puts the same cheat upon us, bestirring himself immensely to keep the secret of his littleness. He spins his most seeming surface directly before the eye, to conceal the universe of his ignorance. To what end his languages, his correspondence, his academic discourses, his printed volumes? Newton said that if this porous world were made solid, *it would lie in a nutshell.*

All our writings are variations of one air. Books for the most part are such expedients as his who makes an errand for the sake of exercise. And for the sincere great men the wisest passages they have writ, the infinite conclusions to which they owe their fame, are only confessions. Throughout their works, the good ear hears the undersong of confession and amazement, the apothegm of Socrates, the recantation of man.

Such is the inaction of men. We have an obscure consciousness of our attributes. We stand on the edge of all that is great, yet are restrained in inactivity and unconscious of our powers, like neuters of the hive, every one of which is capable of transformation into the Queen bee. We are always on the brink, etc.

Much preparation, little fruit. But suddenly in any place, in the street, in the chamber, will the heavens open and the regions of wisdom be uncovered, as if to show how thin the veil, how null the circumstances. As quickly, a Lethean stream washes through us and bereaves us of ourselves.

What a benefit if a rule could be given whereby the mind, dreaming amid the gross fogs of matter, could at any moment EAST ITSELF AND FIND THE SUN! But the common life is an endless succession of phantasms; and long after we have deemed ourselves recovered and sound, light breaks in upon us and we find we have yet had no sane hour. Another morn rises on mid-noon.

* * *

---

* * *

## NATURE [17]

### *Discipline*

In view of the significance of nature, we arrive at once at a new fact, that nature is a discipline. This use of the world includes the preceding uses [commodity, beauty, language], as parts of itself.

Space, time, society, labor, climate, food, locomotion, the animals, the mechanical forces, give us sincerest lessons, day by day, whose meaning is unlimited. They educate both the Understanding and the Reason. Every property of matter is a school for the understanding,—its solidity or resistance, its inertia, its extension, its figure, its divisibility. The understanding adds, divides, combines, measures, and finds nutriment and room for its activity in this worthy scene. Meantime, Reason transfers all these lessons into its own world of thought, by perceiving the analogy that marries Matter and Mind.

1. Nature is a discipline of the understanding in intellectual truths. Our dealing with sensible objects is a constant exercise in the necessary lessons of difference, of likeness, of order, of being and seeming, of progressive arrangement; of ascent from particular to general; of

[17] *Works.* I, (sections V–VIII) 36–8, 40–2; 47–52, 55–60; 60–5; 72–3.

combination to one end of manifold forces. Proportioned to the importance of the organ to be formed, is the extreme care with which its tuition is provided,—a care pretermitted in no single case. What tedious training, day after day, year after year, never ending, to form the common sense; what continual reproduction of annoyances, inconveniences, dilemmas; what rejoicing over us of little men; what disputing of prices, what reckonings of interest,—and all to form the Hand of the mind;—to instruct us that "good thoughts are no better than good dreams, unless they be executed!"

The same good office is performed by Property and its filial systems of debt and credit. Debt, grinding debt, whose iron face the widow, the orphan, and the sons of genius fear and hate;—debt, which consumes so much time, which so cripples and disheartens a great spirit with cares that seem so base, is a preceptor whose lessons cannot be foregone, and is needed most by those who suffer from it most. Moreover, property, which has been well compared to snow,—"if it fall level to-day, it will be blown into drifts to-morrow,"—is the surface action of internal machinery, like the index on the face of a clock. Whilst now it is the gymnastics of the understanding, it is hiving, in the foresight of the spirit, experience in profounder laws.

The whole character and fortune of the individual are affected by the least inequalities in the culture of the understanding; for example, in the perception of differences. Therefore is Space, and therefore Time, that man may know that things are not huddled and lumped, but sundered and individual. A bell and a plough have each their use, and neither can do the office of the other. Water is good to drink, coal to burn, wool to wear; but wool cannot be drunk, nor water spun, nor coal eaten. The wise man shows his wisdom in separation, in gradation, and his scale of creatures and of merits is as wide as nature. The foolish have no range in their scale, but suppose every man is as every other man. What is not good they call the worst, and what is not hateful, they call the best.

. . . . . .

2. Sensible objects conform to the premonitions of Reason and reflect the conscience. All things are moral; and in their boundless changes have an unceasing reference to spiritual nature. Therefore is nature glorious with form, color, and motion; that every globe in the remotest heaven, every chemical change from the rudest crystal up to the laws of life, every change of vegetation from the first principle of growth in the eye of a leaf, to the tropical forest and antedilu-

vian coal-mine, every animal function from the sponge up to Hercules, shall hint or thunder to man the laws of right and wrong, and echo the Ten Commandments. Therefore is Nature ever the ally of Religion: lends all her pomp and riches to the religious sentiment. Prophet and priest, David, Isaiah, Jesus, have drawn deeply from this source. This ethical character so penetrates the bone and marrow of nature as to seem the end for which it was made. Whatever private purpose is answered by any member or part, this is its public and universal function, and is never omitted. Nothing in nature is exhausted in its first use. When a thing has served an end to the uttermost, it is wholly new for an ulterior service. In God, every end is converted into a new means. Thus the use of commodity, regarded by itself, is mean and squalid. But it is to the mind an education in the doctrine of Use, namely, that a thing is good only so far as it serves; that a conspiring of parts and efforts to the production of an end is essential to any being. The first and gross manifestation of this truth is our inevitable and hated training in values and wants, in corn and meat.

It has already been illustrated, that every natural process is a version of a moral sentence. The moral law lies at the centre of nature and radiates to the circumference. It is the pith and marrow of every substance, every relation, and every process. All things with which we deal, preach to us. What is a farm but a mute gospel? The chaff and the wheat, weeds and plants, blight, rain, insects, sun,—it is a sacred emblem from the first furrow of spring to the last stack which the snow of winter overtakes in the fields. But the sailor, the shepherd, the miner, the merchant, in their several resorts, have each an experience precisely parallel, and leading to the same conclusion: because all organizations are radically alike. . . .

## *Idealism*

Thus is the unspeakable but intelligible and practicable meaning of the world conveyed to man, the immortal pupil, in every object of sense. To this one end of Discipline, all parts of nature conspire.

A noble doubt perpetually suggests itself,—whether this end be not the Final Cause of the Universe; and whether nature outwardly exists. It is a sufficient account of that Appearance we call the World, that God will teach a human mind, and so makes it the receiver of a certain number of congruent sensations, which we call sun and moon, man and woman, house and trade. In my utter impotence to test the authenticity of the report of my senses, to know whether the impressions they make on me correspond with outlying objects, what difference does it make, whether Orion is up there in heaven, or some god paints the image in the firmament of the soul? The relations of parts and the end of the whole remaining the same, what is the difference, whether land and sea interact, and worlds revolve and intermingle without number or end,—deep yawning under deep, and galaxy balancing galaxy, throughout absolute space,—or whether, without relations of time and space, the same appearances are inscribed in the constant faith of man? Whether nature enjoy a substantial existence without, or is only in the apocalypse of the mind, it is alike useful and alike venerable to me. Be it what it may, it is ideal to me so long as I cannot try the accuracy of my senses.

The frivolous make themselves merry with the Ideal theory, as if its consequences were burlesque; as if it affected the stability of nature. It surely does not. God never jests with us, and will not compromise the end of nature by permitting any inconsequence in its procession. Any distrust of the permanence of laws would paralyze the faculties of man. Their permanence is sacredly respected, and his faith therein is perfect. The wheels and springs of man are all set to the hypothesis of the permanence of nature. We are not built like a ship to be tossed, but like a house to stand. It is a natural consequence of this structure, that so long as the active powers predominate over the reflective, we resist with indignation any hint that nature is more short-lived or mutable than spirit. The broker, the wheelwright, the carpenter, the tollman, are much displeased at the intimation.

But whilst we acquiesce entirely in the permanence of natural laws, the question of the absolute existence of nature still remains open. It is the uniform effect of culture on the human mind, not to shake our faith in the stability of particular phenomena, as of heat, water, azote; but to lead us to regard nature as phenomenon, not a substance; to attribute necessary existence to spirit; to esteem nature as an accident and an effect.

To the senses and the unrenewed understanding, belongs a sort of instinctive belief in the absolute existence of nature. In their view man and nature are indissolubly joined. Things are ultimates, and they never look beyond their sphere. The presence of Reason mars this faith. The first effort of thought tends to relax this despotism of the senses which binds us to nature as if we were a part of it, and shows us nature aloof, and, as it were, afloat. Until this higher agency intervened, the animal eye sees, with wonderful accuracy, sharp outlines and colored surfaces. When the eye of Reason opens, to outline and surface are at once added grace and expression. These proceed from imagination and affection, and abate somewhat of the angular distinctness of objects. If the Reason be stimulated to more earnest vision, outlines and surfaces become transparent, and are no longer seen; causes and spirits are seen through them. The best moments of life are these delicious awakenings of the higher powers, and the reverential withdrawings of nature before its God.

Let us proceed to indicate the effects of culture.

1. Our first institution in the Ideal philosophy is a hint from Nature herself.

Nature is made to conspire with spirit to emancipate us. Certain mechanical changes, a small alteration in our local position, apprizes us of a dualism. We are strangely affected by seeing the shore from a moving ship, from a balloon, or through the tints of an unusual sky. The least change in our point of view gives the whole world a pictorial air. A man who seldom rides, needs only to get into a coach and traverse his own town, to turn the street into a puppet-show. The men, the women,—talking, running, bartering, fighting,—the earnest mechanic, the lounger, the beggar, the boys, the dogs, are unrealized at once, or, at least, wholly detached from all relation to the observer, and seen as apparent, not substantial beings. What new thoughts are suggested by seeing a face of country quite familiar, in the rapid movement of the railroad car! Nay, the most wonted objects, (make a very slight change in the point of vision,) please us most. In a camera obscura, the butcher's cart, and the figure of one of our own family amuse us. So a portrait of a well-known face gratifies us. Turn the eyes upside down, by looking at the landscape through your legs, and how agreeable is the picture, though you have seen it any time these twenty years!

In these cases, by mechanical means, is suggested the difference between the observer and the spectacle—between man and nature. Hence arises a pleasure mixed with awe; I may say, a low degree of the sublime is felt, from the fact, probably, that man is hereby apprized that whilst the world is a spectacle, something in himself is stable.

2. In a higher manner the poet communicates the same pleasure. By a few strokes he delineates, as on air, the sun, the mountain, the camp, the city, the hero, the maiden, not different from what we know them, but only lifted from the ground and afloat before the eye. He unfixes the land and the sea, makes them revolve around the axis of his primary thought, and disposes them anew. Possessed himself by a heroic passion, he uses matter as symbols of it. The sensual man conforms thoughts to things; the poet conforms things to his thoughts. The one esteems

nature as rooted and fast; the other, as fluid, and impresses his being thereon. To him, the refractory world is ductile and flexible; he invests dust and stones with humanity, and makes them the words of the Reason. The Imagination may be defined to be the use which the Reason makes of the material world. Shakspeare possesses the power of subordinating nature for the purposes of expression, beyond all poets. . . .

3. Whilst thus the poet animates nature with his own thoughts, he differs from the philosopher only herein, that the one proposes Beauty as his main end; the other Truth. But the philosopher, not less than the poet, postpones the apparent order and relations of things to the empire of thought. "The problem of philosophy," according to Plato, "is, for all that exists conditionally, to find a ground unconditioned and absolute."[18] It proceeds on the faith that a law determines all phenomena, which being known, the phenomena can be predicted. That law, when in the mind, is an idea. Its beauty is infinite. The true philosopher and the true poet are one, and a beauty, which is truth, and a truth, which is beauty, is the aim of both. Is not the charm of one of Plato's or Aristotle's definitions strictly like that of the Antigone of Sophocles? It is, in both cases, that a spiritual life has been imparted to nature; that the solid seeming block of matter has been pervaded and dissolved by a thought; that this feeble human being has penetrated the vast masses of nature with an informing soul, and recognized itself in their harmony, that is, seized their law. In physics, when this is attained, the memory disburthens itself of its cumbrous catalogues of particulars, and carries centuries of observation in a single formula.

Thus even in physics, the material is degraded before the spiritual. The astronomer, the geometer, rely on their irrefragable analysis, and

[18] This is a fair sample of transcendental quotation. Kant, speaking of syllogistic inference and without reference to Plato, had remarked that "obviously, the principle peculiar to reason in general, in its logical employment, is: to find for the conditioned knowledge obtained through the understanding the unconditioned whereby its unity is brought to completion" (*Critique of Pure Reason.* A 307, tr. Smith, 1929. 306). Coleridge offered an expanded paraphrase, without reference to Kant, as Plato's definition of philosophy: "The grand problem, the solution of which forms, according to Plato, the final object and distinctive character of philosophy, is this: for all that which exists conditionally (that is, the existence of which is inconceivable except under the condition of its dependency on some other as its antecedent) to find a ground that is unconditional and absolute, and thereby to reduce the aggregate of human knowledge to a system" (*The Friend.* Essay V, sec. II. In *Works.* II, 420). Emerson offers an abridgement of this as a direct quotation from Plato himself. No such statement is to be found in Plato, yet it goes to the mark.—Editor's note.

disdain the results of observation. The sublime remark of Euler on his law of arches, "This will be found contrary to all experience, yet is true;" had already transferred nature into the mind, and left matter like an outcast corpse.

4. Intellectual science has been observed to beget invariably a doubt of the existence of matter. Turgot said, "He that has never doubted the existence of matter, may be assured he has no aptitude for metaphysical inquiries." It fastens the attention upon immortal necessary uncreated natures, that is, upon Ideas; and in their presence we feel that the outward circumstance is a dream and a shade. Whilst we wait in this Olympus of gods, we think of nature as an appendix to the soul. We ascend into their region, and know that these are the thoughts of the Supreme Being. "These are they who were set up from everlasting, from the beginning, or ever the earth was. When he prepared the heavens, they were there; when he established the clouds above, when he strengthened the fountains of the deep. Then they were by him, as one brought up with him. Of them took he counsel."

Their influence is proportionate. As objects of science they are accessible to few men. Yet all men are capable of being raised by piety or by passion, into their region. And no man touches these divine natures, without becoming, in some degree, himself divine. Like a new soul, they renew the body. We become physically nimble and lightsome; we tread on air; life is no longer irksome, and we think it will never be so. No man fears age or misfortune or death in their serene company, for he is transported out of the district of change. Whilst we behold unveiled the nature of Justice and Truth, we learn the difference between the absolute and the conditional or relative. We apprehend the absolute. As it were, for the first time, *we exist*. We become immortal, for we learn that time and space are relations of matter; that with a perception of truth or a virtuous will they have no affinity.

5. Finally, religion and ethics, which may be fitly called the practice of ideas, or the introduction of ideas into life, have an analogous effect with all lower culture, in degrading nature and suggesting its dependence on spirit. Ethics and religion differ herein; that the one is the system of human duties commencing from man; the other, from God. Religion includes the personality of God; Ethics does not. They are one to our present design. They both put nature under foot. The first and last lesson of religion is, "The things that are seen, are temporal; the things that are unseen, are eternal." It puts an affront upon nature. It does that for the unschooled, which philosophy does for Berkeley and Viasa. The uniform language that may be heard in the churches

of the most ignorant sects is,—"Contemn the unsubstantial shows of the world; they are vanities, dreams, shadows, unrealities; seek the realities of religion." The devotee flouts nature. Some theosophists have arrived at a certain hostility and indignation towards matter, as the Manichean and Plotinus. They distrusted in themselves any looking back to these flesh-pots of Egypt. Plotinus was ashamed of his body. In short, they might all say of matter, what Michael Angelo said of external beauty, "It is the frail and weary weed, in which God dresses the soul which he has called into time."

It appears that motion, poetry, physical and intellectual science, and religion, all tend to affect our convictions of the reality of the external world. But I own there is something ungrateful in expanding too curiously the particulars of the general proposition, that all culture tends to imbue us with idealism. I have no hostility to nature, but a child's love to it. I expand and live in the warm day like corn and melons. Let us speak her fair. I do not wish to fling stones at my beautiful mother, nor soil my gentle nest. I only wish to indicate the true position of nature in regard to man, wherein to establish man all right education tends; as the ground which to attain is the object of human life, that is, of man's connection with nature. Culture inverts the vulgar views of nature, and brings the mind to call that apparent which it uses to call real, and that real which it uses to call visionary. Children, it is true, believe in the external world. The belief that it appears only, is an afterthought, but with culture this faith will as surely arise on the mind as did the first.

The advantage of the ideal theory over the popular faith is this, that it presents the world in precisely that view which is most desirable to the mind. It is, in fact, the view which Reason, both speculative and practical, that is, philosophy and virtue, take. For seen in the light of thought, the world always is phenomenal; and virtue subordinates it to the mind. Idealism sees the world in God. It beholds the whole circle of persons and things, of actions and events, of country and religion, not as painfully accumulated, atom after atom, act after act, in an aged creeping Past, but as one vast picture which God paints on the instant eternity for the contemplation of the soul. Therefore the soul holds itself off from a too trivial and microscopic study of the universal tablet. It respects the end too much to immerse itself in the means. It sees something more important in Christianity than the scandals of ecclesiastical history or the niceties of criticism; and, very incurious concerning persons of miracles, and not at all disturbed by chasms of historical evidence, it accepts from God the phenomenon, as it finds it, as the pure and awful form of religion in the world. It is not hot and passionate at the appearance of what it calls its own good or bad fortune, at the union or opposition of other persons. No man is its enemy. It accepts whatsoever befalls, as part of its lesson. It is a watcher more than a doer, and it a doer, only that it may the better watch.

## *Spirit*

It is essential to a true theory of nature and of man, that it should contain somewhat progressive. Uses that are exhausted or that may be, and facts that end in the statement, cannot be all that is true of this brave lodging wherein man is harbored, and wherein all his faculties find appropriate and endless exercise. And all the uses of nature admit of being summed in one, which yields the activity of man an infinite scope. Through all its kingdoms, to the suburbs and outskirts of things, it is faithful to the cause whence it had its origin. It always speaks of Spirit. It suggests the absolute. It is a perpetual effect. It is a great shadow pointing always to the sun behind us.

The aspect of Nature is devout. Like the figure of Jesus, she stands with bended head, and hands folded upon the breast. The happiest man is he who learns from nature the lesson of worship.

Of that ineffable essence which we call Spirit, he that thinks most, will say least. We can foresee God in the coarse, and, as it were, distant phenomena of matter; but when we try to define and describe himself, both language and thought desert us, and we are as helpless as fools and savages. That essence refuses to be recorded in propositions, but when man has worshipped him intellectually, the noblest ministry of nature is to stand as the apparition of God. It is the organ through which the universal spirit speaks to the individual, and strives to lead back the individual to it.

When we consider Spirit, we see that the views already presented do not include the whole circumference of man. We must add some related thoughts.

Three problems are put by nature to the mind: What is matter? Whence is it? and Whereto? The first of these questions only, the ideal theory answers. Idealism saith: matter is a phenomenon, not a substance. Idealism acquaints us with the total disparity between the evidence of our own being and the evidence of the world's being. The one is perfect; the other, incapable of any assurance; the mind is a part of the nature of things; the world is a divine dream, from which we may presently awake to the glories and certainties of day. Idealism is a hypothesis to account for nature by other principles than those of carpentry and chemistry. Yet, if it only deny the existence of matter, it does not satisfy the demands of the spirit. It leaves God out of me. It leaves me in the splendid labyrinth of my perceptions, to wander without end. Then the heart resists it, because it balks the affections in denying substantive being to men and women. Nature is so pervaded with human life that there is something of humanity in all and in every particular. But this theory makes nature foreign to me, and does not account for that consanguinity which we acknowledge to it.

Let it stand then, in the present state of our knowledge, merely as a useful introductory hypothesis, serving to apprize us of the eternal distinction between the soul and the world.

But when, following the invisible steps of thought, we come to inquire, Whence is matter? and Whereto? many truths arise to us out of the recesses of consciousness. We learn that the highest is present to the soul of man; that the dread universal essence, which is not wisdom, or love, or beauty, or power, but all in one, and each entirely, is that for which all things exist, and that by which they are; that spirit creates; that behind nature, throughout nature, spirit is present; one and not compound it does not act upon us from without, that is, in space and time, but spiritually, or through ourselves: therefore that spirit, that is, the Supreme Being, does not build up nature around us, but puts it forth through us, as the life of the tree puts forth new branches and leaves through the pores of the old. As a plant upon the earth, so a man rests upon the bosom of God; he is nourished by unfailing fountains, and draws at his need inexhaustible power. Who can set bounds to the possibilities of man? Once inhale the upper air, being admitted to behold the absolute natures of justice and truth, and we learn that man has access to the entire mind of the Creator, is himself the creator in the finite. This view, which admonishes me where the sources of wisdom and power lie, and points to virtue as to

The golden key
Which opes the palace of eternity,

carries upon its face the highest certificate of truth, because it animates me to create my own world through the purification of my soul.

The world proceeds from the same spirit as the body of man. It is a remoter and inferior incarnation of God, a projection of God in the unconscious. But it differs from the body in one important respect. It is not, like that, now subjected to the human will. Its serene order is inviolable by us. It is, therefore, to us, the present expositor of the divine mind. It is a fixed point whereby we may measure our departure. As we degenerate, the contrast between us and our house is more evident. We are as much strangers in nature as we are aliens from God. We do not understand the notes of birds. The fox and the deer run away from us; the bear and tiger rend us. We do not know the uses of more than a few plants, as corn and the apple, the potato and the vine. Is not the landscape, every glimpse of which hath a grandeur, a face of him? Yet this may show us what discord is between man and nature, for you cannot freely admire a noble landscape if laborers are digging in the field hard by. The poet finds something ridiculous in his delight until he is out of the sight of men.

## *Prospects*

. . . . .

At present, man applies to nature but half his force. He works on the world with his understanding alone. He lives in it and masters it by a penny-wisdom; and he that works most in it is but a half-man, and whilst his arms are strong and his digestion good, his mind is imbruted, and he is a selfish savage. His relation to nature, his power over it, is through the understanding, as by manure; the economic use of fire, wind, water, and the mariner's needle; steam coal, chemical agriculture; the repairs of the human body by the dentist and the surgeon. This is such a resumption of power as if a banished king should buy his territories inch by inch, instead of vaulting at once into his throne. Meantime, in the thick darkness, there are not wanting gleams of a better light,—occasional examples of the action of man upon nature with his entire force,—with reason as well as understanding. Such examples are, the traditions of miracles in the earliest antiquity of all nations; the history of Jesus Christ; the achievements of a principle, as in religious and political revolutions, and in the abolition of the slave-trade; the miracles of enthusiasm, as those reported of Swedenborg, Hohenlohe, and the Shakers; many obscure and yet contested facts, now arranged under the name of Animal Magnetism; prayer; eloquence; self-healing; and the wisdom of children. These are examples of Reason's momentary grasp of the sceptre; the exertions of a power which exists not in time or space, but an instantaneous instreaming causing power. The difference between the actual and the ideal force of man is happily figured by the schoolmen, in saying, that the knowledge of man is an evening knowledge, *vespertina cognitio,* but that of God is a morning knowledge, *matutina cognitio,*

# XVI

# John C. Calhoun

1782–1850

Born at Calhoun Creek, Abbeville district, S. C. Attended academy of his brother-in-law, Moses Waddel, where he received his basic education. Attended Yale for two years, 1802–04, and graduated, 1804. Attended law school of Tapping Reeve and James Gould at Litchfield, Conn., for fourteen months. Admitted to bar and began practicing law at Abbeville, 1807. Member of state legislature, 1808–10. Member of House of Representatives, 1810–17. Secretary of War under Monroe, 1817–25. Vice President of the United States, 1825–32. Senator from South Carolina, 1832–43. Secretary of State under Tyler, 1844. Senator, 1844–50. Candidate for President continuously from 1822 to 1850. Died in Washington, 1850.

The period between 1790 and 1850 was one of rapid expansion and change. The population increased from four to twenty-three million. The number of states increased from thirteen to thirty-one. Throughout the period the federal government was exercising more and more power. According to Calhoun, this tendency began with the Judiciary Act of 1789. It was given continuous emphasis by the Federalist statesmen. It was furthered by the conditions surrounding the War of 1812. Such issues as the tariff and taxation kept it before the eyes of the public. As time went on it became apparent, especially to the southerners, that the federal government was becoming less an organ for the expression of common interests and more a tool of special interests. Calhoun said:

> The system, in consequence of this, instead of tending towards dissolution from weakness, tends strongly towards consolidation from exuberance of strength:—so strongly that, if not opposed by a resistance proportionally powerful, the end must be its destruction,—either by the bursting asunder of its parts, in consequence of the intense conflict of interest, produced by being too closely pressed together, or by consolidating all the powers of the system in the government of the United States, or in some one of its departments,—to be wielded with despotic force and oppression.[1]

[1] *Works.* I, 239.

Political parties had begun to assume importance, adding another complicating factor to the operation of government. Many of those who had previously advocated a strong federal government in order to protect their interests, and favored restrictions on suffrage to assure this protection, now accepted a wider suffrage because they felt the numerical majority was under their control. In political theory, they were less desirous of defending a new governmental system than of seeing that that system be interpreted so as to provide greatest advantage to their own sectional or factional interests. Less was said about "life, liberty and the pursuit of happiness," more about securing adequate legal protection for acquired or assumed rights. Industry was developing rapidly, providing incentive to the emerging conflict between the industrial North and the agricultural South.

Calhoun's political theory must be understood in the light of these prevailing trends, but cannot be dismissed as a defense of partisan interests. He was a southerner, bred in the traditions of the South, but never too southern to prevent reasonably objective judgment on the needs of the country. John Quincy Adams, with whom Calhoun associated closely for many years in friendly and unfriendly relations, spoke of him as

> a man of fair and candid mind, of honorable principles, of clear and quick understanding, of cool self-possession, of enlarged philosophical views, and of ardent patriotism. He is above all sectional and factious prejudices more than any other statesman of this Union with whom I have ever acted.[2]

Calhoun's failure to achieve the Presidency was no reflection upon the alert and discriminating mind which he possessed, for in public and private gatherings, upon the floor of the Senate and as a cabinet member he was commonly regarded as one of the most brilliant and incisive men of his time. He was so incisive in his analyses, in fact, that he wearied many of his compatriots. Senator Dixon H. Lewis, a close friend of Calhoun, wrote in 1840:

> Calhoun is now my principal associate, and he is too intelligent, too industrious, too intent on the struggle of politics to suit me except as an occasional companion. There is no *relaxation* with him.[3]

Had Calhoun's interests been turned in the direction of metaphysical issues, he would undoubtedly have given additional demonstration of

[2] This and other like expressions of admiration appear in Adams's *Diary* from 1818 on. Quoted from Meigs: *The Life of John Caldwell Calhoun.* I, 287.

[3] Ibid. II, 97.

a logical and searching mind. He was not interested in metaphysics, however, restricting his philosophical work to his carefully-hewn political treatises. When charged with being a metaphysician in the state rights debates in 1833, he replied that he hated metaphysics but held in high regard

> the power of analysis and combination—that power which reduces the most complex idea into its elements, which traces causes to their first principles, and by the principle of generalization and combination unites the whole in one harmonious system—then, so far from deserving contempt, it is the highest attribute of the human mind.[4]

His attitude of mind was essentially philosophical in nature but his fame in American thought will rest solely upon his contribution to the philosophy of politics.

The great source of Calhoun's political ideas was human experience, although his reading made him acquainted with some of the world's great thinkers. He read Locke's *Essay* when he was but thirteen, a year younger than Edwards had been at the time of his first study of it. He read Aristotle (for whom he had high regard), Machiavelli, Burke and others, but there is no evidence that any writer or school dominated his thinking. He was not the reader that Jefferson was, but his insatiable desire to analyze and think through each problem with which he was confronted gave him a depth and penetration which probably no other statesman of his time possessed. Timothy Dwight taught him moral philosophy at Yale but there is no indication that Dwight particularly influenced him. He acquired much mental discipline through the moot courts which Gould held at Litchfield, but Gould seems to have had little effect upon his political ideas. Calhoun was an independent thinker, forging upon the anvil of his own mind the principles of government and society in which he came to believe.

As many others were beginning to do at the time in which he lived, Calhoun looked upon government as a social organism. He rejected the doctrine of natural rights. He did not believe in a "state of nature" in which man had been free from social institutions. He was opposed to looking upon government as a social contract. To him, man was a social being. Government was a perfectly natural medium through which the social nature of man found expression. Government was not, therefore, a necessary evil; it was necessary, but evil only when motivated by partisan interests or when improperly administered. Man was not the possessor of inalienable rights which government was instituted

[4] *Works.* II, 231.

to protect; he was to be the recipient of whatever rights he possessed by virtue of his participation in government.

Liberty, according to Calhoun, was not a natural right; it was something to be acquired as a reward for virtuous participation in society. Liberty and security, he held, were basic objectives of government. If liberty were regarded as a natural right social maladjustment would inevitably result. Security was really a prerequisite for liberty. Liberty was meaningful only when interpreted as the freedom to pursue that course of action most beneficial for the happiness and welfare of all, but since man was basically social in nature his security was essential to his liberty. Insecurity would "weaken the impulse of individuals to better their condition, and thereby retard progress and improvement." [5] He was well aware of the tendency of government to confine the sphere properly belonging to liberty and he spent much time in urging restraint in government through constitutional and statutory means in order to provide free rein to liberty, but he held at the same time that liberty could be achieved only in society and through the security which society provided as its basis. Just as he opposed the natural rights theory of liberty, he attacked its interpretation of equality. He did accept the principle of equality before the law, but he made a clear distinction between this and "equality of condition." The latter he felt was an untenable postulate. He argued that men were endowed with varying capabilities and qualities, that they varied in the degree to which they developed these native endowments and that arbitrarily to discount these distinctions would be to restrict the domain of liberty. Liberty and equality, to him, were not Siamese twins. He contended that the more you have of the one the less you have of the other. Equality of circumstance, interpreted either as a natural right or as a moral ideal, he regarded as untenable. To accept equality as a natural right was to overlook the actual facts of human existence; to seek it as a moral ideal was to stifle the natural desire of man for development and improvement. Inequality, to him, was essential for moral and social progress. This was, of course, a far cry from the optimistic equalitarianism of Taylor and Jefferson.

Although Calhoun argued for the necessity of government even to the point of conceiving it as divinely ordained, he was no totalitarian. For Calhoun, the state was an organism, but not one which absorbed the individual. Its purpose was to provide the conditions under which the individual could develop his potentialities to the greatest degree. Calhoun was as much interested in liberty as were Jefferson and Taylor

[5] *Works.* I, 52.

but the frame of reference from which he viewed it was different. They looked upon it as a natural right to be preserved; he looked upon it as a social achievement. To them government was a necessary evil by means of which liberty could be preserved; to him it was a social necessity through which liberty could be acquired and human ideals and personal development could be achieved. At the same time he was well aware of its aggrandizing tendencies and its subsequent despotic character. Government was essential, but it was to be held in leash through constitutional restraints.

Those who were responsible for the Constitution were desirous of protecting the people from domination by the government. To that end they had set up a system of checks and balances, instituted popular election, and defined the powers of the federal government. By the time of Calhoun, however, it had become evident that even with these carefully planned restrictions, it was still possible for government to be the tool of special interests of one kind or another. The growth of political parties meant that party government might succeed popular government. The development of industry made it apparent that the North could exert sectional control over the agricultural South. Incompetence in public office was far less a problem to Calhoun than sectional or factional government defended by a numerical majority. Rule by the numerical majority, he came to believe, was but another form of tyranny. The actual practice of democracy in America led him to conclude

> that the North has acquired a decided ascendency over every department of this Government, and through it a control over all the powers of the system. A single section governed by the will of the numerical majority, has now, in fact, the control of the Government and the entire powers of the system. What was once a constitutional federal republic, is now converted, in reality, into one as absolute as that of the Autocrat of Russia, and as despotic in its tendency as any absolute government that ever existed.[6]

It was said above that experience was the major source of Calhoun's ideas; tendencies at work in his age had much to do with his final conclusions. It would be unfair, however, to say that Calhoun developed a political philosophy to defend the interests of his own section. Rather, his was a political philosophy which sought to defend minority rights of any kind, his own section being at the time the best example of a minority whose rights were being threatened. Calhoun conceived of

[6] *Works.* IV, 551.

democracy less as a system demanding rule by a numerical majority, more as a system to protect the rights of all.

Calhoun's solution for the problem of minority rights was the principle of concurrent majorities. He was opposed to a numerical majority which he associated with absolute democracy. In place of this, he supported what he spoke of as a constitutional democracy where the interests of all would not be dominated by the will of the majority. What he proposed was a system whereby special interest groups would have the right of concurrent action with or veto upon the will of the majority. This theory became one of the chief bulwarks of nullification sentiment when the slavery issue came to the fore. It is well to remember, however, that Calhoun favored the principle of the concurrent majority long before agitation against slavery in the North became a serious threat. As early as 1808, when Calhoun was serving his first term in the South Carolina legislature, he had a hand in setting up a system whereby the House was composed of representatives both of districts and of economic interests. It was a principle whose larger implications became clear to him with the passing of time but which could hardly be said to have been dictated by partisan or sectional interests.

The principle of the numerical majority, according to Calhoun, assumed that the interests of people were all the same; hence a numerical vote would indicate the will of all. To Calhoun this was an invalid simplification. He contended that the interests of people were many and varied; hence, to secure the will of the people, it was necessary to provide those who had one particular interest with the right of the negative upon the will of those who wished to protect other interests. The numerical majority achieved its will in the last analysis by force, while the concurrent majority would achieve its will through compromise. Compromise was one means by which minority groups could prevent oppression; it offered greater chance of protecting the rights of every interest group, less chance for domination by one group. This principle of the concurrent majority, as Calhoun worked it out, had points in common with later political pluralism and corporativism.

Calhoun's real importance in political thought was in attempting to revitalize the democratic system by interpreting it in new terms and by suggesting those practical measures which he felt would restore to the people the power of determining their own destiny, free from the control of special interests, factions, parties and usurping politicians. Calhoun lacked the magnetism of Henry Clay and the rhetorical genius of Webster, but he compensated for these virtues by the possession of a keen and discriminating mind, independent in its thinking, consistent in its logic and forceful in its originality.

## REFERENCES


Calhoun, John C.: *Life of John C. Calhoun: Presenting a Condensed History of Political Events from 1811 to 1843.* New York: Harper and Brothers, 1843. (Although this appeared anonymously, it is now believed to have been written by Calhoun himself.)

Cralle, Richard K.: *The Works of John C. Calhoun.* 6 vols. Columbia, S. C., 1852.

Bancroft, F.: *Calhoun and the South Carolina Nullification Movement.* Baltimore: Johns Hopkins University Press, 1928.

Bradford, Gamaliel: *As God Made Them.* Boston: Houghton Mifflin Co., 1929. (Ch. III, "John Caldwell Calhoun.")

Hunt, Gaillard: *John C. Calhoun.* Philadelphia: George W. Jacobs and Co., 1908.

Meigs, William M.: *The Life of John Caldwell Calhoun.* 2 vols. New York: The Neale Publishing Co., 1917.

Merriam, Charles E.: "The Political Philosophy of John C. Calhoun," in *Studies in Southern History and Politics Inscribed to William Archibald Dunning.* New York: Columbia University Press, 1914. 319–38.

Styron, Arthur: *The Cast-Iron Man: John C. Calhoun and American Democracy.* New York: Longmans, Green and Co., 1935.

Wiltse, C. M.: "Calhoun and the Modern State," *Virginia Quarterly Review* 13 (1937) 396–408.


* * *

---

* * *

## A DISQUISITION ON GOVERNMENT [7]

In order to have a clear and just conception of the nature and object of government, it is indispensable to understand correctly what that constitution or law of our nature is, in which government originates; or, to express it more fully and accurately,—that law, without which government would not, and with which, it must necessarily exist. Without this, it is as impossible to lay any solid foundation for the science of government, as it would be to lay one for that of astronomy, without a like understanding of that constitution or law of the material world,

[7] *Works.* I, 1–9, 24–38, 53–9.

according to which the several bodies composing the solar system mutually act on each other, and by which they are kept in their respective spheres. The first question, accordingly, to be considered is,—What is that constitution or law of our nature, without which government would not exist, and with which its existence is necessary?

In considering this, I assume, as an incontestable fact, that man is so constituted as to be a social being. His inclinations and wants, physical and moral, irresistibly impel him to associate with his kind; and he has, accordingly, never been found, in any age or country, in any state other than the social. In no other, indeed, could he exist; and in no other,—were it possible for him to exist,—could he attain to a full development of his moral and intellectual faculties, or raise himself, in the scale of being, much above the level of the brute creation.

I next assume, also, as a fact not less incontestable, that, while man is so constituted as to make the social state necessary to his existence and the full development of his faculties, this state itself cannot exist without government. The assumption rests on universal experience. In no age or country has any society or community ever been found, whether enlightened or savage, without government of some description.

Having assumed these, as unquestionable phenomena of our nature, I shall, without further remark, proceed to the investigation of the primary and important question,—What is that constitution of our nature, which, while it impels man to associate with his kind, renders it impossible for society to exist without government?

The answer will be found in the fact, (not less incontestable than either of the others,) that, while man is created for the social state, and is accordingly so formed as to feel what affects others, as well as what affects himself, he is, at the same time, so constituted as to feel more intensely what affects him directly, than what affects him indirectly through others; or, to express it differently, he is so constituted, that his direct or individual affections are stronger than his sympathetic or social feelings. I intentionally avoid the expression, *selfish* feelings, as applicable to the former; because, as commonly used, it implies an unusual excess of the individual over the social feelings, in the person to whom it is applied; and, consequently, something depraved and vicious. My object is, to exclude such inference, and to restrict the inquiry exclusively to facts in their bearings on the subject under consideration, viewed as mere phenomena appertaining to our nature,—constituted as it is; and which are as unquestionable as is that of gravitation, or any other phenomenon of the material world.

In asserting that our individual are stronger than our social feelings, it is not intended to deny that there are instances, growing out of peculiar relations,—as that of a mother and her infant,—or resulting from the force of education and habit over peculiar constitutions, in which the latter have overpowered the former; but these instances are few, and always regarded as something extraordinary. The deep impression they make, whenever they occur, is the strongest proof that they are regarded as exceptions to some general and well understood law of our nature; just as some of the minor powers of the material world are apparently to gravitation.

I might go farther, and assert this to be a phenomenon, not of our nature only, but of all animated existence, throughout its entire range, so far as our knowledge extends. It would, indeed, seem to be essentially connected with the great law of self-preservation which pervades all that feels, from man down to the lowest and most insignificant reptile or insect. In none is it stronger than in man. His social feelings may, indeed, in a state of safety and abundance, combined with high intellectual and moral culture, acquire great expansion and force; but not so great as to overpower this all-pervading and essential law of animated existence.

But that constitution of our nature which makes us feel more intensely what affects us directly than what affects us indirectly through others, necessarily leads to conflict between individuals. Each, in consequence, has a greater regard for his own safety or happiness, than for the safety or happiness of others; and, where these come in opposition, is ready to sacrifice the interests of others to his own. And hence, the tendency to a universal state of conflict, between individual and individual; accompanied by the connected passions of suspicion, jealousy, anger and revenge,—followed by insolence, fraud and cruelty;—and, if not prevented by some controlling power, ending in a state of universal discord and confusion, destructive of the social state and the ends for which it is ordained. This controlling power, wherever vested, or by whomsoever exercised, is GOVERNMENT.

It follows, then, that man is so constituted, that government is necessary to the existence of society, and society to his existence, and the perfection of his faculties. It follows, also, that government has its origin in this twofold constitution of his nature; the sympathetic or social feelings constituting the remote,—and the individual or direct, the proximate cause.

If man had been differently constituted in either particular;—if, instead of being social in his nature, he had been created without sympathy for his kind, and independent of others for his safety and existence; or if, on the other hand, he had been so created, as to feel more intensely what affected others than what affected himself, (if that were possible,) or, even, had this supposed interest been equal,—it is manifest that, in either case, there would have been no necessity for government, and that none would ever have existed. But, although society and government are thus intimately connected with and dependent on each other,—of the two society is the greater. It is the first in the order of things, and in the dignity of its object; that of society being primary,—to preserve and perfect our race; and that of government secondary and subordinate, to preserve and perfect society. Both are, however, necessary to the existence and well-being of our race, and equally of Divine ordination.

I have said,—if it were possible for man to be so constituted, as to feel what affects others more strongly than what affects himself, or even as strongly,—because, it may be well doubted, whether the stronger feeling or affection of individuals for themselves, combined with a feebler and subordinate feeling or affection for others, is not, in beings of limited reason and faculties, a constitution necessary to their preservation and existence. If reversed,—if their feelings and affections were stronger for others than for themselves, or even as strong, the necessary result would seem to be, that all individuality would be lost; and boundless and remediless disorder and confusion would ensue. For each, at the same moment, intensely participating in all the conflicting emotions of those around him, would, of course, forget himself and all that concerned him immediately, in his officious intermeddling with the affairs of all others; which, from his limited reason and faculties, he could neither properly understand nor manage. Such a state of things would, as far as we can see, lead to endless disorder and confusion, not less destructive to our race than a state of anarchy. It would, besides, be remediless,—for government would be impossible; or, if it could by possibility exist, its object would be reversed. Selfishness would have to be encouraged, and benevolence discouraged. Individuals would have to be encouraged, by rewards, to become more selfish, and deterred, by punishments, from being too benevolent; and this, too, by a government, administered by those who, on the supposition, would have the greatest aversion for selfishness and the highest admiration for benevolence.

To the Infinite Being, the Creator of all, belongs exclusively the care and superintendence of the whole. He, in his infinite wisdom and goodness, has allotted to every class of animated beings its condition and appropriate functions; and has endowed each with feelings, instincts, capacities, and faculties, best adapted to its allotted condition. To man, he has assigned the social and political state, as best adapted to develop the great capacities and faculties, intellectual and moral, with which he has endowed him; and has, accordingly, constituted him so as not only to impel him into the social state, but to make government necessary for his preservation and well-being.

But government, although intended to protect and preserve society, has itself a strong tendency to disorder and abuse of its powers, as all experience and almost every page of history testify. The cause is to be found in the same constitution of our nature which makes government indispensable. The powers which it is necessary for government to possess, in order to repress violence and preserve order, cannot execute themselves. They must be administered by men in whom, like others, the individual are stronger than the social feelings. And hence, the powers vested in them to prevent injustice and oppression on the part of others, will, if left unguarded, be by them converted into instruments to oppress the rest of the community. That, by which this is prevented, by whatever name called, is what is meant by CONSTITUTION, in its most comprehensive sense, when applied to GOVERNMENT.

Having its origin in the same principle of our nature, *constitution* stands to *government,* as *government* stands to *society;* and, as the end for which society is ordained, would be defeated without government, so that for which government is ordained would, in a great measure, be defeated without constitution. But they differ in this striking particular. There is no difficulty in forming government. It is not even a matter of choice, whether there shall be one or not. Like breathing, it is not permitted to depend on our volition. Necessity will force it on all communities in some one form or another. Very different is the case as to constitution. Instead of a matter of necessity, it is one of the most difficult tasks imposed on man to form a constitution worthy of the name; while, to form a perfect one,—one that would completely counteract the tendency of government to oppression and abuse, and hold it strictly to the great ends for which it is ordained,—has thus far exceeded human wisdom, and possibly ever will. From this, another striking difference results. Constitution is the contrivance of man, while government is of Divine ordination. Man is left to perfect what the wisdom of the Infinite ordained, as necessary to preserve the race.

With these remarks, I proceed to the consideration of the important and difficult question: How is this tendency of government to be counteracted? Or, to express it more fully,—How can those who are invested with the powers of government be prevented from employing them, as the means of aggrandizing themselves, instead of using them to protect and preserve society? It cannot be done by instituting a higher power to control the government, and those who administer it. This would be but to change the seat of authority, and to make this higher power, in reality, the government; with the same tendency, on the part of those who might control its powers, to pervert them into instruments of aggrandizement. Nor can it be done by limiting the powers of government, so as to make it too feeble to be made an instrument of abuse; for, passing by the difficulty of so limiting its powers, without creating a power higher than the government itself to enforce the observance of the limitations, it is a sufficient objection that it would, if practicable, defeat the end for which government is ordained, by making it too feeble to protect and preserve society. The powers necessary for this purpose will ever prove sufficient to aggrandize those who control it, at the expense of the rest of the community.

[*Calhoun goes on to propose suffrage as the primary principle of protection against oppression. He contends, however, that suffrage alone is not sufficient, for people are inclined to group together on the basis of common interests, make concessions and combine forces with other groups until two political parties finally emerge, each striving for control of government in order to benefit the interest groups which support it. To Calhoun, this makes for just as much oppression as an absolute form of government. He suggests, therefore, a second protection against oppression and the abuses of government.*]

As, then, the right of suffrage, without some other provision, cannot counteract this tendency of government, the next question for consideration is—What is that other provision? This demands the most serious consideration; for of all the questions embraced in the science of government, it involves a principle, the most important, and the least understood; and when understood, the most difficult of application in practice. It is, indeed, emphatically, that principle which makes the constitution, in its strict and limited sense.

From what has been said, it is manifest, that this provision must be of a character calculated to prevent any one interest, or combination of interests, from using the powers of government to aggrandize itself at the expense of the others. Here lies the evil: and just in proportion as it shall prevent, or fail to prevent it, in the same degree it will effect, or fail to effect the end intended to be accomplished. There is but one certain mode in which this result can be secured; and that is, by the adoption of some restriction or limitation, which shall so effectually prevent any one interest, or combination of interests, from obtaining the exclusive control of the government, as to render hopeless all attempts directed to that end. There is, again, but one mode in which this can be effected; and that is, by taking the sense of each interest or portion of the community, which may be unequally and injuriously affected by the action of the government, separately, through its own majority, or in some other way by which its voice may be fairly expressed; and to require the consent of each interest, either to put or to keep the government in action. This, too, can be accomplished only in one way,—and that is, by such an organism of the government,—and, if necessary for the purpose, of the community also,—as will, by dividing and distributing the powers of government, give to each division or interest, through its appropriate organ, either a concurrent voice in making and executing the laws, or a veto on their execution. It is only by such an organism, that the assent of each can be made necessary to put the government in motion; or the power made effectual to arrest its action, when put in motion;—and it is only by the one or the other that the different interests, orders, classes, or portions, into which the community may be divided, can be protected, and all conflict and struggle between them prevented,—by rendering it impossible to put or to keep it in action, without the concurrent consent of all.

Such an organism as this, combined with the right of suffrage, constitutes, in fact, the elements of constitutional government. The one, by rendering those who make and execute the laws responsible to those on whom they operate, prevents the rulers from oppressing the ruled; and the other, by making it impossible for any one interest or combination of interests or class, or order, or portion of the community, to obtain exclusive control, prevents any one of them from oppressing the other. It is clear, that oppression and abuse of power must come, if at all, from the one or the other quarter. From no other can they come. It follows, that the two, suffrage and proper organism combined, are sufficient to counteract the tendency of government to oppression and abuse of power; and to restrict it to the fulfilment of the great ends for which it is ordained.

In coming to this conclusion, I have assumed the organism to be perfect, and the different interests, portions, or classes of the community, to be sufficiently enlightened to understand its character and object, and to exercise, with due intelligence, the right of suffrage. To the extent that either may be defective, to the same extent the government would fall short of fulfilling its end. But this does not impeach the truth of the principles on which it rests. In reducing them to proper form, in applying them to practical uses, all elementary principles are liable to difficulties; but they are not, on this account, the less true, or valuable. Where the organism is perfect, every interest will be truly and fully represented, and of course the whole community must be so. It may be difficult, or even impossible, to make a perfect organism,—but, although this be true, yet even when, instead of the sense of each and of all, it takes that of a few great and prominent interests only, it would still, in a great measure, if not altogether, fulfil the end intended by a constitution. For, in such case, it would require so large a portion of the community, compared with the whole, to concur, or acquiesce in the action of the government, that the number to be plundered would be too few, and the number to be aggrandized too many, to afford adequate motives to oppression and the abuse of its powers. Indeed, however imperfect the organism, it must have more or less effect in diminishing such tendency.

It may be readily inferred, from what has been stated, that the effect of organism is neither to supersede nor diminish the importance of the right of suffrage; but to aid and perfect it. The object of the latter is, to collect the sense of the community. The more fully and perfectly it accomplishes this, the more fully and perfectly it fulfils its end. But the most it can do, of itself, is to collect the sense of the greater number; that is, of the stronger interests, or combination of interests; and to assume this to be the sense of the community. It is only when aided by a proper organism, that it can collect the sense of the entire community,—of each and all its interests; of each, through its appropriate organ, and of the whole, through all of them united. This would truly be the sense of the entire community; for whatever diversity each interest might have within itself,—as all would have the same interest in reference to the action of the government, the individuals composing each would be fully and truly represented by its own majority or appropriate organ, regarded in reference to the other interests. In brief, every individual or every interest might trust, with confidence, its majority or appropriate organ, against that of every other interest.

It results, from what has been said, that there are two different modes in which the sense of the community may be taken; one, simply by the right of suffrage, unaided; the other, by the right through a proper organism. Each collects the sense of the majority. But one regards numbers only, and considers the whole community as a unit, having but one common interest throughout; and collects the sense of the greater number of the whole, as that of the community. The other, on the contrary, regards interests as well as numbers;—considering the community as made up of different and conflicting interests, as far as the action of the government is concerned; and takes the sense of each, through its majority or appropriate organ, and the united sense of all, as the sense of the entire community. The former of these I shall call the numerical, or absolute majority; and the latter, the concurrent, or constitutional majority. I call it the constitutional majority, because it is an essential element in every constitutional government,—be its form what it may. So great is the difference, politically speaking, between the two majorities, that they cannot be confounded, without leading to great and fatal errors; and yet the distinction between them has been so entirely overlooked, that when the term *majority* is used in political discussions, it is applied exclusively to designate the numerical,—as if there were no other. Until this distinction is recognized, and better understood, there will continue to be great liability to error in properly constructing constitutional governments, especially of the popular form, and of preserving them when properly constructed. Until then, the latter will have a strong tendency to slide, first, into the government of the numerical majority, and, finally, into absolute government of some other form. To show that such must be the case, and at the same time to mark more strongly the difference between the two, in order to guard against the danger of overlooking it, I propose to consider the subject more at length.

The first and leading error which naturally arises from overlooking the distinction referred to, is, to confound the numerical majority with the people; and this so completely as to regard them as identical. This is a consequence that necessarily results from considering the numerical as the only majority. All admit, that a popular government, or democracy, is the government of the people; for the terms imply this. A perfect government of the kind would be one which would embrace the consent of every citizen or member of the community; but as this is impracticable, in the opinion of those who regard the numerical as the only majority, and who can perceive no other way by which the sense of the people can be taken,—they are compelled to adopt this as the only true basis of popular government, in contradistinction to governments of the aristocratical or monarchical form. Being thus constrained, they are, in the next place, forced to regard the numerical majority, as, in effect, the entire people; that is, the greater part as the whole; and the government of the greater part as the government of the whole. It is thus the two come to be confounded, and a part made identical with the whole. And it is thus, also, that all the rights, powers, and immunities of the whole people come to be attributed to the numerical majority; and, among others, the supreme, sovereign authority of establishing and abolishing governments at pleasure.

This radical error, the consequence of confounding the two, and of regarding the numerical as the only majority, has contributed more than any other cause, to prevent the formation of popular constitutional governments,—and to destroy them even when they have been formed. It leads to the conclusion, that, in their formation and establishment, nothing more is necessary than the right of suffrage,—and the allotment to each division of the community a representation in the government, in proportion to numbers. If the numerical majority were really the people; and if, to take its sense truly, were to take the sense of the people truly, a government so constituted would be a true and perfect model of a popular constitutional government; and every departure from it would detract from its excellence. But, as such is not the case,—as the numerical majority, instead of being the people, is only a portion of them,—such a government, instead of being a true and perfect model of the people's government, that is, a people self-governed, is but the government of a part, over a part,—the major over the minor portion.

But this misconception of the true elements of constitutional government does not stop here. It leads to others equally false and fatal, in reference to the best means of preserving and perpetuating them, when, from some fortunate combination of circumstances, they are correctly formed. For they who fall into these errors regard the restrictions which organism imposes on the will of the numerical majority as restrictions on the will of the people, and, therefore, as not only useless, but wrongful and mischievous. And hence they endeavor to destroy organism, under the delusive hope of making government more democratic.

Such are some of the consequences of confounding the two, and of regarding the numerical as the only majority. And in this may be found the reason why so few popular governments have been properly constructed, and why, of these few, so small a number have proved durable. Such must continue to be the result, so long as these errors continue to be prevalent.

There is another error, of a kindred character, whose influence contributes much to the same results: I refer to the prevalent opinion, that a written constitution, containing suitable restrictions on the powers of government, is sufficient, of itself, without the aid of any organism,

—except such as is necessary to separate its several departments, and render them independent of each other,—to counteract the tendency of the numerical majority to oppression and the abuse of power.

A written constitution certainly has many and considerable advantages; but it is a great mistake to suppose, that the mere insertion of provisions to restrict and limit the powers of the government, without investing those for whose protection they are inserted with the means of enforcing their observance, will be sufficient to prevent the major and dominant party from abusing its powers. Being the party in possession of the government, they will, from the same constitution of man which makes government necessary to protect society, be in favor of the powers granted by the constitution, and opposed to the restrictions intended to limit them. As the major and dominant party, they will have no need of these restrictions for their protection. The ballot-box, of itself, would be ample protection to them. Needing no other, they would come, in time, to regard these limitations as unnecessary and improper restraints;—and endeavor to elude them with the view of increasing their power and influence.

The minor, or weaker party, on the contrary, would take the opposite direction;—and regard them as essential to their protection against the dominant party. And, hence, they would endeavor to defend and enlarge the restrictions, and to limit and contract the powers. But where there are no means by which they could compel the major party to observe the restrictions, the only resort left them would be, a strict construction of the constitution,—that is, a construction which would confine these powers to the narrowest limits which the meaning of the words used in the grant would admit.

To this the major party would oppose a liberal construction,—one which would give to the words of the grant the broadest meaning of which they were susceptible. It would then be construction against construction; the one to contract, and the other to enlarge the powers of the government to the utmost. But of what possible avail could the strict construction of the minor party be, against the liberal interpretation of the major, when the one would have all the powers of the government to carry its construction into effect,—and the other be deprived of all means of enforcing its construction? In a contest so unequal, the result would not be doubtful. The party in favor of the restrictions would be overpowered. At first, they might command some respect, and do something to stay the march of encroachment; but they would, in the progress of the contest, be regarded as mere abstractionists; and, indeed, deservedly, if they should indulge the folly of supposing that the party in possession of the ballot-box and the physical force of the country, could be successfully resisted by an appeal to reason, truth, justice or the obligations imposed by the constitution. For when these, of themselves, shall exert sufficient influence to stay the hand of power, then government will be no longer necessary to protect society, nor constitutions needed to prevent government from abusing its powers. The end of the contest would be the subversion of the constitution, either by the undermining process of construction,—where its meaning would admit of possible doubt,—or by substituting in practice what is called party-usage, in place of its provisions;—or, finally, when no other contrivance would subserve the purpose, by openly and boldly setting them aside. By the one or the other, the restrictions would ultimately be annulled, and the government be converted into one of unlimited powers.

Nor would the division of government into separate, and, as it regards each other, independent departments, prevent this result. Such a division may do much to facilitate its operations, and to secure to its administration greater caution and deliberation; but as each and all the departments,—and, of course, the entire government,—would be under the control of the numerical majority, it is too clear to require explanation, that a mere distribution of its powers among its agents or representatives, could do little or nothing to counteract its tendency to oppression and abuse of power. To effect this, it would be necessary to go one step further, and make the several departments the organs of the distinct interests or portions of the community; and to clothe each with a negative on the others. But the effect of this would be to change the government from the numerical into the concurrent majority.

Having now explained the reasons why it is so difficult to form and preserve popular constitutional government, so long as the distinction between the two majorities is overlooked, and the opinion prevails that a written constitution, with suitable restrictions and a proper division of its powers, is sufficient to counteract the tendency of the numerical majority to the abuse of its power,—I shall next proceed to explain, more fully, why the concurrent majority is an indispensable element in forming constitutional governments; and why the numerical majority, of itself, must, in all cases, make governments absolute.

The necessary consequence of taking the sense of the community by the concurrent majority is, as has been explained, to give to each interest or portion of the community a negative on the others. It is this mutual negative among its various conflicting interests, which invests each with the power of protecting itself;—and places the rights and safety of each, where only they can be securely placed, under its own guardianship. Without this there can be no systematic, peaceful, or effective resistance to the natural tendency of each to come into conflict with the others: and without this there can be no constitution. It is this negative power,—the power of preventing or arresting the action of the government,—be it called by what term it may,—veto, interposition, nullification, check, or balance of power,—which, in fact, forms the constitution. They are all but different names for the negative power. In all its forms, and under all its names, it results from the concurrent majority. Without this there can be no negative; and, without a negative, no constitution. The assertion is true in reference to all constitutional governments, be their forms what they may. It is, indeed, the negative power which makes the constitution,—and the positive which makes the government. The one is the power of acting;—and the other the power of preventing or arresting action. The two, combined, make constitutional governments.

But, as there can be no constitution without the negative power, and no negative power without the concurrent majority;—it follows, necessarily, that where the numerical majority has the sole control of the government, there can be no constitution; as constitution implies limitation or restriction,—and, of course, is inconsistent with the idea of sole or exclusive power. And hence, the numerical, unmixed with the concurrent majority, necessarily forms, in all cases, absolute government.

It is, indeed, the single, or *one power,* which excludes the negative, and constitutes absolute government; and not the *number* in whom the power is vested. The numerical majority is as truly a *single power,* and excludes the negative as completely as the absolute government of one, or of the few. The former is as much the absolute government of the democratic, or popular form, as the latter of the monarchical or aristocratical. It has, accordingly, in common with them, the same tendency to oppression and abuse of power.

Constitutional governments of whatever form, are, indeed, much more similar to each other, in their structure and character, than they are, respectively, to the absolute governments, even of their own class. All constitutional governments of whatever class they may be, take the sense of the community by its parts,—each through its appropriate organ; and regard the sense of all its parts, as the sense of the whole. They all rest on the right of suffrage, and the responsibility of rulers, directly or indirectly. On the contrary, all absolute governments, of whatever form, concentrate power in one uncontrolled and irresponsible individual or body, whose will is regarded as the sense of the community. And, hence, the great and broad distinction between governments is,—not that of the one, the few, or the many,—but of the constitutional and the absolute.

From this there results another distinction, which, although secondary in its character, very strongly marks the difference between these forms of government. I refer to their respective conservative principle;—that is, the principle by which they are upheld and preserved. This principle, in constitutional governments, is *compromise;* and in absolute governments, is *force;* as will be next explained.

It has been already shown, that the same constitution of man which leads those who govern to oppress the governed,—if not prevented,—will, with equal force and certainty, lead the latter to resist oppression, when possessed of the means of doing so peaceably and successfully. But absolute governments, of all forms, exclude all other means of resistance to their authority, than that of force; and, of course, leave no other alternative to the governed, but to acquiesce in oppression, however great it may be, or to resort to force to put down the government. But the dread of such a resort must necessarily lead the government to prepare to meet force in order to protect itself; and hence, of necessity, force becomes the conservative principle of all such governments.

On the contrary, the government of the concurrent majority, where the organism is perfect, excludes the possibility of oppression, by giving to each interest, or portion, or order,—where there are established classes—the means of protecting itself, by its negative, against all measures calculated to advance the peculiar interests of others at its expense. Its effect, then, is, to cause the different interests, portions, or orders,—as the case may be,—to desist from attempting to adopt any measure calculated to promote the prosperity of one, or more, by sacrificing that of others; and thus to force them to unite in such measures only as would promote the prosperity of all, as the only means to prevent the suspension of the action of the government;—and, thereby, to avoid anarchy, the greatness of all evils. It is by means of such authorized and effectual resistance, that oppression is prevented, and the necessity of resorting to force superseded, in governments of the concurrent majority;—and, hence, compromise, instead of force, becomes their conservative principle.

. . . . . .

Herein is to be found the principle which assigns to power and liberty their proper spheres, and reconciles each to the other under all circumstances. For, if power be necessary to secure to liberty the fruits of its exertions, liberty, in turn, repays power with interest, by increased population, wealth, and other advantages, which progress and improvement bestow on the community. By thus assigning to each its appropriate sphere, all conflicts between them cease; and each is made to co-operate with and assist the other, in fulfilling the great ends for which government is ordained.

But the principle, applied to different communities, will assign to them different limits. It will assign a larger sphere to power and a more contracted one to liberty, or the reverse, according to circumstances. To the former, there must ever be allotted, under all circumstances, a sphere sufficiently large to protect the community against danger from without and violence and anarchy within. The residuum belongs to liberty. More cannot be safely or rightly allotted to it.

But some communities require a far greater amount of power than others to protect them against anarchy and external dangers; and, of course, the sphere of liberty in such, must be proportionally contracted. The causes calculated to enlarge the one and contract the other, are numerous and various. Some are physical;—such as open and exposed frontiers, surrounded by powerful and hostile neighbors. Others are moral;—such as the different degrees of intelligence, patriotism, and virtue among the mass of the community, and their experience and proficiency in the art of self-government. Of these, the moral are, by far, the most influential. A community may possess all the necessary moral qualifications, in so high a degree, as to be capable of self-government under the most adverse circumstances; while, on the other hand, another may be so sunk in ignorance and vice, as to be incapable of forming a conception of liberty, or of living, even when most favored by circumstances, under any other than an absolute and despotic government.

The principle, in all communities, according to these numerous and various causes, assigns to power and liberty their power spheres. To allow to liberty, in any case, a sphere of action more extended than this assigns, would lead to anarchy; and this, probably, in the end, to a contraction instead of an enlargement of its sphere. Liberty, then, when forced on a people unfit for it, would, instead of a blessing, be a curse; as it would, in its reaction, lead directly to anarchy,—the greatest of all curses. No people, indeed, can long enjoy more liberty than that to which their situation and advanced intelligence and morals fairly entitle them. If more than this be allowed, they must soon fall into confusion and disorder,—to be followed, if not by anarchy and despotism, by a change to a form of government more simple and absolute; and therefore, better suited to their condition. And hence, although it may be true, that people may not have as much liberty as they are fairly entitled to, and are capable of enjoying,—yet the reverse is unquestionably true,—that no people can long possess more than they are fairly entitled to.

Liberty, indeed, though among the greatest of blessings, is not so great as that of protection; inasmuch, as the end of the former is the progress and improvement of the race,—while that of the latter is its preservation and perpetuation. And hence, when the two come into conflict, liberty must, and ever ought, to yield to protection; as the existence of the race is of greater moment than its improvement.

It follows, from what has been stated, that it is a great and dangerous error to suppose that all people are equally entitled to liberty. It is a reward to be earned, not a blessing to be gratuitously lavished on all alike;—a reward reserved for the intelligent, the patriotic, the virtuous and deserving;—and not a boon to be bestowed on a people too ignorant, degraded and vicious, to be capable either of appreciating or of enjoying it. Nor is it any disparagement to liberty, that such is, and ought to be the case. On the contrary, its greatest praise,—its proudest distinction is, that an all-wise Providence has reserved it, as the noblest and highest reward for the development of our faculties, moral and intellectual. A reward more appropriate than liberty could not be conferred on the deserving;—nor a punishment inflicted on the undeserving more just, than to be subject to lawless and despotic rule. This dispensation seems to be the result of some fixed law;—and every effort to disturb or defeat it, by attempting to elevate a people in the scale of liberty, above the point to which they are entitled to rise, must ever prove abortive, and end in disappointment. The progress of a people rising from a lower to a higher point in the scale of liberty, is necessarily slow;—and by attempting to precipitate, we either retard, or permanently defeat it.

There is another error, not less great and dangerous, usually associated with the one which has just been considered. I refer to the opinion, that liberty and equality are so intimately united, that liberty cannot be perfect without perfect equality.

That they are united to a certain extent,—and that equality of citizens, in the eyes of the law, is essential to liberty in a popular government, is conceded. But to go further, and make equality of *condition* essential to liberty, would be to destroy both liberty and progress. The reason is, that inequality of condition, while it is a necessary consequence of liberty, is, at the same time, indispensable to progress. In order to understand why this is so, it is necessary to bear in mind, that the main spring to progress is, the desire of individuals to better their condition; and that the strongest impulse which can be given to it is, to leave individuals free to exert themselves in the manner they may deem best for that purpose, as far at least as it can be done consistently with the ends for which government is ordained,—and to secure to all the fruits of their exertions. Now, as individuals differ greatly from each other, in intelligence, sagacity, energy, perseverance, skill, habits of industry and economy, physical power, position and opportunity,—the necessary effect of leaving all free to exert themselves to better their condition, must be a corresponding inequality between those who may possess these qualities and advantages in a high degree, and those who may be deficient in them. The only means by which this result can be prevented are, either to impose such restrictions on the exertions of those who may possess them in a high degree, as will place them on a level with those who do not; or to deprive them of the fruits of their exertions. But to impose such restrictions on them would be destructive of liberty,—while, to deprive them of the fruits of their exertions, would be to destroy the desire of bettering their condition. It is, indeed, this inequality of condition between the front and rear ranks, in the march of progress, which gives so strong an impulse to the former to maintain their position, and to the latter to press forward into their files. This gives to progress its greatest impulse. To force the front rank back to the rear, or attempt to push forward the rear into line with the front, by the interposition of the government, would put an end to the impulse, and effectually arrest the march of progress.

These great and dangerous errors have their origin in the prevalent opinion that all men are born free and equal;—than which nothing can be more unfounded and false. It rests upon the assumption of a fact, which is contrary to universal observation, in whatever light it may be regarded. It is, indeed, difficult to explain how an opinion so destitute of all sound reason, ever could have been so extensively entertained, unless we regard it as being confounded with another, which has some semblance of truth;—but which, when properly understood, is not less false and dangerous. I refer to the assertion, that all men are equal in the state of nature; meaning, by a state of nature, a state of individuality, supposed to have existed prior to the social and political state; and in which men lived apart and independent of each other. If such a state ever did exist, all men would have been, indeed, free and equal in it; that is, free to do as they pleased, and exempt from the authority or control of others—as, by supposition, it existed anterior to society and government. But such a state is purely hypothetical. It never did, nor can exist; as it is inconsistent with the preservation and perpetuation of the race. It is, therefore, a great misnomer to call it the *state of nature.* Instead of being the natural state of man, it is, of all conceivable states, the most opposed to his nature—most repugnant to his feelings, and most incompatible with his wants. His natural state, is, the social and political—the one for which his Creator made him, and the only one in which he can preserve and perfect his race. As, then, there never was such a state as the, so called, state of nature, and never can be, it follows, that men, instead of being born in it, are born in the social and political state; and of course, instead of being born free and equal, are born subject, not only to parental authority, but to the laws and institutions of the country where born, and under whose protection they draw their first breath. With these remarks, I return from this digression, to resume the thread of the discourse.

It follows, from all that has been said, that the more perfectly a government combines power and liberty,—that is, the greater its power and the more enlarged and secure the liberty of individuals, the more perfectly it fulfils the ends for which government is ordained.

# XVII

# Jean Louis Rodolphe Agassiz

1807–1873

# and John Fiske

1842–1901

JEAN LOUIS RODOLPHE AGASSIZ. Born in Motier-en-Vuly, Switzerland, the son of a minister. Studied at College of Lausanne and Universities of Zurich, Heidelberg, Erlangen (Ph.D., 1829) and Munich (M.D., 1830). Worked with Cuvier on fossils in Paris, 1830–32. Professor of Natural History at Neuchâtel, 1832–46. Came to the United States in 1846 to deliver Lowell Institute lectures in Boston. Became Professor of Natural History at Lawrence Scientific School at Harvard, 1848. Professor of Comparative Anatomy at Medical College of Charleston, S. C., 1851–53. Returned to Harvard, 1853. Established Museum of Comparative Zoölogy at Harvard, 1858, and Anderson School of Natural History on Penikese Island in Buzzards Bay, 1873. Conducted geological and zoölogical expeditions in Europe and North and South America. Died in Cambridge.

JOHN FISKE. Born in Hartford, Conn., as Edmund Fisk Green. Attended private schools at Middletown and Stamford, Conn., until 1857. Studied under tutors until 1860 when he entered Harvard as a sophomore. Graduated with some difficulty in 1863 after having published articles in the *North American Review* favoring evolution. Entered bar in 1864, but gave up law in order to write. Lecturer at Harvard on philosophy and history, 1869–72. Assistant Librarian, 1872–79, except for one year spent in England where he met Spencer, Darwin and others and finished the *Outlines of Cosmic Philosophy*. Turned to lecturing and the writing of popular history books, 1879. Appointed Professor of American History at Washington University, 1884, but continued to reside at Cambridge. Honorary degrees from University of Pennsylvania and Harvard. Died in Gloucester, Mass.

Since the middle of the nineteenth century American philosophy has been deeply affected by the doctrine of evolution. For some it has been a doctrine either to be renounced or else fitted into the framework of an existing system of thought; for others it has been the starting point for a new way of thinking. The first of these paths, the more conservative, was taken early in the controversy by those who feared traditional religious concepts might be invalidated and by those who felt, like Agassiz, that evolution, properly understood, gave further knowledge of the ways of God and in no sense invalidated orthodox belief. The second path, the more radical, was taken by those who became enthusiastic over evolutionary ideas, particularly Darwinism, developed their thought free from conventional opinion, and only later, if at all, reconciled philosophy with religion. Fiske was one of the first Americans to follow this procedure.

Louis Agassiz was everywhere regarded as one of America's foremost scientists. His work on turtles, fish and a wide variety of species, his establishment of the museum at Harvard and his numerous books were landmarks in the scientific annals of the nineteenth century. Longfellow told Agassiz how highly they regarded him in England, quoting Darwin, for example, as saying, "What a set of men you have in Cambridge! Both our universities put together cannot furnish the like. Why, there is Agassiz—he counts for three." [1] Joseph Le Conte, a student of Agassiz and himself an important scientist, contended that Agassiz had laid the "whole foundation of evolution, solid and broad," going on to say, however, that he had "refused to build any scientific structure on it." [2] Le Conte held that Agassiz would have taken the place of Darwin had not certain religious presuppositions led him to repudiate the logical conclusions to be derived from his own scientific investigations. Despite his scientific work, therefore, Agassiz became the champion of the traditionalists, and his scientific reputation did much to strengthen their position.

Agassiz's science was colored by his religion. As Theodore Lyman said, "Agassiz was a man of an inborn spiritual belief, which made a primary element in his nature, and which entered into all his interpretations of the outer world." [3] His work was also colored by an implicit Platonism which he acquired partly from Schelling and partly from reading Plato in the original. His sense of Plato's finality is illustrated by a story told by President Thomas Hill of Harvard, a close friend of Agassiz. Hill and Agassiz, along with other guests, were in Hill's home. Having made a lengthy tirade against Plato's doctrine of innate ideas, one of the guests paused for a moment, expecting Agassiz's assent. Coolly Agassiz said, "Nevertheless Plato has

[1] Agassiz, E. C.: *Louis Agassiz: His Life and Correspondence.* II, 666.

[2] Le Conte, Joseph: *Evolution and Its Relation to Religious Thought.* New York: D. Appleton and Co., 1889. 44.

[3] "Recollections of Agassiz." 229.

been right." [4] Although Agassiz was hardly a "born metaphysician" as Lyman regarded him, he constantly viewed his scientific studies in the light of philosophical and religious principles. As early as 1845 he was delivering lectures in Neuchâtel on "The Plan of Creation." In his *Essay on Classification* he pointed out that science was valuable in providing us with understanding of the world of thought through knowledge of the world of nature. In his last printed article he said, "Philosophers and theologians have yet to learn that a physical fact is as sacred as a moral principle." [5] What he meant by this was that man could understand the activities of the Divine Mind just as easily through scientific as through moral knowledge. The chief merit of science was that it gave us more precise knowledge of the thoughts of the Creator rather than that it provided an orderly arrangement of physical events or furthered man's control over nature.

It is well to remember that the *Essay on Classification* came out two years before Darwin's *Origin of Species*. It cannot be assumed, therefore, that Agassiz was led to express the ideas incorporated in his book on the basis of a reaction against Darwinism. It is more likely that Agassiz was desirous of warding off the implications of evolution finally brought to light by Darwin. In any case, Agassiz regarded physical events as caused, not by some power within material bodies, but by the Creator from without. Agassiz accepted evolution (he used the word development more often) but defined it as "a law controlling development and keeping types within appointed cycles of growth, which revolve forever upon themselves, returning at appointed intervals to the same starting-point and repeating through a succession of phases the same course." [6] This statement substitutes for the belief in cataclysmic destruction (which was one of the tenets of orthodoxy) a theory of cyclic development similar to that of Vico. With orthodoxy, however, it denies that there is any transmutation of species. He believed in metamorphosis, but of this he said, "The truth is that metamorphosis, like all embryonic growth, is a normal process of development, moving in regular cycles, returning always to the same starting-point, and leading always to the same end. . . ." [7] He charged that Darwin had no basis for his doctrine of transmutation since he admitted that the transition types were all extinct and that transition in living types was too subtle to detect. He contended that

[4] Land: "President Hill of Harvard on Agassiz and Darwin." 795.
[5] "Evolution and Permanence of Type." 95.
[6] Ibid. 92.
[7] Ibid. 98.

Darwin had "not infrequently overstepped the boundaries of actual knowledge and allowed his imagination to supply the links which science does not furnish." [8] Agassiz held that each species was created permanent and unchanging, capable only of carrying through the cyclic development characteristic of its own type, not gifted with power of becoming anything else. There were four main classes of organic nature, Articulata, Molluska, Radiata and Vertebrata; within these four classes were many species, each created by a power from without. Referring to his opponents he said:

> The most advanced Darwinians seem reluctant to acknowledge the intervention of an intellectual power in the diversity which obtains in nature, under the plea that such an admission implies distinct creative acts for every species. What of it, if it were true? Have those who object to repeated acts of creation ever considered that no progress can be made in knowledge without repeated acts of thinking? And what are thoughts but specific acts of the mind? Why should it then be unscientific to infer that the facts of nature are the result of a similar process, since there is no evidence of any other cause? [9]

In another place he said, "It is my belief that naturalists are chasing a phantom, in their search after some material gradation among created beings. . . ." [10] On the one hand, he contended that nature was intelligible as the work of an intelligent Creator, but on the other hand he held it could only be intelligible if creation were understood in terms of intermittent divine intervention. In the first of these contentions he was close to eighteenth-century deism, but in the second he held to a thesis which the deists considered to be in opposition to the intelligible lawfulness of nature. On the whole, Agassiz's idealism was a powerful aid to the supernaturalistic school and probably delayed the acceptance of evolutionary ideas for many years.

While Agassiz had a large following, he was opposed in his philosophical conclusions not only by fellow scientists such as Asa Gray but also by a man of rare and brilliant mind, John Fiske. It was Fiske who came to be recognized as the leading exponent of evolutionism in the United States. Fiske contended that Agassiz's errors were caused "not because he refrains steadfastly from all general considerations, but because he philosophizes—and philosophizes on unsound principles." [11] He went so far as to say in reference to Agassiz's position

[8] "Evolution and Permanence of Type." 94.

[9] Ibid. 101.

[10] *Methods of Study in Natural History*. Preface, iii.

[11] "Agassiz and Darwinism." 696.

that "The refusal to entertain a theory because it seems disagreeable or degrading, is a mark of intellectual cowardice or insincerity." [12]

Fiske was an omnivorous reader. By the time he was ready for Harvard he already had a sizable library of his own including works of Humboldt, Voltaire, Lewes, Fichte, Schlegel, Buckle, Cuvier, Comte, John Stuart Mill, Agassiz, Gray and Darwin. He was deeply impressed by Humboldt's *Kosmos,* disagreed with Agassiz's conclusions in the *Essay on Classification* and regarded Darwin's *Origin of Species* as one of the epoch-making works of the period. It is little wonder, then, that at Harvard he was annoyed by Bowen's classes in philosophy and Agassiz's lectures in geology, and that he took rather to Benjamin Peirce's classes in mathematics and was largely occupied with scientific and historical studies.[13] Comte appealed to him a great deal (although he later denied he was ever much inclined toward Comtean philosophy); he was nearly expelled from college for reading Comte in church, although this charge may have been mainly a means by which the authorities sought to temper his advocacy of organic evolution. His acceptance of Darwinism while an undergraduate made his position uncomfortable at times and prevented him from securing an appointment on the Harvard faculty until the advent of the liberal administration of Charles W. Eliot. He was one of the first subscribers in the United States to Spencer's *First Principles;* this early reading of Spencer led to his acceptance of Spencer's thought and to a cordial life-long friendship between the two. He regarded Spencer as the greatest thinker of the age. His own *Outlines of Cosmic Philosophy* was largely Spencerian, although he amplified certain issues on which Spencer had been inconclusive.

The temper of Fiske's philosophy, although hardly offensive today, was not in accord with the thought of the period. The gap which separated Fiske and his contemporaries can be partly understood in terms of the distinction he made between static and dynamic habits of thought. To him, the world was an ever-changing organism, to be understood only in terms of principles applicable to that type of existence. Knowledge was therefore not static but dynamic; it was relative to the world which it sought to represent. This was out of line with the accepted view that the mind of man was capable of divining the ways of God and nature in definitive and more or less final form. Fiske accepted the distinction between the phenomenal and noumenal worlds, holding that man could know the phenomenal world but

[12] "Agassiz and Darwinism." 697.

[13] Benjamin Peirce was the father of Charles Sanders Peirce.

could never know the noumenal except as it was expressed through the phenomenal. There was no magic faculty which enabled the mind to see beyond the veil of the phenomenal and ascertain the ontological status of things. Man's knowledge was limited to that with which he could empirically deal.

On the basis of this more or less positivistic approach, Fiske held that organic evolution was sufficiently verified to be accepted as true. Making this his starting point, he went on to show, along with Spencer, that the principle of evolution was applicable to the whole of nature, to the earth and the other planets as well as to the origin of man. He traced its application to mind, to intellect, to morality and to society, and worked out the conditions of progress. Although not a scientist himself, he contributed to evolutionary theory in the doctrine of prolonged infancy which he held accounted for the high stage of development in the human species.

Fiske's whole-hearted acceptance of the doctrine of transmutation, which he felt was an inherent part of the theory of evolution, made it impossible for him to give credence to the doctrine of special creation. Four types of evidence, he said, pointed to its falsity. First, the classification of species led to the theory of derivation, not to a belief in arbitrary orders created by divine fiat; here he criticized Agassiz's classification and depended largely upon Lamarck, Darwin, Huxley and Haeckel. Secondly, embryological studies proved the existence of modifications which led over a period of time to the development of new species. Thirdly, morphology established the similarity of all vertebrates, a fact only to be explained on the basis of a common origin. Lastly, the geographical distribution of animals and plants considered in respect both to their likenesses and to their differences led to the conclusion that variations were due to environmental factors. On the basis of these four arguments he said, "I think we may, therefore, without further ado, consign the special-creation hypothesis to that limbo where hover the ghosts of the slaughtered theories that were born of man's untutored intelligence in early times." [14]

With the advent of the evolution controversy positivism, Darwinism, materialism and atheism were all associated in the common mind. Spencer had pointed out the respects in which his system differed from Comte's; Fiske was determined to show that Cosmic Philosophy was in no way to be considered a species of Comtean positivism, materialism or atheism. On almost every major issue with which he dealt in *Cosmic Philosophy* he digressed to point out how his position differed from

[14] *Cosmic Philosophy.* I, 464.

that of Comte. When he dealt with the nature of mind he pointed out that he had no desire to be interpreted as saying that mind was the result of material processes. Spencer had never been clear on this issue, but Fiske definitely took the position of psycho-physical parallelism to avoid the charge of materialism. When he came to the religious implications of his theory, he was equally determined to avoid the charge of atheism for, he contended, even though it be impossible to define the nature of deity this was no indication that deity was non-existent. On the contrary, he took a theistic position, arguing that there must be a Force, or Power, or God, of which knowable objects are a manifestation. Spencer had gone this far, but Fiske's rather spirited presentation of the religious implications of evolution left Spencer non-committal and luke-warm. To Spencer the Unknowable was seemingly unknowable and there was little more to be said; to Fiske the Unknowable was to be regarded as not only existing but essential and important. In *Cosmic Philosophy* he argued for cosmic theism over against anthropomorphic theism. In going this far there is serious doubt whether Fiske was keeping to his empirical and inductive method. Darwin, in writing Fiske to commend him on the book, said that Fiske had expressed ideas which had been lingering in his own mind but that since he had given his life to induction he was unaccustomed to thinking in terms of deductive analysis. Fiske never retreated; on the contrary, he later gave his cosmic theism even more definite form. In his two Concord addresses, *The Destiny of Man Viewed in the Light of His Origin* and *The Idea of God as Affected by Modern Knowledge* he surprised his listeners by the extent to which he went in defending his theistic position. Holding that these addresses were a continuation of his earlier work and not in any sense a turning away from it, he went on to show how increased understanding of evolution had made him see the rhythmic and orderly activity of nature, leading up to a teleological position. Man, after all, was not just a victim of natural forces. He was the end toward which all things moved. God, as the "infinite and eternal Power that is manifested in every pulsation of the universe," was a psychical existence working in and through nature up to man, the highest order of existence. The development of cosmic evolution indicated, to him, that the goal ahead was the further adaptation of man to the circumstances of life and the increasing dominance of mind over body. God was a moral being, "the infinite Power that makes for righteousness." [15] Accepting evolution in its broadest sense, Fiske went on to

[15] *The Idea of God as Affected by Modern Knowledge.* 167.

develop a philosophy of creative evolution, theistic but not anthropomorphic except in a very limited sense. Fiske's theism was hardly the necessary complement of his evolutionary philosophy but he did help to make evolution acceptable and he initiated a way of interpreting it which was a precursor of modern systems of creative and emergent evolution.

## REFERENCES

### LOUIS AGASSIZ

Agassiz, Louis: *An Essay on Classification.* London, 1859. (Originally printed as Part I of *Contributions to the Natural History of the United States of North America.* 4 vols. Boston: Little, Brown and Co., 1857.)

———: *Methods of Study in Natural History.* Boston, 1863.

———: "Evolution and Permanence of Type," *Atlantic Monthly* 33 (1874) 92–101.

Agassiz, Elizabeth Cary (editor): *Louis Agassiz: His Life and Correspondence.* 2 vols. Boston: Houghton Mifflin Co., 1885.

Cooper, Lane: *Louis Agassiz as a Teacher.* Ithaca, N. Y.: Comstock Publishing Co., 1917.

James, William: "Louis Agassiz," *Memories and Studies.* New York: Longmans, Green and Co., 1912. 3–16.

Land, William G.: "President Hill of Harvard on Agassiz and Darwin," *New England Quarterly* 6 (1933) 793–801.

Lyman, Theodore: "Recollections of Agassiz," *Atlantic Monthly* 33 (1874) 221–9.

Marcou, Jules: *Life, Letters, and Works of Louis Agassiz.* 2 vols. New York: The Macmillan Co., 1896. (Contains complete bibliography of Agassiz's papers.)

Riley, I. Woodbridge: *American Thought from Puritanism to Pragmatism and Beyond.* Second edition. New York: Henry Holt and Co., 1923. 172–216.

### JOHN FISKE

Fiske, John: *Outlines of Cosmic Philosophy Based on the Doctrine of Evolution: with Criticisms on the Positive Philosophy.* London and Boston, 1874. (The edition used here is the twelfth. Boston: Houghton Mifflin Co., 1891.)

———: "Agassiz and Darwinism," *Popular Science Monthly* 3 (1873) 692–705.

———: *The Unseen World: and Other Essays.* Boston: Houghton Mifflin Co., 1876.

———: *Excursions of an Evolutionist.* Boston: Houghton Mifflin Co., 1883.

Fiske, John: *The Destiny of Man Viewed in the Light of His Origin.* Boston: Houghton Mifflin Co., 1884.

———: *The Idea of God as Affected by Modern Knowledge.* Boston: Houghton Mifflin Co., 1885.

———: *Darwinism: and Other Essays.* Fourth edition, revised and enlarged. Boston: Houghton Mifflin Co., 1888.

———: *Through Nature to God.* Boston: Houghton Mifflin Co., 1899.

———: *A Century of Science: and Other Essays.* Boston: Houghton Mifflin Co., 1899. (Esp. ch. II, "The Doctrine of Evolution: Its Scope and Purport" and ch. IV, "The Part Played by Infancy in the Evolution of Man." The latter essay is also included in *The Meaning of Infancy.* Boston: Houghton Mifflin Co., 1909. Pt. II.)

Clark, John Spencer: *The Life and Letters of John Fiske.* 2 vols. Boston: Houghton Mifflin Co., 1917. (Contains enlightening material on the whole intellectual setting of Fiske's period as well as an able presentation of Fiske's background, life and work.)

Royce, Josiah: "John Fiske as a Thinker." *Harvard Graduate's Magazine* 10 (1901–02) 23–33.

* * *

---

* * *

LOUIS AGASSIZ

# AN ESSAY ON CLASSIFICATION [16]

## *The Leading Features of a Natural Zoölogical System Are All Founded in Nature*

The divisions of animals according to branch, class, order, family, genus, and species, by which we express the results of our investigations into the relations of the animal kingdom, and which constitute the primary question respecting any system of Zoölogy, seem to me to deserve the consideration of all thoughtful minds. Are those divisions artificial or natural? Are they the devices of the human mind to classify and arrange our knowledge in such a manner as to bring it more readily within our grasp and facilitate further investigations,

[16] Taken from the separate edition of this work issued in 1859. Ch. I, (sec. I) 8–14; (sec. XV) 75–84; (sec. XXXII) 199–206. Not all of Agassiz's footnotes are included here; those which were largely bibliographical and added little to the content of his argument have been omitted.

or have they been instituted by the Divine Intelligence as the categories of his mode of thinking?[17] Have we, perhaps, thus far been only the unconscious interpreters of a Divine conception, in our attempts to expound nature? And when in our pride of philosophy we thought that we were inventing systems of science, and classifying creation by the force of our own reason, have we followed only, and reproduced, in our imperfect expressions, the plan whose foundations were laid in the dawn of creation, and the development of which we are laboriously studying,—thinking, as we put together and arrange our fragmentary knowledge, that we are introducing order into chaos anew? Is this order the result of the exertions of human skill and ingenuity; or is it inherent in the objects themselves, so that the intelligent student of Natural History is led unconsciously, by the study of the animal kingdom itself, to these conclusions; the great divisions under which he arranges animals being indeed but the headings to the chapters of the great book which he is reading? To me it appears indisputable, that this order and arrangement of our studies are based upon the natural, primitive relations of animal life,—those systems, to which we have given the names of the great leaders of our science who first proposed them being in truth but translations into human language of the thoughts of the Creator. And if this is indeed so, do we not find in this adaptability of the human intellect to the facts of creation,[18] by which we become instinctively, and, as I have said, unconsciously, the translators of the thoughts of God, the most conclusive proof of our affinity with the Divine mind? And is not this intellectual and spiritual connection with the Almighty worthy of our deepest consideration? If there is any truth in the belief that man is made in the image of God, it is surely not amiss for the philosopher to endeavour, by the study of his own mental operations, to approximate the workings of the Divine Reason, learning from the nature of his own mind better to understand the Infinite Intellect from which it is derived. Such a suggestion may, at first sight, appear irreverent.

[17] It must not be overlooked here that a system may be natural, that is, may agree in every respect with the facts in nature, and yet not be considered by its author as the manifestation of the thoughts of a Creator, but merely as the expression of a fact existing in nature—no matter how—which the human mind may trace and reproduce in a systematic form of its own invention.

[18] The human mind is in tune with nature, and much that appears as a result of the working of our intelligence is only the natural expression of that pre-established harmony. On the other hand the whole universe may be considered as a school in which man is taught to know himself, and his relations to his fellow beings, as well as to the First Cause of all that exists.

But, who is the truly humble? He who, penetrating into the secrets of creation, arranges them under a formula, which he proudly calls his scientific system? or he who in the same pursuit recognizes his glorious affinity with the Creator, and in deepest gratitude for so sublime a birthright strives to be the faithful interpreter of that Divine Intellect with whom he is permitted, nay, with whom he is intended, according to the laws of his being, to enter into communion?

I confess that this question, as to the nature and foundation of our scientific classifications, appears to me to have the deepest importance; an importance far greater, indeed, than is usually attached to it. If it can be proved that man has not invented, but only traced, this systematic arrangement in nature; that these relations and proportions, which exist throughout the animal and vegetable world, have an intellectual, an ideal connection, in the mind of the Creator; that this plan of creation, which so commends itself to our highest wisdom, has not grown out of the necessary action of physical laws, but was the free conception of the Almighty Intellect, matured in his thought before it was manifested in tangible external forms;—if, in short, we can prove premeditation prior to the act of creation, we have done, once and for ever, with the desolate theory which refers us to the laws of matter as accounting for all the wonders of the universe, and leaves us with no God but the monotonous, unvarying action of physical forces, binding all things to their inevitable destiny.[19] I think our

[19] I allude here only to the doctrines of materialists. But I feel it necessary to add, that there are physicists who might be shocked at the idea of being considered as materialists, who are yet prone to believe, that, when they have recognized the laws which regulate the physical world, and acknowledge that these laws were established by the Deity, they have explained everything, even when they have considered only the phenomena of the inorganic world: as if the world contained no living beings; and as if these living beings exhibited nothing that differed from the inorganic world. Mistaking for a casual relation the intellectual connexion observable between serial phenomena, they are unable to perceive any difference between disorder, and the free, independent, and self-possessed action of a superior mind; and call mysticism, even a passing allusion to the existence of an immaterial principle in animals, which they acknowledge themselves in man. (POWELL'S Essays, etc., p. 478, 385, and 466.) [This reference is to Powell, Baden: *Essays on the Spirit of the Inductive Philosophy.* London, 1855.—Editor's note] I would further remark, that, when speaking of creation in contradistinction with reproduction, I mean only to allude to the difference there is between the regular course of phenomena in nature, and the establishment of that order of things, without attempting to explain either; for, in whatever manner any state of things which has prevailed for a time upon earth may have been introduced, it is self-evident that its establishment and its maintenance for a determined period are two very different things, however frequently they may be mistaken as identical. It is, further, of itself

science has now reached that degree of advancement, when we may venture upon such an investigation.

The argument for the existence of an intelligent Creator is generally drawn from the adaptation of means to ends, upon which the Bridgewater treatises, for example, have been based. But this does not appear to me to cover the whole ground for we can conceive that the natural action of objects upon each other should result in a final fitness of the universe, and thus produce an harmonious whole. Nor does the argument derived from the connection of organs and functions seem to me more satisfactory; for, beyond certain limits, it is not even true. We find organs without functions, as, for instance, the teeth of the whale, which never cut through the gum, and the breast in all males of the class of mammalia. These and similar organs are preserved in obedience to a certain uniformity of fundamental structure, true to the original formula of that division of animal life, even when not essential to its mode of existence. The organ remains, not for the performance of a function, but with reference to a plan,[20] and might almost remind us of what we often see in human structures, when, for instance, in architecture the same external combinations are retained for the sake of symmetry and harmony of proportion, even when they have no practical object.

I disclaim every intention of introducing into this work any evidence irrelevant to my subject, or of supporting any conclusions not immediately flowing from it; but I cannot overlook or disregard here the close connection which there is between the facts ascertained by scientific investigation, and the discussions now carried on respecting the origin of organized beings. And, though I know those who hold it to be very unscientific to believe that thinking is not something

---

plain that the laws which may explain the phenomena of the material world, in contradistinction from the organic, cannot be considered as accounting for the existence of living beings, even though these have a material body, unless it be actually shown that these laws imply by their very nature the production of such beings. Thus far, Cross' experiments are the only ones offered as proving such a result. I do not know what physicists may think about them now; but I know that there is scarcely a zoologist who doubts that they only rested upon mistake. Life, in appropriating the physical world to itself, with all its peculiar phenomena, exhibits, however, some of its own, and some of a higher order, which cannot be explained by physical agencies. The circumstance, that life is so deeply rooted in the inorganic nature, affords, nevertheless, a strong temptation to explain one by the other; but we shall see presently how fallacious these attempts have been.

[20] The unity of structure of the limbs of club-footed or pinnated animals, in which the fingers are never moved, with those which enjoy the most perfect articulations and freedom of motion, exhibits this reference most fully.

inherent in matter, and that there is an essential difference between inorganic and living and thinking beings, I shall not be prevented, by any such pretensions of a false philosophy, from expressing my conviction that, as long as it cannot be shown that matter or physical forces do actually reason, any manifestation of thought is to be considered as evidence of the existence of a thinking being as the author of such thought, and that an intelligent and intelligible connection between the facts of nature must be looked upon as a direct proof of the existence of a thinking God,[21] as certainly as man exhibits the power of thinking when he recognises their natural relations.

As I am not writing a didactic work, I will not enter here into a detailed illustration of the facts relating to the various subjects submitted to the consideration of my reader beyond what is absolutely necessary to follow the argument, nor dwell at any length upon the conclusions to which they lead; but will simply recall the leading features of the evidence, assuming in the argument a full acquaintance with the whole range of data upon which it is founded, whether derived from the affinities or the anatomical structure of animals, or from their habits and their geographical distribution, from their embryology, or from their succession in past geological ages, and the peculiarities they have exhibited during each, believing, as I do, that isolated and disconnected facts are of little consequence in the contemplation of the whole plan of creation; and that, without a consideration of all the facts furnished by the study of the habits of animals, by their anatomy, their embryology, and the history of the

[21] I am well aware that even the most eminent investigators consider the task of science at an end, as soon as the most general relations of natural phenomena have been ascertained. To many the inquiry into the primitive cause of their existence seems either beyond the reach of man, or as belonging rather to philosophy than to physics. To these the name of God appears out of place in a scientific work; as if the knowledge of secondary agencies constituted alone a worthy subject for their investigations, and as if nature could teach nothing about its Author. Many, again, are no doubt prevented from expressing their conviction that the world was called into existence and is regulated by an intelligent God, either by the fear of being supposed to share clerical or sectarian prejudices, or because it may be dangerous for them to discuss freely such questions without acknowledging at the same time the obligation of taking the Old Testament as the standard by which the validity of their results is to be measured. Science, however, can only prosper when confining itself within its legitimate sphere; and nothing can be more detrimental to its true dignity than discussions like those which took place at the last meeting of the German Association of Naturalists in Göttingen, and which have since then been carried on in several pamphlets in which bigotry vies with personality and invective.

past ages of our globe, we shall never arrive at the knowledge of the natural system of animals.

## *Permanency of Specific Peculiarities in All Organized Beings*

It was a great step in the progress of science when it was ascertained that species have fixed characters, and that they do not change in the course of time. But this fact, for which we are indebted to Cuvier,[22] has acquired a still greater importance since it has also been established, that even the most extraordinary changes in the mode of existence, and in the conditions under which animals are placed, have no more influence upon their essential characters than the lapse of time.

The facts bearing upon these two subjects are too well known to require special illustration. I will, therefore, allude only to a few points, to avoid even the possibility of a misapprehension of my statements. That animals of different geological periods differ specially, *en masse,* from those of preceding or following formations, is a fact satisfactorily ascertained. Between two successive geological periods, then, changes have taken place among animals and plants. But none of those primordial forms of life which naturalists call species are known to have changed during any of these periods. It cannot be denied, that the species of different successive periods are supposed by some naturalists to derive their distinguishing features from changes which have taken place in those of preceding ages; but this a mere supposition, supported neither by physiological nor by geological evidence; and the assumption, that animals and plants change in a similar manner during one and the same period, is equally gratuitous. On the contrary, it is known, by the evidence furnished by the Egyptian monuments, and by the most careful comparison between animals found in the tombs of Egypt with living specimens of the same species obtained in the same country, that there is not the shadow of a difference between them for a period of about five thousand years. These comparisons, first instituted by Cuvier, have proved, that, as far as it has been possible to carry back the investigation, it does not afford the beginning of an evidence that species change in the course of time, if the comparisons be limited to the same great cosmic epoch. Geology

22 CUVIER (G.), Recherches sur les ossements fossiles, etc., Nouv. edit.; Paris, 1821, 5 vols., 4to., fig. vol. i, sur l'Ibis, p. cxli.

only shows that at different periods [23] there have existed different species; but no transition from those of a preceding into those of the following epoch has ever been noticed anywhere; and the question alluded to here is to be distinguished from that of the origin of the

[23] I trust no reader will be so ignorant of the facts here alluded to as to infer from the use of the word "period" for different eras and epochs of great length,—each of which is characterized by different animals,—that the differences these animals exhibit is in itself evidence of a change in the species. The question is, whether any changes take place during one or any of these periods. It is almost incredible how loosely some people will argue upon this point from a want of knowledge of the facts, even though they seem to reason logically. A distinguished physicist has recently taken up this subject of the immutability of species, and called in question the logic of those who uphold it. I will put his argument into as few words as possible, and show, I hope, that it does not touch the case. "Changes are observed from one geological period to another; species which do not exist at an earlier period are observed at a later period, while the former have disappeared; and, though each species may have possessed its peculiarities unchanged for a lapse of time, the fact that, when long periods are considered, all those of an earlier period are replaced by new ones at a later period, proves that species change in the end, provided a sufficiently long period of time is granted." I have nothing to object to the statement of facts, as far as it goes, but I maintain that the conclusion is not logical. It is true that species are limited to particular geological epochs; and it is equally true, that, in all geological formations, those of successive periods are different one from the other. But because they so differ, does it follow that they have themselves changed, and not been exchanged for, or replaced by, others? The length of time taken for the operation has nothing to do with the argument. Granting myriads of years for each period, no matter how many or how few, the question remains simply this: When the change takes place, does it take place spontaneously, under the action of physical agents, according to their law, or is it produced by the intervention of an agency not at work in that way before or afterwards? A comparison may explain my view more fully. Let a lover of the fine arts visit a museum arranged systematically, and in which the works of the different schools are placed in chronological order. As he passes from one room to another, he beholds changes as great as those which the palaeontologist observes in passing from one system of rocks to another. But, because these works bear a closer resemblance as they belong to one or the other school or to periods following one another closely, would the critic be in any way justified in assuming that the earlier works have changed into those of a later period, or in denying that they are the works of artists living and active at the time of their production? The question about the immutability of species is identical with this supposed case. It is not because species have lasted for a longer or shorter time in past ages that naturalists consider them as immutable, but because, in the whole series of geological ages, taking the entire lapse of time which has passed since the first introduction of animals or plants upon earth, not the slightest evidence has yet been produced that species are actually transformed one into the other. We only know that they are different at different periods, as are works of art of different periods and of different schools; but, as long as we have no other data to reason upon than those which Geology has furnished to this day, it is as unphilosophical and illogical, because such differences exist, to assume that species do change, and

differences in the bulk of species belonging to two different geological eras. The question we are now examining involves only the fixity or mutability of species during one epoch, one era, one period, in the history of our globe. And nothing furnishes the slightest argument in favour of their mutability. On the contrary, every modern investigation has gone only to confirm the results first obtained by Cuvier, and his view, that species are fixed.

It is something to be able to show by monumental evidence and by direct comparison, that animals and plants have undergone no change for a period of about five thousand years. This result has had the greatest influence upon the progress of science, especially with reference to the consequences to be drawn from the occurrence in the series of geological formations of organized beings as highly diversified in each epoch as those of the present day; and it has laid the foundation for the conviction, now universal among well informed naturalists, that this globe has been in existence for innumerable ages, and that the length of time elapsed since it first became inhabited cannot be counted in years. Even the length of the period to which we belong is still a problem, notwithstanding the precision with which certain systems of chronology would fix the creation of man. There are, however, many circumstances which show that the animals now living have been for a much longer period inhabitants of our globe than is generally supposed. It has been possible to trace the formation and growth of our coral reefs, especially in Florida, with sufficient precision to ascertain that it must take about eight thousand years for one of those coral walls to rise from its foundation to the level of the surface of the ocean. There are, around the southernmost extremity of Florida alone, four such reefs, concentric with one another, which can be shown to have grown up one after the other. This gives, for the beginning of the first of these reefs, an age of over thirty thousand years (nay, probably, over one hundred thousand years); and yet the corals by which they were all built up are the same identical species in all of them. These facts, then, furnish evidence as direct as we can obtain in any branch of physical inquiry, that some, at least, of the species of animals now existing, have been

---

have changed,—that is, are transformed, or have been transformed,—as it would be to maintain that works of art change in the course of time. We do not know how organized beings have originated, it is true; and no naturalist can be prepared to account for their appearance in the beginning, or for their difference in different periods; but enough is known to repudiate the assumption of their transmutation, as it does not explain the facts, and shuts out further attempts at proper investigations. See BADEN POWELL'S Essays, quoted above, p. 412 et seq., and Essay 3rd, generally.

in existence over thirty thousand years,[24] and have not undergone the slightest change during the whole of that period.[25] And yet these four concentric reefs are only the most distinct of that region; others, thus far less extensively investigated, lie to the northward; indeed, the whole peninsula of Florida consists altogether of coral reefs annexed to one another in the course of time, and containing only fragments of corals and shells, etc., identical with those now living upon that coast. Now, if a width of five miles is a fair average for one coral reef, growing under the circumstances under which the concentric reefs of Florida are seen now to follow one another, and this regular succession extends only as far north as Lake Ogeechobee, for two degrees of latitude, this would give about two hundred thousand years for the period of time which was necessary for that part of the peninsula of Florida which lies south of Lake Ogeechobee to rise to its present southern extent above the level of the sea, and during which no changes have taken place in the character of the animals of the Gulf of Mexico.

It is very prejudicial to the best interests of science to confound questions that are entirely different, merely for the sake of supporting a theory; and yet this is constantly done, whenever the question of the fixity of species is alluded to. A few more words upon this point, therefore, will not be out of place here.

I will not enter into a discussion upon the question, whether any species are found identically the same in two successive formations, as I have already examined it at full length elsewhere, and it may be settled finally, one way or the other, without affecting the proposition now under consideration; for it is plain, that, if such identity could be proved, it would only show more satisfactorily how tenacious species are in their character, to continue to live through all the physical changes which have taken place between two successive geological periods. Again, such identity, once proved, would leave it still doubtful, whether their representatives in two successive epochs are descendants one of the other, as we have already strong evidence in

[24] I am now satisfied that the age of this reef is not overstated, if estimated at one hundred thousand years; so slow are the operations of nature.

[25] Those who feel inclined to ascribe the differences which exist between species of different geological periods to the modifying influence of physical agents, and who look to the changes now going on among the living for the support of such an opinion, and not being satisfied that the facts just mentioned are sufficient to prove the immutability of species, still believe that a longer period of time would yet do what thirty thousand years have not done. I beg leave to refer, for further consideration, to the charming song of Chamisso, entitled Tragische Geschichte, and beginning as follows: "'s war Einer dem's zu Herzen ging."

favour of the separate origin of the representatives of the same species in separate geographical areas. The case of closely allied but different species occurring in successive periods, yet limited respectively to their epochs, affords, in the course of time, a parallel to the case of closely allied, so-called, representative species occupying different areas in space, which no sound naturalist would now suppose to be derived one from the other. There is no more reason to suppose species equally allied, following one another in time, to be derived one from the other; and all that has been said in preceding paragraphs respecting the differences observed between species occurring in different geographical areas applies with the same force to species succeeding each other in the course of time.

When domesticated animals and cultivated plants are mentioned as furnishing evidence of the mutability of species, the circumstance is constantly overlooked, or passed over in silence, that the first point to be established respecting them, in order to justify any inference from them against the fixity of species, would be to show that each of them has originated from one common stock, which, far from being the case, is flatly contradicted by the positive knowledge we have that the varieties of several of them at least are owing to the entire amalgamation of different species. The Egyptian monuments further show that many of these so-called varieties, which are supposed to be the product of time, are as old as any other animals which have been known to man. At all events, we have no tradition, no monumental evidence of the existence of any wild animal older than those which represent domesticated animals, already as different among themselves as they are now. It is, therefore, quite possible that the different races of domesticated animals were originally distinct species, more or less mixed now, as the different races of men are. Moreover, neither domesticated animals, nor cultivated plants, nor the races of men, are the proper subjects for an investigation respecting the fixity or mutability of species, as all involve already the question at issue in the premises which are assumed in introducing them as evidence in the case. With reference to the different breeds of our domesticated animals, which are known to be produced by the management of man, as well as certain varieties of our cultivated plants, they must be well distinguished from permanent races, which, for aught we know, may be primordial; for breeds are the result of the fostering care of man: they are the product of the limited influence and control the human mind has over organized beings, and not the free product of mere physical agents. They show, therefore, that even the least important changes which may take place during one and the same cosmic period, among animals and plants, are controlled by an intellectual power, and do not result from the immediate action of physical causes.

So far, then, from disclosing the effects of physical agents, whatever changes are known to take place in the course of time among organized beings appear as the result of an intellectual power, and go therefore to substantiate the view, that all the differences observed among finite beings are ordained by the action of the Supreme Intellect, and not determined by physical causes. This position is still more strengthened, when we consider that the differences which exist between different races of domesticated animals and the varieties of our cultivated plants as well as among the races of men, are permanent under the most diversified climatic influence; a fact which is daily proved more conclusively by the extensive migrations of the civilized nations, and which stands in direct contradiction to the supposition that such or similar influences could have produced them.

When considering the subject of domestication, in particular, it ought further to be remembered, that every race of man has its own peculiar kinds of domesticated animals and of cultivated plants, and that these exhibit much fewer varieties among themselves in the case of those races which have had little or no intercourse with other races, than in the case of those nations which have been formed by the mixture of several tribes.

It is often stated, that the ancient philosophers have solved satisfactorily all the great questions interesting to man; and that modern investigations, though they have grasped with new vigour, and illuminated with new light, all the phenomena of the material world, have added little or nothing in the field of intellectual progress. Is this true? There is no question so deeply interesting to man as that of his own origin, and the origin of all things. And yet, antiquity had no knowledge concerning it: things were formerly believed, either to be from eternity, or to have been created at one time. Modern science, however, can show in the most satisfactory manner that all finite beings have made their appearance successively and at long intervals, and that each kind of organized beings has existed for a definite period of time in past ages, and that those now living are of comparatively recent origin. At the same time, the order of their succession, and their immutability during such cosmic periods, show no causal connexion with physical agents and the known sphere of action of these agents in nature, but argue in favour of repeated interventions on the part of the Creator. It seems really surprising, that, while such an intervention is admitted by all, except the strict materialists, for the establishment of the laws regulating the inorganic world, it is yet denied by so many physicists with reference to the introduction of organized beings at different successive periods. Does this not show the imperfect acquaintance of these investigators with the conditions under which life is manifested, and with the essential difference between the phenomena of the organic and those of the physical world, rather than furnish any evidence that the organic world is the product of physical causes?

### *Recapitulation*

In recapitulating the preceding statements, we may present the following conclusions:—

1st. The connection of all the known features of nature into one system exhibits thought, the most comprehensive thought, in limits transcending the highest wonted powers of man.

2d. The simultaneous existence of the most diversified types under identical circumstances exhibits thought, the ability to adapt a great variety of structures to the most uniform conditions.

3d. The repetition of similar types, under the most diversified circumstances, shows an immaterial connection between them; it exhibits thought, proving directly how completely the Creative Mind is independent of the influence of a material world.

4th. The unity of plan in otherwise highly diversified types of animals, exhibits thought; it exhibits more immediately premeditation, for no plan could embrace such a diversity of beings, called into existence at such long intervals of time, unless it had been framed in the beginning with immediate reference to the end.

5th. The correspondence, now generally known as special homologies, in the details of structure in animals otherwise entirely disconnected, down to the most minute peculiarities, exhibits thought, and more immediately the power of expressing a general proposition in an indefinite number of ways, equally complete in themselves, though differing in all their details.

6th. The various degrees and different kinds of relationship among animals which can have no genealogical connection, exhibit thought, the power of combining different categories into a permanent, harmonious whole, even though the material basis of this harmony be ever changing.

7th. The simultaneous existence, in the earliest geological periods in which animals existed at all, of representatives of all the great types of the animal kingdom, exhibits most especially thought, considerate thought, combining power, premeditation, prescience, omniscience.

8th. The gradation, based upon complications of structure, which may be traced among animals built upon the same plan, exhibits thought, and especially the power of harmoniously distributing unequal gifts.

9th. The distribution of some types over the most extensive range of the surface of the globe, while others are limited to particular geographical areas, and the various combinations of these types into zoological provinces of unequal extent, exhibit thought, a close control over the distribution of the earth's surface among its inhabitants.

10th. The identity of structure of these types, notwithstanding their wide geographical distribution, exhibits thought; that deep thought, which, the more it is scrutinized, seems the less capable of being exhausted, though its meaning at the surface appears at once plain and intelligible to every one.

11th. The community of structure, in certain respects, of animals otherwise entirely different, but living within the same geographical area, exhibits thought and more particularly the power of adapting most diversified types with peculiar structures to either identical or to different conditions of existence.

12th. The connection, by series, of special structures observed in animals widely scattered over the surface of the globe, exhibits thought, unlimited comprehension, and more directly omnipresence of mind, and also prescience, as far as such series extend through a succession of geological ages.

13th. The relation there is between the size of animals and their structure and form, exhibits thought; it shows that in nature the quantitative differences are as fixedly determined as the qualitative ones.

14th. The independence, in the size of animals, of the mediums in which they live, exhibits thought, in establishing such close connection between elements so influential in themselves and organized beings so little affected by the nature of these elements.

15th. The permanence of specific peculiarities under every variety of external influences, during each geological period, and under the present state of things upon earth, exhibits thought: it shows, also, that limitation in time is an essential element of all finite beings, while eternity is an attribute of the Deity only.

16th. The definite relations in which animals stand to the surrounding world, exhibit thought; for all animals living together stand respectively, on account of their very differences, in different relations to identical conditions of existence, in a manner which implies a considerate adaptation of their varied organization to these uniform conditions.

17th. The relations in which individuals of the same species stand to one another, exhibit thought, and go far to prove the existence in all living beings of an immaterial, imperishable principle, similar to that which is generally conceded to man only.

18th. The limitation of the range of changes which animals undergo during their growth, exhibits thought; it shows most strikingly the independence of these changes of external influences, and the necessity that they should be determined by a power superior to these influences.

19th. The unequal limitation in the average duration of the life of individuals in different species of animals, exhibits thought; for, however uniform or however diversified the conditions of existence may be under which animals live together, the average duration of life, in different species, is unequally limited. It points, therefore, at a knowledge of time and space, and of the value of time, since the phases of life of different animals are apportioned according to the part they have to perform upon the stage of the world.

20th. The return to a definite norm of animals which multiply in various ways, exhibits thought. It shows how wide a cycle of modulations may be included in the same conception, without yet departing from a norm expressed more directly in other combinations.

21st. The order of succession of the different types of animals and plants characteristic of the different geological epochs, exhibits thought. It shows, that, while the material world is identical in itself in all ages, ever different types of organized beings are called into existence in successive periods.

22d. The localization of some types of animals upon the same points of the surface of the globe, during several successive geological periods, exhibits thought, consecutive thought; the operations of a mind acting in conformity with a plan laid out beforehand, and sustained for a long period.

23d. The limitation of closely allied species to different geological periods, exhibits thought; it exhibits the power of sustaining nice distinctions, notwithstanding the interposition of great disturbances by physical revolutions.

24th. The parallelism between the order of succession of animals and plants in geological times and the gradation among their living representatives, exhibit thought; consecutive thought, superintending the whole development of nature from beginning to end, and disclosing throughout a gradual progress, ending with the introduction of man at the head of the animal creation.

25th. The parallelism between the order of succession of animals in geological times and the changes their living representatives undergo during their embryological growth, exhibit thought; the repetition of the same train of thoughts in the phases of growth of living animals and the successive appearance of their representatives in past ages.

26th. The combination, in many extinct types, of characters, which, in later ages, appear disconnected in different types, exhibits thought, prophetic thought, foresight; combinations of thought preceding their manifestation in living forms.

27th. The parallelism between the gradation among animals and the changes they undergo during their growth, exhibits thought, as it discloses everywhere the most intimate connection between essential features of animals which have no necessary physical relation, and can, therefore, not be understood otherwise than as established by a thinking being.

28th. The relations existing between these different series and the geographical distribution of animals, exhibit thought; they show the omnipresence of the Creator.

29th. The mutual dependence of the animal and vegetable kingdoms upon each other for their maintenance, exhibits thought; it displays the care with which all conditions of existence, necessary to the maintenance of organized beings, have been balanced.

30th. The dependence of some animals upon others or upon plants for their existence, exhibits thought; it shows to what degree the most complicated combinations of structure and adaptation can be rendered independent of the physical conditions which surround them.

We may sum up the results of this discussion, up to this point, in still fewer words:—

All organized beings exhibit in themselves all those categories of structure and of existence upon which a natural system may be founded, in such a manner that, in tracing it, the human mind is only translating into human language the Divine thoughts expressed in nature in living realities.

All these beings do not exist in consequence of the continued agency of physical causes, but have made their successive appearance upon earth by the immediate intervention of the Creator. As proof, I may sum up my argument in the following manner:

The products of what are commonly called physical agents are everywhere the same (that is, upon the whole surface of the globe), and have always been the same (that is, during all geological periods); while organized beings are everywhere different and have differed in all ages. Between two such series of phenomena there can be no causal or genetic connection.

31st. The combination in time and space of all these thoughtful conceptions exhibits not only thought, it shows also premeditation, power, wisdom, greatness, prescience, omniscience, providence. In one word, all these facts, in their natural connection, proclaim aloud the One God, whom man may know, adore, and love; and Natural History must, in good time, become the analysis of the thoughts of the Creator of the Universe, as manifested in the animal and vegetable kingdoms, as well as in the inorganic world.

It may appear strange that I should have presented the preceding disquisition under the title of an "Essay on Classification." Yet it has been done deliberately. In the beginning of this chapter, I have already stated that Classification seems to me to rest upon too narrow a foundation when it is chiefly based upon structure. Animals are linked together as closely by their mode of development, by their relative standing in their respective classes, by the order in which they have made their appearance upon earth, by their geographical distribution, and generally by their connection with the world in which they live, as by their anatomy. All these relations should, therefore, be fully expressed in a natural classification; and, though structure furnishes the most direct indication of some of these relations, always appreciable under every circumstance, other considerations should not be neglected, which may complete our insight into the general plan of creation.

* * *

---

* * *

## JOHN FISKE

# OUTLINES OF COSMIC PHILOSOPHY[26]

### *The Question Restated*

A synthesis of scientific doctrines has now been fairly constructed, in accordance with the plan laid out in the eleventh chapter of our Prolegomena. We have passed in review the sciences which deal with the various orders of phenomena that make up the knowable universe, and we have contemplated the widest truths which these sciences severally reveal, as corollaries of an ultimate truth. Before proceeding to expound our Cosmic Philosophy in its final results, let us briefly sum up the leading conclusions at which we have arrived.

It has been proved to follow from that axiom of the Persistence of Force upon which all physical science is based, that the mere coexistence of innumerable discrete bodies in the universe, exerting attractive and repulsive forces upon each other, necessitates a perpetual rhythmical redistribution of the Matter and Motion of which the phenomenal universe is composed. It has been proved that this eternal rhythm must of necessity be manifested in alternating eras both general and local, of Evolution and Dissolution,—eras in which now the concentration of Matter and dissipation of Motion, and now the diffusion of Matter and absorption of Motion, predominate,—eras which may be short, as in the duration of a snow-crystal or of a butterfly's life, or long, as in the duration of our planetary system. It has been proved that the process of Evolution, during which Matter is chiefly being concentrated while Motion is chiefly being lost, must, under certain assigned conditions, result in a continuous change from a state of homogeneity, indefiniteness, and incoherence to a state of heterogeneity, definiteness, and coherence.

With the aid of these demonstrated truths of Physics, we have surveyed the history of the knowable universe, intent upon finding some provisional answer to the time-honoured question of Philosophy—whence came we, what are we, and whither do we tend? Throughout all the provinces of nature we have traced that aspect of the stupendous process of Evolution, which consists in the transition from indefinite incoherent homogeneity to definite coherent heterogeneity. We have seen it exemplified in the development of our planetary system from a

[26] II, 367–75; 411–6, 422–9. The first selection is a summary of his conclusions on the meaning of evolution in nature, in society and in human life described more at length in the earlier part of the work.

relatively homogeneous ball of vapour. We have witnessed it as shown in the increasing physical and chemical diversity and interdependence of the various portions of the surface of our cooling earth, and in those wonderful differentiations by which solar radiance is metamorphosed into the innumerable forms of energy manifested alike by winds and waves, by growing plants and animals, and by reasoning men. We have described it in some detail as revealed in the gradual change of a seed into a tree and of an ovum into an adult mammal. We have observed it also in the increasing chemical complexity which at a remote epoch resulted in the formation of living protoplasm; and we have seen how from this earliest protoplasm there have arisen, in the course of ages well-nigh infinite in duration, the myriad forms of animal and vegetable life. The progress toward higher complexity and higher organization has likewise been discovered to be taking place in *processes* as well as in *things*. It has been shown that Life is a process, consisting in a series of adjustments between the organism and its environment; and that Mind, objectively considered, is a special form of Life, consisting in a specialized portion of the series of adjustments. In these wondrous processes we have found the Law of Evolution most beautifully exemplified; the degree of Life, or of Mind, being high in proportion not only to the extent which the adjustments cover, but also to their complexity, definiteness, and coherence. That superadded process known as Civilization or social progress, has also been shown to consist in a series of adjustments between the community and its environment, in the course of which society becomes ever more and more complex and more interdependent in its various elements. That moral sense which underlies social progress and renders it possible has been exhibited as the noble product of the slow organization of those feelings of pleasure and pain which, in highly-developed organisms, are mainly concerned in enhancing the perfectness of the adjustments in which Life consists. And finally we have witnessed the wonderful complication of cooperating processes by which Humanity—the crown and glory of the universe as we know it—has been evolved from a lower type of animal life, in entire conformity to the general law. The direct and relatively-simple processes of physical adjustment became at length almost wholly subordinated to the indirect and relatively-complex processes of psychical adjustment, so that variations in intelligence came to be selected in preference to variations in physique; the increased complexity of psychical adjustments entailed the lengthening of the period required for organizing them; the lengthening of infancy, thus entailed, brought about the segregation, into permanent family-groups, of individuals associated for the performance of sexual and parental functions; the maintenance of such family-groups involved the setting up of permanent reciprocal necessities of behaviour among the members of the group; in this way the ultimate test of right and wrong action came to be the welfare of the community, instead of the welfare of the individual; the long process of social evolution, thus inaugurated, has all along reacted upon individual evolution, by increasing the power of mental representation, and nourishing sympathy at the expense of egoism; and thus, through one and the same endlessly complicated plexus of causes, has arisen the historic Man, with his Intellect and his Moral Sense. Yet endlessly complicated as the process has been, we see that it is throughout definable as the gradual substitution of adjustments that are relatively-indirect, heterogeneous, and highly organized, for adjustments that are relatively-direct, homogeneous, and slightly organized.

Thus we have fulfilled all the requirements laid down in the concluding chapter of our Prolegomena. We have found a hypothesis which is based upon properties of matter and principles of dynamics that have previously been established; which appeals to no unknown agency and invokes no unknown attribute of matter or motion; and which, accordingly, contains no unverifiable element. This hypothesis has been successfully subjected to both deductive and inductive verification. In every department of nature it has triumphantly borne the supreme test of reconciling the order of conceptions with the order of phenomena. And in our sociological chapters, as well as in the chapters on the Genesis of Man, it has enabled us to detect relations among phenomena which had hitherto remained in obscurity.

It remains to add that this grand hypothesis, for the conception and elaboration of which I have ventured to liken Mr. Spencer to the thinker who conceived and elaborated the hypothesis of gravitation, affords in itself a striking illustration of that process of Evolution which it formulates. Considered as an event in intellectual development, this discovery is an immense *extension in time* of the correspondence between the order of human conceptions and the order of phenomena, as Newton's discovery was an immense extension of the correspondence in space. The one has enabled us to adjust our mental sequences to phenomena as distant as the Milky Way; the other carries back the adjustments till they comprehend the birth of the Solar System. The announcement of a verifiable Law of Evolution is but the most recent phase of a process which has been going on from the time when men first began to speculate about the world of phenomena,—

the process of substituting what may be called dynamical habits of thought for statical habits. Clearly the formation of a theory of the universe, whether as expressed in the crude mythologies of barbarians or in the elaborate systems of modern philosophers, is the establishment of a complex group of subjective relations that are either very imperfectly or much more completely adjusted to objective relations. All men now existing, whether civilized or savage, with the exception of idiots and very young children, possess some such theory, however vague and shadowy it may be. Such general statements as may be made by the most ignorant boor obviously imply some dim conception of the world and of his relations to it. Even the beliefs that the moon is about the size of a cheese, or that the devil has bewitched his cattle, are parts of a rudimentary kind of cosmic philosophy. Now among uneducated persons, alike in barbarous and in civilized countries, the crude philosophies current universally imply that the general arrangement of things is everywhere and in all ages substantially the same as it is witnessed by them in their immediate environment. Their theories are not adjusted to remote facts in time and space which only a thorough education could have added to their experience. They take what we may call a statical view of things. Hence they suppose that God created the world a few thousand years ago in nearly the same condition in which we now behold it; traditional observances, such as the keeping of a Sabbath, advanced social institutions, like monogamy, and highly elaborated philosophical doctrines, such as monotheism, are unhesitatingly referred back to the beginning of the world and it is in general taken for granted that the thoughts and feelings current in past ages were like the thoughts and feelings current in our own. Until within the last three or four generations this statical view of things was shared by cultivated with uncultivated people, though with somewhat different degrees of narrowness. On the other hand the dynamic view of things, represented by the Doctrine of Evolution, which regards the universe and all that is in it as presenting a different aspect from epoch to epoch, obviously results from the adjustment of our theories to longer and longer sequences in the past. The progress of geologic discovery, revealing the immense antiquity of the earth, was one of the circumstances which began to arouse in educated people a tendency to regard things as continually though slowly changing; and the theories of Goethe and Lyell, the revolution in biology wrought by Lamarck and Cuvier, and the application of the comparative method to the historic and philologic interpretation of past states of society, deepened and strengthened this tendency. In no other respect is the present age so widely distinguished from past ages as in this habit of looking at all things dynamically. It is shown in the literary criticism of Sainte-Beuve, and the art-criticism of Taine, and in the historical criticism of Mommsen or Baur, no less than in Mr. Darwin's science, or Mr. Spencer's philosophy. In our concluding chapter we shall observe some of the practical bearings of this great difference in mental habit between the eighteenth and nineteenth centuries, with especial reference to the political utopias of Rousseau, and to the attempts of the *Encyclopédistes* to overthrow Christianity. It is enough for us now to bear in mind that this immense widening of the mental horizon which modern times have witnessed; this power of criticizing sympathetically the relatively rude theories, customs, and prejudices of bygone generations; this ability to realize in imagination a time when forms of life now wholly distinct were represented by a common ancestral type, or a time when the material universe existed in a shape very different from that in which it is presented to our senses; this growing tendency to interpret groups of phenomena by reference to other groups of phenomena long preceding; are all alike explicable, in an ultimate analysis, as a prodigious extension in time of the correspondence between the human mind and its environment.

The Doctrine of Evolution, in which this dynamical habit of viewing things is reduced to a system, represents also the most extensive integration of correspondences that has yet been achieved. The continuous organization of scientific truths by philosophy has all along been a progress in this kind of integration. From the very first crude observations and the earliest cosmical theories, it is true that succeeding observations have all along had their results incorporated with the cosmical theories, or else new cosmical theories have been framed, which, by including the results of more mature observation, have superseded the old ones. In this way the progress of philosophy has on the whole kept pace with that of science. But between the earlier systems and the more modern ones there is a marked difference in the extent to which special truths in different departments of science are made to support and illustrate each other. For the gaps in the scientific knowledge synthesized in older systems were so considerable that, in order to make a synthesis at all, it was necessary to incorporate a large amount of hypothetical speculation which was not only unverified but unverifiable; so that the relations between science and philosophy were much less coherent than at present. Today the interdependence is more complete than ever before. Our cosmic theories are rapidly modified by the incorporation of the results of countless new observations in all departments of science; and philosophy, refraining more and more from ontological speculations, is becoming more and more thoroughly identified with cosmology. It is recognizing more and more fully that its proper business is to oversee and coordinate those seemingly separate groups of scientific truths which scientific specialists have not the leisure, and often neither the desire nor the ability, to coordinate. And obviously the philosophy most completely organized after this manner, constitutes the most complete integration of correspondences between the order of conceptions and the order of phenomena. It constitutes an integral body of knowledge, the various members of which are at once more distinctly demarcated from each other and more intimately dependent upon each other than in any previous system.

Thus, in accordance with the expectation held out in an earlier chapter, we find that "from the earliest traceable cosmical changes down to the latest products of civilization," there has been going on, and is going on, a ceaseless process of change, of which the main features are simple enough to be clearly deducible from the known physical properties of the universe, but of which the stupendous grandeur is such as to baffle the most strenuous efforts alike of reason and of imagination to follow it out in all its concrete details. Thus, too, we find ourselves amply rewarded for the hope with which we set out upon our inquiry,—namely, that in henceforth abandoning vain ontological speculation we were by no means about to dethrone Philosophy, but were on the point of winning for it even a goodlier realm than that which metaphysics had assigned to it. For in comparison with the sublime synthesis of truths which the foregoing chapters have but unworthily interpreted, all previous philosophic speculation seems fragmentary, crude and unsatisfying. To no other theory of things yet devised by the wit of man can we so well apply the enthusiastic exclamation of Giordano Bruno:—"Con questa filosofia l'anima mi s' aggrandisce, e mi si magnifica l'intelletto."

## *Cosmic Theism*

. . . . Upon the religious side of philosophy as well as upon its scientific side, the mind needs some fundamental theorem with reference to which it may occupy a positive attitude. According to the theory of life and intelligence expounded in previous chapters, mere scepticism can discharge but a provisional and temporary function. To the frivolously-minded the mere negation of belief may be in no wise distressing; but to the earnest inquirer the state of scepticism is accompanied by pain, which, here as elsewhere, is only subserving its proper function when it stimulates him to renewed search after a positive result. In the present transcendental inquiry it may indeed at first sight seem impossible to arrive at any positive result whatever, without ignoring the relativity of knowledge and proving recreant to the rigorous requirements of the objective method. Nevertheless, as was hinted at the close of the preceding chapter, this is not the case. Although the construction of a theology, or science of Deity, is a task which exceeds the powers of human intelligence, there is nevertheless one supremely important theorem in which science and religion find their permanent reconciliation, and by the assertion of which the mind is brought into a positive attitude of faith with reference to the Inscrutable Power manifested in the universe. The outcome of the present argument is not Atheism or Positivism, but a phase of Theism which is higher and purer, because relatively truer, than the anthropomorphic phase defended by theologians.

This all-important theorem in which science and religion are reconciled, is neither more nor less than the theorem which alone gives complete expression to the truth that all knowledge is relative. In the first chapter of this work it was elaborately proved that as soon as we attempt to frame any hypothesis whatever concerning the Absolute, or that which exists out of relation to our consciousness, we are instantly checkmated by alternative impossibilities of thought, and when we seek to learn why this is so, we are taught by a psychologic analysis that, from the very organization of our minds, and by reason of the very process by which intelligence has been evolved, we can form no cognition into which there do not enter the elements of *likeness, difference,* and *relation,*—so that the Absolute, as presenting none of these elements, is utterly and for ever unknowable. Translating this conclusion into more familiar language, we found it to mean, *first,* "that the Deity, in so far as absolute and infinite, is inscrutable by us, and that every hypothesis of ours concerning its nature and attributes can serve only to illustrate our mental impotence,"—and, *secondly,* "that the Universe in itself is likewise inscrutable; that the vast synthesis of forces without us, which in manifold contact with us is from infancy till the close of life continually arousing us to perceptive activity, can never be known by us as it exists objectively, but only as it affects our consciousness."

These are the closely-allied conclusions which were reached in our opening discussion. But since such abstruse theorems need to be taken one by one into the mind, and allowed one after the other to dwell there for a while, in order to be duly comprehended, it did not then seem desirable to encumber the exposition with any reference to the third statement in which these two are made to unite; nor, indeed, would it have been possible to illustrate adequately this third statement until we had defined our position in relation to the questions of phenomenality, of causation and deanthropomorphization, of the persistence of force, and of the evolution of the phenomenal world. But now, having obtained definite conclusions upon these points, we are at last enabled to present the case as a whole. Having seen that in certain senses the Deity and the Cosmos are alike inscrutable, let us now see if there is any sense in which it may be legitimately said that the Unknowable contained in our first theorem is identical with the Unknowable contained in our second theorem.

Upon what grounds did we assert the unknowableness of Deity? We were driven to the conclusion that Deity is unknowable, because that which exists independently of intelligence and out of relation to it, which presents neither *likeness, difference,* nor *relation,* cannot be cognized. Now by precisely the same process, we were driven to the conclusion that the Cosmos is unknowable, only in so far as it is absolute. It is only as existing independently of our intelligence and out of relation to it, that we can predict unknowableness of the Cosmos. As manifested to our intelligence, the Cosmos is the world of phenomena,—the realm of the knowable. We know stars and planets, we know the surface of our earth, we know life and mind in their various manifestations, individual and social. But, as we have seen, this vast aggregate of phenomena exists as such only in relation to our intelligence. Its *esse* is *percipi.* To this extent we have gone with Berkeley. But underlying this aggregate of phenomena, to whose extension we know no limit in space or time, we have found ourselves compelled to postulate an Absolute Reality,—a Something whose existence does not depend on the presence of a percipient mind, which existed before the genesis of intelligence, and would continue to exist though all intelligence were to vanish from the scene. Without making such a postulate, we concluded that it would be impossible to frame any theory whatever, either of subjective or of objective phenomena. Thus the theorem of the relativity of knowledge, when fully expressed, asserts that there exists a Something, of which all phenomena, as presented in consciousness, are manifestations, but concerning which we can know nothing save through its manifestations.

Let us now take a step further, and turning to the conclusions reached in the first chapter of Part II., let us inquire *what is the Force of which we there asserted the persistence?* "It is not," says Mr. Spencer, "the force we are immediately conscious of in our own muscular efforts; for this does not persist. As soon as an outstretched limb is relaxed, the sense of tension disappears. True, we assert that in the stone thrown or in the weight lifted, is exhibited the effect of this muscular tension; and that the force which has ceased to be present in our consciousness, exists elsewhere. But it does not exist elsewhere under any form cognizable by us. It was proved that though, on raising an object from the ground, we are obliged to think of its downward pull as equal and opposite to our upward pull; and though it is impossible to represent these pulls as equal without representing them as like in kind; yet, since their likeness in kind would imply in the object a sensation of muscular tension, which cannot be ascribed to it, we are compelled to admit that force as it exists out of our consciousness, is not force as we know it. Hence the force of which we assert persistence is that Absolute Force of which we are indefinitely conscious as the necessary correlate of the force we know. Thus by the persistence of force, we really mean the persistence of some Power which transcends our knowledge and conception. The manifestations, as occurring either in ourselves or outside of us, do not persist; but that which persists is the Unknown Cause of these manifestations. In other words, asserting the persistence of force is but another mode of asserting an Unconditioned Reality, without beginning or end." Thus as "a subjective analysis proved that while, by the very conditions of thought, we are prevented from knowing anything beyond relative being; yet that, by these very same conditions of thought, an indefinite consciousness of Absolute Being is necessitated,—so here, by objective analysis, we similarly find that the axiomatic truths of physical science unavoidably postulate Absolute Being as their common basis."

Combining, therefore, these mutually harmonious results, and stating the theorem of the persistence of force in terms of the theorem of the relativity of knowledge, we obtain the following formula:—*There exists a POWER, to which no limit in time or space is conceivable, of which all phenomena, as presented in consciousness, are manifestations, but which we can know only through these manifestations.* Here is a formula legitimately obtained by the employment of scientific methods, as the last result of a subjective analysis on the one hand, and of an objective analysis on the other hand. Yet this formula, which presents itself as the final outcome of a purely scientific inquiry, expresses also the fundamental truth of Theism,—the truth by which religious feeling is justified. The existence of God—the supreme truth asserted alike by Christianity and by inferior historic religions—is asserted with equal emphasis by that Cosmic Philosophy which seeks its data in science alone. Thus, as Mr. Lewes long ago observed, the remark of Comte, that the heavens declare no other glory than the glory of Hipparchos and Newton, and such others as have aided in detecting the order of sequence among celestial phenomena, seems as irrational to the scientific inquirer as it seems impious to the religious mind. The Cosmist may assert, as consistently as the Anthropomorphist, that "the undevout astronomer is mad." Though science must destroy mythology, it can never destroy religion; and to the astronomer of the future, as well as to the Psalmist of old, the heavens will declare the glory of God.

[*Here Fiske digresses to attack the positivistic faith of Comte. He praises Comte for recognizing the necessity of religion, but criticizes him for the anthropocentric religion which he set up. Fiske argues that if Comte's religion of humanity were to prevail it would mean the disintegration of religion since worship was an essential part of religion and always pointed toward something mysterious. By reducing the object of worship to a finite knowable such as humanity, Fiske contends Comte had eliminated the most important aspect of religion. He argues that science should push its research as far as possible, but that it must always acknowledge the existence of a boundless mystery beyond.*]

Thus we begin to realize, more vividly than theology could have taught us to realize, the utter absurdity of atheism. Thus is exhibited the prodigious silliness of Lalande, who informed mankind that he had swept the heavens with his telescope and found no God there,—as if God were an optical phenomenon! Thus, too, we see the poverty of that anthropomorphism which represents the infinite Deity as acting through calculation and contrivance, just as finite intelligence acts under the limitations imposed by its environment. And thus, finally, we perceive the hopeless error of the Positivist, who would give us a finite knowable, like Humanity, for an object of religious contemplation. The reasoning which demonstrates the relativity of knowledge, demonstrates also the failure of all such attempts to bind up religion in scientific formulas.

The anthropomorphic theist, habitually thinking of God as surrounded and limited by an environment or "objective datum," will urge that the doctrine here expounded is neither more nor less than Pantheism, or the identification of God with the totality of existence. So plausible does this objection appear, at first sight, that those who urge it cannot fairly be accused either of dulness of apprehension or of a desire to misrepresent. Nevertheless it needs but to look sharply into the matter, to see that the doctrine here expounded is utterly opposed to Pantheism. Though the word "pantheism" has been almost as undiscriminatingly bandied about among theological disputants as the word "atheism," it has still a well-defined metaphysical meaning which renders it inapplicable to a religious doctrine based upon the relativity of knowledge. In the pantheistic hypothesis the distinction between absolute and phenomenal existence is ignored and the world of phenomena is practically identified with Deity. Of this method of treating the problem the final outcome is to be seen in the metaphysics of Hegel, in which the process of evolution, vaguely apprehended, is described absolutely, as a process of change in the Deity, and in which God, as identified with the totality of phenomenal existence, is regarded as continually progressing from a state of comparative imperfection to a state of comparative perfection. Or, in other words—to reduce the case to the shape in which it was presented in the first chapter of this work—the Universe as identified with God, is regarded as self-evolved. Such a hypothesis, equally with that of the anthropomorphic theist, implicitly limits Deity with an "objective datum," and renders it finite; for, as Mr. Mansel has observed in another connection, "how can the Infinite become that which it was not from the first?" Obviously for the change an ulterior Cause is needed; and thus the pantheistic hypothesis resolves itself into the affirmation of a limited Knowable conditioned by an unlimited Unknowable,—but it is the former, and not the latter, which it deifies.

Hence to the query suggested at the beginning of this chapter, whether the Deity can be identified with the Cosmos, we must return a very different answer from that returned by the Pantheist. The "open secret," in so far as secret, is God,—in so far as open, is the World; but in thus regarding the ever-changing universe of phenomena as the multiform revelation of an Omnipresent Power, we can in no wise identify the Power with its manifestations. To do so would reduce the entire argument to nonsense. From first to last it has been implied that, while the universe is the manifestation of Deity, yet is Deity something more than the universe.

The doctrine which we have here expounded is, therefore, neither more nor less than Theism, in its most consistent and unqualified form. It is quite true that the word "theism," as ordinarily employed, connotes the ascription of an anthropomorphic personality to the Deity. But in this connotation there has been nothing like fixedness or uniformity. On the other hand the term has become less and less anthropomorphic in its connotations, from age to age, and in the sense in which it is here employed the deanthropomorphizing process is but carried one step farther. There was a time when theism seemed to require that God should be invested with a quasi-human body, just as it now seems to require that God should be invested with quasi-human intelligence and volition. But for us to concede the justice of the latter restriction would be as unphilosophical as it would have been for the early monotheists to concede the justice of the former. Just as the early Christians persisted in calling themselves theists while asserting that God dwells in a temple not made with hands, so may the modern philosopher persist in calling himself a theist while rejecting the arguments by which Voltaire and Paley have sought to limit and localize the Deity. Following out the parallel, we might characterize the doctrine here expounded as the "higher theism," in contrast with the "lower theism" taught in the current doctrine. Or in conformity with the nomenclature which has already done us such good service, we may still better characterize it as Cosmic Theism, in contrast with the Anthropomorphic Theism of those theologians who limit the Deity by an "objective datum."

This happy expression of Mr. Martineau's lays bare the anthropomorphic hypothesis to the very core, and when thoroughly considered, lets us into the secret of that superficial appearance of antagonism between Science and Religion which has disturbed so many theologians and misled so many scientific inquirers. Though as an act of lip-homage anthropomorphism asserts the infinitude and omnipotence of God, yet in reality it limits and localizes Him. Though it overtly acknowledges that "in Him we live and move and have our being," yet it tacitly belies this acknowledgment by the implication, which runs through all its reasonings, that God is a person localized in some unknown part of space, and that the universe is a "datum objective to God" in somewhat the same sense that a steam-engine is an "objective datum" to the engineer who works it. I do not say that such a conception would be avowed by any theologian: as thus overtly stated, it would no doubt be generally met with an emphatic disclaimer. Nevertheless this conception, whether avowed or disclaimed, lies at the bottom of all the arguments which theologians urge either against the theory of evolution or against any other theory which extends what is called "the domain of natural law." Take away this conception, and not only do their specific arguments lose all significance, but their entire position becomes meaningless: there ceases to be any reason for their opposing instead of welcoming the new theory. For if "extending the domain of natural law" be equivalent to "extending our knowledge of Divine action," what objection can the theologian logically make to this? Manifestly his hostile attitude is wholly prescribed by his belief, whether tacit or avowed, that the sphere of natural law and the sphere of Divine action are two different spheres, so that whatever is added to the former is taken from the latter. It is assumed that the universe is a sort of lifeless machine, which under ordinary circumstances works along without immediate Divine superintendence, in accordance with what are called natural laws, very much as the steam-engine works when once set going, in accordance with the harmoniously cooperating properties of its material structure. Only by occasional interposition, it is assumed, does God manifest his existence, —by originating organic life, or creating new species out of dust or out of nothing, or by causing prodigies to be performed within historic times for the edification of gaping multitudes. So deep-seated is this assumption—so vitally implicated is it with all the habits of thought which theology nurtures—that we sometimes hear it explicitly maintained that when natural law can be shown to be co-extensive with the whole of nature, then our belief in God will *ipso facto* be extinguished.

Such a position is no doubt as irreligious as it is unscientific; but it is not difficult to see how it has come to be so commonly maintained. Not only is it often apparently justified by the unphilosophical language of scientific men—especially of those shallow writers known as "materialists"—who speak of "natural law" as if it were something different from "Divine action;" but it is also the logical offspring of that primitive fetishism from which all our theology is descended. For as physical generalization began to diminish the sphere of action of the innumerable quasi-human agencies by which fetishism sought to account for natural phenomena, there could hardly fail to arise a belief in some sort of opposition between invariable law and quasi-human agency. On the one hand you have a set of facts that occur in fixed sequences, and so are not the result of anthropomorphic volition; on the other hand you have a set of facts that seem to occur according to no determinable order, and so are the result of anthropomorphic volition. The fetishistic thinker could not, of course, formulate the case in this abstract and generalized way; but there can be no doubt that a crudely felt antithesis of the kind here indicated must have been nearly coeval with the beginnings of physical generalization. Now the gradual summing up and blending together of all the primeval quasi-human agencies into one grand quasi-human Agency, could not at once do away with this antithesis. On the contrary, the antithesis would naturally remain as the generalized opposition between the realm of "invariable law" and the realm of "Divine originality." It would be superfluous to recount the various metaphysical shapes which this conception has assumed, in some of which Nature has even been personified as an intelligent and volitional agency, distinct from God, and working through law while God works through miracle. The result has been that, as scientific generalization has steadily extended the region of "natural law," the region which theology has assigned to "Divine action" has steadily diminished, until theological arguments have become insensibly pervaded by the curious assumption that the greater part of the universe is godless. For it is naively asked, if plants and animals have been naturally originated, if the world as a whole has been evolved and not created, and if human actions conform to law, what is there left for God to do? [27] If not formally repudiated, is he not thrust back into the past eternity, as an unknowable source of things, which is postulated for form's sake, but might as well, for all practical purposes, be omitted?

The reply is that the difficulty is one which theology has created for itself. It is not science, but theology, which has thrust back Divine action to some nameless point in the past eternity and left nothing for God to do in the present world. For the whole difficulty lies in the assumption of the material universe as a "datum objective to God," and in the consequent distinction between "Divine action" and "natural law,"—a distinction for which science is in nowise responsible. The tendency of modern scientific inquiry, whether working in the region of psychology or in that of transcendental physics, is to abolish this distinction, and to regard "natural law" as merely a synonym of "Divine action." And since Berkeley's time the conception of the material universe as a "datum objective to God" is one which can hardly be maintained on scientific grounds. It is scientific inquiry,

27 "Illos omnes Deum aut saltem Dei providentiam tollere putant, qui res et miracula per causas naturales explicant aut intelligere student." Spinoza, *Tractatus Theologicus-Politicus,* vi. *Opera,* iii. 86. "Οὐ γὰρ ἠνείχοντο τοὺς φυσικοὺς καὶ μετεωρολέσχας τότε καλουμένους, ὡς εἰς αἰτίας ἀλόγους καὶ δυνάμεις ἀπρονοήτους καὶ κατηναγκασμένα πάθη διατρίβοντας τὸ θεῖον." Plutarch, *Nikias,* cap. 23. The complaint, it will be seen, is the same in modern that it was in ancient times. Compare Plutarch, *Perikles,* cap. 6; Cicero, *Tusc. Disp.* i. 13, *Opera,* ed. Nobbe, tom. viii. p. 299.

working quite independently of theology, which has led us to the conclusion that all the dynamic phenomena of Nature constitute but the multiform revelation of an Omnipresent Power that is not identifiable with Nature. And in this conclusion there is no room left for the difficulty which baffles contemporary theology. The scientific inquirer may retort upon the theologian:—Once really adopt the conception of an ever-present God, without whom not a sparrow falls to the ground, and it becomes self-evident that the law of gravitation is but an expression of a particular mode of Divine action. And what is thus true of one law is true of all laws. The Anthropomorphist is naturally alarmed by the continual detection of new uniformities, and the discovery of order where before there seemed to be disorder; bcause his conception of Divine action has been historically derived from the superficial contrast between the seemingly irregular action of will and the more-obviously regular action of less complex phenomena. The Cosmist, on the other hand, in whose mind Divine action is identified with orderly action, and to whom a really irregular phenomenon would seem like the manifestation of some order-hating Ahriman, foresees in every possible extension of knowledge a fresh confirmation of his faith in God, and thus recognizes no antagonism between our duty as inquirers and our duty as worshippers. He will admit no such inherent and incurable viciousness in the constitution of things as is postulated by the anthropomorphic hypothesis. To him no part of the world is godless. He does not rest content with the conception of "an absentee God, sitting idle, ever since the first Sabbath, at the outside of his universe, and 'seeing it go;'" for he has learned, with Carlyle, "that this fair universe, were it in the meanest province thereof, is in very deed the star-domed City of God; that through every star, through every grass-blade, and most through every living soul, the glory of a present God still beams." [28]

[28] *Sartor Resartus,* bk. ii. chap. vii; bk. iii. chap. viii.

# XVIII

## Chauncey Wright

### 1830–1875

Born in Northampton, Mass. Graduated from Harvard, 1852. Computer for the *American Ephemeris and Nautical Almanac,* 1852–70. Taught for short time during this period in school for girls which Louis Agassiz had founded. Recording Secretary of the American Academy of Arts and Sciences, 1863–70. Published articles in *North American Review, Mathematical Monthly, Nation* and other periodicals. Delivered University Lectures at Harvard on psychology, 1870. Made Instructor in Mathematical Physics at Harvard, 1874. Died in Cambridge.

Transitional figures often pass into oblivion because their thought lacks the systematization characteristic of those who precede and follow. Chauncey Wright was a man of this type. He frowned upon the Agassiz's, Spencers and Fiskes who sought either to fit science into accepted ideologies or to build new ideologies upon hypothetical scientific knowledge. He opened the way for the development of radical empiricism and naturalism without defining their boundaries or expanding their implications. His critical acumen was probably unparalleled in his generation; his constructive contributions were few. Having critically assailed a passing tendency in thought with acute discrimination he sketched only the outlines of another way of thinking which he felt was more in line with scientific procedure. While the works of Peirce and James and the later empiricists are well known, Wright's essays and reviews have been passed over almost unnoticed. Personal factors have added to this obscurity. He was never interested in developing a system for others to adopt and perpetuate, partly because of natural indolence, partly because of his preference for amiable conversation and discussion over the written word and partly because of his distrust of any philosophy which went beyond the boundaries of scientific inquiry. What essays he did write suffered from his insufficient attention to literary form. They abounded in closely-woven argument and allusion not easily understood because of the unrecorded interludes of his thought.

Wright was more a Socrates than a Plato among his contemporaries. Peirce, in speaking of "The Metaphysical Club" to which he, James, Oliver Wendell Holmes, Jr., Fiske, Wright and others belonged, referred to Wright as "our boxing-master whom we—and I particularly—used to face to be severely pummelled." [1] Fiske and Peirce both considered him to have a mind comparable to that of John Stuart Mill. Fiske referred with keen delight to the long arguments in which they were wont to engage, one at least lasting to the break of dawn, while in peripatetic style they walked back and forth between Fiske's gate and Wright's, not able to terminate such stimulating controversy.[2] He thought Wright's mental powers to be almost unexcelled. He said, "A mind more placid in its working, more unalloyed by emotional prejudice or less solicited by the various temptations of speculation, I have never known. Judicial candour and rectitude of inference were with him inborn." [3] Combined with his acute intelligence was an absence of emotional excitability and of aesthetic interests. Fiske observed after Wright's return from Europe that "he recalled sundry historic streets of London and Paris only as spots where some happy generalization had occurred to him." [4] William James considered him to be a good example of tough-minded empiricism and said of him, "Never in a human head was contemplation more separated from desire." [5] For the major part of his life Wright lived as a bachelor in Cambridge, working on mathematics, physics and biology, with all his studies overarched by an ever-present philosophical urge. His conviction of the necessity of precision in thought comparable to the exactitude of science brought out his exceptional critical powers. He was a man who, above all else, would not be "taken in." No idea was too true to go unchallenged, no principle too certain to go unquestioned.

Emerson was Wright's favorite author in college but he left no permanent influence on his thinking unless it be by reaction. Bacon was more to his later liking; he accepted Bacon's criticism of the inclination to anticipate nature and thought Bacon's chief contribution was the emancipation of science from theological and metaphysical considerations. Sir William Hamilton interested him and here again his attention was called to the fallacy of assuming the

[1] Hartshorne, Charles and Weiss, Paul (editors): *Collected Papers of Charles Sanders Peirce.* V, 8.

[2] Clark, John Spencer: *The Life and Letters of John Fiske.* I, 333.

[3] Fiske, John: *Darwinism: and Other Essays.* 85.

[4] Ibid. 108.

[5] James, William: *Collected Essays and Reviews.* 23.

content of thinking to be descriptive of the order of existence. John Stuart Mill further attracted him to the empirical method and left as strong an impression on him as any philosopher he had read. Then came Darwin whose research he regarded as an outstanding example of real scientific method. He became an enthusiastic Darwinian within a year after the appearance of the *Origin of Species* in 1859.

Science meant to Wright the impartial search for factual knowledge verified by sensory experience. The search for factual knowledge itself was no distinguishing mark of modern science; ever since the early Greeks that search had been common to mankind. What really made possible the superiority of modern science was its diligent resort to verification of all theories proposed for acceptance. Wright's positivism, while not derived from Comte, grew out of the same desire to rescue the pursuit of truth from the vagaries of emotion and tradition. He accepted Comte's classification of thought in three stages (the theological, metaphysical and scientific) but emphasized that only their beginnings were successive and that in any developed culture they coexisted as different modes of approach. He was critical of the traditional distinction between subjective and objective methods. He preferred to speak of subjective and objective motives instead, regarding the attitude of the observer as of great importance in investigation of any kind.

> By a subjective motive we mean one having its origin in natural universal human interests and emotions, which existed before philosophy was born, which continue to exist in the maturity of philosophy, and determine the character of an important and by no means defunct order of human speculation. By an objective motive we mean one having an empirical origin, arising in the course of an inquiry; springing from interests which are defined by what we already know, and not by what we have always felt,—interests which depend on acquired knowledge, and not on natural desires and emotions.[6]

Of Comte's three phases of thought, Wright regarded the third, the scientific or critical, as the only one worthy of serious pursuit. The relationships of philosophy and science were not always clear in Wright's thought. Sometimes he seemed to link philosophy so closely with science as to make them almost identical. At other times he seemed to conceive of philosophy as the criticism of procedures, concepts and principles. At still other times he seemed to regard philosophy as the reflective use of science in the service of man's moral and aesthetic interests. The following statement in which he accepted the

[6] *Philosophical Discussions*. 49.

term positivism for his position (although in other places he made it clear that there were different kinds of positivism and that his was not the same as Comte's in many regards) is perhaps as clear a formulation of his conception of philosophy as can be found.

> Positivism, to be sure, so far as it pretends to be a philosophy at all, is more than the body of the sciences. It must be a system of the universal methods, hypotheses, and principles which are founded on them, and if not a universal science, in an absolute sense, yet must be coextensive with actual knowledge, and exhibit the consilience of the sciences.[7]

Wright attempted to distinguish clearly between the metaphysical mode of thought (which was a defense of theological doctrines) and the scientific mode (which was objective in motive and empirical in method). He thought there was an analogous distinction between poetry and science. Metaphysics and poetry were largely reflections of accepted thoughts and feelings supposedly habitual and useful; science reflected man's curiosity and desire to understand the phenomena of nature as they appeared in the light of observation and repeatable experience. He charged language with being responsible for much of the confusion in metaphysical thinking. Such words as substance, cause, matter and mind were associated in metaphysics with inscrutable powers working upon the world; real existence was to be known through its manifestations in phenomena. This "ontological faith" was "a survival of the barbarian's feelings and notions of phenomena as the outward show of hidden powers in things." [8] Philosophy should give up its unproductive search for first and final causes and content itself with the experiences of nature which it was capable of interpreting. "It is possible that laws exist absolutely universal, binding fate and infinite power as well as speech and the intelligible use of words; but it is not possible that the analytical processes of any finite intellect should discover what particular laws these are." [9] He did, however, regard the universality of physical causation as a basic principle of all science.

> The very hope of experimental philosophy, its expectation of constructing the sciences into a true philosophy of nature, is based on the induction, or, if you please, the *a priori* presumption, that physical causation is universal; that the constitution of nature is written in its actual manifestations, and needs only to be deciphered by experimental and inductive research; that it is not a latent invisible writ-

[7] *Letters.* 141.
[8] *Philosophical Discussions.* 240.
[9] Ibid. 229.

ing, to be brought out by the magic of mental anticipation or metaphysical meditation.[10]

Aside from his positivism, Wright's major contribution to thought was the application of his method to the problem of the nature of mind in "The Evolution of Self-consciousness," one of his later essays. Man, to him, was a natural organism. His existence was to be understood on the same basis as any other object of study in the natural world. Thought was neither the creation of a spiritual entity nor self-created; it was the natural outgrowth of biological functions of a more elementary kind. Animals were gifted with sensation, memory and imagination; consciousness and reflection were not distinct faculties but higher developments of these originally animal powers. The basic distinction between man and the animal was one of degree, not of quality. "For differences of degrees in causes may make differences of kinds in effect." [11] Differences of kind in the study of inorganic and organic matter were terms of classification rather than independent entities; the line of demarcation between one and the other was ill-defined. Instinct and intelligence, while seemingly different in their extremities, were interwoven in general to such an extent as to make it impossible to distinguish between them accurately. Again, he opposed the theories of "idealism" and "natural realism" on the basis that they made too sharp a distinction between subject and object. "Idealism" held that the conscious subject was immediately known, "natural realism" that it was equally known along with the object. While expressing qualified sympathy with "natural realism," Wright held that subject and object were undistinguished in consciousness until by reflection we classified and categorized the originally neutral content of experience.

Thus, the sensations of sound and color and taste and pleasure and pain, and the emotions of hope and fear and love and hate, *if not yet referred to their causes, or even classified as sensations and emotions,* belong to neither world exclusively.[12]

As Kennedy has pointed out, this was a doctrine similar to the concept of "pure experience" which James developed later.[13] Subject and object were only "names of the highest classes, and . . . not the names of inconceivable substrata of phenomena." [14]

10 *Philosophical Discussions.* 131.
11 Ibid. 217. Below, p. 435.
12 Ibid. 231.
13 "The Pragmatic Naturalism of Chauncey Wright." 492–5.
14 *Philosophical Discussions.* 234.

Remembering Wright's positivism and his genetic account of reflection it is easy to understand his opposition to any religious position purporting to give an account of existence. Pointing out that Agassiz had rejected the argument of the *Origin of Species* because it was opposed to his favorite doctrines, Wright contended that its conclusions "render his essay on Classification a useless and mistaken speculation." [15] His own religious position was never clearly defined although its outlines can be found in his correspondence; he expressed agnosticism regarding the existence of deity, discredited belief in immortality and contended that whatever dynamic, incentive and devotion the religions of the past had inspired could as easily be acquired through the pursuit of scientific and practical objectives from the standpoint of experience. When asked by Francis Abbot to write an essay on "The Religious Aspects of Positivism" to be printed in a volume he had projected, he declined the invitation on the ground that such an essay "would not properly come from one who is a positivist in spite of religion; it should rather come from some one who is religious in spite of his positivism." [16]

Convinced of the universality of physical causation, Wright attacked numerous forms of teleology including that of Paley and of the Bridgewater Treatises which Agassiz admired so much. He held that the failure of theology and metaphysics in the past was due to the fact that "Their aim was to *prove* truth, not to discover it,—to reduce opinions and ideas which had the warrant of religious associations to the simplicity and consistency of truth." [17] He doubted the existence of any ultimate coherence in cosmic events. He was inclined to think the rationality of events only temporary, there being basically an eddying back and forth of cosmic forces. The development of reflection, for example, was not a planned order; it was, logically, an accident. The name he gave to this position was that of "cosmical weather," indicating by analogy the uncertainty of cosmic affairs. He rejected the nebular hypothesis as unproved and as a scientific hypothesis by which the theologically-minded hoped to establish the orderliness of the earth's creation. While he accepted Darwin's evolutionary position (which he preferred to call the "derivative hypothesis") and was in thorough accord with Darwin's method, he opposed the doctrine of evolution when applied generally to the universe. He was critical of Spencer whom he felt to be a victim of the emotional desire to dramatize the movement of cosmic affairs in an evolutionary train. The doctrine of eternal prog-

[15] *Letters.* 43.
[16] Ibid. 142.
[17] *Philosophical Discussions.* 53.

ress, associated with evolution, was again an example of man's desire to read into the universe a teleological meaning, whereas the seeming rationality of things was actually only a result of "cosmical weather."

> For it is denied by the physical philosopher that causes and effects in natural phenomena can be interpreted into the terms of natural theology by any key which science affords. . . . The belief on other grounds that there *are* final causes, that the universe exists for some purpose, is one thing; but the belief that science discloses, or even that science can disclose, what this purpose is, is quite a different thing.[18]

This tychistic emphasis in Wright's thinking was perhaps the basis for the more developed tychism of Peirce and James.

There was a decided pragmatic emphasis in Wright. His empiricism was pointed toward consequents rather than antecedents. He argued, in true Baconian style, that the object of education was to provide useful knowledge. Knowledge was useful, however, if it led to other and wider ranges of knowledge and to the discipline of the mind as well as to mere "bread and butter." "What we call the objective value of a science is what should be meant by calling it 'useful knowledge.' "[19]

Although Wright never developed a moral philosophy in systematic form, what he did say to numerous correspondents was thoroughly in accord with his empirical and tychistic position. He was largely influenced by Mill's utilitarianism. Remarks such as the following were common. "There is no other test of what duty is in general, and no higher or more religious motive to it, than that it conduces to the highest good of the greatest number."[20] He preferred the Golden Mean to the Golden Rule. He suggested the proper approach to ethics was through an understanding of man's essential capacities. If it was legitimate in any sense to speak of a final cause in relation to man, its only possible interpretation was in terms of Aristotle's realization of potentialities. The relativism which pervaded his moral thought made him an interesting precursor of pragmatic ethics.

Wright's position was the most thoroughgoing expression of empirical naturalism up to this time in American philosophy. He was always quick to detect any tendency, on the part of his best friends as well as of writers he had read, toward analysis which went beyond the categories of experience. Fiske said, "He went as far as it was possible for a human thinker to go toward a philosophy which should take no

18 *Philosophical Discussions*. 36.
19 Ibid. 281.
20 *Letters*. 118.

note of anything beyond the content of observed facts. He always kept the razor of Occam uncased and ready for use. . . ." [21] This statement may be rather strong but it does indicate, coming from one of Wright's close associates, his positivistic tendency and the rigor with which he held his ground. He had, however, a very sympathetic mind and was ever eager to explain the most difficult ideas in science and philosophy to anyone who desired to understand them. An example of his lively manner and sense of humor is to be found in his letter to Miss Catherine Howard who wished to have him recommend a book on psychology for young ladies. He recommended Dugald Stewart's *Elements of the Philosophy of the Human Mind* as the best book, of many poor ones, for this purpose.

> It is an elegantly shallow treatise, not difficult to understand, because superficial; and it ought to be rather interesting to beginners. Professor Stewart was a good man, and is doubtless now in heaven. He wrote on philosophy in the interest of all that is lovely and of good report. There are no heresies in his book.[22]

Naturalism had a temporary foothold in America during the Age of Reason. From the time of its recurrence after the advent of evolutionary ideas, and particularly from Chauncey Wright on, it has been an increasingly influential factor in American thought. This later naturalism was not simply a revival of the former. There was in general a substitution of agnosticism for deism, of a purely natural world for a natural world still tinged with the supernatural, of systematic observation and verification for reason understood as enlightened common sense, and of tychism for determinism. Through his personal influence, more than through his writings, Wright played an important part in the reëstablishment of this movement.

## REFERENCES

Wright, Chauncey: *Philosophical Discussions: with a Biographical Sketch of the Author by Charles Eliot Norton.* New York: Henry Holt and Co., 1877.

Thayer, J. B. (editor): *Letters of Chauncey Wright: with Some Account of his Life.* Cambridge, 1878. (The best account of Wright's intellectual interests and character is by his life-long friend, E. W. Gurney. 361–83.)

Fiske, John: "Chauncey Wright," *Darwinism: and Other Essays.* New edition, revised and enlarged. Boston: Houghton Mifflin Co., 1888. 79–110.

[21] Fiske: op. cit. 104.
[22] *Letters.* 119.

James, William: "Chauncey Wright," *Collected Essays and Reviews.* New York: Longmans, Green and Co., 1920. 20–5.

Kennedy, Gail: "The Pragmatic Naturalism of Chauncey Wright," *Studies in the History of Ideas.* 3 vols. New York: Columbia University Press. III (1935) 477–503.

* * *

---

* * *

## EVOLUTION OF SELF-CONSCIOUSNESS [23]

It has come to be understood, and very generally allowed, that the conception of the origin of man as an animal race, as well as the origin of individual men within it, in accordance with the continuity of organic development maintained in the theory of evolution, does not involve any very serious difficulties, or difficulties so great as are presented by any other hypothesis of this origin, not excepting that of "special creation";—if that can be properly called a hypothesis, which is, in fact, a resumption of all the difficulties of natural explanation, assuming them to be insuperable and summarizing them under a single positive name. Yet in this evolution, the birth of self-consciousness is still thought by many to be a step not following from antecedent conditions in "nature," except in an incidental manner, or in so far only as "natural" antecedents have prepared the way for the "supernatural" advent of the self-conscious soul.

Independently of the form of expression, and of the false sentiment which is the motive of the antithesis in this familiar conception, or independently of its mystical interest, which has given to the words "natural" and "supernatural" their commonly accepted meanings, there is a foundation of scientific truth in the conception. For the word "evolution" conveys a false impression to the imagination, not really intended in the scientific use of it. It misleads by suggesting a continuity in the *kinds* of powers and functions in living beings, that is, by suggesting transition by insensible steps from one *kind* to another, as well as in the *degrees* of their importance and exercise at different stages of development. The truth is, on the contrary, that according to the theory of evolution, new uses of old powers arise discontinuously both in the

[23] *Philosophical Discussions.* 199–222. This essay originally appeared in the *North American Review* in 1873. Footnotes have been omitted since they added little to the content of the argument.

bodily and mental natures of the animal, and in its individual developments, as well as in the development of its race, although, at their rise, these uses are small and of the smallest importance to life. They seem merged in the powers to which they are incident, and seem also merged in the special purposes or functions in which, however, they really have no part, and which are no parts of them. Their services or functions in life, though realized only incidentally at first, and in the feeblest degree, are just as distinct as they afterwards come to appear in their fullest development. The new uses are related to older powers only as *accidents,* so far as the special services of the older powers are concerned, although, from the more general point of view of natural law, their relations to older uses have not the character of accidents, since these relations are, for the most part, determined by universal properties and laws, which are not specially related to the needs and conditions of living beings. Thus the uses of limbs for swimming, crawling, walking, leaping, climbing, and flying are distinct uses, and are related to each other only through the general mechanical principles of locomotion, through which some one use, in its first exercise, may be incident to some other, though, in its full exercise and perfection of special service, it is independent of the other, or has only a common dependence with the other or more general conditions.

Many mental as well as bodily powers thus have mixed natures, or independent uses; as, for example, the powers of the voice to call and allure, to warn and repel, and its uses in music and language; or the numerous uses of the human hand in services of strength and dexterity. And, on the contrary, the same uses are, in some cases, realized by independent organs as, for example, respiration in water and in the air by gills and lungs, or flight by means of fins, feathers, and webs. The appearance of a really new power in *nature* (using this word in the wide meaning attached to it in science), the power of flight in the first birds, for example, is only involved potentially in previous phenomena. In the same way, no act of self-consciousness, however elementary, may have been realized before man's first self-conscious act in the animal world; yet the act may have been involved potentially in pre-existing powers or causes. The derivation of this power, supposing it to have been observed by a finite angelic (not animal) intelligence, could not have been foreseen to be involved in the mental causes, on the conjunction of which it might, nevertheless, have been seen to depend. The angelic observation would have been a purely empirical one. The possibility of a subsequent analysis of these causes by the self-conscious animal himself, which would afford an explanation of their agency, by referring it to a rational combination of simpler elements in them, would not alter the case to the angelic intelligence, just as a rational explanation of flight could not be reached by such an intelligence as a consequence of known mechanical laws; since these laws are also animal conditions, or rather are more general and material ones, of which our angelic, spherical intelligence is not supposed to have had any experience. Its observation of the conditions of animal flight would thus also be empirical; for an unembodied spirit cannot be supposed to analyze out of its general experiences the mechanical conditions of movement in animal bodies, nor, on the other hand, to be any more able than the mystic appears to be to analyze the conditions of its own intelligence out of its experiences of animal minds.

The forces and laws of molecular physics are similarly related to actual human intelligence. Sub-sensible properties and powers can only be empirically known, though they are "visualized" in the *hypotheses* of molecular movements and forces. Experimental science, as in chemistry, is full of examples of the discovery of new properties or new powers, which, so far as the conditions of their appearance were previously known, did not follow from antecedent conditions, except in an incidental manner,—that is, in a manner *not then foreseen* to be involved in them; and these effects became afterwards predictable from what had become known to be their antecedent conditions only by the empirical laws or rules which inductive experimentation had established. Nevertheless, the phenomena of the physical or chemical laboratory, however new or unprecedented, are very far from having the character of miracles, in the sense of supernatural events. They are still *natural* events; for, to the scientific imagination, *nature* means more than the continuance or actual repetition of the properties and productions involved in the course of ordinary events, or more than the *inheritance* and reappearance of that which appears in consequence of powers which have made it appear before. It means, in general, those kinds of effects which, though they may have appeared but once in the whole history of the world, yet appear dependent on conjunctions of causes which *would always* be followed by them. One experiment is sometimes, in some branches of science, (as a wide induction has found it to be in chemistry, for example,) sufficient to determine such a dependence, though the particular law so determined is a wholly empirical one; and the history of science has examples of such single experiments, or short series of experiments, made on general principles of experimentation, for the purpose of ascertaining empirical facts or laws, qualities, or relations, which are, nevertheless, generalized as universal ones. Certain "physical constants," so called, were so determined, and are applied in scientific inference with the same unhesitating confidence as that inspired by the familiarly exemplified and more elementary "laws of nature," or even by axioms. Scientific research implies the *potential* existence of the natures, classes, or kinds of effects which experiment brings to light through instances, and for which it also determines, in accordance with inductive methods, the previously unknown conditions of their appearance. This research implies the *latent* kinds or natures which mystical research contemplates (erroneously, in some, at least, of its meditations) under the name of "the supernatural."

To make any event or power supernatural in the mystic's regard requires, however, not merely that it shall be isolated and unparalleled in nature, but that it shall have more than an ordinary, or merely scientific, interest to the mystic's or to the *human* mind. The distinctively human or self-conscious interest, or sentiment, of self-consciousness gives an emphasis to the contrast named "natural and supernatural," through which mysticism is led to its speculations or assumptions of correspondingly emphatic contrasts in real existences. For mysticism is a speculation interpreting as matters of fact, or real existences outside of consciousness, impressions which are only determined within it by emphasis of attention or feeling. It is for the purpose of deepening still more, or to the utmost that its interest suggests, the really profound distinction between human and animal consciousness, or for the purpose of making the distinction *absolute,* of deepening this gulf into an unfathomable and impassable one, that mysticism appears to be moved to its speculations, and has imbued most philosophy and polite learning with its conceptions. Mental philosophy, or metaphysics, has, consequently, come down to us from ancient times least affected by the speculative interests and methods of modern science. Mysticism still reigns over the science of the mind, though its theory in general, or what is common to all theories called mystical, is very vague, and obscure even in the exclusively religious applications of the term. This vagueness has given rise to the more extended use and understanding of the term as it is here employed, which indicates little else than the generally apprehended *motive* of its speculations, or the feelings allied to all its forms of conception. These centre in the feeling of absolute worthiness in self-consciousness, as the source, and at the same time the perfection of existence and power. The naturalist's observations on the minds of men and animals are impertinences of the least possible interest to this sense of worth, very much as the geologist's observations are generally to the speculator who seeks in the earth for hidden mineral treasures.

Mysticism in mental philosophy has apparently gained, so far as it has been materially affected by such observations, a relative external strength, dependent on the real feebleness of the opposition it has generally met with from lovers of animals and from empirical observers and thinkers, in whom a generous sympathy with the manifestations of mind in animals and a disposition to do justice to them have been more conspicuous than the qualities of clearness or consistency. For, in the comparisons which they have attempted they have generally sought to break down the really well-founded distinctions of human and animal intelligence, and have sought to discredit the theory of them in this way, rather than by substituting for it a rational, scientific account of what is real in them. The ultimate metaphysical mystery which denies all comparison, and pronounces man a paragon in the kinds, as well the degrees, of his mental faculties, is, as a solution, certainly *simpler,* whatever other scientific excellence it may lack, than any solution that the difficulties of a true scientific comparison are likely to receive.

It is not in a strictly empirical way that this comparison can be clearly and effectively made, but rather by a critical re-examination of the phenomena of self-consciousness in themselves, with reference to their possible evolution from powers obviously common to all animal intelligences, or with reference to their potential, though not less natural, existence in mental causes, which could not have been known to involve them before their actual manifestation, but may, nevertheless, be found to do so by an analysis of these causes into the more general conditions of mental phenomena. Mystical metaphysics should be met by scientific inquiries on its own ground, that is, dogmatically, or by theory, since it despises the facts of empirical observation, or attributes them to shallowness, misinterpretation, or errors of observation, and contents itself with its strength as a system, and its impregnable self-consistency. Only an explanation of the phenomena of human consciousness, equally clear and self-consistent with its own, and one which, though not so simple, is yet more in accordance with the facts of a wider induction, could equal it in strength. But this might still be expected as the result of an examination of mental phenomena from the point of view of true science; since many modern sciences afford examples of similar triumphs over equally ancient, simple, and apparently impregnable doctrines. The history of science is full, indeed, of illustrations of the impotence, on one hand, of exceptional and isolated facts against established theory, and of the power, on the other hand, of their organization in new theories to revolutionize beliefs. The physical doctrine of a *plenum,* the doctrine of epicycles and vortices in astronomy, the corpuscular theory of optics, that of cataclysms in geology, and that of special creations in biology, each gave way, not absolutely through its intrinsic weakness, but through the greater success of a rival theory which superseded it. A sketch only is attempted in this essay of some of the results of such an examination into the psychological conditions, or antecedents, of the phenomena of self-consciousness; an examination which does not aim at diminishing, on the one hand, the real contrasts of mental powers in men and animals, nor at avoiding difficulties, on the other, by magnifying them beyond the reach of comparison.

The terms "science" and "scientific" have come, in modern times, to have so wide a range of application, and so vague a meaning, that (like many other terms, not only in common speech, but also in philosophy and in various branches of learning, which have come down to us through varying usages) they would oppose great difficulties to any attempts at defining them by *genus* and difference, or otherwise than by enumerating the branches of knowledge and the facts, or relations of the facts, to which usage has affixed them as names. Precision in proper definition being then impossible, it is yet possible to give to these terms so general a meaning as to cover all the knowledge to which they are usually applied, and still to exclude much besides. As the terms thus defined coincide with what I propose to show as the character of the knowledge peculiar to men, or which distinguishes the minds of men from those of other animals, I will begin with this definition. In science and in scientific facts there is implied a conscious purpose of including particular facts under general facts, and the less general under the more general ones. Science, in the modern use of the term, consists, essentially, of a knowledge of things and events either as effects of general causes, or as instances of general classes, rules, or laws; or even as isolated facts of which the class, law, rule, or cause is sought. The conscious purpose of arriving at general facts and at an adequate statement of them in language, or of bringing particular facts under explicit general ones, determines for any knowledge a scientific character.

Many of our knowledges and judgments from experience in practical matters are not so reduced, or sought to be reduced, to explicit principles, or have not a theoretical form, since the major premises, or general principles, of our judgments are not consciously generalized by us in forms of speech. Even matters not strictly practical, or which would be merely theoretical in their bearing on conduct, if reduced to a scientific form, like many of the judgments of common-sense, for example, are not consciously referred by us to explicit principles, though derived, like science, from experience, and even from special kinds of experience, like that of a man of business, or that of a professional adept. We are often led by being conscious of a sign of anything to believe in the existence of the thing itself, either past, present, or prospective, without having any distinct and general apprehension of the connection of the sign and thing, or any recognition of the sign under the general character of a sign. Not only are the judgments of common-sense in men, both the inherited and acquired ones, devoid of heads, or major premises (such as "All men are mortal"), in deductive inference, and devoid also of distinctly remembered details of experience in the inferences of induction, but it is highly probable that this is all but exclusively the character of the knowledges and judgments of the lower animals. Language, strictly so called, which some of these animals also have, or signs *purposely used* for communication, is not only required for scientific knowledge, but a second step of generalization is needed, and is made through reflection, by which this use of a sign is itself made an object of attention, and the sign is recognized in its general relations to what it signifies, and to what it has signified in the past, and will signify in the future. It is highly improbable that such a knowledge of knowledge, or such a *re*-cognition, belongs in any considerable, or effective, degree to even the most intelligent of the lower animals, or even to the lowest of the human race. This is what is properly meant by being "rational," or being a "rational animal." It is what I have preferred to call "scientific" knowledge; since the growing vagueness and breadth of application common to all ill-comprehended words (like "Positivism" in recent times) have given to "scientific" the meaning probably attached at first to "rational." This knowledge comes from reflecting on what we know in the common-sense, or semi-instinctive form, or making what we know a field of renewed research, observation, and analysis in the generalization of major premises. The line of distinction between such results of reflection, or between scientific knowledge and the common-sense form of knowledge, is not simply the dividing line between the minds of men and other animals; but is that which divides the knowledge produced by outward attention from that which is further produced by reflective attention. The former, throughout a considerable range of the higher intelligent animals, involves veritable judgments of a complex sort. It involves combinations of minor premises leading to conclusions through implicit major premises in the enthymematic reasonings, commonly employed in inferences from signs and likelihoods, as in prognostications of the weather, or in orientations with many animals. This knowledge belongs both to men and to the animals next to men in intelligence, though in unequal degrees.

So far as logicians are correct in regarding an enthymeme as a reasoning independently of its statement in words; or in regarding as a rational process the passing from such a sign as the human nature of Socrates to the inference that he will die, through the data of experience concerning the mortality of other men,—the data which are neither distinctly remembered in detail nor generalized explicitly in the formula, "all men are mortal," but are effective only in making mortality a more or less clearly understood part of the human nature, that is, in making it one of the attributes *suggested* by the name "man," yet not separated from the essential attributes by the contrasts of subject and attributes in real predication,—so far, I say, as this can be regarded as a reasoning, or a rational process, so far observation shows that the more intelligent dumb animals reason, or are rational. But this involves great vagueness or want of that precision in the use of signs which the antitheses of essential and accidental attributes and that of proper predication secure. There is little, or no, evidence to show that the animals which learn, to some extent, to comprehend human speech have an analytical comprehension of real general propositions, or of propositions in which both subject and predicate are general terms and differ in meaning. A merely verbal general proposition, declaring only the equivalence of two general names, might be comprehended by such minds, if it could be made of sufficient interest to attract their attention. But this is extremely doubtful, and it would not be as a *proposition,* with its contrasts of essential and added elements of conception that it would be comprehended. It would be, in effect, only repeating in succession two general names of the same class of objects. Such minds could, doubtless, comprehend a single class of objects or an indefinite number of resembling things by several names; that is, several signs of such a class would recall it to their thoughts, or revive a representative image of it; and they would thus be aware of the equivalence of these signs; but they would not attach precision of meaning and different degrees of generality to them, or regard one name as the name or sign of another name; as when we define a triangle to be a rectilinear figure, and a figure of three sides.

Only one degree of generality is, however, essential to inference from signs, or in enthymematic reasoning. Moreover, language in its relation to thought does not consist exclusively of spoken, or written, or imagined words, but of signs in general, and, essentially, of internal images or successions of images, which are the representative imaginations of objects and their relations; imaginations which severally stand for each and all of the particular objects or relations of a *kind*. Such are the visual imaginations called up by spoken or written concrete general names of visible objects, as "dog" or "tree"; which are vague and feeble as images, but effective as notative, directive, or guiding elements in thought. These are the internal signs of things and events, and are instruments of thought in judgment and reasoning, not only with dumb animals but also with men, in whom they are supplemented, rather than supplanted, by names. But being of feeble intensity, and little under the influence of distinct attention or control of the will, compared to actual perceptions and to the voluntary movements of utterance and gesture, their nature has been but dimly understood even by metaphysicians, who are still divided into two schools in logic,—the conceptualists and the nominalists. The "concepts" of the former are really composed of these vague and feeble notative images, or groups of images, to which clearness and distinctness of attention are given by their associations with outward (usually vocal) signs. Hence a second degree of observation and generalization upon these images, as objects in reflective thought, cannot be readily realized independently of what would be the results of such observations, namely, their associations with outward signs. Even in the most intelligent dumb animal they are probably so feeble that they cannot be associated with outward signs in such a manner as to make these distinctly appear as substitutes, or signs equivalent to them.

So far as images act in governing trains of thought and reasoning, they act as signs; but, with reference to the more vivid outward signs, they are, in the animal mind, merged in the things signified, like stars in the light of the sun. Hence, language, in its narrower sense, as the instrument of reflective thought, appears to depend directly on the intensity of significant, or representative, images; since the power to attend to these and intensify them still further, at the same time that an equivalent outward sign is an object of attention, would appear to depend solely on the relative intensities of the two states, or on the relations of intensity in perception and imagination, or in original and revived impressions. The direct power of attention to intensify a revived impression in imagination does not appear to be different in kind from the power of attention in perception, or in outward impressions generally. But this direct power would be obviously aided by the indirect action of attention when fixed by an outward sign, provided attention could be directed to both at the same time; as a single glance may comprehend in one field of view the moon or the brighter planets and the sun, since the moon or planet is not hidden like the stars, by the glare of day.

As soon, then, as the progress of animal intelligence through an extension of the range in its powers of memory, or in revived impressions, together with a corresponding increase in the vividness of these impressions, has reached a certain point (a progress in itself useful, and therefore likely to be secured in some part of nature, as one among its numerous grounds of selection, or lines of advantage), it becomes possible for such an intelligence to fix its attention on a vivid outward sign, without losing sight of, or dropping out of distinct attention, an image or revived impression; which latter would only serve, in case of its spontaneous revival in imagination, as a sign of the same thing, or the same event. Whether the vivid outward sign be a real object or event, of which the revived image is the counterpart, or whether it be a sign in a stricter meaning of the term,—that is, some action, figure, or utterance, associated either naturally or artificially with all similar objects or events, and, consequently, with the revived and representative image of them,—whatever the character of this outward sign may be, provided the representative image, or inward sign, still retains, in distinct consciousness, its power as such, then the outward sign may be consciously recognized as a substitute for the inward one, and a consciousness of simultaneous internal and external suggestion, or significance, might be realized; and the contrast of thoughts and things, at least in their power of suggesting that of which they may be coincident signs, could, for the first time, be perceptible. This would plant the germ of the distinctively human form of self-consciousness.

Previously to such a simultaneous consciousness of movements in imagination and movements in the same direction arising from perception, realized through the comparative vividness of the former, all separate and distinct consciousness of the inward sign would be eclipsed, and attention would pass on to the thought suggested by the outward sign. A similar phenomenon is frequently observed with us in successions of inward suggestions, or trains of thought. The attention often skips intermediate steps in a train, or appears to do so. At least, the memory of steps, which appear essential to its rational coherency, has ceased when we revive the train or repeat it voluntarily. This happens even when only a few moments have elapsed between the train and its repetition. Some writers assert that the omitted steps are immediately forgotten in such cases, on account of their feebleness,—as we forget immediately the details of a view which we have just seen, and remember only its salient points; while others maintain that the missing steps are absent from consciousness, even in the original and spontaneous movements of the train; or are present only through an unconscious agency, both in the train and its revival. This being a question of memory, reference cannot be made to memory itself for the decision of it. To decide whether a thing is completely forgotten, or has never been experienced, we have no other resource than rational analogy, which, in the present case, appears to favor the theory of oblivion, rather than that of latent mental ties and actions; since oblivion is a *vera causa* sufficient to account for the difference between such revived trains and those in which no steps are missed, or could be rationally supposed to have been present. The theory of "latent mental agency" appears to confound the original spontaneous movement of the train with what appears as its representative in its voluntary revival. This revival, in some cases, really involves new conditions, and is not, therefore, to be rationally interpreted as a precisely true recollection. If repeated often, it will establish direct and strong associations of contiguity between salient steps in the train which were connected at first by feebler though still conscious steps. The complete obliteration of these is analogous, as I have said, to the loss, in primary forms of memory, of details which are present to consciousness in actual first perceptions.

If, as more frequently happens, the whole train, with all its steps of suggestion, is recalled in the voluntary revival of it (without any sense of missing steps), the feebler intermediate links, that in other cases are obliterated, would correspond to the feebler, though (in the more advanced animal intelligences) comparatively vivid, mental signs which have in them the germ, as I have said, of the human form of self-consciousness. The growth of this consciousness, its development from this germ, is a more direct process than the production of the germ itself, which is only incidental to previous utilities in the power of memory. Thought, henceforward, may be an object to thought in its distinct contrast, as an inward sign, with the outward and more vivid sign of that which they both suggest, or revive from memory. This contrast is heightened if the outward one is more strictly a sign; that is, is not the perception of an object or event, of which the inward and representative image is a counterpart, but is of a different nature, for instance some movement or gesture or vocal utterance, or some graphic sign, associated by contiguity with the object or event, or, more properly, with its representative image. The "concept" so formed is not a thing complete in itself, but is essentially a cause, or step, in mental trains. The outward sign, the image, or inward sign, and the suggested thought, or image, form a train, like a train which might be wholly within the imagination. This train is present, in all its three constituents, to the first, or immediate, consciousness, in all degrees of intelligence; but in the revival of it, in the inferior degrees of intelligence, the middle term is obliterated, as in the trains of thought above considered. The animal has in mind only an image of the sign, previously present in perception, followed now immediately by an image of what was suggested through the obliterated mental image. But the latter, in the higher degrees of intelligence, is distinctly recalled as a middle term. In the revival of past trains, which were first produced through outward signs, the dumb animal has no consciousness of there having been present more than one of the two successive signs, which, together with the suggested image, formed the actual train in its first occurrence. The remembered outward sign is now a thought, or image, immediately suggesting or recalling that which was originally suggested by a feebler intermediate step.

In pure imaginations, not arising by actual connections through memory, the two terms are just the same with animals as in real memory; except that they are not felt to be the representatives of a former real connection. The contrast of the real and true with the imaginary and false is, then, the only general one of which such a mind could be aware in the phenomena of thought. The contrast of thought itself with perception, or with the actual outward sign and suggestion of the thought, is realized only by the revival in memory of the feeble connecting link. This effects a contrast not only between what is real and what is merely imaginary, but also between what is out of the mind and what is within it. The minute difference in the force of memory, on which this link in the chain of attention at first depended, was one of immense consequence to man. This feeble link is the dividing region, interval, or cleft between the two more vivid images; one being more vivid as a direct recollection of an actual outward impression, and the other being more vivid, or salient, from the interest or the motives which gave it the prominence of a thought demanding attention; either as a memory of a past object or event of interest, or the image of something in the immediate future. The disappearance altogether of this feeble link would, as I have said, take from the images connected by it all contrast with any pair of steps in a train, except a consciousness of reality in the connection of these images in a previous experience.

To exemplify this somewhat abstruse analysis, let us examine what, according to it, would be the mental movements in a man,—let him be a sportsman,—and a domestic animal,—let it be his dog,—on hearing a name,—let it be the name of some game, as "fox." The general character of the phenomena in both would be the same on the actual first hearing of this word. The word would suggest a mental image of the fox, then its movements of escape from its hunters, and the thought would pass on and dwell, through the absorbing interest of it, on the hunter's movements of pursuit, or pass on even to the capture and destruction of the game. This would, doubtless, recall to the minds of the hunter and his hound one or more real and distinctly remembered incidents of the sort. Now if we suppose this train of thought to be revived (as undoubtedly it is capable of being, both in the man and the dog), it will be the same in the man's mind as on its first production; except that the name "fox" will be thought of as an auditory, or else a vocal image, instead of being heard; and the visual image of the fox will be recalled by it with all the succeeding parts of the repeated train. But in the dog, either the auditory image of the name will not be recalled, since the vocal image does not exist in his mind to aid the recall (his voluntary vocal powers not being capable of forming it even in the first instance); or if such an auditory image arises, the representative visual or olfactory one will not appear in distinct consciousness. His attention will pass at once from either of these signs, but from one only to the more intense and interesting parts of the train,—to the pursuit and capture of the game, or to actually remembered incidents of the kind. Either the first or the immediate sign will remain in oblivion.

Hence the dog's dreams, or trains of thought, when they are revivals of previous trains, or when they rise into prominent consciousness in consequence of having been passed through before, omit or skip over the steps which at first served only as suggesting and connecting signs, following now only the associations of contiguity, established in the first occurrence of the train between its more prominent parts. The suggested thought eclipses by its glare the suggesting one. The interest of an image, or its power to attract attention and increased force, depends in the dog only on its vividness as a memory, or as a future purpose or event, and very little, if at all, on its relations and agency as a *sign*. Images, as well as outward signs, serve, as I have said, in the dumb animals as well as in man in this capacity; but this is not *recognized* by the animal, since those parts of a train which serve only as signs are too feeble to be revived in the repeated train; and new associations of mere contiguity in the prominent parts of it take their places. All that would be recognized in the animal mind by reflection on thought as thought, or independently of its reality as a memory, an anticipation, or a purpose, would be its unreality, or merely imaginary character.

If, on the contrary, a greater intensity, arising from a greater power of simple memory, should revive the feebler parts in repeated trains of thought, to the degree of attracting attention to them, and thus bringing them into a more distinct and vivid consciousness, there might arise an interest as to what they are, as to what their relations, and where they belong, which would be able to inspire and guide an act of distinct reflection. A thought might thus be determined as a representative mental image; and such acts of reflection, inspired also by other motives more powerful than mere inquisitiveness, would by observation, analysis, and generalization (the counterparts of such outward processes in the merely animal mind) bring all such representative images, together with real memories and anticipations, into a single group, or subjective connection. The recognition of them in this connection is the knowledge of them as *my* thoughts, or *our* thoughts, or as phenomena of the mind.

When a thought, or an outward expression, acts in an animal's mind or in a man's, in the capacity of a sign, it carries forward the movements of a train, and directs attention away from itself to what it signifies or suggests; and consciousness is concentrated on the latter. But being sufficiently vivid in itself to engage distinct attention, it determines a new kind of action, and a new faculty of observation, of which the cerebral hemispheres appear to be the organs. From the action of these, in their more essential powers in memory and imagination, the objects or materials of reflection are also derived. Reflection would thus be, not what most metaphysicians appear to regard it, a fundamentally new faculty in man, as elementary and primordial as memory itself, or the power of abstractive attention, or the function of signs and representative images in generalization; but it would be determined in its contrasts with other mental faculties by the nature of its objects. On its subjective side it would be composed of the same mental faculties—namely, memory, attention, abstraction—as those which are employed in the primary use of the senses. It would be engaged upon what these senses have furnished to memory; but would act as independently of any orders of grouping and succession presented by them, as the several senses themselves do of one another. To this extent, reflection is a distinct faculty, and though, perhaps, not peculiar to man, is in him so prominent and marked in its effects on the development of the individual mind, that it may be regarded as his most essential and elementary mental distinction in kind. For differences of degrees in causes may make differences of kinds in effects.

Motives more powerful than mere inquisitiveness about the feebler steps or *mere* thoughts of a revived train, and more efficient in concentrating attention upon them, and upon their functions as signs, or suggesting images, would spring from the social nature of the animal, from the uses of mental communication between the members of a community, and from the *desire* to communicate, which these uses would create. And just as an outward sign associated with a mental image aids by its intensity in fixing attention upon the latter, so the *uses* of such outward signs and the motives connected with their employment would add *extensive* force, or interest, to the energy of attention in the cognition of this inward sign; and hence would aid in the reference of it and its sort to the subject *ego,*—a being already known, or distinguished from other beings, as that which wills, desires, and feels. That which wills, desires, and feels is, in the more intelligent domestic animal, known by the proper name, which the animal recognizes and answers to by its actions, and is a consciousness of its individuality. It is not known or recognized by that most generic name "I"; since phenomena common to this individual and to others, or capable of being made common through the communications of language, are not distinctly referred to the individual self by that degree of abstractive attention and precision which an habitual exercise of the faculty of reflection is required to produce. But, in the same manner, the word "world," which includes the conscious subject in its meaning, would fail to suggest anything more to such an intelligence than more concrete terms do,—such as what is around, within, near, or distant from consciousness; or it would fail to suggest the *whole* of that which philosophers divide into *ego* and *non-ego,* the outward and inward worlds. A contrast of this whole to its parts, however divided in predication, or the antithesis of subject and attributes, in a divisible unity and its component particulars, would not be suggested to an animal mind by the word "world." The "categories," or forms and conditions of human understanding, though doubtless innate in the naturalist's sense of the term, that is inherited, are only the ways and facilities of the higher exercise of the faculty of reflection. They are, doubtless, ways and facilities that are founded on the ultimate nature of mind; yet, on this very account, are universal, though only potential in the animal mind generally; just as the forms and conditions of *locomotion* are generally in the bodies of plants; forms and conditions founded on the ultimate natures or laws of motion, which would be exemplified in plants, if they also had the power of changing their positions, and are indeed exemplified in those forms of vegetable life that are transported, such as seeds, or can move and plant themselves like certain spores.

The world of self-conscious intellectual activity,—the world of mind,—has, doubtless, its ultimate unconditional laws, everywhere exemplified in the actual phenomena of abstractive and reflective thought, and capable of being generalized in the reflective observations of the philosopher, and applied by him to the explanation of the phenomena of thought wherever manifested in outward expressions, whether in his fellow-men, or in the more intelligent dumb animals. Memory, in the effects of its more powerful and vivid revivals in the more intelligent animals, and especially in the case of large-brained man, presents this new world, in which the same faculties of observation, analysis, and generalization as those employed by intelligent beings in general, ascertain the marks and classes of phenomena strictly mental, and divide them, as a whole class, or *summum genus,* from those of the outward world. The distinction of subject and object becomes thus a classification through observation and analysis, instead of the intuitive distinction it is supposed to be by most metaphysicians. Intuitive to some extent, in one sense of the word, it doubtless is; that is, facilities and predispositions to associations, which are as effective as repeated experiences and observations would be, and which are inherited in the form of instincts, doubtless have much to do in bringing to pass this cognition, as well as many others, which appear to be innate, not only in the lower animals but also in man.

The very different aim of the evolutionist from that of his opponents —the latter seeking to account for the *resemblances* of mental actions in beings supposed to be radically different in their mental constitutions, while the former seeks to account for the *differences* of manifestation in fundamentally similar mental constitutions—gives, in the theory of evolution, a philosophical *role* to the word "instinct," and to its contrast with intelligence, much inferior to that which this contrast has had in the discussions of the mental faculties of animals. For the distinction of instinct and intelligence, though not less real and important in the classification of actions in psycho-zoology, and as important even as that of animal and vegetable is in general zoology, or the distinctions of organic and inorganic, living and dead, in the general science of life, is yet, like these, in its applications a vague and ill-defined distinction, and is most profitably studied in the subordinate classes of actions, and in the special contrasts which are summarized by it. Under the naturalist's point of view, the contrasts of dead and living matters, inorganic and organic products, vegetable and animal forms and functions, automatic and sentient movements, instinctive and intelligent motives and actions, are severally rough divisions of *series,* which are clearly enough contrasted in their extremities, but ill-defined at their points of division. Thus, we have the long series beginning with the processes of growth, nutrition, and waste: and in movements independent of nervous connections, and continued in processes in which sensations are involved, first vaguely, as in the processes of digestion, circulation, and the general stimulative action of the nervous system; then distinctly, as in the stimulative sensations of respiration, winking, swallowing, coughing, and sneezing, more or less under general control or the action of the will. This series is continued, again, into those sensations, impulses, and consequent actions which are wholly controllable, though spontaneously arising; and thence into the motives to actions which are wholly dependent on, or involved in, the immediate controlling powers of the will,—a series in which the several marks of distinction are clearly enough designated in the abstract, as the colors of the spectrum are by their names, but are not clearly separated in the concrete applications of them.

Again, we have the series of voluntary actions, beginning at the connections between perceptions, emotions, and consequent actions, which are strictly instinctive. These, though inherited, are independent of the effects of higher, and more properly voluntary, actions in the individual's progenitors, as well as in himself. When they are not simple ultimate and universal laws of mental natures, or elementary mental connections they are combinations produced through their serviceableness to life, or by natural selection and exercise, that is in the same general manner in which bodily organs, powers, and functions are produced or altered. Such connections between perceptions, emotions, and consequent actions, derived through natural selection, or even those that are ultimate laws, and determine, in a manner not peculiar to any species, the conditions and uses of serviceable actions,—are *instinctive* connections, or powers of *instinct,* in a restricted but perfectly definite use of the word. But following immediately in the series of voluntary actions are, first, the inherited effects of habits, and next, habits properly so called, or effects produced by higher voluntary actions in the individual. *Habits* properly so called, and *dispositions,* which are the inherited effects of habits, are not different in their practical character or modes of action from true instincts; but differ only in their origin and capacity of alteration through the higher forms of volition. The latter, or proper, volitions are connections between the occasions, or external means and conditions of an action, and the production of the action itself through the *motive of the end,* and not through emotions or by any other ties instinctively uniting them. They are joined by the foreseen ulterior effect of the action, or else through a union produced by its influence. The desirableness of what is effected by an action connects its occasions, or present means and conditions, with the action itself, and causes its production through the end felt in imagination. The influence of the end, or ulterior motive in volition, may not be a consciously recognized part of the action, or a distinctly separated step in it, and will actually cease to be the real tie when a series of repeated volitions has established a habit, or a fixed association between them and their occasions, or external conditions. This connection in habits is, as we have said, closely similar to strictly instinctive connections, and is indistinguishable from them independently of questions of origin and means of alterations.

Independently of these questions, the series of voluntary actions starting from the strictly instinctive joins to them natural dispositions, or the inherited effects of habit, and passes on to habits properly so called, thence into those in which the ulterior motives of true volitions are still operative, though not as separate parts of consciousness, and thence on to mere faculties of action, or to those actions in which such a motive is still the sole effective link, though quite faded out of distinct attention, or attended to with a feeble and intermittent consciousness. Thence it comes finally to the distinct recognition in reflective thought of an ulterior motive to an action. The ulterior motive, the end or good to be effected by an action, anticipated in imagination, joins the action to its present means and conditions in actual volitions, or else joins it in imagination with some future occurrence of them in an *intention,* or a predetermination of the will. These ulterior motives, ends, or determinations of an action through foreseen consequences of it, may be *within* the will, in the common and proper meaning of the word, when it is spoken of as free, or unconstrained by an outward force, or necessity; or they may be *without* it, like instinctive tendencies to which the will is said to *consent* or *yield,* as well as in other cases to be *opposed.* The motives within the will, either distinctly or vaguely operative, or completely superseded by forces of habit, constitute the individual's character.

# *PART IV*

# The Emergence of Contemporary Issues

# XIX
## Introduction

During the last quarter of the nineteenth century philosophy assumed in America something like the professional character and academic status which it now has, and a movement began which has generally been regarded as a typical expression of the American spirit. Until then, philosophical instruction in the colleges was largely in the senior year and in charge of the president. He was a clergyman whose postgraduate training had been under theological auspices. In this period, however, by the establishment of graduate schools, the departmentalization of the subjects of college instruction and the introduction of the elective system, philosophy became a study which a student might elect early in his college career and continue with increasing concentration for six or seven years. By the end of the century, it was largely in the hands of lay teachers who had done just that. The lecture method was superseding the textbook and recitation method, dogmatic instruction was rapidly being replaced by historical, comparative and critical study of the writings of the great philosophers, and the philosophical issues of the day were brought into the classroom for discussion. The natural sciences had long since become independent subjects, and in this period psychology and the social sciences followed. This led to a clearer formulation of the problems of philosophy proper, as distinguished from those of psychology and the other sciences. Philosophy had lost its dominance of the curriculum, and as a result of the expansion and multiplication of the subjects with which it had to compete under the elective system, it received a diminishing part of the attention of the college community as a whole, but it was more aggressively and intensively pursued by those whom it did attract. Whether the competition made for the ascendency of a particular type of philosophy as well as for the professionalizing of philosophy in general, is another question. It is at least a plausible conjecture that the spread of pragmatism was due in part to the pressure to make philosophy as live a subject as economics and biology.

The seventies and eighties were the heyday of local philosophical clubs, often made up of and led by enthusiastic amateurs without academic connections. The most conspicuous of these was the St. Louis Philosophical Society, which had a prophet in the immigrant German mechanic, lawyer and politician, Henry Brokmeyer, an organizing genius in W. T. Harris, the superintendent of schools, and an organ in *The Journal of Speculative Philosophy* (1867–93). At Jacksonville, Illinois, there was a Plato Club which met weekly for thirty years or more, and became in 1883 the nucleus of a larger society called The American Acadêmê. Its membership reached 180, including corresponding members from California to Maine and from Canada to the West Indies. Its leader was the platonist Dr. H. K. Jones. There were similar clubs in many other cities, especially in the middle west, with occasional interchange of speakers. In addition to their own regular programs they sponsored lectures by Emerson, Alcott and others who came almost annually from the east.

The Concord School of Philosophy (1879–87) was the flowering of this epoch in our culture. Alcott, the dean, represented the final form of New England transcendentalism. S. H. Emery, Jr., the director, was the leader of the philosophical group at Quincy, Illinois. Two of the principal lecturers, Harris and Dr. Jones, represented the larger movements at St. Louis and Jacksonville, and there was a courteous but obvious rivalry between the Hegelian idealism of the former and the Platonic idealism of the latter. The philosophical interpretation of literature was given a large place on the program, foreshadowing the literary schools which one of the lecturers, Denton J. Snider of the St. Louis group, was soon to direct at Chicago (1887–95) and later at St. Louis. At Chicago a year was devoted to each of the four "literary bibles"—Homer, Dante, Shakespeare, Goethe—and then the cycle was repeated. Snider later looked back on three lectures on psychology by William James at the Concord session of 1883 as prophetic of the era in our culture that was to follow that of the literary schools. Certain it is that all these groups, though masculine in leadership, had a large feminine following, and that as our culture became increasingly dominated by women with their growing leisure, there was a steady drift from philosophy to literature (studied for its 'message' rather than its purely literary qualities) and from literature to psychology.

These local societies and their journals were gradually superseded by organizations and periodicals of a more national or international and a more professional character. The five years which *The Journal of Speculative Philosophy* took for its expiring volume (1888–93) witnessed the first appearance of *The Monist* (1890–1936), *The International Journal of Ethics* (1890—), and *The Philosophical Review*

(1892—). These, with *The Journal of Philosophy* (1904—), have been until recently the chief vehicles for articles, discussions and reviews. The Western Philosophical Association was founded in 1900, and the American Philosophical Association a year later.

In the local societies, in the journals and in the colleges there was widespread preoccupation with the question of what type of philosophy was most congenial to the American spirit and its institutions. *The Journal of Speculative Philosophy* was criticized for the "Un-American character" of its contents. Harris replied that what was needed was not American thought so much as American thinkers, and that we should not have them until the great thinkers of the past—the Greeks and Germans especially—were as thoroughly digested as the works of Herbert Spencer. In the end he thought it would be found, as the poet Walt Whitman was saying, that "Only Hegel is fit for America—is large enough and free enough." Whitman, in fact, saw in Hegel's philosophy "an essential and crowning justification of New World democracy," and was puzzled to account for its appearance in the Old World.

In the eighties and nineties appeared a series of critical expositions of "German Philosophical Classics"—Leibniz, Kant, Fichte, Schelling and Hegel—under the editorial supervision of Professor George S. Morris of the University of Michigan. In the prospectus Morris stated that the aim of the series would be "especially to show, as occasion may require, in what way German thought contains the natural complement, or the much-needed corrective, of British speculation." The authors included, besides the editor, John Dewey, C. C. Everett, Noah Porter, John Watson, W. T. Harris, and J. S. Kedney. Morris had previously written a book on *British Thought and Thinkers,* definitely critical in tone.

President McCosh of Princeton, on the other hand, writing on *The Scottish Philosophy* in 1875, observed that "idealism has never struck deep into the American soil." Several years later, considering "What an American Philosophy Should Be,"[1] he thought the time had come for America to declare her independence in philosophy, and deduced from the Yankee genius for practical observation and invention that "the American philosophy will therefore be a Realism, opposed to Idealism on the one hand and to Agnosticism on the other"—such a realism, in fact, as he himself, like Witherspoon a century earlier, had brought with him from Scotland. When he wrote, however, this realism was

[1] This was the title of his introduction to *Realistic Philosophy: Defended in a Philosophic Series.* New York: Charles Scribner's Sons, 1887. It first came out in 1882.

already on the wane, and by the end of the century various forms of idealism occupied the center of the stage. Idealism in voluntaristic form was represented by Royce at Harvard, in intellectualistic form by Creighton at Cornell, and in personalistic form by Bowne at Boston and by Howison at California. Since then there have been revivals of realism, best represented by two collaborative volumes, *The New Realism* (1912) and *Essays in Critical Realism* (1920), but these have been independent developments, best understood in relation to the intervening idealism and pragmatism rather than to the earlier realism.

It would now be generally agreed, even by those who are most critical of it, that pragmatism is America's most distinctive contribution to philosophy. In it for the first time our standing concern for the practical application of knowledge found adequate expression in a theory of knowledge. Ontological arguments, *a priori* reasoning, dialectical triumphs and logical demonstrations have usually been regarded with suspicion among us, even when no flaws could be discovered in them; and we have tended to judge doctrines rather by the conduct of those who adopt them, and by their fruitfulness in invention and contrivance, organization and exploitation, than by their supposed self-evidence or logical consistency. We have seen that Franklin came to regard his *Dissertation* as "another Erratum," not because he or anyone else had discerned a fallacy in it, but because of the moral *errata* which he thought flowed from it in his own conduct and in that of the friends he had converted to it, so that he "began to suspect that this Doctrine, tho' it might be true, was not very useful." It is of special interest, however, to note the latent pragmatism in the various forms of American idealism. The Puritans, and above all Edwards, as James observed, applied the pragmatic test to religion. Edwards failed to carry his "Treatise on the Mind" beyond the stage of notes, in part at least because its central principle, the denial of material substance, though he never doubted its truth, seemed to have no practical consequences for science or religion. Johnson, on the other hand, was converted to this same doctrine less by Berkeley's arguments than by its practical consequence for religion in restoring the sense of the immediate presence of God. Emerson distinguished three stages of idealism: the academic, the poetic, and the practical. "Every intellection," he said, "is mainly prospective: its present value is its least." W. T. Harris recalled long afterwards how, through Brokmeyer's skill in applying the Hegelian dialectic to the issues of the day, "Philosophy came to mean with us . . . the most practical of all species of knowledge."

No doubt it is a far cry from all this to pragmatism as a clearly defined method and a full-blown theory of meaning, knowledge and truth. It would seem, however, that there was a widespread common attitude toward philosophy, in the light of which it is surprising that the method and theory, when finally stated, should have made almost no headway for a generation. The story in barest outline will suffice to show the importance of a name and a portable formula. The essential doctrine was implicit in the articles contributed by C. S. Peirce to the *Journal of Speculative Philosophy* in 1868, and explicit in his review of Fraser's edition of Berkeley in the *North American Review* for October, 1871. It was developed at length and precisely formulated in his series of six papers in the *Popular Science Monthly* in 1877 and 1878, under the general title, "Illustrations of the Logic of Science." An excellent abstract of these papers, including the formula, appeared in *Mind* in 1879 in an article on "Philosophy in the United States" by G. Stanley Hall, who said they promised to be "one of the most important of American contributions to philosophy." The first two papers, the second of which contained the formula, were also published in French in the *Revue philosophique* in 1879, and in their English form Peirce used them as the point of departure in his lectures on logic at Johns Hopkins University. The formula was extremely cumbersome, however, and it was given no name in the papers as printed or in anything published by Peirce prior to the article "Pragmatism" in the second volume of Baldwin's *Dictionary of Philosophy and Psychology* in 1902.

James's form of the doctrine, variously expressed, may be found in private notes from 1873 on, and in many of his publications from 1878 on, often with a reference to Peirce and sometimes with a quotation of his formula, but always without the label. This is the more remarkable in view of the fact that the doctrine was properly christened at its birth in the Metaphysical Club about 1870, and Peirce had ever since, in private conversation, called it by name. The movement of pragmatism, as distinguished from the doctrine, dates from James's *pronunciamento,* "Philosophical Conceptions and Practical Results," delivered before the Philosophical Union at Berkeley, California, in 1898, in which he gave a streamlined and portable version of Peirce's "principle of pragmatism," distinguished his own variant of it, sketched its antecedents in earlier British philosophy, and applied it to religion.

It is certainly no accident that the Cambridge Metaphysical Club of the early seventies, in which pragmatism was born, had for its most active members three men whose primary training had been in natural science—Wright, Peirce, and James—and three lawyers—Holmes,

Warner, and Green. For it is the method of the laboratory scientist and the working lawyer which the principle of pragmatism most aptly expresses. Its application to science is best seen in Peirce's papers, already referred to. Its application to law is well illustrated by Justice Holmes's address on "The Path of the Law" at the dedication of the new hall of the Boston University School of Law in January, 1897.

> . . . The object of our study, then, is prediction, the prediction of the incidence of the public force through the instrumentality of the courts.
> . . . a legal duty so called is nothing but a prediction that if a man does or omits certain things he will be made to suffer in this or that way by judgment of the court; and so of a legal right.
> . . . You see how the vague circumference of the notion of duty shrinks and at the same time grows more precise when we wash it with cynical acid and expel everything except the object of our study, the operations of the law.[2]

The application of pragmatism to education and to the social sciences generally as instruments of social control and reform, was the work of another group at the University of Chicago under the leadership of John Dewey and G. H. Mead. Dewey had been moving slowly from Hegelian idealism to pragmatism under the influence of evolutionary biology and of James's *Psychology.* After long gestation, the group published in 1903 a volume of *Studies in Logical Theory,* the preface to which acknowledged "a pre-eminent obligation" to James "for both inspiration and the forging of the tools with which the writers have worked." By that time pragmatism had been transplanted to Oxford by F. C. S. Schiller, and was beginning to attract international attention. It was the focus of philosophical controversy through the first decade of the twentieth century, and still provides the best approach to more recent developments in American thought. Its latest monument is Dewey's *Logic: The Theory of Inquiry* (1938). Acknowledging its great indebtedness to Peirce in detail and in the general position taken, it appeared just sixty years after Peirce's "Illustrations of the Logic of Science." No other movement in American philosophy has had so continuous a history, or produced so large a body of literature with a living interest for our own time.

[2] *Collected Legal Papers.* New York: Harcourt, Brace and Co., 1920. 167, 169, 174.

# XX

## Charles Sanders Peirce

1839–1914

Born in Cambridge. A.B., Harvard, 1859; M.A., 1862; B.S. in Chemistry, 1863. U. S. Coast Survey, 1861–91. Lecturer in Logic and Philosophy of Science at Harvard, 1864–65, 1869–71. Lecturer in Logic, Johns Hopkins University, 1879–84. Editorial contributor to the *Century Dictionary,* 1889–91. Died near Milford, Pa., where he had retired in 1887.

Peirce's long life was almost exclusively devoted to science and philosophy. He was America's greatest logician and one of the founders of modern mathematical or symbolic logic. His various researches in the service of the Coast and Geodetic Survey were of permanent importance. He wrote for the six-volume *Century Dictionary* all the definitions of the terms used in logic, metaphysics, mathematics, mechanics, astronómy, and weights and measures. Outside the circle of mathematical and scientific specialists, however, his name was scarcely known. His philosophical speculations, which were of potential interest to a much wider public, were heralded by G. Stanley Hall, we have seen, as likely to be "one of the most important of American contributions to philosophy." James and Royce repeatedly acknowledged their indebtedness to him during his lifetime, and Dewey continues to do so at the present day. But only so much of his thinking as has been assimilated, transformed and transmitted by these men has so far reached its potential audience. Peirce himself was isolated and frustrated by the lack of academic position and of avenues of publication. He was cut off from the latter by his failure to meet the prospective reader half way, and from the former by his inability to work in harness, his irregular hours and forgetfulness of appointments, and his marital difficulties.

Peirce was not only one of the most original and versatile of America's philosophers; he was its most prolific projector and drafter of systems. But for the articulation and elucidation of his final system he needed the stimulus of successive generations of able and interested students. That condition seemed in a fair way to be realized at Johns Hopkins University in the early eighties, where he was associated with G. S. Morris and G. Stanley Hall in the conduct of courses for advanced and postgraduate students, in what promised to become the country's chief center for the serious study of philosophy. The caliber of the students is sufficiently indicated by the fact that Royce received his doctor's degree there in 1878 and Dewey in 1884. The quality of the research done under Peirce's direction is evidenced by the *Studies in Logic* which he edited in 1883. There was a vigorous Metaphysical Club, which attracted students and instructors from other fields, and its roster of active contributors included the names of many who later made their mark in the intellectual life of the country. But the administration of the university decided to promote experimental psychology instead of philosophy, Morris and Peirce left, the Metaphysical Club was discontinued, and academic leadership in philosophy passed to Harvard, Michigan, Cornell, Chicago, Columbia and California. This was the critical turn in Peirce's career, and its consequences were tragic not only for him but for American philosophy. No other university would have him, nor indeed could any other have provided an atmosphere so favorable as that of Johns Hopkins to the flourishing of his special abilities. He became a recluse, his style grew more cryptic and perverse, and he left at his death a mass of unpublished manuscripts which are only now being made accessible to students of philosophy.

Peirce's most characteristic theories—pragmatism, tychism, synechism and agapism—may be traced to two early commitments and two early antagonisms, the combination of which in one mind is probably unique. He was committed almost from the beginning of his career to the methodology of the exact experimental sciences and to a scholastic realism derived from Duns Scotus. He was opposed to the rationalism of Descartes and to the nominalism and individualism of the British empiricists: that is, to the characteristic errors, as it seemed to him, of the two traditions from which all modern philosophy stems. He rejected the Cartesian doctrines that philosophy must begin with universal doubt, that the mind when stripped for action can intuit truth directly, and that the ultimate test of truth is to be found in the individual consciousness. We must begin, Peirce maintained, with the prejudices we actually have, and make no pretense of doubting what we have as yet no positive reason to doubt; we must depend, as the sciences do, upon the multiplicity and variety of experiments and arguments and the resultant approach to agreement in the community of minds, rather than upon the apparent conclusiveness of single arguments.

Peirce was equally opposed to the nominalism which had infected British thought from the beginning. In its extreme form in Berkeley it had asserted that only particulars exist, and that universals have no existence even as mental constructions, since what are called abstract or general ideas are only particular ideas (e. g., names), each used as a sign of an indefinite number of other particulars. Berkeley had been driven in the end to support his atomic sensations by linking them with archetypal ideas in God's mind, but this platonic pseudo-realism was as inadequate for the purpose as the later Scotch realism was for escaping Hume's dissolution of mind as well as matter into mere appearances. Nominalism, with its progeny of sensationalism, phenomenalism, individualism and materialism, was again ascendent in Peirce's day among scientists as well as philosophers. This was due, he thought, to persistent misunderstanding of the opposed doctrine of realism, and to misconceptions of the spirit and method of science on the part even of those expert in the practice of it.

According to Peirce the issue between realism and nominalism was not whether universals existed before or alongside of particular things and might be separate objects of intuition, but whether laws and general types were real. The real was the object of true opinion, i. e., that upon which opinion tended to settle in the long run; it was independent, not of thought in general, but of what any one man or any number of men might happen to think at a given time. But general conceptions entered into *all* opinions, and therefore into true opinions; so types or laws must be real. The only questions were, which ones were real, and real in what way, and in what things they really were. No one seriously doubted, for instance, that such a general character as hardness really was in some things as a habit or disposition or mode of behavior of those things, and that there were in us certain habits of belief and action answering thereto. Not to doubt this was to be, so far, a realist.

One might, however, be in doubt whether this or that in particular was hard, and, if so, how hard, and how it got that way. Thought or inquiry was set going by such actual doubts, and its only function was the production and fixation of belief. There were three traditional ways in which beliefs might be locally and temporarily fixed. (1) There was the method of tenacity, but it involved wearing mental blinkers, and man's social nature was against it. It could not hold its ground indefinitely in practice. The problem was to fix belief, not in the individual merely, but in the community. (2) For this purpose, the method of authority was more effective. But not all individuals could be kept indefinitely from discovering that beyond the reach of authority other beliefs flourished. Sooner or later, therefore, both the wilful adherence to belief and the arbitrary forcing of it upon others must be given up. (3) Under conditions of free trade in opinions, a certain standardization might ensue by the *a priori* method, or the test of agreeableness to reason. But opinions so standardized could be nothing more than intellectual fashions, and intellectual fashions seldom lasted more than a few centuries.

Each of these methods had its advantages, but after all everybody wished his opinions to coincide with the facts, and there was no reason why the results of these three methods should do so. That was the prerogative of a fourth method, the method of science. Only by the practice of it could we be assured that the ultimate conclusion of every man would be the same. What was that method? Its first requirement was that the meaning of the opinion in doubt or dispute should be clear. But there were grades of clearness. The "clear and distinct ideas" of the rationalists were not clear enough. Beyond the grades of familiarity and abstract definition, scientific thinking exhibited a third grade of clearness, though the rule for attaining it had perhaps not as yet been adequately formulated. Peirce's formulation of it in 1878 will be found on p. 461 of this book.

The linguistic clumsiness of the formula, with its employment five times over of derivatives of *concipere,* was due, he later said, to his desire to prevent such misunderstandings as that he was using *meaning* in any other sense than that of *intellectual purport,* or attempting to explain a concept by anything but concepts. In this connection it is noteworthy that his first published statement of the rule in 1871 was used in deprecation of Berkeley's denial that we have any abstract or general ideas.

> A better rule for avoiding the deceits of language is this: Do things fulfil the same function practically? Then let them be signified by the same word. Do they not? Then let them be distinguished. If I have learned a formula in gibberish which in any way jogs my memory so as to enable me in each single case to act as though I had a general idea, what possible utility is there in distinguishing between such a gibberish and formula and an idea? Why use the term *a general idea* in such a sense as to separate things which, for all experimental purposes, are the same? [1]

[1] *North American Review* 113 (1871) 469.

Peirce's exposition of the principle of pragmatism in the following selection laid itself open to the quite different misunderstanding of making action the ultimate end of thought. He attempted to correct this in the article "Pragmatism" in Baldwin's *Dictionary*. Action itself, he said, required an end, and that end must be something of a general description. Beyond the three grades of clearness already named, he now distinguished a fourth and still higher grade, which could be attained only by putting the pragmatic maxim into practice with conscientious thoroughness, but which consisted in the realization that "the only ultimate good which the practical facts to which it directs attention can subserve is to further the development of concrete reasonableness; so that the meaning of the concept does not lie in any individual reactions at all, but in the manner in which those reactions contribute to that development."

This development of concrete reasonableness or embodied ideas was not only the end of human action; it was also the direction of growth in nature itself. Nature acquired laws as a man acquired habits. Law was not primary, absolute and invariable, but derivative and approximate. The doctrine of necessity or determinism was neither a necessary postulate nor a probable conclusion of scientific method. "Try to verify any law of nature, and you will find that the more precise your observations, the more certain they will be to show irregular departures from the law." [2] To this primary tendency toward diversification, this pure spontaneity or fortuitous variation, Peirce gave the name of tychism. But all variations and diversities were united *logically* by continuous scales of degrees, as that between any given two there was an infinite series of possible intermediates, and *ontologically* by the tendency toward order, by "the becoming continuous, the becoming instinct with general ideas." This principle of continuity, in both its logical and its ontological aspects, Peirce called synechism. Ontological synechism in the form of "evolutionary love," familiar examples of which might be found in the love of parents for their children and of thinkers for their ideas, he called agapism. Tychism and agapism were complementary phases of the synechistic law of mind, which was at the same time the law of nature.

Realism, pragmatism, tychism, synechism, agapism—these were but the germinal principles of a vast philosophical system, adumbrated in Peirce's early published papers and slowly filling itself out with precise detail and ingenious nomenclature, but difficult if not impossible to

[2] *Collected Papers.* VI, § 46.

reconstruct at this late date from his alternative and partially conflicting drafts with their endless self-correction. It is not too much to say, however, that the assimilation and criticism of his work is likely to prove one of the most fruitful of the enterprises to which younger thinkers are now devoting themselves.

## REFERENCES

Peirce, Charles Sanders: *Chance, Love, and Logic.* Edited with an Introduction by Morris R. Cohen, a Supplementary Essay on the Pragmatism of Peirce by John Dewey, and a Classified Bibliography of Peirce's Published Writings. New York: Harcourt, Brace and Co., 1923.

Hartshorne, Charles, and Weiss, Paul (editors): *Collected Papers of Charles Sanders Peirce.* 6 volumes so far published. Cambridge: Harvard University Press, 1931–35.

Dewey, John: "Peirce's Theory of Quality," *Journal of Philosophy* 32 (1935) 701–8.

Freeman, Eugene: *The Categories of Charles Peirce.* Chicago: Open Court Publishing Co., 1934.

Hartshorne, Charles: "Continuity, The Form of Forms," *Monist* 39 (1929) 521–34.

*Journal of Philosophy* 13 (1916) 701–37. (Contains articles on Peirce by Josiah Royce, Fergus Kernan, John Dewey, Christine Ladd-Franklin, Joseph Jastrow, and Morris R. Cohen.)

Keyser, C. J.: "A Glance at Some of the Ideas of Charles Sanders Peirce," *Scripta Mathematica* 3 (1935) 11–37.

Morris, Charles W.: "Peirce, Mead, and Pragmatism," *Philosophical Review* 47 (1938) 109–27.

Muirhead, J. H.: "Peirce's Place in American Philosophy," *Philosophical Review* 37 (1928) 460–81.

Nagel, Ernest: "Charles Peirce's Guesses at the Riddle," *Journal of Philosophy* 30 (1933) 365–86.

Perry, R. B.: *The Thought and Character of William James: Revealed in Unpublished Correspondence and Notes, Together with His Published Writings.* 2 vols. Boston: Little, Brown and Co., 1935. Chs. 32, 75, 76.

Townsend, H. G.: *Philosophical Ideas in the United States.* Cincinnati: American Book Co., 1934. 196–224.

———: "Some Sources and Early Meanings of American Pragmatism," *Journal of Philosophy* 32 (1935) 181–7.

* * *

---

* * *

# HOW TO MAKE OUR IDEAS CLEAR [3]

## I

Whoever has looked into a modern treatise on logic of the common sort, will doubtless remember the two distinctions between *clear* and *obscure* conceptions, and between *distinct* and *confused* conceptions. They have lain in the books now for nigh two centuries, unimproved and unmodified, and generally reckoned by logicians as among the gems of their doctrine.

A clear idea is defined as one which is so apprehended that it will be recognized wherever it is met with, and so that no other will be mistaken for it. If it fails of this clearness, it is said to be obscure.

This is rather a neat bit of philosophical terminology; yet, since it is clearness that they were defining, I wish the logicians had made their definition a little more plain. Never to fail to recognize an idea and under no circumstances to mistake another for it, let it come in how recondite a form it may, would indeed imply such prodigious force and clearness of intellect as is seldom met with in this world. On the other hand, merely to have such an acquaintance with the idea as to have become familiar with it, and to have lost all hesitancy in recognizing it in ordinary cases, hardly seems to deserve the name of clearness of apprehension, since after all it only amounts to a subjective feeling of mastery which may be entirely mistaken. I take it, however, that when the logicians speak of "clearness," they mean nothing more than such a familiarity with an idea, since they regard the quality as but a small merit, which needs to be supplemented by another, which they call *distinctness*.

A distinct idea is defined as one which contains nothing which is not clear. This is technical language; by the *contents* of an idea logicians understand whatever is contained in its definition. So that an idea is *distinctly* apprehended, according to them, when we can give a precise definition of it, in abstract terms. Here the professional logicians leave the subject; and I would not have troubled the reader with what they have to say, if it were not such a striking example of how they have been slumbering through ages of intellectual activity, listlessly disregarding the enginery of modern thought, and never dreaming of applying its lessons to the improvement of logic. It is easy to show that the

[3] *Popular Science Monthly* 12 (1878) 286–302. This was the second of six papers under the general head, "Illustrations of the Logic of Science." Reprinted with Peirce's subsequent corrections and annotations in *Collected Papers,* V, §§ 388–410. The original text is used here.

doctrine that familiar use and abstract distinctness make the perfection of apprehension, has its only true place in philosophies which have long been extinct; and it is now time to formulate the method of attaining to a more perfect clearness of thought, such as we see and admire in the thinkers of our own time.

When Descartes set about the reconstruction of philosophy, his first step was to (theoretically) permit skepticism and to discard the practice of the schoolmen of looking to authority as the ultimate source of truth. That done, he sought a more natural fountain of true principles, and professed to find it in the human mind; thus passing, in the directest way, from the method of authority to that of apriority, as described in my first paper. Self-consciousness was to furnish us with our fundamental truths, and to decide what was agreeable to reason. But since, evidently, not all ideas are true, he was led to note, as the first condition of infallibility, that they must be clear. The distinction between an idea *seeming* clear and really being so, never occurred to him. Trusting to introspection, as he did, even for a knowledge of external things, why should he question its testimony in respect to the contents of our own minds? But then, I suppose, seeing men, who seemed to be quite clear and positive, holding opposite opinions upon fundamental principles, he was further led to say that clearness of ideas is not sufficient, but that they need also to be distinct, i. e., to have nothing unclear about them. What he probably meant by this (for he did not explain himself with precision) was, that they must sustain the test of dialectical examination; that they must not only seem clear at the outset, but that discussion must never be able to bring to light points of obscurity connected with them.

Such was the distinction of Descartes, and one sees that it was precisely on the level of his philosophy. It was somewhat developed by Leibnitz. This great and singular genius was as remarkable for what he failed to see as for what he saw. That a piece of mechanism could not do work perpetually without being fed with power in some form, was a thing perfectly apparent to him; yet he did not understand that the machinery of the mind can only transform knowledge, but never originate it, unless it be fed with facts of observation. He thus missed the most essential point of the Cartesian philosophy, which is, that to accept propositions which seem perfectly evident to us is a thing which, whether it be logical or illogical, we cannot help doing. Instead of regarding the matter in this way, he sought to reduce the first principles of science to formulas which cannot be denied without self-contradiction, and was apparently unaware of the great difference between his position and that of Descartes. So he reverted to the old formalities of logic, and, above all, abstract definitions played a great part in his philosophy. It was quite natural, therefore, that on observing that the method of Descartes labored under the difficulty that we may seem to ourselves to have clear apprehensions of ideas which in truth are very hazy, no better remedy occurred to him than to require an abstract definition of every important term. Accordingly, in adopting the distinction of *clear* and *distinct* notions, he described the latter quality as the clear apprehension of everything contained in the definition; and the books have ever since copied his words. There is no danger that his chimerical scheme will ever again be over-valued. Nothing new can ever be learned by analyzing definitions. Nevertheless, our existing beliefs can be set in order by this process, and order is an essential element of intellectual economy, as of every other. It may be acknowledged, therefore, that the books are right in making familiarity with a notion the first step toward clearness of apprehension, and the defining of it the second. But in omitting all mention of any higher perspicuity of thought, they simply mirror a philosophy which was exploded a hundred years ago. That much-admired "ornament of logic"—the doctrine of clearness and distinctness—may be pretty enough, but it is high time to relegate to our cabinet of curiosities the antique *bijou,* and to wear about us something better adapted to modern uses.

The very first lesson that we have a right to demand that logic shall teach us is, how to make our ideas clear; and a most important one it is, depreciated only by minds who stand in need of it. To know what we think, to be masters of our own meaning, will make a solid foundation for great and weighty thought. It is most easily learned by those whose ideas are meagre and restricted; and far happier they than such as wallow helplessly in a rich mud of conceptions. A nation, it is true, may, in the course of generations, overcome the disadvantage of an excessive wealth of language and its natural concomitant, a vast, unfathomable deep of ideas. We may see it in history, slowly perfecting its literary forms, sloughing at length its metaphysics, and, by virtue of the untirable patience which is often a compensation, attaining great excellence in every branch of mental acquirement. The page of history is not yet unrolled which is to tell us whether such a people will or will not in the long run prevail over one whose ideas (like the words of their language) are few, but which possesses a wonderful mastery over those which it has. For an individual, however, there can be no question that a few clear ideas are worth more than many confused ones. A young man would hardly be persuaded to sacrifice the greater part of his thoughts to save the rest; and the muddled head is the least apt to see the necessity of such a sacrifice. Him we can usually only commiserate, as a person with a congenital defect. Time will help him, but intellectual maturity with regard to clearness comes rather late, an unfortunate arrangement of Nature, inasmuch as clearness is of less use to a man settled in life whose errors have in great measure had their effect, than it would be to one whose path lies before him. It is terrible to see how a single unclear idea, a single formula without meaning, lurking in a young man's head, will sometimes act like an obstruction of inert matter in an artery hindering the nutrition of the brain, and condemning its victim to pine away in the fullness of his intellectual vigor and in the midst of intellectual plenty. Many a man has cherished for years as his hobby some vague shadow of an idea, too meaningless to be positively false; he has nevertheless, passionately loved it, has made it his companion by day and by night, and has given to it his strength and his life, leaving all other occupations for its sake, and in short has lived with it and for it, until it has become, as it were, flesh of his flesh and bone of his bone; and then he has waked up some bright morning to find it gone, clean vanished away like the beautiful Melusina of the fable, and the essence of his life gone with it. I have myself known such a man; and who can tell how many histories of circle-squarers, metaphysicians, astrologers, and what not, may not be told in the old German story?

## II

The principles set forth in the first of these papers lead, at once, to a method of reaching a clearness of thought of a far higher grade than the "distinctness" of the logicians. We have there found that the action of thought is excited by the irritation of doubt, and ceases when belief is attained; so that the production of belief is the sole function of thought. All these words, however, are too strong for my purpose. It is as if I had described the phenomena as they appear under a mental microscope. Doubt and Belief, as the words are commonly employed, relate to religious or other grave discussions. But here I use them to designate the starting of any question, no matter how small or how great, and the resolution of it. If, for instance, in a horse-car, I pull out my purse and find a five-cent nickel and five coppers, I decide, while my hand is going to the purse, in which way I will pay my fare. To call such a question Doubt, and my decision Belief, is certainly to use words very disproportionate to the occasion. To speak of such a doubt as causing an irritation which needs to be appeased, suggests a temper which is uncomfortable to the verge of insanity. Yet, looking at the matter minutely, it must be admitted that, if there is the least hesitation as to whether I shall pay the five coppers or the nickel (as there will be sure to be, unless I act from some previously contracted habit in the matter), though irritation is too strong a word, yet I am excited to such small mental activity as may be necessary to deciding how I shall act. Most frequently doubts arise from some indecision, however momentary, in our action. Sometimes it is not so. I have, for example, to wait in a rail-way station, and to pass the time I read the advertisements on the walls, I compare the advantages of different trains and different routes which I never expect to take, merely fancying myself to be in a state of hesitancy, because I am bored with having nothing to trouble me. Feigned hesitancy, whether feigned for mere amusement or with a lofty purpose, plays a great part in the production of scientific inquiry. However the doubt may originate, it stimulates the mind to an activity which may be slight or energetic, calm or turbulent. Images pass rapidly through consciousness, one incessantly melting into another, until at last, when all is over—it may be in a fraction of a second, in an hour, or after long years—we find ourselves decided as to how we should act under such circumstances as those which occasioned our hesitation. In other words, we have attained belief.

In this process we observe two sorts of elements of consciousness, the distinction between which may best be made clear by means of an illustration. In a piece of music there are the separate notes, and there is the air. A single tone may be prolonged for an hour or a day, and it exists as perfectly in each second of that time as in the whole taken together; so that, as long as it is sounding, it might be present to a sense from which everything in the past was as completely absent as the future itself. But it is different with the air, the performance of which occupies a certain time, during the portions of which only portions of it are played. It consists in an orderliness in the succession of sounds which strike the ear at different times; and to perceive it there must be some continuity of consciousness which makes the events of a lapse of time present to us. We certainly only perceive the air by hearing the separate notes; yet we cannot be said to directly hear it, for we hear only what is present at the instant, and an orderliness of succession cannot exist in an instant. These two sorts of objects, what we are *immediately* conscious of and what we are *mediately* conscious of, are found in all consciousness. Some elements (the sensations) are completely present at every instant so long as they last, while others (like thought) are actions having beginning, middle, and end, and consist in a congruence in the succession of sensations which flow through the mind. They cannot be immediately present to us, but must cover some portion of the past or future. Thought is a thread of melody running through the succession of our sensations.

We may add that just as a piece of music may be written in parts, each part having its own air, so various systems of relationship of succession subsist together between the same sensations. These different systems are distinguished by having different motives, ideas, or functions. Thought is only one such system; for its sole motive, idea, and function is to produce belief, and whatever does not concern that purpose belongs to some other system of relations. The action of thinking may incidentally have other results. It may serve to amuse us, for example, and among *dilettanti* it is not rare to find those who have so perverted thought to the purposes of pleasure that it seems to vex them to think that the questions upon which they delight to exercise it may ever get finally settled; and a positive discovery which takes a favorite subject out of the arena of literary debate is met with ill-concealed dislike. This disposition is the very debauchery of thought. But the soul and meaning of thought, abstracted from the other elements which accompany it, though it may be voluntarily thwarted, can never be made to direct itself toward anything but the production of belief. Thought in action has for its only possible motive the attainment of thought at rest; and whatever does not refer to belief is no part of the thought itself.

And what, then, is belief? It is the demi-cadence which closes a musical phrase in the symphony of our intellectual life. We have seen that it has just three properties: First, it is something that we are aware of; second, it appeases the irritation of doubt; and, third, it involves the establishment in our nature of a rule of action, or, say for short, a *habit*. As it appeases the irritation of doubt, which is the motive for thinking, thought relaxes, and comes to rest for a moment when belief is reached. But, since belief is a rule for action, the application of which involves further doubt and further thought, at the same time that it is a stopping-place, it is also a new starting-place for thought. That is why I have permitted myself to call it thought at rest although thought is essentially an action. The *final* upshot of thinking is the exercise of volition, and of this thought no longer forms a part; but belief is only a stadium of mental action, an effect upon our nature due to thought, which will influence future thinking.

The essence of belief is the establishment of a habit, and different beliefs are distinguished by the different moods of action to which they give rise. If beliefs do not differ in this respect, if they appease the same doubt by producing the same rule of action, then no mere differences in the manner of consciousness of them can make them different beliefs, any more than playing a tune in different keys is playing different tunes. Imaginary distinctions are often drawn between beliefs which differ only in their mode of expression;—the wrangling which ensues is real enough, however. To believe that any objects are arranged as in Fig. 1, and to believe that they are arranged as in Fig. 2, are one and the same belief; yet it is conceivable that a man should assert one

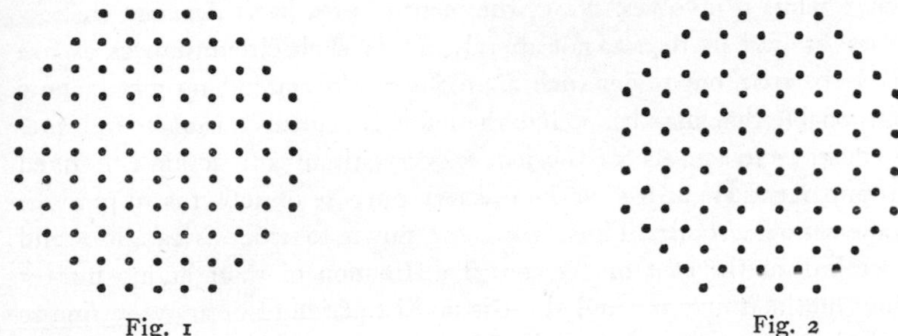

Fig. 1 Fig. 2

proposition and deny the other. Such false distinctions do as much harm as the confusion of beliefs really different, and are among the pitfalls of which we ought constantly to beware, especially when we are upon metaphysical ground. One singular deception of this sort, which often occurs, is to mistake the sensation produced by our own unclearness of thought for a character of the object we are thinking. Instead of perceiving that the obscurity is purely subjective, we fancy that we contemplate a quality of the object which is essentially mysterious; and if our conception be afterward presented to us in a clear form we do not recognize it as the same, owing to the absence of the feeling of unintelligibility. So long as this deception lasts, it obviously puts an impassable barrier in the way of perspicuous thinking; so that it equally interests the opponents of rational thought to perpetuate it, and its adherents to guard against it.

Another such deception is to mistake a mere difference in the grammatical construction of two words for a distinction between the ideas they express. In this pedantic age, when the general mob of writers attend so much more to words than to things, this error is common enough. When I just said that thought is an action, and that it consists in a *relation,* although a person performs an action but not a relation, which can only be the result of an action, yet there was no inconsistency in what I said, but only a grammatical vagueness.

From all these sophisms we shall be perfectly safe so long as we reflect that the whole function of thought is to produce habits of action; and that whatever there is connected with a thought, but irrelevant to its purpose, is an accretion to it, but no part of it. If there be a unity among our sensation[s] which has no reference to how we shall act on a given occasion, as when we listen to a piece of music, why we do not call that thinking. To develop its meaning, we have, therefore, simply to determine what habits it produces, for what a thing means is simply what habits it involves. Now, the identity of a habit depends on how it might lead us to act, not merely under such circumstances as are likely to arise, but under such as might possibly occur, no matter how improbable they may be. What the habit is depends on *when* and *how* it causes us to act. As for the *when,* every stimulus to action is derived from perception; as for the *how,* every purpose of action is to produce some sensible result. Thus, we come down to what is tangible and practical, as the root of every real distinction of thought, no matter how subtile it may be; and there is no distinction of meaning so fine as to consist in anything but a possible difference of practice.

To see what this principle leads to, consider in the light of it such a doctrine as that of transubstantiation. The Protestant churches generally hold that the elements of the sacrament are flesh and blood only in a tropical sense; they nourish our souls as meat and the juice of it would our bodies. But the Catholics maintain that they are literally just that; although they possess all the sensible qualities of wafer-cakes and diluted wine. But we can have no conception of wine except what may enter into a belief, either—

1. That this, that, or the other, is wine; or,
2. That wine possesses certain properties.

Such beliefs are nothing but self-notifications that we should, upon occasion, act in regard to such things as we believe to be wine according to the qualities which we believe wine to possess. The occasion of such action would be some sensible perception, the motive of it to produce some sensible result. Thus our action has exclusive reference to what affects the senses, our habit has the same bearing as our action, our belief the same as our habit, our conception the same as our belief; and we can consequently mean nothing by wine but what has certain effects, direct or indirect, upon our senses; and to talk of something as having all the sensible characters of wine, yet being in reality blood, is senseless jargon. Now, it is not my object to pursue the theological question; and having used it as a logical example I drop it, without caring to anticipate the theologian's reply. I only desire to point out how impossible it is that we should have an idea in our minds which relates to anything but conceived sensible effects of things. Our idea of anything *is* our idea of its sensible effects; and if we fancy that we have any other we deceive ourselves, and mistake a mere sensation accompanying the thought for a part of the thought itself. It is absurd to say that thought has any meaning unrelated to its only function. It is foolish for Catholics and Protestants to fancy themselves in disagreement about the elements of the sacrament, if they agree in regard to all their sensible effects, here or hereafter.

It appears, then, that the rule for attaining the third grade of clearness of apprehension is as follows: Consider what effects, which might conceivably have practical bearings, we conceive the object of our conception to have. Then, our conception of these effects is the whole of our conception of the object.

## III

Let us illustrate this rule by some examples; and, to begin with the simplest one possible, let us ask what we mean by calling a thing *hard*. Evidently that it will not be scratched by many other substances. The whole conception of this quality, as of every other, lies in its conceived effects. There is absolutely no difference between a hard thing and a soft thing so long as they are not brought to the test. Suppose, then, that a diamond could be crystallized in the midst of a cushion of soft cotton, and should remain there until it was finally burned up. Would it be false to say that that diamond was soft? This seems a foolish question, and would be so, in fact, except in the realm of logic. There such questions are often of the greatest utility as serving to bring logical principles into sharper relief than real discussions ever could. In studying logic we must not put them aside with hasty answers, but must consider them with attentive care, in order to make out the principles involved. We may, in the present case, modify our question, and ask what prevents us from saying that all hard bodies remain perfectly soft until they are touched, when their hardness increases with the pressure until they are scratched. Reflection will show that the reply is this: there would be no *falsity* in such modes of speech. They would involve a modification of our present usage of speech with regard to the words hard and soft, but not of their meanings. For they represent no fact to be different from what it is; only they involve arrangements of facts which would be exceedingly maladroit. This leads us to remark that the question of what would occur under circumstances which do not actually arise is not a question of fact, but only of the most perspicuous arrangement of them. For example, the question of *free-will and fate* in its simplest form, stripped of verbiage, is something like this: I have done something of which I am ashamed; could I, by an effort of the will, have resisted the temptation, and done otherwise? The philosophical reply is, that this is not a question of fact, but only of the arrangement of facts. Arranging them so as to exhibit what is particularly pertinent to my question—namely, that I ought to blame myself for having done wrong—it is perfectly true to say that, if I had willed to do otherwise than I did, I should have done otherwise. On the other hand, arranging the facts so as to exhibit another important consideration, it is equally true that, when a temptation has once been allowed to work, it will, if it has a certain force, produce its effect, let me struggle how I may. There is no objection to a contradiction in what would result from a false supposition. The *reductio ad absurdum* consists in showing that contradictory results would follow from a hypothesis which is consequently judged to be false. Many questions are involved in the free-will discussion, and I am far from desiring to say that both sides are equally right. On the contrary, I am of opinion that one side denies important facts, and that the other does not. But what I do say is, that the above single question was the origin of the whole doubt; that, had it not been for this question, the controversy would never have arisen; and that this question is perfectly solved in the manner which I have indicated.

Let us next seek a clear idea of Weight. This is another very easy case. To say that a body is heavy means simply that, in the absence of opposing force, it will fall. This (neglecting certain specifications of how it will fall, etc., which exist in the mind of the physicist who uses the word) is evidently the whole conception of weight. It is a fair question whether some particular facts may not *account* for gravity; but what we mean by the force itself is completely involved in its effects.

This leads us to undertake an account of the idea of Force in general. This is the great conception which, developed in the early part of the seventeenth century from the rude idea of a cause, and constantly improved upon since, has shown us how to explain all the changes of motion which bodies experience, and how to think about all physical phenomena; which has given birth to modern science, and changed the face of the globe; and which, aside from its more special uses, has played a principal part in directing the course of modern thought, and in furthering modern social development. It is, therefore, worth some pains to comprehend it. According to our rule, we must begin by asking what is the immediate use of thinking about force; and the answer is, that we thus account for changes of motion. If bodies were left to themselves, without the intervention of forces, every motion would continue unchanged both in velocity and in direction. Furthermore, change of motion never takes place abruptly; if its direction is changed, it is always through a curve without angles; if its velocity alters, it is by degrees. The gradual changes which are constantly taking place are conceived by geometers to be compounded together according to the rules of the parallelogram of forces. If the reader does not already know what this is, he will find it, I hope, to his advantage to endeavor to follow the following explanation; but if mathematics are insupportable to him, pray let him skip three paragraphs rather than that we should part company here.

A *path* is a line whose beginning and end are distinguished. Two paths are considered to be equivalent, which, beginning at the same point lead to the same point. Thus the two paths, A B C D E and A F G H E (Fig. 3) are equivalent. Paths which do *not* begin at the same point are considered to be equivalent, provided that, on moving either of them without turning it, but keeping it always parallel to its original position, when its beginning coincides with that of the other path, the ends also coincide. Paths are considered as geometrically added together, when one begins where the other ends; thus the path AE is conceived to be a sum of AB, BC, CD, and DE. In the parallelogram of Fig. 4 the diagonal AC is the sum of AB and BC; or, since AD is geometrically equivalent to BC, AC is the geometrical sum of AB and AD.

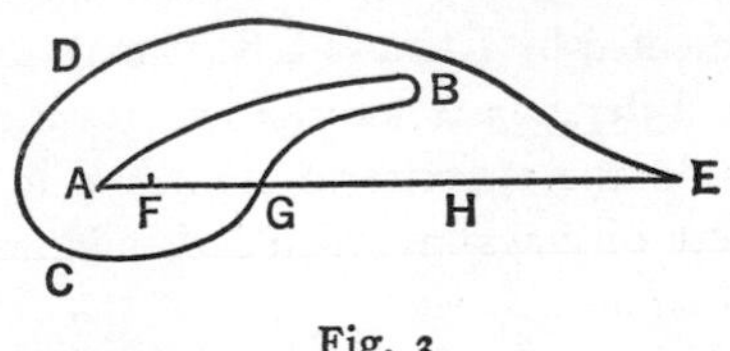

Fig. 3

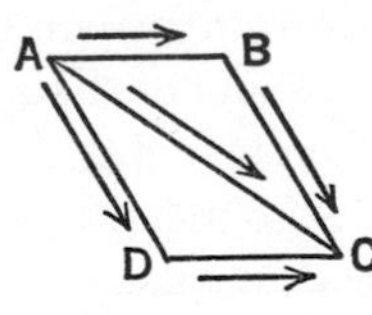

Fig. 4

All this is purely conventional. It simply amounts to this: that we choose to call paths having the relations I have described equal or added. But though it is a convention, it is a convention with a good reason. The rule for geometrical addition may be applied not only to paths, but to any other things which can be represented by paths. Now, as a path is determined by the varying direction and distance of the point which moves over it from the starting-point, it follows that anything which from its beginning to its end is determined by a varying direction and a varying magnitude is capable of being represented by a line. Accordingly, *velocities* may be represented by lines, for they have only directions and rates. The same thing is true of *accelerations,* or changes of velocities. This is evident enough in the case of velocities; and it becomes evident for accelerations if we consider that precisely what velocities are to positions—namely, states of change of them—that accelerations are to velocities.

The so-called "parallelogram of forces" is simply a rule for compounding accelerations. The rule is, to represent the accelerations by paths, and then to geometrically add the paths. The geometers, however, not only use the "parallelogram of forces" to compound different accelerations, but also to resolve one acceleration into a sum of several. Let AB (Fig. 5) be the path which represents a certain acceleration —say, such a change in the motion of a body that at the end of one second the body will, under the influence of that change, be in a position different from what it would have had if its motion had continued unchanged, such that a path equivalent to AB would lead from

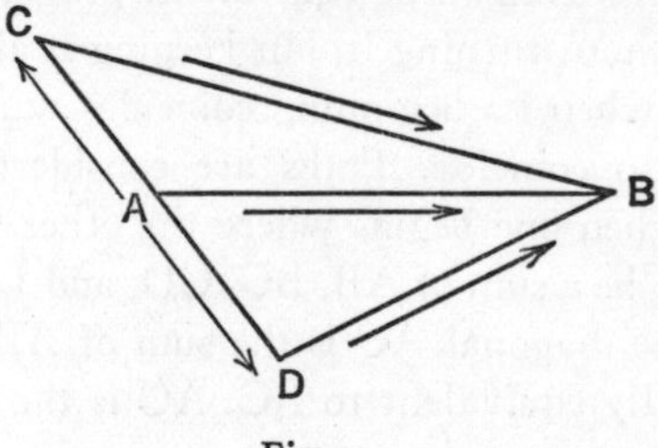

Fig. 5

the latter position to the former. This acceleration may be considered as the sum of the accelerations represented by AC and CB. It may also be considered as the sum of the very different accelerations represented by AD and DB, where AD is almost the opposite of AC. And it is clear that there is an immense variety of ways in which AB might be resolved into the sum of two accelerations.

After this tedious explanation, which I hope, in view of the extraordinary interest of the conception of force, may not have exhausted the reader's patience, we are prepared at last to state the grand fact which this conception embodies. This fact is that if the actual changes of motion which the different particles of bodies experience are each resolved in its appropriate way, each component acceleration is precisely such as is prescribed by a certain law of Nature, according to which bodies in the relative positions which the bodies in question actually have at the moment always receive certain accelerations, which, being compounded by geometrical addition, give the acceleration which the body actually experiences.

This is the only fact which the idea of force represents, and whoever will take the trouble clearly to apprehend what this fact is, perfectly comprehends what force is. Whether we ought to say that a force *is* an acceleration, or that it *causes* an acceleration, is a mere question of propriety of language, which has no more to do with our real meaning than the difference between the French idiom *"Il fait froid"* and its English equivalent *"It is cold."* Yet it is surprising to see how this simple affair has muddled men's minds. In how many profound treatises is not force spoken of as a "mysterious entity," which seems to be only a way of confessing that the author despairs of ever getting a clear notion of what the word means! In a recent admired work on *Analytic Mechanics* it is stated that we understand precisely the effect of force, but what force itself is we do not understand! This is simply a self-contradiction. The idea which the word force excites in our minds has no other function than to affect our actions, and these actions can have no reference to force otherwise than through its effects. Consequently, if we know what the effects of force are, we are acquainted with every fact which is implied in saying that a force exists, and there is nothing more to know. The truth is, there is some vague notion afloat that a question may mean something which the mind cannot conceive; and when some hair-splitting philosophers have been confronted with the absurdity of such a view, they have invented an empty distinction between positive and negative conceptions, in the attempt to give their non-idea a form not obviously nonsensical. The nullity of it is sufficiently plain from the considerations given a few pages back; and, apart from those considerations, the quibbling character of the distinction must have struck every mind accustomed to real thinking.

## IV

Let us now approach the subject of logic, and consider a conception which particularly concerns it, that of *reality*. Taking clearness in the sense of familiarity, no idea could be clearer than this. Every child uses it with perfect confidence, never dreaming that he does not understand it. As for clearness in its second grade, however, it would probably puzzle most men, even among those of a reflective turn of mind, to give an abstract definition of the real. Yet such a definition may perhaps be reached by considering the points of difference between reality and its opposite, fiction. A figment is a product of somebody's imagination; it has such characters as his thought impresses upon it. That those characters are independent of how you or I think is an external reality. There are, however, phenomena within our own minds, dependent upon our thought, which are at the same time real in the sense that we really think them. But though their characters depend on how we think, they do not depend on what we think those characters to be. Thus, a dream has a real existence as a mental phenomenon, if somebody has really dreamt it; that he dreamt so and so, does not depend on what anybody thinks was dreamt, but is completely independent of all opinion of the subject. On the other hand, considering, not the fact of dreaming, but the thing dreamt, it retains its peculiarities by virtue of no other fact than that it was dreamt to possess them. Thus we may define the real as that whose characters are independent of what anybody may think them to be.

But, however satisfactory such a definition may be found, it would be a great mistake to suppose that it makes the idea of reality perfectly clear. Here, then, let us apply our rules. According to them, reality, like every other quality, consists in the peculiar sensible effects which things partaking of it produce. The only effect which real things have is to cause belief, for all the sensations which they excite emerge into consciousness in the form of beliefs. The question, therefore, is, how is true belief (or belief in the real) distinguished from false belief (or belief in fiction). Now, as we have seen in the former paper, the ideas of truth and falsehood, in their full development, appertain exclusively to the scientific method of settling opinion. A person who arbitrarily chooses the propositions which he will adopt can use the word truth only to emphasize the expression of his determination to hold on to his choice. Of course, the method of tenacity never prevailed exclusively; reason is too natural to men for that. But in the literature of the dark ages we find some fine examples of it. When Scotus Erigena is commenting upon a poetical passage in which hellebore is spoken of as having caused the death of Socrates, he does not hesitate to inform the inquiring reader that Helleborus and Socrates were two eminent Greek philosophers, and that the latter having been overcome in argument by the former took the matter to heart and died of it! What sort of an idea of truth could a man have who could adopt and teach, without the qualification of a perhaps, an opinion taken so entirely at random? The real spirit of Socrates, who I hope would have been delighted to have been "overcome in argument," because he would have learned something by it, is in curious contrast with the naïve idea of the glossist, for whom discussion would seem to have been simply a struggle. When philosophy began to awake from its long slumber, and before theology completely dominated it, the practice seems to have been for each professor to seize upon any philosophical position he found unoccupied and which seemed a strong one, to intrench himself in it, and to sally forth from time to time to give battle to the others. Thus, even the scanty records we possess of those disputes enable us to make out a dozen or more opinions held by different teachers at one time concerning the question of nominalism and realism. Read the opening part of the *Historia Calamitatum* of Abelard, who was certainly as philosophical as any of his contemporaries, and see the spirit of combat which it breathes. For him, the truth is simply his particular stronghold. When the method of authority prevailed, the truth meant little more than the Catholic faith. All the efforts of the scholastic doctors are directed toward harmonizing their faith in Aristotle and their faith in the Church, and one may search their ponderous folios through without finding an argument which goes any further. It is noticeable that where different faiths flourish side by side, renegades are looked upon with contempt even by the party whose belief they adopt; so completely has the idea of loyalty replaced that of truth-seeking. Since the time of Descartes, the defect in the conception of truth has been less apparent. Still, it will sometimes strike a scientific man that the philosophers have been less intent on finding out what the facts are, than on inquiring what belief is most in harmony with their system. It is hard to convince a follower of the *a priori* method by adducing facts; but show him that an opinion he is defending is inconsistent with what he has laid down elsewhere, and he will be very apt to retract it. These minds do not seem to believe that disputation is ever to cease; they seem to think that the opinion which is natural for one man is not so for another, and that belief will, consequently, never be settled. In contenting themselves with fixing their own opinions by a method which would lead another man to a different result, they betray their feeble hold of the conception of what truth is.

On the other hand, all the followers of science are fully persuaded that the processes of investigation, if only pushed far enough, will give one certain solution to every question to which they can be applied. One man may investigate the velocity of light by studying the transits of Venus and the aberration of the stars; another by the oppositions of

Mars and the eclipses of Jupiter's satellites; a third by the method of Fizeau; a fourth by that of Foucault; a fifth by the motions of the curves of Lissajoux; a sixth, a seventh, an eighth, and a ninth, may follow the different methods of comparing the measures of statical and dynamical electricity. They may at first obtain different results, but, as each perfects his method and his processes, the results will move steadily together toward a destined center. So with all scientific research. Different minds may set out with the most antagonistic views, but the progress of investigation carries them by a force outside of themselves to one and the same conclusion. This activity of thought by which we are carried, not where we wish, but to a foreordained goal, is like the operation of destiny. No modification of the point of view taken, no selection of other facts for study, no natural bent of mind, even, can enable a man to escape the predestinate opinion. This great law is embodied in the conception of truth and reality. The opinion which is fated to be ultimately agreed to by all who investigate, is what we mean by the truth, and the object represented in this opinion is the real. That is the way I would explain reality.

But it may be said that this view is directly opposed to the abstract definition which we have given of reality, inasmuch as it makes the characters of the real depend on what is ultimately thought about them. But the answer to this is that, on the one hand, reality is independent, not necessarily of thought in general, but only of what you or I or any finite number of men may think about it; and that, on the other hand, though the object of the final opinion depends on what that opinion is, yet what that opinion is does not depend on what you or I or any man thinks. Our perversity and that of others may indefinitely postpone the settlement of opinion; it might even conceivably cause an arbitrary proposition to be universally accepted as long as the human race should last. Yet even that would not change the nature of the belief, which alone could be the result of investigation carried sufficiently far; and if, after the extinction of our race, another should arise with faculties and disposition for investigation, that true opinion must be the one which they would ultimately come to. "Truth crushed to earth shall rise again," and the opinion which would finally result from investigation does not depend on how anybody may actually think. But the reality of that which is real does depend on the real fact that investigation is destined to lead, at last, if continued long enough, to a belief in it.

But I may be asked what I have to say to all the minute facts of history, forgotten never to be recovered, to the lost books of the ancients, to the buried secrets.

Full many a gem of purest ray serene
The dark, unfathomed caves of ocean bear;
Full many a flower is born to blush unseen,
And waste its sweetness on the desert air.

Do these things not really exist because they are hopelessly beyond the reach of our knowledge? And then, after the universe is dead (according to the prediction of some scientists), and all life has ceased forever, will not the shock of atoms continue though there will be no mind to know it? To this I reply that, though in no possible state of knowledge can any number be great enough to express the relation between the amount of what rests unknown to the amount of the known, yet it is unphilosophical to suppose that, with regard to any given question (which has any clear meaning), investigation would not bring forth a solution of it, if it were carried far enough. Who would have said, a few years ago, that we could ever know of what substances stars are made whose light may have been longer in reaching us than the human race has existed. Who can be sure of what we shall not know in a few hundred years? Who can guess what would be the result of continuing the pursuit of science for ten thousand years, with the activity of the last hundred? And if it were to go on for a million or a billion, or any number of years you please, how is it possible to say that there is any question which might not ultimately be solved?

But it may be objected, "Why make so much of these remote considerations, especially when it is your principle that only practical distinctions have a meaning?" Well, I must confess that it makes very little difference whether we say that a stone on the bottom of the ocean in complete darkness, is brilliant or not—that is to say, that it *probably* makes no difference, remembering always that that stone *may* be fished up to-morrow. But that there are gems at the bottom of the sea, flowers in the untraveled desert, etc., are propositions which, like that about a diamond being hard when it is not pressed, concern much more the arrangement of our language than they do the meaning of our ideas.

It seems to me, however, that we have, by the application of our rule, reached so clear an apprehension of what we mean by reality, and of the fact which the idea rests on, that we should not, perhaps, be making a pretension so presumptuous as it would be singular, if we were to offer a metaphysical theory of existence for universal acceptance among those who employ the scientific method of fixing belief. However, as metaphysics is a subject much more curious than useful, the knowledge of which, like that of a sunken reef, serves chiefly to enable us to keep clear of it, I will not trouble the reader with any more Ontology at this moment. I have already been led much further into that path than I should have desired; and I have given the reader such a dose of mathematics, psychology, and all that is most abstruse, that I fear he may already have left me, and that what I am now writing is for the compositor and proofreader exclusively. I trusted to the importance of the subject. There is no royal road to logic, and really valuable ideas can only be had at the price of close attention. But I know that in the matter of ideas the public prefer the cheap and nasty; and in my next paper I am going to return to the easily intelligible, and not wander from it again. The reader who has been at the pains of wading through this paper shall be rewarded in the next one by seeing how beautifully what has been developed in this tedious way can be applied to the ascertainment of the rules of scientific reasoning.

We have, hitherto, not crossed the threshold of scientific logic. It is certainly important to know how to make our ideas clear, but they may be ever so clear without being true. How to make them so, we have next to study. How to give birth to those vital and procreative ideas which multiply into a thousand forms and diffuse themselves everywhere, advancing civilization and making the dignity of man, is an art not yet reduced to rules, but of the secret of which the history of science affords some hints.

# XXI
# William Torrey Harris
## 1835–1909

Born near North Killingly, Conn. Yale College, 1854–57. Teacher in public schools at St. Louis, 1858–66; Assistant Superintendent, 1866–68; Superintendent, 1868–80. Editor, *Journal of Speculative Philosophy,* 1867–93. Resigned Superintendency and moved to Concord, 1880. Concord School of Philosophy, 1879–87. United States Commissioner of Education, 1889–1906, residing in Washington. Editor, Appleton's International Education Series (58 vols.). Editor-in-chief, *Webster's New International Dictionary,* 1909. Died in Providence.

I measure my words when I say that in my judgment Dr. Harris had the one truly great philosophical mind which has yet [1929] appeared on the western continent.—*Nicholas Murray Butler.*

With this singular judgment, which is at the same time a judgment of Peirce, Royce, James and Dewey, a sober historian can hardly concur. Harris was rather our greatest *promoter* of philosophy. He founded and edited the first philosophical journal in the English language, thus providing a medium of publication for the early work of these younger but abler thinkers, and Dewey at least has acknowledged that the encouragement Harris gave him was a determining factor in his choice of philosophy as a career. The journal also widened the range of American philosophy and raised the standard of philosophical scholarship, chiefly through its translations, analyses and criticisms of the works of the great thinkers of Greece and Germany.

Harris owed his philosophical awakening to two quite different men, one scarcely remembered except as the father of *Little Women* and the other long since forgotten. Each had a mind more sensitive, original and profound than Harris's, but lacking his powers of organization and communication. He became the interpreter of each to the other and of both to the philosophical public, and his own position was arrived at partly through this effort of reconciliation.

In March, 1857, Bronson Alcott spent two weeks at Yale College, gave "Conversations" on Plato and Plotinus, was preached against in the college chapel as a representative of "the new philosophical infidelity," and converted Harris to philosophy and idealism. In the following year, Harris met in St. Louis a Prussian immigrant named Henry Brokmeyer, who started him on his life-long study of Hegel. In January, 1859, Harris brought the two men together in St. Louis. He was then twenty-three, Brokmeyer thirty-two, Alcott fifty-nine.

Brokmeyer had come to America at the age of seventeen to escape military service, worked his way from New York through the middle west to Mississippi, settled there in the tanning business and joined the Baptist Church. With the savings of several years he had gone to Georgetown College in Kentucky and then to Brown University in Providence, Rhode Island. In both these Baptist institutions he had disputed theology with the presidents, and at Providence he had drifted from the church and contracted the fever of transcendentalism. In the year in which Thoreau's *Walden* appeared (1854) he had retreated from society into the woods of Missouri. In 1858 he was in St. Louis earning money for hunting and other needed equipment. While still at Providence, he had caught sight of the philosophic luminary (Hegel) who was to restore him to society after his romantic exile and to become the guiding light of the St. Louis movement. F. H. Hedge, the only American transcendentalist who had been from the start at home in German philosophy, was then the Unitarian minister at Providence, and Brokmeyer probably made his acquaintance and certainly read his *Prose Writers of Germany* (1848), with extracts from Hegel and an indication of his system's claim to be the culmination of the whole movement of European philosophy. It gradually dawned upon Brokmeyer that there might be an emancipation from emancipation, a transcending of transcendentalism, and that Hegel had charted the way. Harris, whose transcendental inoculation was still fresh, aroused his tutorial instinct. At his suggestion, Harris ordered from Germany a copy of Hegel's "larger Logic," which was conceded to be the key to his system. Harris and two of his friends, "possessed with a sort of philosophical fury," kept Brokmeyer in St. Louis and paid his modest living expenses for a year while he wrote out for them a labored English translation. These four became the nucleus of a Kant Club, so called because they were working their way back from Hegel through his predecessors to Kant, the first begetter of German idealism, to see precisely what *was* the transcendentalism which Hegel had transcended.

At Harris's invitation, Alcott spent January and part of February,

1859, in St. Louis, in daily association with this group. They were already thinking in Hegelian terms, talked a great deal about "method" and "dialectic," did not admire Alcott's and Emerson's way of simply declaring their intuitions, thought nothing could be understood except through its history, attached less importance to individuals than to institutions and in particular to the state. Back in Concord, Alcott secured two or three simplified accounts of Hegel's philosophy, but neither he nor Emerson could make much of them.

The Civil War brought changes in the membership of the Kant Club and some interruption of its communications with Concord; but it provided the new Hegelianism with a forcing-bed for its maturation. Torn by internal dissension, Missouri was virtually under a dual regime throughout the War, and there was fighting of the fiercest and bitterest nature between Confederate partisans and Union extremists, which, though it had little influence on the outcome of the War elsewhere, brought its issues home to the St. Louis group. As Hegel had fought for a united Germany, Brokmeyer saw in his philosophy the rationale of a reunited America. In the Hegelian dialectic as applied to the state, "abstract right" is opposed by an equally "abstract morality," and the two are reconciled in the culminating "ethical state." To Brokmeyer and his followers, the southern secessionists represented "abstract right," the northern abolitionists represented "abstract morality," and the new union that was to emerge from the tragic conflict was the "ethical state." But this was to come by a genuinely Hegelian synthesis, not by mere conquest and subjection. As a member of Missouri's provisional Union assembly, therefore, Brokmeyer resisted the attempts of extremists to disfranchise southern sympathizers. He applied the fixed formula of triadic movement (affirmation-negation-reconciliation) not only to the struggle as a whole, but to each new development or phase as it arose, both during the war and during the reconstruction period that followed. Harris later recalled how he

> impressed us with the practicality of philosophy, inasmuch as he could flash into the questions of the day, or even into the questions of the moment, the highest insight of philosophy and solve their problems. . . . We studied the "dialectic" of politics and political parties and understood how measures and men might be combined by its light.[1]

Meanwhile, Harris continued his philosophical studies, began writing articles, resumed correspondence with Alcott in 1863, and spent two days with him and Emerson at Concord in 1865. Alcott found

[1] *Hegel's Logic.* xiii.

him "a profound master of Hegel and the German thinkers, able to apply their dialectic to life, literature, art, society, and a man for whom a great future is opening." [2] In January, 1866, the St. Louis Philosophical Society was organized with Brokmeyer as president and Harris as secretary, and in February Alcott came to spend a month as Harris's guest. The new and much larger group included a wider range of talents and a greater variety of interests and views. Two physicians were taking seriously Alcott's doctrine of Genesis and trying to work it out. Other members of the group told him that he was "a Hegelian in spirit if not in form," and Alcott on his side began to respect their concern for form and method. A few weeks later he observed for the first time the unsystematic character of Emerson's thought. Emerson himself was now absorbed in *The Secret of Hegel,* "a rugged book" in two volumes which its author, Hutchison Stirling, had sent him from England; and Alcott's daughter Louisa brought him a set on her return from Europe in July.

Early in the summer Harris submitted an article on Herbert Spencer to the *North American Review*. Charles Eliot Norton, associate editor with James Russell Lowell, asked Chauncey Wright to read it. Wright read it aloud to his close friend E. W. Gurney, Professor of History at Harvard. Gurney pronounced it "a howling wilderness," and Wright reported to Norton that it was "the mere dry husk of Hegelianism, —dogmatic, without the only merit of dogmatism, distinctness of definition." [3] Harris read Norton's letter of rejection to a group assembled in Brokmeyer's law office, and said the time had come for the St. Louis movement to have an organ of its own. In January, 1867, the first number of *The Journal of Speculative Philosophy* appeared, with "Herbert Spencer" as the leading article.

This article was preceded by a page in which the *Journal* introduced itself "To the Reader," and four more in which "The Speculative" was defined as that highest level of apprehension to which Plato's dialogues had pointed the way, and for which Hegel's logic provided the completest discipline. All the great philosophers were agreed "not only with respect to the transcendency of the Speculative, but also with reference to the content of its knowing." This content, which philosophy presented to pure thought, was one with that which art presented to the senses, and religion to fantasy and understanding. It is no occasion for surprise, therefore, to find the *Journal* devoting about

[2] Shepard, Odell: *The Journals of Bronson Alcott.* Boston: Little, Brown and Co., 1938. 373.

[3] Thayer, J. B., (editor): *Letters of Chauncey Wright.* 87.

a third of its space to theories of art, to the nature of the various fine arts, and to discussions of particular works of art. Much less attention was given to religion as such, which had not yet become "a subject for free reflection," but there was no lack of material revealing "the speculative depth" of the great ideas underlying it, and each issue beginning with the third of volume fourteen carried on the cover the motto from Novalis: "Philosophy can bake no bread; but she can procure for us God, Freedom, and Immortality."

The real genius of the movement which gave birth to the *Journal* is better represented, however, by the emphasis in its initial address "To the Reader" upon the movement of the national consciousness out of its phase of "brittle individualism, in which national unity seemed an external mechanism," into a new phase, which needed to be digested and comprehended, in which "each individual recognizes his substantial side to be the State as such." Harris returned to this theme at the end of the article on "The Concrete and the Abstract" with which he opened the fifth volume.

> The depth of a system of thought has an infallible test in the manner it disposes of institutions. When one man, or set of men, get up on the house-tops and proclaim a new doctrine for all mankind, Civilization answers back: "What do you make of my creations—the institutions of realized intelligence—the family, society, the state, and religion?". . . For the forms of civilization—the laws and usages which constitute the warp and woof of its institutions—are not the vain thought of abstract theorists, but the grim necessity in which the human will has made possible the exercise of its freedom. For necessity and freedom are harmonized in institutions alone, and without institutions man is a savage and nothing more. . . .

The St. Louis philosophers were, in fact, institutional men. Brokmeyer was successively colonel of a regiment he had himself recruited, state assemblyman, city councilman, state senator, leader in the state constitutional convention, lieutenant governor, acting governor and corporation lawyer. Harris was superintendent of schools, United States Commissioner of Education, and the most influential figure in American public education for a generation or more. A. E. Kroeger, translator of Fichte and correspondent for the *New York Times,* was city treasurer. J. G. Woerner, for whose treatises on the American law of administration and of guardianship Hegel supplied the philosophical foundations, was probate judge from 1870 to 1894 after holding a continuous series of other public offices for the previous seventeen years. Denton J. Snider and Thomas Davidson were teachers who later pioneered in adult education. Besides these, the group included another judge, a lawyer who wrote on financial, legal and political questions, three school principals and a later superintendent of schools, a leading minister, and three physicians, two of whom played a part in the development of higher medical education.

It is no accident, moreover, that the heyday of the Society, the *Journal's* St. Louis years, the political career of Brokmeyer and the superintendency of Harris, all fell within the period of "The Great Illusion." As early as 1851 there were dreams of St. Louis becoming the greatest as well as the most cosmopolitan city on the continent, but in the sixties and seventies it was, in the grandiose prophecies of Logan Uriah Reavis, "The Future Great City of the World." This was the era of the James B. Eads Bridge and the rise to power of Carl Schurz and Joseph Pulitzer, and the time seemed ripe for removing the national capital to St. Louis. The bubble was pricked by the census of 1880, which put the ascendency of Chicago beyond question. How long the local philosophical movement would have survived the shock if Harris and the *Journal* had remained in St. Louis, it would be hard to say; in any case, both moved to Concord, where the Concord School of Philosophy had already begun its annual summer sessions. This removal and the Concord School itself symbolized the essential kinship underlying the apparent conflict between the transcendentalism of Emerson and Alcott and the Hegelian philosophy of institutions inspired by Brokmeyer. In the comparative leisure of his Concord years Harris completed his synthesis of the two movements, and wrote his major work, *Hegel's Logic,* dedicated to Henry C. Brokmeyer.

## REFERENCES

Harris, William Torrey: *Hegel's Logic: A Book on the Genesis of the Categories of the Mind: A Critical Exposition.* Chicago: S. C. Griggs and Co., 1890. Second edition, 1895.

———: *Introduction to the Study of Philosophy.* Comprising Passages from his Writings, Selected and Arranged with Commentary and Illustrations by Marietta Kies. New York: D. Appleton and Co., 1890.

———: *The Spiritual Sense of Dante's "Divina Commedia."* Revised edition. Boston: Houghton Mifflin Co., 1896. (First edition, 1889.)

———: "The Philosophy of Bronson Alcott and the Transcendentalists," in Sanborn, F. B., and Harris, William T.: *A. Bronson Alcott: His Life and Philosophy.* Boston: Roberts Brothers, 1893. 544–664.

———: *Psychologic Foundations of Education: An Attempt to Show* the *Genesis of the Higher Faculties of the Mind.* New York: D. Appleton and Co., 1898.

Curti, Merle: *The Social Ideas of American Educators.* New York: Charles Scribner's Sons, 1935. (Ch. IX, "William T. Harris, The Conservator.")

Perry, Charles M. (editor): *The St. Louis Movement in Philosophy: Some Source Material.* Norman: University of Oklahoma Press, 1930. (Contains a list of 479 writings of Harris, chronologically arranged, with subject index.)

Schaub, Edward L. (editor): *William Torrey Harris, 1835–1935.* Chicago: Open Court Publishing Co., 1936. (Seven articles on Harris, the St. Louis Movement, and the *Journal of Speculative Philosophy,* with an extensive bibliography of writings about him.)

* * *

---

* * *

# PHILOSOPHY IN OUTLINE [4]

## *Introduction*

*Philosophy is not a science of things in general, but a science that investigates the presuppositions of experience and discovers the nature of the first principle.*

1. Philosophy does not set up the extravagant pretension to know all things. It does not "take all knowledge for its province" any more than geology, or astronomy, or logic does. Geology aspires to know the entire structure of this globe; astronomy, to know all the stars; logic, to know the structure of the reasoning process. Philosophy attempts to find the necessary *a priori* elements or factors in experience, and arrange them into a system by deducing them from a first principle. Not the forms of reasoning alone, but the forms of sense-perception, of reflection, of speculative knowing, and the very forms which condition being or existence itself, are to be investigated.

2. The science of necessary forms is a very special science, because it does not concern itself with collecting and arranging the infinite multi-

[4] *Journal of Speculative Philosophy* 17 (1883) 296–312 (chs. I–VI). The subsequent chapters here omitted are: VII, The Triune Nature of God; VIII, The True Infinite is Free Energy; IX, Freedom, Fate, Individuality; X, The World of Nature and Education; XI, The World of Man and Immortality. The last states his theory of the Invisible Church as the perfect archetype of institutions, which anticipates Royce's doctrine of the community.

tude of particular objects in the world and identifying their species and genera, as the particular sciences do. It investigates the presupposed conditions and ascends to the one supreme condition. It therefore turns its back on the multitude of particular things and seizes them in the unity of their "ascent and cause," as George Herbert names it. The particular sciences and departments of knowledge collect and classify and explain phenomena. Philosophy collects and classifies and explains their explanations. Its province is much more narrow and special than theirs. If to explain meant to find the many, the different, the particular examples or specimens, philosophy would have to take all knowledge for its province if it aspired to explain the explanations offered in the several sciences. But that is not its meaning—to explain means to find the common, the generic principle in the particular. This is just the opposite of that other process which would take all knowledge in its infinite details for its province. To explain all knowledge is not to know all things.

3. To illustrate Philosophic Knowing, and at the same time to enter its province and begin philosophizing, we shall take up at once a consideration of three ideas—Space, Time, and Cause. Space and Time—as the conditions of nature or the world, as the necessary presuppositions of extension and multitude—will furnish us occasion to consider the infinite and the possibility of knowing it. The idea of Cause will lead us to the fundamental insight on which true philosophy rests.

## *Space and Time as Presuppositions of Experience*

4. In all experience we deal with sensible objects and their changes. The universal condition of the existence of sensible objects is Space. Each object is limited or finite, but the universal condition of the existence of objects is self-limited or infinite. An object of the senses possesses extension and limits, and, consequently, has an environment. We find ourselves necessitated to think an environment in order to think the object as a limited object.

5. Here we have, first the object, and secondly the environment as mutually limiting and excluding, and as correlatives. But the ground or condition of both the object and its environment is Space. Space makes both possible.

6. Space is a necessary idea. We may think this particular object or not—it may exist or it may not. So, too, this particular environment may exist or not, although *some* environment is necessary. But Space

must exist, whether this particular object or environment exists or not. Here we have three steps toward absolute necessity: (1) The object which is not necessary, but may or may not exist—may exist now, but cease after an interval; (2) the environment which must exist in some form if the object exists—a hypothetical necessity; (3) the logical condition of the object and its environment, which must, as Space, exist, whether the object exist or not.

7. Again, note the fact that the object ceases where the environment begins. But space does not cease with the object nor with the environment; it is continued or affirmed by each. The space in which the object exists is continued by the space in which its environment exists. Space is infinite.

Let us consider how we know the infinitude of space, for this is a very important concern in philosophy. The doctrine is current that we cannot know the infinite, that we can form no conception of it. Hence the word infinite would be to us without any meaning except a negative one.[5]

8. Space is both divisible (discrete) and continuous. It is composed of parts, each part being again composed of parts. But each part of space is not limited by something else; it is limited only by space. The environment of any finite portion of space is and must be necessarily other portions of space.

9. But if any limited space has space for its environment, it is not limited by it, but continued by it. Any possible limited or finite space is continued by an environment of space, and the whole of space is infinite.

10. This insight into the constitution of Space is a positive knowledge of and an adequate conception of its infinitude, but it is not a mental image or picture of infinite space. Conception in that sense would contradict the infinitude of space, for an image or picture necessarily has limits or environment. But the conception of the infinitude of space is adequate and exhaustive, because it enables us to answer questions relative to the conditions of existence in space—as the science of mathematics shows. A finite object could not exist were it not for this ground or condition which is its own environment. Self-environment is the characteristic of the infinite. The idea of infinite space is therefore the condition of the mental image or picture.

[5] The argument here given I used in 1860 to refute Sir William Hamilton's "Law of the Conditioned." I printed it first as part of a series of philosophical articles in the "Boston Commonwealth" for December 18, 1863. See also, "Jour. Spec. Phil.," vol. iv, p. 279.

11. That which is continued by its environment might be still finite if it could ever arrive at an environment of a different kind, and which, therefore, did not continue it. So Space might be finite were it to encounter an environment that was not space. But such is clearly seen to be impossible by the direct insight which we have into the nature of Space. There can be no object or finite space which does not imply space as the condition of the existence of what is beyond it.

12. As a condition of all change, motion, development, and manifestation, Time is likewise necessary. The object in time is called an event. The event is limited or finite, and has its environment in the form of antecedent and subsequent. The event begins or ends in some other event. But a limited time begins in a time and ends in a time, so that Time is its own environment, and consequently infinite. It is not made finite, but continued by its limits because it is self-limited.

13. Whatever we find to belong to the nature of Time and Space we shall find to have correspondences and correlatives in the laws of things and events in the world, because things and events are conditioned by Space and Time. Hence mathematics, based on this insight into Time and Space, gives us, *a priori,* certain principles which govern things and events.

14. Experience is thus a complex affair, made up of two elements—one element being that furnished by the senses, and the other by the mind itself. Time and Space, as conditions of all existence in the world, and of all experience, cannot be learned from experience. We cannot obtain a knowledge of what is universal and necessary from experience, because experience can inform us only that something is, but not that it must be. We actually know Time and Space as infinites, and this knowledge is positive or affirmative, and not negative. Just as surely as an object is made finite by its limit, just so surely is there a ground or condition underlying the object and its limit, and making both possible; this ground is infinite.

15. The scepticism in vogue, called "Agnosticism," rests on the denial of the capacity of the mind to conceive the infinite; and, strange to say, this very example of the infinite which we find in Space and Time is brought forward to support the doctrine. "I can conceive only finite spaces and times, but not space or time as a whole, because as wholes they contain all finite spaces and times." But agnosticism bases its very doctrine on a true knowledge of the infinity of time and space. For, unless it knew that the environing space was necessarily a repetition of the same space over and over again forever, how could it affirm the impossibility of completing it by successive additions of the en-

vironment to the limited space? It says in effect: "We cannot know Space, because [we know that] its nature implies infinite extent, and cannot be reached by successive syntheses."

## *Three Stages of Knowing*

16. Space and Time have been considered as the presuppositions or preconditions in all experience. Three grades of Knowing have been found by analyzing experience. First, there was knowledge of the object; secondly, of the environment; and, thirdly, of the ground or logical condition which rendered the object and its environment possible. There was the thing in space; secondly, its relation to an environment of things in space; and, thirdly, there was space. There was likewise the event; and its environment of antecedent and subsequent events; and then the underlying logical condition of time.

17. The first stage of Knowing concentrates its attention upon the object, the second upon its relations, and the third on the necessary and infinite conditions of its existence. The first stage of knowing belongs to the surface of experience, and is very shallow. It regards things as isolated and independent of each other. The second stage of experience is much deeper, and takes note of the essential dependence of things. They are seen to exist only in relation to others upon which they depend. This second stage of experience discovers unity and unities in discovering dependence of one upon another. The third stage of experience discovers independence and self-relation underlying all dependence and relativity. The infinite, or the self-related, underlies the finite and relative or dependent.

18. These three stages of Knowing found in considering the relation of experience to Time and Space—object, environment, and logical condition—these elements are in every act of experience, although the environment is not a very clear and distinct element in the least cultured knowing, and space and time are still more obscure. But philosophy, as a higher, special form of reflection, investigates the presuppositions or logical conditions of the objects and environments of our experience, and makes the third stage of experience clear and distinct—far more clear and distinct than the first or second stages, because they relate to contingent and changeable objects, while the insight into the unchanging nature of Time and Space sees the necessary and universal conditions of the existence of all phenomena. The third element of experience which furnishes these logical conditions is the basis of universal, necessary, and exhaustive cognitions.

19. The most rudimentary form of human experience, as it is to be found in the case of the child or the savage, contains these logical presuppositions, although not as a distinct object of attention. Even the lowest human consciousness contains all the elements which the philosopher, by special attention, develops and systematizes into a body of absolute truth.

20. Every act of experience contains within it not only a knowledge of what is limited and definite, but also a cognition of the total possible, or the exhaustive conditions implied or presupposed by the finite object. Hence those vast ideas which we name World, Nature, Universe, Eternity, and the like, instead of being mere artificial ideas, or "factitious" ideas, as they have been called,[6] are positive and adequate ideas in so far as they relate to the general structure of the whole. We know, or may know, the logical conditions of the existence of the world far better than we know its details.

All our general ideas, all our concepts, with which we group together the multitude of phenomena and cognize them, arise from this third stage of experience. It is the partial consciousness of the logical conditions of phenomena which enter as conditions of our experience that enables us to rise out of the details of the world and grasp them together, and preserve them in bundles or unities, which we know as classes, species, genera, processes, and relations. These classes and processes we name by words. Language is impossible to an animal that cannot analyze the complex of his experience so far as to become to some degree conscious of the third element in his experience, the *a priori* element of logical conditions.

21. Another most important point to notice is that these *a priori* conditions of experience are both subjective and objective, both conditions of experience, and likewise conditions of the existence of phenomena. The due consideration of this astonishing fact leads us to see that, whatever be the things and processes of the world, we know that mind as revealed in its *a priori* nature is related to the world as the condition of its existence. All conscious beings in the possession of the conditions of experience—in being rational, in short—participate in the principle that gives existence to the world, and that principle is reason. Time and space condition the existence of the world; time and space we find *a priori* in the constitution of mind or reason. This surprising insight which comes upon us as we consider time and space is confirmed by all our subsequent philosophical studies. We shall find a new confirmation of it in the next chapter, in our study of Causality.

[6] See "Jour. Spec. Phil.," vol. xvi, p. 386.

## *Cause and Self-Cause*

22. Let us return to our study of experience and take account of another presupposition which is necessary to make experience possible, and which is an element far subtler and more potent than Space and Time, because it is their logical condition also. This deeper principle is Causality.

(1) We regard a thing or object as related to its environment as an external existing limit, in which case the ground or logical condition is Space; or (2) we regard the object as an event or process which consists of a series of successive moments with an environment of antecedent and subsequent moments; its ground or presupposition is Time; or (3) we may look upon an object as the recipient of influences from its environment, or as itself imparting influences to its environment. This is Causality.

23. The environment and the object relate to each other as effect or cause. The environment causes some change in the object, which change is its effect; or the object as cause reacts on the environment and produces some modification in that as its effect. The effect is a joint product of this interaction between the so-called active and passive factors or coefficients. For both are active, although one is relatively passive to the other.

24. The principle of causality implies both Time and Space. In order that a cause shall send a stream of influence toward an effect, there must be time for the influence to pass from the one to the other. Also the idea of effect implies the existence of an object external to the cause, or the utterance of influence, and in this space is presupposed. Space and time are in a certain sense included in causality as a higher unity.

25. This principle of causality is so deep a logical condition of experience that it conditions even space and time themselves. For the externality of the parts of space or the moments of time are conditioned upon mutual exclusion. Each now excludes all other nows, and is excluded by them. Each part of space excludes all other parts of space, and is excluded by them. Any portion of space is composed of parts of space, and it is the mutual exclusion of these parts that produces and measures the including whole. Suppose, for instance, that one of the parts of space allowed another part to become identical with it, penetrate it, and did not exclude it; then, at once, the portion of space to which these two parts belonged would shrink by just that amount of space which had admitted the other. The portion of space and all

portions of space are what they are through this exclusion, and this exclusion is a pure form of causality, or an utterance of influence upon an environment. (This seemingly strange conclusion will become more intelligible when the presupposition of cause and effect is investigated.) Time itself is another example of the same exclusion. The present excludes the past, and is excluded by it. Both present and past exclude the future, and are excluded by it. Suppose one of these to include the other, then time is destroyed, but, as time is the condition of all manifestation and expression, the thought of such mutual inclusion of moments of time is impossible. The same implication of causality is found in time as in space.

26. Now, if we examine Causality, we shall see that it again presupposes a ground deeper than itself—deeper than itself as realized in a cause and an effect separated into independent objects. This is the most essential insight to obtain in all philosophy.

(1.) In order that a cause shall send a stream of influence over to an effect, it must first separate that portion of influence from itself.

(2.) Self-separation is, then, the fundamental presupposition of the action of causality. Unless the cause is a self-separating energy, it cannot be conceived as acting on another. The action of causality is based on self-activity.

(3.) Self-activity is called *Causa sui* to express the fact of its relation to causality. It is the infinite form of causality in which the cause is its own environment—just as space is the infinite condition underlying events. Self-activity as *Causa sui* has the form of self-relation, and it is self-relation that characterizes the affirmative form of the infinite. Self-relation is independence, while relation-to-others is dependence.

27. *Causa sui,* or self-cause, is, properly speaking, the principle, *par excellence,* of philosophy. It is the principle of life, of thought, of mind—the idea of a creative activity, and hence also the basis of theology as well as of philosophy.

*Causa sui,* spontaneous origination of activity, or spontaneous energy, is the ultimate presupposition underlying all objects, and each object of experience.

28. We have now before us three of the logical conditions or presuppositions of existence and experience.

I. Object—Environment—Space.

II. Event—Environment—Time.

III. Effect—Cause—*Causa sui.*

## *The Absolute a Personal Reason*

29. Having defined philosophy as the science of the *a priori* factors or elements of experience, which are necessary conditions of existence as well as of experience; having discussed Space, Time, and Causality, and thereby proved and illustrated the reality of this kind of knowledge, whose special object is the logical presuppositions to be found in all other kinds of knowing, no matter how elementary and crude they may be, it is necessary now to consider the bearing of these *a priori* ideas upon the question of the existence of God.

We must ask whether it is not possible to have a world in time and space without a Creator; whether we cannot conceive the Creator, if there is one, as a blind force.

30. To experience, the objects of the world are endlessly diverse. Particularity reigns. Each existence is in some way different from all else. But to philosophy, looking at the *a priori* conditions of experience, there is unity underlying all this diversity. Space conditions the existence of matter, and every physical body must rigidly comply with the geometric laws of space. So, too, all movement and all activity of force must conform to the laws of time. Here we have unity of fundamental condition. In causality there is absolute unity—self-cause being the source of both matter and form in the world. Self-activity is an *a priori* condition, not only of all changes, but also of time and space themselves. The very conception of externality and mutual exclusion involves the act of repulsion or of self-separation such as forms the ultimate element of the idea of cause.

31. The unity of space as the logical condition of matter, and of time as the logical condition of all change and manifestation, prove the unity of the world. The mathematical laws which formulate the nature of space and time condition the existence of all the phenomena in the world, and make them all parts of one system, and thus give us the right to speak of the aggregate of existence under such names as "world" or "universe."

This question of the existence of an absolute as Creator or as Ruler of the universe hinges on the question of the validity of such comprehensive unities as "world" and "universe." If such ideas are derived from experience, it is argued that they are fictitious unities,[7] and do not express positive knowledge, but only our ignorance, "our failure to discover, invent, or conceive." For we certainly have not made any complete inventory that we may call the "universe."

[7] "Jour. Spec. Phil.," vol. xvi, p. 386.

32. Only because we are able to know the logical conditions of experience are we able to speak of the totality of all possible experience, and to name it "world" and "universe." Finding unity in these logical conditions, we predicate it of all particular existence, being perfectly assured that nothing will ever exist which does not conform to these logical conditions. No extended objects will exist or change except according to the conditions of space and time. No relations between phenomena will arise except through causality, and all causality will originate in *Causa sui,* or self-activity.

All co-ordination is based on identity of species, or genera. The Homogeneity of space and time rests on this sort of identity, and ultimately all identity of species is based on the identity involved in *Causa sui,* or self-cause.

33. Self-cause, or eternal energy, is the ultimate presupposition of all things and events. Here is the necessary ground of the idea of God. It is the presupposition of all experience and of all possible existence. By the study of the presuppositions of experience one becomes certain of the existence of One eternal Energy which creates and governs the world.

How does one know that things are not self-existent already, and therefore in no need of a creator? If this question still remains in the mind, it must be answered again and again by referring to the necessary unity in the nature of the conditions of existence—space, time, and causal influence, based on self-cause. The unity of space and the dependence of all matter upon it preclude the self-existence of any material body. Each is a part, and depends on all the rest. Presupposition of experience can only be seen by reflection upon the conditions of experience. The feebleminded, who cannot analyze their experience nor give careful attention to its factors, cannot see this necessity. Indeed, few strong minds can see these necessary presuppositions at first. But all, even the most feeble, in intellect, have these presuppositions as an element of their experience, whether able to abstract them and see them as special objects or not.

34. Let us vary the mode and manner of expressing this insight for the sake of additional clearness. First, let us ask what is the nature of self-existent being—of independent beings, whether there be one or more.

(1.) It is clear that all beings are dependent or independent, or else have, in some way, phases to which both predicates may apply.

(2.) The dependent being is clearly not a whole or totality: it implies something else—some other being on which it depends. It cannot depend on a dependent being, although it may stand in relation to another dependent being as another link of its dependence. All dependence implies the independent being as the source of support. Take away the independent being, and you remove the logical condition of the dependent being, because without something to depend upon there can be no dependent being. If one suggests a mutual relation of dependent beings, then still the whole is independent, and this independence furnishes the ground of the dependent parts.

(3.) The dependent being, or links of being, no matter how numerous they are, make up one being with the being on which they depend and belong to it.

(4.) All being is, therefore, either independent, or forms a part of an independent being. Dependent being can be explained only by the independent being from which it receives its nature.

(5.) The nature or determinations of any being, its marks, properties, qualities, or attributes, arise through its own activity, or through the activity of another being.

(6.) If its nature is derived from another, it is a dependent being. The independent being is therefore determined only through its own activity—it is self-determined.

(7.) The nature of self-existent beings, whether one or many, is therefore self-determination. This result we see is identical with that which we found in our investigation of the underlying presupposition of influence or causal relation. There must be self-separation, or else no influence can pass over to another object. The cause must first act in itself before its energy causes an effect in something else. It must therefore be essentially cause and effect in itself, or *Causa sui,* meaning self-cause or self-effect.

35. (8.) Our conviction, at this stage of the investigation, is, therefore, that each and every existence is a self-determined being, or else some phase or phenomenon dependent on self-determined being. Here we have our principle with which to examine the world and judge concerning its beings. Whatever depends on space and time, and possesses external existence, in the form of an object conditioned by environment, has not the form of self-existence, but is necessarily a phase or manifestation of the self-determination of some other being. If we are able to discover beings in the world that manifest self-activity, we shall know that they are in possession of independence, at least in degree; or, in other words, that they manifest self-existence.

When we have found the entire compass of any being in the world, we are certain that we have within it the form of self-activity as its essence.

36. (9.) We should note particularly that self-activity, or self-determination, which we have found as the original form of all beings, is not a simple, empty form of existence, devoid of all particularity, but that it involves three important distinctions: Self-antithesis of determiner and determined, or of self-active and self-passive, or of self as subject of activity and self as object of activity. These distinctions may be otherwise expressed: (a) As the primordial form of all particularity; (b) the subject, or self-active, or determiner, regarded by itself, is the possibility of any and all determination, and is thus the generic or universal and the primordial form of all that is general or universal; hence the presupposition of all classification; (c) the unity of these two phases of universality and particularity constitutes individuality, and is the primordial form of all individuality.

37. (10.) There is here an error of reflection very prevalent in our time, which does not identify these distinctions of universal, particular, and individual in the absolute existence, but calls this absolute or self-existent being "the unconditioned." It thinks it as entirely devoid of conditions, as simply the negation of the finite. Hence, it regards the absolute as entirely devoid of distinctions. Since there is nothing to think in that which has no distinctions, such an absolute is pronounced "unthinkable," inconceivable, or unknowable. The error in this form of reflection lies in the confusion which it makes between the environment and the underlying presupposition. It thinks the antithesis of object and environment, of object and cause, but fails to ascend to self-limit and *Causa sui* as the ultimate presupposition and logical condition of object and environment.

38. (11.) Plato, in the tenth book of his "Laws," asks, in view of this self-activity which he calls "self-movement": "If we were to see this power (self-movement) existing in any earthy, watery, or fiery substance—simple or compound—what should we call it?" and answers: "I should call the self-moving power Life." Life is the name which we give to such manifestations of self-determination. Aristotle, who is careful not to call this energy "self-movement," but considers it to be "that which moves others, but is unmoved itself," defines it likewise as the principle of life. The tenth book of Plato's "Laws" has, perhaps, been the suggestive source of most of the thinking on the necessity of the divine as the presupposition of the things of the world.

Aristotle has treated the thought again and again; but the seventh and eighth books of his "Physics" and the celebrated seventh chapter of the eleventh book of his "Metaphysics" have furnished theology the most logical form of the intellectual view of this necessity. Aristotle in the latter passage gives his grounds for recognizing in this pure activity of self-determination God "as an eternal and the best living Being." "He possesses the activity of Reason, of pure thinking and of eternal life, and is always his own object."

39. The ground of Aristotle's identification of self-determination, or of energy which moves but is not moved, with Reason or thinking being, becomes clear when we consider that this self-distinction which constitutes the nature of self-determination or *Causa sui* is subject and its own object, and this in its perfect form must be self-consciousness, while any lower manifestation of self-activity will be recognized as life—that of the plant or of the animal. In the plant there is manifestation of life wherein the individual seed develops out of itself into a plant and arrives again at seeds, but not at the same seed—only at seeds of the same species. So the individual plant does not include self-determination, but only manifests it as the moving principle of the entire process. The mere animal as brute animal manifests self-determination more adequately than the plant, for he has feeling and locomotion, besides nutrition and reproduction. But as mere animal he does not make himself his own object, and hence the *Causa sui* which is manifested in him is not included within his consciousness, but is manifested only as species. Man can make his feeling in its entirety his object by becoming conscious, not only of time, space, and the other presuppositions, but especially of self-activity or original first cause, and in this he arrives at the knowledge of the Ego and becomes self-conscious. The presupposition of man as a developing individuality is the perfect individuality of the Absolute Reason, or God.

## *Philosophy, Theology, and Religion*

40. Philosophy is not religion, nor a substitute for religion, any more than it is art, or a substitute for art. There is a distinction, also, between philosophy and theology, although philosophy is a necessary constituent of theology. While theology must necessarily contain a historical and biographical element, and endeavor to find in that element the manifestation of necessary and universal principles, philosophy, on the other hand, devotes itself exclusively to the consideration of those uni-

versal and necessary conditions of existence which are found to exist in experience, not as furnished by experience, but as logical, *a priori* conditions of experience itself.

41. Philosophy finds Time, Space, Causality, Self-activity, and it arrives, in the consideration of self-activity as the only possible basis of time, space, and dynamic influence, at the idea of God as a necessary being. The ideas of time and space, which all conscious beings find as *a priori* factors of experience, justify such general ideas as are expressed by the words "World," "Universe," "Nature," "History," "Society," etc., which are regarded as factitious or artificial by those who have not noticed that all experience possesses, in addition to finite, sensuously present objects, also the universal and logical conditions of that experience. The idea of self-activity is the deepest of these presuppositions which make experience possible, and which make the existence of the world possible.

42. The idea of self-activity is the source of our thought of God. If one lacked this idea of self-activity and could not attain it, all attempts to teach him theology, or even to reveal to him divine truth, would be futile. He could not form in his mind, if he could be said to have a mind, the essential characteristic idea of God; he could not think God as a Creator of the world, or as Self-Existent apart from the world. If the doctrine were revealed and taught to him, and he learned to repeat the words in which it is expressed, yet in his consciousness he would conceive only a limited effect, a dead result, and no living God. But the hypothesis of a consciousness without the idea of self-activity implicit in it as the presupposition of all its knowing, and especially of its self-consciousness, is a mere hypothesis, without possibility of being a fact.

43. A pre-condition of divine revelation is the creation of beings who can think the idea of self-activity. The idea must be involved in knowing as logical condition, although it need not become explicit without special reflection. Philosophy is a special investigation directed to theological conditions of existence and experience, and so likewise theology and religion are special occupations of the soul. The soul must find within itself the idea of the divine before it can recognize the divine in any manifestation in the external world.

44. In discovering and defining the *a priori* ideas in the mind, philosophy renders essential service to religion, because it brings about certain conviction in regard to the objects which religion holds as divine, and conceives as transcending the world although it has not yet learned their logical necessity. It imagines, perhaps, that the mind

can have experience without presupposing in its constitution the divine doctrines which it has received through tradition. But philosophy may arrive at certainty in regard to the first principle, and the origin and the destiny of the world and man, without making man religious. He must receive the doctrine in his heart—that is the special function of religion. To know the doctrine is necessary—that is philosophy and theology; to receive it into the heart and make it one's life is religion.

45. Philosophy has suffered under the imputation of being too ambitious—aspiring to "take all knowledge for its province," or to usurp the place of religion and destroy the Church. We have seen that the mind possesses *a priori* logical conditions which enter experience and render it possible; we have seen, likewise, that the mind, in its first stages of consciousness, does not separate these from experience and reflect on them as special objects. It does not perceive their regal aspect, nor recognize them as fundamental conditions of existence. Nevertheless, it sees what it sees by their means, and may, by special reflection, become conscious of their essential relation. But this higher form of reflection is preceded by many stages of spiritual education, in which partial insight into these *a priori* ideas is attained. Special phases, particular aspects of them, are perceived. In the acquirement and use of language, in the formation of ethical habits, in the creation and appreciation of poetry and art, in the pursuit of science, and especially in the experience of the religious life, these *a priori* presuppositions appear again and again as essential objects under various guises—a sort of masquerade, in which these "Lords of Life," as Emerson [8] calls them, pass before the soul.

46. The knowledge of these *a priori* elements in experience, although a special one, is the most difficult of acquirement. It is not a field that can be exhausted any more than the field of mathematics, or the field of natural science, or that of social science. New acquisitions are new tools for greater and greater acquisition. We must expect, therefore, that the idea of Self-activity, which we have found as the first principle, will yield us new insights into the being and destiny of nature and man, so long as we devote ourselves to its contemplation.

[8] See Emerson's sublime essay on "Experience," in which he describes the soul's ascent through five stages of insight.

# XXII

## Josiah Royce

1855–1916

Born in Grass Valley, Cal. A.B., University of California, 1875. Studied at Göttingen and Leipzig, 1875–76. Ph.D., Johns Hopkins University, 1878. Instructor in English, University of California, 1878–82. Instructor in Philosophy, Harvard University, 1882–85; Assistant Professor, 1885–92; Professor, 1892–1914; Alford Professor of Natural Religion, Moral Philosophy and Civil Polity, 1914–16. Gifford Lecturer, University of Aberdeen, 1899–1900. Hibbert Lecturer, Manchester College, Oxford, 1913. Died in Cambridge.

Philosophical idealism had more devoted followers toward the end of the nineteenth century than did any of its opponents. This was partly because the empirical and naturalistic bias of science had rendered traditional religious concepts suspect whereas idealism provided reformulation of religion without complete rejection of science. It was also partially a result of the powerful influence which German philosophy in the post-Kantian tradition exerted upon leading American thinkers, most of whom felt their philosophical preparation incomplete unless they had spent at least a year in Germany. At all events, the variant expressions of idealism in America served as a restraining influence upon the growing scientific temper. By limiting science to the phenomenal, the idealist could make room for a philosophy which was friendly to religion, a force which had been so prominent in the history of ideas in America. Royce's first major work, *The Religious Aspect of Philosophy,* had the subtitle *A Critique of the Bases of Conduct and of Faith,* indicating his desire to harmonize philosophy and religion. The first paragraph of the preface read:

This book sketches the basis of a system of philosophy, while applying the principles of this system to religious problems. The form and order of the treatment depend on the nature of these latter problems themselves, and are not such as a system of philosophy, expounded solely for its own sake, would be free to take. The religious problems have been chosen for the present study because they first drove the author to philosophy, and because they, of all human interests, deserve our best efforts and our utmost loyalty.[1]

Royce's partiality to religion, common to most idealists, should not be misunderstood as a defense either of a credal expression of religion or of a particular institutionalized form of religion. Looking back upon his own religious training Royce could say, "But without being aware of the fact, I was a born non-conformist." [2] Although he was thus no partisan in the narrow sense of the word, Royce did seek to provide a rational basis for religion and morality and because of this he had a wide and influential following. Santayana's opinion of Royce reflects the bias of his own philosophical inclinations, yet it does indicate the source from which much of Royce's following came.

His reward was that he became a prophet to a whole class of earnest, troubled people who, having discarded doctrinal religion, wished to think their life worth living when, to look at what it contained, it might not have seemed so; it reassured them to learn that a strained and joyless existence was not their unlucky lot, or a consequence of their solemn folly, but was the necessary fate of all good men and angels.[3]

Royce sought to combine social realism and metaphysical idealism, the practical and the theoretical; this synthesis gave him a reputation which extended far beyond the confines of the academic walls where he spent the greater part of his life.

One of the great philosophical friendships in American philosophy was that of Royce and James. In terms of background and training each might naturally have developed the point of view which the other expressed; such was the paradoxical nature of their lives. As Perry aptly states it:

Royce spent his early years in a region where people used their senses, learned by experience, and labored with their hands; his philosophy was rationalistic and *a priori*. James, born and bred among ideas, was the arch-empiricist, turning in his philosophy toward experience and practice. It was James's and not Royce's philosophical world that was "in the making"; it was James's and not Royce's conclusion, that "there is no conclusion." Royce took refuge in "the Eternal," while for James time, flux, and chance constituted the very pulse of the living reality. Royce, feeling his physical impotence in a world of struggle, asked to have the victory written in the stars in order to contemplate and relive it in imagination. James, on the other hand, was the realist. To apply James's own expressions, it was Royce who

[1] v.

[2] *Papers in Honor of Josiah Royce on his Sixtieth Birthday.* 279–80.

[3] Santayana: *Character and Opinion in the United States.* 119.

in philosophy was the "tender-foot Bostonian," though he originated even west of the Rocky Mountains; while James himself, who frequented Boston, Newport, and the capitals of Europe was the philosophical "Rocky Mountain tough." [4]

The relationship between the two ranged from early agreement on the genesis of thought to later cordial but firm disputation when their views took different directions. Their correspondence was full of hearty praise for each other's ability together with favorable and critical comment on their respective theories. Royce lamented that his *Philosophy of Loyalty* had to be a polemic against the philosophy of the man whom he felt had inspired practically everything he had written. James oscillated between exuberant praise to vitriolic criticism of Royce. He could say when Royce was just recovering his health in 1888 that "if you ever *do* relapse, it will be the sorriest shame and suicide that ever disgraced humanity. You must n't, you can't, with your gifts. If you do I'll strangle you with my own hands." [5] He could also say after reading *The Conception of God* that "There is n't a tight joint in his system; not one." [6] James was Royce's senior by thirteen years and had lectured at Johns Hopkins while Royce was doing his graduate work. He was instrumental in securing Royce an appointment at Harvard. He was partly responsible for the voluntaristic emphasis in Royce's philosophy, although Royce's previous knowledge of Schopenhauer and Fichte can hardly be discounted in this connection. James's essay "The Sentiment of Rationality" published in *Mind* in 1879 and Royce's "Mind and Reality" published in the same journal in 1882 were their first contributions to win wide attention and each regarded the other's article as the complement of his own. What they were agreed upon was the importance of volition in thought. James could agree perfectly with Royce on such statements as these:

External reality is something postulated, not given; it is for us because we will it to be.[7]

And finally, all these forms of activity appear as expressions of certain fundamental interests that we take in the world. In each moment we construct such a world because we are interested in doing so. The final basis of our thought is ethical, practical.[8]

[4] Perry: *In the Spirit of William James.* 26–7. By permission of the Yale University Press.

[5] Perry: *The Thought and Character of William James.* I, 802.

[6] Ibid. I, 810.

[7] "Mind and Reality." 52.

[8] Perry: op. cit. I, 788–9.

James could even accept Royce's idealistic interpretation of experience as long as he expressed it only as a postulate and did not make it logically coercive. Later on, when James saw that Royce's Conscious Thought had become the necessary and logical explanation of nature and of finite thinking, their philosophical paths separated, James restricting his consideration to the observed content and structure of every-day experience while Royce continued to concern himself with the ontological basis for that experience.

Royce's philosophical interests developed on the basis of preliminary skirmishes in other fields. In his early teens he spent much time on mathematics. At the University of California he became particularly attached to Professors Edward R. Sill in English and Joseph Le Conte in geology who inspired in him an interest in philosophical questions by the manner in which they treated their subjects. He read Spencer and Mill on the side, and although he had no formal instruction in philosophy he viewed the materials in other fields as amenable to philosophical interpretation. He demonstrated such philosophical acumen in the handling of literary materials as to enlist supporters who made it possible for him to spend a year at Göttingen and Leipzig under Lotze, Wundt and Windelband. His contact with German idealism led him to look upon the analysis of experience as the central issue in philosophical discussion. His dissertation at Johns Hopkins two years later was entitled "Of the Interdependence of the Principles of Knowledge." He quickly arrived at an idealistic position based upon his diagnosis of the limitations and presuppositions of human thinking. In "Mind and Reality" he argued that the finitude of human thought necessitated the postulate of an absolute thought. In the revision of his doctoral dissertation which bore the title of "The Possibility of Error" in *The Religious Aspect of Philosophy* (1885) he argued that the indubitable fact of error was intelligible only on the basis of the existence of an all-inclusive Infinite Thought. Error and truth were finite opposites whose meaning was clear only in reference to their ultimate frame of reference. This Infinite Thought was more than an aggregate of truths, however; it was a rational unity.

It is enough for the moment to sum up the truth that we have found. It is this: *"All reality must be present to the Unity of the Infinite Thought."* There is no chance of escape. For all reality is reality because true judgments can be made about it. And all reality, for the same reason, can be the object of false judgments. Therefore, since the false and the true judgments are all true or false as present to the infinite thought, along with their objects, no reality can escape. You and I and all of us, all good, all evil, all truth, all falsehood, all things actual and possible, exist as they exist, and are known for what they are, in and to the absolute thought; are therefore all judged as to their real character at this everlasting throne of judgment.[9]

No longer, however, was the Absolute simply a postulate. It was a postulate supported by proof, a necessary logical ground for all thought. Returning to this same theme in his later essay "The Implications of Self-consciousness" (originally printed in *The New World* in 1892) he sketched the relationship of the finite thinker to the Infinite Thought, holding that there was an organic connection between them, the Infinite Thought, or the Self, being the one reality of which finite selves were a partial expression. In these works Royce had emphasized the category of thought when speaking of the Absolute, never however without reminding the reader that he had particular reasons for doing so and that the Absolute was a Will as well. In his lecture, "The Conception of God," delivered in 1895 before the Philosophical Union at Berkeley, California, where he debated with Howison, Le Conte and Mezes, he made clear that the Absolute was an organism of interrelated selves and could be spoken of as Thought, Experience or Will with equal correctness. It was the all-inclusiveness of Royce's Absolute that caused Howison in particular to charge that the individual was swallowed up in the Whole and hence that no room was left for freedom or moral judgment. Royce, in turn, argued that the Absolute was composed of individuals, all dependent upon the Absolute and yet free because of the freedom which the Absolute possessed. He considered this a satisfactory handling of the problems both of the one and the many, and of determinism and freedom.

*The World and the Individual* (1900–01) was the most elaborate statement of Royce's position. Acknowledging again his interest in religion, he expanded his previous thought on the philosophical problems basic to religion without greatly altering it. He criticized realism, mysticism and critical rationalism, regarding the latter as an attempt to defend an independent reality through giving universals an objective status as well as having them serve as the ideal structure of thought. He found all three positions unacceptable since they conceived reality in static terms. Over against these theories he defended his own "Absolute Voluntarism." In speaking of the Absolute he here

[9] *The Religious Aspect of Philosophy*. 433.

used the category of purpose. Thought was not representative, but purposive. Ideas possessed two meanings, to which he gave the names internal and external. Internal meaning was the ideal possibility of the object as known by mind, external meaning the definitive character of the object. Internal meaning was the result of the purposive activity of thought; it was realized in the experience of external meaning. Reality was the perfect realization of conscious purposiveness.

What is does in itself fulfil your meaning, does express, in the completest logically possible measure, the accomplishment and embodiment of the very will now fragmentarily embodied in your finite ideas.[10]

The Absolute served three purposes for Royce: it was the fulfiller of ideas, the experiencer of all possible experience, and the Will which gave unity to finite wills. The all-encompassing nature of the Absolute suggested logical difficulties which Royce tried to avoid by conceiving the Absolute to be a completed infinite. Here he relied upon mathematics to establish his case. In the late nineties he had returned to his early interest in mathematics and logic and depended largely upon the work which Peirce had been doing in these fields. He argued that the Absolute was not limited by serial enumeration but was conscious of its own infinity at the same time that it was identical with its own parts which were an unending series of self-representations.

Royce made use of logic as well as of mathematics in the later expression of his thought. Increasingly he felt the necessity of grounding his idealism in the principles of logic which were then coming into vogue. His interpretation of logic was best expressed in "The Principles of Logic," an essay which came out in 1912. He gave the name of "Absolute Pragmatism" to this theory; it was a refutation of logic as a normative discipline, an "Art of Thinking," and a defense of logic as the "Science of Order." Logic as conceived in this latter sense was concerned less with the rules of thought and more with the categories of thought which the norms implied. Logic had objects of investigation in its own right, these objects being systems of intelligibility which were applicable to all fields of knowledge. To pursue logical analysis was to reach out and discover systems of order which were objective and real. This had great similarity to realistic logic, but Royce interpreted it in terms of his idealistic metaphysics. Hypotheses were not to be tested through empirical verifica-

[10] I, 358.

tion but through conformity to the principles of reason. Knowledge was a result of the mind-will in action, checking and verifying its own conclusions through systems of order. Classification was possible only because of a classifying mind, yet the principles discoverable by mind were one with the order systems manifested in nature. Royce had always been interested in logic. His first book was a *Primer of Logical Analysis* which he wrote for his English students at the University of California, the immediate aim of which was "to form and to direct the habit of reflecting upon the meaning of speech." Even at this early date he showed familiarity with symbolic logic and commended the work of Jevons and Venn. The work of Peirce greatly augmented his knowledge in this field. The combination of mathematics, logic and metaphysics which he attempted to effect in his later career was one of the characteristics which distinguished his philosophy from other forms of idealism current at the time.

Something should be said of Royce's ethics, since morality was one of his constant concerns. Reared in a pioneer community Royce early saw the necessity of social order; idealism provided him with a moral philosophy which linked the individual's happiness with that of society. Happiness was not to be achieved by the individual in moral isolation. The individual could realize himself only as he participated in society and furthered social and cosmic harmony. Social forms were necessary for harmony to prevail. One possible form was art, although this was likely to be too individualistic. Another was science, which sought the universally valid. A third was the state, which was the most inclusive. While in his early works he stressed the third form, in his later works he emphasized the second and gave it spiritual content. This is particularly clear in *The Problem of Christianity* (1913). Due to the influence of Peirce his epistemology had shifted so that he could speak of knowledge as a social process by means of which we interpret our experience to one another. The world was a community of minds. The Universal Community took the place of the Absolute. This community was less a social fact than a moral principle; it was a spiritual and intellectual rather than an economic or political order. Man could realize himself only through loyalty to the shared experience of mankind and through loyalty to loyalty itself. As error was a real part of the order of knowledge, so evil was a real part of the moral order. Life was a continuous struggle between good and evil, a struggle in which the good was constantly triumphing. Evil persisted as the enemy for the good to conquer;

both were to be understood in terms of the final good which circumscribed all.

Royce's later thinking was largely an elaboration of earlier ideas. His logic, his doctrine of the community, his idealistic metaphysics all received new treatment and were defended by new arguments, yet there was an essential homogeneity throughout. Royce was important both as a great system-builder and as an assimilator who understood and appropriated with great skill the moving intellectual forces of his day.

## REFERENCES


Royce, Josiah: *Primer of Logical Analysis: for the Use of Composition Students.* San Francisco, 1881.

———: "Mind and Reality," *Mind: A Quarterly Review of Psychology and Philosophy* 7 (1882) 30–54.

———: *Fugitive Essays.* With an Introduction by J. Loewenberg. Cambridge: Harvard University Press, 1925. (Contains many of Royce's early essays.)

———: *The Religious Aspect of Philosophy: A Critique of the Bases of Conduct and of Faith.* Boston: Houghton Mifflin Co., 1885.

———: *The Spirit of Modern Philosophy.* Boston: Houghton Mifflin Co., 1892. (The most popular and readable of Royce's works.)

———: "The Conception of God," *The Conception of God: A Philosophical Discussion Concerning the Nature of the Divine Idea as a Demonstrable Reality.* New York: The Macmillan Co., 1897. 3–53, 135–348. (Co-author along with George Holmes Howison, Joseph Le Conte and Sidney Edward Mezes.)

———: *Studies of Good and Evil: A Series of Essays upon Problems of Life and Philosophy.* New York: D. Appleton and Co., 1898.

———: *The World and the Individual.* Gifford Lectures. 2 vols. New York: The Macmillan Co., 1900–01.

———: "The Relation of the Principles of Logic to the Foundations of Geometry," *Transactions of the American Mathematical Society* 6 (1905) 353–415.

———: *The Philosophy of Loyalty.* New York: The Macmillan Co., 1908.

———: *William James and Other Essays on the Philosophy of Life.* New York: The Macmillan Co., 1911.

———: "The Principles of Logic," *Encyclopaedia of the Philosophical Sciences.* Vol. I. London: The Macmillan Co., 1913. (Translated from the German edition of 1912 by B. Ethel Meyer.) 67–135.

Royce, Josiah: *The Problem of Christianity.* Hibbert Lectures. 2 vols. New York: The Macmillan Co., 1913.

———: *Lectures on Modern Idealism.* New Haven: Yale University Press, 1919.

Albeggiani, Ferdinando: *Il sistema filosofico di Josiah Royce.* Palermo, Sicily, 1930.

Barrett, Clifford (editor): *Contemporary Idealism in America.* New York: The Macmillan Co., 1932. (See dedicatory essay on Royce by George Herbert Palmer. 1–9.)

Creighton, James E. (editor): *Papers in Honor of Josiah Royce on His Sixtieth Birthday.* New York: Longmans, Green and Co., 1916. (Reprinted from *Philosophical Review* 25 (1916) 229–552. The paging is not the same. Good bibliography of Royce's writings by Benjamin Rand.)

Cunningham, G. Watts: *The Idealistic Argument in Recent British and American Philosophy.* New York: The Century Co., 1933. 253–91.

Perry, Ralph Barton: *The Thought and Character of William James: Revealed in Unpublished Correspondence and Notes, Together with His Published Writings.* 2 vols. Boston: Little, Brown and Co., 1935. (Esp. chs. 49–51.)

———: *In the Spirit of William James.* New Haven: Yale University Press., 1938. (Esp. ch. I.)

Santayana, George: *Character and Opinion in the United States: with Reminiscences of William James and Josiah Royce and Academic Life in America.* New York: Charles Scribner's Sons, 1920. (Esp. ch. IV.)

Townsend, H. G.: *Philosophical Ideas in the United States.* Cincinnati: American Book Co., 1934. 160–87.

* * *

---

* * *

## THE IMPLICATIONS OF SELF-CONSCIOUSNESS [11]

### II

Idealism of the post-Kantian type is distinguished by two especially noteworthy features. It first involves a criticism of the inner nature

[11] *Studies of Good and Evil.* 145–68. Originally printed in *The New World: A Quarterly Review of Religion, Ethics and Theology* 1 (1892) 289–310. By permission of D. Appleton-Century Co.

of finite self-consciousness. I, the finite thinker, it says, must be in far more organic and deep and wide relations to my own true selfhood than my ordinary consciousness easily makes clear to me. In essence, then, I am much more of a self than my immediate consciousness, as it exists under human limitations, ever lets me directly know. The true Self is at all events far more than the "empirical" self of ordinary consciousness. This is sure because, upon examination, one finds that the flickering and limited self-consciousness of any moment of my life logically implies far more than it directly contains. I am never fully aware of the content, or of the meaning, of my present self. Unless, then, I am in deeper truth far more of a self than I now know myself to be, I am not even as much of a self as I now suppose myself to be. In other words, it is of the essence of finite consciousness to be, in its logical implications, transcendent of the limited character of its momentary inner contents. This is the first assertion of idealism. Put negatively it runs: Finite self-consciousness never directly shows me how much of a self I am. Therefore finite self-consciousness never directly reveals to me the true nature, or extent, or limitations, or relations of my own personality.

The second feature of our idealistic doctrine appears in its theory of the relation of any finite self to what we call the "external world." The idealistic view here is, that if on the one hand the self of finite consciousness is in any case, by implication, far more than it can directly know itself to be, on the other hand this self, in order to be in true relation to the outer objects which it actually thinks about, must be, by implication, so related to these outer objects that they are in reality, although external to this finite self, still not external to the true and complete Self of which this finite self is an organic part. If the analysis of consciousness has first shown me that my true Self is and must be far more in its essential nature than I can now directly know it to be, the analysis of the definition of "my world of objects" shows that, in order to be *my objects,* in order to be external, as they are, to my finite thoughts about them, "my objects" must be such as my true Self already possesses—objects which it is aware of because they are its immediate objects, and which it knows to be mine because it includes both my meaning and their inner essence.

Uniting these two features we have, as our idealistic metaphysic, this result: The self of finite consciousness is not yet the whole true Self. And the true Self is inclusive of the whole world of objects. Or, in other words, the result is, that there is and can be but one complete Self, and that all finite selves, and their objects, are organically related to this Self, are moments of its completeness, thoughts in its thought, and, as I should add, Wills in its Will, Individual elements in the life of the Absolute Individual.

I begin here at once with the first of these two considerations. It is a familiar assertion ever since Descartes, yea, in fact, ever since St. Augustine, that, whatever else I am doubtful of, I am at least directly sure of my own existence. I am I. What truth, so people say, could be clearer? I exist, and I exist for my own thought; for I doubt, I wonder, I inquire—in short, I think. And in my thinking I find myself, not as a possible dream of somebody else, or as a fiction, or as an hypothesis, or as a matter of doubt, but I find myself existent for myself. Such is one familiar way of stating the initial assurance of human thought.

A popular misunderstanding of the nature of idealism in philosophy supposes that, beginning thus with his own individual existence as somehow a thing very much clearer in nature and in definition than the existence of anything besides himself, every idealist as such must proceed, in a solipsistic sort of way, first to reduce all objective reality to his own ideas, and then to find, among these ideas of his, certain ones which dispose him, on purely subjective grounds, to assume the existence of outer objects. It is historically true, of course, that such methods have been followed by certain students of philosophy. It is also a fact that such methods have a value as means of philosophical analysis, and as preparations for deeper insight. As such I myself have made use of them more than once for purposes of preliminary instruction: not that they constitute the essential portion of the teachings of a metaphysical idealism, of the sort which the post-Kantian thought in Germany developed (for they do not), but merely because they are pedagogically useful devices for introducing us to the true issues of metaphysics.

As a fact, however, before one could undertake, in a serious fashion, to be even provisionally and hypothetically a "solipsist" in his metaphysical teaching, it would be needful to define the Self, the *Ipse,* whose solitude in the world of knowledge the "solipsistic" doctrine is supposed to maintain. The reason why in the end our post-Kantian idealism is not in the least identical with "solipsism," either in spirit or in content or in outcome, is that the definition of the Self, the answer to the question, "Who am I?" is logically prior to the metaphysical assertion that a being called "I" is better known than is any being called "Not I." This assertion itself may be true. But in vain does a doctrine declare that a being called by any name, *x* or *y*, mind or matter, not-self, or Self, obviously and with absolute assurance is known to exist, and is more immediately known to exist than is any other being, unless the doctrine first defines what being is meant under this name. Self-consciousness can only reveal my own substantial existence with absolute, or even with merely exceptional clearness, in case self-consciousness first reveals to me what I mean by myself who am said thus so certainly to exist.

Idealism, then, has no more right than has any other doctrine to fire its absolute assurances "out of a pistol." That I exist is at the outset only known to me in the sense that this thinking, this consciousness, of mine, is no unreality. What reality it is, I shall not know until I shall have reflected long and with success. First, then, to say, "I clearly know myself, but I know not certainly anything beyond myself," and then by analysis to reduce the outer world to "my Idea," and then to say, "Beyond my ideas I can never certainly go"—all this method of provisional and halting reflection, which assumes "the Ego" as something perfectly transparent, may be useful enough as a propaedeutic to philosophy. It is not yet thoroughgoing self-criticism. Nor is it upon such imperfect reflection that the idealistic doctrines of modern philosophy have been built up. Fichte, who is popularly supposed to have done his work in just this way, actually made the Self the central assurance of philosophy only in so far as he also made it the central problem of philosophy. Its very existence is, for him, of the most problematic kind, so that, in the first form of the *Wissenschaftslehre,* the true Self is never realized at all, and exists only as the goal of an *unendliches Streben,* an endless travail for self-consciousness. No sooner has Fichte declared at the outset that it exists—this Self—than he finds the very assertion essentially paradoxical, in such wise that, unrevised, it would become absurd. Moreover, as Fichte insists, the natural consciousness is far from a real self-awareness. "Most men," declares Fichte (Werke, vol. i, p. 175, note), "could be more easily brought to believe themselves a piece of lava in the moon than to regard themselves as a Self." In such a philosophy the *cogito ergo sum* no longer means that I, the thinker, as *res cogitans,* am from the very beginning an obviously definite entity, while all else is doubtful. The first word of such a doctrine is rather the inquiry, *Who, then, am I?* It is the Self which needs winning, and which requires definition, and which is so far unknown, just because it is the object of our reflection.

Beginning thus our consideration—asking, What is the Self whose existence is to appear to a wise reflection as the fact surely involved in our consciousness?—we find of course at once that the larger empirical Ego of the world of common sense is by no means this Self whose truth is to be thus directly certified by the thinking and doubting with which philosophy is to be initiated. I *exist* cannot mean, at the beginning of our reflection, "I—Caius or Titus—I, this person of the world of common sense, calling myself by this name, living this life, possessed of these years of experience—*I* think, and so I am immediately known to exist." For the Self of the world of common sense is inextricably linked with numberless so-called non-Egos. He exists as neighbor amongst neighbors, as owner of these books or of this house, as father of these children, as related in countless ways to other finite beings. As such a creature, self-consciousness does not at first immediately reveal him. As such a being amongst other beings, reflective philosophy, at the outset, must ignore him. His existence is no more immediately obvious at any one moment, at the outset of our philosophical reflection, than is the "lava in the moon." When Fichte's opponents accused him of teaching that Professor Johann Gottlieb Fichte was the only person or reality in existence, and that his students, and even the Frau Professorin, were only ideas that Johann Gottlieb was pleased to create—such critics forgot that *das Ich* at the outset of the *Wissenschaftslehre* is not named Johann Gottlieb, and at this point of the system could not be, and that the beginning of Fichte's philosophy ignores the German professor named Johann Gottlieb as absolutely and mercilessly as it does the castles on the Rhine, or the natives of Patagonia, and knows as yet of nothing but the necessity that a certain pressing and inexorable problem of consciousness, called *das Ich,* must be fathomed, since every possible assertion is found to involve the position of this as yet unfathomed Self.

The Self which constitutes our present problem is, therefore, like Fichte's *Ich* at the beginning of the *Wissenschaftslehre,* a still unknown quantity. Its existence we know only in the sense that, in dealing with it, we are dealing with no unreality, but with a central problem and principle of knowledge.

How much of a Self, then, is clearly to be known to our most direct reflection? If we look a little closer, we next feel disposed to answer that if the Ego, as directly known in consciousness, is not as yet the whole empirical Ego of common sense called in case of any one of us by his proper name, and involved in these external social and personal relationships, then the best account one can give of the immediate subject of the *cogito ergo sum* is, that it is *the knowing Self of this moment.* Here, in fact, is a definition that has become comparatively frequent in philosophy. I myself cannot accept this definition without modification. But it is necessary for us to examine it ere we proceed further. I know directly, so it has often been said, nothing but what is *now* in my consciousness. And now in my consciousness are these current ideas, feelings, thoughts, judgments, and, in so far as I choose to reflect, here am I myself, the subject in whom and for whom are these momentary thoughts. This is what I can directly know. To all else I conclude with greater or less probability; or, again, the rest of reality is an object of my faith, or of my practical postulates. As for myself, I know myself just as the knower of these current thoughts of this moment. Thus, then, is our question to be answered.

Yet once more, is this new answer quite clear? For *how much* does the present Self, the self of this moment, immediately know? And does that which the self of this moment knows belong wholly to this moment? As soon as we try to answer these questions, we enter upon a labyrinth of theoretical problems as familiar, in some sense, as it is intricate. I should not venture to weary the reader with even a passing mention of these subtleties were not the outcome of the necessarily tedious investigation of such importance.

I am to know, then, "this moment," and I am to exist for myself here as "the knower of this moment." Very well, then, shall I, taking this point of view, say that I know immediately the past in time? No, apparently not. I have a present idea of what I now call past time. That must be all that I "immediately know" of that so-called past. Do I immediately know the future? No, again; I have a present idea of what I now call future time. I am limited, then, in "immediate knowledge," to the present in time. This moment is of course, as the present moment, to be cut off from past and future. Very well, then, how large a moment is it, and how long? Is it quite instantaneous, wholly without duration? No, for I must surely be supposed immediately to know, in this moment, a passing of time. My psychological present is a "specious present." It looks backward and forward. It lasts a little, and then insensibly glides over into the next moment. Such at least seems to be the definition that this doctrine of the "present moment" must accept as a good account of what the "present" is.

But, alas! the present, as thus defined, is only the more left undefined. This gliding "specious present," when does it cease to be present? When does it become past? Where are the boundaries?

How much is there of it? For, remember, I am looking for the immediately certain truth. I wanted to know who I am, as an immediately sure reflection shall find or define me. The answer to my inquiry was, "I am the knower of this moment." So much I am to be quite surely aware of about myself. Well, I have tried to define this assurance, and of course, if it *is* immediate assurance, I must be able to give at once its content, i. e., to define just what is contained in this moment. But unfortunately I at once find myself baffled. And as an actual fact, if I look a little closer, I shall always find that, despite the assumption that I do know only the "present moment," I cannot tell reflectively the precise content of my present moment, but can only answer certain reflective questions about the consciousness which is no longer quite my own, because, before I can reflect upon it, it has already become a past moment. As a fact, then, the assumption just made about my knowing fully the content of the "immediately present moment" turns out to be an error. For I know *not* now in full what it is that is present to me, nor who I myself am to whom this is present. And I find out that I do not thus fully know myself at any present moment, just because, when I try to tell what I know, what I tell about is no longer my present, but is already my past knowledge.

This problem about the definition of the "present moment" is one of the most characteristic of the problems of self-consciousness. Let us give some examples of its curious complications. Let the present moment, for instance, be a moment of a judgment. I judge that the paper before me appears extended. This, as it would seem, I just now know immediately, since I chance to notice it. But extension even now already involves, for my consciousness, all sorts of consequences, which will begin to appear upon reflection. If extended, the paper is divisible. In so far as it appears to me as what I call paper, I already begin to think of it as something that I could fold or tear. Yes, upon reflection, I perceive that, even while I saw and felt it as extended, I all the while "sub-consciously" perceived it to be smooth to my hand as I wrote, and also saw it to be white, and knew it to be partially covered by my handwriting, and knew to some extent what letters I was writing, and had furthermore in my mind the train of my more abstract thoughts. All this mass of "mind-stuff" was in me in a more or less latent form. What portion of it was immediately present to me at any moment during the writing of the foregoing half-dozen sentences? Yes, *how much of it all is even now immediately present to my consciousness?* I cannot tell. I know not. "This moment" has ceased to be "this" before I have observed its content, or written down its name. I know all the while that there just now was a present moment; and all the while also I am just coming to know this now flying moment. That is the actual situation. My "immediate knowing" ceases to be immediate in becoming knowledge, and the knowledge that I now have crumbles forever as it passes over into my immediately present state of feeling. I judge what just was my feeling, and feel what may straightway become an object for my judgment.

Enough; I shall never thus define in any precise way who I am. It is here I who ceaselessly fly from myself. My moments as such have no power to define in any sharp fashion their own content. I can therefore only say they must actually have such fleeting content as a perfectly clear and just Reflection would judge them to have. That alone is what I seem to be sure of. For they have *some* content. What it is, however, I can endlessly inquire; but I can never fully and at the same time immediately know. Unless I am an organic part of a Self that can reflect with justice and clearness upon the contents of my moments, these moments contain a great deal that exists *in* me, but *for* nobody. So much, then, for the first result of our inquiry. So much for the effort to define the "Ego" apart from the "external world."

Have I learned anything about myself by this weary and baffling process of reflection? Yes, one thing I have learned. It is the thing that I just stated. It is a difference which I inevitably find myself making between myself as I really am, and myself as I haltingly take myself to be from moment to moment. I am twofold. I have a true Self which endlessly escapes my observation, and a seeking self which as endlessly pursues its fellow. What I really am, even in any given moment, I never find out in that moment itself. I can, therefore, only define my true Self in terms of an ideally just reflection upon the contents of my moment; a reflection of an exhaustive character, such as in fact I in my momentary capacity never succeed in making. I must exist, to be sure, for myself; and as I really am I must exist for myself only. With that consideration one begins in our present inquiry. It is reflection that is to find me. It is my consciousness that is to discover me, if I am ever to be discovered. But the Self for whom I am what I am is not the self at this moment, but is thus far an ideal Self, never present in any one moment. To repeat, then, by way of summary: The Self is never *merely* the self of this moment, since the self of this moment never fully knows who he even now is. It is of his very essence to appeal beyond the moment to a justly reflective Self who shall discover and so reflectively determine who he is, and so who I am. For I am he.

## III

Another way of stating the foregoing result would, therefore, be to say that, unless I am more than the knowing and the immediately known self of this moment, I am not even as much as the self of this moment. For this moment implies more consciousness than I am now fully aware of. That which is just now in me to be known is far more than I just now know. That is the paradox, but it is also the inevitable fact, of my inner life; and thus I already begin to see how large may be the implications of self-consciousness.

But herewith our task is by no means done. We have studied the problem of the Ego viewed apart from a world of "external objects." What we have learned is, that the subject of the *cogito ergo sum* is in the beginning, strange to say, at once the best and the least known of the possessions of our knowledge. I cannot doubt its existence. But I am not yet aware how much of a self it is, nor how much it truly knows, nor whether it is or is not limited to a single series of moments of consciousness and reflection, nor how it stands related to any sort of inner or outer truth. Those who have begun philosophy by saying "The self at least is known," have usually forgotten that the self as known is at the outset neither the empirical Ego of the world of common sense, nor yet merely the so-called "self of the one present moment." It is not the first, because philosophy has not yet at the outset come to comprehend the world of common sense. It is not the second, for the consciousness of the "present moment" can only be defined in relation to a reflection that transcends the present moment; whilst, on the other hand, no human reflection has ever yet fathomed perfectly the consciousness of even a single one of our moments. The self, then, is not yet known to us except as the problematic truth exemplified by the still so mysterious fact of the *cogito* itself. Much less then is the relation of the Ego to outer objects as yet clear.

To this latter relation we must, however, next turn. Perhaps there we shall get a light which is refused to us so long as we confine ourselves to a merely subjective analysis of the inner life of this baffling Ego. The self undertakes to be not merely conscious of its own states, but of outer truth. Is its power in this respect indubitable? And if it is, upon what is founded our assurance that we do know a world of real objects outside the Ego? Possibly in getting a solution of this problem we shall come nearer to a true definition of the Ego itself.

The only way of answering the question about the external world lies in first asking, in a thoroughly reflective way, what is *meant* by a world of objects beyond the Ego. It is useless to try to find the philosophical evidence for the existence of a world of outer objects, unless you first define what an object beyond your consciousness is to mean for you. Amongst the numerous definitions of the meaning of the words *external object,* I may therefore choose three, which seem to me of most importance for our present purpose, and may consider each in its turn. The third will be my own.

1. "The term *outer object* means for me the known or unknown cause of my experiences, in so far as I do not refer these experiences to my own will"—such is a very common account of the nature of the external truth for the Ego. I need not expound this view at great length, since it is so familiar a notion. According to those who hold to this definition, it is somehow perfectly evident to me that my experiences need a cause, and that I myself am not the cause of all or of most of them. The Ego itself is thus definable as that which is conscious of more experiences than it causes, and which therefore looks beyond itself for the causes of most of these experiences. An "external object" means just such a cause, known or unknown.

It is strange that this, the most familiar definition of the nature and meaning of the word "object" should be the most obviously inadequate. In case of my perception of a house, or of a hot iron when I touch it, or of a wind in my face, I do indeed conceive myself as in relation to an object which is causing experiences in me. But most of the external truth that I usually think about and believe in is not truth now perceived by my senses, nor, *as* I think it, is it *now* in any causal relations to me at all. I at present believe in it because I "trust the validity of memory," or "have confidence in the testimony of mankind," or follow some other such well-known criterion of common-sense opinion. When I read my daily newspaper, light-waves are causing retinal disturbances in my eye; but as for me, I am thinking, not about these causes of my experience, but about the news from Europe, about the Russian famine, about the next Presidential canvass, and about other such "external objects," all of which objects I believe in, not because I reflect that my present experiences need causes, but because I trust tradition, or "current opinion," or the "consensus of mankind," or my own memory, or whatever else I am accustomed to trust. Only in the case where I attend to immediate perception, is the object of my belief at the same time the cause of my belief. Our "belief in the reality of an external world" is concretely definable, then, much more frequently as our belief that our experiences have present causes. We all of us believe in the future of this external world of ours. There will come the time called ten years hence, or a million years hence. Something will be happening then, among the things of the physical universe. That future event is an "external reality"; we all accept it as real, however little we know of it. But is it for us a "cause" of our present experiences? We are sure that such an event will come. Does that future event now "cause impressions" in us?

Yet more, were "my object" once defined as that *x* which causes my inner experience, my feeling, *f,* then one would still have to ask, What do I mean by causation? Causation is a relation between facts. I must myself have some inner idea of such a relation before I can attribute to the outer object the character of being a cause. By hypothesis, *x,* the object, is outside me. Its causal relation to my feeling is therefore also, in part at least, external to me. To believe in my object, *x,* as the cause of my feeling, *f,* I must therefore first believe that my notion of causation, derived from some inner experience of mine (e. g., from my own consciousness of my "will" or from my exercise of "power"), does itself correspond to an objective truth beyond me, namely, the outer causation of *x,* as bringing to pass *f.* In other words, I make *x* my object, if all this account is true, only through *first* holding that the inner experience of a relation, called "causation" in me, corresponds to an outer truth, namely, the external causation, whose validity is needed to give me an idea of the very existence of *x.*

But this means that there is here at least *one* external truth, and so one "object" (viz.:—the external fact of the causation itself), which I believe in, not because it is itself the cause of my idea of the causation, but because I trust that my idea of causation is valid, and corresponds to the truth. And it is only by *first* believing in this objective truth, viz., the causation, that I come to believe in *x* the cause.

Hence it follows that even in case of immediate sense-perception, my belief in the external object is always primarily not so much a belief that my experiences need causes, as an assurance that certain inner beliefs of mine are as such, valid, i. e., that they correspond with that which is beyond them.

2. "By *object,* then, I mean that which, beyond me, reduplicates, repeats, corresponds to, certain elements or relations of my own ideas." To this definition the foregoing one, as we have now seen, must lead us, when once properly understood, and when freed from the inadequacies thus far noted.

Here is a definition of what I mean by "outer object"—a definition which is far more true to the facts of consciousness than was the foregoing. My belief in such external objects as the space beyond Sirius, or the time before the solar system was formed out of the primitive nebula, or in the existence of Caesar, or in the presence of monasteries in Thibet, or even in the things that I read about in the newspapers, or learn of daily in conversation—my belief too in your existence, kind reader—all such beliefs are assurances that subjective combinations of ideas have their correspondents beyond my private consciousness. So far then this definition appears adequate. And yet it is really not enough.

For this is not *all* that I mean by an outer object of my thought. It is not enough that beyond my thoughts there should be truths whose inner constitution and relationships resemble those of my thought. For the world of my own external objects is not merely a world which my thought does resemble, but a world which my thought, even as it is in me, intends to resemble. Here I cannot do better for my present purpose than to repeat language that I have used in the Spirit of Modern Philosophy, p. 370. "My object," so I had just been saying, "is surely always *the thing that I am thinking about.* And," as I continued, "This thinking about things is, after all, a very curious relation in which to stand to things. In order to think *about* a thing, it is *not* enough that I should have an idea in me that merely *resembles* that thing. This last is a very important observation. I repeat, it is *not* enough that I should merely have an idea in me that *resembles* the thing whereof I think. I have, for instance, in me the idea of a pain. Another man has a pain just like mine. Say we both have toothache, or have both burned our finger-tips in the same way. Now my idea of pain is just like the pain in him, but I am not on that account necessarily thinking about *his* pain, merely because what I *am* thinking about, namely my own pain, resembles his pain. No, to think about an object you must not merely have an idea that resembles the object, but you must *mean* to have your idea resemble that object. Stated in other form, to think of an object you must consciously *aim at* that object, you must pick out that object, you must already in some measure possess that object enough, namely, to identify it as what you mean."

If this be what is meant by the relation of a self to an outer object, then the relation surely becomes, once more, highly problematic. Unless, namely, the self in question has already its own conscious idea of its object, it cannot formulate its belief in this object. But just in so far as it has its own conscious ideas of the object, the Ego under consideration would seem to possess only inner knowledge. It defines for itself the object of its belief. The definition is internal. The self appears as if cut off from the object. Its ideas shall be "its own." The object, as it seems, is beyond them. The only relation that can exist is so far correspondence. But, alas! this relation is not enough. Another relation is needed. If the self in question is actually thinking of the object, it is already meaning to transcend its own ideas even while it is apparently confined to its ideas. And it is actually meaning, not self-transcendence in general, but just such self-transcendence as does actually bring it into a genuine and objective relation to the particular object with which it means to have its ideas agree. Am I really thinking of the moon? then I not only have ideas that resemble the objective constitution of the moon, but I am actually trying to get my ideas into such correspondence with an external truth called the moon. In other words, whether I succeed or not in thinking rightly of the moon, still, if I am thinking of the moon at all, my thought does transcend my private experience in a fashion which no mere similarity or correspondence between my ideas and other realities can express. The true relation of thought and object needs another formulation.

Shall we attempt such a formulation? In so far as I am fully conscious of my meaning, in any thinking of mine, I am confined to my private ideas. But in so far as I am to be in any relation to an object, I must really be meaning that object without being, in my private capacity, fully conscious that I am thus really meaning just this object. At the moment of my thought of the object, I am conscious only that I am meaning my ideas to be not merely mine, but actually related to some object beyond. Am I, however, actually thus related to a particular outer object, then my present consciousness of my meaning is so related to that which is truly, although at present unconsciously, my meaning, that, were I to become fully conscious of my meaning, the object would no longer be external to my thought, but would be at once recognized as the object that I all along had meant, and would be included in my now more completely conscious thought. Complex as is this formula, it is needed for the sake of expressing the facts.

In other words, the only way in which I can really mean an object that is now beyond me is by actually standing to that object in the relation in which I often stand to a forgotten or half-forgotten name when I seek it, or to the implied meaning of a simple and at first sight obviously comprehensible statement, when, as in studying formal logic, I have to reflect carefully before I discover this meaning. And thus we are led to the following formulation of our own definition of the phrase "my object."

3. "My object is that which I even now mean by my thoughts, although, in so far as the object is beyond my private conscious thought, I cannot at present be fully conscious of this my relation to it. Yet the relation, although just now to me unconscious, must in such wise exist, that a true reflection upon my own meaning would even now recognize the object as actually meant by me. Such a reflection would, however, be an enlargement of my own present thought, a discovery of my own truer self, a consciousness of what is now latent in my consciousness. On the other hand, as a consciousness of my meaning, if complete, could still contain only thoughts, my object, as my object, must even now be a thought of mine, only a thought of which I am not now, in my private capacity, fully aware. In other words, my world of objects, if it exists, is that which my complete self would recognize as the totality of my thoughts brought to a full consciousness of their own meaning."

To sum up both aspects of the foregoing argument, whether you consider your inner life or your supposed relation to a world of objects external to yourself, you find that, in order to be either the self of "this moment," or the being who thinks about "this world of objects," you must be organically related to a true and complete reflective Person whom your finite consciousness logically implies, fragmentary and ignorant though this consciousness of yours is. Thus, then, the essential nature of our idealistic view of reality begins to come into sight. I know not directly through my finite experience who I am, or how much of a personality I truly possess. If, however, I am really a self at all, as even my fragmentary finite self-consciousness implies, then my true Self is aware of its own content and of its own meaning. If directly I cannot through finite experience exhaustively know my own nature, I can examine the logical implications of my imperfect selfhood. And this content and this meaning, which, as I find, are logically implied by even my finite selfhood, must include my whole "world of objects," as well as the whole truth of my inner life. If, then, this analysis of the concept of Personality be sound, there is logically possible but one existent Person, namely, the one complete Self.

Yet perchance to the foregoing argument an answer may be suggested that will seem to some readers, at first sight, conclusive. This idealism it will be said, is, after all, unable to give any notion of the extent, or of the content, or of the magnitude, of this world of the complete Self. What is proved is at best this, that *if* my thought is truly related to objects outside of my finite consciousness, then in so far as this relation exists, that is, in so far as I truly think of these objects, they are in themselves objects possessed by my true or complete Self, whereof this finite consciousness is only an aspect or organic element. But perhaps the assumption that I ever think of objects beyond my finite self is itself an error. How, at all events, can I ever do more than postulate, or hope, or believe, that it is no error? How can the way to an objective knowledge of the objective relations of my finite thought ever be opened to me? How can I ever transcend my finitude, to know that I am really thinking of objects beyond, or that I am implicitly meaning them?

It is at this point that the argument concerning the "Possibility of Error," as I developed it in my chapter so entitled, in the Religious Aspect of Philosophy, becomes immediately important to the present discussion. If, namely, in my finitude, I am actually never meaning any objective truth beyond my finite selfhood, even when I most suppose myself to be meaning such truth, then one must accept the only alternative. I must, then, be really in error when I suppose myself to be referring, in my thoughts, to outer objects. The objective truth about my finite consciousness must then be, that I never really refer to any objective truth at all, but am confined, in a sort of Protagorean fashion, to the world of the subjective inner life as such. I think, let us say, of the universe, of infinite space and time, of God, of an opposing philosophical doctrine concerning these things, of absolute truth, of the complete Self as he is in himself, or of what you will. Well, these are all, it may be supposed, subjective ideas of my finite self. It may be an error to regard them as more. No objects outside my finitude correspond to them. I do not really mean any outer truth by them. I only fancy that I mean outer truth by them. Could I clearly reflect on what I mean by these objects, I should see this illusion, this error, of supposing that I really have in mind outer objects. So our sceptical objector may respond to all the foregoing considerations.

But, once more, if this be true of any of my ideas, if my intent to mean outer truth by them is itself an illusion, then under what conditions, and under what only, is such an error, such an illusion, possible? I err about any specific object only if, meaning to tell the truth about that object, I am now in such a relation to it that my thought fails to conform to the object meant. I cannot be in error about any object, unless I am meaning that object. If, then, when I think of infinite time, or of infinite space, or of the universe in general, or of the absolute truth, I err in supposing that there is beyond my finite self an object corresponding to any of these notions of mine, then my error can only lie in this: that whereas my finite self *means to mean* outer objects, my true Self, possessing a clear insight into what truth really exists beyond my finite self, completing the imperfect insight of my finitude, discovers that what I take to be an outer object is only an idea of mine, and that in the world of the complete insight there exists nothing corresponding to my intended meaning. But thus, after all, we surely change not the essential situation which my finite self must really occupy. For still, whatever its errors, my finite self is an organic element in the correcting insight of the true Self. My notions of time and of space, of truth and of the universe, may be as imperfect, in all specific respects, as you please. Only, in so far as they are erroneous, the complete Self, having possession of the complete truth, corrects them. And even if I do not *mean to mean* an outer truth at any one moment when I imagine myself to be in relation to such truth, even then, this paradoxical situation can only be the objective, the genuine situation, in which my finite consciousness stands, in case my truly reflective Self detects the meaninglessness of my finite point of view in just this case. For, in the case as thus supposed, I am still defined as objectively in error, just in so far as what I *mean to mean,* namely, some particular kind of outer truth, is, from the point of view of the Self that knows my objectively true relations, not in correspondence with what I really mean.

Or, again, to put the case once more in concrete form: I am trying to think of an outer object. I conceive of that object as existent. But I am supposed to be in error. I care not what the supposed outer object shall be—infinite time or infinite space, or any other form of being. If I am in error, then, even now, unknown to my finite self, the objective situation is this, namely, that the world of truth as I should know it if I came to complete self-consciousness, that is, to complete awareness of what I have a right to mean, would not contain this my finite object, but would contain truth such as obviously excluded that object. In any case, then, we cannot escape from one assertion, namely, the assertion upon which the very "possibility of error" itself is based. This is the assertion that there is, even now, the existent truth, and that this exists as the object of my completely reflective Self.

But, finally, does one still object that the completely reflective Self, the possessor of my complete meaning, and of its genuine objects, the Self aware of the world of truth in its entirety, is still, after all, definable only as a possible, not as an actual, Self, namely, as the possible possessor of what I should know *if* I came to complete self-consciousness, and not as the present actual possessor of a concrete fullness of conscious insight? Then we must reply that the whole foregoing argument involves at every step the obvious reflection that, if at present a certain situation exists, which logically implies, even as it now stands, a possible experience, which would become mine if ever I came to complete self-consciousness, then the possibility thus involved is *ipso facto* no bare or empty possibility, but is a present and concrete truth, not, indeed, for me in my finite capacity, but for one who knows the truth as it is. Idealism is everywhere based upon the assertion that bare possibilities are as good as unrealities, and that genuine possibilities imply genuine realities at the basis of them. A merely possible pain, which nobody actually either feels or knows, is nothing. Yet, more, then, is a merely possible reflection, which nobody makes, an unreality. But the foregoing argument has been throughout devoted to proving that the finite consciousness implies the present truth of an exhaustively complete and reflective self-consciousness which I, indeed, so far as I am merely finite, never attain, but which must be attained, just in so far as the truth is even now true.

## IV

Mere outlines are always unsatisfactory. The foregoing argument has been merely a suggestion. There has been no space to answer numerous other objections which I have all the while borne in mind, or to carry out numerous analyses which the argument has brought more or less clearly into sight. My effort has been to make a beginning, and to lead this or that metaphysically disposed fellow-student to look further, if he finds himself attracted by a train of thought to which the whole of modern philosophy seems to me to lead.

Such, at all events, is the path of philosophical idealism. What, now, is the goal? What definition of the complete Self does one thus, in the end, get? I have elsewhere used the tentative definition: "The Self who knows in unity all truth." I have accordingly laid stress upon this character of the divine World-Self as a Thinker, and have labored to distinguish between this his fullness of Being, as idealism is obliged to define it, and those customary notions which define God first of all in "dynamic," rather than in explicitly rational terms, and which, to preserve his almighty power as the director of Nature, and his exalted separateness from our weakness in so far as He is to be our moral Judge, find it necessary, first of all, to make Him other than his world of truth, and only in the second place to endow Him with a wisdom adequate to the magnitude of his "dynamic" business. All such opposed definitions I find, indeed, hopelessly defective. But in insisting upon thought as the first category of the divine Person, I myself am not at all minded to lose sight of the permanent, although, in the order of logical dependence, secondary, significance of the moral categories, or of their eternal place in the world of the completed Self. That they are thus logically secondary does not prevent them from being, in the order of spiritual worth and dignity, supreme. That evil is a real thing, that free-will has a genuine existence in this world of the Self, that we beings who live in time have ourselves a very "dynamic" business to do, that the perfection of the Self does not exclude, but rather demands, the genuineness and the utter baseness of deliberate evil-doing in our finite moral order, and that Idealism not only must face the problems of evil and of moral choice, but as a fact, is in possession of the only possible rational solution for these problems—all these things I have tried elsewhere to show in a fashion which, as I hope, if not satisfactory, is at least sufficiently explicit to make clear to a careful reader that the God of the Idealist is at any rate no merely indifferent onlooker upon this our temporal world of warfare and dust and blood and sin and glory. To my mind, one of the most significant facts in the world is furnished by the thought that all this is, indeed, his fully comprehended world, and that if these dark and solemn things which cloud our finite lives with problems are in and of the universe of the crystal-clear Self, then, whatever the tragedy of our finitude, our problems are in themselves solved; while, as for our own personal destinies, they are, after all, and at the worst, part of his self-chosen destiny. For, as I have elsewhere explained, an absolute Reason does not exclude, but rather implies, an absolute choice; while such a choice does not exclude, but of a necessity implies, as it includes, a finite and personal freedom in us. That this our moral and individual freedom belongs, after the fashion first indicated by Kant, not to the temporal order of our daily phenomenal world, in so far as it is merely temporal and phenomenal, but to a higher order, whereof we are a part, and not unconsciously a part—all this does not militate either against the true unity of the Self, or against the genuineness of the moral order. Every being who is rationally conscious of time, is, by that very fact, living in part out of the world of time. For what we know we transcend. To live in time by virtue of one's physical nature, but out of time by virtue of one's very consciousness of time itself, is to share in the eternal freedom, and to be a moral agent.

# XXIII

## William James

1842–1910

Born in New York City. Educated there, in Newport, and in England, France, Switzerland and Germany. Studied painting with W. M. Hunt in Newport, 1860–61. Studied at Lawrence Scientific School, 1861–64, and at Harvard Medical School, 1864–69 (M.D., 1869), with two interruptions, one of nine months accompanying Agassiz on an expedition to Brazil, the other of eighteen months in Germany studying experimental physiology and reviving his aesthetic interests. Ill health and recovery, 1869–72. Instructor in Anatomy and Physiology, Harvard, 1872–76; Assistant Professor of Physiology, 1876–80; Assistant Professor of Philosophy, 1880–85; Professor of Philosophy, 1885–89; Professor of Psychology, 1889–97; Professor of Philosophy, 1897–1907. Gifford Lecturer, Edinburgh, 1901–02. Hibbert Lecturer, Manchester College, Oxford, 1908. Died in Chocorua, N. H.

A book on American philosophy which must stop short of the present can hardly find a more appropriate terminal figure than William James. More than any thinker of the period between our Civil War and the World War he was regarded by critics at home and abroad as America's most representative philosopher. We have seen that Royce linked him with Edwards and Emerson as typical of an era in our culture. Howison objected that he lacked the technical equipment of a philosopher like Edwards, but classed him with Emerson, Carlyle and Arnold as a great writer. James himself disclaimed and disparaged the system-making bias because it tended to substitute logical manipulation for experience, but in the last decade of his life he began to think of his various theories as constituting a system which deserved exposition as such, and he made some progress in composing it. If he had lived to complete and publish it, the pragmatism for which he is best known would have appeared in it as a methodological postulate leading the way to theories which might have been more difficult to popularize.

James was not interested in the promotion of pragmatism for its own sake, though under the demand for semi-popular lectures he gave it separate exposition. Moreover, he did not intend to develop a distinctively American philosophy. He was by education, taste, friendships and intellectual affinities a cosmopolitan. Probably no American philosopher has enjoyed so many periods of prolonged residence in Europe, or so wide a circle of readers, admirers and correspondents among European philosophers. On the other hand, he ventured west or south of New England and New York only on rare occasions and on professional errands, and even within those narrow limits his first-hand acquaintance with American life was not extensive. To a large degree, in fact, he shared his brother Henry's detachment from the American scene, though he continued to inhabit it. If America has read its own mind in certain of his writings, therefore, this is the result, happy or unhappy, of a series of coincidences and not of a strategic plan.

The interests which went into the shaping of James's philosophy were religious, aesthetic, scientific, and moral. His sense of the reality and importance of religion he owed in large part to his father's lifelong preoccupation with it. His interest in literature and art was developed by his early education and travel and sustained by the achievement of his brother Henry. Seven of their paternal grandfather's descendants became painters, William himself had sketched and painted from boyhood, and he spent a year at Newport under the tutelage of W. M. Hunt before giving up painting as a career. He turned from it to an equally early but hitherto spasmodic interest in science, and acquaintance with Agassiz and his students soon made him see "for the first time how a naturalist could feel about his trade in the same way that an artist does about his." The physical principle of the conservation of energy and the biological principle of evolution were winning wide acceptance, science was assuming a militant tone, religion was on the defensive, and philosophies of a naturalistic and materialistic sort were springing up. James was never really converted to any of these, though he had at first a great enthusiasm for Herbert Spencer, from which he was rescued by Peirce. But after nearly a decade of scientific studies he went through a spiritual crisis (1869–72) brought on by ill health, a sense of moral impotence and an ebbing of the will to live. In its initial stage he wrote to his friend Tom Ward:

> I'm swamped in an empirical philosophy. I feel that we are Nature through and through, that we are wholly conditioned, that not a wiggle of our will happens save as the result of physical laws; and yet, notwithstanding, we are *en rapport* with reason. . . . It is

not that we are all nature *but* some point which is reason, but that all is nature *and* all is reason too.[1]

A year later he was debating whether he should "frankly throw the moral business overboard" or "follow it, and it alone, making everything else merely stuff for it." [2] From this quagmire of indecision he was lifted by the French philosopher Renouvier, who exercised probably the greatest individual influence upon the development of his thought. On April 30, 1870, he wrote in a notebook:

> I think that yesterday was a crisis in my life. I finished the first part of Renouvier's second "Essais" and see no reason why his definition of Free Will—"the sustaining of a thought *because I choose to* when I might have other thoughts"—need be the definition of an illusion. At any rate, I will assume for the present—until next year—that it is no illusion. My first act of free will shall be to believe in free will. . . . I will go a step further with my will, not only act with it, but believe as well; believe in my individual reality and creative power.[3]

This was a conversion to moralism, not to religion, in spite of the fact that one phase of his depression was a pathological state in which he wondered "how other people could live, how I myself had ever lived, so unconscious of that pit of insecurity beneath the surface of life" [4]—a state which gave him first-hand material for his analysis of "the sick soul" thirty years later in his *Varieties of Religious Experience*. The conversion settled at once the issue between monism and pluralism—the religious monism which appealed to the sick soul, and the philosophic pluralism which appealed to the healthy-minded mood which accepted evil not as an illusion to be exercised by reason but as a reality to be overcome by action.

Thus from the early seventies the religious, aesthetic and scientific interests in James were definitely subordinated to the moral. Though he wrote on religious mysticism with the insight of a sympathetic observer, the only God who could have attracted him personally would have been a limited God struggling against evil and needing a helping hand. Though his artistic interest left its mark on his style and was reflected in his standing preference of concrete reality, of feeling and sensation, above intellect, he identified aestheticism with decadence, saw in the philosophy of Santayana the "perfection of rottenness," and advised against permitting oneself to have an

[1] *Letters.* I, 152–3.
[2] Perry: *Thought and Character of William James.* I, 322.
[3] *Letters.* I, 147–8.
[4] Ibid. I, 146–7.

emotion at a concert without expressing it afterwards in some active way. Though he began his career as a scientist, created what best deserves to be called the first laboratory of psychology in America, left as his most impressive achievement a two-volume treatise on *The Principles of Psychology,* and allied himself in philosophy with the empiricism which seemed closest to the temper of science, he deprecated making a fetish of science at the expense of the active and impulsive side of our natures, and he transformed empiricism beyond recognition. An analysis of this transformation will show that the changes were all in the direction of a reading of experience which sets us free for action and reasserts moral responsibility.

(1) Traditional empiricism analyzed experience into atomic bits of sensation which it called ideas or impressions. James emphasized the continuously changing flow of experience.

(2) For traditional empiricism, the relations between things were not given, but mentally supplied by the association of ideas. The inadequacy of this theory had led to the *tour de force* of the Kantian deduction of the categories. For James, the elements of experience were embedded in a matrix of relationships no less given than the elements themselves.

(3) Traditional empiricism set up sharp distinctions between self and not-self, idea and object, of which it was then unable to give a strictly experiential account, so that in the end everything but ideas or impressions was either non-existent or trans-empirical. By unstiffening the distinctions James was able to bring these terms within the range of experience.

(4) Traditional empiricism referred ideas back to the experiences which it supposed had generated them. James referred them forward to the experiences which they foretold and by which they were to be tested. This substitution of a prospective for a retrospective reference reflected his biological interest in functions rather than origins, and involved an application to ideas of the Darwinian theory of the survival of the fittest. It was at this point that James's pragmatism emerged from his general empiricism.

(5) Traditional empiricism, because of its atomic sensationalism and its reduction of ideas to prior experience, tended to be mechanistic and deterministic. James's empiricism allowed for a certain free play in the projection of ideas and in the choice of some for belief and action at the believer's and actor's risk. Though subsequent experience had a selective effect, the projection, choice and risk introduced genuine novelties into experience and modified its course.

(6) Traditional empiricism tended toward positivism and the discrediting of belief that goes beyond, as well as of belief that runs counter to, the available evidence. James, placing thought and belief at the mid-section of the reflex arc, saw that because of the exigencies of action there were forced options of belief in which the evidence was not, and perhaps never could be, sufficient to determine a choice. Confinement of belief within evidence would result in paralysis of action, whereas the function of belief is to facilitate it. The adventure of belief beyond evidence might uncover evidence that would otherwise remain hidden, and at least in the case of belief about a future which depended in some measure upon the will, it might actually create evidence in its own support. This was the fideism of James's *Will to Believe*. Whereas classic empiricism had emphasized the blindness of non-evidential belief to negative evidence, James emphasized its generation of positive evidence.

James's pragmatism and fideism found a common denominator in his theory of truth as a species of goodness, a theory in which his moralism reappeared. The true was what was good in the way of belief, as the right was what was good in the way of action. But beliefs *came* true by *making* good, and there were various ways of making good. Pragmatism applied primarily to such ideas as were made good by the event when the event was uninfluenced by the idea or the action in which it issued; fideism primarily to those which partially determined the event. The reference in both cases was forward.

The differences between Peirce's pragmatism and James's, some of which do not appear in the selection which follows, may here be summarized. In the first place, James's pragmatism was a theory of truth as well as of meaning, whereas Peirce's conception of truth as that upon which public opinion would finally settle was independent of his pragmatism, which was a theory of meaning only. In the second place, Peirce's pragmatism construed the meaning of ideas in terms of conduct; James's, of sensation. Yet it was James who made thought subservient to action, and not Peirce, for whom the value of action was in the life it gave to ideas. In the third place, the meaning of ideas consisted for Peirce in *general* modes of rational conduct in a *community* of selves, for James in *particular* experiences of *individual* selves. Peirce's theories of meaning and of truth were both social and realistic. James's theory of meaning and truth was individualistic, and it was nominalistic in tendency, though Peirce's influence held James back from a thoroughgoing nominalism.

In the fourth and last place, Peirce's pragmatism was absolute and admitted no supplementary fideism. He had, in fact, nothing but contempt for James's "will to believe."

The divergence between the two forms of pragmatism was so great in the end that Peirce rechristened his "pragmaticism," a name so ugly, he thought, as to be safe from kidnapers. Nevertheless the two forms had in common the forward reference of ideas, and also the fact that each was valued by its proponent not on its own account but for the sake of the metaphysical theory in which it seemed to him to issue. For Peirce, however, this metaphysical theory was realism; for James, radical empiricism. There were analogous relations of identity-in-difference between their versions of synechism and tychism.[5] Thus it came about that though James took over more of Peirce's terminology, Royce was closer to Peirce in substantive doctrine.

The fact remains that James's direct influence on subsequent thought was immeasurably greater than Peirce's, and greater even than Royce's. It has been well said that the modern *movement* known as pragmatism is largely the result of James's misunderstanding of Peirce.[6] This movement includes among its diverse expressions in America not merely the absolute pragmatism of Royce and the conceptualistic pragmatism of C. I. Lewis, but the instrumentalism of John Dewey, the operationalism of P. W. Bridgman, behavioristic psychology, and certain aspects of logical positivism. All the varieties of pluralism, most of realism and naturalism, and many of idealism, owe some of their doctrinal content to James. And there is scarcely a current of thought in twentieth-century America which does not derive part of its vitality from the general invigoration of philosophy and psychology which was perhaps James's chief service to it. He offers therefore not merely an appropriate stopping point for such a book as this, but an ideal point of departure for the study of later developments.

## REFERENCES

James, William: *The Principles of Psychology.* 2 vols. New York: Henry Holt and Co., 1890.

———: *The Will to Believe: and Other Essays in Popular Philosophy.* New York: Longmans, Green and Co., 1897.

[5] Perry: Op. cit. II, 411 f.

[6] Ibid. II, 409.

James, William: *The Varieties of Religious Experience: A Study in Human Nature*. New York: Longmans, Green and Co., 1902.

———: *Pragmatism: A New Name for Some Old Ways of Thinking*. New York: Longmans, Green and Co., 1907.

———: *The Meaning of Truth: A Sequel to "Pragmatism."* New York: Longmans, Green and Co., 1909.

———: *A Pluralistic Universe*. Hibbert Lectures. New York: Longmans, Green and Co., 1909.

———: *Some Problems of Philosophy: A Beginning of an Introduction to Philosophy*. New York: Longmans, Green and Co., 1911. (This and the three following volumes were posthumously published.)

———: *Memories and Studies*. New York: Longmans, Green and Co., 1911.

———: *Essays in Radical Empiricism*. New York: Longmans, Green and Co., 1912.

———: *Collected Essays and Reviews*. New York: Longmans, Green and Co., 1920.

James, Henry (editor): *The Letters of William James*. 2 vols. New York: Longmans, Green and Co., 1920.

Baum, Maurice: "The Development of James's Pragmatism prior to 1879," *Journal of Philosophy* 30 (1933) 43–51.

Dewey, John: *Characters and Events: Popular Essays in Social and Political Philosophy*. Edited by Joseph Ratner. 2 vols. New York: Henry Holt and Co., 1929. 107–22, 435–42, 542–7.

Flournoy, Theodore: *The Philosophy of William James*. Authorized translation by E. B. Holt and Wm. James, Jr. New York: Henry Holt and Co., 1917.

Kallen, Horace M.: *William James and Henri Bergson*. Chicago: University of Chicago Press, 1914.

Kraushaar, Otto F.: "What James's Philosophical Orientation owed to Lotze," *Philosophical Review* 47 (1938) 517–26.

Mead, George H.: "The Philosophies of Royce, James and Dewey in their American Setting," *International Journal of Ethics* 40 (1929–30) 211–31.

Moore, George E.: *Philosophical Studies*. New York: Harcourt, Brace and Co., 1922. 97–146.

Perry, Ralph Barton: *Annotated Bibliography of the Writings of William James*. New York: Longmans, Green and Co., 1920.

———: *The Thought and Character of William James: Revealed in Unpublished Correspondence and Notes, Together with His Published Writings*. 2 vols. Boston: Little, Brown and Co., 1935.

———: *In the Spirit of William James*. New Haven: Yale University Press, 1938.

———: *Present Philosophical Tendencies*. New York: Longmans, Green and Co., 1912. (Appendix, "The Philosophy of William James.")

Royce, Josiah: *William James and Other Essays on the Philosophy of Life*. New York: The Macmillan Co., 1911.

Santayana, George: *Character and Opinion in the United States: with Reminiscences of William James and Josiah Royce and Academic Life in America.* New York: Charles Scribner's Sons, 1920. (Esp. ch. III.)

Schiller, F. C. S.: "William James and the Making of Pragmatism," *Personalist* 8 (1927) 81–93.

Wahl, Jean: *The Pluralist Philosophies of England and America.* Authorized translation by Fred Rothwell. Chicago: Open Court Publishing Co., 1925. Bk. III.

* * *

---

* * *

## PHILOSOPHICAL CONCEPTIONS AND PRACTICAL RESULTS [7]

I will seek to define with you merely what seems to be the most likely direction in which to start upon the trail of truth. Years ago this direction was given to me by an American philosopher whose home is in the East, and whose published works, few as they are and scattered in periodicals, are no fit expression of his powers. I refer to Mr. Charles S. Peirce, with whose very existence as a philosopher I dare say many of you are unacquainted. He is one of the most original of contemporary thinkers; and the principle of practicalism—or pragmatism, as he called it, when I first heard him enunciate it at Cambridge in the early '70's—is the clue or compass by following which I find myself more and more confirmed in believing we may keep our feet upon the proper trail.

Peirce's principle, as we may call it, may be expressed in a variety of ways, all of them very simple. In the *Popular Science Monthly* for January, 1878, he introduces it as follows: The soul and meaning of thought, he says, can never be made to direct itself towards anything but the production of belief, belief being the demicadence which closes a musical phrase in the symphony of our intellectual life. Thought in movement has thus for its only possible motive the attainment of thought at rest. But when our thought about an object has found its rest in belief, then our action on the subject can firmly

[7] Address before the Philosophical Union of the University of California, August 26, 1898. We here follow its first printing in *The University Chronicle* I (1898) 289–309 (omitting the first four and the last paragraphs). Reprinted in *Collected Essays and Reviews.* 406–37.

and safely begin. Beliefs, in short, are really rules for action; and the whole function of thinking is but one step in the production of habits of action. If there were any part of a thought that made no difference in the thought's practical consequences, then that part would be no proper element of the thought's significance. Thus the same thought may be clad in different words; but if the different words suggest no different conduct, they are mere outer accretions, and have no part in the thought's meaning. If, however, they determine conduct differently, they are essential elements of the significance. "Please open the door," and, *"Veuillez ouvrir la porte,"* in French, mean just the same thing; but "D—n you, open the door," although in English, *means* something very different. Thus to develop a thought's meaning we need only determine what conduct it is fitted to produce; that conduct is for us its sole significance. And the tangible fact at the root of all our thought-distinctions, however subtle, is that there is no one of them so fine as to consist in anything but a possible difference of practice. To attain perfect clearness in our thoughts of an object, then, we need only consider what effects of a conceivably practical kind the object may involve—what sensations we are to expect from it, and what reactions we must prepare. Our conception of these effects, then, is for us the whole of our conception of the object, so far as that conception has positive significance at all.

This is the principle of Peirce, the principle of pragmatism. I think myself that it should be expressed more broadly than Mr. Peirce expresses it. The ultimate test for us of what a truth means is indeed the conduct it dictates or inspires. But it inspires that conduct because it first foretells some particular turn to our experience which shall call for just that conduct from us. And I should prefer for our purposes this evening to express Peirce's principle by saying that the effective meaning of any philosophic proposition can always be brought down to some particular consequence, in our future practical experience, whether active or passive; the point lying rather in the fact that the experience must be particular, than in the fact that it must be active.

To take in the importance of this principle, one must get accustomed to applying it to concrete cases. Such use as I am able to make of it convinces me that to be mindful of it in philosophical disputations tends wonderfully to smooth out misunderstandings and to bring in peace. If it did nothing else, then, it would yield a sovereignly valuable rule of method for discussion. So I shall devote the rest of this precious hour with you to its elucidation, because I sincerely think that if you once grasp it, it will shut your steps out from many an old false opening, and head you in the true direction for the trail.

One of its first consequences is this. Suppose there are two different philosophical definitions, or propositions, or maxims, or what not, which seem to contradict each other, and about which men dispute. If, by supposing the truth of the one, you can foresee no conceivable practical consequence to anybody at any time or place, which is different from what you would foresee if you supposed the truth of the other, why then the difference between the two propositions is no difference,—it is only a specious and verbal difference, unworthy of further contention. Both formulas mean radically the same thing, although they may say it in such different words. It is astonishing to see how many philosophical disputes collapse into insignificance the moment you subject them to this simple test. There can be no difference which doesn't make a difference—no difference in abstract truth which does not express itself in a difference of concrete fact, and of conduct consequent upon the fact, imposed on somebody, somehow, somewhere, and somewhen. It is true that a certain shrinkage of values often seems to occur in our general formulas when we measure their meaning in this prosaic and practical way. They diminish. But the vastness that is merely vagueness is a false appearance of importance, and not a vastness worth retaining. The *x*'s, *y*'s, and *z*'s always do shrivel, as I have heard a learned friend say, whenever at the end of your algebraic computation they change into so many plain *a*'s, *b*'s, and *c*'s; but the whole function of algebra is, after all, to get them into that more definite shape; and the whole function of philosophy ought to be to find out what definite difference it will make to you and me, at definite instants of our life, if this world-formula or that world-formula be the one which is true.

If we start off with an impossible case, we shall perhaps all the more clearly see the use and scope of our principle. Let us, therefore, put ourselves, in imagination, in a position from which no forecasts of consequence, no dictates of conduct, can possibly be made, so that the principle of pragmatism finds no field of application. Let us, I mean, assume that the present moment is the absolutely last moment of the world, with bare nonentity beyond it, and no hereafter for either experience or conduct.

Now I say that in that case there would be no sense whatever in some of our most urgent and envenomed philosophical and religious debates. The question is, "Is matter the producer of all things, or is a God there too?" would, for example, offer a perfectly idle and insignificant alternative if the world were finished and no more of it to come. Many of us, most of us, I think, now feel as if a terrible coldness and deadness would come over the world were we forced to believe that no informing spirit or purpose had to do with it, but it merely accidentally had come. The actually experienced details of fact might be the same on either hypothesis, some sad, some joyous; some rational, some odd and grotesque; but without a God behind them, we think they would have something ghastly, they would tell no genuine story, there would be no speculation in those eyes that they do glare with. With the God, on the other hand, they would grow solid, warm, and altogether full of real significance. But I say that such an alternation of feelings, reasonable enough in a consciousness that is prospective, as ours now is, and whose world is partly yet to come, would be absolutely senseless and irrational in a purely retrospective consciousness summing up a world already past. For such a consciousness, no emotional interest could attach to the alternative. The problem would be purely intellectual; and if unaided matter could, with any scientific plausibility, be shown to cipher out the actual facts, then not the faintest shadow ought to cloud the mind, of regret for the God that by the same ciphering would prove needless and disappear from our belief.

For just consider the case sincerely, and say what would be the *worth* of such a God if he *were* there, with his work accomplished and his world run down. He would be worth no more than just that world was worth. To that amount of result, with its mixed merits and defects, his creative power could attain, but go no farther. And since there is to be no future; since the whole value and meaning of the world has been already paid in and actualized in the feelings that went with it in the passing, and now go with it in the ending; since it draws no supplemental significance (such as our real world draws) from its function of preparing something yet to come; why then, by it we take God's measure, as it were. He is the Being who could once for all do *that;* and for that much we are thankful to him, but for nothing more. But now, on the contrary hypothesis, namely, that the bits of matter following their "laws" could make that world and do no less, should we not be just as thankful to them? Wherein should we suffer loss, then, if we dropped God as an hypothesis and made the matter alone responsible? Where would the special deadness, "crassness," and ghastliness come in? And how, experience being what it is once for all, would God's presence in it make it any more "living," any richer in our sight?

Candidly, it is impossible to give any answer to this question. The actually experienced world is supposed to be the same in its details on either hypothesis, "the same, for our praise or blame," as Browning says. It stands there indefeasibly; a gift which can't be taken back. Calling matter the cause of it retracts no single one of the items that have made it up, nor does calling God the cause augment them. They are the God or the atoms, respectively, of just that and no other world. The God, if there, has been doing just what atoms could do—appearing in the character of atoms, so to speak—and earning such gratitude as is due to atoms, and no more. If his presence lends no different turn or issue to the performance, it surely can lend it no increase of dignity. Nor would indignity come to it were he absent, and did the atoms remain the only actors on the stage. When a play is once over, and the curtain down, you really make it no better by claiming an illustrious genius for its author, just as you make it no worse by calling him a common hack.

Thus if no future detail of experience or conduct is to be deduced from our hypothesis, the debate between materialism and theism becomes quite idle and insignificant. Matter and God in that event mean exactly the same thing—the power, namely, neither more nor less, that can make just this mixed, imperfect, yet completed world—and the wise man is he who in such a case would turn his back on such a supererogatory discussion. Accordingly most men instinctively—and a large class of men, the so-called positivists or scientists, deliberately—do turn their backs on philosophical disputes from which nothing in the line of definite future consequences can be seen to follow. The verbal and empty character of our studies is surely a reproach with which you of the Philosophical Union are but too sadly familiar. An escaped Berkeley student said to me at Harvard the other day,—he had never been in the philosophical department here,—"Words, words, words, are all that you philosophers care for." We philosophers think it all unjust; and yet, if the principle of pragmatism be true, it is a perfectly sound reproach unless the metaphysical alternatives under investigation can be shown to have alternative practical outcomes, however delicate and distant these may be. The common man and the scientist can discover no such outcomes. And if the metaphysician can discern none either, the common man and scientist certainly are in the right of it, as against him. His science is then but pompous trifling; and the endowment of a professorship for such a being would be something really absurd.

Accordingly, in every genuine metaphysical debate some practical issue, however remote, is really involved. To realize this, revert with me to the question of materialism or theism; and place yourselves this time in the real world we live in, the world that has a future, that is yet uncompleted whilst we speak. In this unfinished world the alternative of "materialism or theism?" is intensely practical; and it is worth while for us to spend some minutes of our hour in seeing how truly this is the case.

How, indeed, does the programme differ for us, according as we consider that the facts of experience up to date are purposeless configurations of atoms moving according to eternal elementary laws, or that on the other hand they are due to the providence of God? As far as the past facts go, indeed there is no difference. These facts are in, are bagged, are captured; and the good that's in them is gained, be the atoms or be the God their cause. There are accordingly many materialists about us to-day who, ignoring altogether the future and practical aspects of the question, seek to eliminate the odium attaching to the word materialism, and even to eliminate the word itself, by showing that, if matter could give birth to all these gains, why then matter, functionally considered, is just as divine an entity as God, in fact coalesces with God, is what you mean by God. Cease, these persons advise us, to use either of these terms, with their outgrown opposition. Use terms free of the clerical connotations on the one hand; of the suggestion of grossness, coarseness, ignobility, on the other. Talk of the primal mystery, of the unknowable energy, of the one and only power, instead of saying either God or matter. This is the course to which Mr. Spencer urges us at the end of the first volume of his *Psychology*. In some well-written pages he there shows us that a "matter" so infinitely subtile, and performing motions as inconceivably quick and fine as modern science postulates in her explanations, has no trace of grossness left. He shows that the conception of spirit, as we mortals hitherto have framed it, is itself too gross to cover the exquisite complexity of Nature's facts. Both terms, he says are but symbols, pointing to that one unknowable reality in which their oppositions cease.

Throughout these remarks of Mr. Spencer, eloquent, and even noble in a certain sense, as they are, he seems to think that the dislike of ordinary man to materialism comes from a purely æsthetic disdain of matter, as something gross in itself, and vile and despicable. Undoubtedly such an æsthetic disdain of matter has played a part in philosophic history. But it forms no part whatever of an intelligent modern man's dislikes. Give him a matter bound forever by its laws to lead our world nearer and nearer to perfection, and any rational man will worship that matter as readily as Mr. Spencer worships his own so-called unknowable power. It not only has made for righteousness up to date, but it will make for righteousness forever; and that is all we need. Doing practically all that a God can do, it is equivalent to God, its function is a God's function, and in a world in which a God would be superfluous; from such a world a God could never lawfully be missed.

But *is* the matter by which Mr. Spencer's process of cosmic evolution is carried on any such principle of never-ending perfection as this? Indeed it is not, for the future end of every cosmically evolved thing or system of things is tragedy; and Mr. Spencer, in confining himself to the æsthetic and ignoring the practical side of the controversy, has really contributed nothing serious to its relief. But apply now our principle of practical results, and see what a vital significance the question of materialism or theism immediately acquires.

Theism and materialism, so indifferent when taken retrospectively, point when we take them prospectively to wholly different practical consequences, to opposite outlooks of experience. For, according to the theory of mechanical evolution, the laws of redistribution of matter and motion, though they are certainly to thank for all the good hours which our organisms have ever yielded us and for all the ideals which our minds now frame, are yet fatally certain to undo their work again, and to redissolve everything that they have once evolved. You all know the picture of the last foreseeable state of the dead universe, as evolutionary science gives it forth. I cannot state it better than in Mr. Balfour's words: "The energies of our system will decay, the glory of the sun will be dimmed, and the earth, tideless and inert, will no longer tolerate the race which has for a moment disturbed its solitude. Man will go down into the pit, and all his thoughts will perish. The uneasy consciousness which in this obscure corner has for a brief space broken the contented silence of the universe, will be at rest. Matter will know itself no longer. 'Imperishable monuments' and 'immortal deeds,' death itself, and love stronger than death, will be as if they had not been. Nor will anything that is, be better or worse for all that the labor, genius, devotion, and suffering of man have striven through countless ages to effect." [8]

That is the sting of it, that in the vast driftings of the cosmic weather, though many a jewelled shore appears, and many an enchanted cloud-bank floats away, long lingering ere it be dissolved—even as our world now lingers, for our joy—yet when these transient products are gone, nothing, absolutely *nothing* remains, to represent those particular qualities, those elements of preciousness which they may have enshrined. Dead and gone are they, gone utterly from the very sphere and room of being. Without an echo; without a memory; without an influence on aught that may come after, to make it care for similar ideals. This utter final wreck and tragedy is of the essence of scientific materialism as at present understood. The lower and not the higher forces are the eternal forces, or the last surviving forces within the only cycle of evolution which we can definitely see. Mr. Spencer believes this as much as any one; so why should he argue with us as if we were making silly æsthetic objections to the "grossness" of "matter and motion,"—the principles of his philosophy,—when what really dismays us in it is the disconsolateness of its ulterior practical results?

No, the true objection to materialism is not positive but negative. It would be farcical at this day to make complaint of it for what it *is,* for "grossness." Grossness is what grossness *does*—we now know *that*. We make complaint of it, on the contrary, for what it is *not*—not a permanent warrant for our more ideal interests, not a fulfiller of our remotest hopes.

The notion of God, on the other hand, however inferior it may be in clearness to those mathematical notions so current in mechanical philosophy, has at least this practical superiority over them, that it guarantees an ideal order that shall be permanently preserved. A world with a God in it to say the last word, may indeed burn up or freeze, but we then think of Him as still mindful of the old ideals and sure to bring them elsewhere to fruition; so that, where He is, tragedy is only provisional and partial, and shipwreck and dissolution not the absolutely final things. This need of an eternal moral order is one of the deepest needs of our breast. And those poets, like Dante and Wordsworth, who live on the conviction of such an order, owe to that fact the extraordinary tonic and consoling power of their verse. Here then, in these different emotional and practical appeals, in these adjustments of our concrete attitudes of hope and

[8] *The Foundations of Belief,* p. 30.

expectation, and all the delicate consequences which their differences entail, lie the real meanings of materialism and theism—not in hair-splitting abstractions about matter's inner essence, or about the metaphysical attributes of God. Materialism means simply the denial that the moral order is eternal, and the cutting off of ultimate hopes; theism means the affirmation of an eternal moral order and the letting loose of hope. Surely here is an issue genuine enough, for any one who feels it; and, as long as men are men, it will yield matter for serious philosophic debate. Concerning this question, at any rate, the positivists and pooh-pooh-ers of metaphysics are in the wrong.

But possibly some of you may still rally to their defence. Even whilst admitting that theism and materialism make different prophecies of the world's future, you may yourselves pooh-pooh the difference as something so infinitely remote as to mean nothing for a sane mind. The essence of a sane mind, you may say, is to take shorter views, and to feel no concern about such chimæras as the latter end of the world. Well, I can only say that if you say this, you do injustice to human nature. Religious melancholy is not disposed of by a simple flourish of the word "insanity." The absolute things, the last things, the over-lapping things, are the truly philosophic concern; all superior minds feel seriously about them, and the mind with the shortest views is simply the mind of the more shallow man.

However, I am willing to pass over these very distant outlooks on the ultimate, if any of you so insist. The theistic controversy can still serve to illustrate the principle of pragmatism for us well enough, without driving us so far afield. If there be a God, it is not likely that he is confined solely to making differences in the world's latter end; he probably makes differences all along its course. Now the principle of practicalism says that the very meaning of the conception of God lies in those differences which must be made in our experience if the conception be true. God's famous inventory of perfections, as elaborated by dogmatic theology, either means nothing, says our principle, or it implies certain definite things that we can feel and do at particular moments of our lives, things which we could not feel and should not do were no God present and were the business of the universe carried on by material atoms instead. So far as our conceptions of the Deity involve no such experiences, so far they are meaningless and verbal,—scholastic entities and abstractions, as the positivists say, and fit objects for their scorn. But so far as they do involve such definite experiences, God means something for us, and may be real.

Now if we look at the definitions of God made by dogmatic theology, we see immediately that some stand and some fall when treated by this test. God, for example, as any orthodox text-book will tell us, is a being existing not only *per se,* or by himself, as created beings exist, but *a se,* or from himself; and out of this "aseity" flow most of his perfections. He is for example, necessary; absolute; infinite in all respects; and single. He is simple, not compounded of essence and existence, substance and accident, actuality and potentiality, or subject and attributes, as are other things. He belongs to no genus; he is inwardly and outwardly unalterable; he knows and wills all things, and first of all his own infinite self, in one indivisible eternal act. And he is absolutely self-sufficing, and infinitely happy. Now in which one of us practical Americans here assembled does this conglomeration of attributes awaken any sense of reality? And if in no one, then why not? Surely because such attributes awaken no responsive active feelings and call for no particular conduct of our own. How does God's "aseity" come home to *you?* What specific thing can I do to adapt myself to his "simplicity"? Or how determine our behavior henceforward if his "felicity" is anyhow absolutely complete? In the '50's and '60's Captain Mayne Reid was the great writer of boys' books of out-of-door adventure. He was forever extolling the hunters and field-observers of living animals' habits, and keeping up a fire of invective against the "closet-naturalists," as he called them, the collectors and classifiers, and handlers of skeletons and skins. When I was a boy I used to think that a closet-naturalist must be the vilest type of wretch under the sun. But surely the systematic theologians are the closet-naturalists of the Deity, even in Captain Mayne Reid's sense. Their orthodox deduction of God's attributes is nothing but a shuffling and matching of pedantic dictionary-adjectives, aloof from morals, aloof from human needs, something that might be worked out from the mere word "God" by a logical machine of wood and brass as well as by a man of flesh and blood. The attributes which I have quoted have absolutely nothing to do with religion, for religion is a living practical affair. Other parts, indeed, of God's traditional description do have practical connection with life, and have owed all their historic importance to that fact. His omniscence, for example, and his justice. With the one he sees us in the dark, with the other he rewards and punishes what he sees. So do his ubiquity and eternity and unalterability appeal to our confidence, and his goodness banish our fears. Even attributes of less meaning to this present audience have in past times so appealed. One of the chief attributes of God, according to the orthodox theology, is his infinite love of himself, proved by asking the question, "By what but an infinite object can an infinite affection be appeased?" An immediate consequence of this primary self-love of God is the orthodox dogma that the manifestation of his own glory is God's primal purpose in creation; and that dogma has certainly made very efficient practical connection with life. It is true that we ourselves are tending to outgrow this old monarchical conception of a Deity with his "court" and pomp—"his state is kingly, thousands to his bidding speed," etc.—but there is no denying the enormous influence it has had over ecclesiastical history, nor, by repercussion, over the history of European states. And yet even these more real and significant attributes have the trail of the serpent over them as the books on theology have actually worked them out. One feels that, in the theologians' hands, they are only a set of dictionary-adjectives, mechanically deduced; logic has stepped into the place of vision, professionalism into that of life. Instead of bread we get a stone; instead of a fish, a serpent. Did such a conglomeration of abstract general terms give really the gist of our knowledge of the Deity, divinity-schools might indeed continue to flourish, but religion, vital religion, would have taken its flight from this world. What keeps religion going is something else than abstract definitions and systems of logically concatenated adjectives, and something different from faculties of theology and their professors. All these things are after-effects, secondary accretions upon a mass of concrete religious experiences, connecting themselves with feeling and conduct that renew themselves *in saecula saeculorum* in the lives of humble private men. If you ask what these experiences are, they are conversations with the unseen, voices and visions, responses to prayer, changes of heart, deliverances from fear, inflowings of help, assurances of support, whenever certain persons set their own internal attitude in certain appropriate ways. The power comes and goes and is lost, and can be found only in a certain definite direction, just as if it were a concrete material thing. These direct experiences of a wider spiritual life with which our superficial consciousness is continuous, and with which it keeps up an intense commerce, form the primary mass of direct religious experience on which all hearsay religion rests, and which furnishes that notion of an ever-present God, out of which systematic theology thereupon proceeds to make capital in its own unreal pedantic way. What the word "God" means is just those passive and active experiences of your life. Now, my friends, it is quite immaterial to my purpose whether you yourselves enjoy and venerate these experiences, or whether you stand aloof, and, viewing them in others, suspect them of being illusory and vain. Like all other human experiences, they too certainly share in the general liability to illusion and mistake. They need not be infallible. But they are certainly the originals of the God-idea, and theology is the translation; and you remember that I am now using the God-idea merely as an example, not to discuss as to its truth or error, but only to show how well the principle of pragmatism works. That the God of systematic theology should exist or not exist is a matter of small practical moment. At most it means that you may continue uttering certain abstract words and that you must stop using others. But if the God of these particular experiences be false, it is an awful thing for you, if you are one of those whose lives are stayed on such experiences. The theistic controversy, trivial enough if we take it merely academically and theologically, is of tremendous significance if we test it by its results for actual life.

I can best continue to recommend the principle of practicalism to you by keeping in the neighborhood of this theological idea. I reminded you a few minutes ago that the old monarchical notion of the Deity as a sort of Louis the Fourteenth of the Heavens is losing nowadays much of its ancient prestige. Religious philosophy, like all philosophy, is growing more and more idealistic. And in the philosophy of the Absolute, so called, that post-Kantian form of idealism which is carrying so many of our higher minds before it, we have the triumph of what in old times was summarily disposed of as the pantheistic heresy,—I mean the conception of God, not as the extraneous creator, but as the indwelling spirit and substance of the world. I know not where one can find a more candid, more clear, or, on the whole, more persuasive statement of this theology of Absolute Idealism than in the addresses made before this very Union three years ago by your own great Californian philosopher (whose colleague at Harvard I am proud to be), Josiah Royce. His contributions to the resulting volume, *The Conception of God,* form a very masterpiece of popularization. Now you will remember, many of you, that in the discussion that followed Professor Royce's first address, the debate turned largely on the ideas of unity and plurality, and on the question whether, if God be One in All and All in All, "One with the unity of a single instant," as Royce calls it, "forming in His wholeness one luminously transparent moment," any room is left for real morality or freedom. Professor Howison, in particular, was earnest in urging that morality and freedom are relations between a manifold of selves, and that under the régime of Royce's monistic Absolute Thought "no true manifold of selves is or can be provided for." I will not go into any of the details of that particular discussion, but just ask you to consider for a moment whether, in general, any discussion about monism or pluralism, any argument over the unity of the universe, would not necessarily be brought into a shape where it tends to straighten itself out, by bringing our principle of practical results to bear.

The question whether the world is at bottom One or Many is a typical metaphysical question. Long has it raged! In its crudest form it is an exquisite example of the *loggerheads* of metaphysics. "I say it is one great fact," Parmenides and Spinoza exclaim. "I say it is many little facts," reply the atomists and associationists. "I say it is both one and many, many in one," say the Hegelians; and in the ordinary popular discussions we rarely get beyond this barren reiteration by the disputants of their pet adjectives of number. But is it not first of all clear that when we take such an adjective as "One" absolutely and abstractly, its meaning is so vague and empty that it makes no difference whether we affirm or deny it? Certainly this universe is not the mere number One; and yet you can number it "one," if you like, in talking about it as contrasted with other possible worlds numbered "two" and "three" for the occasion. What exact thing do you *practically* mean by "One," when you call the universe One, is the first question you must ask. In what ways does the oneness come home to your own personal life? By what difference does it express itself in your experience? How can you act differently towards a universe which is one? Inquired into in this way, the unity might grow clear and be affirmed in some ways and denied in others, and so cleared up, even though a certain vague and worshipful portentousness might disappear from the notion of it in the process.

For instance, one practical result that follows when we have one thing to handle, is that we can pass from one part of it to another without letting go of the thing. In this sense oneness must be partly denied and partly affirmed of our universe. Physically we can pass continuously in various manners from one part of it to another part. But logically and psychically the passage seems less easy, for there is no obvious transition from one mind to another, or from minds to physical things. You have to step off and get on again; so that in these ways the world is not one, as measured by that practical test.

Another practical meaning of oneness is susceptibility of collection. A collection is one, though the things that compose it be many. Now, can we practically "collect" the universe? Physically, of course we cannot. And mentally we cannot, if we take it concretely in its details. But if we take it summarily and abstractly, then we collect it mentally whenever we refer to it, even as I do now when I fling the term "universe" at it, and so seem to leave a mental ring around it. It is plain however, that such abstract noetic unity (as one might call it) is practically an extremely insignificant thing.

Again, oneness may mean generic sameness, so that you can treat all parts of the collection by one rule and get the same results. It is evident that in this sense the oneness of our world is incomplete, for in spite of much generic sameness in its elements and items, they still remain of many irreducible kinds. You can't pass by mere logic all over the field of it.

Its elements have, however, an affinity or commensurability with each other, are not wholly irrelevant, but can be compared, and fit together after certain fashions. This again might practically mean that they were one *in origin,* and that, tracing them backwards, we should find them arising in a single primal causal fact. Such unity of origin would have definite practical consequences, would have them for our scientific life at least.

I can give only these hasty superficial indications of what I mean when I say that it tends to clear up the quarrel between monism and pluralism to subject the notion of unity to such practical tests. On the other hand, it does but perpetuate strife and misunderstanding to continue talking of it in an absolute and mystical way. I have little doubt myself that this old quarrel might be completely smoothed out to the satisfaction of all claimants, if only the maxim of Peirce were methodically followed here. The current monism on the whole still keeps talking in too abstract a way. It says the world must be either pure disconnectedness, no universe at all, or absolute unity. It insists that there is no stopping-place half way. Any connection whatever, says this monism, is only possible if there be still more connection, until at last we are driven to admit the absolutely total connection required. But this absolutely total connection either means nothing, is the mere word "one" spelt long; or else it means the sum of all the partial connections that can possibly be conceived. I believe that when we thus attack the question, and set ourselves to search for these possible connections, and conceive each in a definite practical way, the dispute is already in a fair way to be settled beyond the chance of misunderstanding, by a compromise in which the Many and the One both get their lawful rights.

But I am in danger of becoming technical; so I must stop right here, and let you go.

I am happy to say that it is the English-speaking philosophers who first introduced the custom of interpreting the meaning of conceptions by asking what difference they make for life. Mr. Peirce has only expressed in the form of an explicit maxim what their sense for reality led them all instinctively to do. The great English way of investigating a conception is to ask yourself right off, "What is it *known as?* In what facts does it result? What is its *cash-value,* in terms of particular experience? and what special difference would come into the world according as it were true or false?" Thus does Locke treat the conception of personal identity. What you mean by it is just your chain of memories, says he. That is the only concretely verifiable part of its significance. All further ideas about it, such as the oneness or manyness of the spiritual substance on which it is based, are therefore void of intelligible meaning; and propositions touching such ideas may be indifferently affirmed or denied. So Berkeley with his "matter." The cash-value of matter is our physical sensations. That is what it is known as, all that we concretely verify of its conception. That therefore is the whole meaning of the word "matter"—any other pretended meaning is mere wind of words. Hume does the same thing with causation. It is known as habitual antecedence, and tendency on our part to look for something definite to come. Apart from this practical meaning it has no significance whatever, and books about it may be committed to the flames, says Hume. Stewart and Brown, James Mill, John Mill, and Bain, have followed more or less consistently the same method; and Shadworth Hodgson has used it almost as explicitly as Mr. Peirce. These writers have many of them no doubt been too sweeping in their negations; Hume, in particular, and James Mill, and Bain. But when all is said and done, it was they, not Kant, who introduced "the critical method" into philosophy, the one method fitted to make philosophy a study worthy of serious men. For what seriousness can possibly remain in debating philosophic propositions that will never make an appreciable difference to us in action? And what matters it, when all propositions are practically meaningless, which of them be called true or false?

The shortcomings and the negations and baldnesses of the English philosophers in question come, not from their eye to merely practical results, but solely from their failure to track the practical results completely enough to see how far they extend. Hume can be corrected and built out, and his beliefs enriched, by using Humian principles exclusively, and without making any use of the circuitous and ponderous artificialities of Kant. It is indeed a somewhat pathetic matter, as it seems to me, that this is not the course which the actual history of philosophy has followed. Hume had no English successors of adequate ability to complete him and correct his negations; so it happened, as a matter of fact, that building out of critical philosophy has mainly been left to thinkers who were under the influence of Kant. Even in England and this country it is with Kantian catch-words and categories that the fuller view of life is pursued, and in our universities it is the courses in transcendentalism that kindle the enthusiasm of the more ardent students, whilst the courses in English philosophy are committed to a secondary place. I cannot think that this is exactly as it should be. And I say this not out of national jingoism, for jingoism has no place in philosophy; or out of excitement over the great Anglo-American alliance against the world, of which we nowadays hear so much—though heaven knows that to that alliance I wish a Godspeed. I say it because I sincerely believe that the English spirit in philosophy is intellectually, as well as practically and morally, on the saner, sounder, and truer path. Kant's mind is the rarest and most intricate of all possible antique bric-a-brac museums, and connoisseurs and dilettanti will always wish to visit it and see the wondrous and racy contents. The temper of the dear old man about his work is perfectly delectable. And yet he is really—although I shrink with some terror from saying such a thing before some of you here present—at bottom a mere curio, a "specimen." I mean by this a perfectly definite thing: I believe that Kant bequeaths to us not one single conception which is both indispensable to philosophy and which philosophy either did not possess before him, or was not destined inevitably to acquire after him through the growth of men's reflection upon the hypotheses by which science interprets nature. The true line of philosophic progress lies, in short, it seems to me, not so much *through* Kant as *round* him to the point where now we stand. Philosophy can perfectly well outflank him, and build herself up into adequate fulness by prolonging more directly the older English lines.

# General Bibliography

# General Bibliography

The following list does not pretend to be a complete bibliography of American philosophy. Items included in the reference lists in the body of the volume have in most cases been omitted here. Section V is limited to philosophers who gave expression to their major ideas before 1900 and is arranged according to date of birth. The titles listed in this section have been checked where possible but it is not likely that all errors have been eliminated.

## I. REFERENCE WORKS

Baldwin, James Mark (editor): *Dictionary of Philosophy and Psychology.* 2 vols. New York: The Macmillan Co., 1901–02. Reprinted with corrections, 1925.

*Bibliographie de philosophie* (1937—; section on American Philosophy).

*Biblioteca Americana: A Dictionary of Books Relating to America, from Its Discovery to the Present Time.* Edited successively by Joseph Sabin, Wilberforce Eames and R. W. G. Vail. 29 vols. New York: Bibliographical Society of America, 1868–1936.

Hastings, James (editor): *Encyclopedia of Religion and Ethics.* 12 vols. and index. New York: Charles Scribner's Sons, 1908–27. (Consult especially for articles on Calvinism, Arminianism, Deism, etc.)

Johnson, Allen (editor): *Dictionary of American Biography.* 20 vols. and index. New York: Charles Scribner's Sons, 1928–37.

Seligman, Edwin R. A., and Johnson, Alvin (editors): *Encyclopedia of the Social Sciences.* 15 vols. New York: The Macmillan Co., 1930–35.

## II. JOURNALS HAVING OCCASIONAL ARTICLES ON OR BY AMERICAN PHILOSOPHERS

*Journal of Speculative Philosophy* (22 vols., 1867–93. Edited by W. T. Harris).

*Ethics* (1890——; formerly *International Journal of Ethics*).

*Monist* (1890–1936).

*Philosophical Review* (1892——; index to vols. 1–35, 1927).

*Journal of Philosophy* (1904—; bibliographies for 1933–36).

*New England Quarterly* (1928—; annual bibliography in March number).

*American Literature* (1929—; current bibliographies in each number).

## III. USEFUL BOOKS FOR BACKGROUND READING

Bacon, L. W.: *A History of American Christianity*. New York: The Christian Literature Co., 1897.

Beard, Charles A. and Mary R.: *The Rise of American Civilization*. 2 vols. New York: The Macmillan Co., 1927. Revised and enlarged one-volume edition, 1933.

Boynton, Percy H.: *A History of American Literature*. Boston: Ginn and Co., 1919.

Cargill, Oscar (editor): *American Literature: A Period Anthology*. 5 vols. edited in chronological order by Robert E. Spiller, Tremaine McDowell, Louis Wann, Oscar Cargill, and John Herbert Nelson. New York: The Macmillan Co., 1933.

Cobb, Sanford H.: *The Rise of Religious Liberty in America*. New York: The Macmillan Co., 1902.

Commager, Henry S.: *Documents of American History*. New York: F. S. Crofts and Co., 1934. (Fullest and best collection of source material in one volume. Bibliographies.)

Foerster, Norman: *American Criticism: A Study of Literary Theory from Poe to the Present*. Boston: Houghton Mifflin Co., 1928.

Fox, Dixon Ryan: *Ideas in Motion*. New York: D. Appleton-Century Co., 1935.

Gettell, R. D.: *History of American Political Thought*. New York: The Century Co., 1928.

Jacobson, J. Mark: *The Development of American Political Thought: A Documentary History*. New York: D. Appleton-Century Co., 1932.

Kraus, Michael: *A History of American History*. New York: Farrar and Rinehart, Inc., 1937.

Merriam, Charles E.: *A History of American Political Theories*. New York: The Macmillan Co., 1903.

Morison, Samuel E., and Commager, Henry S.: *The Growth of the American Republic*. New York: Oxford University Press, 1930. Revised and enlarged edition in 2 vols., 1937. (Critical bibliographies.)

Parrington, Vernon Louis: *Main Currents in American Thought*. 3 vols. New York: Harcourt, Brace and Co., 1927–30. (The most brilliant interpretation of American literature in its economic, political, and social setting. Volume I (1620–1800): *The Colonial Mind*. Volume II (1800–1860): *The Romantic Revolution in America*. Volume III (1860–1920): *The Beginnings of Critical Realism in America*.)

Rusk, R. L.: *The Literature of the Middle Western Frontier*. 2 vols. New York: Columbia University Press, 1925.

Santayana, George: *Character and Opinion in the United States*. New York: Charles Scribner's Sons, 1920.

———: *The Genteel Tradition at Bay*. New York: Charles Scribner's Sons, 1931.

Schlesinger, Arthur M., and Fox, Dixon R. (editors): *A History of*

*American Life*. 12 vols. New York: The Macmillan Co., 1929.

Smith, David Eugene and Ginsburg, J.: *A History of Mathematics in America before 1900*. Chicago: Open Court Publishing Co., 1934.

Sweet, W. W.: *The Story of Religions in America*. New York: Harper and Bros., 1930.

Taylor, Walter Fuller: *A History of American Letters*. Cincinnati: American Book Co., 1936. (Conventional textbook, as good as any for reference purposes; chiefly valuable for its more than 200 pages of bibliographies by Harry Hartwick.)

Trent, William P., Erskine, J., Sherman, Stuart P., Van Doren, Carl (editors): *The Cambridge History of American Literature*. 4 vols. New York: G. P. Putnam's Sons, 1917–21. (Strong on colonial and early national periods. Chapters and bibliographies on philosophers, theologians, educators, scholars, economists, and historians.)

Turner, F. J.: *The Frontier in American History*. New York, 1920.

Tyler, Moses Coit: *A History of American Literature during the Colonial Period, 1607–1765*. 2 vols. New York: G. P. Putnam's Sons, 1878. Revised edition, 1897.

———: *The Literary History of the American Revolution, 1763–1783*. 2 vols. New York: G. P. Putnam's Sons, 1897. (Pioneer works, still standard and not likely to be superseded.)

Warfel, Harry R., Gabriel, Ralph H., and Williams, Stanley T. (editors): *The American Mind*. Cincinnati: American Book Co., 1937. (Fullest and most up-to-date one-volume anthology.)

## IV. THE HISTORY OF AMERICAN PHILOSOPHY

### A—*General*

Blakey, Robert: *History of the Philosophy of Mind*. London, 1850. (Vol. IV, ch. VII, "Metaphysical Writers of the United States.")

Carlson, J. C.: *Om Filosofieu i Amerika*. Upsala, 1895.

Cohen, Morris R.: "A Critical Sketch of Legal Philosophy in America," *Law: A Century of Progress, 1835–1935*. 3 vols. New York: New York University Press, 1937. II, 266–319.

Curti, Merle: "The Great Mr. Locke, America's Philosopher, 1783–1861," *Huntington Library Bulletin* 11 (1937) 107–51.

Curtis, Mattoon M.: "An Outline of Philosophy in America," *Bulletin of Western Reserve University* 2 (1896) 3–18.

Hall, G. Stanley: "On the History of American College Textbooks and Teaching in Logic, Ethics, Psychology and Allied Subjects," *Proceedings of the American Antiquarian Society*. New Series. 9 (1894) 137–74.

Jones, Adam LeRoy: *Early American Philosophers*. New York: The Macmillan Co., 1898.

Müller, Gustav E.: *Amerikanische Philosophie.* Stuttgart: Fr. Frommanns Verlag, 1936.

Porter, Noah: "Die Philosophie in Nordamerika," *Philosophische Monatshefte* 9 (1875) 368–75, 424–6, 472–7.

Rand, Benjamin: "Philosophical Instruction in Harvard University from 1636 to 1906," *Harvard Graduates Magazine* 37 (1929) 296–311.

Riley, I. Woodbridge: *American Philosophy: the Early Schools.* New York: Dodd, Mead and Co., 1907.

———: *American Thought from Puritanism to Pragmatism and Beyond.* Second edition with additions. New York: Henry Holt and Co., 1923. (First edition, 1915.)

Townsend, Harvey G.: *Philosophical Ideas in the United States.* Cincinnati: American Book Co., 1934.

Van Becelaere, E. G. L.: *La Philosophie en Amérique depuis les origines jusqu'à nos jours (1607–1900).* New York: The Eclectic Publishing Co., 1904.

Vorovka, Karel: *Americká Filosofie.* Prague, 1929.

White, Henry C.: "The South's Contributions to Philosophy," *The South in the Building of the Nation.* Richmond, Va.: The Southern Publication Society, 1909. VII, 259–68.

## B—*Colonial Thought*

Adams, Brooks: *The Emancipation of Massachusetts.* Boston: Houghton Mifflin Co., 1887. Revised and enlarged edition, 1919.

Adams, J. T.: *The Founding of New England.* Boston: Atlantic Monthly Press, 1921.

Andrews, Charles M.: *The Colonial Period of American History.* 4 vols. so far published. New Haven: Yale University Press, 1934–38.

Fiske, John: *The Beginnings of New England; or, The Puritan Theocracy in its Relations to Civil and Religious Liberty.* Boston: Houghton Mifflin Co., 1889.

Foster, F. H.: *A Genetic History of the New England Theology.* Chicago: University of Chicago Press, 1907.

Hall, Thomas C.: *The Religious Background of American Culture.* Boston: Little, Brown and Co., 1930.

Haroutunian, Joseph: *Piety versus Moralism: The Passing of the New England Theology.* New York: Henry Holt and Co., 1932.

Johnson, Edgar A. J.: *American Economic Thought in the Seventeenth Century.* London: P. S. King and Son, Ltd., 1932.

Jones, Rufus M. (assisted by Isaac Sharpless and Amelia Gummere): *The Quakers in the American Colonies.* New York: The Macmillan Co., 1911.

Kittredge, George L.: *Witchcraft in Old and New England.* Cambridge: Harvard University Press, 1929.

Miller, Perry: *Orthodoxy in Massachusetts, 1630–1650.* Cambridge: Harvard University Press, 1933.

———: "The Marrow of Puritan Divinity," *Publications of the Colonial Society of Massachusetts* 32 (1938) 247–300. (Best analysis of the Federal, or Covenant, Theology.)

———, and Johnson, Thomas H.: *The Puritans.* Cincinnati: The American Book Co., 1938. (Contains the best available bibliography.)

Morison, Samuel Eliot: *The Puritan Pronaos: Studies in the Intellectual Life of New England in the Seventeenth Century.* New York: New York University Press, 1936.

———: *The Founding of Harvard College.* Cambridge: Harvard University Press. 1935.

———: *Harvard College in the Seventeenth Century.* 2 vols. Cambridge: Harvard University Press. 1936.

Osgood, Herbert L.: "The Political Ideas of the Puritans," *Political Science Quarterly* 6 (1891) 1–28, 201–31.

Riley, I. Woodbridge: "Philosophers and Divines, 1720–1789," *The Cambridge History of American Literature.* I, 72–89.

Schneider, Herbert W.: *The Puritan Mind.* New York: Henry Holt and Co., 1930.

Walker, Williston: *The Creeds and Platforms of Congregationalism.* New York: Charles Scribner's Sons, 1893.

Walsh, James J.: *The Education of the Founding Fathers of the Republic.* New York: Fordham University Press, 1935.

———: "Scholasticism in the Colonial Colleges," *New England Quarterly* 5 (1932) 483–532.

Wright, Thomas G.: *Literary Culture in Early New England.* New Haven: Yale University Press, 1920.

## C—*The Age of Reason*

Baldwin, Alice M.: *The New England Clergy and the American Revolution.* Durham, N. C.: Duke University Press, 1928.

Beard, Charles A.: *Economic Origins of Jeffersonian Democracy.* New York: The Macmillan Co., 1915.

Becker, Carl L.: *The Declaration of Independence: A Study in the History of Political Ideas.* New York: Harcourt, Brace and Co., 1922.

———: *The Heavenly City of Eighteenth-Century Philosophers.* New Haven: Yale University Press. 1932.

Brasch, F. E.: "The Royal Society of London and Its Influence upon Scientific Thought in the American Colonies," *Scientific Monthly* 33 (1931) 336–55, 448–69.

Cairns, John: *Unbelief in the Eighteenth Century.* New York: Harper and Brothers, 1881.

Clark, H. H.: "Factors to be Investigated in American Literary History from 1787 to 1800," *English Journal* 23 (1934) 481–7.

Crèvecoeur, St. John de: *Sketches of Eighteenth Century America.* New Haven: Yale University Press, 1925.

Faÿ, Bernard: *The Revolutionary Spirit in France and America: A Study of Moral and Intellectual Relations between France and the United States at the End of the Eighteenth Century.* New York: Harcourt, Brace and Co., 1927.

Hansen, Allen O.: *Liberalism and American Education in the Eighteenth Century.* New York: The Macmillan Co., 1926.

Hibben, John G.: *The Philosophy of the Enlightenment.* New York: Charles Scribner's Sons, 1910.

Jameson, J. F.: *The American Revolution Considered as a Social Movement.* Princeton: Princeton University Press, 1926.

Jones, H. M.: "The Drift to Liberalism in the Eighteenth Century," *Authority and the Individual.* Harvard Tercentenary Publications. Cambridge: Harvard University Press, 1937. 319–48.

Koch, G. Adolf: *Republican Religion: The American Revolution and the Cult of Reason.* New York: Henry Holt and Co., 1933.

Kraus, M.: *Intercolonial Aspects of American Culture on the Eve of the Revolution with Special Reference to the Northern Towns.* New York: Columbia University Press, 1928.

MacIver, R. M.: "The Philosophical Background of the Constitution," *Journal of Social Philosophy* 3 (1937–38) 201–9.

Miller, Samuel: *A Brief Retrospect of the Eighteenth Century. Part First; in Two Volumes: Containing a Sketch of the Revolutions and Improvements in Science, Arts, and Literature during that Period.* 2 vols. New York, 1803.

Morais, Herbert M.: "Deism in Revolutionary America," *International Journal of Ethics* 42 (1932) 434–53.

———: *Deism in Eighteenth Century America.* New York: Columbia University Press, 1934.

Osgood, Herbert L.: *The American Colonies in the Eighteenth Century.* 4 vols. New York: Columbia University Press, 1924.

Riley, I. Woodbridge: "La Philosophie française en Amérique: I, De Voltaire à Cousin," *Revue philosophique* 84 (1917) 393–428.

Sonne, Niels Henry: *Liberal Kentucky, 1780–1828.* New York: Columbia University Press, 1939.

Wiltse, Charles M.: *The Jeffersonian Tradition in American Democracy.* Chapel Hill, N. C.: University of North Carolina Press, 1935.

Wright, B. F., Jr.: *American Interpretations of Natural Law: A Study in the History of Political Thought.* Cambridge: Harvard University Press, 1931.

### D—*Transcendentalism and Evolution*

[Alexander, J. W., and Dod, A. B.]: "Transcendentalism," *Theological Essays reprinted from the Princeton Review.* Series I. New

York, 1846. 608–94. (Originally published in *The Biblical Repertory and Princeton Review* 11 [1839] 37–101.)

*Bridgewater Treatises: Treatises on the Power, Wisdom, and Goodness of God, as Manifested in the Creation.* 12 vols. London, 1834–37.

Brooks, Van Wyck: *The Flowering of New England.* Boston: Houghton Mifflin Co., 1938.

Charvat, William: *The Origins of American Critical Thought, 1810–1835.* Philadelphia: University of Pennsylvania Press, 1936.

Christy, Arthur E.: *The Orient in American Transcendentalism: A Study of Emerson, Thoreau, and Alcott.* New York: Columbia University Press, 1932.

Frothingham, O. B.: *Transcendentalism in New England.* New York: G. P. Putnam's Sons, 1876.

Goddard, H. C.: *Studies in New England Transcendentalism.* New York: Columbia University Press, 1908.

Hawkins, Richmond L.: *Auguste Comte and the United States (1816–1853).* Cambridge: Harvard University Press, 1936.

———: *Positivism in the United States (1853–1861).* Cambridge: Harvard University Press, 1938.

Jenkins, William Sumner: *Pro-Slavery Thought in the Old South.* Chapel Hill, N. C.: University of North Carolina Press, 1935.

Jones, Howard M.: *America and French Culture, 1750–1848.* Chapel Hill, N. C.: University of North Carolina Press, 1927.

Körner, Gustav: *Das deutsche Element in den vereinigten Staaten von Nordamerika, 1818–1848.* Cincinnati, 1880.

Mumford, Lewis: *The Golden Day.* New York: Boni and Liveright, 1926.

Murdock, James: *Sketches of Modern Philosophy, Especially among the Germans.* Hartford, Conn., 1842. (Ch. XV on "American Transcendentalism" reprinted in Townsend, H. G.: *Philosophical Ideas in the United States.* 253–65.)

Nicolson, Marjorie H.: "James Marsh and the Vermont Transcendentalists," *Philosophical Review* 34 (1925) 28–50.

Riley, I. Woodbridge: "La Philosophie française en Amérique: II, Le Positivisme," *Revue philosophique* 87 (1919) 369–423.

### E—*The Emergence of Contemporary Issues*

Adams, G. P., and Montague, W. P. (editors): *Contemporary American Philosophy.* 2 vols. New York: The Macmillan Co., 1930.

Cohen, Morris R.: "A Brief Sketch of the Later Philosophy," *The Cambridge History of American Literature.* III, 226–65. (Bibliography in vol. IV.)

Cunningham, G. W.: *The Idealistic Argument in Recent British and American Philosophy.* New York: D. Appleton-Century Co., 1933.

Garrison, Winfred E.: *The March of Faith: The Story of Religion in America since 1865*. New York: Harper and Brothers, 1923.

Harlow, Victor E.: *Bibliography and Genetic Study of American Realism*. Oklahoma City: Harlow Publishing Co., 1931.

Jones, Howard M.: "The Influence of European Ideas in Nineteenth-Century America," *American Literature* 7 (1935–36) 241–73.

Leroux, E.: *Le Pragmatisme Americain et Anglais*. Paris: F. Alcan, 1923.

Muirhead, J. H.: *The Platonic Tradition in Anglo-Saxon Philosophy*. New York: The Macmillan Co., 1931.

Perry, R. B.: *Philosophy of the Recent Past: An Outline of European and American Philosophy since 1860*. New York: Charles Scribner's Sons, 1926.

Royce, Josiah: "Systematic Philosophy in America in the Years 1893, 1894 and 1895," *Archiv für systematische Philosophie* 3 (1897) 245–66.

Rogers, Arthur K.: *English and American Philosophy since 1800*. New York: The Macmillan Co., 1922.

Thilly, Frank: "La Philosophie Américaine contemporaine," *Revue de metaphysique et de morale* 16 (1908) 607–34.

Warren, Austin: "The Concord School of Philosophy," *New England Quarterly* 2 (1929) 199–233.

Wenley, R. M.: *The Life and Work of George Sylvester Morris*. New York: The Macmillan Co., 1917.

## V. POST-REVOLUTIONARY PHILOSOPHERS NOT REPRESENTED BY SELECTIONS IN THIS VOLUME

Witherspoon, John (1723–1794): Collins, V. L. (editor): *Lectures on Moral Philosophy*. Princeton: Princeton University Press, 1912.

Priestley, Joseph (1733–1804): *Disquisitions relating to Matter and Spirit*. 2 vols. London, 1777.

———: *A Free Discussion of the Doctrines of Materialism, and Philosophical Necessity, In a Correspondence between Dr. Price, and Dr. Priestley*. London, 1778.

———: *Letters to a Philosophical Unbeliever*. Birmingham, England, 1780.

———: *A General View of the Arguments for the Unity of God*. Birmingham, England, 1783.

———: *Discourses on the Evidences of Revealed Religion*. London, 1794; Philadelphia, 1795.

———: *Discourses relating to the Evidences of Revealed Religion*. Philadelphia, 1796–97. (Quite distinct from above.)

———: *Socrates and Jesus Compared*. Northumberland, Pa., 1803.

———: *Doctrines of Heathen Philosophy Compared with Revelation*. Northumberland, Pa., 1804.

Paine, Thomas (1737–1809): Conway, Moncure D. (editor): *The*

*Writings of Thomas Paine*. 4 vols. New York: G. P. Putnam's Sons, 1894–96. (Esp. *Rights of Man* and *Age of Reason*.)

Wilson, James (1742–1798): *Commentaries on the Constitution of the United States of America*. London, 1792. (Co-author along with Thomas MacKean.)

———: Wilson, Bird (editor): *The Works of the Honourable James Wilson, LL.D.* 3 vols. Philadelphia, 1803–04. (Esp. *Lectures on Law*.)

Dwight, Timothy (1752–1817): *The Triumph of Infidelity: A Poem*. Printed in the World, 1788.

———: *The Nature, and Danger, of Infidel Philosophy: Exhibited in Two Discourses, addressed to the Candidates for the Baccalaureate, in Yale College*. New Haven, 1798.

———: *Theology: Explained and Defended, in a Series of Sermons: with a Memoir of the Life of the Author*. 4 vols. Second edition. New Haven, 1823. (Originally published in 5 vols., 1818–19.)

Law, Thomas (1759–1834): *First Thoughts on Instinctive Impulses*. Philadelphia, 1810.

———: *Second Thoughts on Instinctive Impulses*. Philadelphia, 1813.

———: *Thoughts on the Moral System*. Philadelphia, 1833.

Palmer, Elihu (1764–1806): *The Examiners Examined: Being a Defense of the Age of Reason*. New York, 1794.

———: *Principles of Nature: or, A Development of the Moral Causes of Happiness and Misery among the Human Species*. Third edition. New York, 1806.

Hedge, Levi (1766–1844): *Elements of Logick: or, A Summary of the General Principles and Different Modes of Reasoning*. Cambridge: Harvard University Press, 1816.

Beasley, Frederick (1777–1845): *A Search of Truth in the Science of the Human Mind*. Part I. New York, 1822.

———: *A Vindication of the Argument, a priori, in Proof of the Being and Attributes of God, from the Objections of Dr. Waterland*. New York, 1825.

Channing, William Ellery (1780–1842): *The Works of William E. Channing, D.D., With an Introduction*. New and complete edition, rearranged. To which is added, *The Perfect Life*. Boston: American Unitarian Association, 1886.

Shattuck, George (1783–1854): *An Essay on the Influence of Air upon Animal Bodies*. Boston, 1808.

Ewell, Thomas (1785–1826): *The Properties of Matter: Containing the Elements or Principles of Modern Chemistry*. New York, 1806.

Buchanan, Joseph (1785–1829): *Philosophy of Human Nature*. Richmond, Ky., 1812.

———: "Matter and Mind," *Reporter* (Lexington, Ky.), July 21, Aug. 11 and Aug. 25, 1819.

Marsh, James (1794–1842): Torrey, J. L. (editor): *The Remains of the Rev. James Marsh, D.D.: With a Memoir of His Life*. Boston, 1843.

Hickok, Laurens Perseus (1798–1888): *A System of Moral Science.* Schenectady, N. Y., 1853.

———: *Rational Cosmology: or, The Eternal Principles and Necessary Laws of the Universe.* New York: D. Appleton and Co., 1858.

———: *Humanity Immortal: or, Man Tried, Fallen, and Redeemed.* New York, 1872.

———: *Creator and Creation: or, Knowledge in the Reason of God and his Work.* New York, 1872.

———: *The Logic of Reason.* New York, 1874.

———: *Rational Psychology: or, The Subjective Idea and Objective Law of All Intelligence.* New York, 1882. (First edition, Auburn, N. Y., 1849.)

———: *Empirical Psychology: or, The Science of Mind from Experience.* Boston, 1889. (First published as *Empirical Psychology: or, The Human Mind as Given in Consciousness.* Schenectady, N. Y., 1854.)

Wayland, Francis (1799–1865): *The Limitations of Human Responsibility.* Boston, 1838.

———: *Elements of Intellectual Philosophy.* New York, 1866. (First edition, Boston, 1854.)

———: *The Elements of Moral Science.* Boston, 1873. (First edition, Boston, 1835.)

———: *The Elements of Political Economy.* New York, 1878. (First edition, New York, 1837.)

Alcott, Amos Bronson (1799–1888): *Tablets.* Boston, 1868.

———: *Concord Days.* Boston, 1872.

———: *Table Talk.* Boston, 1877.

Mahan, Asa (1799–1889): *Doctrine of the Will.* New York, 1846.

———: *The Science of Moral Philosophy.* Oberlin, Ohio, 1848.

———: *A System of Intellectual Philosophy.* Revised edition. New York, 1854. (First edition, 1845.)

———: *The Science of Logic: or, An Analysis of the Laws of Thought.* New York, 1857.

———: *The Science of Natural Theology: or, God the Unconditioned Cause, and God the Infinite and Perfect, as Revealed in Creation.* Boston, 1867.

———: *The System of Mental Philosophy.* Chicago, 1882.

———: *Autobiography: Intellectual, Moral, and Spiritual.* London, 1882.

Lieber, Francis (1800–1872): *Manual of Political Ethics.* 2 vols. Boston: Little, Brown and Co., 1838–39.

———: *Treatise on Civil Liberty and Self-Government.* 2 vols. Philadelphia, 1853.

Hazard, Rowland Gibson (1801–1888): *The Freedom of the Mind in Willing: or, Every Being that Wills a Creative First Cause.* New York: D. Appleton and Co., 1864.

———: *Two Letters on Causation and Freedom in Willing: Addressed to John Stuart Mill.* New York and Boston, 1869.

Hopkins, Mark (1802–1887): *Lectures on the Evidences of Christian-*

*ity Delivered before the Lowell Institute.* Boston, 1846. (Revised as textbook in 1863.)

Hopkins, Mark: *Miscellaneous Essays and Discourses.* Boston, 1847.

———: *Lectures on Moral Science Delivered before the Lowell Institute.* Boston, 1862.

———: *The Law of Love, and Love as a Law: or, Moral Science, Theoretical and Practical.* New York: Charles Scribner's Sons, 1869.

———: *The Scriptural Idea of Man.* New York, 1883.

———: *An Outline Study of Man: or, The Body and Mind in One System.* Revised edition. New York: Charles Scribner's Sons, 1886. (First edition, 1878.)

Tappan, Henry Philip (1805–1881): *The Doctrine of the Will determined by an Appeal to Consciousness.* New York, 1840.

———: *The Doctrine of the Will applied to Moral Agency and Responsibility.* New York, 1841.

———: *Elements of Logic: Together with an Introductory View of Philosophy in General and a Preliminary View of the Reason.* New York: D. Appleton and Co., 1844.

Hedge, Frederick Henry (1805–1890): *Reason in Religion.* Boston, 1865.

———: *Ways of the Spirit: and Other Essays.* Boston, 1877.

———: *Atheism in Philosophy.* Boston, 1884.

Rauch, Frederick Augustus (1806–1841): *Psychology: or, A View of the Human Soul; including Anthropology.* New York, 1841.

Grimes, James Stanley (1807–1903): *Mysteries of the Head and Heart Explained.* Chicago, 1875. (Originally published as *The Mysteries of Human Nature Explained.* Chicago, 1857.)

———: *Problems of Creation.* Chicago, 1881.

Bledsoe, Albert Taylor (1809–1877): *Examination of President Edwards' "Inquiry into the Freedom of the Will."* New York, 1845.

———: *A Theodicy: or, Vindication of the Divine Glory, as Manifested in the Constitution and Government of the Moral World.* New York, 1853.

———: *An Essay on Liberty and Slavery.* New York, 1856.

———: *The Philosophy of Mathematics.* Philadelphia, 1866.

Peirce, Benjamin (1809–1880): *Ideality in the Physical Sciences.* Boston: Little, Brown and Co., 1864.

Bowen, Francis (1811–1890): *Critical Essays on a Few Subjects Connected with the History and Present Condition of Speculative Philosophy.* Boston, 1842.

———: *On the Application of Metaphysical and Ethical Science to the Evidences of Religion.* Boston: Little, Brown and Co., 1849.

———: *Principles of Political Economy: Applied to the Condition, the Resources, and the Institutions of the American People.* Boston: Little, Brown and Co., 1856.

———: *Treatise on Logic: or, The Laws of Pure Thought: Comprising both the Aristotelic and Hamiltonian Analysis of Logical Terms.* Cambridge, Mass., 1865.

Bowen, Francis: *Gleanings from a Literary Life, 1838–1880.* New York: Charles Scribner's Sons, 1880.

Porter, Noah (1811–1892): *The Human Intellect: with an Introduction upon Psychology and the Soul.* New York: Charles Scribner's Sons, 1868. (Abridged as *The Elements of Intellectual Science.* New York: Charles Scribner's Sons, 1871.)

———: *The Sciences of Nature versus the Science of Man.* New York: Dodd, Mead and Co., 1871.

———: *Science and Sentiment: with Other Papers, chiefly Philosophical.* New York: Charles Scribner's Sons, 1882.

———: *The Elements of Moral Science: Theoretical and Practical.* New York: Charles Scribner's Sons, 1885.

McCosh, James (1811–1894): *The Method of the Divine Government: Physical and Moral.* Edinburgh, 1850.

———: *Typical Forms and Special Ends in Creation.* London, 1855.

———: *The Supernatural in Relation to the Natural.* Cambridge, Mass., 1862.

———: *An Examination of Mr. J. S. Mills' Philosophy: Being a Defence of Fundamental Truth.* London, 1866.

———: *The Scottish Philosophy: Biographical, Expository, Critical, from Hutcheson to Hamilton.* New York, 1875.

———: *The Development Hypothesis: Is It Sufficient?* New York, 1876.

———: *The Intuitions of the Mind Inductively Investigated.* Revised edition. New York, 1882. (First edition, London, 1860.)

———: *Development: What It Can Do and What It Cannot Do.* New York: Charles Scribner's Sons, 1883.

———: *Realistic Philosophy.* 2 vols. New York: Charles Scribner's Sons, 1887. (First published, 1882.)

Stephens, Alexander Hamilton (1812–1883): *A Constitutional View of the Late War Between the States: Its Causes, Character, Conduct and Results.* 2 vols. Philadelphia, 1868–70.

Haven, Joseph (1816–1874): *Mental Philosophy: Including the Intellect, Sensibilities and Will.* Boston, 1857.

———: *Moral Philosophy: Including Theoretical and Practical Ethics.* Boston, 1859.

———: *Studies in Philosophy and Theology.* Andover, Mass., 1869.

Thoreau, Henry David (1817–1862): *The Writings of Henry David Thoreau.* 20 vols. Boston: Houghton Mifflin Co., 1907.

Shedd, William Greenough Thayer (1820–1894): *The True Nature of the Beautiful, and Its Influence upon Culture.* Northampton, Mass., 1851.

———: *Discourses and Essays.* Andover, Mass., 1856.

———: *Lectures upon the Philosophy of History.* Andover, Mass., 1856.

———: *Literary Essays.* New York: Charles Scribner's Sons, 1878.

Stallo, John Bernhard (1823–1900): *General Principles of the Philosophy of Nature.* New York, 1848.

Stallo, John Bernhard: *The Concepts and Theories of Modern Physics.* New York: D. Appleton and Co., 1882.

Le Conte, Joseph (1823–1901): *Religion and Science.* New York: D. Appleton and Co., 1874.

———: *Evolution: Its Nature, Its Evidences, and Its Relation to Religious Thought.* New York: D. Appleton and Co., 1888.

———: *The Conception of God: A Philosophical Discussion Concerning the Nature of the Divine Idea as a Demonstrable Reality.* New York: The Macmillan Co., 1897. (Co-author along with Josiah Royce, George Holmes Howison and Sidney Edward Mezes.)

Wilder, Alexander (1823–1908): *New Platonism and Alchemy.* New York, 1869.

———: *The Symbolic Language.* New York, 1876.

Shields, Charles Woodruff (1825–1904): *Philosophia Ultima.* Philadelphia, 1861.

———: *The Final Philosophy: or, System of Perfectible Knowledge issuing from the Harmony of Science and Religion.* New York, 1877.

———: *Philosophia Ultima: or, Science of the Sciences.* 3 vols. New York, 1888–1905. (These three works bearing similar titles are progressive developments of Shields's philosophy.)

Bascom, John (1827–1911): *Political Economy.* Andover, Mass., 1859.

———: *Aesthetics: or, The Science of Beauty.* Boston, 1862.

———: *The Philosophy of Rhetoric.* Boston, Mass., 1866.

———: *Science, Philosophy and Religion.* New York: G. P. Putnam's Sons, 1871.

———: *Philosophy of English Literature.* New York: G. P. Putnam's Sons, 1874.

———: *Philosophy of Religion: or, The Rational Grounds of Religious Belief.* New York, 1876.

———: *Ethics: or, Science of Duty.* New York: G. P. Putnam's Sons, 1879.

———: *Natural Theology.* New York: G. P. Putnam's Sons, 1880.

———: *The Science of Mind.* New York: G. P. Putnam's Sons, 1881. (Originally printed as *The Principles of Psychology,* 1869.)

———: *An Historical Interpretation of Philosophy.* New York: G. P. Putnam's Sons, 1893.

———: *Social Theory: A Grouping of Social Facts and Principles.* New York: Thomas Y. Crowell Co., 1895.

———: *Evolution and Religion: or, Faith as a Part of a Complete Cosmic System.* New York: G. P. Putnam's Sons, 1897.

Brokmeyer, Henry C. (1828–1906): *A Mechanic's Diary.* Washington, D. C., 1910.

Everett, Charles Carrol (1829–1900): *Science of Thought: A System of Logic.* Boston, 1875.

———: *Theism and the Christian Faith: Lectures Delivered in Harvard Divinity School.* New York: The Macmillan Co., 1900.

Everett, Charles Carrol: *Essays: Theological and Literary.* Boston: Houghton Mifflin Co., 1902.

———: *Immortality: and Other Essays.* Boston: American Unitarian Association, 1902.

Blood, Benjamin Paul (1832–1919): *Pluriverse: An Essay in the Philosophy of Pluralism.* Boston: Marshall Jones Co., 1920.

Mulford, Elisha (1833–1885): *The Nation: The Foundation of Civil Order and Political Life in the United States.* Boston, 1870.

———: *The Republic of God: An Institute of Theology.* Boston: Houghton Mifflin Co., 1881.

Powell, John W. (1834–1902): *Truth and Error: or, The Science of Intellection.* Chicago: Open Court Publishing Co., 1898.

Howison, George Holmes (1834–1916): *The Limits of Evolution: and Other Essays Illustrating the Metaphysical Theory of Personal Idealism.* Revised edition. New York: The Macmillan Co., 1905. (Originally published, 1901.)

———: *The Conception of God: A Philosophical Discussion concerning the Nature of the Divine Idea as a Demonstrable Reality.* New York: The Macmillan Co., 1897 (Co-author along with Josiah Royce, Joseph Le Conte and Sidney Edward Mezes.)

———: Buckham, J. W. and Stratton, G. M. (editors): *George Holmes Howison: Philosopher and Teacher.* A Selection from His Writings with a Biographical Sketch. Berkeley: The University of California Press, 1934.

Hamilton, Edward John (1834–1918): *A New Analysis in Fundamental Morals.* New York: Charles Scribner's Sons, 1870.

———: *The Human Mind: A Treatise in Mental Philosophy.* New York, 1882.

———: *The Modalist: or, The Laws of Rational Conviction.* Boston: Ginn and Co., 1891.

———: *The Perceptionalist: or, Mental Science.* New York, 1899. (First published, 1885.)

———: *The Moral Law: or, The Theory and Practice of Duty.* New York: Funk and Wagnalls Co., 1902.

———: *Perzeptionalismus und Modalismus: eine Erkenntnistheorie.* Leipzig: A. Kröner, 1911.

———: *Erkennen und Schliessen: eine theoretische Logik auf der Grundlage des Perzeptionalismus und Modalismus.* Leipzig: A. Kröner, 1912.

———: *Rational Orthodoxy: Essays on Mooted Questions.* New York: Funk and Wagnalls Co., 1917.

Johnson, Francis Howe (1835–1920): *What is Reality?: An Inquiry as to the Reasonableness of Natural Religion and the Naturalness of Revealed Religion.* Boston: Houghton Mifflin Co., 1891.

———: *God in Evolution: A Pragmatic Study of Theology.* New York: Longmans, Green and Co., 1911.

Montgomery, Edmund Duncan (1835–1911): *Philosophical Problems in the Light of Vital Organization.* New York: G. P. Putnam's Sons, 1907.

Abbot, Francis Ellingwood (1836–1903): *Religion and Science*. New York: D. Appleton and Co., 1874.

———: *Scientific Theism*. Boston: Little, Brown and Co., 1885.

———: *The Way out of Agnosticism: or, The Philosophy of Free Religion*. Boston: Little, Brown and Co., 1890.

———: *The Syllogistic Philosophy*. Boston: Little, Brown and Co., 1906.

Gibbs, Josiah Willard (1839–1903): *Scientific Papers*. 2 vols. New York: Longmans, Green and Co., 1906.

———: Longley, W. R. and Van Name, R. G. (editors): *Collected Works*. 2 vols. New York: Longmans, Green and Co., 1928.

Morris, George Sylvester (1840–1889): *The Final Cause as Principle of Cognition in Nature*. London, 1875. (Reprinted from *Journal of the Transactions of the Victoria Institute, or Philosophical Society of Great Britain* 9 [1875] 176–204.)

———: *Philosophy and Christianity: A Series of Lectures Delivered in New York, in 1883, on the Ely Foundation of the Union Theological Seminary*. New York, 1883.

Davidson, Thomas (1840–1900): *The Philosophical System of Antonio Rosmini-Serbati*. New York, 1882.

———: *The Education of the Wage-Earners*. Boston, 1904.

Snider, Denton J. (1841–1925): *Psychology and Psychosis: Intellect*. St. Louis, Mo., 1896.

———: *Will and Its World: Psychical and Ethical*. St. Louis, Mo., 1899.

———: *Social Institutions in their Origin, Growth and Interconnection: Psychologically Treated*. St. Louis, Mo., 1901.

———: *Cosmos and Diocosmos: The Processes of Nature Psychologically Treated*. St. Louis, Mo., 1909.

———: *A Writer of Books in His Genesis: Written for and Dedicated to His Pupil-Friends Reaching Back in a Line of Fifty Years*. St. Louis, Mo., 1910.

———: *The Biocosmos: The Processes of Life Psychologically Ordered*. St. Louis, Mo., 1911.

Ladd, George Trumbull (1842–1921): *Elements of Physiological Psychology: A Treatise of the Activities and Nature of the Mind, from the Physical and Experimental Points of View*. Revised edition. New York: Charles Scribner's Sons, 1911. (First published in 1889.)

———: *Introduction to Philosophy: An Inquiry after a Rational System of Scientific Principles in their Relation to Ultimate Reality*. New York: Charles Scribner's Sons, 1890.

———: *Philosophy of Mind: An Essay in the Metaphysics of Psychology*. New York: Charles Scribner's Sons, 1895.

———: *Philosophy of Knowledge: An Inquiry into the Nature, Limits, and Validity of the Human Cognitive Faculty*. New York: Charles Scribner's Sons, 1897.

———: *A Theory of Reality: An Essay in Metaphysical System upon the Basis of Human Cognitive Experience.* New York: Charles Scribner's Sons, 1899.

Ladd, George Trumbull: *Philosophy of Conduct: A Treatise of the Facts, Principles, and Ideals of Conduct.* New York: Charles Scribner's Sons, 1902.

———: *The Philosophy of Religion: A Critical and Speculative Treatise of Man's Religious Experience and Development in the Light of Modern Science and Reflective Thinking.* 2 vols. New York: Charles Scribner's Sons, 1905.

———: *Knowledge, Life and Reality: An Essay in Systematic Philosophy.* New York: Dodd, Mead and Co., 1909. (Reprinted, New Haven: Yale University Press, 1918.)

Palmer, George Herbert (1842–1933): *The Field of Ethics.* Boston: Houghton Mifflin Co., 1901.

———: *The Nature of Goodness.* Boston: Houghton Mifflin Co., 1903.

———: *The Problem of Freedom.* Boston: Houghton Mifflin Co., 1911.

———: *Altruism: Its Nature and Varieties.* New York: Charles Scribner's Sons, 1920.

———: *The Autobiography of a Philosopher.* Boston: Houghton Mifflin Co., 1930.

Bowne, Borden Parker (1847–1910): *Studies in Theism.* Cincinnati: Methodist Book Concern, 1879.

———: *Introduction to Psychological Theory.* New York: Harper and Bros., 1886.

———: *Philosophy of Theism.* New York: Harper and Bros., 1887.

———: *Principles of Ethics.* New York: Harper and Bros., 1892.

———: *Theory of Thought and Knowledge.* New York: Harper and Bros., 1897.

———: *Personalism.* Boston: Houghton Mifflin Co., 1908.

———: *Metaphysics.* Revised edition. New York: American Book Co., 1910. (First edition, 1882.)

Ormond, Alexander Thomas (1847–1915): *Basal Concepts of Philosophy: An Inquiry into Being, Non-Being and Becoming.* New York: Charles Scribner's Sons, 1894.

———: *Foundations of Knowledge: in Three Parts.* New York: The Macmillan Co., 1900.

———: *The Concepts of Philosophy.* New York: The Macmillan Co., 1906.

Carus, Paul (1852–1919): *Form and Formal Thought: The Fundamental Problem of Philosophy.* Chicago: Open Court Publishing Co., 1889.

———: *Fundamental Problems: The Method of Philosophy as a Systematic Arrangement of Knowledge.* Second edition. Chicago: Open Court Publishing Co., 1891. (First published, 1887.)

———: *The Soul of Man.* Chicago: Open Court Publishing Co., 1893.

———: *The Foundations of Mathematics: A Contribution to the*

*Philosophy of Geometry.* Chicago: Open Court Publishing Co., 1908.

Carus, Paul: *God: An Inquiry into the Nature of Man's Highest Ideal and a Solution of the Problem from the Standpoint of Science.* Chicago: Open Court Publishing Co., 1908.

———: *Philosophy as a Science: A Synopsis of the Writings of Dr. Paul Carus, Containing an Introduction Written by Himself, Summaries of His Books, and a List of Articles to Date.* Chicago: Open Court Publishing Co., 1909.

———: *The Philosophy of Form.* Chicago: Open Court Publishing Co., 1911.

Marshall, Henry Rutgers (1852–1927): *Pain, Pleasure and Aesthetics: An Essay Concerning the Psychology of Pain and Pleasure, with Special Reference to Aesthetics.* London: The Macmillan Co., 1894.

———: *Aesthetic Principles.* New York: The Macmillan Co., 1895.

———: *Instinct and Reason: An Essay Concerning the Relation of Instinct to Reason.* New York: The Macmillan Co., 1898.

———: *Consciousness.* London: The Macmillan Co., 1909.

———: *The Beautiful.* London: The Macmillan Co., 1924.

Schurman, Jacob Gould (1854–): *Kantian Ethics: and the Ethics of Evolution.* London, 1881.

———: *The Ethical Import of Darwinism.* New York: Charles Scribner's Sons, 1887.

———: *Belief in God: Its Origin, Nature and Basis.* New York: Charles Scribner's Sons, 1890.

———: *Agnosticism and Religion.* New York: Charles Scribner's Sons, 1896.

Fullerton, George Stuart (1859–1925): *The Conception of the Infinite and the Solution of the Mathematical Antinomies: A Study in Psychological Analysis.* Philadelphia, 1887.

———: *A Plain Argument for God.* Philadelphia, 1889.

———: *On Sameness and Identity: A Psychological Study: Being a Contribution to the Foundations of a Theory of Knowledge.* Philadelphia: University of Pennsylvania Press, 1890.

———: *A System of Metaphysics.* New York: The Macmillan Co., 1904.

Baldwin, James Mark (1861–1934): *Mental Development in the Child and the Race: Methods and Processes.* New York: The Macmillan Co., 1895.

———: *Social and Ethical Interpretations in Mental Development: A Study in Social Psychology.* Third edition. New York: The Macmillan Co., 1902. (First edition, 1897.)

———: *Development and Evolution.* New York: The Macmillan Co., 1902.

———: *Fragments in Philosophy and Science: Collected Essays and Addresses.* New York: Charles Scribner's Sons, 1902.

———: *Thought and Things: A Study of the Development and*

*Meaning of Thought, or Genetic Logic.* 3 vols. New York: The Macmillan Co., 1906–11.

Baldwin, James Mark: *Darwin and the Humanities.* Baltimore, 1909.

———: *The Individual and Society: or, Psychology and Sociology.* Boston, 1911.

———: *Genetic Theory of Reality: Being the Outcome of Genetic Logic as Issuing in the Aesthetic Theory of Reality called Pancalism.* New York: G. P. Putnam's Sons, 1915.

Lloyd, A. H. (1864–1927): *Dynamic Idealism.* Chicago, 1898.

———: *The Philosophy of History.* Ann Arbor, Mich., 1899.

———: *The Will to Doubt.* New York: The Macmillan Co., 1902.

# Index of Names

# Index of Names

(1)